PRAISE FOR *SECRET FORMULA*

"A clear, convincing, anecdotal, often fascinating portrayal not just of Coca-Cola's corporate brilliance, but of how it inveighed its way into the center of American, and world, consciousness." —*Financial Times*

"[A] highly entertaining history . . . A juicy look at wheeling-dealing, litigation, global hustling, cola wars and the marketing savvy that carved a niche for Coke in the American social psyche." —*Publishers Weekly*

"At times the book reads like a Russian novel combined with a thriller. It will appeal to the general reader as well as to students of history." —*Library Journal*

"Allen seems to have had unprecedented access to company insiders, corporate archives, and private papers, and he uncovers a trove of information about corporate political clout at home and abroad. . . . Allen successfully contributes to the fascinating lore surrounding this symbol of American culture and enterprise." —*Booklist*

"Eminently readable . . . Contains factual servings derived from previously unpublished corporate papers plus wonderful fat dollops of insider thoughts from 130 interviews." —*Beverage Digest*

"[Frederick] Allen is a terrific writer. . . . He delves into the personalities and movements of the company in an excellent storytelling style." —*Fort Worth Star-Telegram*

"An informative and agreeably anecdotal history . . . An engaging audit of a corporate phenomenon that wisely eschews what-it-all-means analysis in favor of a vivid narrative that can speak for itself." —*Kirkus Reviews*

"If you thought you already knew all you wanted about Coca-Cola, you're wrong. The story of this drink is almost world history, with a special slant on Atlanta people and institutions that longtime residents will recognize and enjoy and newcomers need to know about. It's wonderful." —*The Atlanta Journal-Constitution*

Secret Formula

Secret Formula

FREDERICK ALLEN

OPEN ROAD
INTEGRATED MEDIA
NEW YORK

The author and publishers wish to thank the following for their kind permission to reproduce photographs:

The Coca-Cola Company: photos no. 1, 2, 3, (from a painting by William Kurtz, Sr.), 4, 5, 6, 7, 8, 9, 10, 11, 12, 13, 14, 15, 16, 17, 18, 26, 27, 28, 29, 30, 31, 32, 33, 37, 38, 39, 41, 42, 43, 44, 45, 46, 48, 49, 50, 65, 67, 68, 69, 72, 73, 74, 77, 78, 79 (Arthur Meyerson, Houston), 80, and 81.

Special Collections Department, Emory University: photos no. 19 (Taylor Photo Service, Atlanta), 20, 21, 22, 23, 24 (Brown Brothers, New York), 25 (N. Lazarnick for the White Motor Company, Cleveland), 34 (Reeves Studios, Atlanta), 35, 36, 40, 47 (Leo Barr, New York), 51 (Taylor Photo Service, Atlanta), 52, 53, 54 (Joe Jones), 55, 56 (Gabriel Benzur), 57, 58, 59, 61 (Reeves Studios, Atlanta), 70 (Reeves Studios, Atlanta), 71 (Guy Gillette, Yonkers, N.Y.) and 75.

Atlanta History Center: photos no. 60 (Herbert Jenkins Collection), 62, 63, and 64.

Jay Leviton (Atlanta): photo no. 76

Cover design by Mauricio Díaz

978-1-5040-1985-9

This edition published in 2015 by Open Road Integrated Media, Inc.
345 Hudson Street
New York, NY 10014
www.openroadmedia.com

This book is dedicated to my mother,

Martha Cherrington Allen,

who gave me a love of words and ideas and storytelling.

CONTENTS

Secret Formula

Introduction

RED SCARE

Prince Alexander Makinsky, the Coca-Cola Company's legendary man in Paris, was losing ground quickly.

In the winter of 1950, the French government threatened in all seriousness to outlaw the sale of America's leading soft drink. Makinsky, a Russian aristocrat with a reputation for limitless charm and guile, took charge of the company's defenses. Born in Persia in 1900, raised in Baku on the Caspian Sea by a British nanny who taught him flawless English, educated in Moscow and Paris, Alex Makinsky was a formidable character. He'd spent the years before World War II working for the Rockefeller Foundation as a political operative in France, Portugal, and the United States, making no secret of his close ties with American intelligence. During the war, he helped scientists escape German occupation and flee to the West by an underground route through Lisbon.

At a dinner party in 1946, Makinsky asked the guests in his Paris apartment if he should accept an offer to become Coca-Cola's top overseas lobbyist. "I was the only one who voted no," he joked breezily afterward, "so I took the job."

Makinsky began traveling for the Coca-Cola Company to hot spots in Europe, the Middle East, and South America. With his tidy moustache and tailored suits, wearing the sort of heavy-rimmed glasses that his good friend and neighbor Coco Chanel made famous, he was the very picture of worldliness, as familiar with diplomacy and protocol as a foreign minister. Makinsky prided himself on knowing monarchs and heads of state on a first-name basis. He counted many of them, from Franco to Farouk, as personal friends. Holding court in the elegant back bar of the Ritz Hotel, across the Rue Cambon from Coca-Cola's Paris office, Makinsky loved to smoke slender, elegant cigars, sip champagne, and weave intrigue.

Ordinarily, a showdown with a government was the sort of challenge he welcomed, but this one was different. An unlikely coalition of Communists, winemakers, and intellectual conservatives were united in a desperate struggle to keep Coca-Cola off the French market, and the ferocity of their attack had left Makinsky shaken. The problem was not the product itself. At the moment, the company was selling only a few hundred cases a year in all of France. The average Frenchman in his corner cafe, accustomed to the familiar smells of anisette, strong coffee, and Gitanes cigarettes, had never so much as tasted a "cola."

It was more the *idea* of Coca-Cola that triggered the trouble. Thanks to its familiar red logo and all-American image, Coke had become the lightning rod for a surge of resentment against the United States all across Europe and particularly in France. Makinsky worried that Coke frightened "not only our competitors, but also the great majority of French citizens who do not want to be 'Americanized,' and who consider our advertising as representative of what an 'Americanized Europe' is likely to offer."

By early February 1950, five separate ministries of the French government were conducting investigations of Coca-Cola. Turning up the heat, customs authorities suspended the company's import license, and the police brought criminal fraud charges against Coca-Cola's bottlers in Paris and Algiers. Most ominous of all, the secret police began shadowing Makinsky and his top deputies. Investigators in the French Interior Ministry opened dossiers on them, and there was evidence that someone was tapping Coca-Cola's office telephones and intercepting the mail. One of the company's Parisian lawyers, Pierre Gide, grew so frightened he started using an alias when he called the office.

In an especially chilling incident, Makinsky's number-two man, Alfredo Schvab, got a phone call at the office one afternoon from his wife. A man claiming to be Schvab had called the headmistress of the school where they sent their ten-year-old daughter, Isabelle, and made arrangements to pick her up after classes and take her to the cinema. Suspicious, the headmistress had Isabelle peek out the window from behind a curtain when the man drove up. "No!" the girl said. "That's not my father." As the headmistress and a teacher hid Isabelle inside, Schvab raced to the school just in time to see a sedan pulling away. He got the license number, and a contact in the police department told him it was a counterfeit plate used by a roughneck element in the Communist Party.

Unsettled by the events, the usually buoyant Makinsky warned Coca-Cola's top management that the company was in "imminent peril" of losing the battle of France.

In Atlanta on the afternoon of Friday, February 10, 1950, Pope Brock considered the latest bad news from abroad.

As Coca-Cola's general counsel, the gray-haired, sixty-one-year-old Brock had the unhappy duty of deciding what to do next. A defeat in France, he knew, had the potential of derailing the company's ambition to become a worldwide business. In the years after World War II, Coke had expanded its presence to seventy-six countries, but in most of them it had only a fragile toehold. Its operations in many places were laughably rudimentary. The field man in Colombia, for instance, put $28 on his expense account after he had to buy sneakers for his barefoot sales force.

In the past year, Brock calculated, less than a quarter of the company's $230 million in sales had come from outside the United States. Foreign profits were a meager $3 million. Coke faced intense resistance almost everywhere from the producers of beer, wine, aperitifs, fruit juices, mineral water, and other soft drinks. Every region seemed to have a domestic beverage whose owners were rich and politically well connected, and who made mischief for Coke in the courts and regulatory agencies. If the special interests in France succeeded in banishing Coca-Cola, the dominoes would begin to fall. Europe might be lost for a generation.

The looming disaster in France rattled the top men in Coca-Cola Export, the company's overseas arm headquartered in New York. Much to Brock's disgust, they were issuing memos expressing "alarm" and warning that it might be "a grave mistake" to press ahead.

Like many of the Georgia-born executives at Coca-Cola's boxy, Spartan home office on Plum Street in Atlanta, Brock viewed Export as a maverick operation whose officers got to Manhattan, developed airs, and began to fancy themselves just a little better acquainted with the ways of the world than their country cousins. After growing up dirt poor in the little hamlet of Avalon, Georgia, and working his way through college and law school, Brock carried an ample chip on his shoulder, and his contempt for his counterparts at Export was thorough. He had a particularly dim view of the president of Export, Jim Curtis. A fellow Georgian, Curtis had "gone native" in Manhattan, and his principal hobby was symbolized by the Stork Club ashtray he kept on his desk. Brock understood the dire prospects in France, but this was not the time for panic or self-protection. It was time to show some gumption.

Brock's rumpled appearance, spectacles, and gentle drawl concealed a belligerent temperament that now rose bristling to the surface. The moment had come, he decided, to get off the defensive, raise the stakes, and bring the French affair to an end, win or lose.

All that Friday afternoon and again on Saturday morning, Brock was on the phone, rallying Coke officials in New York and Paris. Brock confided in a memo how he harangued Curtis and Roy Jones, the two top officers of Export: "[I] urged upon both of them the tremendous importance of doing everything humanly possible to win the war that is now going on in France." In war, Brock reminded them, "the only rational thing is to throw all of your strength and all of your resources into it."

There was more to Brock's new strategy than tough talk. He ordered Stephen Ladas, a Greek-born, Harvard-educated lawyer who worked with Export in New York, to fly to Paris with reinforcements. Makinsky's Old World approach wasn't working. Perhaps it was time for something simple and direct. Brock gave Ladas explicit, written instructions to spend whatever amount of money it took to enlist as many "soldiers" as he needed to turn the tide. Ladas had one week to plan the trip and select his targets.

"It may be that we should hire a half-dozen or more influential scientists," Brock wrote Ladas. "It may be that [our lawyer] should associate one—or three—more lawyers. It is possible that one—or a half-dozen—political leaders could be engaged to do legitimate work for us." On the phone with Ladas, Brock suggested other avenues of approach too sensitive to commit to paper, and made it clear there was no upper limit on the blank check.

"This is no penny ante game," Brock warned. "It is the decisive struggle in Europe."

At first glance, Steve Ladas was an odd choice for the French assignment. Shy and bookish, his specialty was international trademark law, not cloak and dagger work. He struck some of his colleagues as a bit naive. Coca-Cola men who worked in South America chuckled over his habit of introducing himself formally by his full name—Stephen P. Ladas—which made it sound as if his family name were *Peladas*, slang in Spanish for "naked."

Brock told Ladas he'd picked him because he was smart enough to improvise in the field, but a better guess was that Ladas was the only one at Export Brock trusted with the company's money.*

Ladas landed in Paris on the morning of Monday, February 20, 1950. In the era of the Lockheed Constellation, an overnight flight from New York took sixteen or seventeen hours, including the refueling stop at Gander, Newfoundland. With the noisy droning of the engines and ceaseless vibration of the propellers, passengers generally arrived exhausted. But Ladas—"full of fighting mood," in his own words—pressed ahead with a busy schedule. With Makinsky off in Algiers finagling a delay in the trial of the Coca-Cola bottler there, Ladas was on his own.

His first order of business was to see the leaders of the various beverage industries. Experience in the United States and elsewhere had demonstrated that Coke did not undercut the sales of other drinks, certainly not liquor. It was simply absurd to think that an American soft drink, selling at eight cents for 6½ ounces, was about to wean the French away from their beloved red table wine, which they could buy for fifteen cents per liter. Yet no amount of persuasion had made the slightest impression. So Coca-Cola wanted to strike a deal.

Ladas described one of his calls: He arrived at the offices of the Radical Socialist Party, where he was greeted by a Mr. Rolland. In spite of its name, the party was actually slightly right of center, and it represented some of the country's wine interests. Ladas repeated the familiar reassurances, which fell as usual upon deaf ears, and then asked if there was anything the Coca-Cola Company could do to appease the vintners. Rolland

---

* It may be a mark of Ladas's guilelessness that he failed to destroy his copies of the confidential letters, memos, and cables detailing the company's highly sensitive maneuvers during the French affair. The Ladas files were discovered in the records of Coca-Cola Export in the late 1980s and later were made available to the author.

paused. Perhaps there was, he replied. The U.S. tariff on French wines was too high. It would be good to cut it in half. And the red tape at the U.S. Food and Drug Administration was impossible. French winemakers would appreciate having direct access to American markets.

Very well, Ladas said. The Coca-Cola Company was prepared to spend $50,000 to engage a lobbying firm in the United States to pursue those very goals, if the wine interests would call off the attack. There might be more help down the road. Rolland shook his head no. He was polite but firm. A generous gesture by Coca-Cola would be welcome, naturally, but he would have to insist on seeing some results before making any commitments. Meanwhile the wine industry had no choice but to remain an adversary.

Ladas found his other stops equally frustrating. The head of the fruit juice syndicate, he notified Atlanta, was a "vicious enemy." The leader of one of France's two soft drink organizations was antagonistic, while the other, claiming to be sympathetic to Coca-Cola, was "secretly aiding our enemies." The General Confederation of Agriculture was implacably hostile. Ladas crisscrossed Paris keeping appointments with lawyers, scientists, bureaucrats, and politicians, asking the same question over and over. Wasn't there something Coca-Cola could do? *Anything?* Everywhere the answer was the same: a Gallic shrug.

As the days passed, Ladas found his spirits flagging and a sense of desperation welling up. He was supposed to be spreading around Coca-Cola's money, he wrote Brock, "but there is really nothing or almost nothing to spend any money on."

Bribery wasn't working.

The company could pinpoint the exact time and place its political troubles were born: October 30, 1949, in the Piazza San Giovanni in Rome. Eight thousand Italian Communists were winding up an event they modestly called the Congress of the Partisans of Peace. The keynote speaker, sent by Cominform, the Bucharest-based propaganda arm of the Party, was a Soviet writer and polemicist named Alexander Fadeyev. Since he spoke in Russian, few in the crowd could understand his remarks, but they did recognize one of the names he spat out—"Coca-Cola"—and many of them booed.

Prodded by the Kremlin, Europe's Communist parties were quick to seize on Coke as a target. "DRINKS COCA-COLA AND DIES," declared a headline in *L'Unita*, the official Italian Communist newspaper, over a story describing how Coke could "turn a child's hair white overnight." A Hungarian magazine ran a picture of teenagers drinking Coke with the caption, "This Is the Way They Debauch American Youth." In France, the Communists warned against "Coca-Colonization" that would turn Frenchmen into *"cocacoliques."*

It might all have been good for a laugh except that the campaign triggered resentments and jealousies far beyond Communist circles, sparking several incidents of violence. Coca-Cola's manager in Vienna was dragged from his car, beaten, and had his tires slashed. The European countryside was still strewn with the physical and psychological wreckage of World War II, and the Marshall Plan was seen in many quarters not just as a way of rebuilding the marketplace, but as a sharp tool meant to pry it open for American goods. The French seethed at the sight of International Harvester tractors in their fields, Chiclet gum wrappers in their gutters, and Frigidaires in their kitchens. It was more than a question of economics. After five years of occupation by the Germans (and more collaboration than they cared to admit), the French were fiercely protective of their culture, and many of them were appalled at the invasion of comic books, the *Reader's Digest*, Hollywood movies, and other American innovations.

In war-weary Europe, with its sapped vitality, the presence of Coca-Cola even carried the undercurrent of a sexual threat. During a visit to the United States, a Swiss newspaper editor explained: "Take your GIs. They made a great impression upon Switzerland. Especially upon the youth of Switzerland. Your GIs came to us after the war, on trips your army organized. They had great success with our girls. Our young men saw that and they didn't like it too much, but it left them with a desire to be as American as possible so the girls would like them better. . . . Now they all drink Coca-Cola."

Company officials did little to discourage the belief that they planned to splash the name of their product on every surface of the Continent in bright red paint. Motorized barges were plying the waters of the Grand Canal in Venice with giant Coca-Cola signs on the side, and anything seemed possible.

Contemplating an onslaught of neon signs, painted walls, billboards, singing commercials, and fleets of red delivery trucks, the ordinarily level-headed editors of the newspaper *Le Monde* warned that the arrival of Coca-Cola represented a menace to "the whole panorama and morale of French civilization."

The contrast with Coca-Cola's position at home in the United States could not have been sharper.

For decades, the men who ran the company had worked feverishly to create a special place for their product in America's social psyche. Coca-Cola was part of the American landscape. In the 1890s and early twentieth century, Asa Candler gave away millions of clocks, paper napkins, thermometers, lighters, watches, watch fobs, pocket knives, pocket books, bottle openers, sterling-silver perfume dispensers, serving trays, change trays, bookmarks, marble paperweights, and Japanese fans—all inscribed prominently with the trademark "Coca-Cola." In time they became *objets*, precious to collectors from coast to coast. Coke's calendars gave American men a pretty girl to look at every month.

Millions of children received school kits with No. 2 pencils, notebooks, blotters, rulers, and spelling primers, all embossed with the trademark. In soda fountains and drugstores, Coca-Cola provided porcelain serving urns, back-bar festoons, window valences, transom bulletins, oilcloth signs, cutout posters, and Tiffany-style stained-glass lampshades. All across America, luncheonettes, candy stores, tobacco shops, and mom-and-pop groceries did business under awnings that carried two names: the proprietor's and Coca-Cola's.

Robert W. Woodruff, the gruff, autocratic Georgian whose family and associates took control of Coke's ownership and management in 1919, drove himself and those around him toward a single goal—to make Coke, as one of his lieutenants put it, "the most American thing in America."

Using the popular artists Norman Rockwell, Haddon Sundblom, and N. C. Wyeth, Woodruff directed an advertising campaign in the 1920s and 1930s that made Coke a familiar, inescapable element of everyday American life. The company's ads even shaped the way Americans imagined Santa Claus: There was no popular vision of Santa as a round, ruddy fellow in a red suit with fleecy white piping until Sundblom invented it in a series of Christmas ads for Coke.

In billboards and magazine ads, posters and jingles, Coca-Cola helped pioneer the art of the soft sell, turning the "pause that refreshes" into an integral part of the national culture. When people thought about Coke, they not only thought about drinking a soft drink, they thought of the activities they undertook *while* they drank it, from small moments like a break at work to serious events like a first date. The company published hospitality booklets that helped housewives entertain at home, donated scoreboards for high school football fields, put coolers in service stations, and filled the vending machines in factories and offices. The amiable side of every new social phenomenon, from the country's love affair with the car, to its discovery of leisure, to the barbecue tongs and cookout lifestyle of its suburbs, was deliberately associated with Coca-Cola. The soda fountain, one ad proclaimed, was "the world's friendliest club—admission 5 cents." Ads never showed what was in Coca-Cola, but instead what Coca-Cola was in: pleasant, poignant scenes of everyday life.

Over time, Coke became part of the ritual of American life. There were "Coke dates" and "Coke clubs" and "Coke parties." When bashful teenagers played spin the bottle, more often than not it was a Coke bottle they spun. For years, no group of little boys could put their empty Coke bottles back in the rack before turning them over to see whose was minted in the farthest city.

During World War II, Woodruff decreed that Coke would be available for a nickel to members of the armed forces wherever they served. Coke went to war with the American GI, and the familiar hoopskirt bottle found its place in the dogface cartoons of Bill Mauldin and the frontline dispatches of Ernie Pyle. The company built bottling plants—sixty-three in all—in every theater of the war, and its Technical Observers delivered cases of Coke everywhere Americans fought, sometimes right into the foxholes. The TOs often faced the same dangers as their military counterparts; three of them were killed in action. The U.S. Navy's last requisition, never filled, was for twenty thousand cases of Coke to be marked "Tokyo."

By forging an association with the nation's sacrifices as well as its pleasures, Coke earned the loyalty of eleven million veterans and their families, and countless other Americans as well. In *God Is My Co-Pilot*, one of the war's best-sellers, Colonel Robert L. Scott wrote, "I don't know exactly what democracy is, or the real, common-sense meaning of a republic. But as we used to talk things over in China, we all used to agree that we were fighting for The American Girl. She to us was America, Democracy, Coca-Colas, Hamburgers, Clean Places to Sleep, or The American Way of Life."

Thanks to the war, Coca-Cola was considered one of the things that defined America. By the late 1940s, according to a document tucked away in Woodruff's private papers, company officials identified their product so closely with the national interest that they were considering a new slogan: "The United Taste of America—Coca-Cola."

But abroad, none of it counted for a thing. At least not yet.

On Thursday morning, February 23, 1950, Ladas visited the American Embassy in the Place de la Concorde.

Shown into the office of U.S. Ambassador David K. E. Bruce, Ladas pulled out a letter accusing the French of acting in "a spirit of persecution, discrimination, and bad faith," and called on the State Department for help. Ladas reminded Bruce that the embassy had interceded on Coca-Cola's behalf many times before.

Just two months earlier, in fact, Bruce had stopped a piece of anti-Coke legislation dead in its tracks in the National Assembly. In December 1949, a deputy named Paul Boulet from Montpellier, in the heart of the wine-producing Hérault region, had introduced a bill giving the minister of health sweeping powers to bar the sales of any beverage he considered harmful. Quickly turning the diplomatic equivalent of a triple play, Makinsky had notified Coca-Cola's Washington lobbyist, Fred Morrison, who alerted his top contact, Under Secretary of State James E. Webb, who in turn dispatched Bruce to see French Premier Georges Bidault. The bill was halted.

Now Ladas was calling again at the embassy, but this time things were not as simple. Along with its political and economic headaches, Coca-Cola was in trouble with the law.

Ever since its birth in 1886 in the hurly-burly of the patent medicine era, Coke had been vulnerable to sporadic outbursts of intense controversy over some of its ingredients, from the trace of cocaine that was finally leached out at the turn of the century, to the caffeine that provoked the first head of the U.S. Food and Drug Administration into fighting Coca-Cola all the way to the U.S. Supreme Court. In postwar Europe, there were scientists—reputable scientists—who sincerely believed that Coca-Cola was toxic and addictive, even that it might contain an aphrodisiac. When none of their suspicions could be proven, they turned the dispute to a technical question about phosphoric acid.

Known as "Merchandise No. 4" in Coca-Cola's celebrated secret formula, phosphoric acid was a clear, colorless liquid used in small amounts for preservation and flavoring. In layman's terms, it put the familiar bite into the taste of Coke. Unfortunately for the company, health laws in most European countries severely restricted or flatly prohibited the addition of mineral acids to beverages. There was no evidence that minor amounts of phosphoric acid in a soft drink were harmful in any way, and the laws were not aimed specifically at Coke—they dated back to the early 1900s—but they nonetheless handed Coca-Cola's enemies a convenient and powerful weapon.

The company had different strategies for dealing with the phosphoric acid problem, depending on the country. In Belgium, Coke hired the services of several prominent scientists, enlisted the full backing of U.S. Ambassador Robert D. Murphy, and slipped through a change in the law. In Switzerland, where the authorities were sympathetic to Coca-Cola and willing to look the other way, Coke's chemists devised a so-called "Swiss formula" that masked the presence of the phosphoric acid. But neither approach was suitable for France. Because of the political climate, there was no way to change the law. And the Swiss formula was out, the company decided, because it was a "thin smoke screen" that might be discovered if the French made a sophisticated analysis.

Up to now in France, the Coca-Cola Company had relied on the simple expedient of stonewalling. French law made phosphoric acid illegal only as an added ingredient, not as a natural by-product of other ingredients, and it was hard to tell the difference in laboratory tests. Company officials, who knew better, assured the French authorities they had no idea about the origins of the phosphoric acid present in Coke. Makinsky, with a jaded flair worthy of Claude Rains in the movie *Casablanca*, advocated maintaining the ruse of ignorance. If he or his people were caught, he said, "we can adopt the attitude . . . that we are greatly shocked and indignant"

But the game was growing more dangerous. The company's bottlers in Paris and Algiers faced charges of criminal fraud, and there was a good chance they would be caught in a lie and convicted.

Ladas wanted the embassy to step in and block the prosecutions. The cases were purely political, Ladas assured Bruce, initiated by the law enforcement arm of the Ministry of Agriculture to protect special interests. The trials "could be stopped entirely," Ladas argued, "if the Prime Minister would merely telephone the Minister of Agriculture and the Minister of Justice, asking them to drop the case." Ladas tried to get Bruce to pressure the prime minister into making the calls.

But Bruce refused to go along. The embassy was happy to help with instances of overt discrimination against American businesses. Bruce would write a letter to the Bidault government warning them again against political harassment of Coca-Cola. But interfering in a criminal prosecution was another matter. If Coca-Cola had violated French law, it would have to face the consequences. The embassy was involved in tense, difficult negotiations with the Bidault government over NATO, the Marshall Plan, a pending trade treaty, and the future of the French military effort in what was then called Indo-China. Bruce made it clear that cleaning up a mess for the Coca-Cola Company was not a high priority with him.

"Bruce is too much of a diplomat," Ladas complained to Brock, "and not aggressive at all." The company was on its own.

Returning from Algiers at the end of the week, Makinsky found Ladas near despair. Everything was "so loose and slippery," Ladas said, "that you do not know where to start from and what to fight."

Makinsky soon discovered that things were even worse than Ladas realized. While Ladas was rushing around Paris trying to make deals, the anti-Coke forces had quietly slipped the Boulet bill back on the agenda in the National Assembly. Ladas had been gulled. The very people he was talking to were busy behind his back plotting another attempt to outlaw Coca-Cola.

Over the weekend, Ladas and Makinsky joined forces and made "frantic" efforts to get the bill postponed, but they failed. It remained Item 9 on the agenda for Tuesday, February 28. Makinsky learned from his spies inside the Cabinet Council that Premier Bidault, free from U.S. Embassy pressure, had no intention of intervening to save Coca-Cola a second time. Bidault and his party, the centrist Popular Republican Movement, had made a great many concessions to the United States to keep aid flowing under the Marshall Plan—the total reached 400 billion francs by the end of 1949—and they chafed under the resulting barrage of criticism from the Communists and Socialists that they were too "pro-American." Here at last was a chance for Bidault to show his independence.

At four o'clock on the afternoon of the twenty-eighth, the Boulet bill came up for debate in the red-carpeted Assembly chambers on the left bank of the Seine. The government's spokesman in the Assembly, Minister of Health Pierre Schneiter, arose and gave an odd talk. His preference, he said, would be to allow Frenchmen to make up their own minds about what they wanted to drink. Smiling and bantering, Schneiter joked about the consequences of a law giving his ministry the responsibility to ban or approve beverages. Perhaps soon, he said, the cafes would have signs saying various drinks were endorsed by the minister of health. "He who will drink too much will say, 'I did it with the authorization of the Minister of Public Health!'" The deputies laughed. Still, Schneiter went on, turning serious, the government understood the politics of the situation. The deputies were free to vote as they wished.

Ninety minutes later, on a vigorous show of hands, they voted over-whelmingly against Coca-Cola.

What happened next caught the company completely by surprise. Like the cavalry in a B-movie Western, the American people came riding to the rescue.

Until the passage of the Boulet bill, few Americans had any idea of Coca-Cola's difficulties overseas. On the theory that it was smarter to work quietly behind the scenes, company officials had done everything in their power to stifle publicity about the resistance Coke was fighting in France and elsewhere. The company was paying a $25,000 annual retainer to the best-known press agent of the era, Steve Hannagan, to keep the hubbub in the European press *out* of the papers in the United States. Business report-ers in New York complained that their phone calls to Export were rarely returned.

In fact, for all its past glories, the Coca-Cola Company of 1950 was in a state of near paralysis. Woodruff's single-minded dedication to a set of fixed standards, once the backbone of the company's success, was beginning to prove more hindrance than help. Business was stagnant, thanks in large part to his stubborn refusal to offer consumers anything larger or more convenient than the traditional 6½-ounce bottles. The company's bottlers, feeling the squeeze of postwar inflation, were up in arms over Woodruff's inflexible allegiance to the 5-cent retail price. Coke's fabled advertising man, Archie Lee, was ill, exhausted, and out of ideas. Woodruff himself was just emerging from a long period of depression, heavy drinking, and spo-radic illness brought on by the suicide of a younger brother. It was hardly surprising that the company shunned attention.

But there was no suppressing a declaration of war on Coca-Cola by the French parliament. The news from Paris raced westward across the Atlan-tic by cable and appeared the next morning above the fold on the front page of the *New York Times*. The Associated Press filed an account that appeared in hundreds of other American newspapers. Radio stations filled the air-waves with word of the strange doings in France. By midday on Wednesday, March 1, 1950, Coca-Cola was the hottest story in the United States.

Most newspapers greeted the bulletin with a mix of puzzled amusement and genuine indignation. The *New York Herald Tribune* proclaimed a "Coca-Colamity," while the *Washington News* complained about "the arrogantly superior French habit of snooting at our beverages, soft and hard, as so much dishwater." The New York *Daily News* raised the threat of cutting off aid under the Marshall Plan.

Commentators could not resist the story. On WCBS radio, Eric Seva-reid reminded his listeners that Coca-Cola had gone to war with the American armed forces and helped liberate France. Across town, in a booth at WNBC, humorist Henry Morgan proposed retaliating with a ban on "French champagne, Schiaparelli, the Eiffel Tower, Napoleon, French poodles, Chanel No. 5, eclairs, Victor Hugo, Simone Simon, and Charlemagne."

At the offices of Coca-Cola Export, up on the eighteenth floor at 515 Madison Avenue, Curtis and his people scrambled to join the fray. Hannagan was brought in to craft a statement for Export's chairman, Jim Farley. A former postmaster general, Democratic Party chairman, and the architect of Franklin Roosevelt's first presidential campaign in 1932, Farley was one of the best-known politicians of his time. He had made one terrible miscalculation in his life—he opposed Roosevelt's bid for a third term—and with his career in eclipse he joined Export in 1940 as a figurehead who traveled the globe constantly, glad-handing diplomats, businessmen, and heads of state. He maintained good relations with the media and his name still had clout.

"I assure you," Farley said of the Boulet bill, "it is the worst bit of political shenanigan I have ever encountered—and that covers a lot of territory at home and abroad!" Farley wondered rhetorically what General Lafayette would have thought, cited the generosity of the Marshall Plan, and closed with the stinging observation, "Coca-Cola was not injurious to the health of the American soldiers who liberated France from the Nazis so that Communist deputies could be in session today." His remarks gained wide coverage.

Thanks to Farley, the story even made it onto the infant medium of television. Sitting at a table at the Stork Club, with Walter Winchell in the next chair, Farley appeared live on CBS on a show featuring the husband-and-wife team of Peter Lind Hayes and Mary Healy. Then as now, TV hosts could be a little vague about their subject matter, and Healy asked, "Wasn't there something in the paper recently about something that happened with the French?" Farley, conspicuously sipping a Coke, took his cue and gave his spiel.

In Atlanta, Woodruff watched with grudging approval as the controversy spread. A man who ordinarily detested publicity of any sort about his company's business affairs, he could see the advantages of joining the Cold War on the American side. Coca-Cola's name was better known than Stalin's, Woodruff told an associate, and certainly more popular.

Ed Sullivan, then a syndicated gossip columnist, recognized the bonanza Coke was reaping. "[The] French Commies' attack on Coca-Cola," he wrote, "is one of those publicity breaks a company dreams about, but rarely gets, huh?" More than headlines, though, the real value to Coca-Cola was the leverage it gained from the growing sentiment in favor of reprisals.

Like Henry Morgan, many Americans thought of retaliating against French products. Unlike Morgan, some were perfectly serious. The Broadway showman Billy Rose announced that his nightclub, the Diamond Horseshoe, would suspend the sale of French champagne. In his syndicated column, "Pitching Horseshoes," Rose (or more likely his ghostwriter) explained the decision in the breathless newspaperese of the day:

From where I cogitate, it boils down to this: John Q. Frenchman is being denied a choice between Coke and vino only
because the Lefties, aided and abetted by the bird-brain
Righties, don't like the country Coca-Cola comes from.
Well, messieurs et mesdames, two can play at boycott as well
as one. So, no French champagne will be sold in my place
until the idiotic ban against our home product is lifted. And
if that doesn't work, we can get really tough and stop buying
your French postcards!

But it did work. Rose's column ran in 417 different newspapers, from
the New York *Daily News* to the *Beaver* (Utah) *Press*, and within a matter of
days, sales of French wines began to drop.

The tide turned swiftly. On March 14, just two weeks after the Boulet bill was approved, the French Embassy in Washington issued a press
release complaining about the anti-French "campaign" under way in the
American media. No actual prohibition of Coca-Cola was in place, the
statement argued, so it was unfair to boycott French products in America.

Two days later, the French ambassador, Henri Bonnet, ushered Farley
and Curtis into his office at the embassy in Washington for a meeting. The
mood had changed. Now it was the French who were asking what they
could do to make things right Moving cautiously, the Export men asked for
a small but vital concession. Coca-Cola's import license was still suspended,
and the company was unable to supply its French bottlers with the concentrate they needed to make Coke. Unless French Customs backed off, it was
a matter of days until Coke would be forced to stop sales. Lift the suspen-
sion, Farley and Curtis said, and they would see what they could do about
soothing anti-French feelings in America.

Ladas, who had returned to New York in disgrace, could feel the company's fortunes (and his own) reviving. He gave Mr. Rolland, the politician with ties to the French wine industry, a taste of his own medicine.
"Unfortunately," Ladas wrote, "events since my departure from Paris have
taken a bad turn." The $50,000 lobbying effort to cut the tariff on French
wines and smooth their distribution, Ladas explained, would have to go on
hold. American public reaction to the Boulet bill had been "simply amazing and extraordinary." Perhaps, if Rolland could help arrange a gesture
of good faith—restoring Coke's import license, for instance—Ladas could
take another look. In the meantime, though, it was no deal. In case Rolland missed the point, Ladas tucked a copy of Billy Rose's column into the
envelope.

Not everyone in France surrendered easily. Just days after the vote
on the Boulet bill, the Communists stormed the speaker's rostrum in the
Assembly chambers and held it by force for seven hours. Their grievances
covered a wide array of issues, not just Coca-Cola. But as one of the deputies was dragged away bodily he cried out against American imperialism

and Coca-Cola, and it made a nice metaphor. One way or the other, calmly or kicking and screaming, the French were giving up ground.

The breaks began going the company's way. The judge in the Paris bottler's case was about to be married and proposed a one-month delay in the trial while he went on his honeymoon. "Why not take two months?" Coca-Cola's lawyer asked. The judge agreed.

Ambassador Bonnet invited Farley back to Washington to apologize for a slight delay in getting Coca-Cola's import license restored. There were still enemies in the French government, Bonnet explained, and he would have to work around them. Farley, accompanied this time by Ladas, assured the ambassador that he understood. The company could wait a few days. But in the meantime, Coca-Cola wanted something else. The Bidault government must guarantee that no further criminal cases would be filed. "Yes, yes," Bonnet agreed, "that would be too much." Good, said Farley. In that event, he was prepared to put out a statement calling on the American people to stop their boycott of French goods. The prosecutions were quietly forgotten.

A final piece of business fell into place a few months later. The company remained anxious for the Ministry of Agriculture to adopt a new, modern health law permitting a small amount of phosphoric acid in soft drinks. Then and only then would Coke be fully protected. An ad hoc "Committee of 21," composed of scientists, health experts, and beverage industry lobbyists, was in charge of drafting the new law. The deputy chairman of the committee, Louis Descamps, the president of the Carbonated Bottlers Syndicate of France—the man Steve Ladas had found so utterly treacherous and hostile she months before—approached Jim Curtis with an offer. Descamps would deliver a majority vote of the committee in favor of the law allowing phosphoric acid. In return, he wished to be awarded the Coca-Cola bottling franchise for the city of Toulouse. Coca-Cola's men had met the enemy, and he was theirs.

Only the details remained to be worked out. Descamps asked for $25,000 worth of equipment and a guaranteed ten-year operating loan. Worried about the propriety of giving him an "outright gift" (especially if it became public knowledge), Curtis countered with the modern charade of leasing Descamps the equipment at no charge and making him a consultant for five years at $5,000 a year, payable in advance.

"It is my view," Curtis explained in a confidential memo to Woodruff, ". . . that if we can settle the problem in France for $50,000, the price would be cheap." As indeed it was.

The lesson of the French affair stuck in Coca-Cola's corporate memory for years to come.

The company's top man in Washington, Ben Oehlert, had the newspaper clippings from the period bound up in three red leather volumes entitled *The French Problem, Publicity*, and he often found occasion to pull them out.

In 1966, for instance, when Coca-Cola granted a bottling franchise in Israel, the thirteen member nations of the Arab League threatened an Islamic boycott. Oehlert promptly arranged an appointment with Mustafa Kamel, the United Arab Republic's ambassador to the United States, showed him the books, and warned him solemnly of the impending "outcry." The American people had a love affair going with Coca-Cola, a romance that defied rhyme or reason, and one interfered with it only at the greatest peril.

Yet corporations are capable of forgetting history, too, and they can be doomed to repeat it. On April 23, 1985, six weeks after Robert Woodruff's death, the company's top officials announced at a jammed news conference in New York that they were changing the formula of Coca-Cola. "The best," said chairman and chief executive officer Roberto Goizueta, "has been made even better." New Coke made its ill-fated debut.

What the management forgot was that Coca-Cola is more than a soft drink—more than a carbonated beverage with definable characteristics that a company lawyer, in his prosaic way, once called "mouthfeel and physical organoleptic properties." Coke has *always* been greater than the sum of its parts, from the very beginning. Back before the turn of the century, thirsty Southerners nicknamed the drink "Dope" in the belief they were getting a little kick from the coca leaf, when in fact they were really getting their lift from sugar and caffeine—four times the amount of caffeine Coke contains today.

There were more than a dozen alterations to Coca-Cola's sanctified secret formula, many of them significant, in the ninety-nine years leading up to the introduction of New Coke. Yet the company kept those changes quiet and jealously guarded the mystique and mythology of the formula. The existence of a lone copy of the original recipe, locked in a vault at the Trust Company of Georgia, unavailable to anyone for any reason except by formal vote of the company's board of directors, was part of the nation's folklore. The *idea* of Coca-Cola was something quite separate and apart from the product. In fact, that was Coke's real secret formula: the inexplicable act of alchemy that elevated a bottle of sugar and water into a national icon. Blindfolded, people were consumers who wanted a new taste. Eyes open, they were Americans who felt betrayed by New Coke.

The backlash against New Coke easily surpassed the French episode of thirty-five years before. Thinking that as many as 5 percent of its die-hard consumers might rebel against New Coke, the management added ten new WATS lines to the seven it already maintained. But the operators were soon handling more than a thousand calls a day, then five thousand, then eight thousand, almost all of them furious. The company put 158 operators to work on 83 lines and eventually answered 400,000 calls. The American public simply refused to accept the notion of a change in Coke, *even if the change was an improvement.* "It was like saying you were going to make the flag prettier," one Coke executive realized later. Eleven weeks after the grand unveiling, the management brought back Coke Classic, and a grateful public rewarded the company with a surge in sales that lasted well into the 1990s.

In a sense, Coca-Cola had surrendered to itself. The company pitted the fact of Coke against the fiction, and the fiction won.

It was exactly how the company got started a century before.

One

STIRRINGS

It took two men to invent Coca-Cola, and they could hardly have been more different.

With his full, flowing black beard and dark eyes, John Stith Pemberton was a familiar figure on the streets of Atlanta in the years after the Civil War. A handsome man, a Confederate veteran and war hero, "Doc" Pemberton was a pharmacist who liked to dabble with patent medicines. In the spring of 1886, stirring up the contents of a forty-gallon brass kettle with a wooden oar, he brewed the first batch of a dark, sugary syrup meant to be served with carbonated water and sold at the city's soda fountains. The most successful soft drink of all time was born.

But it wasn't *Coca-Cola* until it had a name, and it got that from another man. Frank Mason Robinson was a Yankee and a veteran of the Union Army. Standing barely five feet tall, with jug ears, sad eyes, and a drooping moustache, Robinson was an easy man to overlook, as most historians have. He arrived in Atlanta in December 1885, went into partnership with Pemberton, and got the inspiration of naming the new syrup after two of its ingredients, the coca leaf and the kola nut. He liked the alliteration. Robinson changed the K in kola to a C for uniformity's sake, put in a hyphen, and then wrote out a label in longhand in the careful Spencerian script that would become the best-known trademark in the world.

Legend credits Pemberton with being the father of Coca-Cola, but Robinson was the father of the *idea* of Coca-Cola, and it was Robinson who kept the venture going through the early years when it very nearly died. He did so even though Pemberton tried to cheat him out of the business.

Doc Pemberton earned his nickname in 1850, at the age of nineteen, when he paid $5 for a temporary physician's license issued by the board of the Southern Botanico-Medical College in Macon, Georgia.

His studies were in a discipline known as the Thomsonian School, whose founder, Samuel Thomson of New Hampshire, believed that most human ills could be cured by inciting high fevers and forcibly cleansing the digestive system. Thompson advocated vapor baths, strong emetics, and the use of preparations made of herbs, plants, and other vegetable matter. His recommended cure for nephritis, or kidney disease, for instance, was a compound of equal portions of wild carrot seeds, spearmint, milk-weed, juniper berries, queen of the meadow, and dwarf elder. The dose was a pint a day.

Not surprisingly, perhaps, the Thomsonians were considered quacks, even in an era when the state of Georgia still licensed doctors to perform bloodletting and prescribe such remedies as mercury, opium, and blisters. Thomson himself was once indicted for murder in the death of a patient. But for all their foolishness, the Thomsonians nonetheless were knowledgeable about botany and chemistry. Their little two-year college in Macon offered a fairly solid course of training in pharmacology, and Pemberton, providentially for all concerned, was drawn in the direction of the laboratory rather than the practice (or malpractice) of medicine.

Abandoning a career as a doctor, Pemberton settled in the bustling Georgia river town of Columbus and was married in 1853 to a fifteen-year-old girl named Ann Eliza Clifford Lewis. In 1855, he opened a wholesale and retail drug business specializing in *materia medica*. An old ad lists drugs, medicines, oils, paints, glass, dye stuffs, perfumery, fancy articles, brushes, surgical instruments, gold foil, cigars, and burning fluid among the articles for sale at Pemberton & Carter.

Pemberton demonstrated a pair of aptitudes in this early period before the war. He had a knack for mixing up potions in the back room, and he had a habit of borrowing money and not paying it back. The two went together. Pemberton dreamed of making a vast fortune with his inventions, and he was likable and convincing enough to get others to put up the stakes. He managed to cajole the then enormous sum of $10,000 from his wife and her father, Colonel Elbert Lewis. A nephew recalled listening once as Pemberton mused about creating an artificial food that would be based exclusively on the body's needs. On that occasion, Pemberton had laughed at himself: "No chemist," he admitted ruefully, "can improve on milk, eggs, beefsteak, and cornbread." But he did not give up so easily in his other ambitions.

Pemberton's headstrong nature showed itself clearly during the Civil War. He joined the Confederate Army and was commissioned as a lieutenant colonel in the 3rd Georgia Cavalry, but he quit almost immediately because he disliked taking orders. He formed a pair of state militia units he could command himself, and he was wounded by shot and saber defending a bridge during the Battle of Columbus.

After the war, resuming his drug business in Columbus, Pemberton sold nutmeg and pepper to the government and began experimenting again with his kettles and percolators. Often he stayed up tinkering into the wee hours. This was the heyday of the patent medicine era, and Pemberton was anxious to stop selling other people's products and begin selling his own.

The postwar, sharecropper South was a region desperate for remedies of every sort. Most people suffered from inadequate diets, and the poor still subsisted on a so-called white diet of the three M's—meat, meal, and molasses—that led to widespread malnutrition. In rural areas, undrained swamps were like giant petri dishes, crawling with disease. The long, hot Southern summers bred insects, spoiled food, and drove children outside barefoot where they caught hookworm. Many households lacked even the rudimentary sanitation of the outhouse. Confederate veterans returned home with aching, lingering wounds and maladies. On top of it all, the region's poverty and rural isolation led to a grinding, dispiriting boredom that made many Southerners susceptible to the relief found in little brown bottles that contained alcohol or laudanum and other opiates.

There was nothing the least bit funny about the forces of ignorance and impoverishment that scourged the South, but no one with a touch of larceny in his heart could contemplate the various cures and nostrums on the market without an appreciative chuckle and a touch of envy. The sheer audacity of the claims made on behalf of some of the elixirs was breathtaking. A pharmaceutical house in Philadelphia, for instance, was selling something called Stadiger's Aurantii for $1 a bottle and promising in newspaper ads that it would cure torpidity of the liver, biliousness, nervous dyspepsia, indigestion, irregularity of the bowels, constipation, flatulence, eructations and burning of the stomach, miasma, malaria, bloody flux, chills and fever, chronic diarrhea, breakbone fever, loss of appetite, headache, foul breath, irregularities incidental to females, bearing-down pains, and backache. Whole pages of the newspaper were devoted to products and pitches worthy of P. T. Barnum (including some by Barnum himself). If people would buy "Dr. Dye's Celebrated Voltaic Belt with Electric Suspensory Appliances, for Nervous, Debilitated Young Men," surely they would buy anything.

Pemberton wanted to get in on the act. The thing he lacked was capital, and he went looking for it in Atlanta.

In 1870, Pemberton, his wife, and their teenage son Charles, joined the 21,789 souls who were hard at work trying to rebuild Atlanta.

The city was founded in 1837 as the southern railhead of the Western and Atlantic Railroad and was burned to the ground by General Sherman during his march to the sea in 1864. Six years later, it was a study in contrasts: a raw, unfinished place, but one full of towering aspirations. The streets were not yet paved—the city code provided a fine of $100 or thirty days in jail for any merchant who swept paper, fuel, slop, or washings out the door on the dusty downtown boulevards—but the DeGive Opera House was completed in plenty of time for the celebrated actor Edwin Forrest to visit on tour and play Hamlet.

In the agrarian South, other cities moved at the seasonal pace of planting and harvest, but Atlanta was born to the clack of the rails and the fast rhythm of commerce. Atlanta's cash crop was cash. With the collapse of the South's plantation economy, country stores sprouted up in small towns and crossroads communities all across the region, and Atlanta was a natural distribution center for the goods that stocked the shelves. At times it seemed everyone in town was a carpetbagger, ex-sutler, Yankee drummer, immigrant peddler, or former farm boy trying to make himself over into a real-life Rhett Butler.

Nothing symbolized Atlanta's hunger for wealth and respectability more than the hotel that was thrown open to the public on October 17, 1870. Operating mostly on borrowed money, Hannibal I. Kimball, a financier of such aggression he was called "a steam engine in breeches," built the largest public accommodation in the South in a record time of seven months. The six-story Kimball House, topped with a mansard roof and ornamental towers, was the first building in Atlanta with passenger elevators and a central heating plant. There was no particular *need* for a new hotel so huge and grand, but as the *Atlanta Constitution* exulted in a page-one story, it was "a brilliant augury of our assured development and commercial importance." With its $20,000 worth of Brussels carpeting and parlors filled with gold-mounted walnut furniture, the Kimball House stood as an announcement to the world that the city of Atlanta was open for business.

Fittingly, Doc Pemberton ended up in the lobby of the Kimball House. In a city bursting with commercial energy, he found the epicenter and set up shop. In the coming years, Pemberton ran a succession of retail and wholesale drug outlets and formed more than a dozen partnerships and corporations with investors who pumped thousands of dollars into his new sideline of proprietary medicines. Pemberton's fanciful inventions included Indian Queen Hair Dye, Gingerine, Triplex liver Pills, and a blood fortifier called Compound Extract of Stillingia or Queen's Delight His first modest financial success was with a croup cure known as Globe Flower Cough Syrup.

During the 1870s, Pemberton gained prominence. His laboratories were used by the state of Georgia to test agricultural chemicals, and one of his employees became the first state chemist. When the state created an examining and licensing board for pharmacists, Pemberton served as a charter member. By all accounts, Pemberton was a popular and respected figure in the community. A newspaper reporter described his "pleasant, benign face. . .patriarchal beard and kindly eyes."

Yet there was a growing sentiment among a small group of his former partners that Pemberton could not be trusted. A man named A. F. Merrill filed suit in 1876, claiming that Pemberton sold him the rights to Globe Flower Cough Syrup and Compound Extract of Stillingia for $6,000— $4,000 in cash and two notes of $1,000 each—but refused to transfer the formulas and ingredients and later resold the same rights to other people. Other lawsuits leveled similar accusations.

Still, Pemberton was doing well enough in 1879 that he began withdrawing from the drug business to give his full attention to manufacturing proprietary medicines. His next product was his most successful. It involved a new drug with remarkable properties that Pemberton thought gave "a sense of increased intelligence and a feeling as though the body was possessed of a new power formerly unknown to the individual. . . ." Cocaine.

At lunch one day in the summer of 1884, Ulysses S. Grant bit into a peach and felt a stinging pain so sharp he thought he might have swallowed a bee. It was not until autumn that the former president saw his doctor and learned he had cancer of the throat. By then it was too late.

Grant's slow, lingering death became a subject of morbid fascination all across the country. Despite the scandals that tarnished his second term in the White House, Grant was still the most beloved public figure in the United States. He was even admired in the South, whose people he had defeated in war. The newspapers in New York City, where Grant lived, set up a spirited competition to disclose as many lurid details about the old general's suffering as they could. One enterprising reporter bragged about seducing a servant girl in an apartment across 66th Street so he could gain access to a window and spy into Grant's bedroom.

As the months passed, Grant decided to cooperate in the death watch. In the spring he was moved to a cottage at Mount McGregor in the Adirondacks, and on mornings when he felt up to it he would dress in a suit, top hat, and slippers and sit on the porch in a wicker chair while tourists filed by to pay their final respects. Grant gave his doctors wide latitude to disclose the particulars of his worsening condition and even agreed to let selected reporters enter his sickroom and observe him. One account described how Grant, unable to swallow because of the agony, dribbled soup down his chin.

One of the things the American people learned about Grant's illness was that he gained relief from his dreadful, wracking pain by using a new miracle drug called cocaine. Some newspapers were so unfamiliar with the substance they called it "cocoacine," but they explained that it was applied both locally as an anesthetic and internally to provide comfort.

The man who provided the cocaine for Grant, and who made sure through promotions and advertising that as many people as possible knew that he did, was a Corsican-born, Paris-based chemist and entrepreneur named Angelo Mariani. Well before Sigmund Freud wrote his treatise *Uber Coca*, well before Arthur Conan Doyle created Sherlock Holmes and his "seven percent solution," Angelo Mariani was hard at work selling the world on the wondrous properties of the coca leaf.

Peruvians had been chewing coca leaves for stimulation for centuries, of course, but it was only in the mid-1800s that European doctors succeeded in isolating the active alkaloid, cocaine, and found that it made an excellent local anesthetic useful in eye, nose, and throat surgery. One of the pioneers, a Parisian doctor named Charles Fauvel, introduced the drug to his pharmacist, Mariani, who in turn began thinking of ways to get this miracle drug on the market. Mariani tried mixing cocaine with a variety of other ingredients (including tea and pâté) but found his greatest success with a wine-and-cocaine cordial he named Vin Mariani. By the early 1880s, from his sprawling brick factory on the Rue de Chartres in suburban Paris, Mariani was directing a global enterprise.

Mariani's favorite promotion was the use of endorsements by celebrities, and over the years he assembled quite a remarkable roster. President Grant's physicians, Drs. Fordyce Barker, John H. Douglas, and George Shrady, furnished statements praising Vin Mariani. So did Sarah Bernhardt, William McKinley, Thomas Edison, Pope Pius X, Emile Zola, Lillian Russell, Henry Irving, and ex-Emperor Don Pedro of Brazil. Some of the testimonials Mariani collected may have been forged or sent in by underlings, but in all he eventually published fourteen leather-bound volumes containing statements of tribute from hundreds of composers, artists, singers, actors, writers, and other luminaries. Almost all of them sounded genuinely enthusiastic. *

Exactly what Vin Mariani *did* for its devotees is a matter of some guesswork. Mariani's formula called for one-tenth of a grain of cocaine per ounce, and the recommended dosage was a "claret-glass" three times a day, after meals. Assuming a wine glass held five ounces, a consumer would ingest a grain and a half a day, or by modern measure about one hundred milligrams—roughly equivalent to the familiar "line" of cocaine that users were snorting in the form of white powder a century later. There is no scientific measure for determining what constitutes a "buzz," but it seems safe to assume that Vin Mariani provided one, especially at 22 proof.

The popularity of Vin Mariani inspired imitations on both sides of the Atlantic. In the United States, for example, Parke Davis & Company trotted out a Coca Cordial, and in Atlanta, Doc Pemberton created Pemberton's French Wine of Coca.

Pemberton made no pretense of originality. The recipe for wine coca was available from the French Pharmaceutical Codex and other sources, and he admitted later to a reporter that he "followed very closely the most approved French formula." Pemberton did make one slight adjustment, however, by adding in a pinch of another popular new drug, extract of the African kola nut.

Pemberton set up his new operation at 59 South Broad Street in downtown Atlanta, hired a small work force of laborers, and began manufacturing French Wine of Coca in tall, English-style flint bottles for sale at $1 apiece. Sales of French Wine of Coca took off toward the end of 1884, and Pemberton claimed that on one memorable Saturday in the summer of 1885 he sold 888 bottles. At the age of fifty-four, after years of striving, Doc Pemberton had a success on his hands.

---

* By far the most arresting endorsement came from the French sculptor Frédéric-Auguste Bartholdi, creator of the Statue of Liberty, who wrote that if he had discovered Vin Mariani and started using it earlier, "it is very probable that [the statue] would have attained the height of several hundred metres."

To make the most of it, he needed fresh capital and new partners. He started by finding a new landlord. Ed Holland, the son of one of Atlanta's pioneer bankers, was renting out his family's old house at 107 Marietta Street. The two-story redbrick structure, three blocks from the center of downtown on the main east-west thoroughfare, had been overtaken by commercial development and the top floor was run as a boarding house. One observer, describing the impoverished residents in their dark frocks and coats, likened the place to an "old rookery," as if its second story were a perch for blackbirds.

In the closing days of 1885, Pemberton moved into the Holland house. He set up his office and a storage and sales room on the ground floor facing the street and assembled his manufacturing laboratories in the back room and basement He rigged up a funnel between the floors and filled it with fine, white Chattahoochee River bottom sand to filter the French Wine of Coca as it trickled down into a metal trough and settling tank below. The basement contained the forty-gallon brass kettle he used for heating and mixing his other medicines. There was a Matthews bottling machine (which looked like a small Victorian monument set into the middle of a workbench) under a coal shed out in the backyard.

It was a distinctive operation, hard to miss, and Pemberton found that he had no need to go searching for his new partners. They came looking for him.

Frank Robinson and David Doe were strangers in town. They arrived in Atlanta in December 1885 lugging a color printing press, hoping to start an advertising business.

The two men were old friends, natives of Maine who ran a general store together in the years after the Civil War and later headed west. After an up-and-down string of modest successes and bankruptcies in small towns in Iowa, they turned their sights south.

A newspaperman sent Robinson and Doe around to see Pemberton, where they quickly struck an agreement. Pemberton would make his patent medicines, and Robinson and Doe would print the ads and handle the promotional end. The deal made so much sense that Holland joined in as a principal, too, turning over title to his premises in exchange for a share of the business. The Pemberton Chemical Company was incorporated in January 1886.

Robinson gambled everything he had on the venture. Like Doe, he put up his half of the printing press, and he also got his brother Charles to invest $6,500. Their father, J. L., put in another $500, and two friends contributed $6,000.

Trained as an accountant, with a bookkeeper's patient, methodical habits, Robinson made an unlikely entrepreneur. Certainly he did not look or act the part. He was short and solid, and his manner was quiet and polite to the point of timidity. His eyes held a fixed expression that could only be characterized as baleful. An acquaintance once described him as "a little dried-up fellow." Yet his life was dotted with episodes of risk-taking. Born in East Corinth, Maine, in 1845, Robinson was underage when he ran away from home to join the Union Army, where he gained enlistment after rocking upward on the stiff soles of his boots to add a couple of inches to his height. He served until a bout of typhoid fever led to his discharge. Later, going west after the war, he built the first house in Sibley, Iowa, and was elected county auditor.

Robinson threw himself into his new business in Atlanta. Not content with minding the books upstairs, he joined Pemberton in the basement as a sort of sorcerer's apprentice, learning his way around the laboratory and helping to brew the line of medicines.

Most significant, he encouraged Pemberton to experiment with a new product.

There is a common misconception that Coca-Cola evolved from French Wine of Coca. The voters of Atlanta narrowly approved a referendum on November 25, 1885, calling for local prohibition, and it was scheduled to go into effect July 1, 1886. Some historians have speculated that Pemberton, checkmated at his moment of triumph by a law banning alcohol, retreated to the lab, removed the wine from French Wine of Coca, and emerged with a non-alcoholic substitute, Coca-Cola. It makes a tidy theory, but it isn't true. The local law closed the saloons—P. J. Kenny, whose name survived to grace the main alley of the entertainment and retail complex Underground Atlanta a century later, shut his doors and took up selling boots—but other liquor sales were unaffected.

Actually, the impetus behind the development of Coca-Cola was a bit more mercenary. By 1886, Atlanta had five soda fountains operating during the summer months, and the principals of Pemberton Chemical wanted a beverage they could sell by the glass. At 75 cents or $1 a bottle, even the most popular patent medicines had a limited market and tended to appeal to those who were sick or thought they were. But almost everyone could afford a nickel for a soft drink, and the potential clientele included anyone who got thirsty during the frying-pan heat of Atlanta's summer season.

The trick was finding the right formula. Carbonated, fruit-flavored soft drinks had been around since the early 1800s—the *U.S. Pharmacopoeia* of 1820 gave directions for making a sarsaparilla syrup—and by Pemberton's time several proprietary brands were coming on the market, including Hires root beer, Clicquot Club sparkling cider, White Rock ginger ale, and a Boston-based novelty called Moxie.

But there was no such thing as a "cola" soft drink. In fact, there was no such thing as *cola*. Kola was the generally accepted spelling and shorthand name for a species of tree, *Kola acuminata*, found in West Africa. At around the same time European doctors were discovering the remarkable properties of the coca leaf, they also stumbled on the seeds of the kola fruit, and some thought (or at least hoped) they had found another miracle drug.

Commercially, kola burst upon the scene in 1881, thanks to a prominent London druggist named Thomas Christy, who mailed samples to drug houses across Europe and in the United States trying to drum up business. Proponents of the kola "nut" (as the seed was popularly misidentified) began making claims on behalf of their discovery that were even more elaborate than those put forward for cocaine.

The problem, however, was that the kola nut's active ingredient turned out to be caffeine. Unlike cocaine, which proved to be quite a potent drug indeed, kola had no greater curative powers than a cup of tea. In spite of the ardent promotions and exaggerations of die-hard believers, kola failed to catch on with the public as a remedy. But Pemberton had an inspiration. His idea, as he heated and stirred the contents of his brass kettle in the spring of 1886, was to create a soft drink with extract of kola as its base—a soft drink that could, in theory, compete with tea and coffee. In the hot South, a cool, carbonated substitute for the traditionally hot caffeine beverages just might make a fortune.

The stumbling block, Pemberton found, was that liquid extract of kola was extremely bitter and astringent, noticeable and disagreeable even in tiny amounts. He conducted extensive trial-and-error experiments, but one associate who visited regularly during that period recalled that the results he sampled were "an awful mixture." There simply was no way to put in enough kola extract to have an effective amount of caffeine without making a syrup that curled people's lips. People might accept and even appreciate foul taste in a medicine, but not in a beverage.

Eventually, as the weeks passed, Pemberton gave up on kola extract and began working on a different approach. His breakthrough came when he tried cutting the amount of kola extract in the syrup to a tiny drop and substituting synthetic caffeine in its place. "Pure" caffeine, in the form of a dry, white powder, came from several natural sources—tea, coffee, kola, and cocoa, for example—and in Pemberton's case, he turned to the German pharmaceutical house Merck for caffeine obtained by removing the starch, gum, resins, and other constituent elements from kola.

The synthetic caffeine was bitter, too, but not nearly so overpowering as the kola extract. Pemberton discovered that he could mask the taste of the caffeine with sugar and other ingredients, and he began refining a recipe that would please—or at least not assault—the nostrils. At last he stood on the verge of inventing Coca-Cola. Down in the basement of the Holland house, Pemberton filled his forty-gallon kettle with plain water, which he then heated to a boil over an open fire. Using a wooden paddle to stir the solution, he melted in sugar and caffeine. Next, he added caramel for coloring, giving the syrup its dark, distinctive, port-wine color. * To balance the

* Caramel in the form of burnt sugar (not to be confused with the tan-colored, chewy candy that has the same name) was widely used as a coloring agent in patent

sweetness of the sugar and give the syrup its "tang," he added lime juice, citric acid, and phosphoric acid.

Then, as the basic blend cooled, Pemberton turned to the question of flavor. Into the mix went vanilla extract, elixir of orange, and several pungent oils refined from various fruits, herbs, and trees: lemon, nutmeg, spicebush, coriander, and neroli, the last an ingredient in perfumes distilled from the flower of the orange tree. The most exotic component was oil of cassia, also known as Chinese cinnamon, made from the bark of a tree found in the tropical regions of Asia.

And, of course, Pemberton added to this brew the fluid extract of coca leaves. Exactly how much cocaine went into the inaugural batch of Doc Pemberton's new soft drink syrup is impossible to calculate more than a century later, but even a touch of the drug, in combination with the sugar and caffeine—four times the amount in today's Coke, or about the same as a strong cup of coffee—made Pemberton's concoction quite a stimulating beverage.

In April and early May of 1886, Pemberton dispatched runners from his basement to Willis Venable's soda fountain three blocks away with small samples of his concoction for taste tests by the customers. Venable, the self-styled "Soda Water King of the South," operated a popular business (with a twenty-five-foot-long marble counter) on the ground floor of Jacobs' Pharmacy at 2 Peachtree Street, in the exact center of downtown Atlanta known as Five Points. Legend has it that Venable "accidentally" served the new syrup with carbonated water, but actually the plan from the very outset was to squirt it into a glass and sprite it with cold, carbonated water from the fountain. Years later, Frank Robinson recalled that as Pemberton made his adjustments in the formula for the new syrup, "it was taken to Mr. Venable's soda fountain for the purpose of trying it and ascertaining whether it was something the people would like or not." After various modifications, Robinson reported in his dry, undramatic way, "It seemed to be satisfactory."

What it lacked was a name. Each of the four partners in Pemberton Chemical submitted a suggestion, and Robinson carried the day. Not everyone appreciated his cleverness: Venable found the name Coca-Cola so hard to remember, he admitted later, that he had to write it down. Nonetheless, on Saturday, May 29, 1886, the *Atlanta Journal* carried a small block of type on the patent medicine page:

> Coca-Cola. Delicious! Refreshing! Exhilarating! Invigorating! The New and Popular Soda Fountain Drink, containing the properties of the wonderful Coca plant and the famous Cola nuts. For sale by Willis Venable and Nunnally & Rawson.

It was the first Coca-Cola ad.

---

medicines. Among other things, it helped conceal any foreign matter that might fall, crawl, or fly into the vat during preparation.

And it was almost the last.

Pemberton fell ill soon after perfecting Coca-Cola and the whole business foundered. A painful inflammation of the stomach and intestines that had tortured him for years flared up anew, and Pemberton took to his sick bed in the small house—more like a cottage, located a few miles east of town—that he shared with his wife.*

Pemberton Chemical fell quiet. After a promising couple of weeks at Venable's, Nunnally & Rawson's, and the other soda fountains in town, sales of Coca-Cola fell off and its ads abruptly disappeared. During the whole summer, only twenty-five gallons were sold, bringing in less than $50. David Doe gave up. He pulled out of the business and left town, taking the printing press he and Robinson owned with him.

But Robinson stayed. He believed Coca-Cola was a good product. It had an appealing taste (although some said you had to try it a second time to appreciate it fully). It had stimulating properties likely to improve the mood and boost the energy of almost any customer, and a customer could be almost anyone. It was priced right, and it could be sold not just once in a while, but over and over again, several times a day. Its only shortcoming was that few people knew what it was or even that it existed. There was no demand for Coca-Cola, Robinson figured, because nothing quite like it had ever been offered before. It simply had to be advertised.

Robinson set out to give Coca-Cola another chance. He spent months working on the design of the trademark, carefully drawing the flowing script of the letters. He went to a local engraver, Frank Ridge, for a smooth, finished version. In the fall of 1886, he had a woodcut made by the James P. Harrison Company so that the trademark could be printed on cards and distributed. In the spring of 1887, Robinson helped bring Coca-Cola back to life by passing out "sampling" tickets around Atlanta. The trick was to get people to try Coca-Cola, and a ticket was good for two free glasses. Using the city directory, Robinson mailed tickets to the homes of prominent citizens. He arranged for a promotional endorsement of Coca-Cola, on Pemberton's stationery, from Willis Venable: "'Tis growing rapidly in favor; gives pleasure to my customers and profit to myself." Robinson also

---

* One intriguing possibility is that along with gastroenteritis, Pemberton may also have developed a drug habit. Cocaine, swallowed in the form of the liquid extract available from the shelves of his lab, would have provided relief from the intense discomfort of his condition, and he would hardly have been the first pharmacist of his time to sample the wares. In a court case years later, two disgruntled former associates testified that he was, in the phrasing of the time, a "dope fiend." They might have been exaggerating or lying, but there is no question that Pemberton's son was an addict. After ten days of "intense suffering," Charley Pemberton died in 1894 of an overdose of opium.

oversaw the manufacture of an inventory of retail advertising materials, including 500 street car signs, 1,600 posters, 45 tin signs, and oilcloth hangers for the soda fountains, all ready for deployment around Atlanta. Starting April 1, 1887, Pemberton Chemical even signed up a salesman, Woolfolk Walker, who traveled by train to various Southern cities taking orders for the company's line of products.

By early summer, Robinson had logged orders for nearly a thousand gallons of Coca-Cola syrup from druggists and soda fountain operators in Atlanta, Columbus, Birmingham, Memphis, and several small cities in Georgia. It seemed the new soft drink just might be a success after all.

On June 6, 1887, in the midst of this mild boom, Doc Pemberton applied to the U.S. Patent Office to register the label of "Coca-Cola Syrup & Extract." On June 28, the trademark was granted. But there was something a bit unusual about it. It wasn't in the name of the Pemberton Chemical Company. It was in Pemberton's name as an individual.

Pemberton had fallen sick again, and as always he needed money. He decided to sell Coca-Cola to Venable, the soda fountain man, but there was a catch. Venable was broke, too, having just bought a house in Atlanta's West End.

In early July 1887, Pemberton called an old friend, an investor and proprietary medicine salesman named George Lowndes, out to the cottage. Lowndes found him bedridden. "I am sick," Pemberton told him, "and I don't believe I will ever get out of this bed." Pemberton explained what he had in mind, and the two men quickly agreed on a deal. Lowndes would put up the money, Venable would be his working partner, and together they would own two-thirds of the rights to Coca-Cola. In exchange, Lowndes would give Pemberton an interest-free $1,200 loan. On July 8, 1887, the three men signed a contract, and the two outsiders took a controlling interest in Coca-Cola.

The partners in Pemberton Chemical were completely left out When Robinson found out what had happened, he felt he'd been stabbed in the back. Despite his meek manner, Robinson was a man with a vivid sense of right and wrong. He wanted his stake in Coca-Cola restored, and he was willing to fight to get it back.

One day shortly after Pemberton struck his deal, Robinson and Ed Holland, the other injured party, happened to be walking near the Fulton County courthouse in downtown Atlanta. It was a "Sales Day," when foreclosed property was auctioned on the courthouse steps. Naturally, quite a few lawyers were milling around. Holland recognized one of them as an old family friend, John S. Candler, and introduced him to Robinson. As the three men stood talking on the street corner in the hot sun, Robinson spilled out his story and urged Candler to take the case.

Candler, just twenty-five years old but already a prominent attorney in town, did not see much hope. He knew Doc Pemberton and was fond of him, but he also knew Pemberton's reputation in business. Nevertheless he agreed to go see Pemberton on Robinson's behalf.

"I found him lying on a bed," Candler recounted later, "not under cover but his coat off—I remember very well, his wife met me and I went in to see him and told him what they had said."

Pemberton listened quietly while Candler laid out Robinson's and Holland's case. Yes, Pemberton admitted, he had sold the rights to Coca-Cola, but he denied that the rights ever belonged to Pemberton Chemical. Robinson and Holland, he insisted, owned no part of Coca-Cola. Then he added bleakly, "It don't make much difference, though, even if they did have any rights. I don't know how you would get anything out of me." Candler never forgot the exhausted resignation in Pemberton's voice: "That's the way he put it: 'I don't know how you would get anything out of me.'"

A day or two later, Candler showed Robinson into his office and explained that it was pointless to proceed. There would be no lawsuit because there were no assets to recover. Pemberton was penniless. "I don't much care for your case on any contingent fee [basis]," Candler told Robinson, laughingly ruefully. It was time to give up.

But Candler did perform one favor for the little man. He brought Robinson's plight to the attention of his brother, Asa.

The Candlers were one of the most remarkable families in Georgia. John was the youngest of eleven children born to Samuel Charles Candler and his wife, Martha Beall Candler. The father was a planter, miner, developer, and merchant in Villa Rica, a town thirty-six miles west of Atlanta. Their sprawling house, on what was then the fringe of the wilderness, was a place of culture, complete with a private library and grand piano.

Several of the children achieved distinction. The eldest, Milton, was a state legislator, a captain in the Confederate Army, and later a four-term congressman from Atlanta. Another son, Ezekiel, practiced law in Mississippi and sired a congressman who served for years from that state. A third son, Warren, was the leading bishop in the Southern Methodist Church. John Candler went on to serve on the Georgia Supreme Court.

Asa Griggs Candler, the eighth child, was the most exceptional of all. He was born in 1851 and showed an early interest in medicine. But the Civil War interrupted his schooling and stripped his family of their land and most of their wealth. After completing only seven years of formal education, Candler apprenticed himself to two doctors in Cartersville, Georgia, in the early 1870s, and then ventured to Atlanta to make his way as a druggist.

Wearing homemade clothes, Candler arrived in Atlanta on July 7, 1873, with exactly $1.75 in his pockets, and spent the day walking the streets, looking for work. One of his many unsuccessful stops was at Pemberton's store in the lobby of the Kimball House. It was after nightfall when Candler finally landed a menial job with another pharmacist, George J. Howard, who put him to work on the spot until the store closed at midnight.

For a while, Candler slept on a cot in the basement of Howard's store at 47 Peachtree Street. The ceiling of the room was so low he had to stoop when he stood, though he was only five foot six. One of his duties was to answer the doorbell late at night if customers called for emergency prescriptions.

Candler did not intend to stay in the cellar for long, like Pemberton, he had the heart of an entrepreneur. As a teenager, Candler made his first dollar when he chased a wild mink through the woods, cornered it—taking a nasty bite on his right forearm in the process—and sent the skin to market. Soon he organized a mink-trapping operation with several neighbors around Villa Rica. He also made money buying straight pins from Atlanta and reselling them in the country. Unlike Pemberton, Candler had a head for business, and he quickly prospered in Atlanta. Howard soon made him the store's chief clerk, and in 1877 Candler started his own business.

Candler's boldness extended to romance as well as commerce. He is remembered for the prim, wintry rectitude of his later public life, but at twenty-six he was a young swain with wide-set expressive blue eyes and a streak of daring. He fell in love with George Howard's teenage daughter, Lucy Elizabeth, known as Lizzie, and defied all of Howard's desperate attempts to forbid the alliance. Howard bitterly opposed his daughter's marriage to a man who had been his employee, but Candler pushed ahead with their engagement anyway. Howard refused to attend their wedding and for several months would not even speak to the young couple. Eventually, though, he relented. In a formal letter to Asa, more than ten months after the ceremony, Howard offered stiffly to "'bury the hatchet' and be friendly in the future," and in 1882 the two men went back in business together, this time as partners. In 1886, Candler bought out the older man and became the sole proprietor of Asa G. Candler & Company.

By 1887, when he got to know Frank Robinson, Asa Candler was running a flourishing drug business, headquartered in a handsome, three-story brick building on Peachtree Street. He could afford to help a sad-faced, hard-luck character by giving him a little part-time work as a bookkeeper, and he did so. The job helped Robinson feed his wife and daughter.

In mid-July 1887, Lowndes and Venable concluded their deal with Pemberton by paying him $283.29 in cash for the physical assets of Coca-Cola: inventory, ingredients, advertising materials, and equipment, including the forty-gallon brass kettle. They sent a horse-drawn dray to 107 Marietta Street and had the goods carted to the basement of Jacobs' Pharmacy, where Venable leased a 3,000-square-foot space for storage.

Under the partnership agreement, Venable was to manufacture Coca-Cola syrup in his basement and sell it at his fountain on the ground floor, while Lowndes took charge of sales to other fountain operators and druggists in Atlanta and around the South.

"Orders began to come in and I went around to see how Venable was making out," Lowndes recalled later. "To my surprise I found all the material and fixtures set over in the corner of the basement. No effort had been made by Venable to make any syrup."

Venable was selling off the ten gallons of finished syrup that was part of the inventory they'd bought, but he wasn't producing any new syrup. He told Lowndes he was too busy serving customers. They argued, and Venable promised to do better. But a few weeks later, when Lowndes checked again, he found that Venable still hadn't made a drop of Coca-Cola. Venable continued to think the beverage had a promising future, but he discovered he had little enthusiasm for manufacturing it or trying to build a distributorship—and no capital to contribute to the venture in any case. He wanted out. Busy with his own work as a salesman, Lowndes decided to cut his losses and sell his and Venable's two-thirds share of Coca-Cola. He approached several drug proprietors in Atlanta, but all of them turned him down flat. Finally, in desperation, he approached Woolfolk Walker, the salesman at Pemberton Chemical. Like everyone else at the old company, Walker was nearly broke. He was boarding in a room at 107 Marietta Street because he couldn't afford other lodging. "Coca-Cola," he repeated to Lowndes. "Why, I couldn't buy a postage stamp. I haven't got a dollar."

"All right," Lowndes said, "but if you can go out and raise a thousand dollars on the outside, I will sell it to you for one thousand dollars cash and you can pay me the balance out of profits of the company."

Walker was tempted. It was a piece of luck that his youngest sister, Mrs. M. C. Dozier, had recently sold her house in Columbus and moved to Atlanta, planning to spend the proceeds on a new home. Walker asked her for the money. She refused, explaining that she and her husband needed the cash to put a roof over their heads. Her husband would be angry if she gave up the money. But Walker insisted. He was the oldest of seven children, she was the youngest, and he held sway over her. He took $1,200 from her, and on December 14, 1887, he bought Lowndes's two-thirds share of Coca-Cola.

The assets of Coca-Cola were moved back where they started, to the basement of Pemberton Chemical, and placed in storage, as if hibernating for the winter.

Frank Robinson observed the latest twist in the fortunes of Coca-Cola and saw an opportunity.

During the winter of 1888, he pitched Coca-Cola to Asa Candler over and over again. One day Robinson pointed out the window at a wagon full of empty beer kegs and told Candler that someday wagons might roll by filled with kegs of Coca-Cola. Initially, Candler was unenthusiastic. For one thing, his business didn't have a soda fountain. There would be no place to sell a soft drink. Then, too, Candler had ambitions of moving out of wholesale and retail drug sales and into the proprietary medicine field. He had acquired the rights to a tonic called Botanic Blood Balm and a dentifrice named De-Lec-Ta-Lave, along with a toilet water called Everlasting Cologne. He had little interest in taking on a fourth product. He told Robinson no.

Then something happened to change Candler's mind. He suffered from recurrent headaches and dyspepsia, the fruits of his long work hours and tightly wound personality. During a visit to Jacobs' Pharmacy one day, he sampled a Coca-Cola at Venable's suggestion and discovered that drinking it made him feel better. The carbonation in the soft drink alleviated his indigestion and the caffeine gave him relief from his headache. He found the results little short of a miracle.

Within days, Candler seized control of Coca-Cola. He eased Pemberton out, acquiring his one-third share by canceling an old debt of $550. Then he paid Walker and his sister $750 for half of their stake. That gave Candler a majority interest, and the first thing he did was to send Frank Robinson back down to 107 Marietta Street and put him in charge. After a year of struggle, Robinson was back on top.

DOC Pemberton died on August 16, 1888. The enteritis that had savaged his stomach and intestines and kept him in a sickbed claimed him at the age of fifty-seven.

His popularity remained intact among the many Atlantans who had avoided entering into business deals with him, and his fellow pharmacists closed their doors during the hour of his funeral to show respect for one of their own. They met in Asa Candler's office at 47 Peachtree Street to pay tribute to Pemberton, and Candler spoke of "his lovable nature and many virtues." Then Candler sent a one-horse wagon around to collect the physical resources of Coca-Cola and put them under his own roof for good.

Candler was now one of the most prosperous druggists in town. He could be found most days waiting on customers and preparing prescriptions on the ground floor of his business on Peachtree Street. At the age of thirty-seven, he was in his prime. His oldest child, Howard, then nine, could recall seeing his father hoist a twenty-pound, wicker-covered demijohn full of carbolic acid up onto his shoulder and hold it perfectly still while he poured off a measure into a glass graduate.

Along with his business success, Candler was cultivating a reputation for solemnity and personal probity. The rambunctious boy was gone, and in his place stood a teetotaler, an ardent non-smoker and active Sunday school teacher, a stiff man who wore starched collars. Every morning when he awoke, he made it a point to remind himself of Marcus Aurelius's motto, "Rise to a man's job." With his thin, downturned lips, Candler seemed to be greeting the world with serious moral purpose, and perhaps even a touch of parsimony in his heart. His eyes took on an icy glint. He was cursed with a high-pitched voice, yet he had a commanding aura and he made men respect him.

Candler brought Frank Robinson into the business as if he were a member of the family. Robinson was named general superintendent of Asa G. Candler & Company, given a desk in the office, and put in charge of compounding Candler's proprietary medicines down in the basement.

The first order of business was to refine the formula for Coca-Cola. At the beginning of the last season, Robinson had been swamped with complaints from soda fountain operators that the syrup turned rancid in storage. Because it lacked an adequate preservative, Coca-Cola syrup was highly unstable. Among other things, it had a tendency to begin fermenting. In addition, Pemberton had used tin cans as well as glass jars to market it, and the tin provoked a chemical reaction with the phosphoric acid. Experimenting together, Robinson and Candler added glycerine to the mix and found that it worked effectively as a preservative and smoothing agent. They got rid of the tin cans.

Then they began tinkering with the two name ingredients, coca and cola. Each presented a problem. The first stirrings of a national debate had begun over the negative aspects of cocaine, and manufacturers were growing defensive over charges that use of their products might lead to "cocainism" or the "cocaine habit." The full-throated fury against cocaine was still a few years off, and Candler and Robinson were anxious to continue promoting the supposed health benefits of the coca leaf, but there was no reason to risk putting more than a tiny bit of coca extract in their syrup. They cut the amount to a mere trace.

With extract of kola, the difficulty was the taste. Even with the tiny quantity Pemberton used, the bitterness was still noticeable and still disagreeable. Not only that, it was expensive—the dried nuts cost $20 per pound on the wharf in New York. So the extract of kola was cut to a minuscule amount as well. Candler and Robinson found themselves in the interesting position of preparing to market a product that contained very little of either ingredient in its trademark—an irony that would have profound legal implications (and shape an entire beverage industry) in the years to come.

In the interest of secrecy, Candler and Robinson stopped referring to the ingredients in their new formula by name and instead began calling them "merchandises." Merchandise No. 1 was sugar, No. 2 caramel, No. 3 caffeine, No. 4 phosphoric acid, No. 5 the combination of coca and kola extracts, No. 6 glycerine, and No. 7X the super-secret blend of flavoring oils.

Next, Candler tidied up his chain of title, buying out the final one-third share of the rights to Coca-Cola still held by Pemberton's old salesman Woolfolk Walker and his sister, Mrs. Dozier. Candler paid them $1,000, and Walker bade a shabby farewell to the Pemberton era by skipping town for Hot Springs, Arkansas, without saying good-bye or paying his sister back.

On May 1, 1889, at the start of the soda fountain season, Candler ran a big ad in the *Atlanta Journal* proclaiming his company "sole proprietors" of Coca-Cola.

Everything seemed to be in place, yet the success of Coca-Cola was still far from assured, and one reason was that Candler had his doubts about the appeal of the product. He was never entirely sure whether to advertise it as a simple refreshment or a curative patent medicine, and so he tried both, often in the same ad. Coca-Cola was "Delicious!" and "Refreshing!"—and at the same time it was a "brain tonic and nerve stimulant." Mostly, Candler retreated to the familiar, tried-and-untrue patter of patent medicines. He was very much a man of his times, and he was comfortable with the old-fashioned hyperbole of his craft. In a brochure he sent to druggists, Candler touted his top product, Botanic Blood Balm, by saying:

> When your blood is impure, when aches and pains trouble you, when sores break out on your person, when you feel weak, nervous and debilitated, when your appetite fails, when you are troubled with dyspepsia, when there is a general functional derangement of the system, when you feel all broke up and life hardly seems worth living, give B.B.B. a trial, and you will at once begin to grow better and stronger.

He took a similar tack with Coca-Cola. The same brochure contained druggists' endorsements of Coca-Cola as a cure for insomnia, neuralgia, headaches, and mental fatigue, and Candler even echoed the claims of the old French Wine of Coca by promising relief "where the voice has been inordinately excited by singing and speaking."

What really propelled Coca-Cola, in the end, was its ability to sell itself. In addition to advertising, Candler underwrote an aggressive sampling campaign for the drink that gave people a chance to try it for themselves for free. The deal was disarmingly simple. Druggists all across the South were asked to send Candler the names of 128 of their best customers— exactly the number of ounces in a gallon. Candler then wrote the customers directly, enclosing a ticket good for a free glass of Coca-Cola at their local soda fountain. The local druggist was then given *two* gallons of syrup: The first was to be used giving away the samples, and the second was for actual sales to "those who will certainly want more." At a nickel a drink, a druggist stood to pocket $6.40 if he could sell the second gallon. To succeed, of course, the gambit required people to like Coca-Cola, and to ask for it again and again, so that the druggist would reorder a third and fourth gallon and more, and start paying Candler his $2 per gallon wholesale price. It was an expensive proposition, one that went against Candler's grain, and Robinson had to prod him to keep accepting the front-end losses. But it worked.

In the summer of 1890, Candler's second season, sales of Coca-Cola syrup more than quadrupled to 8,855 gallons. In the soda fountains of the South, people were beginning to come in and ask for a Coke.

Early in 1891, Candler announced that he was quitting the drug business to go full-time into manufacturing his proprietary medicines. He and Robinson moved to a makeshift factory on the second and third floors of a three-story brick building at 42½ Decatur Street, in a rough section of Atlanta a block from the railroad tracks. It was not a grand enterprise. Their downstairs neighbors were a secondhand shop, the New York Clothing House, and Bob Parrish's pool hall. Candler's labor force consisted of a nephew, Sam Willard, and a black helper named George Curtwright, who toiled from Monday through Friday mixing Candler's top product, Botanic Blood Balm. On Saturdays they cleaned out the forty-gallon brass kettle and made Coca-Cola.

Production was a mess. Willard and Curtwright broke up wooden boxes for fuel to feed a crude brick furnace, brought the water in the kettle to a boil and heaved in bags of confectioner's sugar, caffeine, and caramel. They used wooden paddles to stir the bubbling syrup and try to keep it from scorching. Sometimes they miscalculated and the kettle boiled over. When that happened, sticky, scalding syrup would leak down the walls and through the ceiling below, and Candler had to pay for ruined clothes and other damages several times. Years later, describing the plant to a gathering of Coca-Cola salesmen, Candler shook his head at the memory. "We had a large copper kettle for boiling the syrup," he said, "and one big-footed Negro to handle the paddles. Boys, it was some equipment."

In the summer months, with no air conditioning, the work was hellishly hot. Willard and Curtwright were awash in sweat, and their feet slipped and slid in the moist sugar that spilled on the wooden platform around the kettle. The thick, sweet smell of molten sugar attracted hundreds of bees and yellow jackets that swarmed through the screenless open windows. On Sundays, the cooled-off syrup was pumped by hand into barrels, where the phosphoric acid, coca and kola, flavorings and glycerine were added, and the final product was, in Willard's phrase, "vigorously shaken and sent on its way." Quality control was invested in Frank Robinson's olfactory nerves: He sniffed and tasted a sample from each batch of syrup before giving it his blessing.

Deliveries of Coca-Cola were made by Curtwright's brother Bill on a dray pulled by a horse called "Ol' Bird." When Candler bought the first brass-mounted harness for the rig, Curtwright took pride in spending his Sunday mornings keeping it polished.

For all the crudeness of Coca-Cola's operations, however, sales continued to rise. In Atlanta and other cities across the South, druggists were beginning to appreciate the benefits of selling Coke. In the summer of 1891, Candler and Robinson sold 19,831 gallons of syrup, more than double the year before. As he reviewed his prospects that autumn, Candler realized that he had to have more money—a great deal more money, perhaps as much as $50,000 in cash—to move the factory, expand the production facilities, hire a sales staff (he had only a single full-time Coca-Cola salesman, George W. Little, who had to share Ol' Bird with Bill Curtwright), and pay for the exponential increases that would be necessary in the costs of advertising, sampling, inventory, and distribution.

Candler did not have that kind of money. Nor did he have enough credit to borrow it. And so, in the fall of 1891, he decided it was time to incorporate Coca-Cola, sell shares, and raise capital. Candler's idea was to keep half the company and sell the other half to major wholesalers in cities up North who would distribute the product. The Coca-Cola Company of Georgia was formed early in 1892, with Candler as president and Robinson as secretary. The corporation issued 1,000 shares with a value of $100 apiece, and Candler took exactly half. He gave ten shares to Frank Robinson and then offered the other 490 shares for sale through stock brokers in Baltimore, New York, Boston, and other cities.

Had all gone according to plan, Candler would have raised $49,000 in fresh capital. But there was a problem. Coca-Cola was a Southern phenomenon, virtually unknown up North, and no one seemed to want to take the risk. Only 75 shares were sold (to F. W. Prescott, a broker in Boston), yielding a meager $7,500 in new principal.

Asa Candler was stuck with the company. He would have to build Coca-Cola by himself.

Two

DOPE

With the failure of his stock offering in 1892, Asa Candler was forced to build the Coca-Cola Company slowly—by word of mouth.

His salesmen, several of whom were his nephews, rode the rails from town to town lugging trunks full of complimentary tickets ("Good for a 5¢ glass of Coca-Cola at the soda fountain of any druggist"), which they pressed on any bypasser who would slow down long enough to take one. From Atlanta, using a pair of stenographers, Candler wrote letters to thousands of people all across the country sending them free tickets and urging them to try his new soft drink. It was the nineteenth-century's version of a direct-mail and street-corner sampling campaign, and it worked. Before long, the company was redeeming $50,000 in tickets a year, good for a million free tastes.

"If you can imagine a small man with a fine voice raising particular Cain about advertising expenses, that little man was Uncle Asa when he would see the figures," recalled one of his nephews, J. J. Willard. "I don't think he ever believed how much this free sampling did to introduce Coca-Cola." Actually, Candler understood perfectly well how successful the strategy was, he simply hated giving away something for nothing. But his nephews and Frank Robinson kept prodding him and he went along. People tried Coca-Cola, liked it, and told their friends.

The company prospered. Coca-Cola survived the Panic of 1893 with surprising ease, demonstrating (as the Great Depression later confirmed) that people generally could afford a nickel for a small treat even in the worst economic times. Sales rose every year during the Gay Nineties and reached 281,000 gallons by the end of the decade. The syrup factory was moved and expanded twice to meet the burgeoning demand. Gradually, steadily, an ever thickening stream of customers went to their local drugstores on spring and summer days, stepped up to the cool marble of the soda fountain and ordered Coca-Cola.

Except they didn't always ask for it by name. More and more often, they were starting to say, "Give me a Dope," or "a Coke" or "a shot in the arm." There was a dark side to Coca-Cola's success story, a whispering campaign that went along with the word of mouth. People believed that Candler must be putting something in his drink, and they thought that something was cocaine.

———

In the summer of 1891, Candler drew a quart of Coca-Cola syrup from a ten-gallon keg and shipped it to Dr. H. R. Slack in LaGrange, Georgia.

Dr. Slack was president of the Georgia Pharmaceutical Association and chemical examiner for the Georgia State Board of Pharmacy. Candler asked him to test the syrup and find out if it had any cocaine.

Yes, Dr. Slack answered, it did. He added, however, "The quantity of cocaine is so small that it would be simply impossible for anyone to form the cocaine habit from drinking Coca-Cola, for it would require about thirty glasses, as usually drawn from the fount, to make an ordinary dose of the drug."

The Slack report presented Candler with a challenge. He and Robinson figured they had removed the cocaine from Coca-Cola, or at least reduced it to an undetectable trace, when they modified the formula three years earlier. It now seemed that no matter how drastically they cut back the fluid extract of coca leaves in the syrup, a sophisticated chemical analysis would find a bit of cocaine. And not just a completely innocent bit: An "ordinary dose" of cocaine, as defined by most pharmacists at the time, was one full grain. If Coca-Cola had one-thirtieth of a grain; it meant that heavy Coca-Cola drinkers might—*might*—feel some effects after several glasses. Candler could not afford the risk of putting even a small amount of cocaine in his drink, certainly not when women and children were among its many enthusiasts.

But neither could Candler take the simple step of eliminating the fluid extract of coca leaves from the formula. Candler believed that his product's name had to be descriptive, and that he must have at least some byproduct of the coca leaf in the syrup (along with some kola) to protect his right to the name Coca-Cola. Protecting the name was critical. Candler had no patent on the syrup itself. Anyone could make an imitation. But no one could put the label "Coca-Cola" on an imitation so long as Candler owned the name. The name was the thing of real value, and the registered trademark was its only safeguard. Coca leaves had to stay in the syrup.

Returning to the laboratory, Candler and Robinson worked anew at modifying the formula, and finally devised a tincture of coca and kola that had almost no active properties at all. The coca leaves and kola nuts were mixed together (in a 3-to-1 ratio) and ground up into powder, packed into a rectangular, watertight wooden box, marinated in grain alcohol, white wine, and lime phosphate for twenty-four hours, then drained with steaming hot water. The resultant bitter liquid had a brilliant, light brown color and was nicknamed "tea" by the factory workers. Officially, in the secret formula, it became the new "Merchandise No. 5." Only an ounce and a half went into each gallon of syrup.

So far as Candler could tell, Coca-Cola was now entirely free of cocaine, and he might have been better off to say so. Candler wanted his beverage to have a good reputation, to be a cut above mere "bellywash," as other soft drinks were called. But for some reason, Candler could never bring himself to abandon the suggestive, overblown language of the earliest promotions for coca and kola as patent medicines.

In his sampling letters, Candler wrote that Coca-Cola was a "scientific combination" of coca and kola, that it cured headaches, calmed the nerves, strengthened the muscles, and provided "mental clearness." He published a brochure saying Coca-Cola renewed "the vigor of the intellect."

It seems that Candler, a man of such exuberant virtue that he began the company's annual meetings by leading the singing of "Onward Christian Soldiers," bent to temptation. He tried to have it both ways. He was quick to denounce accusations that Coca-Cola was addictive. "As you doubtless know," he wrote a preacher, "I do not propose to vend a poison." He told the *Atlanta Daily* World in 1892 that he would abandon the business on the spot if anyone could authenticate a single case of cocaine addiction. Yet there was no flat denial, no categorical statement that Coca-Cola was free from cocaine, and no retreat from the carnival barker's spiel. Candler insinuated that his soft drink had curative, perhaps even intoxicating powers, when it did not.

And people believed him. After all, Coca-Cola *was* invigorating. It gave people a boost. Drinking one was like having a cup of coffee with five teaspoonfuls of sugar. Thanks to the secrecy of the formula, no one knew for certain what was providing the stimulation, but it was easy enough to imagine that it was cocaine. Customers began referring to a glassful of Coca-Cola as "a dose." Even some of Candler's closest friends, among them Joseph Jacobs, whose drugstore was the site of the first serving of Coca-Cola, believed that the drink contained the drug. The idea quickly became an article of faith and part of the folklore, especially in the South. Coca-Cola's double life, myth versus reality, was established.

There were consequences.

When the federal government began its twenty-year war of attrition with the Coca-Cola Company, the immediate issue wasn't cocaine. It was money.

To provide part of the financing for the Spanish-American War, Congress passed a stamp tax on medicines, effective July 1, 1898. The commissioner of Internal Revenue, citing the health claims of the company's advertising, ordered the federal tax collector for Georgia to begin assessing the levy on Coca-Cola. Asa Candler vehemently disagreed. During the three-year life of the tax, he grudgingly ponied up $29,502 and paid the government under protest. Then, even before the formal repeal of the act in 1901, he sued to get back every penny, with interest.

Suing the federal government was a risky proposition, and Candler knew it. From a strictly financial point of view, it was absurd. In December 1898, Candler had stood on the steps in front of Coca-Cola's brand-new headquarters in Atlanta and pronounced the block-long, three-story flatiron building "sufficient for all our needs for all time to come." Just three years later, the company was outgrowing the place. By 1901, Coca-Cola's annual sales had accelerated to nearly 500,000 gallons, and the company's gross revenues were approaching the $1 million mark. Candler built branch factories in Dallas, Chicago, Baltimore, and Los Angeles, and opened sales offices in Philadelphia, New York, and other cities. Though sales were heaviest in the South, Coca-Cola was becoming a national product, available in every state of the union.

Looking ahead to 1902, Candler practically rubbed his hands: "If our collections are as good as last year," he told his family, "this is going to be an excellent year financially." He was selling syrup as fast as he could manufacture it. The company ran out of the cream-colored ceramic urns it awarded to druggists after they sold their first thirty-five gallons of syrup. Business was good. Letting the government keep a few thousand dollars would not have hurt a bit, especially since the tax was only temporary.

But Candler's personality came into play, and one incident in particular from the period may explain how his mind worked. Candler's eldest son, Howard, who was working for the company in New York City, discovered that one of his fellow salesmen was a drunk and reported the matter to his father. Asa Candler sent instructions to the New York office manager to investigate. "I have never allowed any person of bad morals to remain in the employ of this Company in any capacity after discovering his unworthiness," Candler wrote. The man was to be fired, but only if there was "indubitable evidence" and independent corroboration of Howard's accusations against him. Candler would not simply take his son's word for it. The supervisor was ordered to make a judgment of the salesman's fitness and report back. And there was a final instruction. The report, Candler insisted firmly, should be limited to a day wire "of not more than 10 words." Candler, in short, was upright, fair-minded—and also incredibly tightfisted. He simply could not bear the thought of parting with money he believed was rightfully his.

Candler filed suit in federal court in Atlanta seeking repayment of the tax, and the government wasted no time in responding. The Coca-Cola Company was incorporated for the purpose of selling medicine, the Internal Revenue Office claimed, and the product was a "medicinal preparation" with at least three drugs in it, compounded under a secret formula. It was advertised as a cure for headache and exhaustion and other physical ailments. Furthermore, the government said, pointing its sharpest dagger, Coca-Cola contained "the drug and medicine cocaine."

The last accusation was potentially the most dramatic and damaging of the government's claims, but it also turned out to be a bit premature. In preparing for trial, the Internal Revenue Office employed a chemist, Dr. Charles A. Crampton of Washington, D.C., to analyze a sample of Coca-Cola syrup, and after several tries he was unable to establish proof that cocaine was present. The charge wasn't going to hold up.

When Asa Candler took the stand, the government's lawyer, assistant district attorney George L. Bell, handled the cross-examination. At first he made little headway. When he asked why Coca-Cola was advertised as a headache remedy, for instance, Candler responded querulously, "Because it cures headaches." Candler testified that Coca-Cola was made mostly of water and sugar, and said the coca and cola were included because otherwise, "the United States government won't give us copyright." Finally, almost as an afterthought, Bell asked Candler, "There is cocaine in it?"

"A very small portion," Candler answered.

Bell was dumbfounded. "There is?" he repeated,

"Your chemist failed to find it," Candler snapped, a note of satisfaction in his voice, "didn't he?"

Candler's triumph was brief. Bell bored in. Was Asa Candler admitting under oath that *cocaine* was present in Coca-Cola? "It probably is," Candler said, "a very small trace of it. Yes, sir." What had happened, in a wondrous twist of fate, was that the Coca-Cola Company had prepared for trial by hiring an expert witness of its own to rebut the evidence and testimony the government was expected to present. No one at the company dreamed that the government would come up short—nor, of course, did they anticipate that their own man, Dr. George F. Payne, the secretary of the Georgia State Board of Pharmacy, would discover that there was still a trace of cocaine in the syrup. But he did.

Using sophisticated techniques that apparently were unavailable or unknown to his federal counterpart, Dr. Payne calculated that Coca-Cola syrup contained one 400th of a grain of cocaine per ounce. "It was the merest trace," he testified at the trial, ". . .not enough to have any appreciable effect. A man would explode before he could drink enough to affect him."

The expert testimony at the trial quickly shifted to speculation about the possibility of the trace of cocaine making Coca-Cola genuinely dangerous to public health. Dr. Payne thought it would take a hundred glasses of Coca-Cola before a consumer could feel any effect from the cocaine. Candler doubled the figure, saying it would take two hundred glasses. The government put up Dr. J. P. Baird, president of the Medical Association of Georgia, who testified that Coca-Cola definitely was habit-forming. "Persons who take it freely," he said, "seem to become more or less dependent on it." But the cocaine, he added, deflating his thesis, couldn't be the cause of the addiction because there was too little of it.

At last the government's lead chemist, Dr. Crampton, stepped into the witness chair. Coca-Cola syrup was mostly sugar and water, he testified, but it also had cocaine. How much? he was asked. "A small amount," he answered vaguely. When the company's lawyers confronted him during cross-examination and accused him of failing to detect any cocaine at all, Dr. Crampton's testimony quickly disintegrated into a hodgepodge of fragmentary answers. He insisted (contrary to well-established fact) that the only way to test for the presence of cocaine was by tasting it and feeling the results on the tongue. "There is no accurate test," he insisted, "other than the effect upon the system." And had he conducted such a test? Yes, he said. He had boiled down a quart, or at least part of a quart of Coca-Cola syrup, added and extracted various solvents, and then tested the result on his tongue. He implied—but never explicitly stated—that his tongue was numbed by the residue of the Coca-Cola syrup. Then he abruptly left the stand, dismissed by both sides.

There is nothing in the trial record to explain Dr. Crampton's partial and confusing testimony. One plausible theory is that he was an embarrassment to both sides, and that the lawyers decided the best legal strategy would be to hurry him out of the courtroom. In any event, it would not have mattered very much—the jury of twelve loyal Georgians found in favor of the Coca-Cola Company during scant deliberations that lasted less than fifteen minutes—except that Dr. Crampton's testimony was revived several times in subsequent trials, and even found its way into a landmark United States Supreme Court opinion written years later by Oliver Wendell Holmes. Dr. Crampton's testimony was misremembered as convincing evidence that Coca-Cola once contained enough cocaine to numb a man's tongue, and the vivid notion quickly found its way into the public consciousness and later into history books.

Candler got his $29,502 back, but the cost was high. He believed the government's true purpose was to punish him by learning the formula of Coca-Cola and exposing it to the would-be imitators of the world, who would then flood the market with cheap substitutes. Actually, there already were plenty of imitators at work, and they did not need the revelations in the courtroom to brew up syrup that closely resembled Coca-Cola. (If anything, the trial probably confused some of the imitators. At one point, testifying about the ingredients of the syrup, Candler cited "cassia," the Chinese cinnamon, and the court stenographer misunderstood him and transcribed the word as "calcium." Anyone trying to perfect a knock-off of Coca-Cola syrup by adding a pinch of calcium would have found himself at a dead end, and quite a tongue-curdling one at that.) No, the real injury to Candler and Coca-Cola came outside the courtroom, where a seismic shift in public opinion about cocaine was just starting to shake the ground.

Around the turn of the century, a scare over cocaine spread through the South, and as was true of so many other things in the region, the trigger was race. Local prohibition laws were turning large parts of the South dry, and in some instances blacks—like other poor people who couldn't afford bootleg liquor—turned to cocaine as a substitute. *The Journal of the American Medical Association* reported in June 1900 that Negroes in the South were becoming addicted to sniffing cocaine, and in no time wild and wicked stories started making the rounds. A Colonel J. W. Watson of Georgia was quoted in the *New York Tribune* urging legal action against Coca-Cola, charging that "many of the horrible crimes committed in the

Southern United States by the colored people can be traced directly to the cocaine habit." There were reports that cocaine gave blacks—black men in particular—"superhuman" powers, and some Southern police departments abandoned their .32-caliber service revolvers in favor of .38-caliber models that supposedly had the greater power necessary to stop blacks when they were cocaine-crazed.

As if that were not enough, a backlash erupted against kola as well. The promoters of kola had yet to give up their crusade to sell the American consumer on the wonders of their product (or to admit that its active principle was caffeine). In the 1890s, fine-tuning their pitch, they aimed their advertising at amateur athletes and the growing ranks of fitness buffs, especially those who were participating in the new craze of bicycling. Playing on racial mythology, some manufacturers brazenly asserted that kola—native to Africa—was the source of the physical strength of black people. Johnson & Johnson, for instance, launched a hard-sell campaign for its brand of kola extract, Kolafra. "Kolafra," said a company pamphlet published in 1897 (with a woodcut picture of a strapping, bare-chested black man on the cover), "will assuage thirst under any and all conditions. African savages march for miles under a burning tropical sun, with heavy burdens on their heads, without water or food. They stop thirst and hunger by the free use of the wonderful Kolafra."

Not surprisingly, the sensational imaginings that were published on behalf of kola fed the flames of racial alarm, too. One self-proclaimed medical expert warned that kola was a cardiac stimulant that blacks could tolerate but not "white-skinned peoples."

It hardly mattered that Coca-Cola contained nothing but the merest trace of either drug named in its trademark. People were growing frightened. A doctor in Augusta, Georgia, said his city was filling up with "Coca-Cola fiends" whose cravings rivaled those of opium addicts. "Every ingredient [in Coca-Cola] is a poison," the *Wilson* (N.C.) Daily News warned its readers, "and not long hence, each unhappy victim of this pernicious tipple, like the opium fiend of the East, may take his neighbor by the hand, and say, 'Brother, what ailed thee, to seek so dire a cure?'"

All around the country, city councils and state legislatures began restricting or outlawing the use of cocaine in patent medicines. In Virginia, attacks on his soft drink that could safely be ignored just a few years earlier suddenly struck Asa Candler as ominous.

> For some reason I can't understand [he wrote his son, Howard, in August 1902], there seems to be an effort made in Virginia to injure Coca-Cola. We have just had a case investigated where it was charged by a country physician that a man had been driven to suicide by excessive use of Coca-Cola. We gave the case the closest investigation and found what we expected, that the fellow was a constant drinker of

liquor and tea, a user of cigarettes, generally an excessively self-indulgent man, in the habit of drinking Coca-Cola early on Sunday morning to relieve him from the effect of a Saturday and Sunday [debauch]. . . . Our greatest danger now is that our enemies will succeed in having a Law enacted prohibiting the sale of Coca-Cola.

For help, Candler turned to the biggest cocaine manufacturer in the United States. It seemed an ironic choice, but Candler figured that an expert in extracting cocaine from coca leaves might know how to extract *all* the cocaine, leaving a residue safe enough to put in Coca-Cola. In June 1903, Candler boarded a train for New York, went to the offices of the Roessler & Hasslacher Chemical Company, and put a challenge to their top supplier, Dr. Louis Schaefer: Could he produce an extract of coca from which "every vestige" of cocaine was removed? Yes, Dr. Schaefer said, he believed he could.

Schaefer, a German emigré, set up a special operation at the Schaefer Alkaloid Works, one of the four chemical production laboratories he had opened in Maywood, New Jersey, in the 1890s. In making the new Merchandise No. 5, Schaefer created a process that was, in a word, thorough. He began by powdering the coca leaves, mixing them with sawdust and soaking the compound in a bicarbonate of soda. Next he percolated the compound with toluene, a powerful solvent derived from coal tar, and then he blasted the treated leaves with live steam. Finally he added in powdered kola nuts, "exhausted" the mixture with alcohol, and finished up by pasteurizing the results. It seemed unlikely that cocaine (or anything else for that matter) could survive.

From Candler's point of view, the removal of the last discernible trace of cocaine came just in time. The Progressive movement was beginning to sweep the country, and crusading journalists were turning a harsh light on corrupt practices in housing, industry, labor, the railroads, finance, insurance, government, and also public health. The pharmaceutical industry was the target of a series of scathing articles entitled "The Great American Fraud" that began in *Collier's* magazine in December 1905. Samuel Hopkins Adams exposed the use of cocaine in patent medicines—including catarrh remedies and other products meant for children, such as "Mrs. Winslow's Soothing Syrup"—and warned that putting the drug in a medicinal product was a "shameful trade that stupefies helpless babies and makes criminals of our young men and harlots of our young women."

The culmination of the reform movement in nutrition and medicine was the passage by Congress in 1906 of the Pure Food and Drugs Act, which among other things required any manufacturer who used cocaine in a product to disclose that fact on the label. One of the leaders of the fight to gain approval of the act was the chief chemist of the United States

Department of Agriculture, Dr. Harvey Washington Wiley, and when the law took effect in 1907, he became the top federal official in charge of enforcing it.

Dr. Wiley believed that Coca-Cola contained cocaine and other harmful ingredients, and he launched a crusade to drive Asa Candler out of business.

Talking with a business associate one day in 1906, John Candler described the great success and fine profits Coca-Cola was enjoying. "But it's like a big balloon," he warned. "Punch a hole in it and it's gone."

Harvey Wiley meant to do exactly that. Wiley was the Ralph Nader of his day, a tireless and passionate consumer advocate, and a man of intense convictions about the harmfulness of a wide variety of chemicals and food-stuffs in the American diet. He had a charming side and a natural, easy knack for public relations, yet he could be a fierce, absolutely unrelenting warrior once he got it into his head that he was fighting something evil.

In the late spring of 1907, responding to complaints that Coca-Cola contained cocaine and alcohol, the War Department banned the sale of the soft drink at canteens and post exchanges on U.S. Army bases. The company's lawyer, John Candler, protested vigorously. Citing the removal of the cocaine and arguing that the amount of alcohol in the syrup was inconsequential, he brought an appeal, and the War Department turned to Dr. Wiley to conduct tests and resolve the issue.

All through the summer months of 1907, the Candlers waited for Wiley to complete his analysis and, they hoped, give them clearance to resume military sales of Coca-Cola. They waited in vain. Finally, in mid-September, John Candler took a train to Washington to find out for himself what was taking so long. He spent two days stalking the corridors at the Department of Agriculture, he reported later, talking to every official he could buttonhole, "from Wiley down to the office boy." He thought he had the problem figured out. The department's tests had confirmed that Coca-Cola syrup no longer had any cocaine in it and also showed that the trace of alcohol—there to help preserve the flavoring extracts and the Merchandise No. 5—was perfectly harmless. But Wiley had raised a new alarm, complaining that the caffeine in Coca-Cola was a health hazard. The Bureau of Chemistry was conducting tests on a "poison squad" of young, male volunteers, feeding them large doses of caffeine in an effort to estab-lish that it was injurious.

Wiley believed the company was guilty of spreading the "Coca-Cola habit," as he privately called it, across the South. His attitude toward the region had been shaped in part by his experiences decades earlier during the Civil War. As a lowly corporal in the Union Army, Wiley served briefly in a volunteer unit from his native Indiana, spending a few weeks in 1864 guarding a supply depot in Tullahoma, Tennessee. The railroad that passed through Tullahoma was a conduit for the food, clothing, munitions, and reinforcements that were headed south to fuel General Sherman's campaign of total war. Returning trains carried wounded and captured Rebel soldiers.

Far from making him hate the South, the war filled Wiley with pity. When he was off duty, he recalled later, he would spend time at the station talking with the Confederates. "Some of them had lost an arm or had a wounded leg," he wrote later. "When I compared the good uniforms and good food and general appearance of the Union soldiers with the tattered uniforms and emaciated bodies of the Confederates, I realized under what strenuous conditions our Confederate antagonists were fighting." Wiley's experience gave him a view of the South as a benighted, unhealthy place—a view that was advanced when he contracted hookworm and spent his tour of duty wasted by severe, chronic diarrhea that eventually sent him home "more dead than alive," his robust frame shriveled down to a mere 119 pounds.

When the Coca-Cola issue arose, Wiley sent his top deputy, Dr. Lyman Frederic Kebler, on an inspection tour of the South from Richmond to Memphis, and Kebler reported back that the region was a land of Coca-Cola "fiends." In his visits to soda fountains in Atlanta, Kebler wrote, he "personally saw the beverage consumed by children of four, five, and six years of age." In many cases, he said, the soft drink was taken home in pitchers and served like beer to the whole family. Incited by Kebler's dire reports, Wiley believed that Coca-Cola was undermining the health and perhaps even the moral fiber of the South. He had no intention of backing off.

Yet there were other forces at work, and they gave some hope to the men at the Coca-Cola Company. Wiley's greatest weakness was the very thing that made him dangerous—his zeal. He was a crusader against almost all food additives, and he had a habit of badgering people until, in many cases, they decided he was unbalanced and turned against him. Wiley tried to enforce a ban on the use of sodium benzoate in catsup, for instance, and when a food manufacturer argued that the preservative was derived from a natural, God-given ingredient in cranberries, Wiley responded with theocratic certitude that "cranberries would be more wholesome had the Almighty left out benzoic acid."

In one celebrated incident, Wiley launched into a diatribe against the sweetener saccharin during a meeting with Theodore Roosevelt at the White House. It was a terrible mistake. "President Roosevelt turned upon me, purple with anger," Wiley recounted later in his autobiography, "and with clenched fists, hissing through his teeth, said: 'You say saccharin is injurious to health? Why, Dr. Rixey gives it to me every day. Anybody who says saccharin is injurious to health is an idiot!'" It happened that the president, fighting a lifelong battle with his weight, relied on saccharin on the advice of his personal physician, Dr. Presley Rixey, the surgeon general of the navy. Convinced that Wiley was a kook, Roosevelt appointed a Referee Board of Consulting Scientific Experts that oversaw (and often squelched)

Wiley's activities. Wiley's immediate boss, Agriculture Secretary James Wilson, also distrusted him, and refused to forward any of Wiley's cases to the Justice Department for prosecution unless two other officials in the Bureau of Chemistry concurred with the decision.

In October 1907, with the army ban still lingering, the Candlers decided to brave an approach to Secretary Wilson. John Candler checked into the Raleigh Hotel in Washington on the evening of October 10 and saw Wilson the next morning. The meeting went well. Wilson "seems entirely in sympathy with our contentions," Candler reported to his family, "and says that he will. . .request a report from Dr. Wiley on our goods. I feel somewhat encouraged, as he is seemingly inclined our way."

Wilson followed through, and six days later—under pressure—Wiley at last submitted his analysis. Coca-Cola, he conceded, contained no cocaine, and it had only a small, harmless amount of alcohol. The Candlers had won. Before the month was out, the army lifted its ban. Sales of Coca-Cola were resumed on the nation's military bases. But the tone of Wiley's report was menacing. He complained bitterly that he had not been allowed enough time to assemble evidence that the caffeine in Coca-Cola was hazardous, and he made it clear that he intended to continue until he had done so. He also spiced the report with his deputy Kebler's random accusations that Coca-Cola was abused by children and adults alike. A druggist in Atlanta was quoted as saying that soldiers liked to mix liquor with Coca-Cola and make a highball that "drove them crazy."

Reading Wiley's report, Asa Candler was livid. It was, he huffed, "the most unmistakable evidence to me of his unfitness [for] so important an office as he is occupying. The idea of his sending a man over the country picking up such rumors as he refers to and then using them in an official order is enough to stagger the patriotism of a better man than myself." Still, Candler contented himself that the army ban was lifted, and he figured people would forget about the controversy soon enough. The rest of the family urged him to publicize the report's findings and advertise Coca-Cola's victory, but he demurred. The less said, he explained, the more likely Wiley's bruised feelings would be soothed, and the sooner he might drop the matter.

Candler could not have been more mistaken.

In the aftermath of his skirmish with Wiley, Asa Candler began wearying of the business of making and selling Coca-Cola.

The company was regularly netting profits of $2 million and $3 million a year, making Candler the richest man in Atlanta. The city's historian, Franklin Garrett, could recall hearing little boys say, "Who do you think I am? Asa G. Candler?" as they spurned their friends' requests to borrow a dime or a quarter. Just as John D. Rockefeller's name was invoked as the synonym for unimaginable wealth elsewhere in the country, Candler's was in Georgia. Yet he took little satisfaction from his fabulous financial success. The business, Candler said dismissively, was nothing more than "a mere money-getting machine."

As befitted a devout Methodist and Sunday school teacher, Candler had a sort of Old Testament ferocity about the temptations of wealth. "Don't indulge SELF," he admonished his children. "He is a tyrant, never satisfied." Others might revel in buying fashionable clothes or getting tickets to the latest show, Candler once wrote, "but I have not arrived to be stylish." He was notoriously frugal—when mail arrived at the office, Candler would slit the envelopes, unfold them, and save them for scratch paper—and he applied that frugality as earnestly to himself as he did to others. Yet Candler was no simple miser. He did not believe it was entirely proper to save his wealth, either. "I never keep money," he once explained to his brother, Warren, the Methodist bishop. "Money is not meant to be hoarded. Myself and all I have I try to keep righteously active." Certainly Candler saw to it that his family enjoyed a decent life; and his children grew up in a comfortable mansion in elegant Inman Park, Atlanta's first suburb. He was a warm, affectionate father. His daughter, Lucy—his "dear sweet fish," as he nicknamed her—played the piano and he loved to listen and sing along. It was just that he tried to teach his children the value of thrift. When two of the boys wanted tool kits one Christmas, he bought a single set and made them share. He raised chickens in the backyard.

Money, in Candler's view, ought to be properly earned and usefully spent, and it was plain that the profits pouring in from Coca-Cola bothered him on both counts. He was proud of his hard work over the years, but the accumulation of wealth, especially once it became virtually automatic, seemed to scratch a raw spot on his conscience. He wanted to leave a legacy of tangible accomplishment Candler took far more pleasure from his burgeoning real estate empire—he built skyscrapers in Atlanta, New York, and Baltimore, and christened each "the Candler Building"—than he did in the Coca-Cola Company.

And Candler was tired of the assaults on his product's reputation and his family's good name. He might not be terribly proud of selling sugar and water to people for a nickel a glass, but he bristled at the idea that he was a villain peddling poison. The years of controversy had taken their toll. Tom Watson, Georgia's fiery populist and propagandist began denouncing Coca-Cola as "dope" and finally pushed the Southern Methodist Church—the denomination led by Candler's own brother—into dropping the company's ads from its newspaper. Warren Candler sheepishly returned the one share of Coca-Cola stock his brother had given him. Coca-Cola came under attack from all sides. Leaders of the Temperance movement denounced the trace of alcohol in it, while liquor manufacturers suspected Candler of favoring prohibition and plotting to make Coca-Cola the nation's "temperance drink." Candler fumed that some newspaper editors were not above shaking him down for advertising and attacking his soft drink if he refused to buy space.

The idea that Coca-Cola contained cocaine—an idea Candler once subtly encouraged—now enraged him. He came to detest the suggestive nicknames people used in place of Coca-Cola. One of Candler's employees told the story of inviting the old man to join him at the soda fountain and "have a dope," only to have Candler explode, "It is not dope! There is no dope in it! It is *Co-Ca Co-La!*"

Now that he was approaching his sixties, Candler had begun to grow more and more conscious of his own mortality. His father had died young, and Candler feared the same fate. He wanted to devote his final years to charitable works and public service, and that meant getting out of the Coca-Cola Company. The question was how.

In his younger days, Candler had insisted that his sons stay away from the business. Peddling soft drinks, he said, was a pursuit with a "narrow compass." Candler was especially anxious for his eldest boy, Howard, to attend medical school and become a doctor—the career Asa himself had been forced to abandon.

Gradually, though, Asa's resolve weakened and his attitude changed. He grew ambivalent. Howard seemed determined to work for the company during vacations and breaks, and Asa felt flattered in spite of himself at his son's interest in the business. One summer Asa offered Howard a job at the company and in almost the same breath urged him not to take it: "The employment that I offered you will be around our factory, packing, painting, filling, and such work as requires common labor [and] would not be any benefit to your mind." Howard took the position anyway and enjoyed the work.

From that point on, perhaps without fully realizing it, Asa began drawing Howard toward a career with the company. When Howard visited Europe in the summer of 1900, after graduating from college, his father gave him careful instructions to make notes on business conditions and assess Coca-Cola's chances: "We must have ice, hot weather, long summers, etc. You will know what to look for." That fall, when Howard returned to the United States, Asa asked him to begin his medical studies in New York City, where he could also keep tabs on Coca-Cola's sales office. A year later, citing eye strain and overall fatigue, Howard dropped his plans to become a doctor, and his father gave him a full-time job. For the first time, Asa started thinking about the possibility that Howard might succeed him in running the company.

Howard Candler's first permanent assignment for Coca-Cola was to remain in New York and try to bring order to the chaos in the office there. It did not go well. Asa considered New York a "bottomless pit" that chewed up men and money, and he regretted having gone there in the first place. Sidewalk vendors sold flavored soda water for a penny a glass, badly undercutting Coca-Cola's pricing, and the saloons were reluctant to carry the Southern beverage. It is unlikely Howard could have done much to improve the company's fortunes even if he'd displayed an aptitude for business, but as it was the experience unnerved him. Howard was only twenty-three years old, with a nervous disposition, and he found that he disliked commerce. "I really enjoy the office part of the work," he wrote his father, "but I don't like to distribute tickets and sell goods. More, I don't like to have to be sociable with the trade such as is demanded to a certain extent here. I mean that the salesman for an article has to go in frequently and talk to a proprietor and his help of soda-men and clerks. I don't like that."

The confession was remarkable. In a business that relied almost entirely on salesmanship, the boss's son found it distasteful to talk to the people who bought the product Asa brought his son back to Atlanta and tucked him away from the public aspects of the business, putting him in charge of the syrup factory.

It was the happiest period of Howard's career. Years later, using language suited to a religious experience, Howard described his initiation into what he called the "Holy of Holies," when his father entrusted him with the secret formula. There was no written version. Instead, Asa made his son memorize the contents of the various containers that were carefully stored in a locked room with their labels peeled or scratched off. For days, with his father standing watch over his shoulder, Howard practiced making the ultra secret flavoring compound, Merchandise No. 7X, learning to recognize the pungent fruit and vegetable oils "by sight, smell, and remembering where each was put on the shelf when it came in from the supplier," until finally he knew by heart the proper amounts and the exact order in which to mix them.

Howard Candler had a natural aptitude for chemistry, and he might have been better served if his father had left him to the satisfactions of overseeing the Coca-Cola Company's laboratory and manufacturing plant. Shy and uncertain, physically slight at five foot nine and 135 pounds, Howard seemed to run into trouble whenever he encountered the human element in pursuit of his duties. It was becoming obvious that he lacked his father's drive and gumption.

Obvious, that is, to everyone except Asa Candler. As his weariness grew, Asa began to dream of turning the company's affairs over to his son. "As soon as possible," he wrote Howard in the summer of 1908, "I desire that you take the place I have been filling for 20 years." One night after supper, Asa drew out a sheet of writing paper, dipped his pen, and almost begged his son to take a larger role: "As soon as I can lay this Coca-Cola business on your shoulders I intend to do it. I want you therefor [sic] to learn it thoroughly. . . ." Asa promoted Howard to a vice presidency overseeing all of the company's operations and pushed him to take a stronger hand, especially in personnel matters. As the months passed, Asa kept encouraging Howard to think harder about the business, "so that you may thoroughly master its details & carry it on successfully." Reading between the lines, it seemed as if Asa sensed his son's limitations, all the while refusing to admit to himself just how severe they were.

There was another problem. Running the company was one thing, but Asa Candler also *owned* Coca-Cola. He was free to retire and place his son in charge of the company whenever he pleased, no matter what misgivings he might harbor, but that would not resolve the issue of ownership. Asa had four other children. If he left the company to Howard, it would mean disinheriting Asa Jr., Lucy, Walter, and William. That option was unacceptable. But dividing the company into five pieces was a troublesome idea, too. What if the children kept their shares and the company failed? They would be left penniless. What if the children sold their shares? Would strangers come along and gain control? Would they force Howard out of a job?

Candler's dilemma was not just hypothetical. In 1908, he quietly sounded out one of his acquaintances about buying the company. Samuel Brown was a well-to-do cotton broker and banker from Albany, Georgia. He liked to visit the Capital City Club when he was in Atlanta to play a few hands of euchre, and he also liked to keep an eye on the Coca-Cola Company. His son-in-law, Harold Hirsch, was a bright young partner in John Candler's law firm. Yes, Brown told Asa Candler, he would be very interested in the possibility of acquiring the company. Brown came from a German-Jewish family (the name was anglicized from Braun) and maintained connections with a bank in Hamburg. He thought he might be able to arrange the financing in Europe.

What Brown had in mind was a fairly simple, two-step plan. He wanted to buy the Coca-Cola Company from Candler and then turn right around and sell shares in it to small investors all across the South. After all, Coca-Cola's sales were still overwhelmingly concentrated in the region, and the drink was still perceived as a "Southern" product. Brown thought people in the South would have as much enthusiasm about owning part of the company as they did about drinking the product.

The idea suited Asa Candler perfectly. He could be done with the company once and for all. He could take his accumulated profits off the company's books and use the money for the charitable purposes he now ached to fulfill. And in theory, at least, taking the company public promised to provide a solution to the predicament of succession within his family. The other children would receive enough cash to make them secure for life, while Howard would get to remain with the company and run it The new owner would not be an individual or group of individuals anxious to put in their own management, but instead the public would own Coca-Cola, and the people of the South would be happy to have a Candler stay in charge. Indeed, they would *insist* on having a Candler at the top. Howard would be protected.

But there was a snag. Before Brown and Candler could negotiate an agreement, they were interrupted.

———

When Howard Candler returned to work at Coca-Cola headquarters in Atlanta after lunch on the afternoon of October 20, 1909, he was intercepted at the front door by the plant manager.

Two federal officials had arrived unannounced, the manager told Candler excitedly, and were poking around in the basement of the factory. They had refused his request to stop.

Howard Candler raced up the five stone steps into the building, not stopping to remove his hat, and ran down the stairs to the basement. There he found Dr. Kebler perched on the top step of a rickety wooden ladder, peering into one of the giant, 1,500-gallon cypress cooling tanks that hung suspended from the ceiling. A federal inspector, J. L. Lynch, was standing beside the foot of the ladder, scribbling notes.

Candler was familiar with both men. In the two years after the fight over the army ban on Coca-Cola, they had toured the factory several times—but always by appointment and always in the company of a member of the Candler family. Howard had accompanied them himself on a couple of occasions. The exchanges had always been polite, even genial. Kebler had brought his wife along on one visit, as if she were a tourist seeing a local attraction.

This time, however, Kebler and Lynch were snooping around without permission. There were no pleasantries. Candler asked what they wanted. Lynch answered that they required a sample of Merchandise No. 5, the mix of coca and kola extracts. They would be willing to sign a voucher for it. Candler, taken aback, walked uncertainly over to the brick vault that contained the secret ingredients of Coca-Cola, poured out a small sample of No. 5 and gave it to Lynch. Then he went to find his father.

Kebler and Lynch were about to leave the building when Asa Candler rushed in, trembling with anger. He demanded the sample back. Lynch refused. "By God," Candler roared in his high-pitched voice, "if I had been here you would not have got it!"

But they had.

For two long years, Wiley had been aching to bring charges against Coca-Cola, only to be held in check by his superior, Secretary of Agriculture Wilson. Any time Wiley moved to make a case against the company, Wilson would direct the two other members of the department's Board of Food and Drug Inspection to vote no. Wiley lost a succession of 2-to-1 decisions inside his own bureaucracy. Finally wearying of the friction, Wilson wrote Wiley a letter demanding plainly that he drop his efforts against Coca-Cola. But contrary to its intended effect, the letter gave Wiley an opening.

As Wiley recounted the episode later, he received a visit one day from Fred Loring Seely, the publisher of the *Atlanta Georgian*, Atlanta's newest and most crusade-minded newspaper. Seely, who was no friend of the

Candlers, wanted to know why the Bureau of Chemistry had abandoned its prosecution of Coca-Cola. Wiley pulled out Wilson's letter, pushed it across the desk and watched with satisfaction as an "astonished" Seely read the contents. Thus armed, Seely called on Wilson and threatened to disclose the whole affair in an unfavorable light unless the order was withdrawn.*

"It is remarkable," Wiley wrote later with glee, "what the fear of publicity will do!" Wilson struck a compromise. He offered to rescind his letter and allow the prosecution to go forward, but he insisted that the case be brought to trial in a venue close to Atlanta and favorable to Coca-Cola. Chattanooga, Tennessee, was the nearest city involved in interstate commerce with the company, and it happened to be the home of some of Coca-Cola's biggest investors. Wiley wanted to sue in Washington, D.C., but he grudgingly agreed to Wilson's choice of sites. The government seized a railroad shipment of forty barrels and twenty kegs of Coca-Cola syrup in Chattanooga and filed suit in federal court charging the company with criminal fraud.

Preparations for the trial took more than a year.

During the afternoon and evening of Sunday, March 12, 1911, participants from both sides began trooping into Chattanooga, filling up the rooms of the luxurious new Patten Hotel.

Far from being treated as a villain, Wiley was accorded the status of a visiting celebrity. A lifelong bachelor, he had just taken a bride at the ripe age of sixty-six, and he used the Coca-Cola trial as the occasion for his honeymoon. Anna Kelton Wiley, less than half her husband's age, was a handsome, accomplished woman and a well-known suffragette. Arriving by train from Washington, the couple made quite a splash in Chattanooga society, and their activities were faithfully recorded by the local press. (At a Woman's Club meeting in the auditorium of the Unitarian Church, after Miss Emily Watson sang her rendition of "My Wee Bird," the Wileys gave short speeches—hers on suffrage, his on the evils of drugs—and both were applauded enthusiastically before they repaired to an anteroom for a reception.)

When they checked into the Patten, the Wileys were given a room overlooking the Post Office Building, where U.S. District Judge Edward J. Sanford planned to gavel the proceedings to order the next morning.

The government had two main charges against Coca-Cola: It was "misbranded" because its name promised the presence of coca and cola when it contained little if any of either, and it was "adulterated" by the addition of caffeine. It seemed as if Wiley, having failed in his determined efforts to

---

* It is entirely possible that Wiley *summoned* Seely to Washington, briefed him on the background of the story, and enlisted him as an ally, but if so Wiley was wily enough to leave no evidence of his actions.

discover cocaine in Coca-Cola, now wished to punish the company for not having cocaine and for using caffeine in its place. No matter that people had been drinking tea and coffee for centuries without apparent ill result, it was Wiley's unshaken belief that caffeine—especially synthetic caffeine, unbuffered by natural ingredients such as the tannin found in tea and coffee—was injurious to human health. The outcome of the trial was expected to turn on the testimony of the small armies of leading scientists each side had lined up to provide the latest information about the physiological effects of caffeine.

The first witness to take the stand that Monday morning in 1911 was Lynch, the federal inspector the Candlers had found poking around the basement of their syrup factory in Atlanta. A prosecutor asked Lynch to describe the premises. He had inspected the plant several times, Lynch answered, and one visit in particular stood out in his mind. It was in mid-July. The equipment for making the syrup occupied the basement and first floor of the building, and the process began in a large, steam-jacketed copper kettle just inside the front door. Water from the city was piped directly into the kettle, which was surrounded by a wooden platform that held numerous barrels of sugar. A Negro put the sugar into the kettle.

The prosecutor told Lynch to speak louder, and then asked, "This Negro cook that was on the platform and dumping the ingredients into the kettle, could you state how he was dressed?"

"Well," Lynch answered, "very scantily. A dirty undershirt, his shoes were badly broken, the bare feet were sticking out through them in parts, and he had on an old, dirty pair of trousers."

"State whether or not he was perspiring."

"Yes, freely."

"Could you state whether or not he was chewing tobacco?"

"Yes, sir."

"Did he expectorate from time to time, and if so, where?"

"Whenever he happens to want to, just wherever it fell, on the platform and on the floor."

At the defense table, John Candler and the company's other lawyers listened in amazement.

Dr. Harvey Wiley, the most prominent advocate of nutritional reform in the country, the head of the federal agency responsible for safeguarding the purity of the nation's food and drugs, a leader of the Progressive movement, a man of science, a man who was raised in an abolitionist household, who married a champion of women's rights, who was arguably the most liberal and enlightened public official in the United States government—this man was opening his landmark case against the Coca-Cola Company with the revelation that a black worker, doing hard physical labor next to a steaming hot kettle in a factory in the Deep South in the middle of July, was *sweating*.

One of the company's attorneys, J. B. Sizer, approached the bench. "They seemed to dwell on the fact that we had a colored cook there," he complained. "I want to show that we are not guilty of any undue negligence." Sizer launched a tough cross-examination, and a "somewhat flustered" Lynch admitted he had not seen the black employee spitting tobacco into the kettle. Otherwise, though, he stuck to his story.

As the government continued putting on its case, the strategy became obvious. The caffeine question was taking a back seat as the prosecution paraded a string of witnesses whose testimony was designed to horrify the jury and alarm the public at large. One of Wiley's chemists, Dr. H. C. Fuller, said he analyzed a sample of the syrup seized in the forty barrels and twenty kegs, and found that it contained bits of hay, straw, dust and dirt, an insect leg, and "part of a bumblebee." From the defense table, one of the company's lawyers announced gamely in a loud stage whisper, audible to the reporters in the courtroom, "Even the bumblebees love Coca-Cola!"

Dr. Henry H. Rusby, a professor of *materia medica* at the New York College of Pharmacy, gave a vivid account of his experiments on rabbits— Coca-Cola killed them, he said—only to admit under cross-examination that he wasn't feeding them any caffeine at all, but instead mammoth doses of Merchandise No. 5, the coca and cola extract.

When the first day's testimony ended at about two o'clock in the afternoon, Wiley and his wife set off cheerfully to do a little shopping (as she confided in her diary) and then took a tour up Lookout Mountain's famous funicular. The next day, they planned to visit the hallowed grounds of the Chickamauga battlefield.

But 110 miles to the south, in the general offices of the Coca-Cola Company, the mood was not so festive. Asa Candler, who was staying away from Chattanooga on the advice of his brother John and the other lawyers, heard about the government's opening salvo and felt his worst fears confirmed. "I anticipated a mean-nasty case in this," he wrote his son, and he was getting one. Candler was especially inflamed by Lynch's testimony— not only about the sweating workman, but also an allegation that Candler had cursed when he discovered Lynch and Kebler in the basement of the factory. "That *liar*," Candler fumed, "should be prosecuted for perjury."

The next few days did little to soothe Candler's rage. Dr. Kebler, Wiley's deputy, took the stand and seconded Lynch's testimony that the Coca-Cola factory was dirty and that the black laborers were sweating and chewing tobacco. What's more, Kebler said, they were giving off germs.

Finally the prosecution turned to the main issue, caffeine. Starting with Kebler, the government put up more than a dozen Department of Agriculture scientists and outside experts who testified that caffeine masked ordinary, natural fatigue and thus drove users to overextend themselves, leading to exhaustion, overworking of the organs, addiction, nervous collapse, and occasionally even death. Kebler, for his part, said caffeine was a poison that made one patient's heart so hard it couldn't be cut with a knife. The scientists described various experiments with frogs, rabbits, mice, and guinea pigs, all of which they said demonstrated the dangers of caffeine to humans. To the defense, at least, the government's witnesses were not terribly persuasive. The company had its own experts, of course, and they were allowed to remain in the courtroom, seated in rows behind the defense table, during the presentation of the government's case. At one point their response to the evidence was an outburst of snickering and sarcastic remarks so clearly audible that Judge Sanford had to admonish them to stay silent. Asa Candler, monitoring the trial from afar, had a similar reaction. As the trial entered its second week and the government's case wound down, Candler sent a wire to his nephews in the Philadelphia office reporting drily: "Conditions at Chattanooga are about as last week. U.S. has about exhausted its rat, rabbit, and frog evidence." Courthouse regulars agreed that the prosecution's case was weak. But there was a final piece of evidence yet to come.

The key to the government's case was the need to demonstrate that Coca-Cola did, in fact, produce addiction and dangerous side effects. Testimony from expert witnesses theorizing about the soft drink's potential for harm was well and good, but there was no substitute for a genuine Coca-Cola "fiend."

Edwin H. Corry was a thirty-seven-year-old streetcar conductor from Philadelphia. In 1910, he was committed to the Philadelphia Hospital for the Insane, and it was the government's contention that he was driven mad by drinking Coca-Cola. Corry's testimony was taken by deposition since he could not safely be released from his ward and brought to court. It was his habit, Corry swore, to drink as many as a dozen Coca-Colas a day. He found that on several occasions when he went to bed and was about to fall asleep, "the bed would move. I had that sensation. Sometimes the head part of the bed would raise up, and sometimes the hind part."

The company's lawyers were suspicious. They wanted to know more about Corry, so they did some investigating in Philadelphia. Corry, it turned out, had been arrested on a warrant sworn out by his own brother for sexually molesting the brother's minor son. Yes, said Dr. Sherman Clouting, who examined him at the time, Corry was insane. "He said he saw faces of people around him at night, that he heard distant music in his ears," the doctor recounted. "He said he got very melancholy at times and had suicidal ideas, and when I asked him if he saw other visions, he said yes, he had seen the devil once or twice and the devil had touched him once." But it had nothing to do with Coca-Cola. Poor Corry, the doctor said, had been born mad. Another doctor who examined Corry was asked if caffeine could have triggered the condition. "No, sir," the doctor replied. "I do not think that any external thing brought about his mental state." It was congenital.

There were other doctors from Philadelphia prepared to confirm the diagnosis, Coca-Cola's lawyer said, but Judge Sanford had heard enough.

"This case," he said, "is not going to depend on this man's testimony." Yet in a way it did. The government concluded its case without presenting a single victim who could illustrate the underlying idea that Coca-Cola was hazardous to the nation's health. It was a prosecution without a victim. Dr. Wiley's celebrated "poison squad," the dozen men who had made human guinea pigs of themselves ingesting caffeine, were never heard from.

In the middle of the trial's second week, the Coca-Cola Company began putting on its own experts, and they made a convincing chorus in rebuttal. Coca-Cola, they testified, contained 1.2 grains of caffeine per serving, or a little less than the average cup of tea or coffee, and had about the same mild effect.

The government scored a few effective blows against the company. Several of Coca-Cola's experts found themselves impeached by their own previous writings that criticized caffeine, and they learned to fear it when the prosecutor would begin his cross-examination by asking, "Have you ever written a book, or are you the author of any work?" When one doctor said with obvious relief that he had never written anything, he provoked a belly laugh in the courtroom. On a more serious note, the company had a tough time denying that children drank Coke, and most of the experts agreed that caffeine wasn't good for youngsters.

Still, it was clear by the end of the trial's second week that Coca-Cola was getting the better end of things. The company even produced the black laborer whose work habits had been described so dramatically when the proceedings started. James "Jeems" Gaston acquitted himself well, testifying earnestly that in twelve years working for Asa Candler he had never chewed tobacco, and that he did not work in broken, open-toed shoes, "'cause the hot licker might burn my feet." The *Chattanooga Times* reported that the government's optimism was "dwindling" and the prosecutors were hoping at best for a hung jury.

The most emphatic signal of shifting fortunes came with the departure of Dr. Wiley. He did not take the stand himself, and two weeks into the trial he abruptly announced that his presence was required in New York at Cornell University for a series of lectures on sanitation. He left with the same flair that marked his arrival. For one of his last dinners, he asked Houstoun Harper, the Patten Hotel's assistant manager, for some "old-style" Southern cuisine: johnnycake, corn pone, and other staples of "black mammy's cooking." Harper dutifully arranged the services of a black cook, who sent a traditional meal to the hotel. "The head chemist of the government 'set to,'" the *Chattanooga Sunday Times* reported, "just as though he had been accustomed to such things all his life. After he had concluded the ceremonies, even to the last crumb, he pushed back his chair, demanded the recipe, and said he was 'feeling first rate.'" And then he was gone.

Sensing victory, the Coca-Cola Company pressed its advantage through a third week of testimony, putting on the remainder of its eighteen expert witnesses. As the end of the trial drew near, the company's lawyers faced a choice. They could leave the outcome in the hands of the jury and hope, as seemed likely, that a verdict would be reached in Coca-Cola's favor. Or they could first ask Judge Sanford to *direct* a verdict—to rule that the government's case was so feeble that even if the facts it alleged were true, no violation of the law had taken place. There was little evident risk in asking for a directed verdict. If the motion failed, Judge Sanford would simply send the case onward to the jury, and Coca-Cola would still have an excellent chance of winning. Only one member of the defense team, Harold Hirsch, raised a warning voice. The danger, he said, was not in losing a motion for a directed verdict It was in winning. But Hirsch was a junior partner. He was overruled.

The senior lawyers went into court and argued that as a matter of law, the Coca-Cola Company could not be guilty of adulterating its syrup with caffeine, because *caffeine had always been part of the formula*. To violate the Pure Food and Drugs Act, they argued, an ingredient had to be "added," and as an original ingredient caffeine could not legally be considered "added" to Coca-Cola. It was a tricky point to grasp. As John Candler anticipated, Judge Sanford quickly seized on it, but other participants—on both sides—had to strain to follow the reasoning. Sanford called J. B. Cox, one of the prosecutors, to approach the bench. "If you cannot have Coca-Cola without caffeine," the judge asked, "how can you adulterate it by adding caffeine to it? That's the trouble I have." Cox was utterly befuddled and unable to answer.

Sanford patiently spelled out his thinking. In theory, coca or kola could be adulterated with caffeine or any other substance. But the government was not charging that Coca-Cola was a compound made of coca and kola. On the contrary, the government said Coca-Cola was "misbranded" because it contained too little of either. But if Coca-Cola was not a compound made of coca and kola, what was it? It was, Sanford continued, the name of a soft drink with certain familiar characteristics the public had come to expect, including the presence of caffeine.

The judge directed a verdict in favor of the company. There was no mistaking that Coca-Cola had won. "CASE IS PRACTICALLY THROWN OUT OF COURT" trumpeted a headline in the *Chattanooga Times*. But as Harold Hirsch feared, the victory was flawed. Part of the problem was a matter of publicity. It appeared that Coca-Cola had escaped on a technicality. After all the sensational testimony, the jury never got a chance to decide if Coca-Cola really was harmful. The facts remained in dispute. There was no sense of finality, no mark of vindication, no banner of innocence for the company to wave.

The directed verdict left Dr. Wiley free to fight another day. A jury's finding that caffeine was a mild, harmless stimulant might have closed the subject once and for all. Now there was nothing to certify how badly Wiley had failed to prove his case. A food industry journal, applauding the outcome, dismissed Wiley as an "irresponsible faddist," but nothing had occurred to persuade the general public to share that view. Within weeks, he was agitating again as vigorously as ever against the evils of caffeine and Coca-Cola.

Worst of all, there was a legal problem. The government intended to appeal the directed verdict because it threatened to limit the scope of the Pure Food and Drugs Act.

The damaging side effects of the verdict became obvious in August 1911, four months after the trial ended, when Candler and Sam Brown renewed their efforts to negotiate the sale of the company. After several weeks of dickering, they agreed on a price: $8 million. Brown got an option from Candler and set about trying to find backers to raise the money. But he got a rude awakening. His son-in-law, Hirsch, had been absolutely right about the directed verdict. With the appeal pending, investors were reluctant to make a commitment

In March 1912, Wiley resigned from the Bureau of Chemistry and accepted a job in the private sector as editor of *Good Housekeeping*. There was rejoicing in Atlanta. The news, Hirsch exulted, was "almost too good to be true." Yet there was still no chance for a settlement. The lawyers in the Department of Agriculture and the Justice Department cared very little about the caffeine in Coca-Cola, but they flatly refused to accept the limitations that the verdict placed on other prosecutions under the Pure Food and Drugs Act. If necessary, they planned to fight the case all the way to the United States Supreme Court.

In 1913, after more than a year searching fruitlessly for a buyer, Brown gave up. Investors everywhere saw the Coca-Cola Company just the way John Candler had once seen it, as a big balloon. Punch a hole in it, and it was gone. The threat of the appeal was like a sharp, shiny pin, and until it was resolved there would be no sale. The company was having its best year ever, on the way to record revenues of $8.8 million, more than the asking price, yet no one would buy. The true bottom line was that the physical assets of the company—the land, buildings, and inventory—were worth far less. As always, the genuine value was in the popularity of the trademark. An investor could pay $8 million for the company and lose almost all of it overnight if a higher court ruled the wrong way and Coca-Cola lost its name.

Candler grew morose. His nerves were frazzled and his dyspepsia was worse than ever. The vindication he craved for himself and his product eluded him. In the aftermath of the trial, D. W. Griffith, the pioneer filmmaker who later gained notoriety for *The Birth of a Nation*, made a short movie that vividly portrayed the ruination of a man named Campbell who produced a soft drink called Dopokoke. The silent film, entitled *For His Son: The Awful Result of Criminal Selfishness*, depicted a man who gains riches by callously lacing his beverage with cocaine, only to come to terrible justice when his own son falls prey to addiction and dies.

The company published a booklet with the patriotic title "Truth, Justice and Coca-Cola" that insisted plaintively, "There is not one indivisible atom of cocaine in a whole ocean of Coca-Cola. This is absolute and final." Yet the notion persisted. Hirsch, paying a visit to Washington early in 1912, nearly a year after the trial, was surprised to find the capital "pretty thoroughly saturated with the idea that Coca-Cola contained cocaine."

In the summer of 1913, Howard and the other children finally succeeded in packing their parents off to Europe for a grand tour. It brought Asa little joy. "I have forgotten the books I used to read," he wrote home wistfully. "I have lost my knowledge of history in my search for wealth till I can't now understand as I want to the wonderful sights that I see." In a remarkable and disturbing turn of phrase, he described himself as "weary, surfeited as a hog, who is penned up to eat and be made fat for slaughter."

At the age of sixty-one, Candler turned his thoughts to a higher plane. "My days on earth are now too few to be wasted . . ." he wrote. "I am from this time to the close of my life going to give myself to trying to make some contributions to the world's betterment."

He was still the owner of the Coca-Cola Company. But he no longer wanted it, and he tried to put it out of his mind.

Three

DOBBS

Samuel Candler Dobbs was near death. In the summer of 1950, his family checked him out of Emory University Hospital in Atlanta and put him in an ambulance for the three-hour drive to his lodge, The Lichens, in the cool, forested foothills near Lakemont in north Georgia.

At eighty-one, Dobbs was suffering the same dreadful ailment that seemed to haunt many of the men in the Candler family. He'd had a severe stroke, which was keeping his brain from getting enough blood and oxygen. Lying on his sickbed, he kept slipping in and out of delirium.

At times he grew terribly agitated. "He has to get back to Atlanta," his attending nurse explained, describing the recurrent hallucination that drew Dobbs backward into the distant past: "Howard Candler has just been made president of Coca-Cola and he simply can't let the work of years be thrown away in such a manner." The nurse, Eleise Wrenne, would try to calm Dobbs. That was a long time ago, she'd say. The company survived. "He says, 'No, they have just had a special meeting that elected Howard president . . . Howard is not capable of leading such an enterprise up the road as it should go.'"

Again and again, the vivid, fearful memory visited Dobbs, so real that he strained to rise and leave his bed. His first cousin, Howard Candler, had been made president of the Coca-Cola Company. It was a tremendous blunder. Dobbs had to do something before it was too late.

From the very first moment he discovered Coca-Cola, Sam Dobbs was in a fever. There really was no other way to put it. As a green, gangly seventeen-year-old fresh from the farm, he arrived in Atlanta to work for his uncle, Asa Candler, in 1886, the same year the drink was invented. Dobbs tried Coca-Cola for the first time at a soda fountain in the bakery next door and was smitten.

When Candler acquired the rights to Coca-Cola, it was Dobbs who drove the one-horse dray clattering down Marietta Street to Doc Pemberton's old headquarters, loaded up the kettles, percolators, inventory, and handmade advertising signs and delivered them to their new home. He was thrilled. The boys in Candler's laboratory "rejoiced," Dobbs recalled years later, because now "we could get all the Coca-Cola we wanted." And in Dobbs's case, that was a lot: He liked to drink at least a dozen Cokes a day, sometimes as many as fifteen.

Dobbs's excitement was more than just that of a consumer finding a ready supply of his favorite refreshment. Even as a teenager, he had an intuitive feel for the whole business. He wanted to sell Coca-Cola, and he was bursting with ideas how it should be done.

Dobbs was rough around the edges. The son of one of Asa Candler's older sisters, he'd grown up poor in a one-room shack in Carroll County, Georgia, near the Alabama line, during the rock-hard days of Reconstruction. "Sammie" Dobbs, as the Candler family called their country cousin, had finished only six months of formal schooling, and his grammar occasionally grated on the ear. Making a meager salary of $6 a week, sleeping on a cot in the back room, and wielding a broom, he was not expected to volunteer suggestions to his Uncle Asa about the best way to run the company. Yet he did.

There was the matter of bottling, for instance. During one of his visits to Doc Pemberton's ramshackle headquarters, Dobbs spotted the primitive bottling operation under the coal shed out in the backyard, and he was fascinated. The Matthews machine was little more than a wooden table with tubes connected to a generator and a pair of crude metal cylinders. It had hand and foot levers that were used to lower a valve, squirt syrup and carbonated water into a bottle, and secure an internal rubber disk and wire contraption known as a Hutchinson stopper as a seal. The carbonation was provided by the old-fashioned, malodorous method of mixing sulfuric acid and marble dust, and then forcing the escaping gas into water held under pressure in one of the cylinders. The process was "typically unsanitary, dirty, and antique," Dobbs had to admit, yet in the wink of an eye he could see the vast potential of selling Coke in bottles.

After Candler assumed control of Coca-Cola, he sent Dobbs out on the road to sell the new soft drink to soda fountain operators in Georgia, South Carolina, and the rest of the South. Dobbs did as he was told, calling on druggists in towns and small cities all across the region, but he also went his uncle one better and sold syrup to merchants who had back-alley bottling setups similar to Pemberton's. When Dobbs got home, Candler confronted him and told him to stop. Bottling was a primitive, unwholesome craft, in Candler's view. "There are too many folks who are not responsible," he explained, "who care nothing about the reputation of what they put up, and I am afraid the name [of Coca-Cola] will be injured." Bottles with Hutchinson stoppers were notoriously hard to clean and sanitize, and few of the early bottlers even bothered to try. It was not unusual for a bottling machine to be placed in the stable, conveniently near the wagons, on a floor covered with straw and horse manure. Candler told Dobbs to confine himself to selling the syrup solely for use at soda fountains.

As he recounted the episode years later, Dobbs remembered standing up to his uncle and arguing for what he believed: There simply weren't enough soda fountains. The smart move would be to sell Coca-Cola wherever they could, any way they could. A glass, of Coke could be sold only at the fountain, but a *bottle* of Coke could be shipped anywhere, sold anywhere, consumed anywhere. It was the future of the business, and it was limitless. Perhaps young Dobbs, still in his teens, was not quite as bold with his uncle as he enjoyed recalling. Not many men had the gumption to talk back to Asa Candler. Yet there is no question Dobbs was an advocate of bottling Coca-Cola long before others joined him in pushing the same idea. In the popular 1934 movie *Imitation of Life*, starring Claudette Colbert, a character repeats the widespread myth that Asa Candler once paid $50,000 for a two-word piece of advice about Coca-Cola—"Bottle it!"—but the truth of the matter was that Candler got the advice free from his own nephew and simply chose to ignore it for more than a decade.

During the first two full seasons of the Candler era, the summers of 1889 and 1890, Dobbs traveled the South by rail and buggy, ranging as far west as the Mississippi River and as far north as North Carolina. He bragged later (with justification) that he did more than any other individual to introduce Coca-Cola in the region. Then, graduating quickly from life on the road, Dobbs was assigned a desk in Atlanta and took charge of the company's shipping department. It was a job that required a certain degree of precision, since his Uncle Asa would dock his pay if he made a mistake and sent a shipment to Oxford, North Carolina, say, instead of Oxford, Mississippi. But Dobbs handled his chores well. As he grew into manhood in the 1890s, Dobbs completed his apprenticeship. Working side by side with Frank Robinson, he learned every step of the business, from buying the ingredients and making the syrup to keeping the books and packing advertising materials for the other salesmen.

At night, with Bishop Warren Candler as his tutor, Dobbs studied hard and tried to make up for his lack of schooling. In time, he gained polish and a bit of sophistication to go along with his innate sense of self-confidence. The country bumpkin was turning into quite a formidable adult, but the one part of Dobbs's personality that never seemed to mellow, the one rough edge that was never sanded smooth, was his ambition. In a photograph from that period, the striking thing about Dobbs was the look in his eyes: luminous, intense, knowing, needy, somehow almost feral.

The Coca-Cola Company of the Gay Nineties was a business of deceptive simplicity. As late as the turn of the century, when production exceeded a quarter of a million gallons and sales were recorded in every state of the union, the corporate headquarters in Atlanta employed only twenty people. When the new factory was opened in 1898—the factory Asa Candler believed would meet Coca-Cola's needs "for all time to come"—the entire workforce could fit on the front steps to pose for a picture.

While the flow of syrup swelled dramatically with each passing year, the process of making it remained basically unchanged. Water, sugar, caffeine, and caramel were cooked in a kettle, preservatives and flavorings were added in the cooling tanks, and the final product was drawn into jars, kegs, and barrels for shipment by dray and rail. The real challenge and excitement, then as now, lay in selling and advertising, and it was in that direction Dobbs felt himself tugged.

Asa Candler deployed a tiny platoon of salesmen across the American countryside, trying to get dealers to carry Coca-Cola. The efforts were not always successful. One nephew, Dan Candler, delighted in telling the story of a call he made on a druggist in a small town in Oklahoma. The man had never heard of the new soft drink, and when young Candler tried to sell him a fifty-gallon barrel of syrup he laughed out loud. Candler suggested a smaller ten-gallon keg. Still no deal. Finally, a bit exasperated, Candler said, "Well, how about buying a one-gallon jug? Anybody can sell a gallon of Coca-Cola." And the druggist replied evenly, "Well, Mister, you ain't done it yet."

Frank Robinson and Sam Dobbs were working on ways to make those sales easier. In addition to the sampling campaign that deluged soda fountain operators with hundreds of thousands of free tickets good for a Coke "for you and a friend," Robinson and Dobbs concocted a series of promotions designed to make the soft drink familiar and accessible. They got Ed Grant, an independent sign painter in Atlanta, to design an oilcloth banner that could be pinned around the flap of the awnings that adorned most drugstores. The trademark, in red lettering on a white background (with the slogan "Delicious and Refreshing" in blue), reminded people they wanted a Coca-Cola and told them where they could get one. In 1894, an artist named Jim Couden painted Coca-Cola's name on the side of a drugstore operated by Will Young and Evans Mays in Cartersville, Georgia; it was the first of twenty thousand Coca-Cola wall signs that eventually punctuated the American landscape. One year Robinson and Dobbs made it their goal to have "Coca-Cola" painted on every barn in the Midwest. Asa Candler once said he realized his product had gained a national reputation when he saw a Coca-Cola sign in the background of a photograph of President McKinley's funeral cortege as it moved from New York to Ohio in 1901.

For the insides of stores, Robinson and Dobbs commissioned articles known as "dealer helps": keepsakes, posters, trays, and other items that carried the name "Coca-Cola" and were meant to jog a consumer's memory and close a sale before he escaped. The company bought the rights to a photograph of the popular actress Lillian Russell, for example, painted a glass of Coca-Cola near her hand, and printed up five thousand poster-size copies to be displayed at soda fountains. Long before the phrase "impulse buying" became part of the advertising vernacular, Robinson and Dobbs understood instinctively that they had a chance to sell Coca-Cola to people who hadn't planned to drink one when they first walked into the store. To trigger that impulse, the company sent out thousands of ceramic syrup urns, clocks, metal signs, posters, trays, and decals—all to ensure that no matter which way a customer turned, the name "Coca-Cola" would pop up in his or her line of vision.

In time, store owners came to appreciate Coca-Cola because they found it attracted customers who would spend their money on other goods as well.

The company took its promotions out into the streets, too, as the salesmen gave away thousands of blotters, paperweights, calendars, and other novelties to anyone who would take them. The leading item was Coca-Cola's famous Japanese fan. Unfolding to reveal a pretty picture on one side and the Coca-Cola logo on the other, the fans created a subliminal, stroboscopic message whenever a hot, thirsty customer fluttered one in front of her face.

Passing out the fans became something of a rite of passage in the Candler family. When he was working as a salesman during summer vacation one year, Howard Candler recalled being ordered to distribute a hundred boxes of the fans in offices, restaurants, barber shops, and hotel lobbies around Kansas City. He made a practice of stringing the fans on pieces of rope, hitching a string over each shoulder, trudging up to the top floor of every building in town and making his way down, office by office, giving away the fans. (It is perhaps an indication of Howard's intellectual limitations that he did not think to begin the distributions on the ground level and work his way *up* the floors, thereby lightening his load as he went, but in any case he carried out his instructions and "got rid of a tremendous amount of bulk advertising material, as well as practically all of my energy. . . .")

As the 1890s progressed, Dobbs gradually took over the job of sales manager. Though Robinson kept the title, Dobbs eased him aside and assumed the duties of training the salesmen, arranging their trips, filling their orders, and packing their advertising supplies in the metal-bound trunks that were shipped ahead to the railroad stations along their routes. Asa Candler's other nephews watched Dobbs's rise with a mix of trepidation and grudging admiration. In part it was a matter of personality. In dealing with underlings, Robinson was known for his gentle, forgiving tone. If a secretary or a stenographer made a mistake, Robinson typically apologized and said it was his own fault for not making his instructions clear. Like a doting parent, Robinson worried about the health and welfare of his salesmen out in the field and urged them to take care of themselves.

Dobbs had a much harder edge. He was demanding, and he got more out of the men. Among other things, Dobbs expected his salesmen to show soda fountain operators how to prepare Coca-Cola properly, a job that often entailed ducking down and crawling through the dank cobwebs and grit underneath the counter to check the ice chamber and cooling coils, making sure the carbonated water was cold enough. A warm Coca-Cola was a sin.

Following the example set by Asa Candler, Dobbs saw to it that the company recruited men of high personal standards. Bill Trebilcock, the Chicago manager, made a habit of attending Women's Christian Temperance Union meetings to look for candidates for his sales staff. With his flowing, fiery, red moustache, Trebilcock was an arresting sight, but many of the salesmen found the most memorable thing about him the fact that he didn't smoke, chew, drink, or curse—or hire other men who did. In an era when traveling salesmen ("drummers" in the parlance of the day) earned a reputation for card-playing and carousing, Coca-Cola's representatives stood out as exceptions.

In return for their hard work, Dobbs fought for his salesmen's interests at the home office in Atlanta. With the horse-and-buggy era drawing to a close, the men wanted to drive company cars, yet Asa Candler seemed wedded to the old ways and balked at the extravagance. Dobbs spent years breaking down his uncle's resistance and finally arranged the purchase of a small fleet of Locomobiles for the salesmen in New York City. He turned over his own car, a two-seat, Belgian-made Metalurgique, to the men in Chicago.

Along with affection, Dobbs commanded respect and fidelity. Coca-Cola salesmen earned a modest but regular salary of $12.50 a week, plus expenses, and Dobbs made sure they knew he was the one who controlled their livelihoods. (It was the expense allowance that made a job with Coca-Cola especially coveted, since the company paid for three restaurant meals a day, lodging in good hotels, and first-class rail travel whenever a salesman was on the road.) Over time, Dobbs made himself "the only contact point with the home office that the sales force knew," and the salesmen repaid him with their loyalty. One of them later described Dobbs as a natural leader, "an immensely attractive man—a dynamic personality and a brilliant speaker."

Dobbs took up other causes as well. One of a salesman's toughest chores was keeping the merchants from buying cheap, substitute syrup and passing it off as the real thing. The tremendous profit margins built into each level of the Coca-Cola business were supposed to keep everyone happy. It cost the Candlers less than $1 to manufacture a gallon of syrup, which they then sold to a jobber (typically a grocery or drug wholesaler) for $1.50, yielding a return of 50 percent. The jobber sold the gallon of syrup to a retailer for $2, making a quick turnaround profit of one-third. The retailer did best of all, serving about 100 drinks from each gallon at a nickel apiece, pulling in $5 on his $2 investment. But an even handsomer return was available to a retailer if he could buy syrup for less than $2, and as Coca-Cola's popularity rose, so did the number of small-time operators peddling dark, watery imitations that could be passed off as Coca-Cola syrup.

With his keen, high-pitched sense of proper business ethics, Asa Candler railed against the "unscrupulous pirates" and "scoundrels" who were undercutting Coca-Cola's reputation and profits, yet he had only the most rudimentary strategy for fending them off: Candler expected his salesmen to protect the company's interests with their fists. John H. Power, one of the early salesmen hired by Dobbs, recalled that his colleagues would give a soda fountain operator one warning, and "on the next trip if they found the man still substituting, they would. . .take him out the front door on the sidewalk and 'biff' him one. That actually happened." A grocer in Virginia complained to Power that one of the other salesmen routinely took him outside in front of the store "and hit me in the eye." Power, who was physically slight, tried to rely on persuasion instead.

Dobbs found the idea of fisticuffs hopelessly outmoded. As he looked around the company, Dobbs suffered a growing sense of frustration. He saw the need to modernize nearly every facet of Coca-Cola's operations, yet everywhere he turned he found inertia and an instinct to continue doing things in the tried-and-true ways that had served the company well enough so far. The solution to the substitution problem, he believed, wasn't out in the street, brawling, but in the courtroom using the swiftly evolving body of law that provided manufacturers with protection against unfair competition.

The salesmen weren't the only ones who needed legal help. In 1899, ten years after Dobbs first prodded him to do so, Asa Candler finally relented and agreed to let independent operators begin bottling and selling Coca-Cola. All across the country, small businessmen were scraping together money and investing in bottling operations, only to find themselves undercut by competitors mimicking Coca-Cola's name.

Dozens and eventually hundreds of imitators flooded the market with sound-alike soft drinks, among them Afri-Cola, Ameri-Cola, Ala-Cola, Bolama-Cola, Cafe-de-Ola, Carbo-Cola, Candy-Kola, Capa-Cola, Chero-Cola, Christo-Cola, Coke-Ola, Coo-EE-Cola, Curo-Cola, Grap-O-Cola, Its-A-Cola, Kaffir-Kola, Kaw-Kola, Kiss-Kola, Ko-Ca-Ama, Koca-Nola, Ko-Co-Lem-A, Kokola, Klu Ko Kolo, Loco Cola, Luna Cola, Mitch-O-Cola, Mo-Cola, My Cola, Roco-Cola, Toca-Cola, Taka-Cola, Qua-Kola, Uneeda-Cola, Zero-Cola, and Zippi-Cola. In New Bern, North Carolina, a pharmacist named Caleb Bradham was making a drink he called Pepsi-Cola.

The brazenness of the counterfeiters was remarkable (it could almost be said that they showed inventiveness in their plagiarism), but Dobbs found nothing at all amusing about their activities. He yearned to sue them, and in private he complained that his uncles, Asa and John, were content "to allow infringements—some of them most flagrant—to go on undisturbed." While the older Candlers were devoting most of their legal and political energies to the unfolding fight against Dr. Wiley and the government, Dobbs worried that the imitators were infiltrating the market and siphoning off Coca-Cola's sales.

Dobbs was also growing restless over the company's marketing. Advertising was his passion, and as the years went by he became increasingly envious of Robinson's control over the creative end of the business. Like a gifted student surpassing his professor, Dobbs learned from Robinson and then began to want to move faster and try newer ideas and spend more money.

At the turn of the century, Robinson was fifty-four years old and Dobbs thirty-one. A new era was opening—the company placed a $10,000 order for its first magazine ads in 1902, in *Munsey's* monthly—and Dobbs longed to take charge. Robinson and Dobbs started bickering about the size and scope of the company's advertising, and their arguments grew increasingly ugly. Dobbs had been given a directorship of the company, and he began carrying his disputes with Robinson to the board, making Asa Candler arbitrate. At first, Robinson won most of the skirmishes, but then the tide turned.

The incident that sparked Dobbs's final break with Robinson was the employment in 1902 of an outside advertising agency. St. Elmo Massengale, an old friend of Robinson's who ran a one-man shop in Atlanta, was signed up to help design the company's ads. Bringing an innovative touch to the job, Massengale inaugurated the use of endorsements of Coke by sports figures of the age. In 1903, for instance, the champion bicyclist Jack Prince advocated Coke in a newspaper ad. Massengale wrote copy in which the athletes seemed to be speaking directly to the reader. "The other players can drink all the whisky, beer and wine they want," said the baseball star Nap Lajoie, "but none of that for me . . ." Lajoie preferred Coca-Cola.

Massengale created slice-of-life scenes and tried to make Coca-Cola an integral part of the activity. Unlike the earlier, static ads featuring stiff, corseted actresses, Massengale's work showed theatergoers—actual consumers—lining up for a Coca-Cola during intermission. His ads illustrated thirst and fatigue in social settings and showed people using the product. Massengale also recognized the opportunities inherent in the advent of the automobile age. One of his pioneering ads showed a party of motorists stopping at a roadside restaurant, where a white-coated waiter came out and presented a tray full of glasses of Coca-Cola "to refresh the parched throat, to invigorate the fatigued body, and quicken the tired brain." If Massengale had a failing, it was his inclination to depict Coca-Cola drinkers as aristocrats of "discriminating" taste (his men typically wore high hats and his women favored ornate bonnets) when the company's target was people from all social levels.

Dobbs had no quarrel with the switch away from the tone and techniques of old-fashioned advertising. His criticism of Robinson and Massengale was that they didn't go far enough. In Dobbs's view, Coca-Cola advertising ought to "attract the eye with something appealing, in the way of an illustration that in itself tells a story, and then impress that story on the reader with good, catchy phrases [*sic*], giving a reason why they should spend their money with us." Coca-Cola was a beverage, Dobbs conceded, "but isn't it something more than a beverage?"

Marketing differences, however, were not the real issue. The clash between Robinson and Dobbs over advertising came at the same time Asa Candler was beginning to withdraw more and more from the daily operations of the company. By taking a hands-off role and acting as "chief policy maker," Candler was creating a power vacuum in the executive suite, and it became apparent that Robinson and Dobbs were actually competing to see who would run the Coca-Cola Company in the years ahead. Gaining authority over advertising was the key to gaining control of the whole business.

It was possible to be blinded by Dobbs's ambition. Lacking the grace to conceal his longing for power, Dobbs made the mistake of letting everyone in the company and the Candler family know just how badly he wanted to make it to the top. Most of them were repelled. Among his relatives, Dobbs was still known disparagingly as "Sammie," in reference to his humble beginnings in the country. They found something unseemly about his willingness to climb over a man as gentle and loyal as Frank Robinson, and of course they found something fearful in his eagerness to climb over them. His cousins saw Dobbs's assault on St. Elmo Massengale as nothing more than a matter of office politics and naked jealousy: Dobbs was after Massengale's hide because Massengale worked for Robinson, and Robinson was in the way.

Thus it came as a considerable surprise throughout the company when Asa Candler resolved the struggle, in 1906, by making Dobbs the director of Coca-Cola's advertising. The point everyone seemed to miss was that Dobbs, whatever his social shortcomings, had a brilliant mind for the business and a track record to prove it. Candler decided to give Dobbs a chance to show what he could accomplish with the company's ad budget, and Dobbs quickly made the most of his opportunity. He had his selfish reasons for pushing Massengale aside, true, but in picking a replacement Dobbs succeeded in discovering one of the great rising talents of the advertising world, Bill D'Arcy, who would spend the next half-century making history with his work on behalf of Coca-Cola.

William Cheever D'Arcy was working for an agency in St. Louis, selling space for advertising cards on streetcars, when Dobbs first encountered him during a trip through the Midwest in the early 1900s. The two were introduced by the Coca-Cola salesman in St. Louis, Willard Cox, and quickly formed a friendship, discovering they shared a passion for baseball. D'Arcy was anxious to go into business on his own, and Dobbs gave him encouragement.

At the St. Louis World's Fair in 1904, D'Arcy attracted considerable attention with a display he created for George A. Dickel & Company, the Nashville distiller. Piping water up from the Mississippi River, D'Arcy built an eye-catching artificial waterfall to promote Cascade Whiskey, and Dickel agreed to become his first client. Coca-Cola was his second. In the late summer of 1906, in a small suite he rented for $5 a month, D'Arcy opened his own office in downtown St. Louis. Dobbs gave the fledgling D'Arcy Advertising Company a total of $4,602 in billings that first year, including $1,500 for newspaper ads in St. Louis and Kansas City. Then, pleased with the results, Dobbs hiked D'Arcy's budget up to $25,000 the next year, and kept giving him more and more of the company's business.

A native of St. Louis born to parents of Irish ancestry, D'Arcy was a strikingly handsome man who bore himself with immense dignity. He wore starched collars and a pince-nez, and as he walked to his office at the corner of Pine and Sixth streets he resembled a banker or a minister more than a promoter. He was reserved by nature and took a serious approach to his work. He believed in an intimate relationship between agent and client—like a doctor and patient—and formed a close personal and professional bond with Dobbs.

For all his chilliness, Bill D'Arcy was a natural salesman. He shared Dobbs's view that Coca-Cola advertising should create scenes that drew people in and made them part of the pleasant interludes of everyday life. In an ad he placed in the St. Louis classified phone directory, D'Arcy proclaimed, "All classes, ages and sexes drink Coca-Cola," and the sentiment could have served as a manifesto for his approach to the company's advertising. Like Massengale, D'Arcy believed in slice-of-life illustrations, but D'Arcy also had a knack for writing text that reached the common man and brought the illustrations alive. In one of his first newspaper ads for Coca-Cola, D'Arcy showed a picture of the baseball star Ty Cobb at bat, and wrote:

> Something's bound to happen. Everybody on edge—nerves-a-tingle—head whizzing. Crack!! Good boy Ty!! Safe!! And then you shout yourself hoarse. When it's all over you're hot, thirsty and limp. A cold, snappy drink of Coca-Cola will put you back in the game—relieve the thirst and cool you off.

D'Arcy gave a story line to his ads (and a sense of excitement) that outpaced all earlier efforts. His ads had a universal appeal and connected on a simple, emotional level. D'Arcy understood human nature. One of the legendary stories about him involved an ad campaign the agency undertook on behalf of a hosiery company. A staff artist worked up a design for a billboard featuring a breathtaking young woman with long, shapely legs. The account executives who brought the mock-up to D'Arcy's office were nervous about the presentation, thinking they probably had gone a little too far, but to their surprise D'Arcy looked over the drawing and nodded his approval. "Gentlemen," he said solemnly, "I want that artwork finished so that a man walking or riding down the street and passing this poster will desire that woman."

Before D'Arcy took over, the women depicted in Coca-Cola's ads tended to look either girlishly innocent, or, in the case of the professional actresses who endorsed the soft drink, stiff and Victorian. There was a sense of innocence about them that reflected Asa Candler's primness. One of Asa's nephews, Sam Willard, recalled that in the early days, when illustrations arrived from the lithographer, everyone in the Atlanta headquarters would gather around for a close inspection: "If a particularly beautiful portrait was shown, a lovely and discreetly gowned model, Mr. Robinson would say, 'I think Mr. Asa will like this one.' That always called for a general twinkling of eyes." After D'Arcy came on the scene, the models remained fresh and wholesome, but there was a new, unmistakably flirtatious air about them. The company's calendar girls became more accessible, somehow, as if the girl-next-door not only happened to be a smashing beauty but had a coquettish, come-hither personality to boot. D'Arcy introduced the bathing beauty to Coca-Cola's advertising, and with her the idea that a soft drink could have a role in romance.

As he demonstrated with his artificial waterfall, D'Arcy loved innovations and dramatic flourishes. In 1908, he created an animated billboard alongside the Pennsylvania Railroad, and travelers from Philadelphia to New York City were treated to the sight of a white-capped clerk serving what appeared to be genuine Coca-Cola (it was actually water pumped through a two-inch pipe from a nearby city main) from a giant ceramic urn. A year later, D'Arcy hired a dirigible that cruised slowly over Washington, D.C., carrying giant Coca-Cola signs on either side.

The advent of the general circulation magazines, with their high quality paper and four-color presses, gave D'Arcy his greatest chance to shine. He could reach a mass audience with good popular art, and by 1910 the company was giving him $225,000 a year to buy full pages in the *Saturday Evening Post, Collier's,* and *Good Housekeeping.* Poor Massengale saw his role diminish—he was relegated to placing ads in religious publications—until he lost the Coca-Cola account entirely.

Although Dobbs's coup left him in charge of sales and advertising, he quickly turned his attention to the company's other operations as well. In January 1906, Harold Hirsch joined John Candler's law firm as a partner, and he instantly allied himself with Dobbs in the view that the company should be seeking protection in the courts from the onslaught of substitutions and trademark infringement. Just as Dobbs and D'Arcy formed an effective partnership overseeing Coca-Cola's advertising, Dobbs and Hirsch became a force for change in the direction of the company's legal policies. Hirsch was a brilliant and combative lawyer, eager to track down Coca-Cola's enemies and sue them out of existence.

Born into a prominent Jewish family in Atlanta, Hirsch first displayed his competitive streak as a young man, playing center and fullback for the University of Georgia football team and graduating with high honors in 1901. Spurning his family's clothing business, Hirsch earned his law degree at Columbia University in 1904 and came to the attention of John Candler, who was then serving as a justice on the Georgia Supreme Court Candler sensed the need for new energy and scholarship in his practice and made

Hirsch a senior partner (at the tender age of twenty-four) in the firm of Candler, Thomson & Hirsch.

Hirsch, a stocky, powerful man who wore his Phi Beta Kappa key prominently displayed on his vest, brought a renewed spirit of aggressiveness to the defense of Coca-Cola's trademark. As part of the Progressive movement, Congress passed the Trade-Mark Act of 1905 in an effort to bring a measure of reason and logic to the chaotic mix of common law, individual state statutes, and federal case histories that governed the use of proper names and distinctive marks for manufactured products. For the first time, federal trademark law was specifically applied to interstate commerce, giving the company an opportunity to sue infringers in U.S. district court. The older Candlers viewed the new law with uncertainty, worrying that it might be years before the courts finished interpreting it, with no guarantee that the company's exclusive right to use "Coca-Cola" as a trademark would ultimately be upheld. But with Dobbs urging him on, Hirsch brushed aside the misgivings of the older generation and went on the attack.

Discovering a pair of bottlers in South Carolina who were manufacturing an inferior product and labeling it "Coca-Cola," Hirsch sued in federal court and secured his first injunction in the spring of 1906. It hardly mattered that the two bottlers had pocketed only a meager $125 peddling their bogus syrup; Hirsch's point was to send a message that the company no longer intended to tolerate substitutions and infringement Hirsch won judgments in Pennsylvania against the manufacturers of Toca-Coca, in Louisiana against Ko-Kola, and in Illinois against Kos-Kola. Dobbs backed up the new legal strategy with an advertising campaign that urged consumers to insist on "genuine" Coca-Cola.

As the first decade of the twentieth century unfolded, Dobbs continued to cement his role as Asa Candler's top lieutenant. When the company's troubles with Dr. Wiley began in 1907, for instance, Dobbs took charge of lining up political support from the nation's thousands of soda fountain operators. At a convention of druggists in Chicago, Dobbs headed a team of twenty Coca-Cola men who provided transportation, nonstop entertainment, and gentle arm-twisting for the three thousand conventioneers in attendance. He also saw to it that Coca-Cola's Japanese fans were passed out at the final banquet in the First Regiment Armory, where it was so hot the keynote speaker busily waved his fan the whole time he was giving his address. "I saw the President of the Association as he was leaving the hotel," Dobbs reported home, "and, taking hold of my hands, he remarked: 'Dobbs, you and the boys are alright; they did themselves proud this week, and we are all for Coca-Cola.'"

As John Candler and Harold Hirsch prepared the company for its showdown with Wiley in the courtroom, Dobbs emerged as Coca-Cola's most effective spokesman in the equally crucial arena of public opinion. Battling to rid Coca-Cola of the last vestiges of its patent medicine origins, Dobbs maneuvered in 1909 to become president of the Associated Advertising Clubs of America, where he helped launch the "Truth in Advertising" movement. During his two-year term heading the league, Dobbs estimated he traveled 45,000 miles around the country preaching the doctrine of "clean, truthful, honest publicity" (and concurrently associating the Coca-Cola Company with those virtues).* The local committees Dobbs helped organize later evolved into the national system of Better Business Bureaus. Thanks in large measure to Sam Dobbs, a company that had brazenly exaggerated the benefits of its product just a few short years earlier was now busily trying to transform itself into a model citizen.

Dobbs's rise to the top echelon of the Coca-Cola Company was remarkable, considering the lowliness of his starting position, and it was made even more dramatic when measured against the failure of Asa Candler's own children to keep pace. While Dobbs was showing his facility for a variety of executive tasks, Candler's eldest son, Howard, was doing just the opposite. Aside from his enthusiasm for the physical process of making Coca-Cola syrup, Howard proved to be inept at every other chore he was asked to perform.

An episode from 1908 was particularly telling. As the company prepared for battle with Dr. Wiley, Asa assigned Howard the job of traveling to New Jersey to inspect the Schaefer laboratory and make sure that the Merchandise No. 5 manufactured there was free from cocaine and otherwise in compliance with the Pure Food and Drugs Act. Having been surprised before by unexpected and embarrassing test results, Asa was anxious to avoid a repeat performance. When Howard called on Schaefer's agents and asked for an appointment to tour the facilities, however, they told him he was unwelcome. Howard reported back to his father that he was unable to make the inspection. Asa related the news to Sam Dobbs, who expressed amazement at his cousin Howard's timidity. The contract for Merchandise No. 5 was worth tens of thousands of dollars, Dobbs pointed out, and Dr. Schaefer was in no position to refuse a visit from anyone with the Coca-Cola Company, let alone the son of the proprietor. Howard had no need to ask permission to visit the laboratory. He just had to show up, knock on the door, and waltz in. Asa wrote to Howard that night and sent him back to try again.

Given Howard's feebleness, and the lack of aptitude Asa's four younger children displayed for the business (William, the baby of the family, was the only other child on the payroll, and he was an accountant), perhaps it is no surprise that Dobbs came to believe he was destined to succeed his

---

* On the twenty-fifth anniversary of the founding of the movement, in a nice piece of hyperbole (and extended metaphor), the Advertising Federation of America saluted Dobbs for his leadership, saying, "He launched a crusade—at first it seemed almost a lone and personal battle—to drive the infidel Fraud out of the sacred land of advertising. At the end of two years the torch which he carried until it flamed high along the paths of paid publicity passed to other able bearers, to burn undimmed through a generation."

uncle and run the company. In private, Dobbs began referring to Coca-Cola as "our baby" and "my child," and he developed a protective attitude that eventually convinced him he was the only one who could shepherd the enterprise into the next generation. With sales and advertising already tucked in his portfolio, and with more and more control over other operations dropping into his hands every day, Dobbs became a sort of de facto president of the company, lacking only the title (which Asa retained) to complete his authority.

Dobbs was making a salary of $8,000 a year—modest, perhaps, but more than Howard's $6,000 and more than the $5,200 Asa paid himself. It was the top pay in the company. After starting out as a country cousin, Dobbs saw himself as a full-fledged member of the family, worthy of carrying on its purposes. Dobbs had named his son Samuel Candler Dobbs, Jr., which was hardly unusual, but there seemed to be a point in the fact that he called the boy by his middle name.

Dobbs had no way of knowing about the ambitions that Asa Candler harbored deep in his heart on behalf of his own son, Howard. Asa had been urging Howard to broaden his understanding of the business and prepare himself to take over, but those entreaties were passed along in the private conversations and correspondence of a father and his son, not in the open air of the office or in family councils. As Dobbs saw it, he was the company's top executive, and he believed he could count on others to see it that way, too.

For all Dobbs or anyone else knew, Asa shared the widespread view that his eldest son was, as one of the company's salesmen tactfully put it, "quiet, kind, and friendly man," one who might be dedicated to Coca-Cola but plainly lacked the talent to run the company. Despite sharing those apprehensions, though, Asa was gradually persuading himself that Howard should be his successor.

In a confidential letter to his brother, Warren, Asa disclosed his intention to retire completely from the Coca-Cola Company in December 1913, when he turned sixty-two. "Now this is for you and you only to know," Asa added, but his plan was to make Howard the new president. There is nothing in the record to explain in detail why Asa planned to spurn Dobbs in favor of Howard. No doubt the thickness of the blood tie was the decisive factor. Howard wanted the job, and few fathers are capable of inflicting the sort of crushing disappointment on a son that Howard would have suffered in losing the job to his cousin. But there was another element playing a part in Asa's thinking: the matter of temperament.

William Landers was an auditor in the company's Atlanta headquarters, and in his unpublished memoirs he recalled an episode from about 1913, when Dobbs

> was making a pep speech to the employees. As we had had
> an unusually good year, Mr. Dobbs stated with great gusto

that we had now reached a point where we do not have to take off our hats to anybody. I noticed Mr. Candler nervously twiddling his thumbs, as he always did when he did not like something that was being said. He followed Mr. Dobbs with a speech of his own in which he said: "Mr. Sammy Dobbs, in his speech, made the statement that now we do not have to take off our hats to anybody, but I say unto you ladies and gentlemen that I go with my hat in my hand."

Dobbs was headed for a painful awakening. His lifelong goal of becoming president of the company was about to be snatched out of his hands. It was one thing to lose the prize because of an accident of birth, but an even greater cruelty was at work in Dobbs's case. His finest successes on behalf of the company, his triumphs in advertising and marketing, his help in guiding the company through its sternest legal and political challenges, his satisfaction at seeing Coca-Cola making more money than it ever had before—all of these things now seemed to be rubbing Asa Candler the wrong way. Dobbs had groomed himself perfectly for the job of running Coca-Cola, only to find that Asa Candler no longer cared about the qualities that enabled a man to do well in business, or at least disapproved of those qualities if they were not subordinated to a deep sense of humility and selflessness. Weary, nervous, preoccupied with his own mortality, Asa Candler took off for his tour of Europe in the summer of 1913 sounding very much as if he had lost his belief in capitalism itself. "I do not want to make money," the richest man in Atlanta wrote. He wanted to make the world a better place.

As 1913 passed, and then 1914 and 1915, Candler kept postponing his retirement and delaying the moment when Howard would assume the presidency. The old man was growing more and more discouraged about the company's prospects. His hope of selling the company was placed on indefinite hold as Judge Sanford's verdict in the Chattanooga case made its way slowly up the appellate ladder to the United States Supreme Court, where Candler feared he might very well lose. New tax laws were forcing him to distribute the surplus profits he'd grown accustomed to leaving on the company's books. Though the millions of dollars that flowed into his pockets helped pay for his philanthropy, Candler nonetheless worried that the company would not have the capital it needed to grow in the years to come. In the meantime, Candler had witnessed the gathering momentum toward war during his visit to Europe, and he believed the worldwide conflict would eventually reach the United States and wreck business conditions.

The First World War did have a devastating impact on the economy of the American South, as the closing of European markets nearly destroyed the region's cotton farmers. The collapse of cotton prices in the autumn of

1914 gave Candler a chance to demonstrate his new dedication to humanitarianism with a spectacular gesture, as he staked his personal fortune on a $30 million loan guarantee and agreed to purchase the year's cotton crop for the whole state of Georgia. The war "has almost scared the life out of business in this part of the world," Candler wrote one of his nephews, and he meant to relieve that fear and cushion the suffering of his fellow Southerners—single-handedly if necessary.

Thanks to the good financial health of the Coca-Cola Company, Asa Candler was able to give a $1 million cash gift in 1914 to his brother's school, Emory University, to move its main campus from the countryside to Atlanta; a year later he underwrote an entire $3 million bond issue for the state of Georgia, the first time since the Civil War that an offering was covered completely by home-grown capital.

Candler kept the Coca-Cola Company in a state of limbo until January 21, 1916, when he announced tersely at the annual meeting that his son Howard was succeeding him as president. In a book he wrote about his father years later, Howard speculated that the changing of the guard was attributable to a combination of factors, starting with Asa's bitter vexation over the new federal tax laws.* "He felt," Howard wrote of Asa, "that he could no longer conduct his business in the way he believed it should be conducted to assure its best progress and to realize its potential greatness." Howard described his father as extremely discouraged over Coca-Cola's prospects, and he thought perhaps his father was also depressed because he missed Frank Robinson, who retired in 1914 in poor health. The portrait Howard painted of his father's state of mind is noteworthy for the attitude of surrender and hopelessness it depicts. If Asa Candler had any faith that his son was equipped to lead Coca-Cola, or any optimism that the future held promise, certainly he failed utterly to convey it to Howard. Asa seems to have handed his son the reins of an enterprise he believed to be on the brink of decline, possibly disaster.

It appears, in fact, that Candler's abrupt disengagement from the company alarmed some of Coca-Cola's employees and created anxiety in Atlanta's business community. Two weeks afterward, on February 1, 1916, Candler took the uncommon step of issuing a signed public notice that he would remain interested in the company and serve as its chairman. The same statement, apparently designed to provide reassurances about the future of the business, announced that Sam Dobbs would take the title of vice president and manager of sales and advertising, in effect becoming Howard's chief deputy.

---

* In his president's report in 1914, Candler complained that taxes "grow as Hagar's gourd vine and are to us, who must pay them, as offensive as gourd vines in wheat fields," a lament that sounds vaguely biblical but in fact is nowhere to be found in either Old or New Testament, and whose origin remains an unsolved mystery in the Coca-Cola Company's corporate minutes.

Publicly, Dobbs played the good soldier and continued his duties on behalf of the company. But in a clear sign of his private discontent, he began spending as much time as he could away from Atlanta; within a few weeks after Howard's accession, Dobbs notified his Coca-Cola colleagues that henceforth he would be taking his mail at the company's New York office. And he began searching for a way to reverse his fortunes.

So long as Asa Candler owned the Coca-Cola Company, Dobbs had no recourse. At the time Howard became president, Asa held 391 of the 500 outstanding shares and thus maintained absolute, one-man control of what amounted to a closely held family corporation. In the years since Candler chartered the company in 1892, only a handful of outsiders had ever owned stock (mostly jobbers, who distributed Coke in various territories and took a few shares in lieu of cash commissions) and by 1916 Candler had bought all of them out. The remaining 109 shares of the company were owned in small lots by various members of Candler's family and Frank Robinson's. Dobbs held 23 shares, for instance, and Asa's five children, including Howard, owned five shares apiece. Company lore had it that Candler enjoyed dousing the occasional family disagreement by saying, "I vote my shares against that."

Candler's plan to sell the company had remained in a deep freeze for several years, and there is no telling how much longer he might have been content to allow the situation to continue, with his son in charge and the company's affairs flowing along in a gentle, nicely profitable drift, had not events overtaken him. But at long last the day of legal reckoning arrived, and on May 22, 1916, the United States Supreme Court handed down its decision in the Chattanooga case. It reversed Judge Sanford on all counts.

In a withering opinion, one of the last he wrote before resigning from the court to become the Republican nominee for president, Justice Charles Evans Hughes heaped ridicule on the directed verdict from the lower court, just as Harold Hirsch had feared. The government's lawyers had proven implacable in their determination to make sure that the key provisions of the Pure Food and Drugs Act were upheld. The Coca-Cola Company had argued cleverly that caffeine could not be an illegally "added" ingredient since it had always been part of the formula for the soft drink, and Judge Sanford had agreed. Justice Hughes did not. "If this were so," he wrote acidly, "the statute would be reduced to an absurdity. Manufacturers would be free, for example, to put arsenic or strychnine or other poisonous or deleterious ingredients. . .into compound articles of food, provided the compound were made according to formula and sold under some fanciful name."

Hughes was even more scathing in rejecting Judge Sanford's decision on a second vital point, the question of misbranding. Sanford had ruled that the company had a right to call its product Coca-Cola, even though it contained little if any coca or kola, because the two names together were simply a fanciful trademark. (As the company's lawyers liked to point out, Grape-

Nuts cereal had won protection in the courts even though it contained neither grapes nor nuts.) But the Supreme Court spurned this reasoning as well: "To take the illustration suggested in argument," Hughes wrote, "it would permit a manufacturer, who could not use the name chocolate to describe that which was not chocolate, or vanilla to describe that which was not vanilla, to designate the mixture as 'Chocolate-Vanilla,' although it was destitute of either or both. . . ." Judge Sanford had plainly overstepped his authority, the high court ruled. The case should have gone to the jury. The government was entitled to a retrial.

In Atlanta, Howard Candler recalled in his book, the reaction to the Supreme Court's action was "utter amazement, bordering on consternation." Actually, given Harold Hirsch's warnings, the outcome cannot have been as surprising as Howard Candler remembered, but there is no question the decision triggered a renewed urgency on Asa Candler's part in negotiating the sale of the company. The case was headed back to Chattanooga, and Candler had no stomach for a repeat, of the scrap he went through in 1911. Not long after Justice Hughes handed down his decision, Candler reluctantly agreed to run for mayor of Atlanta on a reform ticket (he won), and the last thing he wanted was another legal circus full of sensational accusations against the soft drink he considered virtually synonymous with his good name.

The worst had come to pass, yet oddly enough Candler's asking price for the company went up. It tripled, in fact, reflecting the company's unbroken string of setting new records for sales, revenues, and profits every year since its founding. Candler instructed Harold Hirsch to notify Sam Brown, his father-in-law, that the Candler family would entertain an offer of $25 million for the company. In turn, Brown and Hirsch wired their investors that Coca-Cola was back in play.

The thing that made Candler's proposal so intriguing (and reflected his anxiety) was the unusual nature of the terms he was suggesting: His family would take $15 million of common stock in the reorganized company, but Candler wanted to sell the other $10 million of stock to the underwriters for $5 million in cash. In effect, Candler was offering to *give away* $5 million. He planned to award a fifth of the value of his business, an uncommonly high figure, to the middlemen who handled the transaction. In a way, it was as if Candler had posted a reward offer, the payment of a $5 million bounty to anyone able to settle—or fix—the Chattanooga case.

And as it happened, one of the more savvy operators in national financial circles came to the conclusion that fixing the case was a genuine possibility.

During the sale negotiations that took place from 1911 to 1913, Hirsch and Brown had enlisted the help of Max Pam, a Chicago lawyer who specialized in corporate consolidations, to lobby on Coca-Cola's behalf in Washington. Pam befriended the top chemists and lawyers in the Department of Agriculture and concluded that they did not share Dr. Wiley's adamant opposition to caffeine. There had been no way to keep the government's lawyers from pursuing the Chattanooga case to the Supreme Court, Pam recognized, because they were committed to striking down the precedent it threatened to set. But he thought avoiding an actual retrial might be relatively easy. With Wiley gone, no one seemed hell-bent on putting Coca-Cola out of business. The company might reach a compromise by cutting the amount of caffeine it put in the syrup.

As Pam saw it, the company's prospects were not nearly so dire as some of the Candlers seemed to think. When Asa Candler reopened negotiations in 1916, Pam quickly lined up the backing of Kuhn, Loeb & Company, the New York investment house, and agreed to terms, including the price tag of $25 million.

The sale never took place.

After eight long years of maneuvering to rid himself of the company, with an attractive offer now sitting on the table, Asa Candler suddenly balked. On two separate occasions in 1916, his family met behind closed doors and rejected Max Pam's deal.

Candler failed to leave behind a single word of explanation, but there are several clues that suggest what happened. For nearly a quarter-century, Candler had treated the Coca-Cola Company as a sort of personal corporation; it owned all of his real estate in addition to the soft drink business. Candler's second son, Asa Jr., known to the family as "Buddie," was a wildly eccentric young man who had no interest whatever in Coca-Cola but wanted very much to inherit his father's office buildings, including the handsome skyscrapers in Atlanta and New York that bore the family name. Buddie was a source of constant exasperation to his father: "He is such a child!" Asa Sr. once wrote, when his son complained that his travel plans had been interrupted by the severe medical difficulties his wife suffered during the birth of their daughter. Asa Jr. borrowed money from his father and rarely paid it back; at one point his debt reached $100,000. The young man did have a certain knack for acquiring valuable land, and Candler tried to assuage Buddie's ambitions, first by buying him a 300-acre plot of land for an automobile speedway (land that today forms the nucleus of Atlanta's Hartsfield International Airport) and later by making him a vice president of Coca-Cola in charge of the company's properties.

But Buddie wanted more. Where Howard Candler was a man of gentle disposition and passive ways, Asa Candler, Jr., was full of flair and audacity (and often, it was said, of whiskey). In his later years, he collected rare birds and wild animals, which he housed in specially built cages on the grounds of his twenty-two-room mansion on Briarcliff Road in one of the city's more fashionable neighborhoods. His menagerie eventually included four fully grown adult elephants, which he named Coca, Cola, Pause, and Refreshes, and which he used in harness on one occasion to plow the ground for his kitchen garden. When the neighbors finally succeeded in forcing him to get rid of his personal zoo—one of the many lawsuits he faced was filed by a neighbor who was bitten by a fugitive baboon—he gave the entire collection to the city, thereby founding the Atlanta Zoo. Later still, he opened a dry-cleaning business in the back of the mansion, and when it was gutted by a fire that destroyed the clothes of several prominent citizens, he turned to his final project, the acquisition of Westview Cemetery, where he created turmoil by proposing to raze all the tombstones in favor of a sleek, mowable lawn. His last office was in a windowless building in the middle of the cemetery.

Asa Jr.'s exploits became the stuff of legend in Atlanta in the 1930s and 1940s. He was thought of, not without affection, as the dotty relative who lent color to an otherwise distinguished and even stuffy family. In 1916, however, when he was thirty-five, his idiosyncrasies had yet to reach full flower and his family took his ambitions seriously. He insisted on excluding the Candlers' real estate holdings from the sale of the soft drink business, and his father tried to accommodate him. The minutes of the old Coca-Cola Company are sketchy, but it appears that Asa Candler, Sr., arranged for the other shareholders to set a nominal price and "sell" him the company's real estate, which he then removed from the books of the Coca-Cola Company and placed into a separate corporation run by Asa Jr.

Carving away the real estate effectively scuttled the family's agreement with Max Pam. One reason Pam and his backers were willing to put $5 million of their own cash into the deal was their belief that even if Coca-Cola went into a complete collapse, the company's real estate would still be worth roughly that much and they would have a chance to recoup some or all of their investment. Candler tried to revive the negotiations, but with the most valuable pieces of property off the table, Pam withdrew and the deal was dead.

At first, the consequences of Asa Jr.'s actions did not appear terribly serious. There were others who had reached Pam's conclusion that the Chattanooga case could be settled, and they made it clear to the Candlers that they would be happy to handle the job for a lot less than $5 million. In fact, it seemed the matter could be handled virtually within the family: Sam Brown's son Edward was a member in a New York law firm whose senior partner, Bainbridge Colby, enjoyed the same kind of clout Pam did. Colby, who went on to serve as secretary of state during the last year of Woodrow Wilson's presidency (and who afterward gave the ailing Wilson a sinecure as a partner in the firm), went on several pilgrimages to Washington trying to work out a solution to the company's legal predicament. He, too, was confident that the difficulties could be resolved. On January 15, 1917, Asa Candler and the other stockholders signed a private agreement giving Colby and Ed Brown the job of reorganizing and selling off the company. Their bonus—set at $1 million—looked like a bargain.

But the Candlers soon reneged again, abruptly calling off the deal with Colby and Brown. As before, no explanation was given, only that an unnamed family member triggered the default by refusing to surrender his stock. Furious, Colby was threatening to bring a breach of contract suit for the $1 million fee he'd been promised. There was a risk of bad publicity. Still, all of these machinations might have been of little lasting importance, except for one thing. They created delay. Instead of becoming a publicly owned corporation with Howard Candler tucked more or less safely into the job of president, the Coca-Cola Company now entered a period of uncertainty. A symbolic turning point was reached when Coca-Cola's corporate offices were moved out of the redbrick factory by the railroad tracks and up to the seventeenth-floor penthouse suite of the Candler Building, the tallest skyscraper in Atlanta. The family seemed to be trading the known for the unknown, giving up its familiar physical labors in favor of the thinner air of commerce and high finance.

Candler noticed that his youngest son, William, who had risen from accountant to replace Frank Robinson as Coca-Cola's corporate secretary, rarely ventured to the plant anymore. "I suggested to William that he ought to go occasionally to see what was being done at the factory," Asa wrote drily in a letter to Howard. "I always found that watching by owners was good policy." But the owners weren't watching.

Sam Dobbs was handed the one indispensable tool he needed if he hoped to change his unhappy fate: time.

Before a new deal could be completed, the company found itself drawn into the hardships of war, and for more than a year the legal and financial entanglements took a back seat to a concern over simply surviving.

Even before the United States declared war on Germany in April 1917, the government instituted rationing for a variety of foodstuffs, notably sugar, and later it imposed a special tax on syrup sales—a pair of actions that put a vise-like squeeze on the company. "We are finding it exceedingly difficult to secure sufficient amounts of sugar and other material to keep our plants running," Dobbs wrote one of his salesmen in the spring of 1917, "and even where we are able to obtain raw materials, it is at such prices that practically eliminate all profits."

Asa Candler took a fatalistic attitude. "Don't let lack of material worry you," he advised Howard. "I have become resigned to 'no profits' till after the war is over. If you make any the [government] will confiscate it—then why make it?" But Howard *was* worried. The goal of making money might be temporarily suspended, but the company had millions of faithful customers whose demand for their favorite soft drink continued, war or no war, and Howard scrambled to maintain production. In a touch of irony, the company that had fought so hard defending its use of caffeine now faced a shortage, and Howard had to travel to New York and pay "enormous prices" on the open market for tea waste from the Far East.

Another shortage provided an important early lesson about consumer attitudes. Confronted with a scarcity of caramel, the burnt corn sugar that gave Coca-Cola its distinctive dark color, Howard experimented with a caramel-free syrup and made up an otherwise ordinary one-gallon batch of Coca-Cola—it was straw-colored—to try out in taste tests. With blindfolds on, he reported, people found the flavor to be identical with regular Coca-Cola and perfectly acceptable, but "when the testers tried it with eyes open, the assertion was made that the uncolored product tasted different." It was a parallel discovery to the one company officials made with New Coke nearly seven decades later. Colorless Coke was scrapped.

Dobbs threw himself wholeheartedly into the campaign to keep the company alive. During most of 1917, thanks to repeated visits he and Hirsch made to Washington, the company was awarded sugar allotments equal to the levels it used the year before. Sales actually rose slightly. But late autumn was the canning season in households all across the country, and in anticipation of a heightened demand for sugar, the government's Food Administrator, Herbert Hoover, decreed that syrup manufacturers would be limited to a half quota for the final two months of 1917. The company tried to make up part of the shortfall with beet sugar, glucose, and other substitutes, but its stockpile lasted only ten days, and it became clear by the middle of November that production would have to be severely curtailed. Bowing to the inevitable, Dobbs and D'Arcy collaborated on a brilliant magazine ad, "Making a Soldier of Sugar," in which the company promised with a patriotic flourish to abide by the government's regulations. Dobbs and D'Arcy took the train to Washington to call on Hoover on the day the ad first ran, and D'Arcy recalled later that "Mr. Hoover had a clipping of the advertisement on his desk when we knocked at his door. He opened up completely—conversationally and by his attitude. It was, frankly, a refreshing experience, and when we left his office we felt that we had done well by all."

The episode was a foreshadowing of the strategy that would serve Coca-Cola so well during World War II: Lobby furiously behind the scenes, give in gracefully when the cause is lost, and be sure to associate the product with the highest national interest. It was a "privilege," D'Arcy wrote, for the company to sacrifice its sugar to the American fighting man.

In the spring of 1918, Hoover relaxed the sugar quota and Coca-Cola was allowed to make 80 percent as much syrup as it had the year before. The company's sales dipped from 12 million gallons in 1917 to 10 million gallons in 1918, and profits were as narrow as Asa Candler predicted, but the important point was that Coca-Cola survived. In 1919, after the last restrictions were lifted, the company was able to satisfy a soaring demand that had accumulated during the war years, and sales almost doubled to nearly 19 million gallons, or about two and a half billion servings, enough to provide an average of thirty Cokes a year for every man, woman, and child in the United States. As D'Arcy put it in a triumphant ad, "Victory's Reward Means Volume Restored."

On the surface, at least, it appeared that the Coca-Cola Company had weathered its storms and could look forward to a period of tranquility and renewed profits. An especially encouraging moment occurred on November 12, 1918, one day after the Armistice, when Harold Hirsch finally arranged a settlement of the Chattanooga case. The Department of Agriculture proved willing to accept a face-saving compromise. The company privately agreed to cut the amount of caffeine in Coca-Cola by half, to six-tenths of a grain per serving, and the government responded by dropping all charges. Neither side wanted publicity, and Judge Sanford closed the proceedings with a terse order noting simply that the company had adopted "certain modifications" in its manufacturing process. The company paid court costs, and the government returned the forty barrels and twenty kegs of syrup it had seized nine and a half years earlier. The only objection was raised by Dr. Wiley, who complained bitterly for the rest of his life that the government had abandoned his cause.*

By all outward appearances, life at the Coca-Cola Company went on as it had before. Early in 1919, the Candlers arranged the purchase of a parcel of land at the corner of North Avenue and Plum Street, alongside the railroad tracks a few miles northwest of downtown Atlanta, for the construction of a new factory and office complex. It was to be the ninth home of Coca-Cola, the largest yet by far, reflecting the postwar boom in sales and the apparent good health of the company.

Behind the scenes, however, the Candler family's affairs had grown dangerously complicated. There seemed to be no way of disposing of the Coca-Cola Company that would satisfy everyone in the family, and so on Christmas Day 1917, Candler divided his stock and gave it to his wife and five children, keeping only seven shares for himself. At Coca-Cola's annual stockholders' meeting on February 14, 1918, the new stakes were entered onto the minutes. Candler's wife, Lizzie, had 64 shares. Howard, Asa Jr., Lucy, Walter, and William now owned 69 shares apiece and controlled the company.

Sam Dobbs got nothing. Aside from the 23 shares he already owned—a third of the portion that now belonged to each of his cousins—he did not inherit any of the wealth he had done so much to create.

At the same meeting, the Candlers decided that they did not need outside help in reorganizing the company after all. They simply agreed to rewrite the original corporate charter and exchange their old, cumbersome shares for new, liquid "ownership certificates." The transaction was handled in-house a few weeks later by Central Bank and Trust, the Candler family bank, which issued $25 million of the new paper and divided it on a pro

---

* Using his column in *Good Housekeeping* as a forum, Wiley continued to attack the company for several years to come. In May 1922, he wrote in "Dr. Wiley's Question-Box" that drinking three or four Coca-Colas a day over a period of years would have "very serious" health consequences. "In the case of a growing child," he added, "it would probably ruin his health for life."

rata basis among the family members. The ownership of Coca-Cola was "corralled," as Asa put it, and held by his children. They were free to do whatever they wished with it.

With his legacy distributed, Asa Candler now withdrew even further from the business affairs of the company. He announced that at the end of his mayoral term, on January 1, 1919, he would retire to private life. Along with his many other preoccupations, he had to attend to his wife, who was gravely ill with cancer and had only a few weeks left to live.

Had Asa Candler not been distracted by his grief and weariness, he might have paid more attention to the string of events that unfolded next. At the regular Coca-Cola directors' meeting in May 1919, Sam Dobbs ventured the suggestion that the company consider having its books audited. It might be a good idea, he explained, to let a tax expert make sure the company was paying the proper amount to the federal government. The proposal sounded sensible, and the Candlers readily agreed. Dobbs was authorized to proceed, and he hired the accounting firm of Haskins & Sells to carry out the job.

No one had any way of knowing the real purpose behind the audit, but the truth of the matter was that it had nothing to do with taxes. Dobbs was negotiating his own private deal to sell the Coca-Cola Company, and he needed the audit to verify the financial status of the business. It was vital to Dobbs that his intentions remain secret, because the buyer he had found was a man Asa Candler detested, Ernest Woodruff.

"E. Woodruff," as he signed himself in a thin, economical hand, was the president of Trust Company of Georgia. A hard man, squat and powerfully built, with a bristling moustache and jutting, undershot jaw, Woodruff resembled a bulldog. He looked on the world with small, cold eyes, and he had a reputation around Atlanta as a shrewd and often ruthless trader.

Trust Company's main activity was making deals. It provided the usual financial services for its customers, but by today's standards it more nearly resembled an investment banking house than a commercial bank. Its charter, written by the Georgia General Assembly, gave Trust Company "the right to do almost anything in the world," as one officer cheerfully put it, and Woodruff enjoyed seeing how far he could push the limits. His specialty was the acquisition and consolidation of small businesses, and he used the bank's resources—as if they were his own, some critics said—to put together monopolies in several small industries then emerging in the South. Starting in 1902, Woodruff began buying up companies that delivered ice and coal, and in 1910 Trust Company formed the Atlantic Ice and Coal Company with operations in Georgia, Tennessee, Virginia, and the Carolinas.

Woodruff was known as a man who believed in doing whatever was necessary to protect his interests. Needing land to build a new plant for Atlantic Ice and Coal, for instance, he had the bank buy a row of houses and lots in the red-light district south of the railroad tracks along Atlanta's notorious Collins Street, and then he personally evicted the madams and their girls and spent several nights sitting in a rocker on the front porch of the biggest house, cradling a double-barrel shotgun and shooing off the angry customers. (His partner in the adventure was a young lawyer who handled some of Trust Company's legal business, Robert P. Jones, the father of the celebrated golfer Bobby Jones.)

Woodruff's approach to business was typified by the way he handled the Atlanta Steel Company affair. Founded at the turn of the century to make bands for cotton bales and hoops for turpentine barrels, Atlanta Steel nearly went under during the Panic of 1907, until Woodruff stepped forward and provided $850,000 in new capital from Trust Company. That he did so without bothering to obtain permission from the directors of either concern was a mark of his strong suit, a sense of unflinching self-assuredness. "Suppose the steel company turns you down," one of Woodruff's lieutenants recalled asking him nervously, "or the Trust Company directors won't confirm your purchase?" But Woodruff was undaunted. He believed he could persuade both sides it was a smart move, and he was right. He took control of Atlanta Steel, changed its name to Atlantic Steel, ousted its old management and put his own man in charge. The company began making money again.

Operating from a huge Rand & Leopold rolltop desk in his office on the second floor of the Equitable Building, Woodruff became known as the most aggressive financier in town, the nearest thing Atlanta had to a Wall Street baron. He seemed to like capitalism just for the sport of it, as if besting other men and taking their money were a kind of rugged game, and made no pretense of believing in any higher purpose. He made a bad deal for Trust Company once when he bought a paper mill from a man named Moultrie Sessions in Marietta, Georgia, and later he confided to a friend, "I don't mind losing the money so much as I do having that man beat me in a trade." He liked to haggle and didn't care if he insulted other men by rudely questioning the figures in their financial statements. The directors of Trust Company, some of Atlanta's most respected businessmen, watched in nervous awe as Woodruff made them rich. Yet what set Woodruff apart from the rest of the Atlanta business community was not just his fiercely competitive attitude—for he was hardly unique in that regard—but rather the suspicion he created among his fellow businessmen that he didn't always play by the rules.

One episode in particular put a stain on Woodruff's name, and it helps explain why so many Atlantans distrusted him. Woodruff moved to Atlanta from Columbus, Georgia, in 1893, after his brother-in-law, Joel Hurt, recruited him to help in the family's business enterprises. Hurt was one of Atlanta's busiest early developers, a railroad surveyor by training who settled in the city after the Civil War and threw himself into the task of rebuilding atop the ruins. Among the many activities that earned him the nickname "the Ringmaster," Hurt chartered a mortgage association and an insurance company, built an eight-story skyscraper and helped organize Trust Company of Georgia. He also developed Atlanta's first suburb, Inman Park. Hurt's grandest scheme was a decade-long struggle to gain control of the city's streetcar lines and convert them from mule-power to electricity. He brought in Woodruff, his wife's younger brother, to take charge of day-to-day strategy and maneuvers.

Dubbed the "Second Battle of Atlanta," the streetcar fight pitted Hurt and Woodruff against an alliance of northern investors and local businessmen in a series of skirmishes over franchises, condemnation rights, pricing, and other issues, with the ultimate goal being the establishment of a monopoly on electric power in the city. War was waged in the courts, the city council, the state railroad commission, and also in the Atlanta newspapers, where each side churned out propaganda against the other. Thanks to several bare-knuckle stunts, including the night Hurt and Woodruff had workmen rip up the rails along Capitol Avenue under cover of darkness rather than pay the city's assessment for paving, they got the worst of the publicity and saw their standing in the community plummet

The most damaging smear came when a lawyer for the other side claimed to have found one of Woodruff's monogrammed cufflinks wedged in the bottom of a file in a drawer in his desk. The suggestion that Woodruff had rifled another man's office was devastating, especially since the lawyer in question was Jack Spalding, the founding partner of one of the most respected firms in town, King & Spalding. The accusation was never made public (nor is there any existing documentation to prove it), but it made the rounds of Atlanta's business community via the rumor mill, and the story was still familiar to the law firm's senior partners nearly a hundred years later. Hurt and Woodruff eventually surrendered and sold out to the other side, which evolved into the Georgia Power Company, the state's largest electric utility.

Woodruff's next gambit tarnished his reputation even further. In 1904, two years after the streetcar fight, Hurt fell ill and his doctor, mistakenly diagnosing pneumonia, confined him to his home. Believing that he would never return to active management, Trust Company's directors removed him as president at their next meeting and gave the job to Woodruff, who kept the position even though Hurt recovered fully within a few weeks. Moving quickly to make his mark (while practicing thrift at the same time), Woodruff blacked out Hurt's name on the letterhead of the bank's stationery and used a rubber stamp to put his own imprint, E. Woodruff, just below it. Hurt never forgave Woodruff for what he believed was a palace coup, and relations between the brothers-in-law were strained from then on. Around town, businessmen marveled at Woodruff's brilliance and toughness, but they also whispered that he was not, as one of them put it, "altogether on the up and up."

Asa Candler shared the community's widespread feeling of distaste toward Woodruff, and Woodruff knew it. At one point in 1912, Woodruff told an associate he was interested in acquiring Candler's bank and merging it into Trust Company, and the associate warned him that Candler would never do business with him. So it was understandable that later, when Woodruff's eye turned to the Coca-Cola Company, he decided to keep his involvement a secret "I knew it would not do for me to approach him, or any of his family," Woodruff explained afterward, ". . . and I undertook to do it through other people."

In 1919, Sam Dobbs was a respected member of Atlanta's business elite. He was elected president of the Chamber of Commerce and gave a well-received, wide-ranging talk at the Woman's Club in which he advocated improvement of the public schools, decency in women's fashion, and strict reliance on references in hiring domestic help.

He also counted himself a close friend of Ernest Woodruff, having invested heavily in several of Trust Company's ventures. Dobbs served as a director of the steel company and Atlantic Ice and Coal, and in 1916 he went on the board of the bank itself. When Woodruff asked him about the possibility of buying the Coca-Cola Company, Dobbs recalled later, "I told him I thought probably it could [be done], that I would be willing to sell out—that I would like very much to sell out."

Dobbs agreed with Woodruff that it would be best to keep Woodruff's name out of the deal. To guard against inadvertent disclosure, they decided to hold their meetings in private at the Waldorf Hotel in New York City, where they quickly reached agreement on the major details of the transaction. The information Dobbs provided about the company's financial status, backed up by the findings of the audit, convinced Woodruff that the asking price of $25 million was justified, provided the buy-out could be structured to his satisfaction.

It was not a trade Trust Company could swing on its own. The bank's net worth at the time was a modest $2 million, and it was clear that Woodruff would have to find backers on Wall Street. Relying on partners represented an unhappy complication for the freewheeling Woodruff, but he found a silver lining: The partners could be cloaked with the appearance of being the actual buyers, thereby concealing Woodruff's role. The first order of business was to lock down the right to make the purchase, and to do that Woodruff had to get Candler's offspring to sign options on the ownership certificates they held in the old corporation. They would not sign in defiance of their father, and their father would not sell to Woodruff, so it was vital to suggest to the Candlers that someone else was acquiring the company. Woodruff had just the man in mind.

Eugene Stetson was a native of Hawkinsville, Georgia, who had pursued a banking career in the North, rising to become vice president of the powerful Guaranty Trust Company. Stetson helped Woodruff round up a syndicate of New York investors willing to underwrite the major portion of the purchase, and he also agreed to handle the negotiations with the Candlers. There is no proof that Stetson openly misrepresented himself, but he did leave the Candlers with the plain impression that he was the head of the group of investors who wanted to buy the company, and that his bank, Guaranty Trust, was the lead institution.

Dobbs did nothing to hide his own role in the transaction. On the contrary, he enlisted Harold Hirsch as an ally (Hirsch was also a director of Trust Company), and together they worked to persuade the members of the Candler family that the deal was good for them and also in the best interest of the future of the company.

In late July 1919, an Atlanta lawyer named Robert C. Alston made the rounds and obtained the signatures of Asa Candler's five children on a single sheet of paper—a blank option for the purchase of their stock. There is no easy explanation for the inattention the Candlers paid to the details of the transaction, unless it was their comfort with the understanding that Stetson and his bank were going to receive the option. Howard Candler testified later that he was unsure what interests Alston represented, and it may be that all of the Candlers were weary to the point of indifference after the difficult, fruitless negotiations that had been grinding on for the past several years. What is indisputable, however, is that Alston was not representing Stetson but instead was acting on behalf of his friend and fellow Trust Company director, Ernest Woodruff, and delivered the option to him at the bank. When Asa Candler learned that his children had given Woodruff control of the company, Howard wrote later, "he was profoundly shocked and was particularly chagrined that this had been done without any of them having even consulted him, taken him into their confidence, or sought his advice in determining the details and terms of the proposal."[*]

On August 2, 1919, Woodruff called a special meeting of the bank's board of directors and dazed them with the news that they were going to buy the Coca-Cola Company. With the option in hand, Woodruff was halfway home, but he soon realized he had a lot more hard work to do. Even among a group of men well accustomed to his wheeling and dealing, Woodruff's latest coup was frightening in its scope and ambition. He was proposing that the bank risk all of its resources trying to swallow a com-

---

[*] Candler's only public utterance about the sale, in an interview he granted to the *Kansas City Times* a year and a half afterward, contributed to the aura of confusion that surrounded the transaction. "I have four fine boys," he told the newspaper, "but they are just boys. When I gave them the business it was theirs. They sold out a big share for a fancy price. I wouldn't have done that, but they did, and from a sale standpoint drove a pretty keen bargain." Actually, Candler could not have objected to the sale of the company, since it was a goal he had long contemplated, nor could the price have disturbed him, since he had set it himself during earlier negotiations. His own words notwithstanding, the source of Candler's disappointment could only have been the identity of the buyer.

pany more than ten times its own size. The symbolism was daunting: Trust Company occupied Joel Hurt's old eight-story building; from its top floor the directors could look a block and a half north and see the seventeen-story Candler Building towering over them.

There were immediate objections to Woodruff's plan, chief among them a renewed concern over Coca-Cola's legal status. In February 1919, just three months after the Chattanooga case was finally settled, the United States Circuit Court of Appeals in San Francisco ruled in a civil case (brought by Coca-Cola against an outfit called the Koke Company of America) that the company had no right to protect its trademark from infringement by imitators. Unless the U.S. Supreme Court reversed the decision, hundreds of sound-alike beverages would flood the market and very likely leave Coca-Cola to drown.

Woodruff reassured his colleagues that he had consulted Hirsch and other lawyers, who were confident the company would prevail in the high court, but the board still balked. After a lengthy argument the directors nervously agreed to participate in the purchase, but only upon the unanimous agreement of lawyers representing Trust Company and all of the other partners in the deal that Hirsch was right. And there was another catch. The directors refused to go ahead unless at least half of Trust Company's investment in the syndicate could be secured by "solvent persons, firms, or corporations"—that is, by someone else's cash.

For Woodruff, the board's recalcitrance introduced a new problem into the equation: the element of time. His option on the Candlers' stock was good only until August 28, and that gave him less than a month to arrange the financing, exercise the options, and close the sale. With the Trust Company situation still in limbo, Woodruff sped back to New York by train to continue negotiations with Stetson and his Wall Street partners, a loosely organized group of officers and stockholders in Guaranty Trust and the Chase Securities Company.

The first part of the deal involved the payout to the Candler family, which was fairly simple: The Candlers had agreed to accept $15 million in cash and $10 million in preferred stock that paid 7 percent a year. As Woodruff and the New York bankers saw it, the real bottom line was the immediate requirement of raising the $15 million in cash. In their hard-eyed view, the preferred stock was mere paper, a long-term obligation that could be carried indefinitely (for $700,000 a year) by the company's revenues. The cash was all that mattered. The partners settled on the broad outlines of a plan to form a brand-new, Delaware-based Coca-Cola Company and sell shares to the public. In nice round numbers, they penciled in the figures of 500,000 shares of common stock at a price of $40 a share, calculating that if they sold all the shares at the asking price, they would raise $20 million and net themselves a tidy profit of $5 million.

But Woodruff and his partners made a fateful decision. Instead of turning a quick profit and walking away, they wanted to keep a stake in the company. Woodruff believed Coca-Cola had a promising future, and he was positive he could find ways to squeeze higher revenues—much higher revenues—out of its operations. Meeting day after day in New York with Stetson and the other bankers, Woodruff and his assistants worked out a complicated (and highly secretive) plan that would allow them to keep as much stock as they could while raising the cash needed to pay off the Candlers. Specifically, the group calculated that if they sold exactly 417,000 shares of the common stock, clearing $35 per share (after subtracting $5 in handling fees and the cut for the brokers), they could afford to "sell" the remaining 83,000 shares to themselves for a nominal price of $5 per share. They would own a large chunk of the company virtually for nothing.

The arrangement was perfectly legal, but it was essential that it not be made public for the simple reason that it would create immense resentment on the part of the people who were about to pay $40 per share—people who in many instances would be friends and neighbors of Woodruff and the other deal-makers, and who would never understand why they were paying eight times more money for their investment in Coca-Cola than the organizers of the transaction.

Having settled on the figure of 83,000 shares as their stake in the deal, Woodruff and his New York partners next began thrashing out the division of the spoils. Woodruff found himself handcuffed by the restrictions imposed by his board of directors back in Atlanta, and at one point he rattled off a telegram to Trust Company's executive committee complaining, "Impossible to undertake to continue an exchange of views at this long range." He demanded—and received—nearly complete autonomy in negotiating the fine points of the deal, but the board was adamant in holding Trust Company's overall participation in the sale to $4.5 million, or a little more than twice its net worth. And the board stuck to its stipulation that half the bank's participation had to be underwritten by liquid assets. As a result, Woodruff somehow had to scrape together more than $2 million in cash, and he had a deadline that was quickly approaching.

What happened next provided the basis for some of the great family fortunes in Atlanta, but at the time the mood was one of haste and uncertainty. Woodruff and the board decided to raise the $2 million through a subscription among Trust Company's stockholders. On August 19, 1919, just nine days before the option was due to expire, a letter marked "Strictly Confidential" was mailed to each Trust Company stockholder, asking him to put up $195 for every share he held of the bank's stock. The bank planned to pool the money and hold it as a reserve during the Coca-Cola offering. Afterward—assuming all went well—the stockholder would be repaid and participate in an otherwise unspecified "distribution" of Trust Company's proceeds from the transaction.

It is difficult to imagine what the bank's shareholders must have thought when the letter was delivered. For one thing, it was the first many of them had heard of the impending sale of the Coca-Cola Company, the town's most important commercial enterprise, and the news undoubtedly came as a shock. Then, too, the letter had a breathless tone to it—which was hardly surprising since Woodruff had drafted it off the top of his head.

"This is a large transaction, involving a large sum of money, and we have made a large commitment in connection with the financing of the enterprise," the letter said, leaving no doubt that it was a large deal indeed. Most of all, perhaps, the recipients would have been excited and confused. They were told virtually nothing about the terms of the transaction, only that "it will be necessary to make the financial arrangement immediately and before the details can be worked out." They had five days to respond.

Meanwhile an unexpected problem erupted in New York. Woodruff discovered that the men in Atlanta were not the only ones suffering from a sudden attack of unsteady nerves. Stetson and his colleagues now wanted to put the deal on hold, and Woodruff was in a rage. If the deadline slipped by, it was highly unlikely the sale could ever be revived. The Candlers were now fully aware he was a principal in the deal, and that knowledge alone probably was enough to scuttle any chance of future negotiations. If Woodruff did not exercise his option by August 28, he was finished. As they headed off one morning for a meeting with the New Yorkers, Woodruff's top assistant, a Trust Company vice president named William Wardlaw, noticed a familiar look on his boss's face, one that could freeze other men in their tracks. He called it Woodruff's "stop, look, and listen" expression. Twenty years later, Wardlaw remembered the scene vividly. He and Woodruff

> met with the representatives of the Chase and Guaranty groups and they were rather insistent on delay. [Woodruff] said, "Gentlemen, don't forget this is my deal and it is going to be handled my way. We will be back here at 12 o'clock, and in the meantime you can decide whether you will go along or whether you count yourselves out of the business." We went back at 12 o'clock and the deal went through as he planned it. To see those bankers who were accustomed to telling others to lie down, roll over and play dead, when someone else started putting on the show, was most interesting.

Woodruff left the meeting, Wardlaw recalled, with a tight smile of satisfaction on his face. At the same time, Trust Company's shareholders in Atlanta were answering Woodruff's call with a remarkable show of support Whatever their apprehensions, they seemed to be swept along by the appeal of becoming part owners of the fabled Coca-Cola Company. Joining the undertaking in huge numbers, they raised nearly $2 million, and they raised it quickly. Just forty-eight hours after the letter of solicitation was mailed, Trust Company's board expressed satisfaction with the level of the response and voted to exercise the Candler options. Making Woodruff's triumph complete, his most cautious colleague, J. Carroll Payne, offered the motion.

At last events began flowing smoothly. The Atlanta newspapers reported the sale of the Coca-Cola Company to the Trust Company syndicate under banner headlines, and Woodruff and his partners settled back to see how the public offering of common stock in the new company would go. On August 26, 1919, they opened their books for a one-day subscription by brokers and banks around the country and were rewarded by a stampede. By three o'clock in the afternoon, all 417,000 shares had been reserved, and there were additional orders for another 140,000 shares. Once all the paperwork was completed in a few weeks, the brokers would be turning around and offering the shares to the public, and there was every reason to anticipate the same high level of enthusiasm. People were going to buy the stock of the new Coca-Cola Company, and they were going to pay $40 a share, maybe a little more. The deal was going to work.

In all the hoopla, it was easy to miss some of the fine print In the prospectus Trust Company put out there was a reassuring section that said, "The present management [of Coca-Cola], which is responsible for the remarkable growth and successful operation of the Company, will continue and will also be interested through the ownership of a substantial amount of the stock of the Company." To the unpracticed eye, the statement sounded very much like a commitment that the Candlers would still be running things.

But that was not exactly the case. Howard Candler was being brushed upstairs to serve as chairman of the new Coca-Cola Company's board of directors. The board, however, would not have final authority over the company's affairs. In fact it would have very little authority at all because the syndicate, in the interest of assuring "continuity," had quietly vested all the rights of ownership in a Voting Trust. The three members of the Voting Trust would hold what amounted to a proxy for all 500,000 shares of Coca-Cola's common stock, giving them complete power within the company. Two of the trustees were Ernest Woodruff and Gene Stetson.

The third was Coca-Cola's new president, Sam Dobbs. For the second time in his life, thirty-one years after carting its inventory across town in a dray, Dobbs was responsible for delivering the Coca-Cola Company.

Four

BOTTLED-UP ANGER

The new Coca-Cola Company began life in a conference room at a law office on lower Broadway in New York City.

Howard Candler had been blissfully unaware of the urgent scheming that led up to the sale of his father's business, but now his cooperation was vital. If he raised a ruckus, if he so much as whispered a quiet word suggesting foul play, he would create panic among investors and disrupt the public offering of common shares of Coca-Cola. He could ruin everything.

There was no question he was upset. He was the president of the company, yet he had been told nothing about the transaction, nothing about the Voting Trust, nothing about the men who were behind the deal, and nothing, of course, about losing his job to his cousin Sam Dobbs. "I had nothing to do with the syndicate," he recalled later. "I didn't know it existed until the thing was all closed up. I was told about it."

In late August and early September of 1919, after Ernest Woodruff and the directors of Trust Company exercised their option to buy the Candler family's stock, a campaign was begun to win back Howard's trust and convince him to join the new team and play along. One source of reassurance was the placement of his brother-in-law, Thomas K. Glenn, on the board of the new company. Howard's wife, Flora, was Tom Glenn's sister, and Glenn was one of Ernest Woodruff's closest associates. Glenn was an open, jovial man with the kind of round, ruddy face that invited confidence, and he worked to persuade Howard that in spite of his reputation Woodruff was not really a bad fellow at all.

There were also powerful financial inducements to keep Howard from making trouble. His share of the $15 million purchase price (after various expenses and other obligations were subtracted) came to $1.85 million in cash, and he also got $1.38 million in preferred stock whose value was tied directly to the company's continuing good performance. His sister and three brothers each had the same stake. Rocking the boat could jeopardize their fortunes. And it was not Howard's nature to act boldly or cause a disruption or stand up to another man in a test of wills. In the end, though, what finally secured Howard's cooperation was the simple promise that he was still needed and would still have a job to do.

The directors who gathered at 61 Broadway on the morning of September 16, 1919, represented a mix of investors from Atlanta and Wall Street, an uneasy alliance of strong-willed men who were just beginning to feel each other out. The Wall Street contingent was led by Gene Stetson and E. V. R. Thayer, the president of Chase National Bank, while Woodruff headed a group that included Dobbs and Glenn, Harold Hirsch, and one of the biggest individual investors from Georgia, an old friend of Woodruff's from Columbus named W. C. Bradley. One of the company's main sugar suppliers, Robert W. Atkins, joined the board, and so did Bill D'Arcy. Given the wide variety of interests in the room, a clash over the direction of the company was possible—actually it was inevitable—but the first order of business, the one goal that overrode all others, was taking care of Howard Candler.

The directors quickly elected him chairman, which had been the plan all along, and then took the unusual step of formally amending their brand-new by-laws to stipulate that Candler's authority would be "co-extensive" with that of the new president, Dobbs, that his salary would be the same as Dobbs's—$25,000—and that he would remain in direct charge of the company's manufacturing operations.

Candler tested his strength immediately, interrupting the meeting to question some of the interim decisions Woodruff and Dobbs had made during the four weeks since the option was exercised. Trust Company had bought a chemical laboratory, for instance, and Candler argued that most of its assets were unneeded. He made a motion to sell off the greater part of the lab's equipment, and the board agreed. Then he made a motion to move the materials that remained, and the board agreed again. The board agreed with everything Candler had to say that morning, and they did so with the utmost courtesy. Whatever he wanted was fine, at least for a few more days.

The first step in the public offering of Coca-Cola stock, the subscription by brokers, had gone flawlessly, with all the shares reserved in a single day. Now the second step was under way, and the brokers were reselling the stock to individual investors. If people would buy the shares at the asking price of $40, Woodruff and his partners stood to make a great deal of money.

In fact, Woodruff stood to make money in so many different ways it was hard to keep track. First, there was his bank. As manager of the syndicate, Trust Company was paid a custodial fee for transferring the 417,000 shares of common stock that were sold through brokerage houses. In addition, Trust Company's board authorized more than $3.4 million in loans to brokers and individuals who bought those shares, and the bank also acted as a commercial brokerage itself, taking 50,000 shares to sell directly to the public. Finally, and most important, Trust Company kept 24,900 of the little-known $5 shares as its portion of the syndicate's profit. Federal law no longer allows a bank to play so many roles in the same transaction, but at the time it was all perfectly legal: Trust Company was buyer, seller, lender, and middleman, making money on each step.

Woodruff had a personal stake in the transaction, too. He got 2,000 of the $5 shares to tuck away as a permanent investment, and the bank's directors rewarded him for masterminding the whole deal by allotting him 20,000 shares of Coca-Cola common to put on the market himself.

If the numbers were confusing, Woodruff's behavior made the point with absolute clarity: He wanted, *needed* to sell shares in the new Coca-Cola Company to as many people as he could at the highest price possible. Acting like a merchant with a new shipment of goods, he hawked his wares on the corner of Edgewood Avenue and Pryor Street under the stone archway that formed the entrance to the bank, personally pulling dozens of Atlanta's citizens inside and selling them stock. "He would meet 'em walking up and down the street," a retired Atlanta banker recalled, and he'd "take 'em to the loan discount window and say, 'Lend this fellow $10,000'—or $20,000 or whatever he decided to put this fellow in for—and the teller just lent it to him. The bank officers and the Finance Committee, they didn't even know about it 'til the next day. They'd say, 'Who the hell put this note through?' And [then] they'd say, 'Oh! Well, that's fine!'"

Price Gilbert, Sr., a justice of the Georgia Supreme Court, remembered Woodruff calling him on the phone and asking him to come by the bank. When Gilbert arrived, Woodruff greeted him with the paperwork for a $50,000 loan already completed. "Price," Woodruff said, "sign this note. I'm going to buy you some Coca-Cola stock." Gilbert, whose wealth came from his wife's family, said he would have to talk it over at home. His wife was nervous about the proposition, but the next day he returned to the bank and agreed to go in for $25,000.

The same story was repeated dozens of times. At Woodruff's urging, several of his closest associates made huge investments in Coca-Cola stock. William Clark Bradley—"Uncle Will" to his friends—was the wealthiest businessman in Columbus, Georgia, with interests in cotton production, banking, steamships, and other enterprises along the Chattahoochee River. He staked a large part of his fortune on Coca-Cola even though he had never so much as tasted a sip of the soft drink. (He found it "very palatable," he said later.) James H. Nunnally, the candy-maker whose landmark soda fountain in downtown Atlanta sold Coca-Cola by the gallons, also bought thousands of shares. So did the coal mining heir, John Bulow Campbell. And it was not just the well-to-do who jumped into the game. Employees of Trust Company and the Coca-Cola Company took part of their salary in Coca-Cola stock. Hundreds of smaller investors scraped together their savings or borrowed money and bought as many shares as they could afford.

When Ernest Woodruff and the other principals closed the books on the offering, every share had been sold at the asking price of $40 or slightly higher. Nearly half the sales were in the Atlanta area, where an estimated 1,500 individuals participated, and the rest were scattered among the customers of dozens of brokerage houses on Wall Street and around the country. The undertaking was counted a phenomenal success. Coca-Cola common stock was listed on the New York Stock Exchange as "KO" and the designation seemed entirely appropriate. It was a knockout.

No one had the faintest idea that the Coca-Cola Company was on the brink of ruin.

The problem was sugar.

Coca-Cola syrup was half sugar, and by 1919 the company had become the largest consumer of granulated cane sugar in the world, using nearly 100 million pounds a year.

For two decades, the company had taken the availability of cheap sugar for granted, rarely paying more than four or five cents a pound. Even during World War I, when sugar was rationed, the government had fixed the price at an affordable 9 cents a pound. But price controls were due to be lifted on December 1, 1919, and in the weeks after the sale of the company the cost of sugar futures began to rise, slowly at first and then with alarming speed. Speculators were cornering huge segments of the world's sugar supply, driving prices higher and higher. Sugar jumped to 16 cents a pound and then to 20 cents, and it kept going up. There was no telling how expensive it might become.

The company was caught. The cost of manufacturing syrup more than doubled in a matter of weeks. Sugar purchases began eating up all of the company's revenues. Yet public demand for Coca-Cola was at an all-time high and had to be met, no matter what. There could be no cutback in production.

Ernest Woodruff had not planned to give Howard Candler or Sam Dobbs much authority in the new company. As soon as the public stock offering was safely concluded, Woodruff convened another meeting of the Coca-Cola board of directors and set up a powerful executive committee with final control over corporate decision-making. It was the way Woodruff liked to operate. He had no desire to oversee the day-to-day operations of any of the companies he acquired (and rarely set foot inside them), but he insisted on having the last word in matters that were likely to cost him money. In the case of Coca-Cola, he installed W. C. Bradley as president of the committee, which then took charge of the company's legal and financial affairs.

When it came to making syrup, however, Woodruff and his fellow directors still relied on Howard Candler. Candler had been in charge of production for more than a decade, and it was the one area of the Coca-Cola Company's activities in which his expertise was thought to be unassailable. As the price of sugar began soaring, Candler was given a green light to corner as much of the supply as he could.

Woodruff and his partners felt they had no choice. They adopted a policy of maintaining at least a sixty-day supply of sugar in inventory, even though it meant going deep into debt. The new owners arranged a $1 million line of credit with Gene Stetson's bank, Guaranty Trust—giving the only existing copy of the top-secret Coca-Cola formula as collateral. The most celebrated trade secret in American business history was placed in an ordinary envelope, sealed, and locked away in a vault in New York City. As Woodruff saw it, the company's one possible salvation was to spread the misfortune down the line to its independent bottlers. Bottling now accounted for 40 percent of the company's syrup sales, and Woodruff believed the bottlers could afford to pick up the slack. He intended to make them do it.

The company's arrangement with its bottlers was highly unusual.

In 1899, two young lawyers from Chattanooga, Benjamin Franklin Thomas and Joseph Brown Whitehead, arranged an introduction to Asa Candler, traveled to Atlanta, and made a pitch for the rights to put the soft drink in bottles.

At first Candler was unenthusiastic. Bottling was still a back-alley business, in his view, and there was a danger that Coca-Cola's reputation might suffer if he allowed them to go ahead. Still, Candler told his visitors, he had no interest in keeping the bottling rights for himself and his company. "Gentlemen," he recalled telling the two Chattanoogans, only half in jest, "we have neither the money, nor brains, nor time to embark in the bottling business." Investing in bottling equipment—the machinery, conveyors, bottles, boxes, dray teams, and real estate—was more than he cared to handle.

After mulling it over, Candler asked Thomas and Whitehead to consider a deal in which they would guarantee the quality of the product, with the Coca-Cola Company retaining the right to cancel the contract if the quality proved to be poor. In exchange, Candler said, he would sell them syrup and give them the nationwide rights to bottle Coca-Cola—free. The only exceptions were the six New England states, where Candler's fountain wholesaler held a dormant bottling option. (The states of Mississippi and Texas were held out temporarily, but later included as part of the transaction.) Astounded at the offer, Thomas and Whitehead quickly accepted. Thomas hastened back to his room at the Piedmont Hotel in Atlanta and drew up a six-hundred-word contract, which Candler duly signed on July 21, 1899. Candler did not send his partners off with much of an endorsement. "If you boys fail in this undertaking," Whitehead recalled Candler admonishing them, "don't come back to cry on my shoulder, because I have very little confidence in this bottling business."

For a time it seemed Candler's dour assessment might prove prophetic. Thomas and Whitehead had a magnificent opportunity—a "stunner," Candler called it—yet they had very little money. Thomas scraped together several hundred dollars and opened a bottling plant in Chattanooga within a few weeks, but it was "crude in the extreme," as one worker later recalled. Fitted into a narrow space on the ground floor of an abandoned pool hall in one of the city's poor neighborhoods, the plant had a jury-rigged "contrivance" that lifted a ten-gallon keg overhead, allowing gravity to feed syrup down a rubber tube to a small, foot-powered bottle filler. One day a pulley broke, sending the keg crashing to the floor and showering the plant manager, Billy Hardin, with sweet, sticky syrup. And that was not the only hazard. The bottles occasionally exploded under the pressure of carbonation; early workers learned to wear narrow-mesh wire face masks that made them look as if they were outfitted to go fencing.

Customers faced a different sort of danger: spoilage. The Hutchinson bottle was sealed by a rubber gasket held in place by a long, looping wire. Soda pop got its nickname from the "pop" that resulted when the wire and stopper were pushed down into the bottle. Because the mechanism was internal, the bottles were difficult to clean and impossible to sterilize, and Thomas and Whitehead soon discovered that in hot weather their product had a shelf life of only ten days or two weeks before it turned rancid.

As they looked ahead to 1900 and the challenge of fulfilling their contract, Thomas and Whitehead realized there was no way they could afford the time and money it would take to open plants across the country one by one by themselves. Their only hope, they concluded, was to become "parent" bottlers, recruiting other men and giving them franchises to build the actual facilities and sell Coca-Cola in the surrounding territories.

Thomas, slightly older and better established than Whitehead, was ready to get started. But Whitehead was broke. One of his immediate obligations under the contract with Candler was to open a bottling plant in Atlanta, and he couldn't afford to do it. With a wife and two infant sons to feed, Whitehead decided he had to find a new partner with pockets deep enough to carry him through the early years. He and Thomas agreed to split up—literally. They drew a line across a map of the United States and divided the country in two. Thomas took the Northeast, Atlantic states, and West Coast, and Whitehead picked the South.

In the spring of 1900, Whitehead formed a partnership with J. T. (for John Thomas) Lupton, a crusty veteran of the patent medicine era who enjoyed bragging about the small fortune he'd made during the 1890s selling Black Draught and other concoctions for the Chattanooga Medicine Company. In exchange for a half-share in Whitehead's region of the country, Lupton put up $2,500, and Whitehead moved to Atlanta and used the money to open the first Coca-Cola bottling plant in the soft drink's home town.

The two "parents" began working their separate sides of the national street, searching for prospects willing to, become Coca-Cola bottlers. Response during the first couple of years was slow, and the Coca-Cola bottling enterprise might very well have died in its infancy, little more than a handful of grubby, unprofitable plants scattered here and there across the country, had it not been for a remarkable breakthrough in technology. A mechanical engineer in Baltimore named William Painter perfected and patented a new kind of closure—the bottle cap—that made the Hutchinson bottle obsolete and allowed for striking advances in mechanized washing and sterilization.

The use of crown caps led to an immediate improvement in the quality of bottled Coca-Cola, and sales rose dramatically. The Coca-Cola bottler in Athens, Georgia, ran into Asa Candler one day and showed him his figures. "What are you doing with all that syrup?" Candler asked in amazement. "Pouring it into the Oconee River?"

After their discouraging start, Thomas, Whitehead, and Lupton found themselves assembling a national network of Coca-Cola bottlers with gathering speed. In 1902 alone, the Whitehead-Lupton parent company opened plants in nearly two dozen Southern cities from Savannah, Georgia, to Meridian, Mississippi, while the Thomas company dotted the rest of the country with plants from Buffalo to Kansas City to Los Angeles. The parent bottlers opened 32 plants in 1903, 47 in 1904, and a record 80 in 1905. They took on new partners, divided the country into smaller regions, and hastened to fill in the grid with a bottler in every city and town.

Bottled Coca-Cola went on sale in markets across most of the country. In the choking, sticky heat of the textile mills of the Deep South, vendors would roll a "dope wagon" with an ice-water tank through the aisles past the looms and slubbers, and the sweating, lint-covered workers would pay their nickels and steal a minute to gulp down a cold Coke. In New York City, where Coca-Cola was slow to catch on, the local bottler was surprised at the robust sales he enjoyed in the Italian neighborhood around Mott and Mulberry streets—until he learned that his customers, a vegetable store, barber shop, undertaker, and harness maker, all had secret card-rooms in back where the men liked to mix Coke with chianti and stay up late gambling. In New Orleans, the bottler used a low-slung river bark, the *Josephine*, to deliver Cokes in the bayou country.

The bottling venture was proving to be a huge success, but the hard work took its toll. Whitehead's constant travel exhausted him, and in 1906 he developed a severe cold he couldn't seem to shake. He set off for a rest in his wife's home town of Thaxton, Virginia, but developed pneumonia and died there at the age of forty-two. Ben Thomas had a short life as well. He suffered a stroke in 1914 and died soon afterward while trying to recuperate in Atlantic City. He was fifty-two.

The Coca-Cola bottling system passed to a new generation. Whitehead's widow, Lettie, and his partner, Lupton, turned over responsibility for the day-to-day operations of their parent company in Atlanta to a twenty-four-year-old bookkeeper named Veazey Rainwater. Thomas, who died childless, left control of his company in the hands of a twenty-seven-year-old nephew, George Hunter, in Chattanooga.

The two younger men came into power at the parent companies at a time when it was far from clear exactly what they were expected to do. The original goal of the parent bottlers was to recruit actual bottlers to do the work, yet for the most part that job was finished.

By 1909, there were 397 Coca-Cola bottling plants in the United States, enough to inspire a convention. Gathering at the Aragon Hotel in Atlanta, a hundred Coca-Cola bottlers compared notes, posed in white sailor caps for a group photo, listened to speeches from Asa Candler and other luminaries, and held a smoker (complete with a "Joke Contest") before leaving town. They even had their own monthly magazine, *The Coca-Cola Bottler*, published by Candler's nephew Joe Willard, full of professional tips and social tidbits. The business had matured in the short space of a decade.

In most cities, a franchise to bottle Coca-Cola was now considered a license to make money. (Expressing the point explicitly, the bottler in San Antonio printed up a letterhead that depicted a Coke bottle spurting dollar signs, over the slogan, "There is money in it.") Many bottlers found demand so heavy they divided their territories and assigned their rights to a new genus of *sub*-bottlers who built smaller, more efficient plants. There was no need to recruit new bottlers, because applicants were beating down the company's door and begging for the opportunity.

The parent companies were left without a clearly defined role. Syrup was shipped from the Coca-Cola Company's factories directly to the actual bottlers, so the parents were not even acting as genuine middlemen. They simply sat back and took a royalty on every gallon, even though they never handled a drop. The parents paid the Coca-Cola Company 92 cents a gallon for syrup, then turned around and "resold" it to the actual bottlers at a generous markup, usually $1.20 a gallon. It was all done on paper.

Supervising the operations of the actual bottlers required some effort, but frankly not that much. Not long before he died, Thomas received a worried letter from his bottler in Jackson, Tennessee, wondering why sales had taken a dramatic downturn in the middle of a warm snap in August. "WATERMELONS, YOU DUMBBELL!" Thomas wired back. By the eve of World War I, the combined royalty payments to the parent companies were approaching $1 million a year, yet the organizations had few serious responsibilities.

Not surprisingly, perhaps, the growing wealth of the parent companies kindled a fair degree of resentment at the Coca-Cola Company's headquarters in Atlanta. Sam Dobbs, for instance, considered Lupton a venal old meddler whose "entire business life has been spent in getting all that he could put his hands on." (When the first bottlers' convention was proposed to Lupton, his wary response was, "Who's going to pay for it?") Hunter was judged to be a slow mover, while Whitehead's two sons, growing up in Atlanta, developed reputations around town for heavy drinking and skirt-chasing and showed no inclination to follow their father into the business.

Over the years it has become an article of faith at the Coca-Cola Company that Asa Candler's seemingly mindless giveaway of his bottling rights was actually an act of genius, since it spurred a quick profusion of plants that otherwise might have taken decades to develop. But the truth is, Candler really *did* throw away something of tremendous value. He and his family could easily have acted as parent bottlers themselves, recruiting the actual bottlers and providing them with financing. Or they could have built plants on their own, skipping the parent stage entirely. Candler had more money than Thomas, Whitehead, and Lupton put together. He simply didn't believe in bottling. Some of his associates—Frank Robinson, Dobbs, Harold Hirsch—ached to get into the bottling business and pleaded for the chance, but Candler refused to let them, leaving them to watch sullenly as others grew rich. The problem was not just that the parents were making more money on bottled Coca-Cola than the Coca-Cola Company itself, but that they were doing so without having to lift a finger.

The exception was Veazey Rainwater, the new chief of the Southern parent company. A wiry man with small, bright eyes and jug ears, Rainwater invented a fresh job for himself as a hardworking liaison between the actual bottlers and the Coca-Cola Company. He could see that the business was changing, and he believed the greatest challenges in the future would be legal and political. The company and its bottlers would have to join forces and present a united front if they hoped to survive—but Rainwater could see it was not going to be easy. His bottlers were a stubborn, independent lot, and many of them regarded the company with deep suspicion, almost as an enemy. Asa Candler's diffidence toward bottling had rubbed them the wrong way from the beginning, and over the years they had accumulated a set of petty grievances. They thought the company's advertising favored Coca-Cola at soda fountains over Coca-Cola in bottles. They complained that the company didn't do enough to police its fountain wholesalers and stop them from selling syrup to pirate bottlers.

Part of the trouble was a difference in values. One year at the bottlers' convention, Bill D'Arcy was describing his latest advertising campaign and giving a pep talk. Hoping to make a vivid point, he took a twenty-dollar bill out of his wallet, tore it up and threw the pieces on the floor. Sitting out in the audience, Arthur Montgomery, the surly old bottler who ran the Atlanta plant, flew into a rage. He had never seen anything so stupid in his life, he declared, and from that day on he refused to buy any of D'Arcy's advertising materials from the company. Even in his later years, when he was nearly blind, Montgomery would run his hands over the company's annual advertising contract and make his assistants swear that there was no commission in it for D'Arcy. All of the bottlers had substantial amounts of capital tied up in their equipment—the cost of a top-of-the-line plant in a big city had risen to more than $100,000—and they tended to view Dobbs and the younger Candlers as a clan who had made their money and could afford to fiddle around. If the Coca-Cola business came to an overnight halt—if the bubble burst, as John Candler had put it—the Candlers would still be rich. The bottlers would be ruined.

But the way Rainwater saw it, all the friction was a minor matter compared to the threat the bottlers and the company faced together from out-side forces. State legislatures were forever taking up bills aimed at taxing soft drinks or outlawing various ingredients, and Rainwater organized his bottlers into a potent lobbying battalion that fought back, most of the time successfully. He and Hunter, his counterpart in Chattanooga, formed a close alliance with Harold Hirsch and agreed to split the expenses of these statehouse skirmishes. Correspondence from the period contains a variety of enigmatic invoices from Coca-Cola's cashier: a bill for $500 in 1911, for instance, for Rainwater's share of the $2,000 it had cost Hirsch to resolve "some trouble" with the Texas legislature. Similar charges were forwarded for lobbying efforts in Virginia, Louisiana, and Mississippi.

The grandest campaign, of course, was the company's long struggle with the federal government. When Dr. Wiley first filed his charges against Coca-Cola in 1909, one of the company's bottlers, Crawford Johnson of Birmingham, Alabama, took Hirsch aside. "Harold," he asked worriedly, "can you keep us going for three years?" Yes, Hirsch replied, he thought he could. A decade later, when Hirsch finally settled the case in Coca-Cola's favor, the parent bottlers gratefully paid their half of a legal bill that had reached $250,000.

The bottlers came to rely on Hirsch as their champion in the court-room. One of the biggest headaches they confronted was a spate of lawsuits by people claiming to have found "strange elements" in bottles of Coca-Cola. Many of the allegations were plainly fraudulent—two bottlers dis-covered they had paid hush-money to the same woman, who claimed she'd found a frog in a bottle—and in 1914 a group of bottlers met in Hirsch's office in Atlanta and formed the Coca-Cola Bottlers' Association to pool their resources and fight the cases in court. Hirsch oversaw the defense efforts. On those occasions in which a startled consumer really did find a bug in a bottle of Coca-Cola, Hirsch would arrange for the services of expert witnesses. (In later years, the company used a museum curator from Atlanta named Perry Wilbur Fattig, who was famous for demonstrating the harmlessness of insects by eating them in front of the jury.)

Rainwater earned the company's gratitude, meanwhile, by working to improve the standards of his bottlers. A stickler for quality control, he sent teams of inspectors around to check sanitary conditions in the plants in his region, and if a bottler was making an inferior product he would threaten to shut him down unless he made improvements. Some of the bottlers bridled at the interference, but Rainwater was smart enough to ally himself with the most successful operators in his region, and they backed him up.

The growing sense of unity between the company and the bottlers cul-minated with the success of a project Rainwater and Hirsch spearheaded for the design of a distinctive Coca-Cola bottle. At most retail outlets of the period, bottled soft drinks were sold in large tubs filled with ice water. Coca-Cola's bottlers used the same ordinary, straight-sided bottles everyone else used, and thirsty customers had to roll up a sleeve and fish around in the murky depths without any way of knowing what brand they were grabbing. Even when they pulled a bottle up into the daylight, the confusion continued, because the labels typically came unglued and slid down to the bottom of the tub. Putting Coca-Cola in a specially shaped bottle would help tremendously with marketing. It would also give Hirsch another tool—a trademarked package—to use in fighting the competition in court. And if the new bottle should be a little *smaller* than normal, if it were 6 or 6½ ounces, say, instead of the usual 8 ounces, that would mean higher profits. At Hirsch's urging, Rainwater chaired a committee of bottlers charged with picking a model.

The choice they made resulted from a felicitous mistake. In Terre Haute, Indiana, in the late summer of 1913, a heat wave shut down operations at the Root Glass Company, one of Coca-Cola's bottle suppliers. Taking advantage of his free time, plant manager Alex Samuelson began playing around with ideas for the new bottle and was struck by an inspiration. He sent one of his employees, an auditor named Clyde Edwards, off to the city library to look up information on coca leaves and kola nuts. It was Samuelson's thought that a bottle shaped like one of the original ingredients in Doc Pemberton's formula would be unique, which was true enough, but somewhere along the line he and Edwards got crossed up. Perhaps the difficulty was Samuelson's poor command of English—he was a native Swede—or it might have been Edwards's fault, but in any case they ended up on the wrong page of the *Encyclopedia Britannica*. They designed a bottle whose vertical striations and curved, bulging middle bore no resemblance whatsoever to the coca leaf or kola nut, but instead was a dead ringer for the totally unrelated seed pod of the *cacao* tree, the source of chocolate. Thus was born one of the most familiar shapes in product history.

Rainwater, cheerfully ignorant of the error that inspired it, loved the new design. He arranged for a prototype to be tested in secret at several Coca-Cola bottling plants, and after a few technical modifications he got the bottlers' committee to adopt it for exclusive use at all of the company's plants. He also won a protracted dispute with Hunter over the color of glass to use, prevailing with light green over brown. The new bottle was an immediate hit. Hirsch proposed giving C. J. Root, who held the patent, a royalty of 25 cents per gross on all the bottles his company and others manufactured. Root generously demurred, asking for only a nickel a gross—and ended up the wealthiest man in Indiana anyway.

By the time the Candlers sold Coca-Cola in 1919, Veazey Rainwater and his bottlers were accustomed to doing business with the company on a handshake. They trusted Hirsch—so much so that they had him serve as their lawyer at the same time he was the company's general counsel. They saw no conflict of interest.

When the sale went through, Rainwater gladly accepted Hirsch's reassurances that the old management would remain in place, and that the new owners would bring new capital to the table and build the business to new heights. Hunter, a more cautious soul who kept a wary eye on the company's doings from his perch up the road in Chattanooga, wired Hirsch during the negotiations, asking plaintively, "I wish you would take a few minutes and write me what is actually going on." Hirsch responded soothingly, "Powerful interests are taking this proposition over and will make a big go of it, but the bottlers' rights will be absolutely protected. . . ."

The matter had never been addressed in any formal way, but Rainwater and Hunter both believed that their contract with the company, the old document signed by Asa Candler twenty years earlier, was perpetual and unbreakable. As they saw it, the company was legally obliged to sell them syrup at 92 cents a gallon, which they were then free to sell to their actual bottlers at whatever price they could command. They believed Hirsch concurred in their interpretation.

In November 1919, when the price of sugar began soaring, Rainwater and Hunter received a panicky letter from Sam Dobbs asking their permission for the company to begin buying as much sugar as it could in the newly uncertain marketplace. Howard Candler would handle the emergency purchases, Dobbs wrote, and the company and the bottlers could sort out the finances later. Anxious to help ease the pressure, and secure in the ultimate strength of their position, the two parents readily gave their assent. Rainwater and Hunter had agreed to two minor, temporary increases in syrup price during the war, when the government fixed sugar prices at 9 cents a pound, and they were willing to help out again. Only this time they were dealing with Ernest Woodruff.

On December 15, 1919, when the company's newly formed executive committee met in New York, W. C. Bradley opened a letter from Hirsch proposing a compromise in which the company and the parents would share the burden of the higher costs. Woodruff objected. He saw no reason to approach the parent bottlers on bended knee. His lawyers had looked over the original contract, he announced, and in their view the company could cancel it at will. Perhaps something could be worked out with the parents, he said, but it would be on the company's terms. If the bottlers didn't like it, they would be out of luck. It was a very hard line, one that made Dobbs and Howard Candler extremely uncomfortable, but Woodruff controlled the committee and refused to yield.

Back in Atlanta, Hirsch summoned Rainwater and Hunter to his law office in the Candler Building. "Boys," he said, "I have called you up here to tell you bad news." The directors of the Coca-Cola Company, he said, planned to meet and cancel the contract. Rainwater was, as he put it later, "completely dumbfounded." Surely, he argued, the new owners were not serious. Surely Woodruff was angling for a better position in working out a compromise.

Hirsch seemed unsure himself just what Woodruff had in mind, but he set to work with Rainwater trying to fashion a new proposal that might pass muster. The days of the parent companies' 28-cent-per-gallon royalty were over, obviously, but perhaps Woodruff would allow them a more modest margin. Hirsch and Rainwater drafted a document spelling out in detail the exact price and proportion of every "merchandise" in the Coca-Cola formula, along with the company's expenses for labor, cooperage, freight, advertising, and overhead. If the company and the parents would agree to a profit of 10 cents each per gallon, they calculated, syrup could be sold to the actual bottlers for $1.35 per gallon—a big jump from the $1.20 they were accustomed to paying, but still affordable, especially in light of the ongoing sugar emergency.

Dobbs and Howard Candler favored the settlement, and as president and chairman of the board of the company they expected their judgment to prevail. But they hadn't counted on the iron will of Ernest Woodruff. During a bitter, all-night session in February 1920, Woodruff made it clear once and for all that he was in charge. All decisions would be made by the executive committee, which he controlled. The compromise drawn up by Hirsch and Rainwater was unacceptable. At Woodruff's direction, Candler wrote a letter to the parent companies informing them that their contract would be terminated on May 1, 1920.

Dobbs seemed especially surprised and agitated at discovering this new, harsh side to the man he'd considered his partner. Woodruff, he wrote a friend, obviously intended "to emasculate and supersede" the authority of the board of directors—Dobbs included. Dobbs had been president of the Coca-Cola Company for all of five months, and already his relationship with Woodruff had turned into an ugly battle of nerves, one he was afraid he was losing. Woodruff was guilty of "constant butting-in and interfering" with the company's business, Dobbs complained, and "seems too disposed to tell us all what we ought to do and is very much outraged when we don't agree with him." Dobbs was no particular fan of the parent bottlers, but he believed the smart business move was to reach an accommodation with them. Woodruff grudgingly gave him one last chance.

Dobbs, Candler, and W. C. Bradley convened a negotiating session in Atlanta with Rainwater, Hunter, and Lupton, and laid out the Coca-Cola Company's final offer. The parent companies could have a royalty of 7½ cents a gallon, period, take it or leave it. Rainwater and Lupton reluctantly accepted on behalf of their parent company. But Hunter refused the ultimatum, stormed out of the meeting, and went home to Chattanooga. He asked himself, he said later, what his uncle Ben Thomas would have done, and he believed his uncle would have chosen to fight. A few days later, Hunter called a council of the Thomas company's bottlers, who now numbered nearly six hundred. Most of them came to Chattanooga, and they listened as Hunter, furious, vowed darkly that if he went down he intended to pull the whole Coca-Cola business down with him.

Lupton and Rainwater withdrew their acceptance and prepared for war.

———

The first thing the parent companies required was a lawyer, and by a stroke of pure coincidence they ended up with one who detested Ernest Woodruff.

A year earlier, the Whitehead family had placed the law firm of King & Spalding on retainer. There was no pressing legal business at stake. It was simply that Joe Whitehead's younger son, Conkey, had turned twenty-one and wanted a lawyer to look after his inheritance while he pursued the life of the playboy around Atlanta. He picked King & Spalding more or less by chance, unaware that the firm's founding partner, Jack Spalding, was the old warhorse who had faced off against Woodruff and Joel Hurt in the bitter streetcar fight back before the turn of the century.

Spalding relished the chance to step back in the ring with his old opponent, but he was sixty-three years old and in poor health, so he picked one of his firm's toughest young litigators to handle the case for him. John A. Sibley had come to the firm a couple of years earlier from Milledgeville, Georgia, where his successes in the courtroom brought him statewide attention. Sibley had a round face and soft country accent that concealed a sharp, competitive nature. He was a dangerous opponent in the court-room, capable of skinning a witness. It was a mark of Spalding's faith in his abilities that he picked Sibley as lead counsel for the Coca-Cola case over another partner in the firm—his own son, Hughes Spalding.

Sibley joined forces with the lawyers Hunter had retained on behalf of the Thomas parent company, and on April 14, 1920, they filed suit against the Coca-Cola Company in Fulton County Superior Court in Atlanta. Even by the typically belligerent language of lawsuits, the petition was notable for its bristling tone and accusations of betrayal. After years of honorable conduct, it said, the Coca-Cola Company had been taken over by certain "promoters and high financiers" who manipulated the stock and duped the public and pocketed millions of dollars in quick, undeserved profits. Wood-ruff and his associates, the suit said, were men of "cupidity and avarice and greed." The local newspapers picked up the story and reported the out-break of hostilities as if the most prominent family in town were engaged in a dirty, no-holds-barred divorce, which in a way was exactly what was happening.

Rainwater believed the outcome of the fight depended as much on pub-lic opinion as it did on the law. It was vital to him to maintain the allegiance of the hundreds of Coca-Cola bottlers across the country. If Dobbs and Woodruff could convince the bottlers it was in their best interest to elimi-nate the middleman and deal directly with the company, the parent bottlers would be in serious trouble. The way to keep that from happening, Rain-water calculated, was to paint Dobbs and Woodruff as sly, dishonest men who would gouge the bottlers and the public with higher prices if they ever got the chance.

Dobbs could see Rainwater's strategy unfolding. The parent bottlers were "moving heaven and earth to prejudice the actual bottlers against us," he wrote his friend and fellow director Bill D'Arcy a few days after the suit was filed. "Everything that has been sent out . . . is along the line that the Coca-Cola Company [is] trying to confiscate the bottlers' property." Dobbs tried to calm the apprehensions triggered by the lawsuit and the lurid headlines, but he felt overwhelmed. When he gave an interview to the *Atlanta Constitution* claiming the Coca-Cola Company was under the same old management that had been running things for years, Rainwater answered by disclosing the existence of the Voting Trust. The public had been led to believe the Candler family still controlled Coca-Cola, Rainwater said, but all the power actually rested in the hands of Ernest Woodruff—the kind of man, he added archly, who "needs no introduction to this community."

Hearings in the case began just a week after the suit was filed. A special commissioner took testimony, presiding in a makeshift courtroom that was set up in King & Spalding's offices in the Empire Building. Dobbs was one of the first witnesses called, and before he knew it he found himself answering embarrassing questions about how he had come to be president of the company. Under the lawyers' prodding, Dobbs divulged all the details of the transaction that had taken place the previous fall—the clandestine meetings with Woodruff in New York, the blank option that Asa Candler's children had signed, the Trust Company syndicate, the Voting Trust, even the existence of the $5 shares.

Harold Hirsch tried—and failed—to stem the damage. At one point during Dobbs's testimony, Hirsch noticed that a lawyer for the parents, Ben Phillips, had picked up the company's minutes book and taken it over to his table, where he and Sibley were leafing through its pages, reading about the activities of Coca-Cola's executive committee in rapt fascination. When Phillips began to recite excerpts of the minutes into the record, Hirsch jumped to his feet, rushed across the room, and tried to grab the heavy leather volume out of Phillips's hands. Phillips held on desperately and the two men began huffing and heaving in a tug of war. "It is not going in the record," Hirsch called out, "and I demand the book back. *Give me my book back!*" Phillips answered, breathlessly but with perfect lawyerly formality, "I will have the commissioner report that Mr. Hirsch physically takes the book!" Eventually order was restored and Hirsch recovered the book, but not before everyone in the room got the clear message that the Coca-Cola Company had secrets it wanted to hide.

There were further humiliations inflicted on Hirsch. One of the juiciest morsels that emerged during the hearings was the disclosure that the Candlers had been forced to honor their old contract with Bainbridge Colby and Edward Brown, from the aborted sale of 1917, and had paid the New York lawyers $1 million in cash from the proceeds of their eventual sale to the Woodruff syndicate. The news had not come out before, and it created quite a stir, especially since Colby was now the U.S. secretary of state.

Mustering all his powers of insinuation, Sibley asked Hirsch to explain how his brother-in-law, Brown, had managed to profit so handsomely from this "manipulation." Hirsch, who had done nothing improper in connection with the affair, was bound by his obligation of confidentiality to the Candler family. Even though his silence seemed highly incriminating, he refused to answer.

Day after day the testimony continued, as the participants explained the complicated twists and turns of the banking transactions Woodruff had carried out, where the money went, who got it and how much. The details could be numbing, but Veazey Rainwater made a very effective witness when he observed simply that Woodruff and his associates made a bigger profit on the Coca-Cola Company in one day than he and his bottlers had made in twenty years.

The hearings lasted two weeks, and they put a fatal strain on the brittle relationship between Dobbs and Woodruff. Every detail of the company's business was coming out publicly in the worst possible light, and Woodruff was in a towering rage.

"I had to tell him," Dobbs reported to D'Arcy, "that the lawyers were trying the case and that I was not going to interfere and he shouldn't, and if he felt the lawyers were not handling the case properly to call a meeting of the board and I would submit the matter to them."

Dobbs was becoming increasingly contemptuous of Woodruff—the man was "as busy as a mangy dog with fleas," he wrote D'Arcy—and he yielded to the dangerous temptation of allowing his contempt to show. He complained to W. C. Bradley that Woodruff was impossible to deal with, and Bradley answered that he simply couldn't understand why they were having such difficulties, except that his old friend Woodruff was an intensely demanding man. In all the years he had known him, Bradley said, Woodruff had never been satisfied with what he got. Dobbs agreed. Woodruff struck him, Dobbs said, as the sort who expected to get back $101 when he cashed a check for $100, and complained if he didn't get it.

The lawsuit entered a new phase, and for a time it appeared the company's fortunes might be improving. Once the plaintiffs got through presenting their case, Hirsch had a chance to fight back, and while there was little he could do to repair the damage to the company's reputation, he did manage to score several sharp points in assailing the parent companies' legal position. He discovered evidence suggesting that hundreds of bottlers were operating under an "exclusive license" directly with the Coca-Cola Company, and Dobbs observed gleefully that "when this fourteen-inch shell fell into the ranks of Hunter and Rainwater they were certainly panic-stricken."

Dobbs exaggerated, but it was true that the parent bottlers were growing nervous about the outcome of the trial. In spite of their success in embarrassing the company and winning the allegiance of the actual bottlers, Hunter and Rainwater had no assurance of prevailing on the legal issues. Asa Candler had testified on the company's behalf, swearing that he never intended the bottling contract to be permanent, and his word had clout. Thomas and Whitehead were no longer alive to contradict him.

The judge, John Pendleton, began dropping hints that he planned to rule in favor of the company, which was, after all, the most powerful and influential business in town. (Rainwater and Hunter noticed with some trepidation, too, that the judge's grandson had just signed on with Hirsch's law firm as its newest junior partner.) Rather than wait for a verdict, the parent bottlers decided to stage a strategic retreat. On the last day of May 1920, they abruptly withdrew their suit, pulled out of Georgia, and refiled their petition in federal district court in Delaware—thereby guaranteeing that the dispute would drag on for many more weeks.

The prospect of delay was intensely disheartening to the company. All during the spring of 1920 the sugar problem kept worsening, until finally the price reached a record high of 28 cents a pound in the first week of May, in the midst of the trial. Desperate to ensure a continuing supply, Howard Candler exercised a series of contracts with several large refineries and importers, locking in deliveries of thousands of tons of sugar—a half-year's supply—at exorbitant prices. Candler figured the company was losing nearly $200,000 a month selling syrup to the bottlers at the old contract price, and the bottlers reluctantly agreed that they couldn't go on indefinitely paying only 92 cents a gallon for syrup that now cost more than $1.50 a gallon to manufacture. Rainwater and Hunter did not, after all, wish to bankrupt the company.

On June 10, 1920, under the supervision of U.S. District Judge Hugh Morris in Delaware, the two sides agreed to a temporary compromise. For the next five months, which figured to be the period it would take to try the case, the parent bottlers would pay the company $1.57 a gallon, which Howard Candler certified was the actual cost of manufacture.

The two sides settled into an uneasy truce, and peace was restored to the Coca-Cola family—but only for a moment. Sam Dobbs still had a company to run, and he intended to keep marketing Coca-Cola to a thirsty American public. Dobbs's closest ally on the board of directors continued to be Bill D'Arcy, and the two men shared the view that in spite of the financial pinch it was vital to keep advertising the product.

"If I used my own judgment I would start a vigorous advertising campaign the first of September," Dobbs wrote D'Arcy. Traditionally, the end of the summer season brought a decline in soft drink sales and a corresponding reduction in the advertising budget. But Dobbs meant to keep the demand high year-round, and he proposed spending a generous $100,000 a month on newspaper ads through the fall.

Dobbs's ambitions brought him into another unpleasant clash with Woodruff. The two men no longer made even a pretense of trying to get along. At an executive committee meeting in New York in July 1920, Woodruff made it plain that the company's first obligation was to pay dividends to its stockholders. In Dobbs's colorful phrasing, Woodruff and E. V. R. Thayer, the leader of the Wall Street investment group, were "tearing their hair, howling for retrenchment, because they want dividends." Woodruff scuttled the advertising plan, and Dobbs threatened to convene a meeting of the full board of directors to resolve the impasse and decide once and for all who was running the company.

Before that could happen, however, another economic blow shook Coca-Cola. In early August of 1920 the world sugar market collapsed almost overnight. The price plummeted to about 10 cents a pound.

The company found itself in a crisis, committed to spending $8 million on sugar that was suddenly worth only half that much. Howard Candler had made a costly mistake. In signing the long contracts, he'd gambled that sugar prices would remain high indefinitely. Instead they'd tumbled. Candler told a colleague years later that he actually prayed for a tropical storm to sink one of the steamers, the *Hilton*, which was carrying a 4,100-ton shipment of high-priced sugar from Java. But the ship docked safely at Brunswick, Georgia. All of the company's deliveries came through and had to be honored. "For a considerable period of time," Coca-Cola's auditor said, "it looked like the company might not be able to carry on."

The balance of power shifted decisively away from Sam Dobbs. For the foreseeable future, all the company's efforts would have to be bent toward saving money. Except for D'Arcy, no one on the board had any appetite for an expensive advertising campaign.

Still, Dobbs persisted in forcing a showdown. Among other things, he badly misunderstood the practicalities of stock ownership. "Woodruff and Bradley are very fond of talking about how much stock they own," he wrote D'Arcy. "They, however, seem to overlook the fact that Howard Candler and I represent $10,000,000 of Preferred Stock, which makes the combined holdings of the executive committee. . .look like thirty cents." Actually, the preferred stock carried no voting power, a harsh fact of life Dobbs ought to have remembered since he helped engineer the deal in the first place. Further weakening his cause, Dobbs counted on support from board members he should have known would remain loyal to Woodruff. For instance, Dobbs counted Tom Glenn in his corner—Tom Glenn who worked for Ernest Woodruff at Trust Company and served him as head of the Atlantic Steel Company. By some woeful miscalculation, Dobbs convinced himself that he could muster a majority of Coca-Cola's directors, when in fact he stood almost alone.

On October 4, 1920, Dobbs returned to Atlanta from a lengthy business trip visiting the company's salesmen in the western states. As he stepped off the train, a messenger greeted him and asked him to go directly to the Candler Building to see Harold Hirsch. When Dobbs emerged from Hirsch's office, he went to his desk and wrote out his resignation as president of the Coca-Cola Company. His tenure had lasted just one year and two weeks.

In describing the chain of events to his confidant, D'Arcy, Dobbs was guarded in explaining why he quit, "other than to say to you that under present conditions as I found them upon my return here, I could not remain with the company and retain my self-respect." The best guess is that Woodruff had gathered enough support from the board to whittle down Dobbs's authority. During an executive committee meeting in late September, Woodruff and Bradley made a show of counting up the company's advertising and publicity expenses, portraying Dobbs as a big spender, and it appears they planned to take away his control of the budget. Certainly they succeeded in checkmating his plans for an aggressive advertising campaign. In any case, Dobbs made no secret of his feelings. He could retire comfortably, he told D'Arcy, and "I am in a position where it will not be necessary for me to act either as Mr. Bradley's valet or Woodruff's office boy."

In a stroke of wicked irony, the board asked Howard Candler to return as president of the Coca-Cola Company, thus making Dobbs's worst nightmare into a reality for the second time. Bradley stepped in to take Candler's place as chairman of the board. And Woodruff ruled the roost.

As Dobbs packed his bags and loaded his shotguns for an extended hunting trip in western Canada, he left behind a company moving closer and closer to collapse.

Word of Dobbs's resignation and rumors about what might have caused it fluttered through Wall Street, driving the stock to a new low of 27⅛. The *Atlanta Journal* reported—accurately—that the board was planning to skip the next payment of the quarterly dividend of $1 a share on common stock.

On November 1, 1920, the temporary agreement between the company and the parent bottlers ran out, and to the amazement of the bottlers (and most investors) the company announced that its cost of manufacturing syrup had gone *up*, all the way to $1.81 a gallon, despite the drop in sugar prices. It was clear the backlog of high-priced sugar was far higher than previously believed, and that the company's losses would take much longer to pay off—if they could be paid off at all. A week later, Judge Morris in Delaware ruled in favor of the parent companies, holding that the old contract was perpetual. The company planned to appeal, but in the meantime there would be no shifting of the burden of the sugar losses onto the backs of the bottlers. Coca-Cola stock took another nose dive.

And there was another peril looming. On November 18, 1920, the United States Supreme Court began hearing oral arguments in a trademark case that would determine whether Coca-Cola had a right to protect its name.

It was impossible to exaggerate the importance of the Koke case. The ten-year battle with Dr. Wiley had established that Coca-Cola was legally made and that its name did not constitute a criminal fraud on the public. But trademark infringement was a matter of *civil* law, and the courts had yet to decide once and for all whether Coca-Cola was entitled to sue its imitators and put them out of business.

Hirsch had brought dozens of suits against Coca-Cola copycats in federal district courts across the country, and he had prevailed in almost every instance. But when the Supreme Court reversed the Chattanooga verdict in 1916, an element of confusion was introduced. Even though the company successfully settled the Chattanooga case and got the old charges dismissed, judges were left to wonder anew if Coca-Cola was a legal trademark.

The test case, fittingly enough, involved a nearly forgotten character from Coca-Cola's early days. J. C. Mayfield was Doc Pemberton's last partner, a hard-luck fellow who thought he'd bought the rights to Coca-Cola in 1888 only to learn that Pemberton had already sold them. Mayfield spent a season in Atlanta trying to sell a taste-alike product named "Yum-Yum," but soon went out of business.* Eventually Mayfield wound up manufacturing a soft drink he called Koke, and when he incorporated his operation as the Koke Company of America and tried to register his trademark, Hirsch sued. For the sake of thoroughness (and to harass Mayfield with steep legal expenses), Hirsch brought actions in Washington, D.C., and in four different states where Koke was sold.

The lower courts sided with Hirsch and the Coca-Cola Company. Generally speaking, trademark cases were a matter of common sense. A product could not be made and marketed with the intent of creating and exploiting confusion with another product. Koke syrup was colored to look like Coca-Cola, sold in similar red kegs and barrels, marketed openly as a cheaper substitute, and of course its name was more than just confusingly similar to Coca-Cola, it was a homonym for Coca-Cola's popular nickname "Coke," indistinguishable to the ear. Few infringement cases have ever been as open and shut. "There is no use of mincing words in describing [Mayfield's] plan of operation," one of Coca-Cola's lawyers said. "It is a cheap and common swindle." The courts agreed. But trademark protection could not be given to any product that was itself fraudulently made or marketed, and when the Supreme Court overturned the Chattanooga verdict, Mayfield's lawyers suddenly had a new weapon for their appeals to the higher courts.

One of the cases Koke lost was in Arizona, and the appeal was heard by the Ninth Circuit Court of Appeals in San Francisco. Citing the Supreme

---

* Mayfield and his wife, Diva, claimed they learned Coca-Cola's secret formula from Pemberton, but there is scant evidence to support their assertion. They later divorced, and Diva Brown, as she was known after she remarried, became a minor celebrity in the South around the turn of the century peddling copies of the "authentic" formula. Although a trade journal labeled her "a humbug and a fake," she had many takers.

Court's ruling, the appellate court held that in spite of Mayfield's obvious guilt as an infringer, the Coca-Cola Company was ineligible for relief because of its own "deceptive, false, fraudulent, and unconscionable conduct. . . ." According to the Ninth Circuit judges, Coca-Cola had lost the right to protect its trademark because it had contained "the deadly drug cocaine" for many years, and because the caffeine in its syrup came from sources other than kola. This was the ruling that had frightened the directors of Trust Company so badly when Woodruff asked them to approve his, plan to buy the Coca-Cola Company. Hirsch and the other lawyers were confident the company would prevail on appeal to the Supreme Court, but as both sides gathered in Washington for final arguments in the late fall of 1920 the outcome was far from certain.

The days before the Supreme Court ruled in the Koke case marked a low point for the Coca-Cola Company. Common stock fell to 17⅜, less than half its offering value the year before, as panicky investors dumped their holdings. The stock might have dropped even further except that it became hard to find buyers at any price, especially in Atlanta. Hundreds of Georgians were stuck with shares that couldn't be sold, whose dividends were suspended indefinitely. They had borrowed money from Trust Company and other banks to buy the stock, and now they were unable to repay the loans. Businessmen would encounter Asa Candler, take him aside and ask him to do something to save the company—to save *them*—and he would explain gently that he was retired and no longer involved with Coca-Cola. But they "do not seem to want to understand," he complained sadly, and he found that he could not sleep at night.

On December 6, 1920, in an opinion written by Justice Oliver Wendell Holmes, the Supreme Court rendered its decision. It was a triumph for the Coca-Cola Company. In an elegant phrase that captured the precise point of the company's argument, Holmes called Coca-Cola "a single thing coming from a single source, and well known to the community."

The trademark, Holmes explained, was widely recognized by American consumers as the name of a familiar soft drink—not as a chemical compound made up of coca leaves and kola nuts. Perhaps Coca-Cola had once contained a small amount of cocaine, Holmes conceded. Perhaps, as a government chemist once suggested, it was even enough to numb a man's tongue and create a habit. But those days were long gone. The company had inaugurated a "drastic process" that removed the cocaine from the coca leaves, and it had "advertised to the public that it must not expect and would not find cocaine" in Coca-Cola. The word "cola," he added, conveyed little if any meaning to most consumers.

The trademark "Coca-Cola" did not fool consumers into thinking they were buying something they were not, Holmes concluded. On the contrary, the trademark identified a soft drink millions of Americans knew and liked. "It hardly would be too much to say that the drink characterizes the name as much as the name the drink," Holmes wrote. Coca-Cola was fully entitled to protection against Koke, which Holmes called a "palpable fraud."

The outcome of the case was an enormous relief to the members of the Coca-Cola family, naturally. The *Atlanta Journal* reported "a distinct feeling of optimism in local business and financial circles." Today one can find the words ". . . a single thing coming from a single source, and well known to the community . . ." etched in marble in the foyers of hundreds of Coca-Cola bottling plants around the world. The phrase has become something like the motto on a coat of arms, an emblem of victory and honor won by an ancestor on a glorious field of battle.

Yet the decision did not by any means mark the end of the company's troubles. Had the court ruled differently, the business would have failed in a matter of days. As it was, the company could look forward to surviving into 1921, but how far it could survive into the new year remained an open question. The price of stock rose a few points, then stabilized just above $20 a share and refused to budge. Sixteen million pounds of sugar, most of it purchased at high prices, still clogged the inventory. Sales were flat and beginning to trend downward. Most ominous of all, the fortunes of the company were in the hands of Howard Candler and Ernest Woodruff, two men who didn't understand or trust each other.

On the last day of January 1921, Howard Candler was in New York City, making calls on sugar suppliers and asking them to defer some of their deliveries. He hated the city—hated its weather and people and its ways of doing business. It was raw and wet outside his hotel room, snowing but not sticking, and he missed Atlanta.

"I still find it quite difficult to accomplish anything here," he wrote his father, upset that a supplier was making him stay overnight before giving him an answer. "People here don't seem to go straight to a conclusion. Endless delays are encountered." The president of the Coca-Cola Company, forty-two years old, sounded more than a little like a homesick schoolboy.

Making Coca-Cola syrup had always given Howard Candler a feeling of satisfaction; running the company left him intensely frustrated and deeply unhappy. He agreed to resume the presidency because he felt a sense of familial duty in a time of trouble, but with Dobbs gone he found that he had too many duties, too many obligations in areas of the business that were alien to him. And making a difficult situation even worse, he had Ernest Woodruff looking over his shoulder criticizing his every move.

Woodruff called one of the company's vice presidents to his office at Trust Company and complained that Candler was disrupting the wage scale of Atlanta by paying Coca-Cola's factory laborers 5 cents an hour more than unskilled workers received elsewhere around the city. When word got back to Candler he was furious. He *knew* how to make syrup, and he was proud of the abilities of his work force. "We do not employ, and cannot use, so-called common labor," he wrote in a private memo that he tucked away in his files. "It is necessary that we employ semi-skilled labor, or labor with more intelligence than the riff-raff and drift-wood of the streets."

Candler complained that Woodruff's "continued picayunish interference" with the company's management was driving him to distraction. It bothered Woodruff that Coca-Cola cost more at restaurants and clubs and on the train than it did at the corner grocery store, and he badgered Candler to do something about it, though Candler couldn't imagine what. On a related front, Woodruff was pressing Candler to subsidize selected retailers in every market and compel them to sell Coke for a nickel, thereby putting pressure on other retailers to cut their prices as well. Candler thought the policy was "distasteful" and refused to implement it.

For his part, Woodruff found Candler impossibly naive. As winter turned to spring in 1921, investors in Atlanta and New York were putting Coca-Cola common stock into play, beginning a tense financial and psychological struggle for control of the company. Woodruff was the key player, and he wanted a president who would help him, not one who called things distasteful and balked at every move.

The price of Coca-Cola common began creeping back up, and the reason was simple: Speculators were gambling on the possibility that Coca-Cola might survive after all. Huge blocks of Coca-Cola shares were changing hands, and most of the buying was coming from New York. It appeared a battle might be shaping up between Wall Street and Atlanta—between North and South.

Woodruff's use of the Voting Trust to maintain control of the company's affairs was in jeopardy, partly because the legality of such trusts was under attack, and partly because many of the stock transfers were going unrecorded, with ownership passing into unknown hands. Woodruff tried to explain to Candler that if new owners came along and gained control, the old management probably would be shown the door. But Candler could not or would not recognize the threat. He told Woodruff he couldn't see why anyone would want to get rid of him.

At one board meeting, Candler wanted to talk about expanding the company's fledgling overseas business. He began urging the directors to think about establishing branches in other countries, until Woodruff rudely cut him off and signaled for an adjournment. Daydreaming about Coca-Cola's future was fine, Woodruff said, but it was a fool's luxury. What mattered was the present. There wasn't much point planning foreign operations if the company was about to fail, or if someone intended to sneak up and snatch it out from under them. If Candler had his heart set on pursuing the subject, if he *had* to waste the board members' time, Woodruff suggested, then he ought to write them a letter—which is just what Candler was reduced to doing.

In the meantime, Woodruff turned all of his considerable wiles to the challenge of trading against the New York investors. During the spring of 1921, he made a flurry of moves, many of them secret, most of them difficult to interpret, all of them designed to improve his position. There is no question he engaged in insider-trading practices that would be illegal today (as did the other side). At one point, Woodruff tried to bully Candler into releasing a patently false report exaggerating the company's progress in digesting its supply of high-priced sugar. At other times he leaked contradictory rumors, sending the stock price down, apparently so that he could buy shares at a reduced price.

On one occasion when Woodruff made a visit to New York, Candler took note of a "very rapid and unusual advance" in the price of the company's stock, even though "nothing has occurred in the status of the business to justify such advances." Candler was certain Woodruff was providing confidential information, some of it falsified, to the financial press in New York. He even summoned the gumption to challenge Woodruff about his activities during a face-to-face meeting, but Woodruff answered coolly that he had no idea what Candler was talking about and ended the conversation.

For a time, at least, it appeared Woodruff was willing to sell out. In a strange episode in April 1921, he told Candler that an unnamed investor in New York was offering to buy a block of 150,000 shares of stock. According to notes Candler made at the time, Woodruff said he wanted to make the sale and had put together a pool of 100,000 shares toward that end. He wanted Candler's help in assembling the other 50,000 shares. If true, it was a significant moment in Coca-Cola's history—the Trust Company crowd meant to cut their losses and surrender the controlling interest in the company, whose headquarters might well be moved out of Atlanta and up to New York. New management and directors would take over. Yet there is no certain way of knowing the truth of the matter, because Woodruff routinely hid his real motives behind a cloak of misdirection. In any case, Candler refused to participate unless the buy-out offer was extended to the holders of all 500,000 shares, and he believed his opposition had the effect of killing the deal.

Wall Street learned to treat Woodruff with suspicion. Once, at Woodruff's direction, Candler put out a formal statement denying that the expensive sugar had been exhausted and insisting that there were no plans to resume paying dividends, yet the market responded to this gloomy report by sending Coca-Cola up, as the stock reached its highest price of the year. A consensus was forming among investors that in spite of Woodruff's bluster and bluffing and broken-field running, the company's chances of pulling through were improving. And they were right.

In the midst of all the financial maneuvering, an act of startling good sense took place in the federal courthouse in Philadelphia.

The company had appealed the verdict in the bottlers' case, and in May 1921 a panel of judges on the Third Circuit Court of Appeals convened to hear oral arguments. Ignoring the legal niceties, the presiding judge called the lawyers for both sides up to the bench and urged them to reach a settlement. Performing the judicial equivalent of knocking their heads together, he emphasized the great likelihood that both parties would suffer if either side "won," and said that only a compromise would do. It was sound advice. Taking it to heart, each side put forward a senior man—Gene Stetson for the company and Jack Spalding for the bottlers—and they hastened off to Atlantic City to meet in private and work out the details.

A little more than a month later, a deal was struck and the parent companies agreed to a syrup royalty of 12½ cents per gallon. The war with the bottlers was over. One way of looking at it was that sheer willfulness on both sides had very nearly destroyed the whole business over a matter of pennies. As a practical matter, though, the settlement was good news, and when word got out the price of Coca-Cola stock zoomed even higher. There was no single magic moment when the survival of the Coca-Cola Company suddenly became a certainty, but the settlement of the bottlers' suit, which was ratified by the board on July 25, 1921, came as close as anything.

Over the next several months, the company gradually reduced its stocks of overpriced sugar. Its debt dropped. Sales began to climb again, revenues picked up, and on December first the $1 per share dividend was resumed. Ten days later, the price of Coca-Cola common completed its long recovery and closed at 41⅜, back to its starting point after two long years. When the books were closed on the tumultuous year of 1921, it turned out that sales were a relatively healthy $28.5 million—off only a little from the year before despite the lingering postwar recession and all the company's internal difficulties. In his annual report, Candler chided the company's bottlers "who allowed themselves to become discouraged and get into a state of lethargy in so far as pushing the sales of Coca-Cola was concerned." But that lethargy was now gone. The wounds of the fight were healing (though they would never be repaired completely), and the prospects for 1922 looked promising.

The one question that remained unresolved was control over the ownership. If he had briefly entertained the thought of selling out, Woodruff's mind was now very much changed. The *Wall Street Journal* reported a "steady accumulation" of Coca-Cola stock by New York investors, and Woodruff bent himself to the task of taking it out of their hands. He said nothing publicly, but bank records and Woodruff family documents disclose that he spent the next few months buying up large blocks of Coca-Cola stock for himself, his family, and the bank. He got several associates from Trust Company to join him in the venture, and together they amassed a new stake of thousands of shares.

Meanwhile, with the power of the Voting Trust dwindling, Woodruff also began looking for a new way of exercising domination over the other owners. If he planned to maintain his ultimate authority over the management of the Coca-Cola Company's affairs—and he most assuredly did— then he would have to devise a means of circumventing a board of directors that was growing increasingly responsive to the interests of the Wall Street investors. In the spring of 1922, Howard Candler tried to send an official from the company's New York office to Central America on a ninety-day assignment, only to be blocked by a pair of major shareholders who wanted to keep the official in town and threatened to make trouble if he left. Woodruff cared nothing about the particulars of the incident, but the display of strength by the Wall Street men annoyed him. He decided to show them who was boss. During the summer and fall of 1922, Woodruff quietly organized a holding company, the Coca-Cola International Corporation, and traveled around the state of Georgia asking hundreds of Coca-Cola stockholders in Atlanta and Columbus and other cities to convert their Voting Trust certificates into shares in Coca-Cola International.

The holding company proved to be a brilliant device. In spite of the heavy buying in New York, Georgians still owned more than half of the 500,000 outstanding shares of Coca-Cola common stock, and as far as they were concerned, Woodruff's proposal seemed perfectly reasonable. It was strictly a paper transaction: A share of Coca-Cola International represented ownership of an underlying share of stock in the Coca-Cola Company, with the same dividend and market value. Most shareholders were happy to make the switch. But the new company had its own set of directors, ready to take control as soon as a majority of the shares of Coca-Cola were in hand—and that moment arrived in the late fall of 1922.

When the Coca-Cola Company's board of directors gathered in Atlanta for their regular meeting on November 27, 1922, the members were surprised to see a pair of new faces in the room. One of the visitors was Frank Dick, representing the E. F. Hutton organization of New York. The other was Ernest Woodruff's eldest son, Robert. According to the *Atlanta Journal's* description, when the two men took seats at the table alongside the directors, "there was speculation among observers as to their mission." But the puzzlement did not last long.

Ernest Woodruff disclosed that he had formed Coca-Cola International, and that the new holding company now controlled a majority of Coca-Cola common stock. Then he named the directors of the new company: Tom Glenn, Jim Nunnally, W. C. Bradley, E. F. Hutton, and Robert Woodruff. There was an awed silence. Woodruff had staged a coup. His son, three of his closest associates, and a new partner from New York would now be running the Coca-Cola Company. The board had no choice but to authorize the necessary paperwork to complete the transfer of stock.

The New Yorkers were stunned. The Southern group had gained what amounted to a proxy, with the ability to vote a majority of Coca-Cola stock in any showdown over policy. Woodruff's old ally, Gene Stetson, registered his opposition to the new arrangement, but was utterly powerless to prevent it. The Wall Street investors complained bitterly, and even went so far as to block trading in Coca-Cola International stock on the New York Stock Exchange, yet there was nothing they could do to change the outcome.

Woodruff had beaten them. And he had an even bigger surprise in store next.

Five

"GET YOUR READINESS"

When he was a very old man—when he had been running the affairs of the Coca-Cola Company for more than sixty years and had turned its trademark into the most familiar symbol in the world, when he was heralded as one of the most successful businessmen of his generation, and after he'd made and given away hundreds of millions of dollars—even then Robert Woodruff maintained the myth.

He could not bear to have anyone think his father gave him the job. And so he created an elaborate fable to explain how he rose to the presidency of Coca-Cola: Ernest Woodruff was such a terror, and so monumentally inept at operating the company, that the other members of the board went behind his back and arranged to hire his son—his strong-willed, defiant son—to be the new president. That was the story. When no one else would stand up to Ernest Woodruff, the board brought in the one man who could tame the lion and bring order to chaos.

The way Bob Woodruff told it, the way he genuinely seemed to remember it after all the retelling over the years, was that three of his father's closest friends, including W. C. Bradley, came to visit him in New York City during the winter of 1923. The Coca-Cola Company was about to go broke, they told him. He had to come back to Atlanta and take charge of the management and save their investments. He held a stake in the company, too, they reminded him. He had borrowed heavily and gone into debt to buy Coca-Cola stock, and now the value of that stock was in dire jeopardy.

Responding to the urgent persuasion of his visitors, the younger Woodruff reluctantly agreed to return home. According to a statement he later placed in the company's archives, the board elected him president at a special meeting in April 1923, even though his father objected strongly and then stalked out of the room and abstained from voting. "The only reason I took that job," Woodruff liked to tell people, "was to get back the money I had invested in Coca-Cola stock. I figured that if I ever brought the price of stock back to what I had paid for it, I'd sell and get even."

It made a fetching tale, tidy and plausible, and eventually every account of the company's history repeated it in one version or another. Only it wasn't true.

In 1923, the Coca-Cola Company was like a patient recovering with surprising swiftness after a terrible accident. In spite of the bruised feelings and distrust between the company and its bottlers, there was a grudging realization on everyone's part that the smart course would be to return to business as usual, because business as usual meant profits.

When hundreds of bottlers and fountain salesmen assembled in Atlanta on the evening of Tuesday, March 6, 1923, for a convention aimed at hastening the healing process, one of the first things they saw was a huge, life-size mock-up of a village in the warehouse section of the Coca-Cola factory. It looked like something from a movie set. The display of shop fronts along "Main Street" showed a "Right Side" and a "Wrong Side," and while it was designed to illustrate the right and wrong ways of merchandising Coca-Cola—window signs should be big but uncluttered, painted with a pattern or blueprint, and never drawn freehand—it also served as a perfect metaphor: The company intended to do things the right way from now on.

Over the course of two full days of meetings, the bottlers heard pep talks from every official in the Coca-Cola hierarchy. In every case the message was the same. The business was back on track. The national economy was emerging at last from its lingering postwar doldrums, and the company intended to follow suit. Ernest Woodruff made his first (and last) public appearance before the bottlers, as Veazey Rainwater introduced him and signaled that it was time to let bygones be bygones because the principal owner was now completely committed to the grand crusade of selling Coca-Cola. Woodruff's top lieutenant, Tom Glenn, urged the bottlers to buy Coca-Cola stock—Trust Company would be happy to lend them the money to do so, he said—and the plain if unspoken point was that whatever manipulations might have taken place before, a share of Coca-Cola stock was now a long-term investment in a company that was going back to work.

The star of the convention was the company's new vice president for sales, Harrison Jones. Standing six foot two, with a wild crown of unruly silver-brown hair that made him seem even taller (and with bulging eyes that often made him look as if he were about to burst), Jones was a remarkable physical specimen. He was a natural arm-pumper and back-slapper, a robust and captivating man with an evangelical public speaking style that left his listeners absolutely riveted.

After starting with the company in 1910 as a lawyer helping gather evidence in the Chattanooga case, Jones switched to the management side as an assistant to Howard Candler and then rose to the top sales position on the strength of his ability to dazzle and inspire the company's salesmen and especially its bottlers. Jones once bragged to a younger associate that he could pick up a copy of the *Saturday Evening Post*, open the magazine to any page at random, glance at a sentence, and instantly give an hour-long declamation on the subject "And he was damn near right," the associate said.

Jones's speeches were legendary, a blend of flowery oratory and towering profanity delivered with the stagecraft of an actor. Jones never sat on the dais but always at the back of the hall, and when he was introduced he made a point of sauntering toward the front with exquisite, theatrical stateliness. "Sometimes it would take him fifteen minutes to get to the podium," a colleague said with admiration, "just strolling down there big and handsome as he was, breathing hellfire and damnation, and the bottlers loved it."

On the morning the convention opened, Jones was at the very top of his form. His voice filled the warehouse and billowed out over the men in their seats next to the Main Street exhibit. Yes, Jones said, there were rumors and fears and bad feelings. But that no longer mattered. The company was back together, and everyone must begin pulling as one. He knew the fountain salesmen and the bottlers often clashed, often saw each other as competitors, but they had to remember that they were actually Siamese twins, forever joined in the larger glory of selling Coca-Cola. Jones had a special message for the bottlers. They were the wave of the future. They were not delivery men, not mere truck drivers, he told them—they were *Coca-Cola salesmen*, a special breed. And their employees had to be special, too.

"We want men of energy," Jones said, beginning the climb to his first crescendo. "We want men whose record proves that they will put out! We want men with guts, who will stand the gaff and won't holler—who will stand up and not lay down, who will take orders and carry them out *wholesouled . . . red-blooded . . . HE-MEN!*"

Jones had the bottlers back in the fold before the first day's session broke for lunch. It was more than just his gift for delivering a sermon. He had news for the bottlers, too. He told them the company intended to match their efforts and mount a new advertising campaign that would surpass anything they'd ever seen before. Instead of pocketing their renewed flow of dividends, Jones announced, the board of directors planned to spend an extra $1 million on advertising in 1923, and it was going to be a record year for profits.

With Jones adopting the role of master of ceremonies, the company's top men trooped one after another to the lectern to spin a picture of the challenges and opportunities that lay ahead. Bill D'Arcy came in from St. Louis to report on his plans for placing ads—hundreds of pages of ads, the highest number ever—in newspapers, farm publications, women's magazines, railroad bulletins, and most important of all in the general circulation magazines that now served as the leading medium of national influence.

Already the company had unveiled its new slogan, "Thirst Knows No Season," in the *Saturday Evening Post* (accompanied by an illustration of an exceptionally pretty girl in a very short skirt skiing smartly past a bank of snowdrifts). The new advertising budget was intended to put muscle behind the strategy of selling Coca-Cola year-round. There were 110 million people in the United States, D'Arcy said, and when he looked at them he saw 110 million parched throats that were thirsty in autumn, winter, and spring as well as summer.

Charles J. Carmody, whose company designed most of Coca-Cola's outdoor advertising, reminded the bottlers that one American in five now owned a car. To reach the driving public, he said, the bottlers needed to make use of a new art form that was beginning to spring up along the roadside of the country's thousands of miles of new highways. It was the 24-sheet poster (so named for the 24 individual sheets of reinforced paper, each 28 by 42 inches, that were glued together to form a mosaic 25 feet long and 11 feet high)—better known as the billboard. Billboards were the way to sell Coca-Cola to the nation's twenty million motorists.

The bottlers should be prepared, Carmody warned, to join the fight to fend off critics—usually irksome society dowagers with nothing better to occupy their time—who were complaining that billboards were an eyesore and campaigning to make them illegal. In his home state of Pennsylvania, Carmody confided, the outdoor sign lobby was already spending $15,000 to $20,000 every year, "just to ride back and forth to Harrisburg," the capital, to kill off restrictive legislation.

Carmody closed his remarks with a description of the giant sign he was building for the company in Times Square in New York City. It was going to be sixty-five feet tall—six and a half stories!—with four thousand electric light bulbs that would illuminate the famous script of the Coca-Cola logo in brilliant white against a deep red background. Coca-Cola was going to see its name in lights on Broadway, Carmody said. He left the stage to a standing ovation.

The company men were willing to admit they still had some problems. There was no denying it. Jones and his engineers had designed a carry-home carton, a rudimentary six-pack made of heavy, buff-colored paper board, in the hope of creating a household market for Coca-Cola. The company was testing the new package in Miami, Tampa, Mobile, New Orleans, Shreveport, Oklahoma City, Birmingham, and Asheville. But sales were dismal. There simply wasn't enough home refrigeration to inspire housewives to lug the bottles home from the grocery store. It might be years before people got used to the idea of drinking Coca-Cola at home.

On another front, the long fight with Dr. Wiley and the government had raised doubts about the healthfulness of Coca-Cola, and those doubts had yet to be entirely dispelled. "There is hardly a day goes by," complained Walter Bellingrath, the president of the Bottlers' Association, "but what some man asks me something about Coca-Cola, and if it is not dangerous and whether it will kill you, and if it is not wrong for your children to drink it."

Ross Treseder, who handled sales and advertising in the company's Chicago office, had just been to a Pure Food and Health Show in Louisville. It was a good thing he went, he said, because he found a couple of ladies running a Women's Christian Temperance Union booth and passing out flyers that said, "Do Not Drink Coca-Cola." Their pamphlet, he said, made Coke sound worse than Alabama Shinny! Luckily he was able to talk some sense into them and get them to stop.

Despite the few notes of defensiveness, though, the overall tone of the convention was vigorously positive. The speakers were delivering a sort of collective state of the company address, and they wanted it known that the state of the company was sound.

As the bottlers wrapped up the second day of the convention and prepared to head back to their plants, their mood was upbeat. The bleakest days, the days of overpriced sugar, collapsing stock prices, looming court decisions, and combat with management, seemed to be receding into the past.

"If there are no other questions," Harrison Jones said, bringing the final session to an end, "I will tell you a little story." Then he interrupted himself. "First let me ask—if you are asked to come again, will you?" He was rewarded with cries of "Yes! Yes!" and an ovation, and after a suitably dramatic pause he returned to his farewell story:

"Down in a little town in Alabama they don't have a train caller, but an old Negro woman that works in the station constitutes herself train caller and everything, and this is what she says. 'Dat air train from Bumminham am showin' himself. Get your readiness.'

"This year 1923 is showing herself, and trees are in bloom in Atlanta! Get your houses in order! Get your readiness! *Good-bye and good luck!*"

Severe, chronic hearing loss ran as a physical trait through the Woodruff family. Ernest Woodruff's father, George Waldo Woodruff, used an old-fashioned ear trumpet, and it was so much a part of his appearance and daily routine that once when he sat for a formal portrait he held it in his hands and had the photographer include it in the picture. Most of his children and grandchildren inherited the problem, just as they did his stout physique and strong jaw line.

Not so obvious, but just as prevalent, was another family characteristic: stubborn persistence.

The Woodruffs traced their lineage to an Englishman named Matthew Woodruff who crossed the Atlantic in 1636 and became a Connecticut Yankee, settling as a pioneer in the area around Farmington. Six generations of flinty New Englanders later, George Waldo Woodruff moved to the South and started a corn, wheat, and flour milling operation on the Chattahoochee River in Columbus, Georgia. In the years before the Civil War, George Waldo made a considerable fortune, and his faith in his adopted region of the country proved to be so strong that he insisted on investing everything he had (with the exception of a lone ten-dollar gold piece) in Confederate currency.

The war ruined George Waldo, leaving him broke and reducing his mill, which he had used to help feed the Confederate Army, to a charred patch of ground. Yet during Reconstruction he managed to scrape together enough borrowed money to start anew, and before long Empire Mills was making a steady stream of handsome profits again, using the modern "Complete Gradual Reduction Roller System" to produce a line of flours that included Snow Flake, Silver Leaf, and Pearl Dust.

George Waldo was demanding of his son. Ernest turned eighteen in 1881, and soon afterward his father put him to work as a salesman for the mill riding a circuit that covered southwestern Georgia, northern Florida, and parts of Alabama. Ernest spent weeks on end on the road, making trips he came to dread, especially in the summer when the heat was almost unbearable (though the drenching rains of February were scarcely any better). Journeying through the countryside of the American South before the turn of the century was an arduous, bone-wearying task. Most nights Ernest stayed in boarding houses, since hotels were rare in the small towns and crossroads settlements that dotted the region. He drove his own buggy and usually traveled with a shotgun and hunting dog and brought home food for the dinner table.

Life in Columbus was not much easier. When he was home, Ernest worked at the mill, and his father often sent him down to supervise operations at night. All in all, the prospect of a career in the flour business struck Ernest as unappealing, and he seized every opportunity he could to slip away from Columbus and stay with his older sister, Annie Bright, and her husband, Joel Hurt, up in Atlanta.

During one of his visits to see the Hurts, in 1883, Ernest met the girl next door, Emily Winship. "Miss Ernie," the daughter of Robert and Mary Frances Winship, had just celebrated her sixteenth birthday. She was slender and petite, shy and physically frail, given to occasional bouts of dark moods, and Ernest found himself hopelessly smitten. He sent her flowers, along with a note asking if he could take her out for an afternoon stroll along Atlanta's fashionable Ponce de Leon Avenue. Her parents need not worry, he wrote, because "I will take the best care of you."

Rather than worry, the Winships forbade the date. Ernie was entirely too young for a romance, her parents felt, and they tried to discourage her from taking an interest in her new suitor. They returned one of Ernest's letters unopened, making it clear to him that his pursuit of their daughter was unwelcome. But Ernest was unfazed. He kept seeing Emie on his trips to Atlanta, kept writing her, kept wooing his "precious little girl" in the stiff, Victorian fustian of the day:

> I admit that a lady should always be on her guard least she over-steps the bounds of propriety, but on the other hand, don't think she should be so reserved as to permit her lover to believe that she had not the utmost confidence in him. If your father objects to our union it is very unfortunate, but why should you be cool to the man who *adores* you at the *very* time he would most appreciate your love?

Other than their daughter's age, and the lack of enthusiasm they might have felt over the idea of her moving to another town, there is nothing in the record to explain the Winships' disapproval of Ernest Woodruff as a prospective groom for Emie. The Winship family was in several respects a carbon copy of the Woodruffs. Emie Winship could trace her roots back to England and a seventeenth-century ancestor who emigrated to Massachusetts just a few years after the landing of the *Mayflower*. Her father's father, Joseph Winship, moved to Georgia in the early 1800s and started several businesses, among them a successful operation manufacturing cotton gins, before settling in Atlanta in 1853 and opening an iron foundry.

During the Civil War, the Winship Machine Company made munitions for the Confederacy. As Sherman neared Atlanta in 1864, Ernie's parents fled the city—her mother to the safety of Madison, Georgia, which was spared in the march to the sea, and her father to a railroad camp where the men hid from the Union armies and relied on catching squirrels for their food. When the Winships returned, they found their home had been looted and their factory razed during the burning of Atlanta. (Their dining room sideboard, a magnificent, hand-carved piece topped by a staghead with a perfect set of antlers, was stolen; they later found it at a public auction and bought it back for $5.) Like the Woodruffs, the Winships rebuilt their business after the war, making agricultural equipment that included cotton gins and presses, self-feeders and condensers, and saw and grist mill machinery.

If there was a difference between the clans that caused friction, it might have been the greater gentility of the Winships. They were a quiet, soft-spoken crowd who displayed little of the eccentricity and fierce ambition associated with the Woodruffs. Whatever their misgivings, however, Ernie's parents were no match for the perseverance and ardor of Ernest Woodruff. He proposed marriage and sent Ernie a ring, guessing correctly that since it fit his little finger it would be the right size for her ring finger. "Now my dear little girl," he wrote her at one point, bearing down literally and figuratively with a firm hand, "you ought not to trifle with me on this subject."

Eventually he prevailed. Ernie agreed to marry him, and her parents, forced to be satisfied with having postponed the event for two years until she turned eighteen, finally relented and gave their blessing. Ernie and Ernest were married on April 22, 1885, and went to the Grand Central Hotel in New York on their honeymoon.

The new couple settled in Columbus. Ernest assumed a vice presidency in his father's business and curtailed his grueling life as a traveling salesman. Ernie and Ernest's first child, a son, was born on December 6, 1889, and they called him Robert Winship Woodruff, after Ernie's father.

The fact that the boy carried both family names began to seem more and more appropriate as he grew up. It was plain even in his early years that he had inherited all of his father's willfulness and determination, but he also showed signs of shyness and brooding, tenderness and melancholy—traits that ran in his mother's family. He was a complicated child.

In 1893, just before Robert Woodruff turned four, his parents moved to Atlanta. Ernest accepted Joel Hurt's invitation to join him and help run his burgeoning empire in banking, real estate, streetcars, and electric power. As Ernest's career advanced in the new city, his manner turned more brusque and domineering. He encouraged his employees and associates to call him "the Chief," and he gained the reputation, as one newspaperman put it, of being an "exacting master." Growing a close-cropped moustache, he altered his physical appearance and managed to make himself look more imposing. At five foot eight he was stocky and powerfully built.

At Trust Company, Woodruff showed little patience for office comradery or small talk. He liked to eat a huge breakfast at home and then skip lunch at the bank so he could work. If visitors called on him when he was busy, he had the habit of handing them a small leather pouch full of collections of jokes and stories, so they could occupy themselves until he had time for them.

(One palm-sized booklet Ernest gave out was called "Wisdom of the Sages." It contained peppy aphorisms—"The man who watches the clock will always be one of the hands"—and corny two-liners: "Teacher: 'Why don't you like our school, Willie?' Willie: 'Oh, it's not the school so much as it is the principal of the thing.'" Reading a copy decades later, it is hard to escape the conclusion that Woodruff felt contempt for other men and expected them to amuse themselves while he made money.)

Woodruff's frugality was the stuff of legend. He collected hotel soap. He refused to pay more than $2 for a white shirt. At the bank, he tried to block Christmas bonuses for the employees. Once, while he was off on a trip, a junior officer ordered modern telephones and had them installed in the bank's offices; when Woodruff returned, he had them torn out and the old upright phones restored.

On one celebrated occasion, Woodruff and Tom Glenn took the train to Baltimore to pick up several hundred thousand dollars' worth of streetcar bonds. Refusing to spend $200 on insurance and express shipping, Woodruff led Glenn back up to their hotel room, where the two men stripped down to their underwear, wrapped the bonds around their bodies, and concealed them under their clothes. They sat up rigidly all night riding the train home, and later—many years later—they laughed at how they'd crackled like diplomas every time they budged. Glenn was one of Woodruff's few unabashed admirers, but even he had a cautionary explanation of why they got along: "Because I always let him have his own way, and it is usually the right way."

More and more, though, Woodruff's way had a mean edge. He had his first falling-out with Joel Hurt over plans for the basement of Hurt's skyscraper, the Equitable Building. Hurt wanted to open a cafe where businessmen could get a quick bite at lunch instead of going home and having a heavy midday meal followed by a nap. It would be more productive if the men could stay downtown, Hurt thought, and better for the city. But Woodruff didn't care. He argued for a saloon and pool hall that would make more money.

On his thirty-fourth birthday, Ernest's mother wrote him a stark, disturbing letter that chided him for failing to keep the Sabbath. He was far too involved, she warned him, in "the strife for Earthy [*sic*] treasures."

At home, Woodruff remained devoted to Miss Ernie, the "main spring" of his life. After Robert, she and Ernest had a second son, Ernest Jr., who died of spinal meningitis in 1896. They then had two more sons who survived, George and Henry, and Ernest spent $20,000 building a fine, rustic-style English house for them in Inman Park, Hurt's suburb east of Atlanta. A newspaper account of the time remarked on the modern facilities in the house and marveled that "Mrs. Woodruff has only to touch certain buttons, turn little handles and knobs and. . .the electric globes, bulbs, and blossoms burst into golden bloom, window shutters stand at attention, doors come open and servants come forward to receive commands."

The house had all the amenities of the era, including a hot water heater, an anthracite-burning furnace, and a specially designed icebox that could hold an oversized, two-hundred-pound block of ice. With its tiled porches, marble bathrooms, and wainscoting finished in Antwerp oak, it was certainly a handsome place.

By all outward appearances, the three Woodruff boys grew up in idyllic circumstances, surrounded by the considerable luxuries that were available to well-to-do families around the turn of the century. Ernest was one of the first men in Atlanta to buy a car, a big black Oldsmobile that arrived by rail from Detroit and created quite a stir. On Sundays, the family typically climbed in it and rode out to the exclusive Piedmont Driving Club, where they could swim and bowl and play tennis. The Woodruffs had servants, including a formidable-looking black woman named Mammy Lou who favored severe white turbans and looked after the boys.

Ernest was determined not to spoil his sons. Even as he provided them with the rewards of his wealth, he tried to teach them the importance of thrift and honesty, self-discipline and hard work in school. But with his eldest son, Robert, it seemed the lessons were failing to take hold. Robert— or "Buddie," as his younger brothers nicknamed him—was a spirited boy, growing up lanky and good-looking, with an ability to attract the attention and affection of his teachers and other children. He was not, however, a good student. When he was ten and his parents were on a trip, he wrote them, "Our class had an arithmetic examination today. I think I got four on it."

Not that Robert was dull-witted. Far from it. Lively and sociable, he enjoyed having other children around him so much that when he had exhausted his mother's patience for throwing parties he would invite his friends over to an aunt's house and entertain them there. He had a definite touch of Tom Sawyer about him. When his father gave him a small allowance to pay for boarding the pony he rode to school, he pocketed the money and talked the chief hostler at Asa Candler's stables into keeping the animal for no charge. It was Robert's favorite childhood story—the first time he outfoxed his father.

In the classroom, though, Robert was miserable and self-conscious. In hindsight, it seems highly likely that he was suffering from undiagnosed dyslexia. As an adult he had an aversion to reading, and his associates noticed that on those rare occasions when he was forced to decipher a letter or memo, he had to stop and look at each word individually and allow it to register before he moved on haltingly to the next. As a schoolboy, he complained that his homework gave him trouble with his eyes and often made him feel ill. His grades were poor and he required tutoring and summer school. His parents had no idea what might be wrong, except the strong suspicion that he was not applying himself.

Robert had a wretched physical problem, too, a severe underbite his parents sought to remedy by sending him to a dentist who experimented on him with the newest type of fixed braces. The wires and bands caused him a great deal of discomfort, especially when they were tightened twice a week, and prevented him from participating in athletics. Photographs from the period show a handsome young man, but one who was never caught smiling.

As he grew into adolescence, Robert was made well aware that his father was disappointed in him and concerned over his inadequacies. During Robert's teenage years, his first cousin from Columbus, George C. Woodruff— "Kid" Woodruff, a year older and soon to become the star quarterback and captain of the University of Georgia football team—was in boarding school in Stone Mountain, just outside Atlanta. Ernest regularly invited Kid Woodruff to spend weekends and vacations with the family, and made it no secret that he felt a greater admiration for his brother's son than his own.

In 1906, when he was sixteen, Robert flunked out of Boys High School. His father responded by sending him where many families sent sons who frustrated them, to a military boarding school, in this case the Georgia Military Academy just south of Atlanta in College Park. Like most proprietary military academies of the time, GMA placed a higher premium on teaching discipline than scholastics.

Robert remained an indifferent student, yet in every other respect he blossomed in cadet gray. He discovered that he was a natural leader. Kept from playing sports by his dental woes, he joined every other activity he could find and rose to take charge of many of them. He was manager of the football team, manager of the basketball team, manager of the Dramatic Club, manager of the school paper, the *Gamilicad*, and manager of the school annual, *Parade Rest*. He was even manager of a board of other managers.

Robert joined the Alpha Theta Literary Society, the Painter's Club, and the bugle corps, and was initiated into a fraternity, Sigma Chi, at 3:13 one Saturday morning under the school's grandstand. He became first lieutenant in the Corps of Cadets. When someone proposed raising money to buy instruments and start a school band, Robert took on the project. "As long as I was out trying to raise money for the band, I didn't have to go to classes," he joked years later. But there was more to it than that. He enjoyed taking on challenges and working out deals and testing his budding skills as a salesman.

Perhaps the most remarkable thing about Robert Woodruff's career at GMA was the profound, lasting impression he made on so many of the people who came in contact with him. His roommate, Dick Gresham, was utterly devoted to him. Gresham grew up to be a preacher, and for the rest of his life he wrote long, thoughtful letters to Woodruff in the form of private sermons. The Sunday school teacher at GMA, Mrs. Alonzo Richardson (known to one and all as "Sweetheart") wrote him an amazing letter years later describing a dream she'd had in which he saved her life during a terrible storm, carrying her through swirling, muddy water—"confident, so strong and sure"—reaching dry ground without getting a smudge on his fine, white suit.

When Robert graduated from GMA in 1908, the school's headmaster, Colonel John C. Woodward, had a private talk with Ernest. "Don't send Robert to school anymore," he warned. "You'll ruin him."

Woodward was right, but understandably Ernest Woodruff disagreed. The plan was for Robert to go to college and earn a degree and become a banker, and Ernest was not about to give up so easily on the course he had set for his son.

In the fall of 1908, under his father's prodding, Robert set off for Emory College, then a small Methodist institution with about three hundred students in Oxford, Georgia, a little village about thirty-five miles east of Atlanta. For a time, at least, Robert went through the motions of applying himself to his studies, which pleased his parents. He was, he wrote his father, "nearly studying my head off." As a reward, Robert regularly beseeched his parents for permission to visit home, and whenever they agreed he was elated. On one occasion, writing in the dreadful doggerel he had begun to affect, Robert tried to articulate his gratitude:

> This afternoon when I received your letter,
> It made me feel a great deal better
> To see, how kind and considerate
> You are to a son who is so illiterate.

My great appreciation is most unbounded
And when I here a good footing have founded
You will be proud you sent me to Emory
Because I will try and do credit to the family.

But it soon became clear that he was not doing credit to anyone. As summer stretched into autumn in his freshman year, Robert's parents discovered that his awkward, touching expressions of diligence were nothing but a con job. Robert was not studying his head off; he was barely studying at all. The feeble scholarship of GMA had left him completely unprepared for the rigors of Emory's modest curriculum, and rather than batter himself against a hopeless challenge he was devoting his time to the pursuit of pleasure. Instead of attending classes, he was spending his time hanging around the Kappa Alpha fraternity headquarters upstairs at Stone's Store in Oxford. And downstairs at Stone's, he was racking up the bills, charging his account for more than he could ever hope to cover with his $40 a month allowance.

Robert's fervor about visiting home turned out to have less to do with his devotion to his parents than it did his love of girls and parties and his desire to escape the dullness of Oxford for the bubbling social scene in Atlanta. Young women, it turned out, found Robert very attractive. He had grown tall—six feet—and was lean as a stalk. He had the dark eyes and good looks of the male line of Winships. A pretty debutante named Helen Payne told Ernie Woodruff at a reception one afternoon that she was crazy about Robert and wished he would call on her more often. A lot of girls felt that way.

Ernie could understand her son's appetite for fun. "I trust I shall always be a comfort to you," Robert once wrote her, and for the most part he was. Mother and son were extremely close, and she sympathized with his struggles at learning. The two shared a predilection for illness brought on by nervous fatigue. During Robert's years at GMA, when he suffered headaches and pain from his braces and other occasional disorders including severe indigestion, she monitored his condition closely by telephone and oversaw his treatment and medication. She wanted him to be happy, and she tried to protect him from his father's wrath.

Ernest thought it was all nonsense. He believed his wife spoiled their son. Once when she came down with one of her sick headaches, he told Robert it was probably because she had overworked herself planning a party for him. In Ernest's view, finishing college was a simple question of will. If Robert tried, he would succeed.

In October 1908, during Robert's first term at Emory, Ernest and Ernie made a trip to Denver for a banking convention. Stopping off in Colorado Springs, Ernest picked out a postcard that neatly expressed his view of his son's travails. It showed a cowboy riding a bucking bronco. "Hope you have held on until it comes easy," he wrote Robert at school. "That's how this fellow did."

When the postcard arrived at Emory, Robert was gone. Taking advantage of his parents' absence, he had sneaked back to Atlanta and was spending a long weekend at home enjoying himself, openly defying his parents' emphatic instructions not to leave the campus again before Thanksgiving. In light of his father's strict discipline, it was a reckless act. Yet Robert made no attempt at all to cover up his tracks. On the contrary, he went to Trust Company and borrowed money from one of his father's clerks, used his father's charge account to buy clothes at a store, and raided his father's closet before returning to college Tuesday evening. His behavior seemed calculated to provoke an explosion, and it did.

Arriving home and learning of Robert's mischief, his father hastened to his desk, drew out a sheet of stationery, and began writing swiftly with a quill pen. "It was a source of <u>mortification</u> and <u>regret</u> that you disobeyed me and came to Atlanta again," Ernest wrote, underlining the occasional word for emphasis.

> I had hoped that I had made it clear to you that you must apply yourself and not leave Emory without permission; such willful disobedience and extravagance as you are guilty of is inexcusable and will not [*sic*] longer be tolerated; the sooner you change your habits the better it will be for you, your conduct is wholly [*sic*] inexcusable and will not be tolerated.

After finishing the letter, venting his anger to the extent of repeating himself, Ernest discovered the evidence of Robert's rummaging in his clothes closet. He returned to his desk, jerked the letter back out of its envelope, and resumed writing in a cold fury. In a postscript set down with a pencil in blunt, heavy slashes, Ernest continued:

> I note that you have carted off my cane and two of my valices [*sic*] and I know not what <u>else now.</u> You will do me the kindness to return all of my property you have carried off to College the <u>first passing.</u> If you have not worn the new suit of clothes you ordered <u>charged</u> to me at <u>$35.00</u> I would advise you to return them as I <u>positively decline to pay for them.</u> When I am ready to tender to you the use of my <u>credit</u> and <u>bank account</u> I will let you know. If you think the object in going to College is to spend money and play "big Ike" you had better quit and learn to earn your own living. I am doing all I can for you and to make a man of you but my patience is nearly exhausted; and I beg that you will not force me to harsh measures to <u>save you from yourself.</u>

It scarcely seemed possible that the relationship between Robert and his father could go downhill from that point, but it did. The Christmas holidays, in Ernest's view, were a long, unproductive waste of time that allowed Robert to slack off and lose the last traces of his meager momentum as a student.

Returning to Emory, Robert complained of toothaches and eye troubles and sought to postpone taking his written examinations. Deeply exasperated but unsure what else to do, his father wrote the president of Emory, Dr. James E. Dickey, and suggested that perhaps Robert might benefit from resting his eyes for a week or ten days before deciding whether to try to continue with his second term at the college. Dr. Dickey wrote back to say that Robert's problem was not one likely to be cured by a period of rest.

"I do not think it advisable," Dr. Dickey wrote, "for him to return to college this term as he has not done satisfactory work and cannot therefore make up what he would lose before returning again. He has never learned to apply himself, which together with very frequent absences makes it impossible for him to succeed as a student." In other words, Robert was being dismissed. He returned home to the house on Edgewood Avenue and found his father at wit's end. He always remembered what Ernest said to him: "Damn it, boy, it's only three generations from shirtsleeves to shirtsleeves. Learn something." And Robert remembered what he answered back. "I'll take the shirtsleeves now."

In February 1909, Robert Woodruff put on a pair of overalls and started work shoveling sand at the General Pipe and Foundry Company for 60 cents a day. He had to walk the six blocks to and from work because his father sold his horse to help pay off his debts.

Before long, Robert graduated from the shop floor and began an apprenticeship as a machinist, learning to handle molten metal and run a lathe. Though he was earning less than his college allowance, he seemed to enjoy the hard labor. "Good old muscle jobs," he said later, "aren't so bad." A photograph taken at the time shows him wearing a denim cap at a jaunty angle, standing with his hands cocked on his hips.

In the summer, perhaps in a final bid to remind his son of the good things of life that would be lost to a member of the working class, Ernest included Robert on a trip out west. Borrowing the private Pullman car of his friend Charles A. Wickersham, the president of the Atlanta & West Point Railway, Ernest packed up Ernie and his three sons and an assortment of nephews, cousins, aunts, and uncles, and set off on a deluxe, two-month trip across the country to California and down into Mexico. The party visited Chicago, Salt Lake City, Seattle, San Francisco, Los Angeles, and Mexico City, and took a tour by stagecoach through Yellowstone National Park.

If a lesson was intended, however, it did not take. Robert returned home, shrugged off the memories of his vacation and resumed his job with General Pipe and Foundry. He showed no interest at all in changing his mind and furthering his education. He would never have a college degree. But he did prove to be a willing worker. He pleased and impressed his employers, and after a year he gained a promotion to assistant stock clerk in the foundry's parent company, the General Fire Extinguisher Company. Not long after that, in 1911, he was made a salesman, peddling fire extinguishers to the scores of textile mills in and around Atlanta. He did well and his territory was enlarged.

The next year, Ernest called a truce. His son was twenty-two years old, and it was time to bring him back into the fold, forgive his rejection of higher education and help him with his career. Robert was beginning to show signs of settling down. After years of playing the field, he was finally serious about a girl and it looked as if he might be getting married. Nell Hodgson was a plump, pretty brunette from a large, prominent family in Athens, Georgia, the eighth of nine children born to Edward R. "Prince" Hodgson, a well-to-do businessman who ran a wholesale grocery and manufactured fertilizer and cottonseed oil. Ernie and Ernest considered Nell Hodgson a fine catch and were anxious for Robert to get engaged. Ernest arranged to have Robert hired as a purchasing agent for one of his companies, Atlantic Ice & Coal, at a salary of $150 a month, with the prospect of a generous raise to $250 a month if he took Nell as his wife.

But maintaining an agreeable relationship between father and son proved impossible. Ernest couldn't help demanding absolute control over Robert, any more than Robert could help fighting for independence. Years later, Robert described a Saturday morning when he and Nell and some friends were setting off from Atlanta in a convertible to drive up to Asheville, North Carolina, to play golf. With the sky darkening and thunder rumbling menacingly in the distance, his father warned him not to attempt the trip. Robert insisted on going anyway, and his father exploded. "You try to buck everything that gets in your way," he admonished his son, "but boy, you can't buck the elements!" Robert smiled and patted him on the arm and answered, "Good-bye!"

The serious trouble began when Robert went off to the national automobile show in New York. Wandering the aisles, indulging his fascination with the newest and best the automotive industry had to offer, he soon came to the White Motor Company's display area, where he met Walter White, the scion of the family. White Motor was known for making high-quality trucks, and Walter White quickly persuaded young Woodruff that Atlantic Ice & Coal would be smart to put its mule teams out to pasture and switch to a fleet of modern, motorized White delivery trucks. As purchasing agent for his father's company, Robert agreed to buy fifteen White trucks. And he made a good bargain. In exchange for a low price, he suggested that White keep the trucks on display for the rest of the show and exhibit them as the largest fleet ever sold to a Southern company. Perhaps, Robert said, other Southerners would be inspired to buy White trucks, too.

What Robert failed to do was consult his father about the deal. Predictably, Ernest was furious, believing that the old way of delivering ice and coal was perfectly adequate and that the acquisition of a fleet of trucks was a wild, irresponsible extravagance.

On October 17, 1912, Robert married Nell Hodgson in a fancy ceremony—the "most brilliant social event of the season," according to the *Atlanta Journal*—at her parents' house in Athens. Ernest gave the bride and groom a gift of a check for $1,000, but he did not come through with the $100-a-month raise Robert thought he'd been promised. Robert went to his immediate boss, a man named Baker, and asked if it was true that Ernest had blocked his raise. Yes, Baker said, it was. "Then you can tell him," Robert announced, "that I will always love him, but I'll never do another lick of business with him as long as I live."

Robert quit Atlantic Ice & Coal and went to work for Walter White. His father was surprised and disturbed by his decision and tried to talk him out of it. "He thought I was making a mistake [and] told me that I had no sales ability and was sure to fail," Robert reported later. His father also reminded him of the low social esteem and reputation for shaky ethics associated with car and truck salesmen and urged him to reconsider and go into banking. Bitter and angry, Robert snapped at his father that as far as he knew, the Atlanta Federal Penitentiary had no automobile executives behind its bars, though it held quite a few bankers.

Walter White had a practical reason for hiring Bob Woodruff. The young fellow knew everyone in Atlanta—knew how to open doors and gain access in a town that was still a bit provincial and distrustful of outsiders. The way White had it figured, Woodruff could do the Cleveland-based trucking company a great deal of good just by arranging introductions, even if he eventually made up with his father and went into banking.

But Woodruff surprised White. He turned out to be a good salesman. Woodruff sold trucks to several companies in Atlanta and then traveled across Georgia calling on county commissioners, convincing them to buy sturdy, reliable White trucks that could survive the ruts and bumps of the state's mostly unpaved roads. He learned that the counties run by lone commissioners were his best bet, because the decision to buy was in the hands of one man. "I don't waste any time with the wrong fellows," he once told an associate, explaining that it paid to get to know the top people in an organization—the decision-makers—rather than spend time with their underlings.

And he showed initiative. One of the things that had struck Robert on his trip out west with his father was the lazy pace and discomfort of the horse-drawn stagecoaches that carried groups in and out of Yellowstone Park. Thinking that White buses would be an improvement, he called on the company that ran the tours and tried to get them to switch. It turned out the tour operators liked the slow, old-fashioned method because they also ran the lodge near Old Faithful where tourists had to pay to spend the night. When they declined to buy buses from him, however, Woodruff refused to accept their answer. He took his case all the way to the federal parks commission in Washington, and won.

Woodruff was promoted quickly from salesman in White's Atlanta office to manager of sales and service for the state of Georgia and then to manager of sales in the Southeast, overseeing North and South Carolina, Georgia, Alabama, and Florida. In 1916, at the age of twenty-six, he was making $300 a month plus expenses and a 25 percent commission on his sales. He lived well. He hired his first valet, James Roseberry, and joined several clubs around town. He played golf with his friend Bobby Jones (soon to be America's premier amateur golfer) and went hunting occasionally with Ty Cobb. At Christmas, as a peace offering, his parents gave him the deed to a house and lot behind the family home on Edgewood Avenue. Whatever their differences, they wanted him nearby.

The most striking aspect of Woodruff's early career at White was his natural ability to command the respect of the men who worked for him. Just as he had at the military academy, he drew people to him and elicited surprisingly powerful feelings. In January 1917, he organized a trip for his salesmen, first to Cleveland to see a demonstration of the company's new 16-valve engine and then to New York for the auto show. When they got home, his men sent him an extraordinary letter:

It remains only for us to express now our hearty thanks for our own Chief and renew our pledges of loyalty in thought and action, to the man who matches every ounce of loyalty with a pound of appreciation; every foot of initiative with a yard of cooperation; every pint of "Pep" with a gallon of Tabasco and every man-power of push with one-hundred horse-power of pull—that's Bob Woodruff, the good pal of our play, and the leader of our work, to whom we are bound by a chain that may lengthen but can never break.

He answered his employees' tribute by giving a supper and presenting each of them a gold medal stamped with the legend, "Woodruff gives credit to his men." A newspaper photograph taken on the day they departed shows Woodruff standing in the midst of the group on the back platform of the train. The others are waving but he is not. With a cigar stuck firmly in his mouth, he looks serenely confident and completely in charge.

When World War I came along, Woodruff discovered a new way of applying his energies for the company's benefit. He lobbied for assignment to the army's ordnance department, where he helped design a special truck body meant for transporting troops by road instead of rail. The specifications he drew for the 18-man carrier just happened to require the use of a White Motor Company chassis—a bit of capitalist chicanery worthy of Ernest Woodruff himself. By war's end, Major Robert Woodruff had participated in the design of several military vehicles, all of them dependent on parts and assemblies manufactured by the White Motor Company. His standing with Walter White, already high, rose higher.

After the war, Woodruff stretched to enlarge his circle of friends and especially to cultivate older men who knew their way around the board rooms of New York. Thanks to Walter White, Woodruff was invited to join Norias, a hunting club near Thomasville, Georgia, whose members included some of the most prominent businessmen in the country. He found that his personal magnetism was just as potent with men above him as below. Bill Potter, the chairman of New York's Guaranty Trust, arranged for his bank to lend Woodruff money so he could begin accumulating an investment portfolio. Walter C. Teagle, the powerful president of Standard Oil of New Jersey, made a point of befriending Woodruff and treating him as a protegé.

In a sense, Woodruff chose to bypass his own father. He found there were other men who could help him just as much as Ernest could—perhaps more—and they did so without stirring up all the old frictions and resentments of years gone by. Robert kept a portrait of his father over his bed and ached for his respect and approval, but at the same time he had no intention of relying on him for advancement. Living nearby, Robert tried to maintain cordial relations with his father, but he found they couldn't help testing each other, trying for the upper hand. Many years later, when he was on his deathbed, Ernest confided to a nurse that he loved his son but was jealous of him. Robert, he believed, was doing all the things he wished he had done, and he felt envy.

Ernest continued to chide Robert for his extravagant standard of living, so much so that even as an adult Robert felt the need to conceal some of his activities. Occasionally the results were amusing. Robert and a friend named Abie Cowan once slipped off to Havana for a few days to visit the nightclubs and play the casinos, and when they returned they brought back a supply of fine, 50-cent Cuban cigars. Ernest encountered Cowan on the street in Atlanta a few days later, admired the cigar he was smoking, and asked suspiciously where he got it. Afraid to admit where he and Robert had been, Cowan waved toward an Atlanta tobacco shop and mumbled something about a shipment of nickel cigars. "At that price it's a damn fine cigar," Ernest said, pulling a $50 bill out of his wallet. "Go back and buy me a thousand."

More often than not, however, the give and take between father and son had an ugly side. "Ernest Woodruff used to treat [Robert's wife, Nell] like dirt," one of her nephews recalled. "He'd borrow her new Chevrolet which they'd just bought, and. . .he'd put pigs in the back seat and take 'em out to his farm and get [the car] dirty and muddy. And also he would use their servants unmercifully and never pay 'em anything."* Once, when they were traveling together on a train, Ernest tried to awaken Robert in the lower berth by flicking him with a razor strop, only to find he'd slapped and badly startled a woman Robert had volunteered to give his place. Ernest had to apologize profusely, and Robert thought it served him right.

At the height of their tug of war, Ernest and Robert even fought over the allegiance of Robert's younger brother, George. A plodding, dependable sort who bore a close physical resemblance to Ernest, George dutifully studied engineering in college and was rewarded afterward with a job as a draftsman at Atlantic Steel, one of his father's companies. Robert promptly snatched him away, giving him a more glamorous position with White Motor.

In August 1921, Robert was promoted to a vice presidency of White. His success stirred a good deal of attention around Atlanta because it was unusual, at a time when sectional prejudices still ran strong, for a Southerner to rise to the top of a major national corporation headquartered in the North. One of Robert's childhood friends, his Sunday school classmate Harrison Jones, wrote him a friendly note of congratulations and said the Coca-Cola Company would make it a policy to buy all of their trucks from White, giving Robert the commissions. Good to his word, Jones had Coca-Cola order thirty White trucks for $100,000 later in the year.

Robert and Nell left Atlanta and began shuttling back and forth between apartments in Cleveland and New York. Robert opened an office in Manhattan and continued to expand his set of acquaintances and business contacts. Within a year, he moved up a final notch to the number two spot at White Motor, securing his position as Walter White's alter ego and heir apparent. With his career soaring, Robert told a friend he felt as if he had the world by the tail on a downhill string. He had no intention of coming home.

For the first time, his father seemed to realize that he was in danger of losing his son.

Robert was not aware of the first step his father took in the tricky, complicated process that drew him back to Atlanta.

In the spring of 1922, Ernest was traveling around Georgia buying up

---

* Robert told the story of sending his chauffeur, Lawrence Calhoun, down to the station to pick up Ernest and his luggage. After getting home, Ernest stalled and patted his pockets, saying, "I know I have a quarter here someplace," and Calhoun supposedly shot back, "Mr. Ernest, if you ever had a quarter I know you've still got it." Actually, no black employee of that period would have dared speak so insolently to a man of Ernest Woodruff's standing; Calhoun's remark was probably what he later told Robert he *wanted* to say. What makes the story revealing is that Robert recounted it—frequently—to portray his father as a skinflint.

all the Coca-Cola stock he could find, preparing for the showdown with his Wall Street partners over control of the company. At one point, when he laid hands on a block of three thousand shares, Ernest signed the securities over to his three sons without bothering to tell them, Robert became the owner of a thousand shares of Coca-Cola and didn't even know it.

In fact, for all his claims to the contrary later in his life, the truth was that Robert had no idea how much Coca-Cola stock he owned and little interest in finding out. Unlike his father, Robert was not born with the instincts of a financier. His aptitude was for sales and promotions and managing men, not for the hard-eyed work of playing the stock market. He borrowed money and bought securities and then tended to leave them in a desk drawer, dusty and forgotten.

During the first three years of his father's involvement with the Coca-Cola Company, Robert played no role at all in the business. He picked up a few blocks of Coca-Cola stock here and there, some of it in the form of the special $5 shares available to the shareholders and directors of his father's bank, Trust Company, but he was not a very big investor. It was not until the fall of 1922, when Ernest formed his holding company, Coca-Cola International, that Robert bought additional shares and took a hand in the enterprise, and even then he merely volunteered his name as one of the five directors loyal to his father.

There is no way of pinning down the precise moment it occurred to Ernest that he wanted to make Robert the president of Coca-Cola. Yet there is no doubt it was Ernest who made the decision. The pretense that he was a passive bystander, or that he somehow objected to Robert getting the job, is simply absurd. After defeating his Wall Street rivals, Ernest Woodruff enjoyed immense, virtually unfettered power over the affairs of the Coca-Cola Company, and nothing was done—nothing *could* be done—without his knowledge and approval. According to a letter discovered in Robert Woodruff's private papers, written to him by one of his father's closest associates, the issue of giving him Coca-Cola's presidency was a matter of intense discussion for several weeks—but only because Ernest worried that people would think Robert was elected "just because you were his son." The concern was over the appearance of nepotism, that is, not the wisdom of placing Robert in the job.

Certainly Ernest was ready to replace Howard Candler, who was just as eager to go. Relations between the two men were as strained as ever. Candler continued to detest the pressures and disagreements of the executive suite. He hated traveling on company business, and he counted the trips he had to make to New York—nine in 1920, five in 1921, six in 1922—as if they were part of a prisoner's sentence to be served and crossed off the calendar. His official duties, he admitted years later, were a "burden" he was hoping to lay down.

Then, too, the Candler name was losing some of its magic. In the autumn of his life, Asa Candler stumbled into a lurid personal scandal that threatened to destroy the reputation he'd spent so many years building up. Just a few days after his children agreed to sell the Coca-Cola Company in 1919, Asa attended a huge Confederate reunion in Atlanta's Piedmont Park. ("Welcome, Gallant Wearers of the Gray!" announced a full-page newspaper ad taken out by a local department store, as an estimated ten thousand visitors arrived and set up a tent city.) On the night before the reunion opened, a group of society matrons from New Orleans honored the "Lost Cause" with a Grand Ball of the Sons of Confederate Veterans at the City Auditorium, and it was there that the recently widowed Candler met one of the chaperones, Onezima de Bouchel, and fell in love.

Mrs. de Bouchel was a dark-haired, dark-eyed beauty, and while she was not quite as exotic as her name and her French and Spanish heritage might have suggested to some, nonetheless she was a Roman Catholic, a divorcée and a suffragette, which was more than enough to set tongues wagging in Atlanta's straitlaced social circles. Asa's children and other family members were appalled, especially when they learned that he planned to marry her, and they set out to break things off. They hired a private detective who investigated Mrs. de Bouchel and claimed to have found a pair of unidentified men willing to say they had "visited her at her room in a hotel in Atlanta, at night, on her solicitation." Asa reluctantly called off the engagement.

Mrs. de Bouchel, who appears to have been entirely falsely accused, vowed to fight to protect her reputation as a "pure, chaste, and virtuous woman." In February 1923, right in the midst of the period of change that was buffeting the Coca-Cola Company, she filed a sensational breach of promise suit against Asa Candler asking for $500,000. Atlanta's greatest citizen became the source of mockery. When Mrs. de Bouchel released a cache of thirteen of his love letters, a rapt newspaper audience learned that he called her "My Very Precious Sweetum." Schoolboys ran in the streets chanting, "O-nah-zee-mah dee Boo-shell! C'mon, Asa, give 'em hell!"*

Under the circumstances, there was little call for retaining Howard Candler as the president of Coca-Cola or for naming any of his relatives as successor. During the past two years, the company had been purging many of the men who were loyal to Sam Dobbs. "Every one that was very close to me in the Coca-Cola Company is being penalized," Dobbs wrote plaintively to a friend who was let go as a salesman. The "accumulated jeal-

---

* A year later, after a trial that made frontpage news in Atlanta for a week, a jury found in favor of Asa Candler; it was discovered that Mrs. de Bouchel had neglected to complete her divorce from a previous husband and thus was ineligible to marry anyone else. By then Asa had furthered his family's humiliation by giving the slip to his guardians and marrying a young widow, May Little Ragan, a stenographer who worked in his building. She provoked a new round of headlines when she was arrested in a police raid in the company of two male acquaintances, drinking liquor and having what she described as "a little party."

ousies" of years were at work, he said, and there was nothing he could do to help. Dobbs still owned a large block of stock and served on the board of directors, but he rarely went near the office and freely admitted he knew "little of what is going on there." Some of Asa Candler's other nephews continued in middle management, but no thought was given to promoting any of them.

Nor did anyone else in the current management seem right for the top job. The logical choice was Harrison Jones, who made no secret of his desire for the promotion or his confidence that he could handle it. The problem with Jones was his flamboyance. Who could forget his performance in front of the bottlers in New York a few years earlier? Arguing the vital importance of sterilizing bottles, he had thundered in his grand style:

> The bottles before returning to the owner are frequently used for every purpose where a liquid-holding receptacle is necessary, from obtaining gasoline to clean mother's skirt, to the collection of a specimen of pathological urine for examination by the local doctor. And there are bottles which have been emptied directly by the lips of tubercular persons or by lips sore with some loathsome infectious disease, and bottles salvaged from garbage cans and from the city dump—of such does the flotsam returned to the bottler consist.

If it was possible for a man to be just a little too eloquent for his own good, that was Harrison Jones. There would always be a place for him in the Coca-Cola Company, but it would never be the presidency.

With no obvious choice in sight, Ernest Woodruff decided to give the job to Robert. He sounded out his closest allies on Coca-Cola's board of directors and they encouraged him. W. C. Bradley in particular had a high regard for Robert and urged Ernest to go forward. The one part of the myth of Robert's return that was more or less true was that several of his father's friends thought he would make a good pick, not so much because they believed he could stand up to his father—no one expected that—but because they thought he might bring peace to the organization. Bradley did make a trip to New York, along with Tom Glenn and Charles Wickersham, to urge Robert to accept.

Robert's friends thought he should take the job, too. Hoping to give his confidence a boost, Walter Teagle, the Standard Oil baron, took Robert out for a round of golf and promised to hire him in any job he wanted, and at any salary he cared to name, if things didn't work out in Atlanta. The important thing was to try. Robert had a chance, Teagle argued, to unite the factions at the Coca-Cola Company and bring stability to the organization.

Yet Robert was reluctant. As he often said later, "I didn't know any more about the soft drink business than a pig knows about Sunday." He was not at all sure his skill at selling trucks would translate to the very different challenge of selling Coca-Cola. Nor was he confident that he knew how to be a good executive. He liked to hire men who appealed to him and put them to work without worrying about titles and chains of command. "Hang the chart," he once explained to Walter White, "these men are here to sell trucks!" What he really liked, it seemed, was having everyone report directly to him, a management style that might not work at the Coca-Cola Company.

Then there was the question of compensation. Thanks to a surge in commissions, Robert calculated that he had earned about $85,000 in 1922, far more than he had ever made before, and far more than the $36,000 his father and the board of Coca-Cola were offering him to return to Atlanta. Robert tried making a counteroffer—a straight, 5 percent commission on any increase in Coca-Cola sales over current levels—but his father vetoed the idea. If he came home, he would have to accept a reduction in income of nearly $50,000 a year.

In later years, Robert claimed he accepted the job to recover losses he had suffered investing in Coca-Cola stock. Yet that was plainly not so. As he contemplated taking the presidency of Coca-Cola, the company's stock was hitting an all-time high of $75, nearly double the original offering price of $40, and he could easily have sold out for a handsome profit. Robert's personal portfolio was in fine shape—not that he was following the ticker tape very closely: "I am . . . having a very difficult time figuring out how much Coca-Cola stock I have and how much Coca-Cola International stock I have and where it is," Robert wrote his secretary early in 1923, asking for help in tracking down his stock certificates. Looking over his dividend deposits, Robert figured out he must own 3,537 shares, and later he learned to his surprise from Ernest's secretary that his father had given him gifts totaling another 1,500 shares. Had he wished, Robert could have sold out then and there for more than a quarter of a million dollars.

Further contradicting Robert's memory, the company was not in the dire financial straits he recalled. The crisis was over. The loans securing the high-priced sugar were nearly paid off, the dividends on common stock had been restored (and had been hiked from $1 to $1.50 a share per quarter), and the company had $4 million in cash sitting in the treasury. The simple truth was that much as he wanted to believe so, Robert was not being called to the rescue. He was being called home by his father. And the reason he accepted the job was to prove to his father that he could do it.

The first problem Robert faced was an angry insurrection in Howard Candler's family.

Howard was content to step aside, but Flora, his wife, was beside herself. This was the second time Ernest Woodruff had plotted to shove her husband out of his rightful place as president of the Coca-Cola Company, and she had no intention of going along. The fact that her brother, Tom Glenn, was a party to the scheme just made it that much worse. At her urging,

Howard told the Woodruffs that if they wanted him out as president, he would gladly go, but he also planned to resign from the board of directors and withdraw completely from the company's affairs.

Returning to Atlanta, Robert hastened out to Callanwolde, Howard Candler's mansion on Briarcliff Road, to confront the angry couple. The last thing Woodruff wanted was a flood of publicity suggesting that the Candlers were being purged from the Coca-Cola Company. The transition needed to be smooth. Woodruff urged Howard to remain on the board and to take the chairmanship of a new advisory committee that would help set policy for the company and determine its long-range strategy.

That Howard and his wife bought the idea is perhaps a measure of the mastery Woodruff had achieved in the art of persuasion. There was little in his proposal to mask the fact that Howard was being shunted aside to a powerless sinecure. Yet Woodruff argued forcefully that he needed Howard at his side if he hoped to run the company successfully. In fact, Woodruff swore—and there is no indication he was bluffing—that he would refuse to take the presidency unless Howard agreed to stay on and lend him his personal support. "I need help," Woodruff remembered telling Howard Candler, "I need your help and support." Genuinely convinced, Howard agreed.

Others in the family had a hard time believing Howard could be so easily mollified. His brother William, in particular, was anxious to protest the change of command. William had served as corporate secretary of the Coca-Cola Company until the previous fall, when he resigned in the wake of Ernest Woodruff's victorious showdown with the New York interests. Now William was threatening to create a scandal on Howard's behalf, and Howard worked quickly to dissuade him. "As frequently happens," Howard wrote a mutual friend, "William did not get a right reflection of the situation and was inclined and, in fact, declared it to be his purpose to adopt a policy which would be, if I am unable to control him, very embarrassing to me."

Howard was able to calm his brother by assuring him that "it is entirely wrong for anybody to think for one minute that I am going to be put out of the Coca-Cola Company. . . . Mr. Robert Woodruff has made it a condition upon his coming into the company that I stay with it."

With Howard on board, the path was nearly clear for Robert's election as president. As a preliminary step, at a Coca-Cola stockholders' meeting in February 1923, Ernest put through a slate of new directors that included Robert and Walter White. He also put Robert on the company's powerful executive committee.

One hurdle remained. Howard and his immediate kin might be satisfied, but the same could not be said for others in the top ranks. While no one was careless enough to leave proof of an insurrection, company records strongly suggest that Ernest Woodruff had to accept a final deal with several other board members before gaining their acceptance of Robert as president. Sam Dobbs, Bill D'Arcy and Harold Hirsch all viewed Robert's accession with a measure of skepticism, and it appears they insisted on a trade-off: Hirsch was to be made a vice president of the company, and his firm, Candler, Thomson & Hirsch, was to be named general counsel. In that way the smart and seasoned Hirsch could keep an eye on the new president, who after all had never sold a glass of Coca-Cola in his life.

At eleven o'clock on the morning of Saturday, April 28, 1923, the board met in special session at the Coca-Cola Company's headquarters in Atlanta. Twelve of the fifteen directors showed up. Ernest and Robert Woodruff were there, along with their staunch allies Tom Glenn and Walter White, and loyal Atlanta investors Jim Nunnally, Bulow Campbell, and W. A Winburn. W. C. Bradley came up from Columbus with his son-in-law, D. Abbott Turner, who went on the board the same time Robert Woodruff did. Elsewhere around the table were Dobbs, D'Arcy, and Howard Candler. The only members who failed to attend were the New Yorkers, E. F. Hutton, Gene Stetson, and Charles Hayden, who no longer had much say in running the company.

Howard Candler tendered his resignation as president and nominated Robert Woodruff as his successor. The vote in favor was unanimous. According to the minutes, Ernest Woodruff did not object or abstain or leave the room.

In his first days as president of the Coca-Cola Company, Bob Woodruff did what many new chief executives do. He redecorated his office and started hiring his friends.

Coca-Cola's home base in Atlanta was a boxy, three-story brick building at the corner of North Avenue and Plum Street, completed in 1920 and meant to house the corporate offices on top of the syrup factory. Yet until Woodruff arrived, there was little sense of the place as a headquarters. Ernest operated as always from his rolltop in the Equitable Building halfway across town, while Harold Hirsch and most of the Candler clan retained their handsome suites atop the Candler Building. The two top floors of the Plum Street building, partially unfinished and occupied mostly by shipping clerks and junior men who worked in advertising and promotion, seemed dreary and far removed from the real center of power.

Woodruff was determined to make Plum Street his base of operation. He had workmen install oak paneling and glass partitions in each office along the main corridor of the second floor, lending an atmosphere of privacy to what had been little more than an open space full of desks and chairs. Choosing a corner office for himself, Woodruff settled in behind a sturdy leather-top desk, stuck a spittoon on the floor to catch his cigar ashes (some of them, anyway), and gave the signal that from now on, Coca-Cola's business would be conducted from the Coca-Cola building.

For years afterward, Woodruff liked to tell the story that his first official act as president of the company was to give a lifetime job to Jim Key, the hostler who ran Asa Candler's stables. Key was about to be fired, now that the company had switched from horse-drawn drays to trucks, when Woodruff intervened. Remembering Key's kindness in boarding his pony years before, Woodruff arranged to keep him on the payroll, explaining vaguely to those who asked that he was making the old black man a "staff vice president."

It was a nice tale, one that illustrated how different Robert Woodruff's way of doing business would be from his father's. Part of the mythology surrounding Woodruff was the notion that he raced into the Coca-Cola Company at a gallop, cracking his whip and bringing the fusty old enterprise out of a long snooze. Actually, he moved with deliberation, and it was not so much a case of his reawakening the company as it was his starting to rethink some of the assumptions that guided it.

Woodruff had tremendous curiosity about his new enterprise. As he set about the task of discovering Coca-Cola's secrets, one of his first revelations came in the unlikely setting of Moose Jaw, Canada. Making a cross-continental train ride in early winter, Woodruff passed through Moose Jaw, a small city in Saskatchewan Province, on a day when the temperature plunged unexpectedly to 35 degrees below zero. He saw people in the station drinking Coca-Cola, and he was struck by the thought that the soft drink had no natural boundaries of culture or climate. Someone sitting in woolens beside a hot stove in winter was just as likely to get overheated and thirsty as a sunbather at the beach in July. Reading reports from the company's branch offices, Woodruff noted with interest that the consumption of Coke was nearly as high in Montreal as it was in New Orleans.

Coca-Cola's potential seemed limitless. A couple of years earlier, some of the directors of the D'Arcy agency had calculated that for all the millions of gallons of syrup the company was selling, it had barely begun seeping toward its saturation point. Across the United States, the average per capita consumption of Coca-Cola was a relatively meager three servings a month. "We got to talking about it," one of the D'Arcy men reported. "Some of us used our pencils, and we were amazed to discover that if we could enlarge the monthly per capita consumption of Coca-Cola by just a fourth of a drink, it would mean. . .3.3 million additional gallons of syrup [annually]." Even the most modest increases in consumption would translate into great leaps forward in production and profits.

Woodruff recognized, as Asa Candler never had, the importance of Coca-Cola in bottles. The company was quickly approaching the day when sales of syrup to the bottling companies would exceed sales to fountain outlets. More and more, customers were insisting on the convenience of having Coca-Cola come to them instead of vice versa. The number of soda fountains serving glasses of Coca-Cola had peaked at about 115,000; nearly four times that many retail outlets offered bottled Coke, and more were being added every day. "An arm's length from desire" was the florid phrase Harrison Jones coined to describe the ubiquity offered by bottled Coca-Cola, and Woodruff liked the ring of it. He wanted Jones to continue his efforts at mending fences with the bottlers, and he wanted the bottlers to work harder.

He also seemed determined to discover and preserve the aspects of the business that had made it successful in the past, beginning with a new emphasis on the importance of quality. At the age of thirty-three, Woodruff was three years younger than Coca-Cola itself. He had a keen appreciation of just how unusual it was for a soft drink to have lasted so long. The White Motor Company was known for the reliability of its trucks, and Woodruff thought the Coca-Cola Company should exploit its own reputation for making a consistently superior beverage.

Before he could begin making changes or setting new policies or thinking up new ways of selling an old product, though, Woodruff first had to establish his authority over the people around him. Before he could lead, he had to prove he was a leader.

He began by asserting his presence at the company's Plum Street headquarters. Sanders Rowland, who was working nights at Coca-Cola and supervising the cleaning staff while he put himself through Georgia Tech, remembered how startled he was one evening to discover Woodruff staying late. Rowland had instructed one of the janitors, Tom Freeman, to replace a leaking Icy-0 cooler outside Woodruff's office; seeing later that the job hadn't been done and that melted ice was pooling under the box, Rowland gave Freeman a sharp dressing down.

Rowland recounted, "Someone tapped me on the shoulder and said, 'That's right, Sanders, give 'em hell if they don't do what you tell them to.' It was Woodruff. He was with someone else, passing through his quarters and overheard what I said. I was flabbergasted that he caught me fussing at Tom—and even more amazed that he knew my name."

Woodruff had learned certain basic tricks of command. He did not make the mistake of trying to befriend his employees. He maintained his distance, cultivating a stern expression and demeanor—a "mean squint," in the words of a nephew—that were meant to intimidate underlings and usually did. The cigar with the red-hot tip that he kept clamped in his teeth made him seem a little unsafe to approach physically. When he gave orders, he never asked if they had been carried out; that way no one could give him an excuse.

As he'd shown before, Woodruff enjoyed the intangible quality of making men want to please him. Joseph Jones, who served him for fifty arduous years as a traveling companion, personal aide, and later as chief of staff, and who was on call twenty-four hours a day, every day of every year during the entire time (and who endured two divorces as a result), tried to explain Woodruff's appeal: "People asked me over the years, why do you do what you do? Why do you put up with it? Hell, I *wanted* to. . . . It never occurred to me that I was being imposed upon. Whatever was necessary, whatever was required, to the extent I could do something I thought he would like or maybe was thinking about, I just went on and did it." Others felt the same way.

Woodruff assembled an inner circle of close associates who gathered most mornings in his office at Plum Street to receive their daily marching orders. They styled themselves the "Eight O'Clock Club" in honor of their regular meeting time and soon developed the same sort of esprit de corps that had characterized the men who worked under Woodruff at White Motor. (Woodruff's formal name for the group, reflecting the purpose for which he intended to use them, was the Board of Control.)

The new president's strong suit was selling, and he moved quickly to put his own team in the company's sales department. He chopped the United States into four zones and picked the men he wanted to run them. An old Atlanta friend named Carl Thompson, a former star athlete at Georgia Tech who had pitched two seasons for the New York Yankees, took the Western region headquartered in San Francisco. Eugene Kelly moved over from White Motor to run the Central region out of Chicago, while Hamilton Horsey, an insurance executive, took up a post in New Orleans to supervise the South and Southwest. The Eastern region went to one of Asa Candler's ablest nephews, Sam Willard, in Baltimore. Another old hand, Neal Harris, was appointed to oversee the whole sales effort.

Next, Woodruff bent to the difficult task of establishing dominion over the company's senior men. There was friction between Woodruff and Harold Hirsch right from the start. Hirsch had no role in marketing or sales or the other commercial activities of the business, but he expected to have a free hand in guiding the company's legal affairs. Woodruff thought otherwise.

When Woodruff arrived on the scene, Hirsch was preparing a final settlement of Coca-Cola's long-running feud with the proprietors of Chero-Cola, a look-alike, sound-alike soft drink made in Columbus, Georgia. Seeing the terms of the settlement, Woodruff was surprised and disappointed. Instead of fighting the issue in court and putting Chero-Cola out of business, Hirsch was proposing a compromise that would allow the other beverage to call itself "Cherokola."

It seemed to Woodruff that Hirsch, once the staunchest defender of the trademark in the company, was giving in too easily. Woodruff held up the settlement, demanding terms more favorable to the Coca-Cola Company and forcing a reluctant Hirsch to reopen the negotiations. At Woodruff's insistence, the makers of Chero-Cola agreed to drop the word "Cola" from their name and market their product simply as "Chero," a decision that eventually drove them out of business.*

---

* The proprietor of Chero-Cola, a dour-faced pharmacist named Claud A. Hatcher, attended his company's bottlers' convention in 1923 wearing a cape and a plumed hat, and later published a little booklet, the *Chero-Cola Booster*, whose cover showed an orange Chero-Cola truck bouncing up the road toward "Prosperity." Actually sales fell off sharply after the settlement and the soft drink, once very popular in the South, disappeared entirely during the Depression.

Woodruff won a different kind of showdown with Harrison Jones. The two were almost the same age; they had been neighbors and Sunday school classmates for years and were related by marriage. (One of Jones's brothers was married to Nell Woodruff's little sister, Dorothy.) Jones found it hard to accept the fact that an old friend—one who had never worked a day in his life in the soda pop business—was now his boss. A quarrelsome man at the best of times, Jones began complaining loudly and frequently to almost anyone who would listen that Woodruff was in over his head, until finally his father, Sam Jones, who knew and liked Woodruff, stepped in and advised him to cool off.

"What is your title?" Sam Jones asked his son.

"Vice president."

"And what is Bob's title?"

"President."

"I'd suggest," Sam Jones replied pointedly, "that you remember it."

Bit by bit, Woodruff took charge. He operated quietly, behind the scenes, but there was no mistaking his intention of putting his own stamp on Coca-Cola. His first goal was to restore one of the company's greatest assets, its secret formula, to the position he believed it deserved.

Over the years, the Candlers had made several changes in Coca-Cola syrup, from eliminating the cocaine to adjusting the levels and kinds of sweeteners, to experimenting with different sources for the acids and caffeine. During World War I and its aftermath, the company tinkered with the formula to compensate for shortages in various ingredients, notably sugar, and tried a variety of substitutes. On the eve of Woodruff's arrival, the amount of caffeine, which had been halved to six-tenths of a grain per serving in the settlement of the Chattanooga case, was reduced again, to four-tenths of a grain.

Company officials had not publicized the alterations, naturally. Yet neither had they focused on the importance of protecting Coca-Cola's reputation for quality and consistency. Consumers appreciated quality, Woodruff believed, but just as important they responded to the *idea* of quality. They wanted to buy products from companies that were known to be committed to high standards. In Woodruff's view, changing the syrup was dangerous, not so much because consumers were likely to notice a difference in the taste, but because they might think the Coca-Cola Company was cutting corners and lowering its standards if they found out.

Woodruff decided to adopt a policy that there would never again be a change in the formula, no matter what. He got in his car, he later said, and drove down to Columbus to see W C. Bradley, the chairman of the board. Woodruff asked Bradley point blank to agree that from now on adjusting the formula was "not acceptable." Bradley went along.

The new president inaugurated a Quality Control division to perfect the syrup, sent inspectors out to improve conditions at the bottling plants, and staked the company to a public promise that it would make every single serving of Coca-Cola taste exactly alike. The idea, as Woodruff explained it, was "to sell the company as an institution as a guarantee of the product itself." He approved a new slogan, "The Charm of Purity," and commissioned an ad pointing out proudly that Coca-Cola had been sold during the terms of eight presidents.

Woodruff then turned his attention to retrieving the lone copy of the formula.

The sheet of paper was still sitting in a bank vault in New York, its home since serving as collateral for the company's sugar loans. As a practical matter, of course, having the written recipe was unnecessary for the conduct of business. At least four people in the company, and probably several more, knew how to make Coca-Cola syrup. Howard Candler, Sam Dobbs, and Sam Willard all had been in charge of production at one time or another, and Ernest Woodruff had hired a chemist, W. P. Heath, specifically for the purpose of learning the formula from the Candlers. Any one of them could have jotted down a fresh version. Yet there was huge symbolic importance in regaining custody of the original. Woodruff planned to begin a campaign to give an air of sanctity to the secret formula, and that would hardly be possible if the company casually abandoned the document. With the board's permission, he arranged to have it returned.

During a trip to New York, Woodruff sent a representative over to Guaranty Trust, where a group of vice presidents came forth and ceremoniously turned over a blue envelope closed with sealing wax. Woodruff carried the envelope home to Atlanta on the train, had the contents examined and certified as genuine by Dr. Heath, and then placed the formula in a safe deposit box, marked with a red flag for careful handling, at Trust Company. The formula was back in a bank vault, only this time it was in the Trust Company of Georgia—the Woodruff bank.

Woodruff's attitude toward the formula was more than just a matter of careful stewardship of one of the most valuable trade secrets in American business. He gloried in the process of secrecy itself, setting up elaborate procedures that seemed to be designed to call attention to the formula as much as they were to protect it. At Woodruff's direction, the company established a rule that no one could see the formula without the formal permission of the board, and then only in the presence of the chairman, president, or corporate secretary. Furthermore, the rule said, only two company officials would be allowed to know the formula at any given time, and their identities were never to be disclosed for any reason. The company then publicized the policy.

Over time, Woodruff's dramatic, cloak-and-dagger treatment of the formula had the effect of elevating it to the status of a cult object. During the era of air travel, the company's policy was amended to forbid the two officials who knew the formula from flying on the same plane; that rule, too, was widely broadcast The existence of the most mysterious of the ingredients, the blend of flavoring oils called Merchandise No. 7X, was teasingly admitted—even while its composition was guarded as carefully as a state secret.

The strategy seemed to spring directly from Woodruff's personality. He had become an intensely secretive man. Even by the standards of caution and reticence that marked the way many businessmen presented themselves to the public, Woodruff stood out. In direct contrast to the warmth and magnetism he exuded dealing in private with friends and colleagues, his public demeanor was stiff and guarded.

His return to Atlanta to run the Coca-Cola Company triggered a wave of news stories, yet he ducked every opportunity for personal publicity. In the single in-depth article that appeared, a profile in a Sunday edition of the *Atlanta Journal*, he protested to the reporter, "I've just been lucky. I'm not at all the kind of person to write about. I never knew my lessons at school. I've never done any of the things the books say you should." Woodruff disliked being interviewed, disliked making speeches, disliked exposing himself in any manner to the scrutiny or judgment of others. He had a terrible fear, apparently rooted in the misery of his school years, that he would not be able to express himself properly. He worried about being misunderstood.

If Woodruff could think of a way to escape a public obligation, he did so. Once, at a formal dinner in Cleveland for the executives of the White Motor Company, Walter White leaned over and asked him to get up and make a few remarks. What subject? Woodruff asked. Anything you like, White answered. "Well," Woodruff whispered after a moment, with a deadpan expression, "I guess if I *must* talk, maybe the subject I'm most qualified to discuss is the one these boys are the most interested in—you. I bet I can tell 'em some interesting things that maybe they don't know." White never called on him.

When a public encounter was inescapable, Woodruff escaped anyway, taking refuge behind a wall of banalities that concealed his true thinking. The early statements he made after taking the presidency of Coca-Cola are models of empty, sanitized bromides that could have been found (and possibly were) in a book of sayings. "You don't have to blow your own horn," he told a nationally syndicated business writer. "Ability shows." Reporters complained that he interviewed *them*, sending them off feeling flattered but carrying notebooks full of blank pages.

In any communication likely to become part of the record, Woodruff retreated to the safety of cardboard sentiment In an early issue of the *Friendly Hand*, one of the Coca-Cola Company's in-house publications, the editors offered an article entitled, "Thoughts from President Woodruff." It began with Polonius's advice—"To thine own self be true"—and concluded, "To change the thought of Shakespeare a little, with each and all of us honest with ourselves, it follows that the Coca-Cola organization will be beyond question the kind of organization that makes us proud of it. . . ."

Digging out the real man was extremely difficult. Woodruff's desire for privacy—or, more accurately, his desire to protect himself from being observed and judged by people who were beyond his control—bordered on an obsession. He was cryptic by nature. He made up a code so that he and other Coca-Cola officials could communicate by telegram without divulging the company's secrets. His private papers contain a manual setting out five-letter designations for a variety of different messages. If the combination "YAIGZ" appeared, for instance, it meant sales were off. "BLERZ" indicated that the conditions were right for setting up a Coca-Cola factory. All businesses have confidential information to guard, of course, but Woodruff seemed to like secrecy for its own sake: When he traveled, he would routinely wire back "DEGIG." It meant he'd arrived safely.

The same flair for the clandestine marked Woodruff's private business dealings as well. When he set up a personal holding company, Acmaro Securities, he meant its name to be a puzzle. Only a few insiders figured it out: The "Ac" stood for Woodruff's accountant, Arthur Acklin, the "ma" was borrowed from his secretary, Mattie Lott, and the "ro" represented the first two letters of his own name, Robert.

A psychology buff might find fertile ground speculating about the origins of Woodruff's enigmatic temperament. Certainly it would not be unusual for a boy who continually displeased his father to develop a variety of defenses, including emotional camouflage. Several of Woodruff's friends and associates guessed in hindsight that he found it necessary to conceal a tender side he inherited from his mother. He was not as tough as his father, they thought, but he was fully capable of acting as if he were, which was the next best thing.

Whatever the reasons for it, Woodruff placed a complicated and occasionally deceptive persona into the service of a company whose very purpose was to lead a dual existence—to make its name familiar while keeping its formula obscure.

It might be true that any halfway competent chemist could manufacture an imitation of Coca-Cola syrup good enough to fool the palate of an expert, but as long as people *thought* Coca-Cola was special they would continue demanding it. In Asa Candler's day, his insinuations of black magic about Coca-Cola—the fanciful health claims, the flirtation with cocaine—eventually came very close to destroying the company. Woodruff was from a different generation with a vastly different perspective, and he was extremely cautious about Coca-Cola's reputation. He placed the greatest emphasis on the virtues of quality and consistency.

But in his own way, Woodruff, too, meant to give Coca-Cola an aura of mystique. He wanted to tantalize the American consumer with the idea that Coca-Cola had unique, slightly exotic properties, and thanks to the attention he directed toward the secret formula, he succeeded.

There was one other area of the company's business that Drew Woodruff's keen interest: advertising.

Woodruff did not get along well with Bill D'Arcy. Older by sixteen years, and with nearly two decades of experience creating highly successful ads for Coca-Cola, D'Arcy thought he knew what was best for the company and had a habit of telling Woodruff so.

Years later, Woodruff told a nephew that he often had to stand up to D'Arcy and say, "No, Mr. D'Arcy, we're going to do it *this* way." Actually, Woodruff preferred to avoid confrontations and found it easier to sidestep D'Arcy. He soon discovered that he could work more smoothly with one of the agency's junior men, Archie Lee, who was handling the Coca-Cola account on a day-to-day basis.

Archie Laney Lee did not fit anyone's stereotype of an advertising man. Born in Monroe, North Carolina, and educated at Duke University, Lee was thoughtful and quiet, full of spiritual and philosophical musings, but also ambitious. An eager student of human nature, he wanted to write great books one day. "I want my life to be complete in itself," he wrote his mother when he was a young man. "I feel that to work just for money's sake would be a desecration. I want to do something really worthwhile. I would die happy if it should be just one recognized and lasting thing." He hungered for success. "A man who can see life in its colors and describe it in words," he added in the same letter, "can gain fortune and fame. Fortune and fame! They make a lot of difference. I can never be happy as a commonplace man."

Lee moved to Atlanta in 1908, fresh out of college, and started work on the *Atlanta Georgian*, the newspaper whose editor caused Asa Candler such grief during the Chattanooga trial. Lee covered the celebrated Leo Frank murder trial in 1912, when a wave of anti-Semitism convulsed the state of Georgia, and proved himself to be a graceful writer. During the war, he joined the infantry and served as a captain in France. He displayed an unusual knack for being able to dismantle and reassemble rifles and pistols, even in complete darkness, and was sent home to the United States to become an instructor.

Mustered out after the Armistice, Lee returned to his job at the newspaper. Not long afterward, he did a flattering profile of Sam Dobbs, the new president of Coca-Cola, and as such things often transpire Dobbs offered him a job at a higher salary writing ads. Lee took it. He joined the D'Arcy agency in St. Louis and quickly became one of the top men churning out Coca-Cola copy.

The quality of Lee's work was apparent to D'Arcy and everyone else in the agency. Even after his mentor, Dobbs, was ousted from power, Lee continued to take on more and more responsibility for the Coca-Cola account until finally, doing "the best work I have ever done in my life," as he proudly put it, he single-handedly wrote an entire Coca-Cola campaign.

On a gray Saturday late in October 1921, Lee sat alone in his seventh floor office and wrote his father a long letter. The sky was wintry, he said, and it was so dark the lights were on at three o'clock in the afternoon. He and D'Arcy had just returned from a business trip to Atlanta, where they had met with Howard Candler and the other top brass of the Coca-Cola Company. The agency had prepared more than fifty pieces, most in full color. "Mr. Candler said it was the best material that had ever been presented to them," Lee wrote. "That made me feel proud because I had had a big part in preparing it."

As he continued writing his letter, Lee began daydreaming, sharing his innermost feelings with his father. His job, he believed, was to furnish ideas—to think. And it was hard work. Thomas Edison kept a quotation from the English portraitist Sir Joshua Reynolds hanging on a wall in his private office, Lee told his father. It said, "There is no expedient to which a man will not resort to avoid the real labor of thinking." Lee expanded the thought and added his own view: "Being too lazy to think is the cause of religious prejudice—the cause of Republican administrations, threatened railroad strikes, prohibition, bad roads and divorces. People have plenty of ability to act intelligently if they would only think."

The man who pitched Coca-Cola to the world was a complicated fellow indeed, and that gave him something in common with Robert Woodruff. The two men had met and formed a casual friendship in Atlanta during Lee's newspaper days. They renewed their acquaintance in the summer of 1922 when Woodruff gave White Motor Company's advertising to the agency. A year later, after taking the reins at Coca-Cola, Woodruff turned to Lee and put him in charge of the account.

The work Archie Lee did for Coca-Cola was remarkable. It was not just the technical excellence of the advertising, although that was certainly a factor. Lee hired the best illustrators of the day and got them to paint attractive, original canvases. More important, though, he put his fertile mind to work on a philosophy that would give the company's ads a purpose.

Lee and Woodruff spent hours together talking about the challenge that confronted them. "We wanted to promote Coca-Cola not just as a soft drink or even as 'the leading' soft drink," Woodruff recalled. "We wanted to promote it as something bigger than just the answer to thirst. We wanted to make it a thing apart. . .to sell it to all segments of the social structure as one of the pleasant things of life."

The ad campaigns that eventually stitched Coca-Cola into the fabric of American society had their origins in the long conversations Woodruff and Lee held during the early days of Woodruff's presidency. They talked in Woodruff's office and on the golf course, went hunting together, took long walks, and sometimes rode horses far out into the countryside. They grew close, so much so that Lee asked Woodruff to be the best man at his wedding. They enjoyed pondering the grand imponderables, wondering with each other about the meaning of life and the existence of God when they weren't actively calculating how to sell more syrup. Lee once told Dick

Gresham, the preacher who had been Woodruff's roommate, that the discussions he had with Woodruff "bridged the gap" and helped him find faith.

Haddon Sundblom, the gifted illustrator who later created Coca-Cola's Santa Claus ads (and who was already famous for inventing Aunt Jemima and the Quaker Oats Man), did his first canvas for Lee in 1924. "At the time I hadn't the slightest idea of the philosophy of Coca-Cola advertising," Sundblom said later, but he soon learned that in addition to painting pictures he was expected to undergo what he called an "indoctrination" into Lee's thinking. Coca-Cola's primary color was red, of course, dating back to the bright paint Asa Candler chose for sprucing up the old beer kegs and barrels he used to ship his syrup. The familiar script of the company's logo was almost invariably rendered in white on a red background. As Lee saw it, though, there was a problem with red: It was a hot color, when the whole point of Coca-Cola was refreshment—cool, icy, thirst-quenching refreshment. (Sam Dobbs had grappled with the same dilemma years earlier. He couldn't use the red background in bathing beauty ads, he said, because "red is not a very cool-appearing color on a hot day.") There was no way to eliminate the venerable red, but Lee decided to soften the effect by adding green and white to the mix.

"I learned," Sundblom reported, "that the red, white and green combination was much more than a temporary device of harmonious color. It had been planned carefully and thoughtfully—much as a nation might plan its flag . . . RED for energy, WHITE for pure wholesomeness, GREEN for refreshing coolness." Sundblom's first illustration was a girl in a creamy white "garb" at a soda fountain against a green background. The colors were envisioned as a sort of emblem for Coca-Cola, he said. In time, a simple poster showing a bottle of Coke in a snowdrift against a green background would be sufficient to convey everything the company wanted to say about its product without a single word of text.

Like most advertising men, Lee believed in repetition. Certainly there was no lack of familiarity with the name Coca-Cola. In one recent year alone, the company had passed out a million calendars, 17 million paper napkins, 75,000 "Ice Cold" signs, 6,000 gross of pencils, 50,000 oval serving trays, 15,000 oilcloth signs, 100,000 streetcar signs, and three million blotters, all with the trademark prominently displayed. But Lee wanted a greater sense of uniformity, an overriding theme to the ads and promotions that would have, as one D'Arcy executive put it, a "family resemblance." Lee came up with the idea of putting the trademark in a rectangle and later devised the round red sign with the white logo that eventually became the best-known commercial symbol in the world.

Along with simplicity and familiarity, Lee wanted Coca-Cola's advertising to convey meaning. He believed a product could come alive and take on a sort of animate personality if it had the right advertising. He once described how he was struck by his five-year-old daughter's capacity for believing that her Winnie the Pooh doll was a living creature. "'Pooh' is as much alive in her life and in the sphere around her as any god on Olympus ever was to the Greeks," Lee observed with wonderment "And 'Pooh' has come to influence the conduct of the whole family."

Lee had nothing less in mind for Coca-Cola. Early in 1925, he pulled together all of his new ideas and created the "Ritz Boy" ad. It showed a handsome bellboy in a crisp, white uniform carrying a tray with a bottle of Coca-Cola and a glass. The background was dark green and the trademark appeared in a rectangle at the upper right; the text said, "6,000,000 drinks a day." Appearing on more than five thousand billboards in towns and cities across the country, the ad imparted a subtle but clear message. The bellboy, who got his nickname because his outfit resembled the fancy costumes worn by pages at the Ritz hotels, conveyed a sense of elegance and social distinction. Yet he seemed to be stepping forward and serving the Coca-Cola directly to the consumer standing in front of the scene, as if to say the drink (and all the elegance associated with it) was readily available to everyone. For the initiation fee of a nickel, the ad suggested, a customer could enjoy a Coca-Cola—and along with it the reassurance that he or she was worthy of sitting in the lobby of a Ritz Hotel being waited on by a servant in livery.

In selling Coca-Cola, Lee once told Woodruff, "you are dealing with something almost as broad and subtle as promoting an idea like free enterprise or democracy." It was not enough to describe Coca-Cola as a quality product, not enough to say it tasted good or quenched thirst or even that it restored energy to the tired and downtrodden. For years, the company's advertising had described Coca-Cola as a pleasing, helpful product associated with activities and events that caused thirst, excitement or fatigue. Lee now moved a step beyond. He unabashedly linked Coca-Cola with "American youth and romance," writing copy that appealed to the human craving for popularity and sociability. For the first time, ads not only showed boy-meeting-girl, but suggested pointedly that boy and girl somehow were meeting *because* of Coca-Cola.

Lee was masterminding one of advertising's first great "brand image" campaigns, investing Coca-Cola with an appeal that went far beyond its function as a product. Tremendously pleased, Woodruff had him promoted to account executive and waited to see what he would think of next.

Six

SHORT SALES

In October 1924, Robert Woodruff summoned one of the Coca-Cola Company's top men and dispatched him on a secret mission overseas.

Since taking the presidency of the company a year and a half earlier, Woodruff had grown increasingly eager to sell Coca-Cola in foreign markets. The soft drink's popularity in Canada was a proven fact, and Woodruff thought similar results ought to be attainable elsewhere. He was especially eager to introduce Coca-Cola in Europe, with its crowded urban centers and convenient distribution systems.

The company had been taking small, tentative steps onto foreign turf for more than two decades, beginning with Asa Candler's decision to send a salesman into Cuba and Puerto Rico in 1899 after the Spanish-American War. Coca-Cola "followed the flag" to Hawaii, the Philippines, and Panama, and pioneering sales efforts were undertaken in a variety of ports of call from Bermuda to Shanghai. Howard Candler, ordinarily so timid in his guidance of the company's affairs, had nagged the board until it granted him permission to look for bottlers and start awarding franchises in Central America and Western Europe.

The problem was that except in Canada, the vast majority of people who ordered and drank Coca-Cola in foreign lands were Americans—soldiers, tourists, diplomats, businessmen, and expatriates who'd learned to look for Coca-Cola's logo as a familiar reminder of home. The millions upon millions of people who *lived* in other countries were almost entirely oblivious to Coca-Cola. Sales were confined for the most part to military canteens and the bars and restaurants of luxury hotels. Local markets were barely being scratched. The "invasion" of the world Asa Candler once grandly promised had never happened.

One grim episode typified the company's hapless performance on the international stage. Just after the end of the war, with the blessing of the home office, an American entrepreneur named R. A. Linton launched a promotional campaign in France, supplying dozens of dubious cafe and restaurant owners with bottled Coca-Cola to offer their customers. Unfortunately, Linton and his French partner, George Delcroix, knew little about sanitation and production. In a terrible comedy of errors, they used stale ingredients, unrefined sugar, and unsterilized tap water to make their syrup, mixed it with carbonating gas full of beer esters from a brewery, and capped the product with untreated cork crowns that quickly sprouted cultures of virulent bacteria. Everyone who tried a sip got violently ill. For years afterward Coca-Cola salesmen reported being chased out of various Parisian establishments by infuriated proprietors, in one instance by a shouting, red-faced man wielding a butcher's knife.

Woodruff wanted to expand the company's efforts beyond the American colony and tap into the native populations of the rest of the world. And he wanted to do it right, using the refined technology and sales techniques the company had developed in the United States. He was confronted, however, with a distinct lack of enthusiasm on the part of his father and some of the other big shareholders on the board of directors. The company was making money quite nicely, they felt, without risking big losses on experiments with the tastes and habits of strange people in strange lands.

In hopes of proving his doubters on the board wrong, Woodruff picked the most promising, culturally compatible target he could imagine—England—and sent a trusted lieutenant, Hamilton Horsey, to find out what it would cost and how long it would take to build a market there for Coca-Cola. Horsey sailed from New York, spent six weeks in London and gave his confidential report to Woodruff the day after returning.

Horsey tried hard to be encouraging. Recommending an immediate campaign to introduce Coca-Cola in Great Britain, he predicted confidently that the English would be receptive to the soft drink. They liked mineral water, after all, and were accustomed to caffeine from drinking tea. Horsey called them the key to unlocking Europe. The news was exactly what Woodruff wanted to hear.

But when Woodruff began reading the details of Horse's written report, he could see that the prospects were actually extremely discouraging. The list of potential difficulties was long and daunting, beginning with the absence of soda fountains in England. Unless they planned to take the syrup home and carbonate it themselves, Horsey pointed out, the English would have to enjoy Coca-Cola in bottles—and those bottles would be warm, because refrigeration was virtually unknown and the English had a deep-seated, traditional dislike for chilled beverages. It probably would take at least three years and $500,000 worth of advertising just to create a "limited" demand, Horsey said, and even then the company's prospects were further clouded by the likelihood of a backlash if its ads were considered too brazen. The English, he noted, disliked the "show of pomp and 'braggadocio' attitude which sometimes distinguishes the American manufacturer in foreign markets."

Given the bleak prospects of the venture, there was simply no way Woodruff could pry a half million dollars out of his father and the other conservatives on the board. It was not that Ernest and Will Bradley and the rest were opposed to doing business overseas; they willingly gave Robert the authority to begin start-up operations almost anywhere he pleased. They just wouldn't give him the kind of money he needed to do a first-class job of getting Coca-Cola off the ground. At about the same time Horsey was returning on the boat from England, for instance, the board of directors gave Robert the green light to start selling Coca-Cola in Mexico. But they also set a strict cap of $150,000 on expenditures and took the unusual step of making the limit part of the formal corporate minutes.

As with so many things in his life, Woodruff later painted a veneer of myth over his early activities on the international front. When his father and the board tried to block his efforts at overseas expansion, he claimed that he defied them and set up a clandestine Foreign Department that carried out his plans anyway.

The truth, as usual, was a good deal more complicated. Woodruff did set up a Foreign Department, but he acted with the knowledge and permission of his father and the board. It was hardly a secret Early in 1926, the company rented space in New York at 111 Broadway, and Ham Horsey was placed in charge of a five-member team assigned to foreign sales. (The office's male secretary, known for his machine-gun loud typing, was Jimmy Curtis, later the head of Coca-Cola Export. Curtis had served the Woodruff family as a personal retainer, knew Ernest well, and hardly would have been picked for the job if Robert had intended to deceive his father.)

Horsey's men went about their business openly and, at times, with inventive flourish. One of their targets was the passengers on the great ocean liners that steamed in and out of New York harbor. The ship stewards considered soft drinks a "steerage-class" product and were reluctant at first to stock Coca-Cola. Even after the company developed a special export bottle with emerald-green glass and gold foil that looked like a split of champagne, the stewards balked at ordering more than a case or two at a time. Finally one of the salesmen, Chuck Swan, had a brainstorm. Attending the bon voyage parties that were held aboard the ships the nights before they sailed, he would order a dozen or more bottles of Coca-Cola, gulp down the contents and scatter the empties on tables throughout the salon. Orders picked up immediately.

Swan and his colleagues developed contacts at the U.S. Commerce Department and at the Customs House in New York's Battery who would tip them off when American trade commissioners or consuls were passing through on visits home. The diplomats often were happy to put in a good word for Coca-Cola with local distributors when they returned to their postings. Gradually a modest demand was stirred in several countries, and the Foreign Department held a small celebration when an order for a full freight-car load of cases was received from the Dutch East Indies.

The company added bottling operations in Guatemala and Honduras in 1926 and expanded the next year with franchises in Mexico, Burma, Colombia, Newfoundland, Italy, Belgium, and South Africa. Woodruff instituted a pair of helpful new practices: He cut shipping prices dramatically by removing much of the water from the syrup, distributing it instead in the much lighter form of concentrate. And he approved the use of beet sugar (rather than cane) as the sweetener in Coca-Cola sold overseas, allowing the company to save money by taking advantage of the cheap, plentiful harvests that flourished in the beet fields of Europe after the war.

In many ways, though—especially by the standards of sophistication that characterize the Coca-Cola Company's international dealings today—the Foreign Department was a decidedly amateurish operation. Horsey's men would get lists of distributors from the import-export houses in New York and then write to them cold, trying to solicit interest in Coca-Cola bottling franchises. They wrote to one Brazilian company in Spanish, thereby confusing and offending the Portuguese-speaking businessmen who received the letter. Horsey himself spoke only English and required an interpreter when he went traveling to drum up business.

Horsey tried to do too much too quickly. He often awarded franchises to inexperienced men who didn't have enough capital to absorb losses as they built up their markets, and several of them went bankrupt. They discovered it was easier to give away calendars with pretty girls than it was to sell Coca-Cola in places where no one knew what the product was. Within a few years, operations closed down in Burma, Colombia, Newfoundland, and most cities in Mexico. Many of the company's European bottlers allowed production to dwindle to a meager trickle. One month the total sales in all of France amounted to the paltry sum of $94.22.

Contrary to his recollections, Woodruff did little to reverse the company's faltering efforts overseas. In the spring of 1925, he undertook a major expedition to Europe, but he acted more like a man on a pleasure cruise than a serious business trip. After a sumptuous bon voyage party at the Barclay Hotel in New York, where the members of the Eight O'Clock Club presented him with a movie camera as a gift, he and Nell boarded the S.S. *Berengaria* and sailed for England. They were accompanied by a young company employee named Frank Harrold, who was instructed to draw an advance large enough to cover six weeks' worth of expenses. Harrold brought $1,000 in cash, which he exhausted paying the bill at Claridge's Hotel in London after the first week. By the time the Woodruffs finished visiting France, Belgium, the Netherlands, Switzerland, Germany, and Monte Carlo, they had spent more than $5,000, and the company's business office took months to unravel their expense account

The highlight of the trip was a dramatic incident that took place at the elegant casino in Monte Carlo. Woodruff was playing roulette and hit a winning number. Instead of paying off, though, the croupier swept up Woodruff's chips, pushed them into another player's pile and started to resume play. When Woodruff objected, the croupier ignored him and spun the wheel. Woodruff stood, reached over, grabbed the roulette ball and put it in his pocket. "Sorry," he said, "but you won't spin this wheel again until you pay me."

The story contributed to Woodruff's swiftly growing reputation as a man of nerve, but it also pointed up the lack of business results from the trip. It was the only accomplishment of note he could claim. The board gave Woodruff power of attorney to set up operations in England during his visit, but apparently he did nothing more than oversee the registration of Coca-Cola's trademark. By all accounts he passively accepted the tight restrictions placed on him by his father and the other directors.

Coca-Cola, it seemed, was destined to be a North American phenomenon, at least for the foreseeable future.

As he guided the Coca-Cola Company through the Roaring Twenties, Woodruff gave every appearance of a man content with his job and his life.

His hope of building an overseas empire was on hold, but at home his company was in the midst of a booming recovery. Sales were soaring. Coca-Cola men loved to talk about numbers, and the reason was easy to understand: The growth of their business was genuinely impressive. "The cash register rang two *billion*, four hundred *million* times in 1924 because of Coca-Cola," Harrison Jones announced in thunderous tones to the bottlers at their annual meeting early the next year. He continued:

> If every drink of Coca-Cola were put in a bottle and put end to end they would extend 296,000 miles, more than eleven times around this world. If they were put in cases, 24 bottles to the case, they would cover five square miles. You would have to have a warehouse of 3,200 acres to take care of the quantity of the product. If they were piled top on top, together they would extend 12,600 miles into the air. Pikes Peak is . . . 14,000 feet, and I am talking about 12,000-odd miles!

Insiders called these calculations "gee-whizzers" because of the reaction they provoked. They came from the company's new Statistical Department, which Woodruff created to track the company's progress and find ways of speeding it up. Woodruff believed selling was as much a science as an art, and he bent to the task of modernizing the company's marketing programs to take advantage of the changes that were sweeping the country.

Few places were beyond the reach of the automobile any longer, a point that was illustrated vividly one day when John Power, one of Coca-Cola's salesmen, drove into the remote hamlet of Williamson, West Virginia, and got caught in a crossfire between the Hatfields and the McCoys, narrowly dodging a bullet. Woodruff ordered an exhaustive study of the nation's traffic patterns, and the Statistical Department pinpointed the busiest intersections in scores of cities and towns across the map. Placing its advertising at strategic spots, the company became the heaviest user of billboards in the country.

In 1927, as the number of households with radios passed the six million mark, Coca-Cola sponsored its first program on the airwaves, a romantic serial of sorts (on the fourteen stations of the fledgling NBC network) featuring a pair of characters named Vivian and Jim whose courtship was meant to epitomize the love affair between Coca-Cola and the public. The company also sponsored a prize contest, awarding $10,000 to Miss Mabel Millspaugh, a stenographer from Anderson, Indiana, for her essay extolling the "Six Keys" to Coca-Cola's popularity—taste, purity, refreshment, sociability, price, and thirst.

Within the company, the most memorable of Woodruff's moves came one afternoon when he assembled all of the company's soda fountain salesmen and had them "fired," then rehired them as "servicemen." It was more a gimmick than a genuine threat of job loss, but the men took the point. In addition to selling syrup, they were expected to teach their customers how to serve Coca-Cola the right way.

Woodruff settled in at Plum Street. He had a fourth floor added to the company's headquarters and moved into a spacious new office. The solid, heavy furniture, which included the rolltop desks that had belonged to his grandfathers, Robert Winship and George Waldo, Woodruff, lent the space an air of permanence. He installed his secretary, Mattie Lott, known as "Bitsy" in tribute to her considerable girth, to serve as a friendly but diligent gatekeeper outside his door. The corridor beyond was lined with men he'd hired and promoted—men who were intensely loyal to him, and whose loyalty he returned. At a board meeting in 1925, when one of the directors stood up and proposed giving him a $25,000 bonus for a job well done, Woodruff declined the money unless the directors added another $75,000 to be distributed among his top officers.

"My prosperity," one of the members of Woodruff's inner circle, Gene Kelly, wrote to him, "has enabled me to brighten the evening of my good mother's life with a few luxuries which she had never before enjoyed. When I gave her a car and chauffeur the other day she thanked me. I told her she need not thank me but you who had made it possible."

With regular dividends restored, Coca-Cola common stock began a sharp, steady rise until it passed $160 a share, more than quadruple its original offering price. It was split two-for-one early in 1927 and continued to gain in the bull market that inflamed Wall Street. The company paid off all of its outstanding loans, retired the $10 million in preferred stock held by Asa Candler's children, and built a surplus in the treasury.

Robert and Ernest Woodruff both profited handsomely from the company's success. All of Coca-Cola's shareholders did well, naturally, but the Woodruffs and some of their closest associates at Trust Company did even better, thanks to a pool Ernest operated that speculated in Coca-Cola stock. Practicing the sort of insider trading that was widespread at the time (and is illegal today), Ernest typically bought shares for himself, Robert, Tom Glenn, and a few others in advance of news that was likely to drive up the price. They made a big buy in October 1926, for instance, just before the stock split was announced, and enjoyed a run-up of $16 a share in less than two weeks.

Ernest's syndicate also had a way of taking advantage when the company hit an occasional downturn. If he and the others anticipated a temporary dip in the value of Coca-Cola stock, they would execute a short sale—that is, they would sell a block of Coca-Cola stock but delay delivery of the shares until a point in the future, gambling that prices would fall. Later they would complete the transaction with cheaper shares and have cash left over. (A short sale could be ruinously expensive if the price of the stock went up, of course, but in the Woodruffs' case their inside knowledge of the company's affairs protected them from guessing wrong very often.)

The existence of Ernest's syndicate was fairly well known in Atlanta business circles, but gaining access to it was difficult. One of Ernest's lawyers, Dan Rountree, told the story of visiting him in his office at Trust Company one morning and asking casually if it was a good time to buy Coca-Cola. No, Ernest replied, shaking his head with evident sincerity, it was not. The very next day, glancing on the desk at his stockbroker's office (and reading upside down), Rountree spotted a large buy order for Coca-Cola signed by Ernest Woodruff himself. Hurriedly scraping together all the capital he could find, Rountree bought heavily and made a killing.

By the spring of 1927, Ernest's holdings of Coca-Cola stock had swollen in value to more than $4 million, making him one of Atlanta's wealthiest men. At the age of thirty-seven, Robert, too, could count himself a millionaire, albeit just barely.

On March 5, 1927, Robert and Nell set off on a grand cruise around the coast of South America, and this time there was no pretense of working on company business. It was a pleasure trip, pure and simple, designed as a reward for the triumphs Robert had achieved in four short years as Coca-Cola's president. "It was the only time in my life," he liked to say later, "that I felt rich."

Only a handful of close associates saw the clues that Robert was growing dissatisfied—that he was, in fact, on the verge of quitting the Coca-Cola Company and risking almost everything he had on a dangerous business venture.

There was no question he had an appetite for gambling. He played poker and roulette and liked betting on sporting events of all kinds: prizefights, horse races, the World Series, college football games, and golf matches. He even made wagers with his vice presidents over the company's quarterly sales and production figures. The stakes were usually fairly modest—$10 to $100, sometimes a suit of clothes—but he liked the excitement.

And he felt lucky. Everything seemed to be turning to his advantage, including his misadventures. On his trip to South America with Nell, when their ship ran aground off Bahia, Brazil, Woodruff placed bets with several fellow passengers that he could beat them home. Rather than wait for the ship to be refloated, he and Nell hopped a tramp steamer, sailed to Europe via the Canary Islands, toured the Continent, and still made it back to New

York in time to collect their wagers. Along the way they stopped in Paris and joined in the celebration of Charles Lindbergh's historic transatlantic flight.

At work, Woodruff began dropping hints that he was becoming restless. He told Joseph Bennett, one of the aides who traveled with him, that in another ten years or so he might want to try his hand at something new. The remark left Bennett with "a sort of empty feeling," along with the suspicion that change might be coming much sooner.

Still, no one expected Woodruff to act as quickly as he did, or as rashly, or with such far-reaching consequences.

In the autumn of 1927, Walter White, Woodruff's good friend and mentor, began trying to gain a controlling interest in his family's business. White Motor Company was going through a difficult period. Sales were off because buyers no longer felt it necessary to pay a premium for top-quality trucks now that more and more roads were paved. Walter White found himself in the odd position of needing to retool his factory to make cheaper trucks, an idea that met resistance from some of his family and other members of his board. Hoping to attain the same kind of ownership control the Woodruffs enjoyed at Coca-Cola, White planned to buy back half of the 800,000 outstanding shares in White Motor, which was a publicly held corporation, and take it private. He asked Woodruff to be one of his partners in the venture.

The idea of resuming a career in the truck industry hit a responsive chord in Woodruff. He liked the notion of going back into business with Walter White. His friendship with White had deepened over the years to the point that they were planning to buy a plantation together in south Georgia. They had decided to quit the Norias Club, where the formal cocktail hours and black-tie dinners kept them cosseted indoors too much of the time. They wanted to build their own operation instead and were looking for land where they could hunt quail and dove and wild turkey to their hearts' content, from dawn to dusk if they wished, free from social distractions and game wardens alike.

Getting together again at White Motor made sense to Woodruff. He admired White, who was thirteen years his senior, and considered him a sound businessman, tough and sagacious. One of his favorite stories about White was an occasion when the two of them went riding with a guest over the grounds of Gates Mills, White's estate outside Cleveland. As they stopped by the stables, the guest asked White how many horses he owned. Considering the question impolite and not wishing to give a direct answer, White replied off-handedly that he didn't know. "You've got twenty-nine," a groomsman piped up, "and a couple of colts are on the way." The next morning White told Woodruff he had to run an errand down at the stables. "I'm going to fire that son of a bitch," he explained. "He knows too much."

Woodruff tried to model his own conduct on White's example: discreet, commanding, hard-edged when necessary, a man's man.

As long as Woodruff remained at the Coca-Cola Company, he would be subject to the whims of his father. They were getting along reasonably well at the moment, true, but there was no guarantee that their relationship would stay smooth. Nor, for that matter, was there any guarantee that his father and the Trust Company crowd would keep the company. Above all else Ernest Woodruff was a financier, a profit-and-loss man who wouldn't hesitate to sell out his interest in Coca-Cola if he thought the time was right. The way Robert saw it, he had completed his job. He had proven himself to his father, and now the time was ripe to demonstrate once and for all that he could make it on his own in the field he loved best.

The stakes were enormous. The price tag on White's buy-out plan was more than $10 million, and the other partners, including Walter Teagle, the Standard Oil tycoon, had substantial resources at their command. Woodruff, very much the junior man, would have to strain to come up with the money to participate.

He decided to do it. On October 11, 1927, Woodruff instructed his New York stockbroker, Hornblower & Weeks, to execute a short sale of 4,600 shares of Coca-Cola common stock, raising $560,000 in cash. He was risking half his personal fortune on the deal, gambling that the value of the shares would drop sharply in the near future. He planned to cover the sale for a great deal less money, leaving a sizable profit he could use to pay for his purchases of White Motor stock.

Woodruff took elaborate steps to conceal his role in the transaction, operating through dummy corporations and using surrogates to sign the actual papers. What he was doing was not strictly illegal, but even by the lax standards of the era it was considered unethical for the president of a company to make short sales of his personal stock. In effect, Woodruff was betting against his own company when he was in a position to damage its performance—a direct conflict of interest.

As it happened, there is no evidence that Woodruff intended to sabotage the company. He had reasons for thinking the deal would turn out the way he hoped without any interference from him. After several years of national prosperity, his Statistical Department was warning of an impending recession, and Coca-Cola sales had fallen off during the summer, showing a "pronounced weakness" that suggested tough times might be coming.

A confidential, in-house list of "company problems" cited the proliferation of new state taxes (including a ruinous one-cent sales tax on soft drinks in South Carolina), continuing hostility from temperance organizations, resistance by parents and teachers to children drinking Coca-Cola, and rising competition in the "5-cent market" from candy, ice cream, cakes, and other beverages. The solicitation for advertising by some publications, especially in the nutrition field, was "closely akin to blackmail," the report added, while the federal government was stirring concern again over some of Coca-Cola's ingredients. Congress, in a protectionist mood, was toying with a substantial hike in the tariff on imported sugar.

The most immediate threat to the company was a rising international movement, centered in the League of Nations, for tighter control over traffic in narcotics. Congress was contemplating legislation that would forbid the import or export of coca leaves or any of their by-products, no matter how thoroughly decocainized. The company faced the prospect of losing its supply of coca leaves for making Merchandise No. 5 and also of being barred from shipping its syrup out of the country. The situation was considered so desperate that Woodruff secretly leased a cocaine plant in Lima, Peru, and placed it on standby—an arrangement fraught with the potential for embarrassment if it came to light publicly.*

In spite of all the signs pointing to a downturn, however, Coca-Cola's sales swiftly rebounded, as did the company's stock prices. As the autumn of 1927 deepened, it began to grow more and more evident that Woodruff was losing his gamble. Demand for Coca-Cola was strong all across the country. The bottler in New Orleans, A. B. Freeman, became the first member of the company's "Quarter of a Million Gallon Club," using that much syrup in less than a year. Instead of falling back, the company was headed for record profits.

In the words of a close friend, Woodruff had made "a sad guess," and he started to feel the squeeze. He refused to take any steps to hurt the company or help himself. To meet the obligation of his short sale, he was going to have to come up with 4,600 shares of Coca-Cola stock, either by buying them on the open market or by surrendering them from his own holdings. Both options looked increasingly painful.

His father was appalled. Robert had acted without his knowledge or blessing and had blundered terribly. Ernest had traded Coca-Cola stock up and down from the day he bought the company nine years earlier, but he had never taken a risk as dangerous as Robert's. Working with blocks of a few hundred shares at a time, Ernest treated the market as a hobby while keeping the main corpus of his Coca-Cola fortune safely in the vault, along with his Liberty bonds and treasury notes and other conservative investments. His son was gambling half his fortune on a single cut of the deck, a winner-take-all proposition that was turning out the wrong way. Ernest chided Robert for his folly and admonished him to "learn to resist

---

* Woodruff disguised the lease by assigning it to the Rohawa Company, a subsidiary whose name was another of his riddles. The "Ro" stood for Robert, but the source of the other letters is unclear. The "ha" probably represented Harold Hirsch, and the "wa" may have come from Walter White. Rohawa's main purpose was to serve as the anonymous intermediary when the Coca-Cola Company wanted to buy out independent Coca-Cola bottlers who were doing a poor job. Eventually it owned and operated several bottling operations in the United States and a handful overseas.

the temptations and evil influences that never fail to accompany success and wealth."

Yet Ernest was not about to abandon his son in a time of crisis. If there was a soft side to Ernest Woodruff's personality, it was the forgiveness he occasionally displayed toward friends and family who made mistakes. He was rarely surprised to see others fall short of his example, and when they did he took a measure of satisfaction in helping them. An associate once said of Ernest, "He always comes through handsomely in every emergency. He will give you the devil to keep you from getting in a fix, but when you get in a fix he is the first one to help you out."

Ernest now applied that principle to his son. In the final days of 1927 and the early winter of 1928, Ernest and several of the other major Coca-Cola shareholders at Trust Company took steps to put Coca-Cola stock in play, apparently with the idea of driving down the price and rescuing Robert. Ernest personally took a short position of 3,400 shares of Coca-Cola common. As always, Ernest's manipulations were undertaken with the greatest secrecy, and the precise strategy and eventual outcome he had in mind can never be known. What is certain, though, is that for one of the few times in his career he found himself outsmarted. Instead of dropping, as he anticipated, the price of Coca-Cola stock mysteriously began to rise.

Someone was covering the short sales made by the Woodruffs and Trust Company. Someone was gambling that the Coca-Cola Company was a wise long-term investment and was paying a premium to snap up all the shares that came into the marketplace. In early March of 1928, as the price of Coca-Cola common reached $130 a share and began heading toward $140, Wall Street's financial press grew curious about all of the unexplained activity.

B. C. Forbes went to see Robert Woodruff for an interview and came away complaining that his friend was even more reticent than usual. "He is a walking interrogation mark," Forbes wrote in his business column. "Each time I asked him something, he plied me with questions—on the plea that as I had been traveling all over the country, I must know a lot more than he!"

Had Forbes been a mind reader, he would have understood the extreme awkwardness of Woodruff's position. With his company prospering and its stock soaring, Woodruff should have been in the jauntiest of moods. Instead, Coca-Cola's good fortunes were threatening to bankrupt him. The few seemingly bland quotes he gave Forbes were laced with irony. "So far as our company is concerned," Woodruff told him, "I constantly expect trouble. At the opening of each year I say to myself that something is pretty sure to happen to prevent us from equalling the progress made in the previous year." Forbes recorded that Woodruff then smiled and added, "Maybe it's because we're constantly on the lookout for trouble that we have been able, so far, to avoid it."

In the first week of April 1928, Coca-Cola common closed at an all-time high of 146¾, and Wall Street's curiosity burst into a buzz of speculation about the identity of the speculators. R. L Barnum, a syndicated financial columnist, took notice of the unusual rise in Coca-Cola and concluded that whoever was making the short sales seemed to be suffering "terrific punishment."

But who was doing the buying and selling? Barnum didn't know. No one on Wall Street knew. On April 9, 1928, the Associated Press reported a "sensational climb" of Coca-Cola common as the stock hit another record high, soaring to more than $160 a share. A war was under way, and the combatants were still nameless.

The next day, the buyer came forward.

Lindsey Hopkins grew up poor in Reidsville, North Carolina, in a wood frame house with rocks holding up the front porch. He started out as a printer's devil with the *Greensboro Patriot* making $2 a week, graduated quickly to selling oil, and soon displayed a knack for making vast sums of money by investing in new ventures. He had a habit of losing his shirt almost as often.

"When in doubt, take a chance" was his motto, and he lived by it. Hopkins moved to Atlanta in 1909, made a fortune selling Overland automobiles, and then promptly squandered everything by gambling prematurely on commercial aviation. He bought a Curtiss biplane in 1911, flew the first piece of airmail into Atlanta, sponsored the first air meet at Candler Field, and went broke. He recouped by financing the movie *Death of a Nation*, the sequel to D. W. Griffith's *Birth of a Nation*, in 1916, and then began playing the market in cotton, railroads, rubber, and shipping. When Coca-Cola stock was at a low point in 1921, he started buying, and by the spring of 1928 he was a major shareholder.

Hopkins stood a shade under six feet tall. He was lean, balding, sharp-featured, gregarious, partial to dapper clothes and, so far as anyone could tell, completely without fear. In the words of a friend, Hopkins had a "divine spark of push, go-aheadness, and an acquisitive spirit that would broach no stopping." He believed the Coca-Cola Company had "barely scratched the surface of the possibilities before it," and he was pretty sure Ernest Woodruff was trying to sell it short. He meant to stop him.

On April 9, 1928, Hopkins leaked a story to the Associated Press in New York disclosing his role as the investor who had been buying Coca-Cola stock and pushing up its price. Then he walked into the main branch of Chase National Bank in New York, signed a six-month note and borrowed $1 million in cash so he could buy more. For the next three weeks, he and the Woodruffs fought a desperate battle over the future of the company. Ernest and Robert and their allies at Trust Company launched a new round of short sales, hoping to depress the price of the stock, while Hopkins spent his million dollars buying up their positions and keeping the value high.

It is a piece of folklore in Atlanta business circles that Ernest tried to arrange a truce at one point. He reportedly picked up the phone at Trust Company, called Hopkins and said, "Lindsey, I want to see you. Can you come down?" And Hopkins answered evenly, "Ernest, I'd be glad to see you anytime. The door to my office is always open." There was no meeting.

Hopkins next demanded a list of the names and addresses of all the company's shareholders, intending to write them and pitch his belief that their stock was worth keeping as a permanent investment. When the company refused to give him the list, Hopkins got angry and went public with a sensational accusation. The source of all the short selling, Hopkins told the *Atlanta Constitution*, was the insider crowd at Trust Company, who were scheming to "deflate" the price of Coca-Cola stock for their own benefit. He labeled Ernest Woodruff as the ringleader.

Hopkins's charge created an uproar in Atlanta and on Wall Street. The directors and major stockholders of the company were caught flat-footed in the glare. It was one thing for Ernest and his friends to run a syndicate that traded Coca-Cola stock for fun and small profits. It was another thing altogether for them to be accused of trying to wreck the company's prospects by driving down the value of its stock. Ernest was forced to attempt a strategic retreat.

Much to the surprise of Hopkins and everyone else in Atlanta, Ernest spun around completely and decided to sell the company—for good.

Up to now, Ernest and his allies at Trust Company had disposed of very little of their actual holdings of Coca-Cola stock. They had covered their short sales by digging into their pockets and buying shares in the marketplace, paying what amounted to a monetary fine for having guessed wrong as the price went up. They were all tens of thousands of dollars poorer, but they still owned and controlled a giant block of Coca-Cola stock—nearly half the outstanding shares—through the Coca-Cola International Corporation, the holding company Ernest had organized five years earlier when he seized power from his New York partners.

On April 16, 1928, one week after Hopkins turned up the heat on him, Ernest directed the president of Trust Company, Tom Glenn, to mail a letter to all of the stockholders of Coca-Cola International recommending that they pool their shares and sell out together.

The letter was front-page news in Atlanta. Signed by Ernest and the other major investors associated with the Trust Company of Georgia, including Jim and Charles Nunnally, Bulow Campbell, Charles Wickersham, and J. N. Goddard, its message was plain: Ernest Woodruff's crowd—the insiders—meant to get out of the Coca-Cola Company entirely and were assembling an attractive package that would place control of the company in the hands of anyone who cared to buy from them. If such a sale went though, Lindsey Hopkins would be left high and dry, a minority stockholder in a company being run by a new owner.

There was, however, one highly conspicuous absence from the list of names on the letter. W. C. Bradley, the chairman of the board of the Coca-

Cola Company, did not sign it. The omission was significant It suggested strongly that Ernest was facing dissent within the inner circle over his plan to sell out. When a newspaper reporter approached Bradley for an explanation, he fueled the suspicion that he opposed the sale. "Let the other fellows do the talking," he grumbled. "I have nothing to do with it. That's all being handled by the Trust Company of Georgia."

On the morning of Monday, April 30, 1928, the Coca-Cola Company's directors assembled in Atlanta in a mood of high tension.

Their only piece of official business was a unanimous vote raising the dividend on Coca-Cola common stock from $5 to $6 a year. First quarter profits for 1928 were up, and the move appealed to all factions, giving those who wanted to keep their shares a higher rate of return while enhancing the value of the holdings of those who wanted to sell. It gave Ernest Woodruff and his group a chance to demonstrate that they were no longer interested in trying to knock down the price of the stock.

But the dividend was the only thing the directors could agree on. Lindsey Hopkins asked for permission to attend the meeting and address the board, and much to Woodruff's disgust a majority of his fellow directors voted to hear from the maverick investor. Hopkins spoke of his confidence in the company and its future and made a fervent appeal for harmony on the board. He called for a four-for-one split in the common stock that would cut the price per share and allow smaller investors to buy the company's stock, thereby distributing its ownership across a broad spectrum of people.

Hopkins's unspoken message—one plainly understood by every director in the room—was a sharp rebuke to Ernest Woodruff, delivered directly in his face. By urging widespread ownership of the company's stock, Hopkins was saying in effect that Woodruff's group at Trust Company had failed to act in the best interests of Coca-Cola and that the man in the street could be trusted to do a better job. Hopkins was insulting Woodruff face-to-face in the boardroom of his own company, an act few men had the temerity to try. More remarkable still, several of the other directors seized the occasion to praise Hopkins, saying his trading activities had helped the company.

Woodruff and his group sat in silence through the meeting. Later, a reporter approached Tom Glenn and asked for a comment. "I have nothing to say," he answered, tight-lipped. The Trust Company crowd still hoped to sell the company, only now it was clear they might very well have a revolt brewing on the board.

As always, Ernest kept his plans to himself. Two days after the meeting, he was spotted boarding a Pullman car on the *Crescent Limited*, Southern Railway's opulent new passenger train to New York City. The Atlanta newspapers speculated that he was off to find a buyer for Coca-Cola International's huge block of stock, as indeed he was.

When he got to Manhattan, Ernest held a series of hush-hush meetings with Gene Stetson, the Guaranty Trust banker who had helped him buy the

Coca-Cola Company from the Candlers in 1919. Stetson was a large individual shareholder in the Coca-Cola Company, a member of the board, and he continued to be the point man in Coca-Cola's dealings with Wall Street. Woodruff and Stetson did not always see eye to eye on questions of how to run the company and its financial affairs, nor did they completely trust each other, but they maintained a close relationship based on mutual respect.

"I consider him," Stetson once said of Ernest, "the greatest trader I have ever known." The trade Stetson had in mind at the moment was the merger of the Coca-Cola Company and Canada Dry Ginger Ale, Incorporated, into the biggest soft drink business in the world. Stetson had joined Canada Dry's board three years earlier, partly in anticipation of just such a consolidation, and he was ready to begin confidential negotiations with Canada Dry's president, P. D. Saylor, right away. Ernest gave him the green light.

Canada Dry was a Prohibition drink that had outgrown its origins as a mixer to become a popular soft drink. In what one writer called a "fairy tale" of success, annual sales of the ginger ale spurted from 1.7 million bottles in 1922 to more than 50 million just four years later. The officers of the company saw the merger as a chance to gain access to Coca-Cola's 1,250 bottlers and half-million retail outlets, allowing them to reach a vastly wider market than ever before.

It was not so easy to see why the Coca-Cola Company would be interested in the deal, especially since Canada Dry was envisioned as the surviving corporate entity. One business publication later labeled the notion of Canada Dry swallowing up the far larger Coca-Cola Company as "fantastic." Nonetheless, Woodruff and Stetson began talks with Canada Dry's Saylor aimed at arranging a liquidation of Coca-Cola International. They agreed to make a public offering of stock in the new enterprise once the consolidation was completed.

On the afternoon of Tuesday, May 8, 1928, rumors of the negotiations began swirling around the brokerage houses of Wall Street. Heavy trading in the stock of both companies took place just before the New York Stock Exchange closed for the day. Without knowing any details of the planned merger, the investment community rendered a quick verdict that Canada Dry would be getting the better end of the deal, and its stock shot up more than $7 a share to $85.

After the story broke in the financial press, the *Atlanta Constitution* reported that several Coca-Cola directors were heading to New York to join in the discussions. Actually, the directors were speeding to New York to find out what Woodruff and Stetson were doing, since most of them were completely in the dark. They had heard rumors, nothing more. A company spokesman issued a statement professing ignorance of any of the dealings going on in New York.

The very next day the deal was dead. Canada Dry's president, Saylor, made the announcement in New York, saying negotiations were "definitely off" because of an impasse over the terms of the merger. No one would give a public explanation of the real reasons for the collapse of the deal, but later reports disclosed that some of Coca-Cola's biggest shareholders, including members of Ernest Woodruff's inside circle at Trust Company, had stepped in and put a stop to it. Woodruff returned from New York, declined comment, and went home.

In a quiet signal of surrender a few weeks later, Tom Glenn wrote another letter to the shareholders of Coca-Cola International, dissolving the pool. Several offers had been received for their stock, he said, but none was attractive enough to take. They would keep their holdings.

Hopkins had the final word. The board granted him permission to include a personal letter along with the second-quarter dividend payments that were mailed out to shareholders in June of 1928. Coca-Cola, he reminded them again, was a good permanent investment. He paid off his $1 million loan from Chase National Bank, with interest, and placed the canceled receipt in his scrapbook as a trophy.

A few days after the collapse of his father's campaign to dispose of the company, Robert Woodruff boarded the ocean liner *Ile de France* for his annual vacation in Europe with Nell.

He tried to behave as if nothing had happened. When he returned home, he resumed his duties at Plum Street and pretended to go about business as usual. His lone concession to the scent of scandal that had brushed his family was to pose for a publicity photo donating a camera to a Boy Scout from a local troop in Atlanta, a small act of charity staged for the benefit of the newspapers. He appeared wooden and ill-at-ease.

In private, Woodruff's associates could tell he was preoccupied. It was difficult to get him to make a decision. One of the company's bright young engineers, John Staton, came up with a solution to the age-old problem of getting retailers to sell Coca-Cola in cold, clean bottles. Using a wooden box and insulation made of Celotex dipped in asphalt, Staton invented a cooler that could chill three cases of Coke with just a nickel's worth of ice. It cost only $12.50 and took a scant fifteen minutes to assemble. Staton's cooler offered a way out of "the Stone Age," as one enthusiastic bottler put it, but Woodruff kept balking at giving the go-ahead for distribution to dealers. Finally Gene Kelly had to venture up to Asheville, North Carolina, and interrupt Woodruff's summer retreat to get his reluctant blessing.

During a meeting of his sales committee in September 1928, Woodruff gave a pep talk about the need for everyone in the company to work harder, then left the room while his top men were still struggling over design changes in the six-pack for the home market. (One of them wanted to try a paper bag with handles, just big enough to hold six loose bottles, an idea the others ridiculed and quickly killed.) Hamilton Horsey tried to get Woodruff's okay for a new bottling arrangement in Germany and France, but reported that the boss was too busy to see him, tied down with "a great number of matters not related to Coca-Cola."

The truth was, Woodruff still wanted to rejoin the White Motor Company. "I have gotten poor," he wrote Walter White, yet he went ahead with their plan to buy land together for the plantation in southwest Georgia. He suggested jokingly that White might have to pay for both their halves, then mustered the bravado (and borrowed the money) to pay for his share. He joined the board of directors and executive committee of White Motor and kept buying stock along with the other partners.

Woodruff's financial position was not nearly as dire as it might have been, thanks to a postponement of the day of reckoning for his short sales of Coca-Cola stock. Having no wish to see the president of the company reduced to insolvency, especially in the public spotlight, Tom Glenn and Harold Hirsch agreed to lend him more than $1 million worth of Coca-Cola common stock from their own portfolios to cover his position with the brokers. The loans were indefinite, which meant Woodruff could take as long as he needed to make good his sizable losses. In the meantime he was able to keep borrowing.*

"I have many troubles and afflictions," Woodruff wrote a friend, "and one of them—not the least—is bankers." Yet he turned to the bankers for a line of credit that would allow him to pursue his dream, and they gave it to him.

By February of 1929, Woodruff and Walter White and their partners were halfway to their goal of gaining control of the ownership of White Motor. Woodruff's spirits began to improve. He and White started spending time together on their land, a 30,000-acre patchwork of old farms and natural woods in Baker County that they named Ichauway (pronounced *Itch*-away), after the Creek Indian phrase for "where deer sleep." With its stands of longleaf pine and ground cover of scrub oak, broom sedge, and wire grass, the plantation was a perfect gray-green habitat for quail and other fowl. Woodruff and White spent days on horseback ranging over the property with their hunting dogs, flushing coveys and testing their skills as shooters.

The two men had a genial debate about what kind of lodge to build. White wanted a grand mansion on top of a limestone bluff overlooking the dark water creek that cut through the property, but Woodruff disagreed. Reminding White that they were quitting the Norias Club precisely because it encouraged too much social life indoors, Woodruff drew up plans for a sturdy, wood-frame house with seven sparely furnished bedrooms—a handsome but not especially comfortable dormitory for men whose interests were hunting, eating and drinking, card-playing, and little

---

*   Woodruff's circumstances also were eased in January 1929 when the board voted an unusual one-for-one stock split in the form of a million shares of Class A stock worth $50 apiece. Stockholders who needed cash could sell their Class A (as Woodruff eventually did) while others could choose to hold it, thereby avoiding capital gains taxes. It paid a handsome annual dividend of $3, or 6 percent.

else. Woodruff's idea prevailed, and construction was begun on the house, along with stables, kennels, an overseer's cottage, and other outbuildings around a half-mile circle on a section of flatland away from the river.

As the summer of 1929 passed, Woodruff seemed to take more of an interest in Ichauway than he did in his business obligations. He began learning about life in a section of the country that had been utterly bypassed by prosperity, and the experience affected him. In Baker County, as in much of the rural South, people survived hand-to-mouth, sharecropping on tired land or working for pitiable wages or, in some cases, making moonshine in the deep woods. While rich men from the North hunted quail for sport on the area's grand plantations, poor men, black and white, poached on the land and hunted for food for their families. Hard currency was hard to come by. One of Woodruff's first lessons was in rudimentary economics: Hoping to attract more game birds to the plantation by culling their natural predators, he posted a reward notice offering a bounty of 25 cents for snakes and 50 cents for skunks and blue hawks, and then watched in amazement as folks from all over the county brought in a heap of corpses that ended up costing him more than $50.

The backwardness of the region made a keen impression on Woodruff. For the rest of his life, he told the story of the day one of his tenants, an elderly black man, walked up to him on the circle at Ichauway to pay his respects, only to topple to the ground in a shuddering fit. Woodruff stepped back, alarmed. "Malaria," explained his overseer. More than 40 percent of the people in the area suffered from the disease, and Woodruff quickly ordered a supply of quinine to be distributed in pharmacies and general stores all across the county. Decades later, old-timers on Ichauway still remembered the summer the "barrel of pills" arrived, how the quinine tasted bitter and how grateful they were to have it.

The poverty and suffering he saw around him brought out a new side in Woodruff. Just a few months earlier, handing the camera to the Boy Scout in Atlanta, he'd been stiff and uncomfortable. Now his acts of charity seemed to be drawn from a deeper well. One of the young black men who lived on Ichauway, Bud Walker, had lost a leg several years earlier in a shooting accident, and Woodruff paid to send him to Atlanta to be fitted with a prosthesis. "Mr. Woodruff is very liberal and free-hearted," the *Baker County News* reported, "and the way he has help [*sic*] the poor people of the county is greatly appreciated by them and especially the Negro boy, who has been trying to work and save his money to get him a cork leg."

Woodruff did not give up his own enjoyment of the good life, of course. In Atlanta, he was in the midst of a brief spurt of interest in thoroughbred horses, and he still traveled extensively, venturing to California to play the dramatic golf course at Pebble Beach and taking his regular month-long vacation to Europe in August. The change in Woodruff was subtle, but there was no mistaking that something was happening. His old military academy roommate, Dick Gresham, the Baptist minister, was disappointed in a church assignment and asked Woodruff to lend him a small sum of money so he could afford to refuse the posting and take a trip to Scotland. Uncharacteristically, Woodruff refused. "Get on top of your job first," he told Gresham. "Then you can go."

It was the kind of gruff advice Woodruff's father was accustomed to giving—the kind Woodruff, on the eve of his fortieth birthday, had spent his life ignoring.

Walter White was driving to work in Cleveland on the morning of Saturday, September 28, 1929, when he smashed into another car in a head-on collision, shattering both his legs and suffering severe internal injuries. In spite of four blood transfusions, he died a day later.

The accident threw the White Motor Company into turmoil. No one had been groomed to succeed White, and his death triggered a sudden scramble for power among various members of his family and the management. An emergency meeting of the board of directors was convened within the week.

Hoping to quell the feuding, and also to preserve his own options for the future, Woodruff rushed to Cleveland and arranged, to have himself elected president in White's place. White's widow, Virginia, gave Woodruff her backing, as did Walter Teagle and the other partners who had been trying to gain control of the company.

For public consumption, at least, Woodruff described his new duties as temporary and announced that he would continue to serve as president of the Coca-Cola Company. "I'll live in a Pullman car, I guess," he told the *New York Times*, adopting a deliberately unruffled tone. His dual corporate presidencies—at age thirty-nine—made headlines across the country and even merited an item in the popular new weekly magazine, *Time*.

Woodruff tried to reassure investors and truck buyers alike that operations at White Motor would go on as usual during the search for a permanent successor. He made sure he was seen at a couple of World Series games in Chicago, as if to signal that both of his companies were running smoothly without the need for day-to-day supervision. The *Cleveland Plain Dealer* endorsed his stewardship, informing its readers that Woodruff was "more thoroughly representative of the new style Southern industrial leader than any other man."

But there was no calming the skittishness of Wall Street over the future of White Motor. The company's stock price began to slip and then to tumble. The killing blow came less than a month later, on October 24, 1929, when "Black Thursday" struck the stock market and triggered the crash that led eventually to the Great Depression. Stock prices plummeted across the board. White Motor, already weakened, lost a third of its value.

At the White Building in Cleveland, a mood of desperation took hold. Woodruff arrived one morning in early November for a meeting of the company's branch managers and saw the fearful expressions in the men's eyes.

He commandeered a large room on the sixth floor, had all of the telephones removed, and posted a guard at the door with orders to turn away everyone who tried to enter, no matter how urgent their business. He had a workman tack sales charts and advertising proofs on the walls. From eight o'clock in the morning until well past six that night, pausing only long enough for lunch, Woodruff delivered the inspirational talk of his life. It was not enough. Sales went up for a day, then slumped again.

Woodruff's plan to gain control over the company's ownership collapsed under the strain of the falling market. With stock prices plunging, the banks began demanding more and more collateral from Woodruff and the other partners to secure their loans, yet fresh collateral was nowhere to be found. Deeply in debt and utterly dejected, Woodruff grudgingly gave up and dissolved the pool he and White had formed to pursue a majority interest. "I must say it was not a 'howling success,'" Woodruff wrote Walter Teagle, outlining the problem sadly but succinctly. "A careful analysis shows that all we did was to buy a lot of stock at the high and when it started downward we got cold feet."

Whatever hope Woodruff had of returning to the trucking business disappeared along with the fading fortunes of White Motor.

He never discussed Walter White's death, but after the crash Woodruff helped found a traffic safety council in Atlanta. He also had a courtesy sign painted on the back panel of every truck in the Coca-Cola Company's fleet saying, "Sound Your Horn, This Truck Will Pull Over."

He became a slow, scrupulously cautious driver. Even at night, when there were no other cars on the roads, he made a point of stopping at every traffic light, stop sign, and railroad crossing. A friend once asked if he always obeyed the rules of the road. "Of course," he replied. It was the only way to avoid a tragic accident.

Woodruff decided to get on top of his job at the Coca-Cola Company.

By any standard measure, the business was having a banner year in 1929. Revenues were up, profits were up, gallon sales of syrup were up. The price of its stock dipped during the crash but quickly recovered. When Woodruff reported the company's numbers at the end of the year, the *Chicago Daily News* gushed, "Corporation presidents in their happiest moments dream of making annual reports like the one presented today by R. W. Woodruff."

The public face of Coca-Cola reflected the breezy, modern spirit of the Jazz Age. Coca-Cola's calendar girl had long since bobbed her hair and thrown off her bustles and corset; now she wore a flapper's dress with a low neckline and looked ready to jump off the page and start dancing the Charleston.

With his uncanny knack for tapping the temperament of the American people, Archie Lee had come up with a brilliant new catch-phrase for Coca-Cola: "The Pause That Refreshes." Premiering in a series of ads in the *Saturday Evening Post*, the slogan meshed neatly with the emerging notion that working men and women were entitled to brief, regular breaks during the business day. One illustration showed a secretary pushing her chair back from her typewriter and smiling as she rested her tired fingers and sipped a bottle of Coca-Cola. Per capita consumption in the United States jumped by half.

Behind the scenes, however, the company found itself snarled in a growing crisis, one that seemed to spring directly from a dark page in Coca-Cola's past. A group of chemists in the U.S. Food, Drug and Insecticide Administration in Washington conducted a test on a batch of Merchandise No. 5 and found traces of ecgonine, an alkaloid in the coca leaf that could be synthesized to create cocaine. The administration's director of regulatory affairs, W. G. Campbell, said he ordered the lab work because of a suspicion that "there must be something besides caffeine in Coca-Cola to cause the very noticeable Coca-Cola addiction of large numbers of persons."

Nearly two decades after Dr. Harvey Wiley quit the government, his protégés were still at work. In Wiley's day, ecgonine had been difficult to detect, but advances in chemical analysis gave his followers new tools to carry on his crusade, and they were doing so. Alerted to the results of the test—and deeply alarmed—Harold Hirsch assigned the Coca-Cola Company's own chemist, William Heath, to double-check the procedure for making No. 5.

Heath hurried to New Jersey, where the Maywood Chemical Works still prepared No. 5 under contract. To his dismay, he discovered that in spite of all the rigors of the decocainizing process, it was true that a tiny bit of ecgonine remained in the residue, even if the distillation was performed twice. Not only that, but sophisticated testing could detect a microscopic trace of cocaine itself in some of the samples. By Heath's calculation, the amount of ecgonine was infinitesimal: no more than one part in 50 million. In an entire year's supply of 25-odd million gallons of Coca-Cola syrup, Heath figured, there might be six-hundredths of an ounce of cocaine. But the findings were perilous nonetheless.

The merest whisper of the word "cocaine" was a public relations calamity in the making. After beating Dr. Wiley in Chattanooga, the company had published a booklet that proclaimed, "There is not one indivisible atom of cocaine in a whole ocean of Coca-Cola." How would it look to have to admit there was an atom of cocaine in an ocean of Coca-Cola? What would the company's enemies and competitors have to say about that? What fresh blaze of rumors and controversy would be ignited?

More ominous still, there were serious legal ramifications at hand. It seemed unlikely the government would prosecute in the U.S. courts, given the minuscule amounts of cocaine and ecgonine involved, but company officials could not be sure. And they grew especially nervous about the risks of continuing to ship Merchandise No. 5 to their overseas bottlers. Federal law was adamant in forbidding the export of narcotics to other countries. The government chemists had forwarded their findings to Colonel Levi

Nutt, the head of the enforcement division of the Federal Narcotics Control Board, and it appeared possible he might order a seizure.

Then, as if the other accumulating pressures were not enough, one of the company's men made a mistake, a serious error in judgment that threatened to create a full-scale international incident. Woodruff gave the go-ahead for production of Merchandise No. 5 at the cocaine plant the company was secretly leasing in Peru. His idea was to ship No. 5 directly to the company's overseas bottlers, thus avoiding the risk of exporting it from the United States. He did not expect the young man who was supervising the operation to sell the cocaine that was extracted as a by-product during the process, but that is exactly what happened. Claude Gortatowsky, a cost-conscious employee of the Coca-Cola Company, sold 19 kilograms of pure cocaine to a narcotics broker in Paris for $1,152. He dutifully sent the money to the home office in Atlanta.

There was no way to undo the transaction. If word of it ever leaked out, the company would have a lot more than an atom of cocaine to explain—it would have nearly 42 pounds, to be precise. Already, agents of the Permanent Central Opium Board, the anti-narcotics bureaucracy of the League of Nations, were asking questions about Coca-Cola's Peruvian operation. If they learned of the sale, they would be sure to accuse the company of drug trafficking.

The company also confronted a dicey predicament involving imports. Federal law made it illegal to import coca leaves into the United States except for scientific and medicinal purposes. In the past, the prohibition had been no hindrance: Since Maywood Chemical Works was one of the country's largest legitimate manufacturers of cocaine, it simply imported the leaves it needed to produce cocaine and used the decocainized residue in making Merchandise No. 5. But Coca-Cola's growing success and popularity were creating a need for No. 5 that outstripped the amount Maywood could legally supply. For the past two years, Coca-Cola had been forced in effect to buy a cocaine allowance from another legitimate manufacturer, Merck & Company, to get enough coca leaves. Now even Maywood and Merck together were unable to obtain enough coca leaves to meet the demand.

By the end of 1929, Woodruff was facing a deadline. His production managers informed him that unless new arrangements could be made immediately, the Coca-Cola Company would run out of Merchandise No. 5 on February 1, 1930. The news focused Woodruff's attention in a way his associates had not seen in several years. His air of distraction was banished.

"Mr. Woodruff has been phoning us two or three times a day about what progress is being made on No. 5," Harrison Jones wrote another company officer, describing the atmosphere at Plum Street. "He feels very acutely the seriousness of the situation, in which feeling we all share. The fact that we know nothing definitely, the fact that time is so short, and the fact that we have taken no concrete steps and February 1 is when our supply in American plants is exhausted, is enough to make us all gray-headed."

Snapping back into action, Woodruff orchestrated a lobbying effort whose goal was nothing less than a special exemption for the Coca-Cola Company from the narcotics laws of the United States. Congress was just beginning one of its periodic revisions of the nation's drug codes, and Woodruff set himself to the challenge of making sure they were amended in a way that protected the interests of his soft drink company.

First, Woodruff dispatched Harold Hirsch to Washington to see Colonel Nutt, who agreed to hold off any legal action pending adoption of the new legislation. Next Woodruff lined up a pair of allies from Georgia, Representative Charles Crisp and Senator Walter George, who agreed to plead the company's case in their respective chambers. Trickiest of all, Woodruff got the leader of the reform movement, Representative Stephen G. Porter of Pennsylvania, to listen to Coca-Cola's plight with a sympathetic ear.

Porter, the chairman of the House Foreign Affairs Committee, had an ambitious agenda. He had been crusading for almost a decade for tighter controls on worldwide production and distribution of opium, heroin, and cocaine, and he had spearheaded a movement in the United States for the humane treatment of addicts in recovery "farms" rather than prisons. The Porter Bill, which was making its way through Congress in the early weeks of 1930, sought to toughen U.S. narcotics laws and centralize enforcement in a new Bureau of Narcotics in the Treasury Department.

In a private conversation with Representative Crisp, his House colleague, Porter agreed to amend his bill to allow the unlimited importation of coca leaves into the United States as long as they were processed beforehand to remove the cocaine and ecgonine. The amendment was plainly aimed at rescuing the Coca-Cola Company, and when hearings on Porter's legislation began in the House Ways and Means Committee on March 7, 1930, several members objected. One went so far as to raise questions about the recent test of Merchandise No. 5 and the government's findings. But Porter proved to be an ardent defender of the company, ridiculing the idea that Coca-Cola contained cocaine or any other active alkaloid. With the nation's leading drug fighter acting as the company's advocate, congressional opposition dried up. The House passed the Porter bill with the amendment intact, and the Senate was prepared to concur.

In the State Department, however, the special exemption ran into a roadblock. The government had been trying for years to attack narcotics at their source by discouraging the cultivation of opium poppies and coca leaves. In international negotiations at the League of Nations and elsewhere, U.S. delegates had argued that the best way to curtail drug trafficking was to prevent the manufacture of the drugs in the first place. The United States was particularly anxious to pressure the British into a firmer stance against the smuggling of opium from India into China. Now the

Coca-Cola Company wanted the government's legal blessing for the pres-ervation and expansion of a huge market for Peruvian coca leaves, an obvi-ous contradiction of U.S. policy.

Congressman Crisp learned that the State Department planned to fight the amendment in the Senate. He sent a warning to Harrison Jones in Atlanta, who passed the news along to Woodruff. The choices seemed bleak. Trying to ram the amendment through the Senate in the face of State Department opposition would invite bad publicity. The company probably would lose, and even if it won the language of the amendment was less than ideal: Before importing its coca leaves, the company would have to remove all of the cocaine and ecgonine, a process it had yet to perfect.

But giving up would mean changing the secret formula, and that was unacceptable. An outsider might have found the company's anguish amus-ing, somewhat akin to the famous *New Yorker* cartoon that conjured up the day a bar of Ivory soap sank at Procter & Gamble. To Woodruff, though, it was no laughing matter. Coca-Cola without the coca was unthinkable, even if the coca in question was a tiny dollop that was powdered, percolated, steamed, double-distilled, pasteurized, and otherwise exhausted until not one consumer in a million would have noticed its absence. The point was Coca-Cola's mystique, the cult of the formula. If word got out that the coca was gone, people might *think* they tasted a difference, and that could be ruinous.

A subtler dynamic was at work as well. Nearly half a century after the first glass was served at Willis Venable's soda fountain, the idea persisted that Coca-Cola had special restorative powers—not cocaine, of course, but nonetheless something more than just a simple, mundane mix of sugar and caffeine. Years of advertising and promotion had produced a kind of com-mercial magic trick, an act of levitation in which the product kept up its allure even as it became familiar and trusted and commonplace. Taking away one of the ingredients threatened to burst the illusion.

Woodruff found a shrewd solution. He called in a big favor from one of his older friends at the Norias Club, Senator Walter Edge of New Jersey. Edge, a wealthy publisher and banker from Atlantic City and one of the most influential Republicans of his day, persuaded acting Secretary of State J. P. Cotton to accept an entirely new approach to the company's dilemma. In a complete reversal of position, the Hoover administration unexpect-edly declared that it would permit the importation of an unlimited amount of untreated coca leaves into the United States, provided the Coca-Cola Company agreed to destroy any cocaine or other alkaloid in the leaves under the supervision of the newly established Bureau of Narcotics.

The new policy allowed the State Department to accommodate the Coca-Cola Company while maintaining an anti-drug posture. The com-pany would still be underwriting a huge coca harvest in Peru, but at least the processing of the leaves would take place on U.S. soil, with federal agents guaranteeing the destruction of any resultant narcotics, so that there would be little chance of illicit cocaine finding its way into the marketplace. Fulfilling its end of the bargain, the company quietly agreed to suspend the use of its plant in Lima.

Both houses of Congress gave quick approval to Coca-Cola's special exemption and made it part of federal law. The company's steady supply of coca leaves resumed. Syrup production returned to normal. With enforcement shifted into other hands, Dr. Wiley's disciples abandoned their investigation and decided to wait for another day to pursue the cause.

In Atlanta, Harrison Jones calculated that the cost of manufacturing Merchandise No. 5 would be a bit higher now—$1.11 a pound—because of new taxes and additional processing expenses. But he and Woodruff agreed the price was worth paying.

Woodruff was keeping an impossible schedule, trying to run the Coca-Cola Company and White Motor at the same time.

He spent three days a week on the train, riding back and forth between Atlanta and Cleveland, six hundred miles at a stretch, lunching on sardines and saltines, napping in the afternoons, sitting up late into the night in his Pullman car working, draining the energy of the men who traveled with him.

Until he found a new man to run the White Motor Company, Woodruff was determined to shepherd his old business through the rough times it confronted. It was a source of pride to him that while he had to cut production, working hours, and take-home pay, he was able to avoid laying off any White employees.

There was no question, though, where Woodruff's allegiance belonged. He intended to stay at Coca-Cola—and to stay in charge. Others might envy Coca-Cola's annual report, but it would not remain rosy for long if he allowed things to slide, and the place to start, he believed, was with the troubled effort on the international front.

The situation in Germany was so tangled it seemed possible someone might end up in jail. Ham Horsey had gone into business there with an expatriate Atlantan named Ray Rivington Powers, giving him a standard contract to bottle Coca-Cola in Essen, the major city of the Ruhr Valley. Powers had spun a grand vision of his dream, how he planned to supply America's favorite soft drink in the canteens of the huge Krupp, Thiessen, and Stinnes industrial works, where tens of thousands of German laborers worked up a fierce thirst every day. He expected to have bottling plants up and running in no time throughout the Ruhr and along the Rhine, and then he wanted to become a parent bottler and expand into Hanover, Westphalia, Hesse-Nassau, Hohenzollern, Baden, Wurttemberg, and the Saar. He was looking at a potential market of twenty-three million people, almost as many as there were in the American South, squeezed into an area half the size of Georgia. He painted a promising, convincing picture, and Woodruff approved the deal when Horsey brought it to him.

When Powers started up his business in the spring of 1929, however, it quickly became clear that he was a better dreamer than doer. His capital was a few thousand dollars he borrowed from his wife and a German partner, and his bottling plant consisted of a hand-operated, six-spout filler and a horse-drawn cart. At one stage during the height of the summer season, his sales were a meager ten cases a week. Working by himself, he had no time to recruit other bottlers for the rest of his territory.

Powers peppered the home office with excuses. He was "struggling along blindly," he wrote Horsey, trying to figure out how to refrigerate his Coca-Cola. The proprietors of Essen's cafes, restaurants, and *trinkhallen* were willing to take a sample case or two, but they served the drink warm. The only source of ice was the beer brewers, and they had little interest in helping sell an American soft drink. Waiters refused to handle the product unless they were bribed. It was almost impossible to get anyone to put up outdoor signs. The Germans were going to love Coca-Cola, Powers was certain, but creating the market was going to be a long, slow, expensive process, and he was going to need help.

In December 1929, Powers paid a visit to Atlanta, where he called on Woodruff and made a pitch for money from the company. As ever, he displayed a gift for weaving the tale of a can't-miss opportunity. The Germans responded to Coca-Cola "even more favorably" than Americans, he argued. The vital element was time. It would take time to establish the market in Germany, just as it had in the United States and Canada, but success was inevitable.

Powers was a born storyteller. He liked to describe the afternoon he saw a huge workman push through the doors of a tavern, stride to the bar and bark out, "*Eine!*"—One! Powers dreamed of the day consumers in Germany would order Coca-Cola the same way they ordered beer, the way an American might say, "The usual!" Then it turned out the man *was* ordering a Coca-Cola. The barmaid put a cold bottle in front of him, and he gulped it down. He was the "principal Coca-Cola drinker" of the neighborhood, the barmaid explained. In time, Powers believed, thousands of Germans would be doing the same thing.

Woodruff sent Powers back to Germany, saying he wanted to think it over. Two months later, on February 10, 1930, he summoned Powers to a meeting at the Biltmore Hotel in New York and outlined the deal he was prepared to make. To get the Essen bottling plant operating again in time for the 1930 season, Woodruff would give Powers a loan of $10,000. In exchange, he wanted a first mortgage on the property. Powers accepted, and they signed the papers on the spot. As deals go, the terms and the amount of money involved were entirely unremarkable. What was unusual about the contract was that Woodruff executed it in the name of the Rohawa Company, the subsidiary he used for covert operations.

The act of rebellion that Woodruff remembered occurring in his creation of the Foreign Department was actually the deal he made with Ray

Powers. He had no intention of trooping in front of his father and the board of directors to get permission for a modest $10,000 loan to the pioneer Coca-Cola bottler in Germany, so he closed the transaction on his own and tucked it away from view.

As it happened, though, there were complications arising from the contract In Germany, as in almost every other nation in Europe, various laws severely limited the rights of foreigners to own property, sell products, or otherwise conduct business. If Powers failed, the mortgage on his bottling plant would revert to the Rohawa Company. Rohawa was a U.S.-based corporation. It could not legally own or operate a business on German soil.

As they examined the question, Woodruff and Harold Hirsch discovered that there was more than a mere technicality involved. For the past few years, they learned, Ham Horsey had been signing up bottlers all around Europe without paying attention to the niceties of the laws involving foreign ownership. While Woodruff was preoccupied with his other affairs, the Coca-Cola Company had bought and sold property and equipment, signed contracts and employed personnel, all without the proper licenses or permission from the host governments. Every one of the company's bottlers was in some degree of jeopardy. So was the company's trademark. In Horsey's stark admission, he and the company had been "operating illegally."

Scrambling to repair the damage, Woodruff and Hirsch created a new entity, the Coca-Cola Export Corporation, owned by Rohawa with Woodruff as president, and sent Horsey off to the Continent on a mad dash to create a labyrinth of new corporations, including foreign holding companies headquartered in Luxembourg and the Netherlands, that would pass legal muster as links in the chain of ownership. Powers was brought to Atlanta, where his arrangement was restructured to conform with the new proprieties.

The flurry of activity came to Ernest Woodruff's attention, and naturally he took a dim view. Yet he made no move to intervene. He had begun to find it "very distasteful," in his phrase, to have to oppose his son on matters of company policy. When they clashed at board meetings, the other members squirmed with discomfort. It could not accurately be said that Ernest was mellowing, but he was almost sixty-seven years old and he liked spending time on his farm outside Richmond. More and more, when items came up that were likely to pit him against Robert, he decided it was easier to boycott the meetings and let Robert have his way. He did so now.

At first, Powers did little to reward Robert Woodruff's faith in him. As soon as he returned to Essen he began a drumbeat of requests for more money. It turned out he had been forced to give half the loan proceeds to his German partner, who was threatening to sue him. He ran through the other $5,000 in less than a month and demanded $5,000 more. "Lord knows I have plenty to do," he wrote Harrison Jones, "without cabling daily about funds and having the worry of wondering where the money is coming from." Woodruff grudgingly okayed another loan.

When Woodruff sent an accountant to look at Powers's books, the report came back that they were in "appalling" condition. Powers had filed false tax returns with the German government, the accountant said, and might be facing arrest. The municipal authorities in Essen were threatening to slap him with a steep fine for putting up excess outdoor advertising. But there was one inescapable fact that overrode all other concerns. Sales had doubled. Powers was a wretched businessman and an infuriating partner—"I advise you to scrutinize very closely any claims that he files," Horsey warned the home office—yet it seemed his faith in the German appetite for Coca-Cola was well placed. He was a good salesman. In spite of his red ink and bad books and other shenanigans, Woodruff drew up papers creating a parent bottling company in Germany, with Powers as a part owner and general manager, and had the company invest another $100,000 in the venture.

Then Woodruff relieved Horsey of command over Coca-Cola's European operations. Horsey's limitations, especially his careless inattention to the bottom line, made him expendable. If the company was going to risk large sums of money developing the market in Germany and the rest of Western Europe, it became imperative that a man of rigid discipline be placed in charge as a watchdog.

Gene Kelly was such a man. Tall, lean, ramrod straight, he could still do one-handed pushups in his forties. With his clipped moustache and shock of salt-white hair, he looked every inch the colonel he'd been in the Great War. Kelly ran the company's Canadian operations from Toronto and made a tidy profit every year by imposing a strict set of rules on every aspect of the system. Before the term was much in vogue, he prided himself on being an efficiency expert, and Woodruff relied on him to give basic training to the promising young men who came into the company.

In a small trunk that opened up like a portable desk, Kelly kept manuals he'd written on the best (and cheapest) ways of doing every job in the business, from soaking the scrubbers to buying advertising to filling a cooler (egg-sized chunks of ice in three inches of water). His compulsive penny-pinching was legendary. Kelly put governors on the accelerators of his delivery trucks so the drivers would use less gasoline. Once, after a trip across town on company business, he put through an expense account for the streetcar fare of a nickel.

Numbers mattered to Kelly. He kept a record of every round of golf he'd ever played and figured out his running average at the end of every year. While other Coca-Cola men guessed that it might be hotter indoors in winter than it was outdoors in summer, Kelly went roving around Canada with a thermometer and calculated that it was *exactly* 7.5 degrees hotter.

Oddly enough, Kelly's stinginess did not extend to his personal life, at least not to his wardrobe and social pursuits. He dressed impeccably, favoring custom-fitted suits from London, shirts with dickey fronts from Belgium, French ties, and Italian shoes. He drank only Veuve Cliquot champagne. A bachelor and unabashed ladies' man, he encouraged the rumor that he had once been forced to leap from a married woman's bedroom into a thorn bush below, narrowly escaping serious injury.

When it came to the company, though, Kelly was a miser and a stickler for procedure, and his mission in Germany was to inflict those qualities on Ray Powers. They met for the first time in Cologne, where the new parent bottling company was headquartered. As Powers later described the scene, he drove over from Essen to greet Kelly when his train arrived. After introducing himself, Powers reached out to take Kelly's luggage and was startled when Kelly rudely brushed him aside. "I never trust my suitcase to anybody," he said. Their relationship never got any warmer.

Kelly imposed order on the German operation. He developed a device the company's German salesmen later nicknamed the *Seufzertasche*, or "case of sighs," a leather briefcase with a tinplate lining that held six bottles of Coca-Cola in ice. Powers and his salesmen lugged the heavy case from tavern to tavern, making sure the samples they peddled were ice-cold. Their instructions were to find the proprietor, "and see him before sitting down to order a drink, as this saves the price of the drink if he happens not to be in." Kelly enumerated the standard points to be made in the sales pitch: Coca-Cola was natural, wholesome ("used in many hospitals"), thoroughly tested, sanitary, delicious, and refreshing. And he added a thought that was rarely expressed openly in the United States—that Coca-Cola was a first-rate hangover cure, especially for beer drinkers.

Powers complained bitterly to Woodruff, Harrison Jones, Hirsch, and anyone else in the home office who would listen about the rigors of life under Kelly's tutelage, but there was no disputing the results. Powers was a hard worker, and once his work was tamed and focused it led to greater sales and revenues. In March of 1932, the Essen plant sold 4,000 cases of Coca-Cola. For the year, sales in Germany topped 60,000 cases. The company was on the way to its first success beyond North America.

Some days Woodruff's job was easy. One of the men in the Chicago office wrote him a note suggesting the company market Coca-Cola golf balls. Woodruff said no.

Other problems were more challenging, and some threatened to remain insoluble until fundamental change arrived in the way Americans lived. Home sales of Coca-Cola would be meager until home refrigeration was widespread, a day that awaited the advent of cheap electricity and affordable appliances. In the meantime, Coca-Cola was sold mostly at soda fountains and retail outlets. Drivers with tongs and shoulder pads continued to deliver fifty-pound blocks of ice to Coca-Cola's dealers, much as they had since the last century, and many of those dealers continued to defeat the purpose by wrapping the ice in newspaper so it wouldn't melt.

Trying to guess what the future held could be risky. The major gas companies were discouraging their attendants from selling Coca-Cola at service stations because, as Harrison Jones explained it, "they did not desire their employees, who were there to serve oil and gas, to fool with other articles." But Jones did not think installing vending machines was a good alternative. Drivers, in his view, would not be willing to go to the trouble of getting out of the car, walking a few steps, putting a coin in the slot, and pulling the lever.

Jones served the company as "Mr. Outside" to Woodruff's "Mr. Inside," and it was easy to assume, wrongly, that Jones wielded significant power. In the phrasing of a *Fortune* magazine writer, "It is Mr. Jones who listens to the white folks' troubles, and who gets the colored folks out of jail." That much was true, perhaps, but it was Woodruff who called the shots. In a time of uncertainty and change, with the nation slipping deeper into the worst depression anyone had ever known, it fell to Woodruff to gauge the future and decide on the company's course.

By the closing days of 1931, nothing loomed larger on the company's horizon than the anticipated repeal of Prohibition and the widespread feeling that people would cut back on drinking Coca-Cola once they could buy beer and liquor again legally. On Wall Street, rumors shot through the financial community that Coca-Cola's earnings were falling off, and like a self-fulfilling prophecy the company's stock prices began to drop.

In a bid to publicize the argument that Coca-Cola's prospects would be unaffected by the undoing of the Volstead Act, Woodruff had favorable articles planted in *Barron's*, the *Wall Street Journal*, B. C. Forbes's newsletter, and other publications. But the strategy backfired, fueling the suspicions of trouble. A new wave of selling broke out, sending the price of Coca-Cola common stock spiraling down toward $100 a share, half its high-water mark during the trading war of 1928.

Much to his chagrin, Woodruff was forced to turn to his father one final time for help. It scarcely seemed possible that after eight straight years of robust growth in sales and profits, after a record of success that defied all attempts at reversal (even those instigated by the Woodruffs themselves), the Coca-Cola Company was back in the kind of dizzying downward spiral that nearly brought ruin a decade earlier. Yet the numbers clacking in on the afternoon ticker tape were irrefutable.

Drawn out of his semi-retirement, Ernest Woodruff returned to his big desk at Trust Company, revived his Coca-Cola stock syndicate, and began buying shares of common stock with the same headlong fury he'd exhibited trying to sell them just a few years before. Denouncing the "lower class 'tip-ster sheets'" that were predicting doom for Coca-Cola (as if he had never engaged in such practices himself), Ernest and his inner circle vowed to buy every share of common stock that came on the market.

"We were all sweating blood," Tom Glenn recalled later. One Friday afternoon, with the price of the stock still tumbling, Ernest put through a buy order for 15,000 shares. Glenn asked him where he was going to get the money. "I don't know," Ernest replied. Somehow he managed to cover the purchase and arrange another. He convinced banks in New York to assume several million dollars' worth of loans so that Trust Company and other institutions in Atlanta could step up their lending and relieve some of the company's biggest shareholders. Ernest personally lent stock to Robert and others who were in debt, bolstering the shrinking value of their collateral to keep them from foreclosure.

Thanks to the syndicate, the drop in the price of Coca-Cola common was gradual. More people in Georgia had money invested in the Coca-Cola Company than any other enterprise in the South, and a sudden collapse of the stock price, in the words of one Atlanta financier, "could have resulted in nothing short of a sectional panic." As if to reflect the keen apprehension gripping everyone involved in the matter, one of the company's newspaper ads showed a worried businessman, evidently a stockbroker, clutching a telephone in one hand and a bottle of Coca-Cola in the other. "Break the tension," the ad copy advised, "with a pause."

The tension did break. By the spring of 1932, the worst of the scare was over. The bottom wasn't touched until the end of the year, when Coca-Cola common reached 68½, down fully two-thirds of its value, yet there was no panic because the shareholders knew Woodruff's syndicate would always step in to buy if necessary. "These past few days have been about the most strenuous I have ever contended with," Ernest wrote his son, "but I have in a way enjoyed it. . . ." He even managed to do a little trading along the way. He made a short sale of 5,000 shares during the summer, explaining to Robert that "there was considerable disposition on the part of some insiders to undertake to trade in and out while we are 'holding the bag.'" Some things never changed.

For Robert Woodruff, the price of relying on his father was high: a renewed stream of suggestions—vigorous suggestions—on how to run the company. In particular, Ernest began demanding sharp cuts in pay for all of the company's employees, top to bottom, a step Robert resisted with all his heart. W. C. Bradley, still serving as chairman of the board, finally stepped in on Robert's behalf. "Frankly, Ernest," he wrote his old friend, "I do not concur with some of your views on Coca-Cola management, and can not agree with your position that we should make any sort of drastic reduction in the salaries of our officers and employees, for the reason that they have given us extraordinary efforts, and our net results during 1929, 1930, and 1931 do not justify any such action."

Bradley helped Robert stand up to his father. A man of immense bashfulness himself—once, dedicating a new theater in Columbus, he was able to say only, "My friends," before turning beet red and sitting down—Bradley acted as a go-between and tried to help father and son communicate. "Confidentially," he wrote Ernest at one point, "I spent two or three hours in conference with Bob on last Tuesday and found him more nervous and depressed over the situation than I had ever seen him before, and I feel perfectly safe in making the statement that he needs your approval and cooperation more now than he ever has before. . . ."

One day at the height of the troubles, Robert had a visit in his office at Plum Street from his friend Gresham, the minister, and their old Sunday school teacher, Mrs. Richardson. As he walked them down the glass-lined corridor to the elevator, Woodruff confided, "I am trusting God more than you think, really I am." Yet it was not prayer that held Ernest in check. It was the board of directors, rallying under the guidance of Will Bradley. Ernest's demands for pay cuts and other sharp reductions in expenses were defeated, as were most of his other attempts at interference. Like Sam Dobbs a decade before, Robert believed that the worse the economy was, the more the company should spend, especially on advertising. Unlike Dobbs, Robert had the bloodlines and the backing of enough directors to make his point stick in the face of his father's disapproval.

In November 1932, in the pit of the Depression, with sales tailing off and many of the company's small dealers either closed or so strapped for cash they had to buy their supply of syrup a half day at a time, Woodruff announced that the company would put an extra $1 million into advertising in 1933.

And he made one other crucial decision. Congress was on the verge of allowing the sale of beer with a 3.2 percent alcohol content—so-called near beer—as an interim step before the impending repeal of the Eighteenth Amendment. Many in the company feared the return of beer would cut into Coca-Cola's sales, and Harrison Jones proposed a solution: Coca-Cola Beer. With 1,250 independent bottlers and nearly a million retail outlets, the company was ideally positioned to distribute its own brand from coast to coast. Some of the bottlers might have "scruples" about going into the brewing business, Jones conceded, but others would do so whether the Coca-Cola Company wanted them to or not. "It would be my idea," he wrote, "that we manufacture a beer, both in bulk and in bottles, and that we make all the accepted forms, both light and dark, [so] that we might have a full line and meet the demands of a varying population and varying taste."

Something told Jones his suggestion might not capture Woodruff's fancy. "I have just hit the high-spots in this memorandum," he concluded, "so that you may think this matter over and shoot it full of holes." Which is just what happened. It was Woodruff's conviction that the Coca-Cola Company make and market one product, and one product only. He could not have believed more profoundly in Oliver Wendell Holmes's words, "a single thing coming from a single source, and well-known to the community," if he had written them himself. He had no intention of allowing the trademark to represent anything other than the soft drink. There would be no Coca-Cola beer.

As 1932 drew to a close, no one could know if Woodruff's decision was the right one. But three days before New Year's, Sam Dobbs wrote to a friend. "If I had a million dollars in cash to-day to invest, I would not hesitate a minute to put it all in Coca Cola. . . ."

Seven

PEPSI

During the worst of the Depression, when most businesses stopped paying for outdoor advertising, some billboard owners gave space to the Coca-Cola Company for free. Rather than expose mile after desolate mile of blank, peeling displays, they preferred showing the cheery pictures created by Archie Lee's stable of artists and illustrators. It was one more way Coca-Cola had of penetrating the mind's eye of America.

Lee understood that a special bond was forming between the soft drink and the American people. In the popular novel *Ann Vickers*, published in 1933, Sinclair Lewis described a character drinking a Coca-Cola as part of her daily routine. "I see a great significance in such things," Lee wrote Woodruff. The author was trying to create "a typical, normal American situation," Lee explained, and had included Coca-Cola "as naturally as he would a telephone."

In the early 1930s, the name Coca-Cola appeared on 20,000 walls, 160,000 billboards, and five million soda fountain glasses across the country, and the company's ads were reproduced on more than 400 million individual newspaper and magazine pages a year. Depicting people from every walk of life—young men at Princeton, tourists visiting Old Faithful, a pair of nicely dressed women shoppers, a motorcycle cop clicking bottles in a toast with a young school-crossing monitor—Coca-Cola's illustrations cloaked the product with a degree of prestige and acceptance no soft drink, no "bellywash," had ever before enjoyed. Coca-Cola ads looked like Norman Rockwell paintings, in many instances because they were.

The company distributed tens of thousands of little booklets called "When You Entertain," by the hostess Ida Bailey Allen, who advised housewives on etiquette, including the proper way of serving Coca-Cola at afternoon social gatherings. At a time when other soft drinks were still considered vaguely disreputable, one of the company's illustrators noted, "The Junior League were drinking Coke in the drawing room." Lee's "pause that refreshes" became part of the nation's vernacular.

The interest people took in Coca-Cola's advertising was simply remarkable. William Forbes, a socially prominent Boston lithographer who printed the company's posters and calendars, wrote Woodruff one summer to say that a preview of the annual bathing beauty had earned the applause of the city's Brahmin set. "Mrs. Wigglesworth, who is one of the conservative family of that name, was so delighted in it that she begged it of me to show her boys," Forbes reported with satisfaction, and it seemed that Coca-Cola had met a high standard indeed.

On another level, one that was not so innocent, the company and its bottlers pursued a strategy aimed at the country's children. As a matter of policy, no one under the age of about twelve appeared in Coca-Cola's ads, but marketing was directed at youngsters as soon as they turned six and entered the first grade. In Dayton, Ohio, for instance, the bottler distributed company-made "Coca-Cola Nature Study Cards" in the 198 schools in his franchise area and worked at cultivating the goodwill of the PTA by distributing toy gliders, packages of needles, pencils, rulers, balloons, thermometers, billfolds, and other items (including a Coca-Cola scooter and an electric corn popper) for sale at school bazaars. Tours of bottling plants were encouraged.

The market for Coca-Cola was like a conveyor belt, a company official observed, with the obstetrician at one end and the undertaker at the other. The goal was to win customers when they were young and keep them for life. In Kansas City, the bottler provided a gaily colored bus for school outings and broadcast a weekday radio program called "Brother John's Kiddie Club."

Nothing exemplified the combination of gentle charm and mercenary purpose in the company's advertising better than the series of Christmas illustrations that Haddon Sundblom began painting for Coca-Cola in December 1931. In an earlier ad for the company, another artist had depicted Santa Claus as a mere mortal, a man in a costume in a department store pausing to refresh himself amid the crush of children and adult shoppers. But Lee wanted to create a fantasy, a vivid portrait of the "real" Santa Claus enjoying Coca-Cola on the job. Sundblom captured the idea with perfection. His Santa was jolly and rotund, a ruddy Dutch uncle who glowed with a luminous warmth and loved to drink Coca-Cola while delivering presents from the North Pole.

The genius of Sundblom's ads was that Santa never tried to force Coca-Cola on anyone, child or parent. Instead, Santa simply enjoyed the soft drink while he cobbled toys in his workshop or slipped down the chimney to make deliveries. One year Sundblom's ad depicted a grateful Santa discovering a bottle of Coca-Cola on a family's mantel alongside a stocking and a child's roughly scribbled note: "Dear Santa, Please Pause Here—Jimmy."

Sundblom, who was not nearly as sentimental a man as his art suggested, later explained that Lee's instructions to him were to show Santa "on his fanny being served by kids." Bluntly expressed, that was exactly the point. The company would never be caught (at least not red-handed) exploiting the faith and fable of Santa Claus by soliciting children as customers and pushing the product directly at them. Yet the company would do almost anything to make Coca-Cola part of the narrative mythology of American life, for Americans of every age—including the very young.

In the crisis over Repeal, as ever, the company's top men looked after their interests with hard-eyed realism. Coca-Cola's advertising director, Turner Jones (no relation to Harrison), designed a campaign specially tailored to compete with beer and the resumption of liquor sales in general. As Jones saw it, the company had to modify its pitch by putting an emphasis on what he called "the stimulating characteristics of our product." He wanted to portray Coca-Cola as a pick-me-up and to suggest, without saying so directly, that beer led to inebriation and drowsiness and was fattening as well.

The result was the "Back to Normal" series of magazine ads, an eerie, sophisticated set of illustrations in 1933 that showed people's faces as masks of dull fatigue that could be whisked off after a sip of Coca-Cola, revealing eager, animated expressions underneath. "Put your best face forward," admonished one ad that depicted a woman pushing aside her own frowning likeness. "Refresh yourself and be alert."

Recognizing that a direct appeal to adults and adult moods might jeopardize Coca-Cola's standing as a beverage suitable for children, Jones charged the D'Arcy agency with responsibility for "a frequent changing of pace to keep the innocent, wholesome, healthy child viewpoint alive." A memo from the agency's archives indicates that the challenge was taken seriously. "There is a large market for Coca-Cola among young children," an account executive named E. C. Bolton reported to Archie Lee:

> This market is rather seriously hampered by an apparently
> widespread belief among parents that the carbonated water
> and caffein [sic] in Coca-Cola are harmful for children. Much
> could be done, in my opinion, to overcome this sales obstacle
> by a campaign in parents' magazines . . . and in the major
> medical journals. The campaign would also serve another
> worthwhile purpose in acting as a foil against any possible
> fear or ill-will that might conceivably be caused by the pres-
> ent and proposed stimulation campaign.

Woodruff gave his blessing to a strategy that trumpeted the benefits of Coca-Cola "as a means of relieving fatigue of various kinds," a pitch typified by an ad in the *Ladies Home Journal* that showed a pair of trim, athletic women on a diving board under a headline that proclaimed, "Keeps You Feeling Fit." After years of scrupulously avoiding any hint of curative powers, the Coca-Cola Company was returning to its roots.

As the company delved into the business of trying to manipulate the national psyche, an echo of Asa Candler's distant voice could be heard repeating the blandishments of the patent medicine era. Only this time the spiel promised purity and came equipped with the glamour of Hollywood. "If it's good for the stars, it's good for you," declared an endorsement of Coca-Cola by the cast of the movie *Dinner at Eight*. Lionel Barrymore,

Wallace Beery, Jean Harlow, Marie Dressler, Billie Burke, and the other stars of MGM's popular comedy, along with director George Cukor, all lined up on the set between scenes and posed for a photograph with bottles of Coca-Cola in their hands, sipping the soft drink through straws and smiling gamely.

Expressing the point of the campaign explicitly, the text of the ad proclaimed that Coca-Cola "banishes drowsy yawns and hot, thirsty faces. It's the way to snap back to normal and be alert. . .because an ice-cold Coca-Cola is more than just a drink. It combines those pleasant, wholesome substances which foremost scientists say do the most to restore you to your normal self."

The backlash Woodruff and others feared never materialized. The lone voice raised against Coca-Cola in the early 1930s came from a doctor in Illinois who wrote the *Journal of the American Medical Association* to warn that teenagers were dissolving aspirin in Coca-Cola to create an "intoxicating" beverage with addictive properties that were as bad as "narcotic habituation." The company studiously ignored the report in hopes it would sound ridiculous and fade away, as it eventually did. The prevailing view, that Coca-Cola was a mild, benign refreshment, as familiar and harmless a part of American life as tea was to the English, took a deeper hold.

In a neat coda that signaled the success of the campaign, Harold Hirsch conducted a round of quiet negotiations with the editors of *Good Housekeeping*, the magazine that had once given Dr. Wiley a forum to attack Coca-Cola, and secured the coveted Seal of Approval.

As for the return of liquor, the company survived with effortless ease. Archie Lee had never believed beer posed a genuine threat to Coca-Cola, and he was right. "I just can't see," he once told Woodruff, "how a taste for Coca-Cola can accept beer as a substitute." His puzzlement was justified. If anything, the nation's failed experiment with Prohibition ended up helping Coca-Cola by putting thousands of saloons and corner taverns out of business and encouraging a much higher level of home consumption of beverages of all kinds.

Investors, seeing their fears were groundless, began a two-year run of heavy buying that pushed the stock price of Coca-Cola common back above $100 a share, then above $200, and finally, in the summer of 1935, to a record mark of $224.75—the highest figure on the New York Stock Exchange. The recovery was complete.

But by then the company had another problem: Pepsi.

For more than a decade, the playing field had belonged to Coca-Cola almost exclusively. The U.S. Supreme Court frightened off most of the manufacturers of copycat soft drinks in 1920 with its decision against the Koke Company of America, and the collapse of sugar prices that same year drove many of the rest into bankruptcy.

In the years since, Harold Hirsch had assembled a team of lawyers in the company's Legal Department who scoured the land protecting Coca-Cola's trademark, hunting down violators, and filing hundreds of lawsuits that produced a blizzard of orders, injunctions, decrees, and judgments against defendants big and small.

The company's vigilance became a matter of legend and eventually of criticism. No one questioned Coca-Cola's right to its good name, of course. Some of the infringement cases were flagrant, with the guilty parties' intent to deceive as plain as the names they put on their bottles. The makers of Co-Cola and Coke-Ola, for example, deliberately chose homonyms for the way many Southerners pronounced Coca-Cola, and were summarily put out of business.

But other cases were not so obvious, and in time the Coca-Cola Company's relentless opposition to the use of the word "cola" by anyone else began to seem like an unwarranted bid for a monopoly on an entire category of soft drinks. In the eyes of the federal courts (and the general public, too) the notion was growing that "cola" was a generic term—meaning a dark-colored, sugar-based, carbonated soft drink containing caffeine—and that the Coca-Cola Company did not have an exclusive right to make and market the lone brand of it. A lot of people saw how immensely profitable Coca-Cola was and resented the company's refusal to share the wealth.

Nothing did the company's reputation and legal standing more harm than the activities of its Trade Research Department, a euphemistically named group of investigators—mostly Pinkerton detectives and beefy ex-football players from Hirsch's alma mater, the University of Georgia—who threatened reprisals against soda fountain proprietors suspected of palming off cheap syrup in place of Coca-Cola. Even though the practice of substitution was illegal, the specter of a rich, powerful corporation sending a private police force into candy stores, restaurants, and mom-and-pop shops to enforce its favored position looked like unnecessary bullying.

The company men issued no-nonsense warnings: When a customer ordered Coca-Cola, the shopkeeper was obliged to serve the genuine article. If the warnings were ignored, other investigators followed up with legal action. Working in pairs, they would enter a place a few minutes apart, pretending not to know each other. While one observed and surreptitiously took notes, the other would order a glass of Coca-Cola, slip a sample of the beverage into a medicine bottle, and seal it for testing by a chemist. Or the investigator would demand a sample of syrup straight from the dispenser and take it by sheer force of intimidation. Either way, if the syrup was fake the company would file suit and the investigators would testify in support of each other. Sometimes the company ran the drill a half-dozen times or more at a single fountain, just to accumulate evidence.*

---

* The regional Federal Records Center outside Atlanta, a sprawling government warehouse, still stores boxes containing some of the vials of dark liquid that Hirsch's men collected and carefully closed with sealing wax—forgotten, dust-coated exhib-

Over time the investigators came to think of themselves almost as law enforcement officers. With the encouragement of Hirsch and the rest of the company's management, they developed a certain swagger and prosecutorial zeal, a cocksure certainty that whatever they did on behalf of Coca-Cola was not merely in the interest of the company but of simple justice itself. It was a situation tailor-made for overstepping the bounds, as soon happened.

Charles Guth made candy for a living, but no one who met him ever made the mistake of thinking he was a sweet man.

The son of German immigrants, Guth grew up in Philadelphia before the turn of the century and started learning the confectionery business as an apprentice when he was fourteen. He moved to Baltimore in 1900, opened a shop of his own, and after a series of ups and downs finally prospered making a chocolate drink with the unlikely name of Mavis.

His reputation as a tough customer was cemented in 1913 when he shot and killed his chauffeur, who allegedly attacked Guth with an axe and beat him with his fists in a fierce assault after Guth fired him.

In the late 1920s, Guth operated out of an office on the fourth floor of the Candler Building in Baltimore, where he was a neighbor of the executives in the Coca-Cola Company's eastern regional headquarters. The Coca-Cola men came to dislike Guth intensely because of his habit of approaching the company's bottlers and bribing their salesmen (with gifts of gold watches, in one instance) to produce and market Mavis as a sideline.

Guth worked at presenting a baronial image to the world. He owned a pair of expensive Pierce Arrow cars and wore a big ring with a diamond. His outer office was filled with ornate furniture, including gold-brocaded chairs with museum-style streamers across the arms to prevent anyone from sitting down in them. His private office was set up to give the impression of a throne room. Guth sat behind a huge desk on a raised platform and gazed down on his callers from a height. One visitor remembered him as a large man, even though he stood only five foot six and weighed 150 pounds.

"He wore spats and had a derby hat," one of the Coca-Cola Company's lawyers recalled years later. "A debonair guy, but he had the eyes of a snake."

Guth's temper was notorious, as was his lack of trustworthiness. Many of his associates learned too late mat they should have been more careful doing business with him, a group that included the Loft family. The Lofts were the proprietors of a chain of candy stores that bore their name in New York City. They made a stock deal with Guth, trading shares in their company for an ownership stake in Mavis, and soon found themselves on the losing end of a proxy fight. Guth seized the presidency of Loft, Incor-

---

its from lawsuits that were brought against various pharmacists and shop owners around the South in the 1920s and 1930s.

porated, and assumed control of their stores. By 1931 Guth had taken over two other chains, the Happiness and Mirror candy stores, and was running 225 outlets in New York, most of which had soda fountains that served Coca-Cola.

It was Guth's firm belief that he deserved a discount on the 30,000 gallons of Coca-Cola syrup his stores in New York were buying each year. With the figure of $15,000 in mind, he called on the company's top man in Baltimore, Neal Harris, to press his case. Harris declined, reciting the company's strict policy of selling syrup only through authorized wholesalers and never directly to the retailer. When Guth demanded that Harris treat him as a jobber to make him eligible for the reduced price, Harris flatly refused. Furious, Guth ordered all of his candy stores to stop serving Coca-Cola.

Guth started looking for a substitute cola, and as it happened he knew exactly where to turn. Pepsi-Cola had just gone bankrupt for the second time in its existence, and it was little trouble for Guth to talk the company's handful of creditors into letting him buy the trademark and formula for $12,000. The formula was of no interest to him at all, but the trademark was virtually priceless: By an accident of history, it had never been challenged by Coca-Cola, and no court had ever ruled that it was an infringement.

Pepsi had begun life around the turn of the century in New Bern, North Carolina, the creation of a pharmacist named Caleb Bradham who first called it "Brad's Drink" and later got it registered under the trademark Pepsi-Cola. There is little question Bradham was inspired by Asa Candler's success with Coca-Cola, but Pepsi differed at least slightly in composition: It contained pepsin, a digestive enzyme, and was marketed in its early days mainly as a stomach soother. Bradham enjoyed a considerable success with Pepsi around the Carolinas and Virginia, and by 1915 he claimed to have nearly three hundred franchise bottlers in twenty-four states.* Bradham built a fine mansion in New Bern and had five live-in servants, but he was one of the many soft drink entrepreneurs ruined by sugar after World War I.

Why the Coca-Cola Company failed to include Bradham and his drink among the hundreds of suits they filed against imitators cannot be fully explained. Harold Hirsch once remarked that he wanted to make Pepsi a target in the very early days, before he and Sam Dobbs took charge of the company's legal policies, but was overruled by John Candler. Later, Hirsch underwent a curious change of heart and testified under cross-examination in an infringement case against another soft drink that he did not believe the name Pepsi-Cola infringed on Coca-Cola's trademark. The likeliest

---

* One sign of success was that Pepsi drew imitators of its own. J. C. Mayfield, the old partner of Doc Pemberton who created such mischief for the Coca-Cola Company peddling Koke, also put out a product he called Pepsi-Nola.

possibility is that by the time Hirsch got the opportunity to sue Pepsi, the rival drink was so well established he feared he might lose the case.

The point appeared moot, of course, when Pepsi went out of business. But the existence of an unchallenged trademark proved to be a temptation. In 1923, the makers of Taka-Kola lost an infringement suit, tried again with Takola and lost, and were on the verge of defeat in a third suit, with Vim-Kola, when they bought the rights to the name Pepsi-Cola. For a time, they used Taka-Kola syrup to bottle and sell a product they called Pepsi-Cola. They, too, gradually went bankrupt, but not before drawing the notice of Charlie Guth.

Fully aware of Pepsi's odd past and future promise, Guth believed he had the perfect weapon to inflict a costly lesson on Neal Harris and the Coca-Cola Company. He had one of Loft's chemists mix up a syrup that tasted more or less like Coca-Cola's, then christened it Pepsi-Cola, and began serving it at the fountains in his candy stores.

Taking the bait, the Coca-Cola Company retaliated. At first, the reprisals had a frisky, fraternity-boy air. Posing as legitimate customers, some of the company's investigators went into Loft, Mirror, and Happiness stores, ordered a Pepsi, took a sip and loudly spat it out, saying it tasted awful. When that failed to work, Hirsch sent other investigators around who set to work in deadly earnest trying to prove that Guth's soda fountains were illegally substituting Pepsi in place of Coke.

The problem, from the Coca-Cola Company's point of view, was that Guth knew his law. He understood perfectly well that if a customer asked specifically for Coca-Cola, another product could not be served in its place without the customer's okay. Warned by Guth to be careful, most of his soda jerks dutifully explained to customers that the cola they were getting was Pepsi-Cola, not Coke. (It was the origin of the ritual caveat—"No Coke! Pepsi!"—that eventually became the subject of a recurring skit on the television show "Saturday Night Live," with John Belushi playing a counterman in a diner who barked the phrase at his customers over and over in a thick accent.) But there were inevitable slips, and Coca-Cola's investigators kept returning again and again until they had accumulated what they claimed were several hundred instances of substitution.

Anticipating the impending lawsuit and court battle, Guth tried a publicity gimmick aimed at securing the high ground. He told the New York newspapers he was offering a $10,000 reward for information leading to the detection of any substitution of Pepsi on calls for other soft drinks at any of his stores. Answering in kind, Hirsch had the Coca-Cola Company make a formal claim on the money, asserting that clerks were cheating in all of the Loft, Happiness, and Mirror stores.

The dispute over the reward money captured the fancy of New York's tabloid press and guaranteed heavy coverage for what happened next. The Coca-Cola Company filed suit in Wilmington, Delaware (where both companies were incorporated), charging a pattern of repeated substitution and asking that Guth be barred from selling Pepsi in his stores. Guth responded by filing a series of countersuits in New York alleging harassment and seeking $10 million in damages. The Coca-Cola Company, Guth claimed in one of the suits, had threatened him with "destruction."

With a keen interest in the showdown between the two soft drink companies (and with blind prescience) the editors of the *New York Journal* reported the story under a headline calling the dispute the "BEVERAGE BATTLE OF THE CENTURY." So it would prove to be.

The first courtroom engagement in what came to be known as the Cola Wars took place in Chancery Court in Wilmington, Delaware, in the first week of June 1933. Hirsch called wave after wave of his investigators to the stand to describe episodes in which soda jerks in Guth's stores had served Pepsi-Cola when Coca-Cola was ordered. He also called more than a hundred former Loft employees, badgering them about their activities. As the parade of witnesses continued, the judge, Chancellor J. O. Wolcott, grew increasingly exasperated. It was plain that some substituting had occurred, perhaps even widespread substituting, but Guth's side presented convincing evidence that the store managers had instructed their employees not to do so. The Coca-Cola investigators had zeroed in on a few repeat offenders, returning time and again to make hundreds of "trap orders" meant to compound the offenses and exploit them. It was overkill.

Chancellor Wolcott ruled in Guth's favor. If the Coca-Cola Company had evidence that some of the fountain clerks in the Loft, Happiness, and Mirror stores were guilty of substitution, the judge said, the proper response would have been to notify Guth and complain to him in writing, thus allowing him an opportunity to intervene with his employees and correct the problem on his own. Instead the company had concentrated on accumulating evidence from stores where the offense was most common, and rather than warn Guth of the situation it had done the precise opposite.

The ruling was a great victory for Guth, but it was also a costly one. Showing he was not completely credulous, and that he understood Guth was no innocent schoolboy, Chancellor Wolcott ordered the Loft stores to pay the court costs of the case, which had reached the substantial level of about $60,000. By inflicting pain on both sides, Wolcott ensured that the struggle between them would continue, and that it would be conducted with a new sense of rancor.

For his part, Guth decided to begin competing with Coca-Cola on a far grander scale. He moved beyond New York City in his marketing to cover most of the Northeast and Atlantic Coast, and he inaugurated bottling operations, moving the contest out of the soda fountains and into the increasingly lucrative arena of grocery stores and other retail outlets.

At first, Guth struggled. He tried putting Pepsi in 6½-ounce bottles, the same size as Coca-Cola's, and found he could not compete. He tried doubling the size of the bottle and the price—12 ounces for a dime—and got nowhere. In the last months of 1933, facing defeat, he even extended a feeler to Atlanta to see if the Coca-Cola Company had any interest in buying him out. It did not.

Then Guth hit upon a brilliant idea. What about doubling the size of the bottle while holding the price at a nickel? Pepsi could not begin to match the prestige of Coca-Cola, but it could sell twice as much for the same price, a concept any thirsty consumer could grasp in an instant and appreciate, especially as the grip of the Depression continued to squeeze the country. The additional costs would be negligible since most expenses—filling, capping, packaging, labor, handling, transportation, and advertising—would remain the same. Doubling the ingredient amounts would require only a relatively minor increase in outlay.

Almost overnight, sales of Pepsi—in clunky, used, 12-ounce beer bottles—began to rise. In New York and the other urban centers of the Northeast in particular, where Coke had never engendered the popularity and product loyalty it enjoyed elsewhere, Pepsi-Cola moved quickly into the kitchens (if not the drawing rooms) of families who had to watch their money and get the most they could for a nickel. In 1934, Guth sold $450,000 worth of Pepsi-Cola and cleared revenues of about $90,000.

In Atlanta, the emergence of a competing soft drink, even one whose sales were approximately one-hundredth the size of Coca-Cola's, provoked anger and a cold sweat. Woodruff truly believed that Guth was a common thief trying to steal Coca-Cola's good name. Just as Asa Candler once denounced the "unscrupulous pirates" who copied his soft drink, Woodruff growled darkly about "chiselers" who traded on the reputation he and others had built so arduously for Coca-Cola. Woodruff could not bring himself to speak the word "Pepsi," and for many years, well into the 1960s, the company's internal communications referred to the rival soft drink only as "the Imitator," as if it were the villain in a morality play.

Woodruff's contempt for Guth was transformed into a sharper emotion, vengefulness, in the summer of 1934, when Pepsi-Cola began doing business in Canada. It was bad enough that Guth coveted Coca-Cola's great success in Montreal and other Canadian cities and wanted to snatch a share of it, but the way he went about the campaign was designed to enrage Woodruff: Guth hired away one of the Coca-Cola Company's top men in Europe, D. S. Hawkes, to be Pepsi's Canadian general manager. Woodruff prized loyalty above all other virtues, and the defection ensured that he would pursue total victory over Guth and Pepsi at almost any cost.

Before Woodruff could pace off the steps and have his duel with Guth, there was an urgent need to bring order to the Coca-Cola Company's own house.

In most respects, surviving the Depression and the threat of Repeal made the Coca-Cola Company a vastly stronger institution. Certainly it was richer. The multiplying value of Coca-Cola stock relieved the distress of the company's major shareholders, saving their fortunes and turning them into millionaires once again. Woodruff was able to pull himself out of debt at long last and cover the remaining losses from his short sales. His father, hastening to beat the imposition of new federal gift and inheritance taxes, divided the major portion of his estate between Ernie and his three sons and gave each of them more than $1 million in securities, mostly Coca-Cola stock.

But the company's affairs were more tangled and complicated than ever, marked—and in some ways scarred—by Robert Woodruff's unyielding determination to take complete control of every aspect of the business. Being president was not enough. After years of painful clashes with his father and others, Woodruff set himself toward a goal of absolute authority over everyone in the company, from the board of directors down to the janitors. He wanted the final say on every decision, major and minor, and he no longer had much tolerance for people who disagreed with him.

Woodruff's bid for total power took an important turn when he lost patience with J. T. Lupton, the parent bottler from Chattanooga, who kept pestering the home office with suggestions about selling Coca-Cola. Lupton's advice often was flawed (he disapproved of the company's "Pause That Refreshes" slogan and protested vehemently against the Sundblom Santa) and he had the irritating habit of referring to his own brilliance in making a fortune selling Black Draught during the Panic of 1893, as if that provided a model for marketing Coca-Cola four decades later. He routinely refused to heed the advice of his own chief administrator, the highly respected Veazey Rainwater.

Lupton constantly belittled Woodruff's top officers as "the kindergarten" and demanded the right to devise his own advertising materials. He distrusted the company's soda fountain salesmen and repeatedly accused them of trying to undercut his bottlers. He might have been dismissed as a harmless old mossback, except that he kept threatening litigation.

In order to rid himself of Lupton, Woodruff began negotiating with J. B. Whitehead's widow and sons to buy their half of the parent company—a strategy that at first glance yielded little hint of how it might promote harmony or improve the company's relations with its bottlers or strengthen Woodruff's hand in any other way. Lettie Pate Evans, as she was known after remarrying, was a complaisant, affable woman, but her two sons were hellions, a pair of hard-drinking men with disagreeable natures and track records spotted with scandal and divorce.

The younger son, Conkey Pate Whitehead, carried a particularly bad reputation. He first married Julia Murphy, the daughter of a prominent Atlanta banker, then divorced her and took up with a pretty young actress from New York named Frances Porter. When he threw Miss Porter over, she tracked him down to his yacht in Havana harbor, clambered aboard, and went after him with a slipper and a hatpin, driving him ashore. He demanded that the Cuban authorities deport her; she responded by filing charges of false arrest, imprisonment, and assault and battery, along with a $250,000 breach of promise suit.

By the time the matter came to trial, Whitehead was remarried. A photograph from the period shows a smug, dapper fellow in two-tone shoes and a blazer, perched next to his bride atop a pillowed sofa, petting a lapdog. Marian Hughes, the new Mrs. Whitehead, did not last long. Whitehead was an alcoholic, given to bouts of drinking so fierce that a private detective had to follow him around trying to keep him from harming himself and others. One night, during a late-hours party at the old Atlantan Hotel, the detective discovered Whitehead passed out on the floor, turning blue, and sent for a doctor. The examination revealed that Whitehead was lying in his own vomit, turning the color of the dye in the carpet.

Jack Spalding, the founder of King & Spalding, assigned his son, Hughes, to look after Whitehead's interests—and then questioned how Hughes could tolerate the assignment Whitehead "is so thoroughly demoralized and debauched and has such a big streak of mean in him," Spalding once wrote his son, "that I wonder sometimes how you have ever gotten along [with him] as well as you have."

For all their considerable shortcomings, though, the Whiteheads had one quality that appealed tremendously to Woodruff: They had not the slightest interest whatsoever in working for a living. They never tried to interfere in the Coca-Cola Company's business—never gave advice, never second-guessed a decision, never so much as asked a question. They simply wanted to get and spend their royalty from syrup sales, and as long as the money came in they were, after their own fashion, happy. (Hughes Spalding once visited Conkey Whitehead and his mother when they were staying in a suite at the Hotel Pierre in New York; they were "guarded and protected from outside influence," he observed, "as if they were royalty.")

The Whiteheads agreed to sell their stake as parent bottlers back to the Coca-Cola Company in exchange for common stock. From their point of view, the trade was of little consequence. Instead of a royalty, they would begin receiving roughly the same amount of income in the form of regular dividends. But for Woodruff, the deal had several significant aspects. First, it gave him the leverage to force Lupton to sell out, too. As an equal partner, Woodruff now had the ability to checkmate Lupton on any matter that provoked a disagreement, and rather than spend his remaining years fighting the home office the old man quietly surrendered. He traded his rights in a stock deal similar to the Whiteheads' and retired.

Second, the deal marked a turning point in Woodruff's relationship with his father. Characteristically, Ernest Woodruff opposed the deal with the parent bottlers—or, to put it more precisely, he kept up a steady barrage of criticism of the way Robert was negotiating the deal. From his farm outside Richmond, Ernest launched a fusillade of letters, telegrams, and phone calls to his son and other officers and directors of the company, warning that they were being out-traded and paying too much and were likely, as he said in one letter, to find themselves "in a jam."

Refusing to bend to his father's will or heed his prophecies of doom, Robert pushed the deal through with the support of Will Bradley and the other directors, including Ernest's long-time deputy, Tom Glenn. As was his increasingly frequent habit, Ernest boycotted the board meeting when the deal was approved, but his sullen recalcitrance no longer seemed to carry much weight. With the company making profits again, the board had renewed confidence in Robert's judgment, and the deal with the parent bottlers marked the beginning of the end of any further serious efforts by Ernest to challenge his son over matters affecting the company.

Finally, and most important, Robert Woodruff's negotiations with the Whiteheads brought him back into close contact with John Sibley the lawyer at King & Spalding who had won the parent bottlers' bitter suit against the Coca-Cola Company back in 1920. Sibley's firm still represented the Whiteheads, whose large block of Coca-Cola common stock now gave them a voice in the company's ownership.

Woodruff found that he liked Sibley. There was a tremendous amount of resentment and bad blood directed at Sibley by some of Coca-Cola's officers and directors, especially by Harold Hirsch, who had been so badly humiliated by Sibley during the trial, yet it was one of Woodruff's qualities that he was willing to befriend men who had bested him in order to take advantage of their abilities. Woodruff came to appreciate Sibley's temperament—his utter discretion, his innate conservatism and common sense and especially his competitive, often combative nature, one that was very much like Woodruff's own. For ten years, Woodruff had been trying to assemble a team of his own to run the company exactly as he wanted it run, and in Sibley he found the final piece in the mosaic.

In the months before and after the Whitehead deal was closed, Woodruff cultivated an intimate bond with Sibley that lasted until the two men were in their nineties. Sibley rose in a very short time to become Woodruff's top adviser in the company, shaping decisions not only in matters of law but in the areas of personnel, politics, advertising, and general business strategy. Sibley became Woodruff's personal lawyer. He handled Woodruff's taxes and fought the IRS for him, spent time with him at his plantation, traveled to Europe with him, and got a car from him as a Christmas present. Before long he became Woodruff's choice as heir apparent for the presidency of the company.

It was not a relationship of equals. Woodruff dominated Sibley just as he did every other man and woman who ever worked for him. Georgians who remember Sibley in his later years as perhaps the most distinguished man of public affairs in the state, chairman of the famous Sibley Commission that brokered the peaceful desegregation of the public schools, might have blinked in disbelief had they seen him back in the 1930s at one of Bob and Nell Woodruff's anniversary parties, dressed in a Western costume, singing this doggerel tribute:

I'm a Woodruff fan,
And I like his plan.
He's a sho' nuff friend
And a real he-man.
As a legal guide
I can give advice,
But it must be right,
'Cause he don't ask twice;
When I'm slow to act
Well, he don't act nice—
Yippi-I-Oh-Ki-A,
Oh, Yippi-I-Oh-Ki-A!

When Sibley, a widower whose first wife had died in a car accident, got remarried in a service in suburban Philadelphia, Woodruff called up the governor of Pennsylvania and insisted on arranging a conspicuous motorcade through several small towns from the bride's home to the church, led by three motorcycle policemen in full regalia. "John didn't like it a bit," his partner Hughes Spalding recalled, "but he couldn't do anything about it."

Nonetheless, Sibley came as close as anyone ever did to serving Woodruff as a right-hand man, and his influence on Woodruff's thinking changed the course of Coca-Cola's history.

Sibley's ascendancy put an indelible stamp on the company, and the reason was that for all his considerable talents in other disciplines, at the end of the day he was first and foremost a lawyer—an advocate. In the second half of the decade of the 1930s, as it faced heightened competition from Pepsi-Cola and other soft drinks, the Coca-Cola Company arrived at a fork in the road. It could compete in the marketplace, using the tools of advertising and salesmanship, building upon the reservoir of goodwill it enjoyed from the American people, or it could compete in the courtroom, using lawyers. Largely because of Sibley, the company took the second course.

Harold Hirsch's days as the Coca-Cola Company's general counsel were numbered as soon as Sibley came on the scene.

For public consumption, Hirsch's eclipse was explained as a matter of geography. Late in 1934, fearful that Georgia Governor Eugene Talmadge was about to impose heavy taxes on securities held by the wealthy, Woodruff moved the corporate headquarters of the Coca-Cola Company to Wilmington, Delaware, where he and several other officers established legal residency.

Hirsch was reluctant to abandon Atlanta, where he was the senior partner of his law firm and president of Scripto, the big pen and pencil manufacturing company, and his refusal to move to Wilmington, it was said, led to his replacement by Sibley.

Yet that was not quite so. Woodruff's move to Wilmington was partly a charade. He rented a house there and had his office furniture shipped to a modest, two-room suite of offices in the Du Pont Building, leaving the fourth floor at Plum Street looking "a little queer and forsaken," in the words of a secretary who stayed behind. But Woodruff continued to spend a great deal of time in Atlanta—he would buy tickets and reserve train seats between Wilmington and Atlanta for days on end, just to be sure he and his men could travel back and forth at their convenience— and he offered Hirsch wide leeway in attending to his interests at home.

The deeper problem, aggravated by personal friction, was Sibley's fundamental disagreement with the way Hirsch was conducting the company's legal business, from tax planning to political lobbying, from renewing the patent on its bottle to formulating the strategy for fighting off competitors.

Hirsch wanted to finish the fight with Pepsi. "It was my desire," he said later, "to try out the question, without any secondary questions or other matters being involved, as to whether Pepsi-Cola was an infringement of Coca-Cola." Hirsch conceded that it was far too late to challenge Pepsi-Cola's trademark in the United States, where it had been used in various incarnations for several decades. Instead he came up with the idea of a flanking maneuver—an attack on Pepsi in Canada, where Guth had just begun doing business. One of the key tests of a trademark's validity was how long it had been established, and in Canada, unlike the United States, Pepsi was a newcomer little known to the buying public.

Sibley took a dim view of Hirsch's brainstorm. Even if it proved successful, he reasoned, it would be of no help in the United States. And there was no guarantee that it would be successful. Sibley scrounged around in the Coca-Cola Company's legal archives and found a transcript of the testimony Hirsch had given years earlier when he said he did not believe Pepsi-Cola was an infringement of Coca-Cola's trademark. Sibley also found a letter Hirsch once wrote to one of the Coca-Cola Company's directors giving the same opinion. If Guth's lawyers were clever enough to discover and produce either document, Sibley figured, the potential for embarrassment in the courtroom was huge.

Using the issue of residency in Wilmington as a wedge, Sibley pushed Hirsch aside as Coca-Cola's general counsel and took over the reins of the company's legal affairs. But, as if to grant Hirsch one last favor for his three decades of faithful service, Woodruff and the board gave him the green light to sue Pepsi in Canada.

———

On May 30, 1936, Coca-Cola's Canadian subsidiary filed suit against Pepsi in the Court of the Exchequer in Ottawa.

Trial began a few months later, and at first it appeared Hirsch had been right after all. Guth was embroiled in a separate lawsuit back in the United States with Loft, Incorporated, over the ownership of Pepsi and was either too preoccupied or too poor to mount a first-rate defense in the Canadian case.

His counsel, W. D. Herridge, became the butt of a string of caustic remarks from the bench. Endeavoring to explain why Guth had introduced Pepsi in Canada, Herridge wandered into a dense soliloquy and had trouble extricating himself. "It is true," he noted, "that within the last three or four years the soft drink business through the continent has boomed in an amazing way, really out of keeping with the general recovery in merchandising. Precisely why that is, I do not know. It may be on account of prohibition, or something. . . . Montreal is a tremendous soft drink center, in some respects the greatest soft drink center in the world. Why that should be I do not know, but it is. . . ." Interrupting him, Justice A. K. MacLean snapped, "There is a lot about it you don't know!"—an observation that proved keen as Herridge went on to assert mistakenly that coca comes from the coconut.

Completely outmatched, Herridge had all he could do to fend off the judge, let alone mount a challenging case against Coca-Cola. Though the formal ruling would not be handed down for several months, it was clear the court sided strongly with Coca-Cola. In fact, if one listened carefully enough, it almost seemed that history was repeating itself. Justice MacLean sounded a great deal like Edward Sanford, the federal judge in Chattanooga who had directed a verdict in Coca-Cola's favor a generation earlier.

As a younger man with a better ear for nuance, Hirsch had taken alarm at the ease of Coca-Cola's victory over Dr. Wiley, anticipating the difficulties that would arise on appeal. This time he failed to hear the warning signals. With Hirsch's blessing, the company's Canadian lawyer, Russel Smart, decided not to present any evidence showing that consumers were deceived by the name Pepsi-Cola. Fearful of taxing the judge's patience, perhaps, or still stinging from the accusations of overkill in their legal assault on Guth and Pepsi in the substitution case in the United States, Smart and Hirsch opted for a quick, two-day trial in which they relied on what they believed was the inescapable obviousness of Guth's desire to steal Coca-Cola's business by peddling a confusingly similar product.

But they blundered. Trademark law is a knotty subject, yet there is one important principle at the heart of it that is quite simple: It is designed to protect the public as well as the manufacturer. In layman's terms, the law says consumers have a right to get what they expect when they ask for a product with a familiar trademark. What complicates the issue is determining just how similar a rival product can be before it crosses the line and improperly confuses the public. The question is highly subjective, of course, and the Coca-Cola Company's legal files bulge with the tortured attempts of various trademark examiners and federal judges who tried to sort out right and wrong and often succeeded only in sounding faintly ridiculous.

Many judges took the position, in effect, that they might not be able to define infringement but knew it when they saw it. An examiner in one case held that Ko-Co-Lem-A was an infringement and then (in a literal reversal) volunteered parenthetically that he thought Lema-Koco would not have been. A federal judge in one jurisdiction found Mitch-O-Kola to be an infringement while another elsewhere gave a clean bill of health to Roxa-Cola.

The one protection Coca-Cola had against the caprices of these judicial rolls of the dice was the presentation of evidence that ordinary citizens found a competing product so similar that they were confused by it. Since the interest of the public was at stake, the opinion of the man and woman in the street counted. And other evidence was admissible as well: If another product used similar packaging or colors, or the same Spencerian script, or if its salesmen openly likened it to Coca-Cola, those facts could also be used in arguing the intent to infringe.

In the Canadian case, by forfeiting the chance to lard the record with testimony from people who said they mistook Pepsi for Coca-Cola, the company left the question of infringement solely up to the judge—and thus vulnerable to the second-guessing of the appeals courts. Hirsch's final victory for Coca-Cola was a shaky one, a verdict that would be wide open to whim and, as it proved, to whimsy.

Woodruff was not a humorless man, but the members of his staff had a very hard time working a smile out of him during the months that the fate of the trademark hung in the balance.

The one who tried hardest was Ralph Hayes, an eccentric fellow who came to the fore during the period of exile in Wilmington. Hayes joined the company as secretary and treasurer in 1933 and seemed destined from the start to act as a natural foil for Sibley and the grim seriousness of the company's legal business.

Hayes prided himself on teasing Woodruff, trying to keep him from becoming completely overbearing. On one occasion when Woodruff agreed to sit for a portrait, Hayes snapped off a quick memo urging him to change his mind. "Anyone who thinks you could be induced to sit still long enough to get a portrait painted is a dim-witted crackpot," Hayes wrote. "Any artist painting what he saw during a half dozen sessions with you would have to label the result 'St Vitus, Dancing.'"

It was a better idea to pose for a photograph, Hayes added. "I want to see the documentary chaos that surrounds you; those stacks of home work behind you that make the place look like a hoo-rah's nest in a hurricane; your old pipe reclining where you last left it; your collar a little askew; a half-empty glass of Coca-Cola; your spectacles lying in front of you—none of this pretending you don't need them. . . ."

Balding, bow-tied, pixie-faced, with a twinkle in his eye, Hayes was part humorist and part historian, a natural writer and twirler of tales—the only one of his time who understood what a good story Coca-Cola was. By training, Hayes was a banker, yet his real calling was in public relations. He was interested in having fun, and he tried to make Woodruff join him.

Even more than Archie Lee, Hayes appreciated the affection the American people felt for Coca-Cola, and he believed it was imperative to encourage that affection to grow. "We have an opportunity, if we are equal to it, to make Coca-Cola the national beverage, the great American drink," he preached to Woodruff. The phrase "as American as Coca-Cola" was gaining currency, in venues as diverse as the *Washington Post* and the *Music News*, and Hayes clipped every such reference and added it to a file he kept pushing under Woodruff's nose.

In Hayes's view, the company's fiftieth anniversary in 1936 was the perfect occasion to burnish Coca-Cola's image as an American institution. He commissioned the D'Arcy agency's writers to prepare a booklet saluting the history of Coca-Cola, and when their effort proved weak he gave Ralph McGill, who was then writing a sports column for the *Atlanta Constitution*, a $500 commission to try another version. Neither pleased Hayes entirely and eventually he did the job himself. The result was a delightful piece of puffery.

"Kings have abdicated, wars have raged, thrones have toppled, the map of the world has changed and rechanged," Hayes wrote (or rather, overwrote), "since that one-horse wagon rattled down Marietta Street carrying all there was of Coca-Cola in a single load on a lonely journey to a basement home. . . ." Hayes was determined to invest Coca-Cola with the proper portent, to mark its place in history and anchor it in the grand scheme of things. He went back in time to look at the world of 1886: Grover Cleveland was married in the first White House wedding, Queen Victoria celebrated the start of her Jubilee Year, gold was discovered in the Transvaal, a French company broke ground for the Panama Canal, and brilliant minds invented the typewriter, the streetcar, laces for shoes, and Coca-Cola.

With a fine, strong cadence, Hayes ticked off the many ways Coca-Cola had announced its name to the world in the half-century since then—"blown into glass, lettered in paint, moulded in metal, embossed on fibre, fashioned in flowers, burned in wood, engraved on gold, built with brick, flung into the waves of the air and thrown in smoke against the sky."

Hayes wanted to throw open all of the Coca-Cola Company's windows, air out the mustiness and shout his message from coast to coast. He was the one man in the organization, besides Woodruff, with a truly national perspective, and he yearned to tug the company's center of gravity away from the "quieter and pleasanter back-waters" of Atlanta and Wilmington toward the beckoning bright lights of New York City. To flourish, he believed, Coca-Cola belonged in the nation's cultural and financial capital. Naturally, he and Sibley became adversaries.

Hayes had devoted his life to escaping the drudgery and misfortune of his childhood. He came from Crestline, Ohio, the youngest son of a railroad engineer father and a mother so unhappy she made all ten of her children swear they would never marry. None ever did. When his mother died at forty-two, his father abandoned the family and Hayes was raised by an older sister. Two of his siblings died as infants and three others died in their twenties. He was the first in his family to attend college. He learned to be happy in spite of it all.

After earning a Phi Beta Kappa key from Western Reserve College in Cleveland, Hayes became a protegé of Newton Baker, then the city's mayor, and followed him to Washington when Baker was named secretary of war in the Wilson administration. After enlisting as a private and rising to become a lieutenant in World War I, Hayes went to work at the Cleveland Trust Company, the prototype community trust bank. He and Woodruff got to know each other during that period, and Woodruff later said he knew he wanted to hire Hayes in some capacity within a half-hour of meeting him.

Before their paths crossed professionally, though, Hayes went to work for the motion picture industry, joining the office that helped police the moral content of the movies and tried to fend off government censorship. For a time, Hayes lived in a tiny, bohemian town house in Greenwich Village in New York, a three-story, 9½-foot-wide space that had once belonged to Edna St. Vincent Millay. He became a prolific letter writer, one of the last of a breed of formal correspondents who kept up a running exchange of news and ideas with public figures from almost every walk of American life. One of his many pen pals (and an occasional dinner partner) was the writer Edna Ferber.

Hayes was running the New York Community Trust when Woodruff recruited him to begin spending part of his week working for Coca-Cola in Wilmington. For the next several years, Hayes divided his time between hotel suites in New York and Delaware, commuting in and out of the company's offices, serving as a combination jack-of-all-trades and jack-in-the-box, using his charm—and contacts—on behalf of the company.

Unlike Sibley, who often took a brass-knuckles approach to Coca-Cola's affairs, Hayes preferred humor and honeyed words as his weapons, which he demonstrated when he solved an unfinished piece of business left over from the crisis involving Merchandise No. 5. Thanks to Woodruff's lobbying of Congress, the company had succeeded in rewriting federal law to allow the importation of coca leaves, but in 1934 a lawyer in the Federal Bureau of Narcotics unexpectedly raised questions about the legality of exporting No. 5 because of its coca residue. Before the company could intervene, the new head of the bureau, the celebrated anti-drug crusader Harry J. Anslinger, issued a ruling that barred the company from shipping No. 5 out of the United States. Woodruff assigned Hayes to solve the problem.

Hayes complained loudly and frequently to Woodruff about the difficulty of the job. "This assignment of mine," he wrote at one point, "is as full of maggots as any piece of work I ever saw." Yet Hayes's technique was as smooth and sure-footed as a career diplomat's. He befriended Anslinger and began a long, intricate campaign to sweet-talk him into reversing his decision. Shameless in his flattery, Hayes bombarded Anslinger with compliments about the bureau's performance. "Not only has there been built up in this country what the rest of the world regards as a model agency," Hayes wrote Anslinger, "but domestically it has won the commendation of every element of the public, and that is a comforting and heartening thing, in spite of the long, hard labor it has entailed. More power to you!" Hayes did political favors for Anslinger, too, making sure that the Coca-Cola Company's nationwide network of employees and bottlers gave his agency support whenever it was needed.

Nor was Hayes above shading the truth if it suited his purposes. When Anslinger made inquiries about the rumors that cocaine from the company's processing plant in Peru had once been sold in the open market, Hayes responded reassuringly (and completely misleadingly) that the byproducts had been "disposed of with care."

In time, Anslinger came around to the company's view and issued a new ruling stating in effect that Merchandise No. 5 did not contain any derivative of coca—an assertion that was harmless enough, given the tiny amount of residue actually involved, but remarkable nonetheless because it ignored the truth and pronounced what Hayes called the "benediction" of the federal government on the Coca-Cola Company's use of coca leaves.

Woodruff was so pleased at the outcome he gave Hayes a brand-new Studebaker as a reward. Irreverent as always, Hayes thanked him politely but later suggested that "if you had wanted to make up for the wear and tear you had caused you would have had to give me the factory."

All through the late 1930s, as Sibley moved the company closer and closer to a showdown with Coca-Cola's competitors over the trademark, Hayes served as a counterbalance. He was an insouciant suitor, forever courting Woodruff's favor and trying to nudge him in a different direction. Where Sibley was serious to the point of fierceness, Hayes was bouncy and blasphemous, constantly looking for a way to provoke a chuckle and with it a shift in the corporate attitude. Instead of clashing with the company's enemies, he wanted to win them over.

Hayes made his point with perfection in one memorable instance when his friend William Allen White, the small-town newspaperman from Kansas whose editorials in the *Emporia Gazette* had earned him a Pulitzer Prize and made him a national celebrity, posed for a photograph in *Life* magazine on his seventieth birthday sipping a Coca-Cola. Hayes wrote a note of thanks for the free plug, and White responded with a letter whose words of praise remain familiar today to every member of the Coca-Cola Company's extended family. Coca-Cola, White wrote, is "a sublimated essence of all that America stands for, a decent thing honestly made, universally distributed, conscientiously improved with the years."

White's description became a mantra within the company, yet it was the little known second half of his letter that illuminated the problems Coca-Cola suffered because of management's frequently heavy-handed approach to business. A few years earlier, White told Hayes, the company had pulled its advertising out of the *Gazette* after he wrote a column with a mildly derogatory reference to Coca-Cola. White was open-minded enough to excuse the incident, but others who received rude treatment were not so quick to forgive and forget.

It would be an exaggeration to say that Sibley and Hayes were locked in a fight over the company's future. They rarely engaged in direct corporate combat, and when they did Hayes usually danced away before damaging blows were exchanged. (Once, when Sibley accused him of "harshness and trickiness" during a minor dispute, Hayes answered that Woodruff had accosted him that very day for being "a sentimental softie and a gullible pushover," a discrepancy in opinion that "must have given the gods a giggle.") Yet the two men came to symbolize a conflict that was dividing the company and threatening to give it a split personality.

Woodruff was keenly aware of the friction between Sibley and Hayes. In many ways he encouraged it, as a means of testing and assessing their visions of what the company was and what it should become. Coca-Cola was enjoying a phenomenal success. The common stock was split 4-for-1 after reaching its record high in 1935 and the price kept right on climbing. The company's market value grew to more than half a billion dollars, twenty times what Ernest Woodruff had paid for it in 1919. Syrup sales doubled between 1933 and 1937. With annual revenues passing the $50 million mark and heading steadily upward toward $100 million by the end of the decade, Woodruff's first responsibility, like a doctor's, was to do no harm. But how to keep the Coca-Cola Company healthy was a tough question to answer.

Like most businessmen, Woodruff kept a wary eye on the Roosevelt administration and groused about the New Deal's flurry of new agencies, regulations, codes, and taxes. "We are contending," he complained to a friend early in Roosevelt's first term, "[with] almost every imaginable kind of interference, or I might say distraction, from one's real business as well as one's pleasures." Determined to protect the company's interests—and profits—Woodruff made sure his friends in Washington maintained a state of virtual military preparedness so they could respond within a matter of hours to any change in political circumstances.

At times the company's defense mechanisms worked with impressive, clinical efficiency, as the events of late May 1936 demonstrated. Woodruff's closest ally in Washington was Senator Walter F. George—"George of Georgia," as he was known—the senior senator from Coca-Cola's home state and chairman of the Senate Finance Committee. Woodruff and George were personal friends. The senator's hometown of Vienna, Georgia, was near Ichauway, and Woodruff often stopped by the senator's modest, five-room house to visit on the way back to Atlanta from the plantation. The two would sit in a pair of white metal rocking chairs with green cushions on George's screened-in porch, discussing business and politics and what they could do for each other.

The senator was a man of immense courtliness, an old-fashioned Southerner with a manner so formal his wife, Miss Lucy, called him "Mr. George" and never by his first name, not even when they were alone. Once when Woodruff arrived for Sunday dinner George greeted him warmly and said, "Bob, come back in my room a minute. There's something I want to show you." George reached into a bureau drawer, pulled out a bottle of bourbon, and poured them each a drink. "I apologize for doing it this way," he explained, "but you know, Papa wouldn't approve." The senator's father, a teetotaler, lived with him, and he believed in showing his father respect.

George was about as far removed from the image of a back-scratching, hand-in-the-pocket politician as a man could get, yet the fact was that he became deeply obligated to Woodruff, and he did so in the time-honored way. According to a file of confidential documents in Woodruff's private papers, the Coca-Cola Company gave the senator a series of off-the-books loans totaling $8,000 during the Depression, apparently to help him save his farm. And the senator responded by looking after the company.

On the morning of Saturday, May 23, 1936, George learned that officials in one of Roosevelt's New Deal agencies, the Agricultural Adjustment Administration, were planning to push for a ½-cent per pound processing tax on sugar. Knowing the tax would affect the Coca-Cola Company, with its huge inventory of sugar, George obtained a copy of the proposal, slipped it in the mail to Woodruff, and urged him to wire his response. The letter arrived in Wilmington on Monday morning, May 25, and Hayes quickly calculated that the tax threatened to cost the company $2 million. Hayes phoned Atlanta, alerted Woodruff and Sibley to the situation, and then hopped the train to Washington, arriving in time to see George as the Senate was adjourning for the day. Hayes made it clear the company required his help.

Hayes spent the evening with George's aides, feeding them facts and arguments for the senator to use with his colleagues in trying to defeat the proposal in the Finance Committee. George had a subcommittee meeting the next morning at 9:30, which seemed to be the perfect time to nip the idea in the bud. Woodruff and Sibley arrived in Washington by overnight train from Atlanta with minutes to spare. Reading Hayes's briefing papers in a car as they sped to the Capitol, they arrived in time to give George final instructions and a pep talk before he went into the meeting. When he came out, the sugar tax was dead. Its life span had been seventy-two hours.

No hint of the company's role in the lobbying effort came out publicly, but insiders could guess what had happened. In St. Louis, Bill D'Arcy dropped Woodruff a note with a backhanded compliment: "I can see your fine Italian hand," he said, "as I read the conclusions as to what is [happening] in tax matters."

The company's influence on the media was often just as Machiavellian. In the days before the opening of the 1933 Chicago World's Fair, the fair president, Major Lenox Lohr, committed the dreadful blunder of refusing to give free tickets to the newspapermen who arrived to cover the event, thereby provoking a wave of bad publicity. The Hearst newspapers were especially critical, and there was even a brief worry that the fair wouldn't be able to open. With a major exhibit planned and hopes of selling a small ocean of Coca-Cola, the company responded quickly. Harrison Jones called Hearst's headquarters in New York, reminded the top editors that the company had just signed an advertising contract worth nearly a million dollars, and the coverage turned positive overnight.

Within the company, meanwhile, Woodruff's power was becoming almost absolute. After the annual stockholders' meeting one year, in a gesture of homage, Howard Candler walked up to him, shook his hand, and thanked him for "the splendid status of our business, due chiefly to your ability and efforts." The other directors felt the same way. Woodruff arranged what amounted to a series of retirement ceremonies for his father, signaling a changing of the guard. He had Sibley organize a black-tie dinner in honor of Ernest and Jack Spalding at the Capital City Club in Atlanta, and the two old antagonists buried the hatchet amid long-winded speeches and toasts from the city's business elite that went on past midnight

Less publicly, Woodruff made it clear to his father that speculating in Coca-Cola stock was no longer an acceptable activity. Stung by the consequences of his own missteps as a trader (and having narrowly survived a criminal investigation by the IRS as a result), Woodruff grew adamant that he and his family and the company's other major owners ought to hang on tight to their holdings as permanent investments. He never again sold a single share.*

Among the company's employees, Woodruff's stature grew to outsized proportions. His refusal to cut the payroll during the Depression earned him tremendous loyalty. Elizabeth Patterson, who went to work in Coca-Cola's traffic department in 1934, recalled vividly the way she and her

---

* Decades later, when Woodruff started giving away his fortune, becoming the greatest philanthropist the city of Atlanta has ever known, his stockbroker marveled at the antiquity of the stock certificates that emerged from the vault "dirty old pieces of paper, really filthy and dog-eared." They hadn't been disturbed in almost half a century.

coworkers felt about him: "That he was God." Others stopped well short of deifying him, but even Harrison Jones, who was not accustomed to sharing credit for the company's good fortune, gave Woodruff high marks for his "very skillful navigating" through an intensely difficult period.

When the directors voted everyone on the staff an extra month's wages as a bonus at the end of 1936, one of Woodruff's secretaries in Atlanta reported, "This office was about the happiest place. . .you have ever seen. After the first shouting died down everybody was going around with a broad smile. And I think you could have counted every tooth of every porter." Woodruff was remote from most of the men and women who worked for him, traveling constantly, coming and going by private elevator when he visited his Plum Street office, typically striding the corridors with his head down, rarely making eye contact. Yet it didn't matter. He was held in awe.

The pinnacle of the post-Depression euphoria that swept through the company came with the celebration of Harrison Jones's fiftieth birthday, a nightlong exercise in excess that took place at the Brookhaven Country Club in Atlanta on May 25, 1937. The guests, Coca-Cola's top fifty executives, had boutonnieres pinned on their lapels by pretty flower girls as they arrived. Mint juleps were served from an ice display on the terrace. The dinner table was a giant oval with a lily pool in the center. Perry Bechtel's band played and a female chorale sang popular songs of the day, including "Rhythm Is Our Business." There was a flaming dessert, followed by the presentation of a birthday cake filled with live birds. Next a group of actors played out vignettes of the honoree's life while the guests sang a spoof called "Old Man Jones."

In the grand finale, a line of black waiters paraded in through a door carrying gifts high above their heads as if they were porters on safari. They circled the ballroom twice to the sound of a trumpet fanfare, and then deposited their largesse, including cured hams, cases of wine, a sculpture made of petrified wood, and a complete set of Lenox china, in a pile at Jones's feet.

With his affinity for axioms, Woodruff liked to tell his men, "It's easy to see down into the valley and up the slope, but it's tough as hell to see over the next hill." Trying to foresee the company's future became a near obsession with him. He grew more restless than ever—moody, dissatisfied, demanding, full of conflict. The company's prosperity brought him anxiety, not satisfaction.

In a rare moment of introspection, Woodruff described his inability to achieve peace of mind: "I belong to the discontented," he said. "Maybe I was born that way. I'm never satisfied with the status quo." No one around him had any doubt of it. Giving orders in what one of his secretaries called his *"big* voice," Woodruff loaded all of the top officers in the company, including himself, with extra work.

The first man to crack under the strain was Arthur Acklin, the company's top administrator. A tall, long-faced accountant and former IRS agent,

Acklin served as a one-man clearinghouse for all of the company's major business dealings and also handled many of Woodruff's personal affairs. He was Woodruff's go-between in the turf wars and his sounding board whenever a tough decision had to be made—the human "crossroads" of the whole company, as Hayes put it Acklin relieved the pressure by drinking, which got out of hand from time to time, and eventually he suffered a mild nervous breakdown.

Hayes warned Woodruff that he was developing "a pretty tough reputation for wearing out the hired hands," but Woodruff seemed incapable of letting up on himself or anyone else. He told Acklin to take it easy, then began heaping him with duties again in a matter of days. "Thank goodness Bob Woodruff is out of town!" Hughes Spalding once exclaimed. "I like him very much, but he can talk to you two or three hours, and give you two or three months' work."

Woodruff's own health suffered from the battering. He, too, was a heavy drinker and found he had to force himself to go on the wagon or on beer-only regimens occasionally. He acquired a habit of literally worrying himself sick, starting with an episode during the Depression when a head cold deteriorated into an illness so severe he had to recuperate at White Sulphur Springs, the spa in West Virginia. His teeth bothered him terribly and he underwent a series of painful extractions. His eyesight worsened. A trick knee would slip in and out of place, especially when he was tired, leaving him hobbled. An acquaintance, A. D. Whiteside, the president of Dun & Bradstreet, ran into Woodruff on the sidewalk in New York one day and reported that he was "twitching" with fatigue and "looked like the devil."

Friends began noticing a deep change in Woodruff in the mid-1930s, what his old friend Gresham the minister described as an "urgent, wistful need" for some kind of faith or philosophy to give him comfort and a sense of purpose. His family urged him to spend more time going to church and reading the Bible, but Woodruff was unable to find solace in the conventions of religious worship. If prayer was so helpful, he liked to ask, then why did so many people engage in it only once a week?

Woodruff endured a succession of personal losses that left him yearning for answers. His wife, Nell, was unable to have children, and a favored young cousin they had virtually adopted was killed in a car accident at the University of Georgia when he was just twenty years old, full of promise. And the worst blow of all: Woodruff's mother, Ernie, began to suffer terribly from a condition that was misdiagnosed for quite a while as neuritis or neuralgia but turned out to be cancer.

A nurse who attended Ernie Woodruff during her drawn-out fight with the disease remembered how her son would come to visit her in the hospital and sit at her bedside, "just like a little boy, you know, with his arms folded on the bed, and her patting him on the head." Woodruff had long talks about life and its purposes with Ralph McGill, who was fast becoming an intimate friend and confidant, as they sat in the swing on the porch of

Woodruff's house in Atlanta or rode horses together in the predawn still-
ness at Ichauway.

One of Woodruff's nieces, Martha Ellis, recalled her uncle standing in
front of the fireplace at her house one evening, with his hand on the mantel, saying with feeling, "If I don't develop a philosophy I'm going crazy."
Friends worried that he would, or at least that he might be on the brink of
some sort of breakdown.

Nor was Ernest Woodruff much help. Inevitably, perhaps, Ernest found
it impossible to disappear gracefully from public life. Just a few months
after the fine testimonial dinner that marked his retirement, he was held
up at gunpoint in his office at Trust Company by a man who claimed—
convincingly—that Ernest had cheated him in a business deal.

The episode seemed to crystallize all of the elements, from physical
courage to reckless parsimony to unpopular politics, that had gone into
creating Ernest's reputation over the years. William Moyers was the director of the Georgia chapter of the Liberty League, a highly conservative
political organization dedicated to fighting Roosevelt and the New Deal.
He swore that Ernest Woodruff had arranged to give him the job and to
pay him a commission on any contributions he raised. When the money
failed to materialize, Moyers barged into Ernest's office, waved a loaded
pistol at him, demanded $30,000 in cash, and tried to take him hostage.

Ernest, then seventy-three, flatly refused to budge. He had only a few
good years left, he announced evenly, and was willing to die on the spot. He
unbuttoned his vest and invited Moyers to shoot. Instead, Moyers got the
money from Tom Glenn, fled the bank and escaped on foot into a crowd
that had gathered to watch a four-alarm fire blazing through a nearby
building.

For four days, Robert managed to keep the story out of the local newspapers. Then the FBI captured Moyers. Defying his son's good advice one
final time, Ernest insisted on pursuing criminal charges, which guaranteed
that Moyers's account would gain wide coverage. Moyers was convicted
of robbery, but only after a highly publicized trial in which he described
Ernest's duplicity in thorough, humiliating, and completely believable
detail. The affair was a "one hundred percent mess," according to Hughes
Spalding, one that left Robert feeling more unsettled than ever.

The pace of work at the company quickened. Woodruff talked about
delegating some of his responsibilities but never did so. Sibley and Hayes
and the other top men learned that when Woodruff urged them to show
initiative and make decisions on their own he didn't really mean it. "Some
day," Woodruff once told Hayes with exasperation, "somebody is going to
make an admirable suggestion and put it in effect without telling me . . .
and I'm going to be shocked and surprised, but greatly pleased." And Hayes
shot back, "The cemetery is full of the headstones of people who went
barging ahead with what they were pleased to regard as admirable ideas

without consulting you." The only safe way to proceed, Hayes added, was by obtaining "an affirmative or negative grunt" from Woodruff.

And it was true. For all his protests to the contrary, Woodruff insisted on calling the shots, from items as minor as buying a new truck for the New Orleans office to the critical issue of what to do about the competition.

At a board meeting not long after the Pepsi trial in Canada, Harold Hirsch withdrew once and for all from the company's legal affairs and turned the job over to Sibley.

Just as Hirsch had once proven to be far more aggressive than John Candler in pursuing the company's interests in court, Sibley now drew up a battle plan with the air of Armageddon about it, charting an all-out assault on Coca-Cola's competitors. He had nothing less in mind than wiping Pepsi-Cola and its cousins off the market.

Rather than shrink from the tough tactics the company had been using in accumulating evidence against other manufacturers, Sibley redoubled the efforts of the Trade Research Department and turned the company's inspectors into a team of hard-nosed detectives willing to push the limits to make a case. In one notable instance, he sent a dozen of them to Chicago to run a sting operation against the vendors of Royal Crown Cola.

As the company geared up for a final resolution of the trademark issue, however, not everyone saw the wisdom of fighting. Hayes found he had allies in his crusade to stay out of court. Gene Kelly, for one, thought Coca-Cola's competitors were making inroads not so much because they cheated or did anything illegal but simply because "they give more goods for the money." Pepsi and Royal Crown and some of the other new colas were "quite palatable," Kelly warned Woodruff, especially to "the lower classes who are not very discriminating." The name was not the issue, he added, as one could see by looking at the steady progress of Dr Pepper.

Harrison Jones thought competition was inescapable. Coca-Cola created a demand, he explained in his usual colorful way, "and the bed-bugs just crawl in." Rather than waste time in court, he believed the company would be smarter to prepare for a war of commerce, using its skills to compete in the marketplace.

At the D'Arcy agency, Archie Lee and his writers found themselves hamstrung by an impossibly rigid set of rules compiled by Sibley and Coca-Cola's other lawyers to provide maximum protection for the trademark. The first rule (in a memo that ran two and a half pages) was never to split the name Coca-Cola on two lines of text. The second rule was, "Any change in the style, color, or use of the trademark must have legal approval." On and on it went, including Rule 24, which in hindsight had a fine irony: "Never refer to Coca-Cola as 'it.'"

The dicta that were handed down by Sibley and his Legal Department could be as impenetrable as a medieval theological treatise. One of Lee's copywriters once submitted a piece of text that referred to the birth of Coca-Cola, saying, "A new kind of beverage was born. It tasted so good that more and more people grew to like it." For reasons best known to himself, Sibley sent back an amended version that read, "A soft drink with a distinctive taste was born. It was so good that more and more people grew to like it."

Sibley was determined to fight anyone who misused the trademark, inside the company or out. He understood how difficult it might be to win, but he didn't care. He detested the imitators who were "filching" Coca-Cola's name and "pirating its reputation." In all the trademark-related business that crossed his desk, the lone instance in which he recommended not suing for infringement involved a group of students at Bucknell University who put a sign on the door of their basement playroom that said "Coca-Cola Night Club." Sibley let them off the hook. In every other case, he urged litigation. He averaged filing a lawsuit a week.

With the company dividing into rival factions, a decision had to be made, and in due course Woodruff made it. He sided with Sibley.

Those who were surprised by Woodruff's choice, who wondered why he was preoccupied with the law when he might have been better off building on the company's fifty-year record of successful and often brilliant advertising and marketing, failed to take into account his complicated attitude toward the product Woodruff had a genuine reverence for Coca-Cola, a belief that it transcended the ordinary push and shove of American commerce and occupied a special place that deserved constant, diligent protection.

Of all the company's legal rules, the strictest was an absolute prohibition on any use of the word "Coke," and it came straight from Woodruff. Based on his interpretation of Justice Holmes's decision in the Koke case, Woodruff believed—wrongly, as it turned out—that the Supreme Court's protection extended only to the full trademark, Coca-Cola, and not to the familiar nickname millions of Americans used in ordering the soft drink. There was no legal basis for Woodruff's position, just a rigid adherence to past practice that bordered on superstition.

One episode in particular illustrated the way Woodruff's mind worked. It was an open secret within the company that Coca-Cola syrup went stale if it sat in a fountain proprietor's back room too long. The natural inclination of the company's salesmen and jobbers over the years had been to get shopkeepers to buy the big fifty-gallon barrels of syrup, but the practice created a problem with small retailers who took months or even years to use up their supply.

Woodruff was fully aware of the problem—he kept a file in his private papers marked "Fresh Syrup and More of It"—but he was also acutely sensitive to the potential for damage if any word of the issue was breathed in public. He quietly agreed to a new pricing policy designed to promote faster turnover by providing equal discounts for smaller units of syrup, yet it was not a subject he cared to discuss, as a group of officers in the Fountain Sales Department discovered one morning when he blew his top during a meeting in his office in Wilmington. Woodruff "very definitely expressed himsel:," one of the participants recorded,

> that during the past year there had been far too much discussion about tests, analyses, ingredients, et cetera, all having to do with the quality of Coca-Cola. Mr. Woodruff took the position that the quality of Coca-Cola today is, as always, above reproach and offered as evidence the fact that the company is a healthy one and has shown a rather good experience throughout the years, and *that it could not have done so if the quality of the product, broadly speaking, had not been good.*

Woodruff operated on the thesis that Coca-Cola represented an ideal, a view he was able to hold with complete conviction at the very same time he took steps that were necessary to make it better. Far from being simpleminded, his philosophy demanded an almost metaphysical approach to running the business. Facing competition, most executives thought about making changes, yet for Woodruff that avenue was closed. In his view, there could never be such a thing as a "new and improved" Coca-Cola, for the plain and inescapable reason that Coca-Cola was already considered perfect.

The sanctity he accorded the product knew few bounds. When Haddon Sundblom did his illustrations for the company's ads, for instance, he was under strict orders to deliver the canvases unfinished so that a draftsman with a fine eye for detail could paint in the image of the soft drink itself. Sundblom's broad, creamy brush strokes and evocations of inner warmth were fine for creating impressions and moods, but the bottle of Coca-Cola in the picture had to be an exact, flawless reproduction, right down to the tiny lettering of the trademark and patent registrations. Sundblom was free to reshape the popular concept of Santa Claus, that is, but not to tamper with Coca-Cola.

In a way, Woodruff found himself trapped by history. By creating an idea of the product that went far beyond its actual, utilitarian function—that of quenching thirst and providing a mild lift from sugar and caffeine—the company had elevated Coca-Cola to an ethereal plane that had little to do with how it tasted or the size of the bottle it came in. The point wasn't to compete with other soft drinks or to insist that Coca-Cola was "better," but to hold tight to the precious illusion that Coca-Cola was something completely different, above and apart.

And, of course, to sue anyone who disagreed.

On July 17, 1938, more than a year after the trial, Justice MacLean finally handed down his decision in the Canadian case. As expected, he ruled in favor of the Coca-Cola Company.

Sibley was pleased with the verdict, not so much because it was a victory but because it played into his strategy for escalating the fight. As badly as he wanted to do battle with Pepsi in the United States, he had been unable to find an opening that would let him go on the attack. Now, he believed, Pepsi would do his work for him. Guth and his lawyers were bound to respond to the Canadian verdict somehow, and Sibley was certain they would slip up and give him a chance to counterattack. With serene confidence, he assured Woodruff that "usually an unprincipled concern, if given an opportunity, would make a fundamental mistake."

As if to prove him right, Pepsi's lawyers rushed headlong into court in Queens, New York, and filed suit accusing the Coca-Cola Company of trying to create a monopoly through "intimidations and threats" and various other types of improper harassment. For good measure, they even petitioned the U.S. Patent Office to cancel the registration of Coca-Cola's trademark.

Unfortunately for Sibley, though, his adversary in the looming show-down would not be Guth. A few days after the Canadian case was decided, in a twist of luck, a judge in Delaware ruled that Guth had acquired Pepsi improperly, and ownership was restored to Loft, Incorporated. Instead of fighting Guth, who could be portrayed as an almost cartoonish villain, the Coca-Cola Company suddenly found itself up against a smooth, sophisticated investor named Walter Mack, who had been buying up shares in Loft for several years. Pepsi had become a valuable prize by 1938, with sales of almost $10 million a year, and Mack had captured it

Sibley's investigators were in the process of compiling a remarkable dossier on Guth, a 308-page looseleaf notebook that set out in vivid detail every dark secret of his life, including unsubstantiated rumors that he arranged to have his enemies beaten up by thugs. The shooting of his chauffeur was reexamined in depth (in a separate chapter entitled "Guth Kills His Negro Chauffeur") even though all evidence pointed to his innocence. Private eyes interviewed Guth's neighbors and collected gossip, including a story that Guth once gave his son-in-law a $3,000 wedding check that bounced. Sibley was preparing to destroy Guth in court, but all of it went for naught. Guth was now out of the picture.

Walter Mack was a respected businessman, a prominent member of New York's Jewish community, and active in Republican politics. His circle of friends extended from Mayor Fiorello La Guardia to the Ochs family, publishers of the *New York Times*. He was a graduate of Harvard. The worst that could be said of Mack was that he was a bit of a self-promoter, and that he associated himself with "hardheaded" businessmen who specialized in finding weak corporations, turning them around and taking a profit. It hardly seemed surprising when one of Mack's partners turned out to be an old friend of Ernest Woodruff's: They were in the same line of work.

Slashing away at Mack held little promise, and Sibley was forced to shift his attention and revise his tactics. As Sibley saw it, the company's fortunes depended on severely restricting the right of other manufacturers to use the word "Cola" in their trademarks or advertising. Leaving the Pepsi case on a back burner, he began assembling a monumental pile of evidence for a pair of suits he hoped would prove his point. One target was Dixi-Cola Laboratories, a Baltimore company that sold a line of drinks including Dixi-Cola, Kola Special, Lola Kola, Apola-Cola, and MarBert Cola. The other was Nehi, Incorporated, the manufacturer of Royal Crown Cola. If Sibley could get the courts to agree that those two businesses were guilty of infringement, he would be well on his way toward building a powerful wall of protection around Coca-Cola's trademark.

Sibley spared no expense preparing the suits. He wrote brilliant, book-length briefs setting out the company's position in fine, elegant detail. He had Harry Nims, a New York lawyer who specialized in trademark law, conduct a survey of hundreds of consumers to find out if they thought of Coca-Cola when they heard the word "cola." They said they did. Scores of soda jerks, waitresses, and bartenders were interviewed and asked the same question. Edward Rogers, the country's premier trademark lawyer, was retained to argue the cases in court.

The work was exhausting, and it exacted a price. On a Saturday morning in early November 1938, Sibley keeled over in a dead faint in his office and lay unconscious for about five minutes. Badly upset by the episode, he feared he'd suffered a heart attack and asked Woodruff if he could take some time off. Woodruff told him to rest up for a day or two and then get back to work, but Sibley insisted on taking a leave of absence of sixty to ninety days.

The incident shook Woodruff's confidence in the wisdom of Sibley's strategy. Here was a risky, terribly expensive, highly aggressive plan of attack, and its commanding general, didn't seem to have the stomach to carry it out. Even after Sibley recovered, Woodruff was left to wonder if he should settle with Pepsi out of court. Walter Mack, who knew Woodruff slightly, had initiated contact, sounding Woodruff out about a possible resolution of Coca-Cola's legal differences with Pepsi now that "we have our friend Guth out of the way." Woodruff put off answering but jotted down his inner thoughts on a sheet of paper: "We should go forward with a minimum of acrimony."

Meanwhile the other cases proceeded. By his own admission, Sibley's argument was a long shot. He conceded that the fight over the use of "cola" as a generic term was all but lost. Other manufacturers could make a soft drink that resembled Coca-Cola in appearance and taste, and they could call their product a cola. But, he contended, they could not sell that product by trading on the familiarity and popularity of the word "cola," because the Coca-Cola Company had single-handedly created all of the meaning and commercial value the word conveyed.

The problem was that Sibley's theory had a hard time meeting the test of common sense. True, the word "cola" might make people think of Coca-

Cola, just as the word "beer" might make one person think of Budweiser or another think of Pabst Blue Ribbon. Legally speaking, though, that did not matter. The Coca-Cola Company had to prove that hearing the word "cola" made people think *only* of Coca-Cola and of no other product or company. And that was no longer the case. People did not go into soda fountains and say, "Give me a 'Cola'" if they were ordering Coca-Cola. They asked for a Coke or a Coca-Cola, precisely because they had learned that if they didn't they might get something else. (And many of them *wanted* something else, Pepsi or Royal Crown or Dixi-Cola, because they knew they would get more cola for their money.)

The feebleness of the Coca-Cola Company's legal position was exposed during the Royal Crown trial when a surprise witness testified that he had overheard one of Coca-Cola's investigators coaching a bartender to swear on the witness stand that he had never tasted or even heard of such a thing as a "cola" soft drink. It was an absurd position, one that was hard to maintain with a straight face.

A slow collapse of dominoes was coming, and it began when the Canadian Supreme Court reversed Justice MacLean's decision in the Pepsi case. With no other evidence or testimony to guide their deliberations, the Canadian jurists relied solely on the subjective test of comparing the names Coca-Cola and Pepsi-Cola. "The general impression on the mind of the ordinary person," the court held, ". . . would be one of contrast, rather than similarity." Pepsi did not infringe.

With the Coca-Cola Company's trademark fight stuck in legal limbo, Walter Mack took advantage of the opportunity to show off his talents as a master salesman.

Pouring money into Pepsi's promotional budget, he gave out college scholarships, opened "Junior Club" recreation centers, assigned a team of skywriters to cross the country filling the air with his soft drink's name, and published a comic strip whose characters, "Pepsi" and "Pete," appeared in 205 newspapers and soon ranked third behind the Old Dutch Cleanser girl and the Planters Peanut man in public recognition. His most effective idea by far was a simple, 15-second jingle for radio:

> Pepsi-Cola hits the spot
> Twelve full ounces, that's a lot
> Twice as much for a nickel, too
> Pepsi-Cola is the drink for you.

Sung to the catchy tune of an old English pub song, "John Peel," the ditty proved so popular that listeners began calling stations and asking them to play it free. Mack calculated that by the end of 1940, it had been aired some 300,000 times on hundreds of stations from coast to coast. Sales rose accordingly. From a standing start seven years earlier, Pepsi seized a tenth of the soft drink market in the United States.

Capturing the mood of chagrin at Plum Street, *The New Yorker* ran a cartoon showing three men in Coca-Cola uniforms manning a machine gun, trying to shoot down one of Pepsi's skywriters. What galled the elders of he Coca-Cola Company most was the success of Pepsi's radio campaign. For reasons they could not fully understand, Coke's advertising on radio lad been mediocre at best, and more often just dismal, ever since the medium caught the public fancy toward the end of the Depression. By 1939, there were twenty-eight million families listening to radio, yet Coca-Cola was unable to make much of an impression on them. The company's ads were "as sound as parsnips," in Ralph Hayes's assessment, "but are hey any more inspiring?"

Little had changed since the start of the decade, when Woodruff pronounced himself "not wholly sold" on radio. He ruled out placing the company's ads on news shows or drama programs, believing their serious tone was incompatible with Coke's upbeat mood. Archie Lee vetoed comedies, arguing that the comedian always "steals the show." That left music and variety, and the company's track record in choosing popular performers vas unenviable, as typified by its sponsorship of Singin' Sam, the self-styled "homey Hoosier" who crooned for housewives during the day, and Andre Kostelanetz, whose orchestra played bland classical music during he "Coca-Cola Concert" on Sunday afternoons.

The underlying difficulty was that Coca-Cola, whose glory lay in the allure created by its visual art, had no message that could be easily communicated in words or lyrics alone. It had no answer to Pepsi's offer of twice as much for the same price, except to emphasize the idea of quality. And that idea was in jeopardy. In the summer of 1940, the editors of the magazine *Consumers Union Reports* ran a blind taste test pitting Coca-Cola against its rivals and found that no one could tell the difference between Coke and Royal Crown, Lime-Cola, or Double Cola. (A few of the tasters detected a slight difference between Coke and Pepsi: With a third more sugar, Pepsi tasted a little sweeter.)

"For the interesting fact that Coca-Cola can continue to charge twice as much as other brands and stay in business," the magazine said, "there seems to be a two-fold explanation. For one thing, there is the deceptiveness of Coca-Cola's well-known bottle. By using a 'wasp-waist' and fancy paneling, the Coca-Cola Company contrives to make six ounces look like much more than that. More important is the power of Coca-Cola's prodigious advertising, which has led people by the millions to form the habit of asking for Coca-Cola without even thinking of any competing beverage."

With that habit under attack, Coca-Cola began relying more heavily than ever on its social cachet, so much so that its ads risked crossing the line into snob appeal. For the first time since the turn of the century, when St. Elmo Massengale handled the chores, Coca-Cola's advertising took on an air of superiority. An ad in the *Ladies Home Journal* showed a patrician bride holding a bouquet of calla lilies in one hand and a bottle of Coca-Cola in the other, along with the suggestion, "There's always a moment for the pause that refreshes," as if a society wedding were likely to grind to a halt while the bridal party had a Coke.

In a story typical of the kind of publicity the company was generating, the *New York Sun* took note when the celebrated debutante Brenda Frazier introduced a new concoction, milk and Coca-Cola, to the 1,500 guests she'd invited to a grand ball at the Ritz-Carlton Hotel.

Hayes, for one, was alarmed. "I hope we shan't ever forget so much as an hour," he warned Woodruff, "that our great market is 'across the tracks.' While Coca-Cola is fortunately capturing the Union League and the Junior League, I hope the glamour of those conquests will never blind us to the fact that it is the man in the overalls who has enabled us to come as far as we have—and who could turn us back if we lost his favor." In fact, in the places where quantity counted, in factories and at construction sites, and in home sales in cartons, Pepsi was already outselling Coca-Cola. Disturbed at the trend, Harrison Jones thought it might be necessary for the company to begin marketing a cheap, 12-ounce drink of its own that would undercut Pepsi—admittedly a "far-reaching and drastic" step.

In the midst of this soul-searching, a second legal domino came clattering down. Against all odds, Sibley and his litigators had won the Dixi-Cola case at the trial court level. The verdict, like others that came before it, was a testimonial to the skills the Coca-Cola Company's lawyers brought to the courtroom. But like the others it failed on appeal. In January 1941, the Fourth Circuit Court of Appeals overturned the trial judge's decision and ruled that Coca-Cola had no inherent right to bar a competitor from using the suffix "-Cola" in a trademark, so long as the prefix did not unduly resemble "Coca-."

For many years, the judges noted, top officials of the Coca-Cola Company, starting with Asa Candler, had sworn under oath that kola was an essential ingredient in the soft drink, one of the important flavoring agents that gave the syrup its unique taste. They were the ones responsible for turning "cola" into the only word available to describe the kind of soft drink Coca-Cola was. Now, in a 180-degree reversal, the company was trying to insist that the amount of kola was minuscule, so tiny it could not be detected by modern science, and thus not really descriptive at all. But the judges said it was too late. The beverage had come to be called cola "in much the same fashion as other soft drinks are named for a small quantity of flavoring ingredients rather than the large quantities of sugar and water that mainly compose them."

Cola was as generic as ginger ale.

When he learned of the decision in the Dixi-Cola case, Sibley sent a telegram to Woodruff. "quite disappointing," it said. "means much more hard WORK."

It also meant more risk and more expense, without any certainty of success. At the rate Sibley was going, Ralph Hayes joked sharply, it wouldn't be long before the company's officers ended up in prison. "Do you suppose," he asked pointedly, "they have turkey on Christmas at [Sing Sing]?"

Sibley wanted to press ahead and go to trial against Pepsi-Cola in New York, but before he could do so Woodruff decided to apply the brakes. Mack had telephoned him a number of times, had even paid him a visit in person, asking about a settlement. So far, Woodruff had insisted on Pepsi-Cola dropping the "-Cola" from its trademark, which Mack refused to do. Now, with Coca-Cola's position badly weakened, Woodruff was no longer quite so adamant. When Mack made a new offer—to play down the word "Cola" in his advertising and put the focus on "Pepsi"—Woodruff asked for a written, off-the-record proposal: Mack sent one to Atlanta with his secretary.

Sibley hit the roof. If the overture from Mack were accepted, he said, it would permanently cripple the company's right to protect its trademark. The company had to keep fighting, "militantly" if necessary, or face disaster. But Woodruff rejected his plea. He gave Sibley a direct order to proceed with negotiations for a settlement, and Sibley did the only thing he believed he could: He went to his office, sat down at a typewriter, and carefully drafted his resignation as general counsel. The company was adopting a policy of "appeasement," he wrote, using one of the most loaded words of the era, and he would not be a party to "the infection of compromise." Then he put on his hat, got on the Marietta Street trolley, and leaded back to his law office downtown, thinking he was leaving the Plum Street building behind for good.

Woodruff personally concluded the settlement with Mack, as the two men agreed to drop all legal proceedings against each other in the United States and abroad. In the future, they agreed, their rivalry would be confined to the marketplace. Signaling the start of the new era, Woodruff gave the go-ahead for use of the well-known nickname "Coke" as a second trademark for his soft drink.

Sibley's farewell gesture might have made the perfect ending to the Coca-Cola Company's long legal drama, only the fates conspired to add a final indignity. Sibley had appealed the Canadian Supreme Court's decision to the Judicial Committee of the Privy Council, the body in Great Britain's House of Lords that reviewed cases from the lower courts throughout the Commonwealth. Believing he had a good chance to win a reversal, Sibley ventured to London himself, surmounting the considerable difficulties of wartime travel, to help with the oral arguments. It was his last chance to prove that his legal reasoning was sound.

On the appointed day, Sibley found himself in a committee room in Parliament before a panel of five law lords. Much to his amazement he learned that the principal legal test they planned to apply to the case consisted of looking up "cola" in the dictionary.

On behalf of his peers, Lord Russell of Killowen explained that "while questions may sometimes arise as to the extent to which a Court may inform itself by reference to dictionaries there can, their Lordships think, be no doubt that dictionaries may properly be referred to in order to ascertain not only the meaning of a word, but also the use to which the thing—if it be a thing—denoted by the word is commonly put. . . ." He wheezed on at some length, but his meaning was plain. If "cola" was in the dictionary, the Coca-Cola Company could have no proprietary right to the use of it. And so their lordships ruled.

They applied a second test to determine if Pepsi-Cola's trademark unduly resembled Coca-Cola's. They took copies of the two trademarks and turned them upside down—as if they were Chinese characters, in the analogy of one of the lords—to see if the general impression they made was similar. Despite "the tendency of words written in script with flourishes to bear a general resemblance to each other," the lords concluded, it would be "difficult, indeed impossible" for the word "Pepsi" to be mistaken for the word "Coca." They found in favor of Pepsi on all counts.

Thus the Coca-Cola Company's decade-long attempt to put Pepsi-Cola out of business came to a close in utter failure, with five mystified men in powdered wigs holding two soft drink labels upside down, wondering how in the world such a silly affair had ever begun.

Eight

WAR

In Brussels, on the afternoon of Monday, May 13, 1940, Carl West called together the employees of the Belgian Coca-Cola Company and asked them an urgent question. Would they be willing to join him in trying to escape the German invasion and flee to France?

It would be dangerous, West explained. They would have only a day to gather their families, pack a few personal belongings, and form a convoy of trucks for the eighty-mile trip to the border. The Blitzkrieg was three days old. German armies were racing into Belgium, France, and the Netherlands. No one knew what was happening, only that the lines of defense were crumbling with dismaying speed as the Germans swept over the countryside. West, the Norwegian-born manager of Coca-Cola's operations in Belgium, wanted to evacuate as much as he could of the company's equipment and inventory before Brussels was overrun. His workers said they would go with him.

Working feverishly all that day and the next at Coca-Cola's bottling plant and warehouse, West and his men loaded syrup and raw materials, including two tons of sugar, onto a hastily assembled caravan made up of five flatbed trucks, three paneled vans, and a passenger car. Most of the bottling equipment and the company's main supply of sugar had to be left behind. West closed out the company's bank account, advanced everyone a month's salary, and then hid the rest of the cash, 106,000 francs, the equivalent of several thousand dollars, under his clothes, "next to my skin."

The preparations took longer than expected and it was not until one o'clock Wednesday morning that the group finally got rolling. There were sixty-four people in all, about a third of them children. The oldest member of the party was over seventy, the youngest just eleven months. They made it safely to the French border and continued on toward Paris. There the news from the front persuaded them to keep going. The Netherlands had surrendered, Belgium was all but lost, and France was expected to fall, perhaps in a matter of days. Like tens of thousands of others, West and his group headed for the French coast, desperate to stay ahead of the Panzer divisions and the Luftwaffe, hoping somehow to escape across the English Channel.

They didn't make it. They got as far as Boulogne, a small harbor city on the channel just south of Calais and Dunkirk, when the German front line overtook them. After two nights stuck in the middle of what West called a "full-dress bombardment," his convoy was left in tatters. Caught in the street-fighting, strafed by *machine-gun fire during air attacks, four of his trucks were knocked out and most of their cargo was lost. The miracle was that none of his people were killed.*

With no means at hand of crossing to England, West reluctantly concluded that the best chance of survival lay in returning to Brussels. As he turned his group around to begin the long trip back, the trucks that were still running towed the others, and the little expedition looked very much like what it was—a band of hobbled refugees, limping home to submit to an army of occupation.

The onset of the Second World War confronted the Coca-Cola Company with an acute irony. For all their dogged efforts at building an overseas empire during the past decade and a half, Woodruff and his team could point to only one country that was a complete, unqualified success: Nazi Germany.

Ray Powers, the colorful American pioneer, set new sales records every year in Germany during the 1930s—100,000 cases in 1933, more than a million in 1936—and every year he watched with mounting alarm as the belligerence and ugliness of the Nazi movement quickened. At first he'd displayed an almost jaunty irreverence toward Hitler and his followers. It was not unusual, Powers reported to the home office, to see the tables in German taverns covered with bottles of Coca-Cola, "and back of each bottle a Nazi in his brown uniform." Hitler was agitating against the Jews, Powers noted, but it seemed to be mostly talk. That was 1933.

By 1937, Powers was worried. Coca-Cola's popularity had spawned competition in Germany, just as it did in the United States, and the tactics employed by some of Coca-Cola's rivals were tied directly to the anti-Semitism that was seeping through the country like acid. The most aggressive of the competitors, Blumhoffer & Company, the makers of a look-alike soft drink called Afri-Cola, began spreading a rumor that the Coca-Cola Company was run by Jews. Visiting a Coca-Cola bottling plant on a trip to New York, one of Afri-Cola's executives spotted a billing form with Hebrew lettering, slipped it in his pocket, and later made thousands of copies that he sent to restaurant and tavern owners—and Nazi Party members—all across Germany.

Coca-Cola's German salesmen began encountering open hostility. After several of them were pushed into fistfights in taverns and beer gardens, Ralph Hayes went to the Whitehall Building in Manhattan and saw Dr. Hans Borchers, the German consul general, to complain and ask for his help in squelching the rumor campaign. Nothing was done. "Hitler's brownshirts were getting to feel their oats pretty good," one of the company's American executives remembered, "and they were unpleasant to foreigners. They'd literally elbow you off the sidewalks into the streets."

In the spring of 1938, Ralph McGill and his wife took an extended trip through Europe to survey the political situation and sample a last taste of life on the Continent before it changed forever. At Woodruff's urging, McGill looked up Powers when he got to Essen, and the two men quickly formed a friendship. By surface appearances, at least, things were going well. Sales were still high despite the rumor campaign, and Powers had organized the first major convention in Germany for the company's bottlers and salesmen. He put on a memorable show: A stage was decorated to resemble the North Pole, with the bow of the "Good Ship Coca-Cola" serving as a platform for the various speakers and singers and comedians. But the most striking thing in the theater, McGill reported, was a giant picture of Hitler that covered the entire back wall—a picture that inspired frequent stiff-armed salutes and shouts of "*Heil, Hitler!*"

Doing business in Germany was becoming increasingly difficult and dangerous. Currency regulations made it impossible for the company to remove any of its earnings from German soil, and Powers relied on deceptive bookkeeping to conceal the extent of Coca-Cola's profits. The German government also placed severe restrictions on imports, making it hard for Powers to get an adequate supply of the secret ingredients needed to make the syrup. The company briefly considered setting up an illicit pipeline to smuggle Merchandises 5 and 7X into Germany through a trader in Constanta, a Rumanian port city on the Black Sea, before deciding the risk was too great.

As their visit drew to a close, Powers took McGill aside and confided in him. Coca-Cola's success in Germany had made him a rich man, Powers said, thanks to the royalty he got as the parent bottler for the country. But his wealth was in Reichsmarks. His money was stuck, by law, in Germany. Powers could see that the time was coming when he would have to leave Germany, and he'd already made plans to move to Paris with his family and continue his trailblazing work for the company there. He did not want to leave his fortune behind. "In Berlin, I'm a millionaire," he told McGill, "but in Paris I'm a pauper." He asked McGill to help him smuggle some of his money to France.

Many years later, McGill recalled the ensuing train trip vividly. He was riding in a compartment with his wife and a carefully concealed package stuffed with thousands of marks. Two large, uniformed guards came in and poked around, made a cursory search, and left, seemingly satisfied. Ten minutes later one of them returned unexpectedly and told McGill he had some questions he wanted answered. McGill felt his pulse pounding so hard he thought he might be having a heart attack. As it happened, the guard merely wanted to know what Norfolk, Virginia, was like because he had a cousin working there. "But in the meantime," McGill admitted, "I nearly died."

Powers was unable to escape Germany. He died in Berlin in the autumn of 1938, the victim not of Nazi menace or anti-American feeling, but of complications from the injuries he received in a mundane traffic accident when his car was hit by a fifteen-ton truck. His death left the affairs of the Coca-Cola Company entirely in the hands of Max Keith (pronounced "Kite"), a thirty-five-year-old German who had risen quickly to become

Powers's deputy. After joining Coca-Cola in 1933, Keith had impressed the executives in the home office with his hard work, his flair for recruiting other men, and the way he helped impose order on Powers's chaotic business practices.

In the winter of 1939, Woodruff and Arthur Acklin invited Keith to Atlanta to discuss the logistics of import and export trade and to get a "little better understanding" of his plans for the future. They let him know they were trusting him to look after their interests in the uncertain days and years ahead. They had no other choice.

On the same day the German armies swept into Western Europe, a bureaucrat in the Federal Trade Commission in Washington sent a form letter to the Coca-Cola Company asking for a wide variety of information about the product, from its advertising to its contents.

It was the kind of communication the men at Plum Street had learned to greet with intense uneasiness: a vague, impersonal demand, unknown in origin, quite possibly innocent but potentially the opening fanfare of a crusade that would play itself out in the courts and newspapers and inflict, great damage on the company.

As it happened, the complaint arose from a recent broadcast of the radio program "Larry and Sue" in Chicago. An announcer had advised listeners, "Give your children Coca-Cola often—the drink that doctors recommend." There might be a problem, the FTC warned, unless the Coca-Cola Company was prepared to prove that the soft drink was good for children and that doctors recommended it.

One of the Coca-Cola Company's recurring headaches was back, and it brought up an interesting question. What if the company *could* prove that Coca-Cola was good for people? Through its bottlers, the company had assembled a list of more than a thousand hospitals and medical centers where Coca-Cola was served. What if that list could be expanded to include doctors who recommended Coca-Cola for their patients? Nutritionists who advocated Coca-Cola as a source of quick energy? Everyone liked Coca-Cola. Few people thought it was harmful. Why not drop the defensive posture and fight?

The issue provoked a heavy debate at the top levels of the company. The Legal Department in particular warned that it was dangerous to make therapeutic claims on behalf of the product. But one of the younger lawyers seized on a different point. Ben Oehlert had joined the company in 1938, recruited from the legal staff of the State Department to handle lobbying chores in Washington and help guide the company through the diplomatic intricacies of getting established in foreign lands. Oehlert had demonstrated an irreverent, contrarian streak from the very start: When Woodruff gave him a bonus at the end of his first year, he expressed his thanks and in the same letter argued that such payments were inherently unfair and ought to be discontinued immediately.

As he contemplated the FTC inquiry, Oehlert found himself looking ahead and seeing a larger picture. Europe was now engulfed in war, and the United States was sure to be drawn into the hostilities. If the company had learned anything from World War I, if a prediction could be made with utter certainty, it was that war would bring shortages and curtail business. Nonessential products would face cutbacks and quotas, and Coca-Cola would suffer, perhaps drastically. But not if the government could be persuaded that Coca-Cola was vital to the war effort.

The FTC eventually dropped its complaint, but for Oehlert the episode was just a beginning. He was completely serious about building a case that Coca-Cola was an essential product in wartime. Hoping to find allies, he sent a memo to Harrison Jones asking for material in support of the company's age-old contention that factory workers and office workers alike benefited from "one or two brief rest periods or pauses" during the workday. Jones replied that the whole idea was sheer lunacy, likely to backfire.

Next Oehlert tried Ralph Hayes. "There is not the slightest doubt in my mind, and I am sure there is none in yours," he wrote Hayes, "that our product makes a very real contribution, not only to the normal economy of the nation but also to its emergency and wartime economy, as well as to the morale of both the civilian population and the armed forces." The company, Oehlert said, should begin pushing the government for official designation as an essential industry.

Hayes promptly dubbed the project "Oehlert's Folly." Yet he had to admit the young lawyer made an intriguing argument. Hayes was aware that many military leaders viewed Coca-Cola as a desirable alternative to beer and other alcoholic beverages for their troops. It was a difficult point to exploit, Hayes thought, but certainly one worth keeping in mind. He quietly instructed the D'Arcy agency to begin compiling endorsements of Coca-Cola by commanding officers at army training camps around the country.

Oehlert's gambit began to pick up momentum. In the spring of 1941, an American reporter in London named Eddie Gilmore sent a cable to Coca-Cola's New York office: "WE, MEMBERS OF THE ASSOCIATED PRESS, CAN NOT GET COCA-COLA ANYMORE. TERRIBLE SITUATION FOR AMERICANS COVERING BATTLE OF BRITAIN, KNOW YOU CAN HELP, REGARDS." The request captured Woodruff's imagination. After checking to make sure the wire was genuine, he ordered the Export Corporation to send a relief supply. Woodruff decided that Oehlert was right. Coca-Cola was a sort of "morale food" necessary for the war effort.

A major breakthrough came when the U.S. War Department asked the company to supply Coca-Cola to the American troops who were being sent to Iceland to set up a staging operation in the North Atlantic. Woodruff had believed for years that it was in the company's best interest to make Coca-Cola available to the armed forces, both to boost the company's association with patriotic themes and to spur product loyalty among the servicemen. Even if the company lost money, he thought it was a smart policy to guarantee that all those in uniform could buy a Coca-Cola for the stateside price of a nickel no matter where they were posted.

Woodruff gave a green light for the shipment of 17,000 cases of Coca-Cola to Reykjavik. He also approved a War Department request for the soft drink to be made available at American bases in the Pacific. That was how four Coca-Cola coolers came to be part of the rubble at Hickam Field after the Japanese attack on Pearl Harbor.

The United States went to war, and just as Oehlert anticipated, the government acted to impose strict restraints on business. Only it was worse than he'd imagined. Six days after Pearl Harbor, the federal Office of Production Management issued an order that threatened to cut Coca-Cola's volume in half.

The target was sugar. Hoping to prevent hoarding, the OPM placed a limit on sugar users of 80 percent of their 1940 levels. It seemed a reasonable standard, but as 1941 ended the Coca-Cola Company was closing the books on the most successful year in its history. Demand was up sharply. By Oehlert's calculations, as he looked ahead to 1942, the quota meant the company stood to lose one sale for every one it made. Not only that, the OPM outlawed large inventories of sugar. The company had diligently stockpiled enough sugar to last for years, and now it was being asked to sell a million hundred-pound bags of sugar back to the government at cost.

Woodruff led a contingent from Atlanta to Washington to protest. Starting with A. E. "Red" Bowman, chief of the OPM's Sugar Section, Woodruff appealed the order straight up the line, all the way to the office of Vice President Henry Wallace. There was no budging the government. The sugar order took effect on January 1, 1942, and its impact was felt almost immediately. The company began rationing syrup. Within days, the public was complaining about the shortage of Coca-Cola.

The sugar order chafed at Woodruff like a piece of sandpaper. He grudgingly agreed to obey it (and ordered his bottlers not to cheat), but he thought it was unfair. Archie Lee prepared a series of print and radio ads explaining the scarcity of Coke, including a folksy speech by Singin' Sam, who told housewives, "As all you ladies know, the war has made it necessary for the government to ration the use of sugar for everybody. I said, 'Everybody' And that, naturally, includes Coca-Cola." When he heard it, Woodruff angrily ordered the ad off the air. Somehow it made drinking Coca-Cola sound unpatriotic.

Oehlert and Hayes collaborated on a marvelous piece of propaganda, an oversize booklet with stars and stripes and an American eagle on the cover, entitled "Importance of the Rest-Pause in Maximum War Effort." Its bellicose text argued that "the grim and ruthless laboratory of War brings new and cogent evidence reaffirming the importance and significance of [the] relationship between fatigue, rest-pauses, refreshment and work output." It even quoted Ovid: "Alternate rest and labor long endure."

In the company's view, the government had a legitimate claim on the sugar needed to make high-nutrition molasses for the armed forces and industrial alcohol for munitions. And a priority was justified for the sugar used in processing dairy products and preserving fruits, vegetables, meat, and other vital foods. But the Coca-Cola Company deserved its fair share, too. Soft drinks, Oehlert argued, occupied a "paramount place" in American life. Hayes called Coca-Cola nothing less than "a part and symbol of a way of life for which a war is being waged."

None of these breathless imprecations had much effect on the government's administrators. In most other respects, the company's political clout was as strong as ever: With Senator George leading the charge, Congress killed a proposed national sales tax on soft drinks and also amended the Roosevelt administration's wartime excess-profits tax to save Coca-Cola some $8 million a year. The company even managed to slip one of its executives, Ed Forio, into a job with the War Production Board. But nothing could shake the quota on sugar.

There was, however, one very large loophole in the sugar order—an exemption for any sales of Coca-Cola to the military. Sugar used in syrup for military sales could be replaced without limitation. Oehlert bombarded the OPM with broad and inventive definitions of what constituted a "military" sale, arguing for the inclusion of post exchanges, National Guard units, USO clubs, the Red Cross, arsenals, ordnance plants, navy shipyards, Veterans Administration hospitals, troop trains, and ultimately any and every plant and office building in the country designated as part of the defense industry.

Coca-Cola's main interest was in serving the huge training camps that began dotting the map, many of them in the South, as the nation's general mobilization got under way. A small town like Fayetteville, North Carolina, with a population of 5,000, suddenly became a market of 60,000 or 100,000 thanks to the soldiers stationed at Fort Bragg. Oehlert managed to talk the government into dropping the sugar quota in the 250 fastest-growing counties in the country, and bottlers in those areas rushed to meet the demand. The commanding officer of the sprawling army base at Chester, South Carolina, sent the local bottler a map of maneuvers and a break schedule every morning so the truck drivers could meet his men in the field and serve them ice-cold Cokes.

Thanks to the military, Coca-Cola's volume in early 1942 was off only 16 percent from the year before, a far cry from the drastic drop originally feared. Revenues declined only slightly, and Harrison Jones worried that the company might be embarrassed if the public learned how little it was suffering financially after all its objections. When it came to lobbying in Washington, he warned, "we are too much in sight and too much in mind."

Still, the company fell way behind the burgeoning civilian demand, and complaints about shortages at soda fountains and retail outlets continued to frustrate Woodruff and his men. Making matters worse, the Pepsi-Cola Company was largely unaffected by the sugar order. Pepsi sold concentrate to its bottlers, who added the sugar in their plants. Most of Pepsi's bottlers were able to find supplemental supplies of sugar, in many instances by curtailing their production of other soft drink lines to meet the demand for cola. Pepsi's sales rose by a third, largely at Coca-Cola's expense.

Trying to think of a way around the sugar shortfall, one of Woodruff's outside advisers, Robert Mizell, the business manager of Emory University, recommended marketing Coca-Cola without sugar. He argued that even though it would taste bad, consumers were desperate enough to give it a try.

Woodruff declined that unappetizing piece of advice, but he did give his reluctant okay for the use of a small amount of sugar substitute in the syrup. "Of course you know I am very leery about these things," he told Arthur Acklin, "and much prefer not to do anything of the kind, except as a matter of life and death."

Other shortages vexed the company as well. Caffeine was down to less than a month's supply and the price shot up from $1.50 a pound to more than $7.50. Hayes, who was placed in charge of procurement, suggested making synthetic caffeine from uric acid and bat guano, another idea Woodruff vetoed. But Woodruff quietly approved a temporary cutback in the amount of caffeine in the formula. And he authorized a new process for Merchandise No. 5 that sharply reduced the need for coca leaves, after telling the chemists at Maywood "to be *very* careful not to change the flavor."

The company's harried attempts to secure a wartime supply of oil of cassia, the most exotic of the secret ingredients, took on the earmarks of a spy mission. The source of the oil was the bark of the rare *Cinnamomum cassia* tree, which grew only in the interior of the southern provinces of China. In 1937, as Japan pursued its relentless military campaign against the Chinese, Jimmy Curtis slipped across the border from Hong Kong and traveled by sampan and on foot to a remote village where the peasants harvested the rare tree and processed the oil. Curtis, who had risen from his job as secretary in the Coca-Cola Export office to become a field agent, spent the night under armed guard to allay the fears of the villagers, then managed to swipe a small supply of seeds and cuttings, which he smuggled to the Philippines. There Curtis hired a botanist to cultivate a crop, only to see the daring venture go for naught when the Philippines fell to the Japanese.*

Everything seemed to be in short supply: gas, glass, cardboard for car-

---

* With its crop in enemy hands, the company apparently had to rely on a temporary substitute for oil of cassia. According to Ralph Hayes's private papers, oil of cassia was dropped as part of the formula's ultra-secret Merchandise No. 7X, then was assigned a new, separate number, Merchandise No. 12, when supplies resumed after the war.

tons, tinplate for bottle caps. Eventually the company even ran out of rubber bands and other office supplies. "We are really having a hell of a time," Woodruff wrote a friend.

The company's fledgling European operations ground to a halt. In England, the Food Ministry echoed the cruel indifference of the Privy Council and ordered Coca-Cola and Pepsi to save costs by combining operations and making a joint product for the civilian market to be called simply "American Cola." Rather than "mingle our ingredients," as one of Coca-Cola's lawyers fastidiously put it, the company suspended business in Britain.

Meanwhile, the German government placed Max Keith in charge of Coca-Cola's properties in the occupied countries, and he sent word through the Coca-Cola bottler in neutral Switzerland that he would try to keep the enterprises alive. But with no means of getting ingredients, Keith stopped making Coca-Cola and began marketing an entirely new soft drink he called "Fanta," a light-colored beverage that resembled ginger ale. The executives in Atlanta doubted his loyalty. "I don't suppose," one of them said, "we even own the business anymore."

Keith was a man given to imperious gestures. His chauffeur made a practice of opening elevator doors for him, then racing upstairs on foot to hold the door when he got off. In cold weather he wore a greatcoat tossed over his shoulders like a cape, and it was not hard to imagine him as a Wehrmacht field marshal. For all anyone at Plum Street could tell, Keith and the company's German lawyer, Dr. Walter Oppenhoff, had joined the Nazi Party and confiscated the company's assets.

With business suffering at home and abroad, it became clear that sales to the U.S. military were the only means of expanding the company's market. But how to pursue that objective was a tricky proposition. According to the company's mythology, Woodruff simply put down his cigar one morning and barked at his underlings, "See that every man in a uniform gets a bottle of Coca-Cola for five cents, wherever he is and whatever it costs." The reality was a bit more complicated.

For one thing, the company had a hard time finding shipping space. Carrying out Woodruff's policy had been fairly easy before the United States was drawn into the war. But now a wide variety of munitions and foodstuffs took precedence over Coca-Cola in the cargo holds of the nation's Merchant Marine. And when a shipment did get through, critics sometimes complained about misplaced priorities. After a six-week supply of Coca-Cola arrived in Australia in May 1942, for instance, Martin Agronsky observed pointedly in a commentary on NBC Radio that there was a far greater need for "guns and planes."

There was doubt within the company, too, about the wisdom of writing a blank check. Supplying Coca-Cola to domestic bases was cheap. Sending it to the front lines when American forces went on the attack would be very expensive. As late as the summer of 1942, the issue was being reexamined. Oehlert wrote a long, thoughtful report to Woodruff urging him to proceed. Coca-Cola, he argued, "must be an inseparable part" of the war effort. If it were, he said, an affection for the soft drink "will carry through the lives of the young men now in the Army and through them will be reflected in generations to come." The company should "strain every resource to get and keep all of this Army business which it possibly can," he added, "regardless of the cost."

Woodruff agreed. "Anywhere for a nickel" remained the company's official policy. But even then, logistical headaches threatened to make it a hollow promise. The product was simply too bulky to send in bottles. A single month's supply of bottled Coca-Cola took up thousands of cubic feet of precious cargo space, and the empties had to be returned to the United States to be refilled.

To reach American GIs overseas in significant numbers, the company would have to build bottling plants where the fighting was going on, in the combat theaters. And it would have to be summoned there by the commanders in the field.

The first invitation came from Dwight Eisenhower. On June 29, 1943, he sent a classified cable from Allied Headquarters in North Africa asking for ten bottling plants and enough syrup to provide his men with six million bottles of Coca-Cola a month.

"I had them make a survey to see just what the men wanted," Eisenhower explained later, "and more of them voted for Coca-Cola than beer." That suited the general perfectly. He thought beer was bad for them, and Coca-Cola had been his favorite soft drink since boyhood. "I wish I could be home and go down to the cafe this morning and have a Coke with the gang," Eisenhower wrote a friend. "I can't do that here."

The cable triggered a frenzy of activity at the Export Corporation's headquarters in New York. Jimmy Curtis scoured the countryside badgering the company's bottlers for heavy equipment and assembled supplies of syrup and CO_2 gas and other materials, including a start-up stock of three million bottles. Then he went to the War Production Board in Washington and got a prized AA-3 priority for shipment.

Not surprisingly, the Pepsi-Cola Company cried foul. In a complaint filed with the Office of the Quartermaster General, Pepsi contended that allowing the military to order soft drinks by brand name would give Coca-Cola a monopoly. But General George C. Marshall, the army chief of staff, backed up Eisenhower. In the interest of morale, Marshall gave theater and area commanders full discretion to set up soft drink bottling operations and to specify the brand they wanted.

Marshall also gave commanders the right to ask for personnel to operate the bottling plants, and the Coca-Cola Company responded by sending technical observers (TOs) off to war. Curtis recruited an engineer named Albert Thomforde from the company-owned plant in Hartford and assigned him to the task of shepherding the bottling machinery to North Africa. As Thomforde recalled it later, he didn't get much of a briefing. "Al," Curtis told him, "I'd like to tell you what if s all about, but you'll just have to play it by ear. We don't know what's going to happen." The equipment and supplies would be sent over, Curtis said. "And you just pick it up from there."

It was early September 1943 when Thomforde received the necessary clearances and boarded a military cargo plane for a hop-and-refuel flight from New York to Maine, Newfoundland, and finally into Prestwick, Scotland. Flying at night through a hailstorm with almost no heat, Thomforde thought he might freeze to death, and when he landed he asked for a stiff drink instead of a Coca-Cola. Then he was loaded onto a blacked-out army DC-3, cheek-by-jowl with a Russian military observer sporting a large sidearm, for another long flight over the Atlantic to Marrakesh, Morocco. From there, in a plane so jammed the aisles were piled chest-high with luggage and crates, Thomforde was ferried into Algiers, the headquarters of the North African theater.

His reception did not go smoothly. In an office overlooking the Mediterranean, the commander of the army's Exchange Service, Colonel H. S. Robertson, offered him an "African" Coca-Cola—a warm dollop of bootleg syrup in a glass with a splash of tap water—and Thomforde spurned it, saying that on his watch Coca-Cola would be served properly or not at all. The colonel replied stiffly that if Thomforde thought he could do better, he was free to try.

Thomforde learned that most of the stateside bottling equipment was either still en route or was scattered, often in unmarked boxes, in army storage dumps all across the region. For the next few weeks, he darted around North Africa on a sort of scavenger hunt looking for the Coca-Cola Company's equipment and supplies. The army depot guards were helpful and occasionally let him have spare machinery, including some vitally needed chlorinating equipment for the water. Eventually, using Italian prisoners of war for labor, he got bottling plants up and running in a handful of cities in Algeria and Morocco.

The value of Coca-Cola to the war effort was not an article of faith with everyone. Quite a few commanders questioned the judgment of giving up valuable shipping space for a soft drink, especially in combat zones. One quartermaster said his transportation facilities were meant for "bullets, guns, tanks, and food"—period. Even Thomforde had his doubts, as he recalled after the war:

> I went over there realizing that there was a war on and there was a lot of privation, lots of trouble, lots of need of efficiency, and I was not sure in my own mind that taking Coca-Cola to the boys was a very worthwhile cause, except that

I had been told that they wanted it, that the army felt that
there were a lot of men who did not care about hard liquor
but they wanted that touch of home that Coca-Cola brought
to them.

No one expected the gush of raw emotion that Coca-Cola aroused in
the American armies. The familiar bottle and trademark and taste turned
out to be a poignant reminder of home for hundreds of thousands and
eventually millions of young soldiers who found themselves in strange
places facing terrible danger. For all the hype the company concocted in
Washington in lobbying for favorable treatment, it turned out that the GI
on the front lines had an affection for Coca-Cola that was deep and long-
lasting and absolutely genuine. Soldiers wanted four things from home:
mail, cigarettes, chewing gum, and Coke.

One of the first American casualties in the war had been a young pilot
from Kansas City who crashed his Spitfire during training with the American Expeditionary Force over Scotland. He'd ended up in a hospital with
a fractured skull, a broken leg, and a face full of hemstitching, and his first
request had been for a Coca-Cola. His wing commander had flown to London to get him one. That story, or a close version of it, was repeated over
and over again as the American involvement in the war escalated. When
Thomforde got the bottling plant in Casablanca running in time to serve
wounded Americans Coca-Cola for Christmas 1943, the good news was
reported in the army newspaper, *Stars and Stripes*.

In the early days of 1944, Thomforde arrived in Naples and set up a
bottling plant to begin supplying Coca-Cola for the first time to frontline
troops engaged in active combat. The American forces that were dug in
for the bloody siege and bombardment of Monte Cassino, the German
redoubt that blocked the way to Rome, got Coca-Cola to drink in their foxholes. Photographers with the War Picture Pool captured classic scenes of
unshaven U.S. soldiers holding up bottles of Coke, beaming, and for weeks
American newspapers were filled with pictures of hometown boys posing
with their favorite soft drink.

Capturing the phenomenon with gentle wit, cartoonist Bill Mauldin
drew a combat photographer telling a dogface, "Congratulations. You're
the 100th soldier who has posed with that bottle of Coca-Cola. You can
drink it."

At first, soldiers were limited to a ration of two Coca-Colas a week,
and they quickly established a black market in which the price of a bottle
soared far above a nickel. Ernie Pyle, the war correspondent, sent home
a dispatch describing a lottery in which a field-artillery sergeant in Italy
raised more than $1,000 for charity selling a single bottle of Coke. Soldiers
began writing to the company, often in extremely moving language, about
the feelings Coca-Cola inspired. A sergeant from Kansas wrote his parents,
"It's the little things, not the big things that the individual soldier fights for

or wants so badly when away. It's the girl friend back home in a drug store over a Coke, or the juke box and the summer weather. The average soldier wants to come home, get back in those old clothes, and do the things he always did."

The enemy did its part, too, singling out Coca-Cola as an American symbol. Otto Dietrich, the German press chief, was quoted as saying, "America never contributed anything to world civilization but chewing gum and Coca-Cola," which he called a menace. Japanese radio warned, "With Coca-Cola we imported the germs of a disease from American society." And Tokyo Rose taunted the American troops in the Pacific: "Wouldn't it be nice to have an ice-cold Coca-Cola! Can't you just hear the ice tinkling in the glass?"

When he crept back into Brussels with his small party of employees and their fami-lies, Carl West found the Coca-Cola plant intact, with some forty tons of sugar still on hand, undiscovered by the Germans.

He tried to resume selling Coca-Cola but quickly realized it would be impossible to operate under the rules of the German occupation. He was rarely able to obtain gas coupons or a driving permit, and in any case the Germans soon confiscated his trucks for military use. He ran low on ingredients. He fashioned a small fleet of jury-rigged tricycles that held a dozen or so cases of Coca-Cola at a time for his salesmen to push around their routes. Two of the men quit, and as sales dropped to nearly nothing West had to lay off the others. He was nearly broke.

Then something odd happened. The Germans reimbursed him for his trucks in cash. So did the industrial giant, Siemens, which took half his warehouse space for a plant that built electric parts for submarines. With the money he got from the Germans, West was able to begin manufacturing a simple, orange-flavored soft drink he called "Cappy," which immediately proved popular. He rehired most of his workers. And he discovered that for some reason he could operate freely on the black market, getting all of the extracts, crowns, cork, and citric acid he needed.

It seemed he had a protector in high places.

One day Max Keith turned up in Brussels to pay West a visit. He explained that he'd been placed in charge of the Coca-Cola Company's European properties. As much as he could, Keith said, he would help West stay in business. He began administering West's books, sheltering his assets and earnings. He arranged for West to buy Dulcine, an artificial sweetener, at the government's official price of 300 francs per kilogram when its cost on the black market was more than ten times higher. Under Keith's patronage, West secretly installed a new semiautomatic bot-tling machine and set up an illicit wood-burning generator nicknamed "the Spit-fire" to run it. He got hold of coal, oil, tires and inner tubes, wagons and trucks. He made a modest profit.

When West came within an eyelash of arrest, Keith pulled strings to save him. Fearing the German military detectives would find his cache of sugar, West and a handful of employees set out to disguise it, mixing it with food coloring and caramel until they had more than twenty tons of black, sticky paste, which they funneled into bags and stacked eight feet high in a remote warehouse, covered with cases of empty bottles. Someone informed on West, but before the inspectors could complete their search and seize the small mountain of contraband Keith intervened with the authorities and squelched the affair.

Keith did similar favors in other quarters of Western Europe. He kept the organization intact and made sure the men had jobs and could feed their families. In many ways he was a savior. The only question was whether he was doing it for the Coca-Cola Company or for himself. No one could answer that until the war was over.

The Coca-Cola Company wanted to be part of the Normandy invasion.

Getting permission to cross the English Channel with the Allied forces was an extremely difficult proposition, and it was made no easier when Ralph Hayes hatched a publicity stunt that nearly undid all of the hard work that had gone into establishing Coca-Cola's legitimacy as a part of the war effort.

In the fall of 1943, anticipating the next stage of the conflict, the Export Corporation assigned Paul Bacon to go to London as chief TO and make preparations for participating in the liberation of Europe. Bacon, a native Atlantan who had spent his whole career with the company, starting in the mailroom before rising to become a bottling supervisor on the West Coast, was anxious to leave immediately. But red tape held him up and Hayes summoned him to Atlanta.

Showing Bacon into Woodruff's office, Hayes outlined a special assignment. A few weeks earlier, Winston Churchill's daughter Mary had visited Fort Oglethorpe, Georgia, on a goodwill tour. "I'd like to take Papa a Coca-Cola when I go back," she'd told the newspapers good-naturedly. "I am drinking all I possibly can while I'm here and can get them." Hayes meant to take Mary Churchill at her word and exploit the opening. Already he'd attempted to ship a case of Coca-Cola to the British prime minister, only to be frustrated by wartime regulations. Now Hayes instructed Bacon to pay a personal call at 10 Downing Street when he got to London and take Churchill a case of Coca-Cola as a gift.

Bacon got clearance to fly to England early in 1944. He set up operations in a two-room suite at the Savoy Hotel and began lobbying British and U.S. Army officials, trying to persuade them to loosen their restrictions and allow wider distribution of Coca-Cola among the American and Canadian servicemen stationed there. He made some progress when the authorities agreed to bend the rules and install Coca-Cola fountain operations at hospitals and convalescent centers, military airfields, supply depots, and Red Cross centers.

Then, on April 27, 1944, Bacon took a case of Coca-Cola and a box of La Corona cigars and dropped by unannounced to see the prime minister. For good measure, he rounded up several copies of Churchill's portrait in hopes of getting them signed for Woodruff, Farley, Hayes, Curtis, and others among the company's top brass. But Churchill and his daughter were out, and the next day a messenger icily informed Bacon that in wartime the prime minister did not give autographs or accept commercial gifts. Undeterred, Bacon returned the next week, trying again for a personal meeting, only to be told that Churchill was in an emergency meeting with Eisenhower, Charles de Gaulle, and General Bernard Montgomery, and would be unable to interrupt the session to receive the Coca-Cola Company's emissary.

In the end, the best Bacon could do was arrange for Mary Churchill to christen an American bomber with a bottle of Coke, a small ceremony that seemed to highlight the frivolousness of the whole undertaking. Bacon established courteous relations with the Army Exchange Service, whose officers knew how much the GIs liked Coca-Cola, but the Quartermaster Department, which was responsible for transporting munitions and supplies, adamantly opposed giving up any shipping space for a soft drink. For the invasion of Europe, Bacon asked for a requisition of 400,000 cases of Coca-Cola in wooden crates, 50,000 pounds of CO_2 gas in 50-pound cylinders, one and a half million bottle caps, 1,800 ice coolers, five bottling plants, and a million gallons of syrup, all to be packed for amphibious landing. The quartermaster for the European Theater said no.

When D-Day arrived, Bacon was stuck in London. Try as he might, he was unable to shake the quartermaster's rigid quarantine of the company's equipment and supplies. A month after the beaches of Normandy were stormed, Bacon was in Brighton, on the southern coast of England, where he'd been reduced to trying to round up a spare LST and make it across the channel to Cherbourg on his own.

Then Eisenhower intervened. Slashing through the red tape, the supreme Allied commander ordered Coca-Cola's payload to be ferried across the channel. Bacon and his team of TOs were dispatched to France to begin operations. Within days they were riding around Normandy serving Coca-Cola right off the back of two-ton trucks, using so-called "jungle units"—portable dispensers that were developed for use in the Pacific—to fill the canteens of GIs who were still involved in the fighting.

As the Allies secured various cities, Bacon and his TOs rode in behind the American forces and began looking for the remains of the company's prewar operations. Sometimes the old plants were intact. In Rennes, France, for instance, they found Coca-Cola's bottler still in business, putting out an ersatz mineral water. He was happy to resume making Coca-Cola for the American troops. Other places had not fared so well. Bacon cajoled an army colonel into putting him on a "red-ball" Jeep express into Paris the day after the liberation, where Bacon found "the damndest bottling operation I ever saw in my life." The company's plant on Rue Felix Faure had been stripped down to a hand-powered rinser, a foot-powered crowner, and a creaking old rotary filler with an output of no more than 150 cases a day. It would hardly be able to supply a single battalion.*

To meet the demand of the thousands of American GIs who were pouring into the city every day, Bacon figured he would need a much bigger building and new, high-capacity bottling machinery. In the suburb of Puteaux, Bacon secured the use of an old municipal garage that had been used for repairing buses. With a 55,000-square-foot concrete floor, it was perfect for the heavy equipment the company was sending. Only no one seemed to know where that equipment was. A complete bottling plant—a giant, 35-ton Meyer-Dumore soaker and a 60-spout Liquid filler, worth some $250,000—had arrived at Le Havre and promptly disappeared.

The soaker was eventually discovered sitting on the docks, where army officials had abandoned it after concluding it was too heavy to transport. Bacon arranged to borrow a tank evacuator, which proved durable enough to get the soaker to Paris, where it was lifted up on house jacks and installed in the new plant. The filler was nowhere to be found, and Bacon assigned John Talley, one of his TOs, to go to Le Havre and trace it. Talley tracked down the original cargo ship, where a mate explained that a cable had snapped during unloading, sending the crate holding the filler crashing down on the corner of a barge. The crate had split open and pitched the contents overboard. The filler was somewhere in the mud at the bottom of the harbor a quarter-mile offshore.

After several days of trying, Talley found an army crew who agreed to dive and look for the filler. Making repeated searches of the harbor floor, they reported spotting boats, tanks, Jeeps, and trucks before finally discovering the filler. One of the divers told Talley they knew when they'd found it "because it was the only thing down there that didn't look like something else." Already badly rusted, the filler was damaged further by the grappling equipment used to raise it, but eventually it was repaired and installed, and the Paris plant began production.

Around the globe, as the United States and her allies were winning the war, Coca-Cola's TOs went to remarkable lengths to make sure their soft drink was never far from the front lines. Fred Cooke shepherded a convoy of eleven army trucks that carried a complete Dixie bottling plant "over the hump" from Calcutta into Kunming, China, on the Burma and Stilwell roads, a trip that took twenty days, most of it in low gear climbing mountain switchbacks and crossing pontoon bridges. During MacArthur's return to the Philippines, Gene Braendle set out from Manila, ventured within three hundred yards of Japanese lines under intense shelling to repair a set of jungle units, and served the GIs Cokes in the midst of combat.

---

* As a temporary measure, Bacon set up a fountain operation at the Red Cross Rainbow Corner in the Hotel de Paris. He watched in amazement as the line of soldiers waiting for a taste of Coca-Cola grew until it wrapped all the way around the block.

Coca-Cola became a commonplace in the pugnacious narrative of war reporting. "A six-man Japanese patrol attempted to infiltrate the lines of the 383rd regiment of the 96th infantry division early today in an attempt to blow up an ammunition dump," the United Press reported from Okinawa. "They missed the ammunition but did destroy a large can of Coca-Cola syrup. Angry doughboys killed them all." A newspaper in Wheeling, West Virginia, carried the story under the headline, "NO WONDER!"

In Europe, the company's men followed the advance of the Allied troops. Brussels was liberated by English tanks on September 3, 1944, and a contingent of TOs reached Carl West a few days later. He still had fifteen cases of Coca-Cola on hand, the last of a dwindling supply he'd been doling out bit by bit to protect the trademark since the war began. With syrup provided by the TOs, he resumed production for the troops.

West reported that he hadn't seen Max Keith in several weeks, not since the German evacuation after D-Day. The Germans had pulled out of Belgium in "pitiful condition," West said, abandoning their stalled trucks and moving on in farmers' carts, on bicycles, and on foot, tugging their belongings behind them. Some had pulled children's wagons.

When the Allies crossed the Rhine, the TOs were among the first to see the destruction English and American bombers had inflicted on Germany's cities. In Frankfurt, the roofless building housing the Coca-Cola plant was the only structure left standing for blocks around. Bacon arrived to discover an army lieutenant in the basement already working on the equipment, trying to get the bottling operation up and running. In Stuttgart, bombs had blown away the side walls of the company's plant and thousands of yellow jackets were swarming around pools of spilled syrup.

Some of the heaviest bombing had been directed at Essen, home of the Krupp works and the other industries of the Ruhr Valley that formed the heart of the German war machine. When Germany surrendered and the city fell to the Allies in May 1945, Bacon, John Talley, and another TO, Ward Wells, bought an old Buick in Paris and set out to find Max Keith.

The trip took three days. The Buick conked out along the way and the party borrowed an armored command car to continue their journey. They arrived in Essen on the morning of May 18, 1945, and set out for the old Coca-Cola plant, which was in the British occupation zone. All they found standing amid the rubble was an empty door frame, with a handwritten note pinned to it directing callers to an address on the outskirts of the city. The destruction was so heavy they couldn't find their way, until a bedraggled civilian guided them to their destination in exchange for a few cigarettes.

Bacon was unsure what to expect. He had known Keith before the war. They had trained together in New Haven, learning how to load a delivery truck and work a route the company way. Bacon thought of him as a friend. Yet the home office's doubts about Keith and his wartime activities were well known to Bacon and the TOs. The army officially considered Keith one of the enemy and issued a strict order against fraternizing with him. Bacon's military supervisor, Lieutenant Colonel Robert Mashburn, the commander of the Army Exchange Service in Europe, warned him against speaking to Keith or even shaking his hand.

When Bacon and his party drove up, Keith stepped out the front door to greet them. In fluent English, he welcomed them to Essen, said it was time to forget the war and its hostilities, and invited them inside. He put out his hand. Each man stiffly shook it, but there were no pleasantries. "I told him," Bacon said, "not to think us peculiar if we acted according to our instructions." Bacon asked to see Keith's books, which showed a modest profit for each of the war years. Then the TOs had a tour of the plant and saw the bomb shelter Keith had dug into the hillside next door. Keith opened a cupboard, took out a bottle of schnapps and a set of shot glasses, and proposed a toast to his colleagues from America. The men had a drink with him but refused his offer of a place to spend the night.

Before leaving, Bacon told Keith the company would be taking over his bottling plants and rebuilding them to make Coca-Cola for the American troops. If Keith would cooperate, it would be greatly appreciated. But because he was a German, he would no longer be in charge.

Given the obvious high standing he had enjoyed in wartime Germany, Keith probably should have understood the company's caution. Instead he was angry and deeply offended, and he shrank from further contact with the TOs and Export Corporation officials who came to visit, heightening the ill will on both sides.

Jimmy Curtis made a trip to Frankfurt hoping to see Dr. Oppenhoff, Coca-Cola's German lawyer, and grew suspicious when he was unable to arrange a meeting. Curtis thought Keith and Oppenhoff might be deliberately trying to duck him.

Eventually the company sent an investigator to Germany to examine Keith's war record, and the findings came as a considerable surprise. Keith had not been a Nazi. In fact he and Oppenhoff had resisted intense pressure to join the party and had endured hardships as a result.

When the war began and the company's property came under government control, the makers of Afri-Cola had asked to be named administrators of their archrival, a move that almost certainly would have resulted in the dismantling of Coca-Cola's German operations. But Keith and Oppenhoff had stepped in and persuaded the office of the *Reichskommissar* to entrust Coca-Cola's affairs to them. They had been pressured to name top Nazi officials to the German Coca-Cola company's board of directors and had refused.

Keith could easily have manufactured Fanta in his own name and kept the profits for himself, the report concluded, yet he had conducted the business on behalf of the Coca-Cola Company. He had scrupulously protected the company's property, even to the extent of arranging storage for an evening coat with a mink collar that belonged to Ray Powers's widow.

Oppenhoff had maintained a complete set of books, which he stored underground in a bank vault in Wurzburg. Thanks to Oppenhoff's intervention, Coca-Cola's trademark had survived in every occupied country in Europe save Denmark. And, thanks to Keith, many of the Coca-Cola men in those countries had survived as well.

Almost as impressive as his loyalty was Keith's ingenuity in keeping the German bottling plants operating during the ferocious pounding of the Allied bombing runs. The Essen building alone was destroyed and rebuilt three times, and all forty-nine of the company's German plants suffered damage of some sort. Keith arranged for workers at each plant to remove one bottling machine and store it in what he called a "siding," a spot outside the center city—an old farmhouse or a dairy—that was unlikely to be hit. These reserve operations were used whenever a main plant was knocked out, and as a result the sale of Fanta was never interrupted for long.

The truth, Curtis was forced to conclude, was that at the end of the war Coca-Cola's operations in Germany were "more satisfactory than we possibly could have contemplated."

When they learned the full extent of Keith's exploits, some of the Coca-Cola men in Atlanta were embarrassed at the way he'd been treated. The company arranged to have him named civilian administrator of Coca-Cola's bottling operations during the military occupation of Germany, in effect restoring him to his previous position.

Keith went back to work with enthusiasm, repairing plants and scrounging up bottles and wooden cases and other supplies. He assigned his employees to help the TOs run the machines and stock the warehouses, and before long he was turning out thousands of cases of Coca-Cola a day, satisfying the thirst of the U.S. Army.

When the war ended, the Coca-Cola Company had sixty-three overseas bottling plants in operation, in venues as far-flung as Egypt, Iceland, Iran, West Africa, and New Guinea.

The Export Corporation had borrowed $5.5 million to pay for the venture, and in many respects it was the smartest investment the company ever made. After gulping down more than a billion servings of Coca-Cola, eleven million veterans were returning with a lifelong attachment to the soft drink. The editors of *American Legion* magazine took a survey and found that GIs preferred Coke over its nearest competitor, Pepsi, by a factor of more than eight to one. Coca-Cola's place in American life seemed as secure and tightly woven as the stars and stripes in the flag.

Yet the adventures and glories of the war years had done little to resolve the fundamental business problems that were gnawing at the company in the marketplace back home. When the Pepsi suit was lost, Bill D'Arcy wrote a letter of warning: "We are starting a new industry," he said—one that would have to compete in a modern, mass society.

Before going off to war, one of the company's brightest young men,

Price Gilbert, Jr., the advertising director, wrote a long, angry report accusing Woodruff and the other elders of Plum Street of ignoring the new realities. It was sheer fantasy, Gilbert said, to think that Coca-Cola could survive the challenge of Pepsi and the other colas by sticking to the same policies that applied "before we had any real competition."

The son of one of Ernest Woodruff's original investors, Gilbert owned enough Coca-Cola stock to make him a millionaire many times over, and he vented his frustrations with an abandon born of personal wealth. From the moment Pepsi began offering twice as much for the same price, he said, Coca-Cola's share of the market had begun to shrink, and the trend was threatening to accelerate. So far, the company's only response had been to advertise Coca-Cola as a superior product. The problem was that a lot of people didn't care. They wanted a bargain.

"Everything we do helps [the] competition as much as it helps us," Gilbert argued, "because they are supplying the demand for our product at a lower cost. Every time we sell a cooler, open a new dealer, or teach a new customer to drink Coca-Cola—we help them." And that was assuming people continued to believe Coca-Cola was better. "If the day ever comes when the public says, 'I really prefer the other drink,'" Gilbert continued, toying with heresy, "then we really have something to worry about."

The company had no empathy with the American housewife, Gilbert went on. By offering exactly one package, the six-ounce bottle, Coca-Cola was telling women, "No matter how much you want, you must take it home six ounces at a time. You may want five gallons of punch for a children's party, but you will have to open a hundred bottles of Coca-Cola to get it."

Two wooden cases containing forty-eight six-ounce bottles of Coca-Cola weighed several dozen pounds, Gilbert said. The company's drivers had a hard time loading and unloading their trucks; most of them were better weight lifters than salesmen. Did the company expect homemakers to perform that sort of physical labor? Why not offer bigger bottles? Cans? "We say to the public, 'When you drink Coca-Cola you must drink six ounces, no more, no less. No matter how hot tired, and thirsty you may be.' That's not true of coffee or tea or milk or anything else, but with Coca-Cola it is six ounces, take it or leave it. Minimum quantity, maximum price, maximum trouble and inconvenience."

Gilbert's reward for his frank assessment of Coca-Cola's shortcomings, when he returned to the company after the war, was banishment to internal exile. He got an office and his old salary back but no duties, and before long he quit. Without paying the same harsh penalty, others, too, learned that there was a limit to Woodruff's tolerance for criticism and appetite for change. One of Woodruff's friends, Louis Marx, the toymaker, urged him to develop other flavor lines—"Lima-Cola," for example, or "Orana-Cola"—and Woodruff replied that he saw no reason at all to offer any new flavors. He could sell ten times as much Coca-Cola, he said, with the same effort. When Marx admonished him lightly that successful men occasionally overplayed their old, established methods, Woodruff answered him firmly, "I don't agree with you."

As to the larger bottle size, Woodruff was gambling that economic factors would allow him to keep selling six ounces of Coca-Cola for a nickel while Pepsi and the others began to feel the squeeze of selling twelve ounces for the same price. One afternoon toward the end of the war, driving Woodruff back to San Francisco after a round of golf at Pebble Beach, a couple of his West Coast executives summoned up their nerve and suggested going to a bigger bottle. Nonsense, Woodruff said. Pepsi and Royal Crown and the others were headed for bankruptcy.

It was not that Woodruff refused to face the future. On the contrary, he was trying as hard as ever to see over the next hill. He surprised his staff one day with a flat prediction that within twenty-five years, foreign sales of Coca-Cola would surpass those in the United States. It was a simple matter, he said, of 2 billion mouths versus 130 million. But as ever, the question of how to reach those customers provoked fierce contentiousness within the company. And as always, the disputes were resolved single-handedly, with stubborn finality, by Woodruff himself.

In 1939, with his mother dying, Woodruff had tried to relieve himself of some of his day-to-day responsibilities. He picked Arthur Acklin, the company's top administrator, to replace him as president, only to spend the next few years second-guessing most of Acklin's decisions as the man drank himself into a second nervous breakdown, a serious one that required a lengthy convalescence and forced him to resign. As the war ended, Woodruff found himself back in the president's chair, still coping with the minutiae of the business. He was fifty-five years old, anxious to choose a successor, yet unwilling or unable to relinquish control.

Woodruff's friend Mizell, the Emory business manager, warned him that he would never find a satisfactory replacement because he was looking for a younger version of himself. "I don't understand," Woodruff replied. "I don't get it." Yet in a way he did. One of the stories Woodruff enjoyed telling on himself was the time he had dinner and a few drinks with L. F. McCollum of the Continental Oil Company. Half in jest, McCollum expressed an interest in the Coca-Cola presidency. "You're hired," Woodruff said. Then, as McCollum described how he would make all the decisions and call all the shots, Woodruff added, "You're fired."

As he conducted the search for a new company president, Woodruff insisted he wanted a strong-minded, independent operator, not a puppet. No one had any idea if he meant it, with the result that some of the men jockeying for the job worked at displaying self-reliance while others played up to Woodruff and flattered him shamelessly. One, a little-known lawyer named Bill Hobbs, managed to do both, and on May 5, 1946, Woodruff stunned the Coca-Cola family by choosing him as the new president

Hobbs's path to the top was unorthodox, to say the least.

In the late 1930s, the fertilizer and cotton oil business run by Nell Woodruff's uncles in Athens, Georgia, was losing money at a $10,000-a-month clip and falling rapidly into bankruptcy. Anxious to rescue his wife's family and preserve their livelihoods, Woodruff assigned Hughes Spalding to straighten out the company's affairs.

Joining Hodgson's, Incorporated, as an outside director, Spalding discovered a mess. A tenth of the company's stock was listed in the name of the Lord, reflecting the Hodgson family's devotion to the Baptist church, and it seemed their accounts receivable books were based on faith as well. Ned and Harry Hodgson underpriced their fertilizer, sold it on credit, and rarely managed to collect what they were owed.

With commercial banks in Athens and Atlanta refusing to renew the company's loans, Woodruff and Spalding decided the only way to keep Hodgson's going was to obtain new financing from the federal government. At Woodruff's prompting, the Hodgsons applied for a loan from the Atlanta office of the Reconstruction Finance Corporation. They were turned down. Spalding then traveled to Washington, where he encountered a bright young RFC lawyer named Bill Hobbs. In short order, Hodgson's, Incorporated, was the recipient of a five-year, $450,000 loan. As Spalding explained it to the Hodgsons, with biblical glee, "We blew the trumpets, the walls of Jericho have fallen down and we have entered into the Promised Land, overflowing with financial milk and honey."

Either out of gratitude, or more likely to ensure that the RFC loan would be renewed in the years to come, Spalding invited Hobbs to move to Atlanta and join King & Spalding as a partner, which he did. Hobbs was an engaging man, and before long Spalding developed a genuine admiration for his abilities.

King & Spalding took care of a great many chores for Coca-Cola and enjoyed a correspondingly large flow of legal fees. In hopes of bolstering the relationship, Spalding persuaded Woodruff to hire Hobbs as an assistant counsel in the company's Legal Department where, presumably, he would be able to guard the firm's flank.

Hobbs made a fine first impression, especially on the department's secretaries. He was tall and good-looking, full of charm, the sort who would break into a soft shoe and make the young women giggle. He worked his magic on Woodruff as well. "Hobbs was a great listener," recalled Howard Kurtz, Jr., who served as his aide, "and frankly he was a sycophant. Woodruff [liked] him, and Hobbs saw to it that that appeal was strengthened."

One of the lawyers in the department described Woodruff as becoming "enamored" with Hobbs. A nephew put it more bluntly: "There were people who knew how to work [Woodruff], who played on his goodwill and affection, people—real ass-kissers, to use a common term—who advanced through it." Hobbs, the nephew believed, was one of them. Within a year, Woodruff promoted Hobbs to vice president and made him manager of the Legal Department, with a mandate to reorganize the operation.

There were signs of trouble from the start. In a power play that ruffled everyone's feathers, Hobbs assigned his assistant, Kurtz, to open all of the department's mail, even letters addressed by name to the other lawyers. As deferential as Hobbs was with Woodruff, he showed a cruel streak with underlings. Ralph Hayes, who regarded Hobbs warily, nicknamed him "Legree," only partly in jest. Many of the veteran hands at Plum Street viewed Hobbs's rise with alarm, an attitude he helped inflame by referring to them collectively and dismissively as "the old farts."

In one respect, though, Hobbs succeeded quite well. His charge from Woodruff was to cut costs in the Legal Department, and he did so. In the aftermath of the Pepsi decision, Woodruff saw little point in continuing the company's policy of aggressive litigation. Not long after John Sibley resigned as general counsel, his place was taken by another King & Spalding partner, Pope Brock, who promised Woodruff he would hold down the expenses. Brock criticized his colleague Sibley for having put Coca-Cola "through what is, so far as I know, the most disastrous campaign of litigation ever experienced by any party in the history of the world." He canceled several of the company's appeals, calling them fruitless, and Hobbs saw to the resultant layoffs of staff lawyers and investigators as the Legal Department was downsized.

As Woodruff's enthusiasm for Hobbs grew, some of the company's senior men warned him to go slowly and test Hobbs's abilities more carefully. But Woodruff pushed ahead, giving Hobbs a prize stepping-stone, the presidency of the Export Corporation, in 1945. Once again there were danger signals. During an inspection tour of the company's field operations in Europe, Hobbs astonished Paul Bacon and the other technical observers by complaining that too much Coca-Cola advertising material was on display in the post exchanges and other military outlets where the soft drink was served.

Bacon, who was posted in Paris, had worked day and night installing ice coolers full of Coca-Cola in army barber shops, garages, hangars, ordnance shops, snack bars, billets, and school installations, and he'd plastered the walls with the company's signs and posters, thinking they added "a touch of home" and were good for business as well. "Mr. Hobbs saw so many signs that it was embarrassing to him," Bacon recalled later. "He felt that it was playing too big a part in the show over there and that we should soft-pedal it a bit." The criticism struck Bacon as highly peculiar, coming from a Coca-Cola man, and he refused to carry out Hobbs's orders to cull the material.

Hobbs and Bacon clashed on another matter as well. Many of the TOs wanted to remain in Europe and hoped to be awarded bottling franchises to supply the huge civilian markets that beckoned once the occupation ended and economic restrictions were lifted. Bacon had applied for the territory of Paris and its suburbs and was told he would receive consideration. But expansion was going to be monumentally expensive. Knowing how much capital would be needed, the company devised a formula calling for franchisees to put up $1 for every person in their territory, an amount far beyond the modest means of the TOs. Instead of letting Bacon down gently, Hobbs asked him coldly, "Where're you going to get six million dollars?" Bacon, who had served the company ably and at times with courage throughout the war, never forgave the slight.

Woodruff gave no evidence that he was bothered by any of these disquieting portents. When Hobbs flew back to New York from his tour of Europe in the spring of 1946, Woodruff called him on the phone and asked, "Are you ready to go to work?" Hobbs said he was. At the age of forty-two, with fewer than four years of experience in the business, none of it in marketing and sales, he became president of the Coca-Cola Company.

Aware of the resentment and apprehension the senior men felt toward Hobbs, Woodruff took steps to signal that the choice was firm and final. He made a point of leaving Atlanta for a long trip out west, so that no one could complain to him or approach him to overturn the new man's decisions. In a crafty gesture, Woodruff asked one of the company's top vice presidents, Burke Nicholson, to do a favor and find a pair of felt-sole rubber boots, size nine, that he could take along on his fishing trip. It was a way of deflating Nicholson and telling him and all the company's other doubting Thomases that Hobbs would be handling the important matters while they were reduced to running errands.

For his own part, Woodruff resisted the temptation of interfering, at least at first. Though he had "a slight touch of the jitters," as he described it to a friend, he spent the summer and most of the fall traveling while Hobbs worked to establish his authority within the company. Woodruff told the company's publicity agents to put the focus on Hobbs, saying, "I have retired, you know." An item was planted in Hedda Hopper's column calling Hobbs "Mr. Coca-Cola," a ludicrously premature declaration.

Plum Street fell into a tentative, wary mood as Hobbs and the old hands circled each other. Reporting to Woodruff after attending a budget meeting, Harrison Jones passed along the pallid reassurance that the other officers were cooperating with Hobbs "by and large," a phrase that suggested quite the opposite. Hobbs guaranteed a rocky start by ordering his colleagues to give up their company cars. He fought and lost a needless skirmish trying to cut off Pope Brock's access to the board of directors. And he failed to establish a comfortable working relationship with Archie Lee.

Sensing that Hobbs was in trouble, Woodruff took the unusual step of making a formal speech at one of the company's sales meetings. Standing on his feet for nearly an hour in the ballroom of the Brookhaven Country Club in Atlanta, he gave an ardent pep talk about Coca-Cola and then went "off the record," as he put it, to discuss Hobbs. "Mind you," he said,

"I'm not singing a swan song. I expect to be around here for a long time. I'll tell you a secret—and it's no secret to a number of you—but one of the greatest struggles I'm having is restraining myself from jumping in and trying to run the business. That job, as I've told you, has been handed to Mr. Hobbs. . . ."

Some of the listeners took Woodruff at his word, but others heard an echo of doubt. If Hobbs was doing a good job, they wondered, why did Woodruff have to speak up for him? And if Woodruff was so well pleased with Hobbs, then why was he having such a struggle letting go? The speech had a curiously contradictory effect. Though Woodruff reaffirmed explicitly that Hobbs would continue as president, he also seemed to be making an admission of sorts that Hobbs had been a flawed choice. It was an invitation for uncertainty within the company, a signal that Hobbs's authority was limited and suspect and that his decisions were open to questioning and even subversion.

Woodruff ended his period of exile and began roaming the fourth floor at Plum Street again, cigar glowing, dropping into offices and checking up on people. He presented a commanding figure—"the Boss," as he was known to one and all—whose age and experience (and absolute control over the board of directors) made Hobbs look juvenile and feeble by comparison. Soon a new office joke was making the rounds: "The trouble with Hobbs," it went, "is he thinks he's president."

Aware of the undermining effect his renewed presence had on Hobbs, Woodruff asked his friends and advisers if he was doing the right thing. Not surprisingly, they reassured him he was. After two decades, it was second nature for most of the company's executives to depend on Woodruff for guidance, and he welcomed their reliance.

"One of the mistakes that Hobbs made," recalled Joe Jones, Woodruff's chief of staff, "was he didn't check in with Mr. Woodruff. It was fine for Woodruff not to be calling him up every day, but he damn well expected to hear from Hobbs, and that didn't happen."

Eventually Hobbs grew gun-shy and began ducking decisions. Ralph Hayes went to him with an idea for an advertising campaign, for instance, and complained that he couldn't get Hobbs to give a thumbs up or down. "You are the top knocker around here," he admonished Hobbs angrily, "and I think you ought to be either for or against it, instead of just letting it get kicked up and down the hall until it's done to death."

As the months passed, Hobbs's standing with Woodruff became an open question in the company. One night on a trip to New York, Hughes Spalding watched in intense discomfort as Woodruff and Hobbs started drinking heavily at dinner and fell into an ugly argument, one that degenerated as they got progressively tipsier until Hobbs began cursing and calling Woodruff names. Spalding, who was on the wagon, feared his protégé had burned his bridges. The next morning Woodruff had trouble remembering the particulars of the spat and asked Spalding, "What did he say about me?"

Spalding replied, "I'm not telling you." An immediate firing was averted, but it was plain that Hobbs had moved permanently to Woodruff's bad side.

The simplest solution might have been to replace Hobbs. But Woodruff was reluctant to admit he'd made a mistake, especially so soon after Acklin's collapse. He hated dismissing people. And in one important respect the presence of a weakened president suited him perfectly well. It discouraged change. Woodruff wanted to keep Coca-Cola exactly the same as it had been for sixty years—same taste, size, package, price, and image. A debilitated management team was one surefire method of keeping innovation at bay. So Hobbs stayed on, hobbled.

The company slipped deeper into a state of paralysis, with painful consequences. Frustrated, feeling he'd been reduced to a vice presidency "in charge of Fourth Class mail," Ralph Hayes took Woodruff aside one morning and said he was quitting. Ben Oehlert left the company, too. Coca-Cola faced daunting challenges in production, procurement, foreign expansion, marketing, and advertising, Oehlert complained, and Woodruff's response had been to go outside the family, spurning the men who had proven themselves during the war, to bring in a new president who knew nothing about any of those things.

And there was a third resignation as well. Alfred Steele, the company's flamboyant vice president of merchandising, walked out of Coca-Cola's New York office and joined Pepsi, the enemy.

Al Steele was a showman. Everything about him seemed to be part of a costume, from his thick horn-rimmed glasses to the big boutonniere he stuck in his lapel, even the gap between his front teeth. He called people "Pal" and liked to slap them on the back, hard. In the straitlaced atmosphere of the Coca-Cola Company, his vulgarity stood out like an act of sacrilege. So did his brilliance.

Among the other jobs he'd held in a quicksilver career, Steele once worked for a circus, and he enjoyed telling the boys at Coca-Cola about all the carny tricks he learned on the midway. The reason the shelf at the ticket window was so high, he often explained, was so the customers couldn't see it. If they paid with a $20 bill, the cashier would put their tickets and small change on one side but leave the $10 they were owed a little apart, where they wouldn't feel it and might forget and leave it behind. The story struck many people as summing up Steele's business philosophy, as if he admired petty larceny as an art form.

Steele was a native of Nashville who acquired a worldly air growing up in Tokyo, Manila, London, and other cities where his father, an international secretary of the YMCA, had postings. After college, Steele tried his hand at several occupations before discovering a flair for marketing. As a young salesman for the Union Bed & Spring Company, he devised something he called a "Sono-Meter" that purported to measure the energy people lost while they tossed and turned sleeping on a bad mattress. Union's sales shot up 80 percent in the next nine months, and Steele's career was launched. He went into advertising and eventually joined the D'Arcy agency as a Coca-Cola account executive.

His work came to Woodruff's attention, and in 1943 Steele was dispatched to D'Arcy's New York office with instructions to liven up the company's perennially dreary radio advertising. One evening he wandered into the Savoy Plaza Hotel, where he discovered Morton Downey, the famous tenor, once one of the highest paid performers in the country, singing in the lounge. Obviously down on his luck, Downey was eager to accept a sponsorship from Coca-Cola, and Steele moved quickly to sign him up.

Steele drew Woodruff into the glamorous, wartime world of New York's cafe society. Woodruff and Downey and Downey's agent, Sonny Werblin, became fast friends, along with Coca-Cola's public relations man, Steve Hannagan, and his fiancée, the actress Ann Sheridan. They became fixtures on the nightclub circuit, hobnobbing with the likes of Xavier Cugat and Guy Lombardo and dropping in at Toots Shor's and the 21 Club. A photograph from the period shows Woodruff's wife, Nell, sitting primly in a booth at the Stork Club next to the stunning Sheridan, whose looks had earned her the nickname "the Oomph Girl."

Pleased with Steele's efforts, Woodruff hired him away from the D'Arcy agency and made him a vice president in Coca-Cola's New York office with responsibility over sales, merchandising, advertising, and promotions. Steele began running the company's sales meetings and bottlers' conventions, staging productions that dazzled everyone with their Broadway qualities. In Atlantic City one year he filled an exhibit hall with vignettes from an imaginary trip around the world. Travelers alighted from the Pan Am Clipper and discovered Coca-Cola in various exotic venues, including a thatched hut where pretty girls in grass skirts served Cokes while a band played island music. The awed executives from Plum Street nicknamed Steele "the Maestro," and Hannagan began calling him "Tent Pole," a tribute to his circus background (and a sly reference to his reputation as a ladies' man).

In addition to his gifts as an impresario, Steele demonstrated a solid understanding of the evolving position of soft drinks in the marketplace. The D'Arcy agency did a survey during the war and discovered that fully half of Coca-Cola's sales were now for home consumption, a sharp climb that validated many of Price Gilbert's warnings about the need to tailor the company's advertising and marketing toward housewives. The battlefields of the future, Steele recognized, would be shelf space in supermarkets, coin-operated vending machines at service stations, and cup dispensers in factories, fast-food outlets, theaters, and ballparks. Steele foresaw the social landscape of the 1950s—the rise of suburbs and shopping centers, the birth of family entertainment on television, the liberating concept of leisure time. He had bold ideas about making Coca-Cola part of it all, more ideas, an associate said, "than a dog has fleas."

But Steele was a man whose flaws were as spectacular as his talents. When it came to running an office, he was not just poorly organized and forgetful; his behavior bordered on out-and-out corruption. He liked to tell his underlings that when they filled out an expense account, they should add up all the items and then put a "1" in front of the total.

During Hobbs's troubled presidency, Woodruff decided Steele needed closer supervision and moved his office from Manhattan to Atlanta. Plum Street was not quite the informal, intimate clubhouse it had once been. There was an office manager now, a meticulous fellow named W. G. Lamb, who sent out stern memos ordering employees to "refrain from placing empty glasses on the window sills, propping your feet against the walls and radiators, placing your hands on the walls in going up and down the stairs, and striking the doors with the toes of your shoes in opening them." Workers were instructed to park neatly when they arrived and to turn off their lights and unplug their fans before they left for the day. Executives were expected to live within their budgets.

To say that Steele chafed under the tight rules and close scrutiny of the home office would be a considerable understatement. He was utterly miserable. "Pal," he complained to an old friend at the D'Arcy agency, "I've been here for a whole goddam week and I have nothing to do. I am absolutely going crazy."

With Hobbs out of the loop, the responsibility for day-to-day decisions at the company fell into the hands of Burke Nicholson, who took a dim view of Steele and made no secret of it. Nicholson was a man of breeding, a courtly, dignified Georgian who took great pride in his descent from Scottish nobility. He had held many of the top jobs in the company and was passed over for the presidency only because Woodruff thought he lacked a hard edge. Tall, slightly stooped, pipe-smoking, he looked every inch an elder statesman, which was how he was treated around the company. But he was not toothless. He thought Steele's spending was wildly extravagant—$150,000 or more for some of his stage productions—and wanted to choke it off. He got his chance when Steele slipped out of town for a few weeks to establish residency in Las Vegas and get a divorce. While Steele was gone, Nicholson slashed his budget once and for all.

Seeing a bleak future in Atlanta, Steele moved back to New York and began looking for other prospects. On a breezy day in March 1949, he accepted an invitation to have lunch in the Oak Room of the Plaza Hotel in Manhattan with four of the directors of the Pepsi-Cola Company. Over martinis and filet of sole, they offered him the executive vice presidency of their company, which he accepted. He never returned to 515 Madison Avenue.

Steele's departure from the Coca-Cola Company was not unexpected, of course, but his decision to join Pepsi shocked his old colleagues and frightened them badly. Steele carried away priceless inside information. He knew most of their secrets, all of their weaknesses. To hear him tell it, he even knew the formula. "That sweet-smelling son of a bitch," Woodruff fumed, remembering Steele's cologne.

The immediate victim of Steele's defection was Walter Mack. After running Pepsi for more than a decade, Mack had simply run out of ideas. He was still using skywriters to scrawl Pepsi's name in the skies, still holding prize contests and putting on square dances.

Of greatest concern, Mack was losing money. Woodruff's prediction of a steady postwar climb in the price of ingredients turned out to be accurate. Sugar rose from 2 cents a pound at the outset of the war to more than 8 cents afterward. Bottles, caps, and crates all went up. Wages doubled. Mack hiked the price of concentrate, and his bottlers responded by raising their wholesale prices. Retailers were forced to abandon the nickel and started charging customers 6 cents or more per bottle.

Soon the famous Pepsi jingle had to be amended: "Twice as much for a nickel, too," became an unconvincing, "Twice as much 'and better,' too." Pepsi's sales fell off, while Coca-Cola's increased. Mack was obliged to borrow money and cut the dividend on Pepsi-Cola common stock, whose value tumbled from a high of $40 a share in 1947 all the way down to $7 just two years later.

The directors who asked Steele to lunch were plotting a coup. Within months of installing him as the second in command, they booted Mack upstairs and gave Steele his job, the presidency, with a free hand to try anything he thought might reverse Pepsi's sagging fortunes. Steele began by hiring away dozens of his old colleagues from the Coca-Cola Company, promising them a relaxed, shirt-sleeves workplace, the liberation of pursuing new ideas, and, most appealing of all, far higher salaries.

Moving quickly, displaying a sense of discipline that had remained under wraps during his tenure at Coca-Cola, Steele put Pepsi's books in order, hired a biochemist to test the formula and improve quality control, and set out to win back the company's disgruntled bottlers. The inflation of the late 1940s had siphoned off the bottlers' profits, leaving them angry with Mack and distrustful of the home office. "The time has come for you to stop driving around in lousy Fords," he told the bottlers in one memorable meeting. "I'm going to put you in Cadillacs."

The underlying problem, as Steele saw it, was that Pepsi had been marketed for years as a cheaper imitation of Coca-Cola. People assumed it was inferior because Pepsi's own ads essentially said as much. Moving off the nickel had been disastrous because it removed Pepsi's only sales pitch, quantity. When "twice as much for a nickel" disappeared, so did the public's reason for buying the product. Pepsi did best with poor people—working-class whites in the big cities of the Northeast, blacks in the South, and children, the "kid trade." The reason Pepsi enjoyed strong home sales was that housewives poured it into glasses in the kitchen and then served it as Coca-Cola in the parlor.

Steele had to find a new pitch, a new reason to buy Pepsi now that it was no longer the bargain it used to be. Checking the reports of his bio-chemist, he discovered what most consumers already suspected: Pepsi was sweeter than Coke. It had more sugar. One reason Pepsi slipped off the nickel before Coca-Cola was that a 12-ounce Pepsi contained more than twice as much sugar as a 6-ounce Coke. Hoping to turn a negative into a positive, Steele had the inspiration of marketing the extra sugar in Pepsi as a plus for consumers. He concocted a wickedly clever ad campaign claiming that Pepsi had "More Bounce to the Ounce" than other soft drinks.

The new Pepsi campaign earned a sniffy "no comment" from the Coca-Cola Company for public consumption but provoked quite a bit of concern internally. Coca-Cola's in-house chemists stepped up their own testing of Pepsi samples and reported finding significant fluctuations in the levels of sugar, caffeine, and phosphoric acid—results that one official said "could build up a reasonably damning indictment of the competitive product for use if. . .necessary."

Before an escalation of the cola wars was triggered, however, the "More Bounce" campaign turned out to be a dud. Much to Steele's surprise (and Woodruff's), the public proved indifferent to the idea of Pepsi-Cola or any other soft drink as an energy supply. Mothers, it happened, were not look-ing for additional sources of sugar to feed their children, and adults seemed to appreciate soft drinks as a refreshment and a way to quench thirst, not as a source of quick calories. The way to satisfy a sweet tooth was a candy bar, they believed, not a cola.

The failure of Steele's first advertising campaign became obvious at the end of 1950 when the annual sales figures were compiled. Pepsi brought in a meager $40 million, down almost 50 percent from three years earlier. Some of Pepsi's bottlers went out of business. The Pepsi plant in Princeton, New Jersey, was sold and remodeled into a factory that produced Maid-enform bras, leading several Coca-Cola executives to joke that now there would be even less bounce to the ounce than before.

Adding to the surge of confidence at Plum Street, Pepsi's difficulties coincided with the remarkable burst of public affection for Coca-Cola that swept the country during the French episode, when the Communists and winemakers and intellectuals attacked the American soft drink and tried to push a ban on it through the National Assembly. In the spring of 1950, *Time* magazine ran an unprecedented cover depicting the smiling face of an animated red Coca-Cola disk with a little arm holding a bottle of Coke to the parched lips of a thirsty, grateful globe. "World and Friend" was the title of a cover story that lavished praise on the company's efforts to expand internationally and help export the "American way of life."

For the frustrated executives in Pepsi's Export Sales office, the *Time* cover was the last straw. It looked to them like an issue of Coca-Cola's in-house magazine, the *Red Barrel*. Henry Luce was favoring one of his big advertisers, they believed, and ignoring the fact that Pepsi now competed with Coke in sixty-seven foreign markets, often quite successfully. Complaining of unfair treatment, the *Bulletin*, Pepsi Export's newsletter, reprinted a snide comment from one of Walter Winchell's columns: "*Time* mag usually pummels its Front Cover subject. But Coca-Cola is given the Kid Glove Treatment. Moral: It Pays to Advertise."

The response to Pepsi's outburst was a perfect illustration of the attitude that prevailed at the Coca-Cola Company at the time. Joe Copps, one of Hannagan's top men, advised Woodruff to say nothing. "I feel we are in the role of a fine, genteel lady," Copps explained, "who must control her temper and hold her tongue, particularly when taunted by people of less breeding, position, and culture who would like nothing better than to irk her into an open street brawl, which would not reflect to her credit but rather to their dubious advantage." There was a word for such thinking: arrogance.

Woodruff remained certain that Pepsi had committed a "fatal error" at the very outset by offering a twelve-ounce drink. Pepsi's men sometimes scoffed at Coca-Cola as the "half as much for a nickel, too, crowd," but that was precisely the point. Higher ingredient prices were bleeding Pepsi to death. If the Coca-Cola Company and its bottlers could hold the nickel price, even though their own profit margins were being severely pinched, they could simply sit back and watch the Pepsi-Cola Company die. That, in a nutshell, was Woodruff's strategy. Keep selling Coca-Cola at six ounces for a nickel and not even the great Al Steele could save Pepsi.

Bill Hobbs, who had increasingly large periods of time on his hands to contemplate the economy and the changes that were taking place in American social life in the early 1950s, wasn't so sure. One morning he glanced over a newspaper clipping that described how the nickel was beginning to disappear as a familiar, independent unit of commerce. The 5-cent fare for subway rides was gone. So was the 5-cent cup of coffee. Telephone companies were beginning to charge a dime a call.

Maybe, Hobbs thought, the Coca-Cola Company was trying to hold the Alamo.

Nine

BLACK AND WHITE

For a guest at Ichauway, Robert Woodruff's plantation in southwest Georgia, a winter day would begin shortly after dawn with a sharp knock on the bedroom door. A black servant entered on cat's feet. "Mornin', suh," he said in a soft drawl, "care for a fire?" He took the tin screen off the fireplace, struck a kitchen match, and dropped it on the wad of newspapers under the dry wood. In seconds the flames leapt up with a loud whoosh and the walls of the big, cold room began dancing in orange light. The heat inched its way through the chilly air toward the bed.

A pot of hot black coffee was served while the guest hurriedly threw on his hunting clothes and headed downstairs to breakfast. In the kitchen, Mattie Heard had been up for hours, cooking. When the bell rang, the guests seated themselves around a long table in the dining room, and a line of servants in white porter's jackets filed through the kitchen door carrying platters of sizzling, crisp bacon, sausage, scrambled eggs, grits, buckwheat hoecakes with Georgia cane syrup, and biscuits with homemade mayhaw jelly. Sometimes Mattie fried up a couple of fat catfish from the black waters of the Ichauway-Notchaway Creek, the meat steaming fresh and fleecy inside the brown breading.

One small oddity of house etiquette was that Woodruff, seated at the head of the table, was always served first. He woke up hungry and liked to eat quickly and get on with organizing the day's activities. As befitted a man of wealth and power, Woodruff had several residences. He leased and later bought a duplex in the opulent River House overlooking the East River in Manhattan, owned Buffalo Bill Cody's old ranch in Wyoming, and had a fine, white-columned Georgian mansion on Tuxedo Road in Buckhead, the most exclusive section of Atlanta. Yet the place he felt truly at home was Ichauway, where he was lord and master of a 30,000-acre estate and the three hundred people, most of them black, who lived on it.

The guests gathered after breakfast on the bright green rye grass in the half-mile circle in front of the lodge, stretching and chatting under the moss-draped live oaks while the handlers finished assembling the elaborate equipment and cast of characters that went into a traditional quail hunt. Halfway around the circle, the horses were led from their stables and saddled. The bedding in their stalls was raked back so the ground could dry out during the warmth of the day.

Two big roan-colored mules in brass fittings were harnessed to the hunt wagon, a specially built dray that rolled on high iron wheels painted Coca-Cola red. Amid a chorus of yelping, the dogs were released from their kennels (where each had a bed and a dish of its own) and loaded into a set of wooden boxes with wire-mesh windows on the back of the wagon. The pointers were sleek and powerful, thanks to their feeder, Edgar Duncan, who gave them a special diet of raw meat, chopped vegetables, shredded wheat, and an occasional treat of canned salmon. If a guest asked him how many dogs Woodruff owned, Duncan always said he didn't know. "It's my job to feed 'em," he would explain, "not count 'em."

As the entourage of men and animals made its way around the circle to the lodge, the plantation overseer handed out light shotguns, mostly 20-gauge over-and-unders, to the guests who had not brought their own weapons. Everyone was given a morning's supply of shells. If a guest did not bring his own hunting clothes, he was fitted with a pair of chaps to keep the sharp brambles from tearing his pants to shreds.

Once his guests were mounted, Woodruff led the hunt party off to one of the dozen old farms that formed his property. There was not much conversation. "I never heard the Boss overtalk," one of his overseers recalled.

The best quail hunting was in fields of wiregrass, between the stands of longleaf pine, where a shin-high, gray-green carpet of foliage provided cover for the coveys. When a likely spot was reached, the handlers stopped the wagon, opened up a dog box, and let out a pair of pointers. The dogs raced ahead, crisscrossing the fields, ranging back and forth as the handlers gave them commands by blowing whistles and shouting the dogs' names— "Yaw! Sally!"—until suddenly a dog would stop and lock into a rigid point, its form utterly frozen from the sharp tip of its nose to its tail held high and straight.

In silence, the two nearest hunters would slide off their horses, load their shotguns, and tiptoe quickly through the broom sedge and scrub oak to the dog's side. When the covey broke, a hunter heard and felt the wild fluttering of wings a split second before he saw the birds explode into a mad dash for the horizon, like so many small players in an airborne game of capture the flag. The fluttering shifted seamlessly to include the hunter's own heart as he aimed instantly without thinking and fired twice, hoping for a "double"—a plump, brown bird with each shot.

It was not hard to understand why Woodruff loved the hunt so much. Simply being outdoors in the pristine air of the country was a tonic anyone could appreciate. For a man like Woodruff, who enjoyed being in command, the hunt was a grand ritual in which he got to direct traffic. Guests, servants, dogs, and horses all responded to his wishes. And he could keep score. For all its gentility, Ichauway was a highly competitive place. At the end of every day, Woodruff asked his guests the same two questions: "How many birds did you kill? How many times did you shoot?" The hunt was a test of skill and, by subtle extension, of manliness. A gifted shot himself,

Woodruff often took his limit without a single wasted shell. Answering his pair of questions could be an uncomfortable exercise for those who had missed.

Finally, Ichauway allowed Woodruff to be generous and to benefit at the same time from generosity's dark cousin, the creation of a sense of obligation on the part of the recipients. Woodruff gave his visitors souvenirs of neatly cleaned filets of quail and jars of mayhaw jelly and usually sent them off with a hearty farewell, laughing and saying, "Well, you drank up all my liquor, ate all my food, and shot all my birds! Time for you to go!" It was said with a smile, but the message was plain. A trip to Ichauway was a gift, a precious gift bestowed by the owner.

One of the few guests bold enough to tease Woodruff, Max Gardner, the former governor of North Carolina, thanked him once for his "dogmatic hospitality," a nice phrase that captured the spirit of the household perfectly. Another guest recalled walking along the plantation's main road one day and finding an arrowhead. He showed it to Woodruff, who said, "If you like it, I'll give it to you."

It was at Ichauway that his friends and associates from the company could see the depths of Woodruff's innate resistance to change. For all his worldliness, his comfort walking into the Stork Club or the White House or dining at the Wilmington Club with the du Ponts, Woodruff was a native Southerner who loved the South and its ways of life. His father, Ernest, had been born during the Civil War, and in rural Georgia nearly a century later those ways had scarcely changed a bit.

After dinner most Saturday evenings at Ichauway, a choir of sharecroppers and servants would line the stairwell to the second floor of the lodge and sing spirituals for the Woodruffs and their guests. Led by the chief wagon driver, Leroy Williams, a fine tenor, they rendered slow, sweet versions of "A Closer Walk with Thee" and other gospel classics that occasionally left their listeners in tears. The black men had a baseball team, the Ichauway Crackers, whose members played in the Georgia-Florida League and got paid on the "forty-sixty" plan—40 cents if they lost, 60 if they won. The plantation provided their uniforms.

Ozzie Garrett, who started work at Ichauway in 1942, was a pitcher on the team, "pretty good at what I did," by his own account, with a curve ball that "came in and dropped down, hard to hit." Garrett worked in the stables, cleaning out the horse stalls in the morning, putting in fresh bedding, feeding the mules, hauling litter, and filling the water troughs. One morning, he recalled, Woodruff called him up to the big house. "You got my horses in pretty good shape," Woodruff told him, reaching into a pocket and handing him a crumpled $100 bill. "'Bout knocked me off my feet when I saw what it was," Garrett related, adding that he figured maybe from then on he ought to start brushing the horses' teeth.

Many years later, retired and still living on the plantation in a small one-story house on a cinder-block foundation, Garrett reflected on the question of Woodruff's paternalism. "He didn't just take it and throw it at you," Garrett said after a while. "He was one of the gentlest white men I've ever known."

Woodruff's secretary, Lucille Huffman, went to Ichauway every year and took a census, making a list of all the members of the plantation's families and their clothing sizes. At Christmas, Nell Woodruff, known to one and all at Ichauway as "Ole Miss," passed out boxes full of brand-new outfits—pants and shirts, dresses for the women, underwear, shoes, socks, gloves, coats, and caps for every adult and child living on the property. It was remarkable, old-timers agreed, how much trouble was taken to make sure all of the articles fit properly. "Mr. Woodruff," one of them said proudly, "didn't settle for 'dat'll do.'"

The reverence his black tenants felt for Woodruff was based on more than docile gratitude. In the summer of 1933, four years after he opened Ichauway, there was a lynching right outside the plantation's general store. A mob of white men marched into the little white-frame building, seized a black sharecropper, dragged him outside onto the sandy ground, shot him five or six times with a pistol, and once more with a shotgun, then strung him up on a nearby tree and left him hanging. When word of the incident reached Woodruff in Atlanta, he hired several Pinkerton detectives and dispatched them to Ichauway, where they spent the summer working undercover, posing as white farmers. They fooled no one, of course. But the news that a plantation owner would go to such lengths to prevent harm to his black people quickly made the rounds of Baker County, and Ichauway's residents were rarely harassed in the years afterward.*

Among the many things money could buy was an illusion that time stood still. Woodruff spent upward of $60,000 a year underwriting Ichauway's expenses, and in exchange he and his guests were lavished with the ministrations and deference that black servants of the old school knew how to impart with perfection. His stand against lynching, highly unusual for its time and place—a "foolish idea," in the candid assessment of one of his white deputy overseers—earned him the undying allegiance of his black tenants, who gladly indulged his baronial manner. Once, when a one-room black church on Ichauway burned to the ground, he paid to have it rebuilt on the condition that the parishioners not embarrass him by thanking him. Instead they wrote a letter thanking God and sent him a copy.

---

* The Pinkerton men concluded that a white bootlegger was responsible for the lynching. According to reports the detectives sent to Woodruff, a mysterious black man called Bee Aienty killed the bootlegger's brother-in-law in a dispute during a crap game near the old abandoned dam on the Ichauway-Notchaway Creek, and the bootlegger took revenge on Aienty's friends and relatives. No charges were brought, and the detectives could find no trace of Aienty, whose identity may have been nothing more than a phonetic rendering of a nickname, "Big, ain't he?"

The blacks at Ichauway forgave Woodruff his eccentricities, chief among them the cemetery he maintained for his favored hunting dogs. Woodruff's dogs were buried in caskets, under headstones that carried their photographs mounted on porcelain plates, along with their names, dates, and a sentimental inscription. Occasionally there were elaborate funeral ceremonies. When a prize setter named Lloyd George died, several dozen black mourners marched in a torchlight procession to the grave, leading the other dogs on leashes and singing "Swing Low, Sweet Chariot."

Woodruff provided his dogs with expert medical care, including surgery if they were injured, and indulged his favorites with indoor privileges and scraps from the table. "Now, chew this thoroughly," he'd say, tossing a bone to one of his Labradors. "Don't gulp it." Sometimes Woodruff asked an overseer to drive the four hours to Atlanta just to deliver a dog, so he could enjoy canine companionship when he had to be in the city.

It did not escape the notice of the blacks on Ichauway that in some respects the dogs lived better lives than they did, yet for the most part they were bemused rather than resentful. When Woodruff was away, they would invite their friends over to see the cemetery and the dining room in the kennels, and their friends would laugh and shake their heads in disbelief.

The old ways were still very much in evidence when Edgar Bergen came to visit in the late 1940s and early 1950s. The famous ventriloquist was the most recent addition to Coca-Cola's lineup of celebrities, and he was always willing to put on a show for the servants and the members of Ichauway's choir. He did routines with his puppets, Charlie McCarthy and Mortimer Snerd, but it was his magic show that fascinated the plantation audience the most.

One year the *Atlanta Constitution* carried a feature story describing Bergen's performance, how he threw his voice and made his wide-eyed listeners believe it was coming from inside the chimney. Claiming he had a "truth bell" that rang one time when people lied and twice when they told the truth, Bergen asked questions of Ichauway's staff and provoked peals of laughter sounding the bell as they answered. The next day, according to the newspaper, one of Ichauway's girls told her boyfriend, "I ain't going to listen to you no more until I get me one of them truth bells."

If, by the sensibilities that evolved afterward, it all sounded achingly outdated and paternalistic, that missed the point. No one thought so at the time. No one. The, author of the *Constitution's* account was one of Ichauway's regular guests, Ralph McGill, who loved to listen to Negro spirituals, as he called them, who found himself deeply moved when an old blind man on the plantation, Joe, no last name, would strum the guitar and sing "Yonder Comes Day," and who like almost every other Southern white man of his day thought of rural black people as subordinate and childlike—the same McGill who won a Pulitzer Prize several years later for the grace and courage of his writing in support of the civil rights movement.

McGill had no idea how far he and his friend Woodruff were about to travel in their thinking.

For Woodruff, the path started with a speech Jim Farley made in Tampa, Florida, in November 1950.

As usual, Farley was ignoring the Coca-Cola Company's business in favor of a political stemwinder, in this case an urgent appeal to President Truman to drop his fight for civil rights legislation before the Democratic Party was permanently damaged in the South.

Farley's speech came to Woodruff's attention courtesy of an organization called the National Fair Play Committee, based in Harlem, New York, which called for a boycott of Coca-Cola. The Coca-Cola bottler in New York employed not a single black salesman, distributor, clerk, or stenographer, the committee noted, an "ugly fact" that apparently reflected the attitude of Farley and the company's executives in Atlanta.

Woodruff had already begun to recognize that his company was vulnerable on the issue of race in a way that he, personally, was not. Even in the infancy of the movement, when vast numbers of white people all across the country rejected the idea of equal rights for blacks, Southerners found themselves, their region, and their institutions on the defensive, especially when lynchings and other acts of overt racial hostility grabbed the headlines. Woodruff asked his press agent, Steve Hannagan, for advice, and Hannagan warned him that the company's leaders, "by the very drop of a Southern-accented word," identified their origins and invited the assumption that they held backward views.

Assessing the situation with dry practicality, Hannagan argued that the company's officers should espouse progressive beliefs, if for no other reason than the good of the business. Any other approach, he said, putting the matter bluntly, would be "detrimental to an international product because of a sectionalism that has outlived its usefulness." Ralph Hayes, who stayed on the payroll as a part-time "special employee" after quitting as an officer of the company, and whose duties mostly included advising Woodruff on strategy, echoed Hannagan. He cautioned that Coca-Cola "has been too timid in integrating and upgrading Jewish people and colored ones in the Company's organization."

Under Woodruff's prodding, the New York bottling plant hired its first black salesman, Fred Graham, and the *New York Courier* applauded the company for having "opened its ears to the rhythm of democracy." The boycott was averted.

The pragmatism behind the company's steps was obvious. As Hayes never tired of pointing out, there were as many blacks in the United States as there were Canadians in Canada. Blacks were a huge market of more than 15 million whose patronage meant profits. Pepsi already had captured a significant share, not only by offering a cheaper product but also by embracing enlightened attitudes on race. Walter Mack made sure some of Pepsi's college scholarships were directed to black students in segregated states in the South. Calling him "a businessman with a conscience," *Pageant* magazine related an incident from 1946 in which Mack stormed out in protest when a hotel in Chicago denied lodging to a black member of Pepsi's scholarship board.

Mack hired a black sales executive and launched a "Leader in His Field" advertising promotion in which prominent blacks including Dr. Ralph Bunche were profiled in black-oriented newspapers.

Casting a wary and envious eye on the competition, Woodruff asked Hayes, who still served as director of the New York Community Trust, to begin doing "a little bit more" for blacks in the way of charity. Woodruff maintained a private account at Hayes's institution, Special Fund No. 9, which he used to make grants that were officially anonymous but whose source could be made known to the recipients. Hayes suggested setting up a $1,000 annual award for the National Urban League to give to a black honoree for distinction in music, the arts, or public service. Woodruff also. pushed his advertising department to come up with a program like Pepsi's that would attract black customers.

The problem, from the company's point of view, was that pitching Coca-Cola to blacks was not an activity that took place in a vacuum. In the South in particular, there was the very real threat of a backlash by white racists. In April 1949, the company-owned baseball team, the Atlanta Crackers, scheduled a three-game exhibition at Ponce de Leon Park against the Brooklyn Dodgers, whose star second baseman, Jackie Robinson, had broken baseball's color line two years earlier. The grand dragon of the Ku Klux Klan in Georgia responded by calling for a boycott. "The Atlanta baseball club is breaking down traditions of the South," Dr. Samuel Green warned, "and the club will pay for it".

As it happened, the games went off without incident, drawing a record gate of 49,309 fans, and the Crackers won the final game, 8-4. Robinson played safely despite the KKK's threats of personal harm. Yet the specter of retribution for racial moderation continued to haunt the company for years. Lester Maddox, a vitriolic white supremacist who chased black customers from his Atlanta restaurant wielding a pick handle (and who later embarrassed the state of Georgia by winning the governorship), once sent the Atlanta Coca-Cola bottler a warning against "weakening" in the resistance to desegregation. The name of Maddox's group, the People's Association for Selective Shopping, suggested its purpose: boycotts against companies sympathetic to civil rights.

The safest way to proceed, as Mack had demonstrated, seemed to be for Woodruff himself to get involved in charitable ventures on behalf of the black community, but for news of his gestures to be relegated to the black press, far from the eyes of whites in the South and elsewhere, who might be offended. Again relying on Hayes's connections, Woodruff arranged to join the board of the Tuskegee Institute, the Alabama school founded by Booker T. Washington, whose philosophy of social separatism for the races and vocational education for blacks found favor with many whites who liked the idea of a slow, even glacial approach to change.* The press release announcing Woodruff's membership was sent to sixty-three black publications and the beverage trade press, but not to the nation's daily newspapers.

The company began advertising in black magazines and retained a black public relations counselor, Moss Kendrix of Washington, D.C., to make the rounds of black conventions. Lionel Hampton and Graham Jackson were hired to play on Coca-Cola's behalf at various functions. When it came to hiring significant numbers of blacks as full-time employees, though, the company's policy was marked by extreme timidity. According to an in-house memo prepared late in 1951, a plan to recruit blacks was abandoned, "temporarily at least," for fear it would be interpreted by the NAACP and other black groups as a "capitulation" to the threat of a boycott.

In the meantime, Woodruff continued his efforts at personal diplomacy, occasionally with eventful results. In the late fall of 1952, as a participant in a drive to raise $25 million for the United Negro College Fund, Woodruff invited two dozen of the nation's leading bankers and industrialists and their retinues to come to Atlanta for a formal dinner before traveling overnight by private train to Tuskegee. Unfortunately, one of the arriving guests turned out to be black, and not even Woodruff could prevail on the Capital City Club to allow the group to break bread under its roof. Woodruff had to put his party on the train three hours early and feed them in the dining car as they traveled west to Alabama.

Ivan Allen, Jr., later the mayor of Atlanta, made the train trip as a young civic leader assigned to help look after the important guests, who included John D. Rockefeller III, Richard K. Mellon, and Harvey Firestone, Jr. After dinner, Allen recalled, Woodruff called on Winthrop Aldrich, the chairman of Chase National Bank, to make a brief speech. Trying to be heard over the noise and the clacking of the wheels, Aldrich grew exasperated and finally yelled at Woodruff, "Bob, I can't hear myself talk!" Woodruff ordered the train stopped on a siding, and as flagmen ran up and down the track setting out flares Aldrich finished his talk. When he was done, Wood-

---

* In his famous speech at the Cotton States and International Exposition in Atlanta in 1895, Washington called agitation for social equality between the races "the extremist folly," adding, "no race can prosper till it learns that there is as much dignity in tilling a field as in writing a poem. It is at the bottom of life we must begin and not the top." He called for blacks and whites to live side by side but apart: "In all things that are purely social we can be as separate as the fingers, yet one as the hand in all things essential to mutual progress." Woodruff kept a copy of the speech in his private papers. His personal view, which he once shared with Tom Glenn, was that blacks ought to be helped and built up gradually, "instead of pampering them and spoiling them with a lot of money and 'hooey.'"

ruff barked, "Start the train," and the trip was resumed. The next morning, bundled up in overcoats against an unseasonably chilly breeze, the band of millionaire businessmen carried their own bags off the train and went to tour Tuskegee.

Counting the trip a success and anxious for coverage in the black media, Woodruff had his publicity adviser, Kendrix, arrange a major story and photo spread that appeared inside the February 1953 issue of *Ebony* magazine. The cover, designed as if it were intended to capture and preserve forever the era's eager, strained attempts at racial goodwill, carried a photograph of Eleanor Roosevelt under the headline, "Some of My Best Friends Are Negroes."

One of Woodruff's best friends was William B. Hartsfield, the mayor of Atlanta. Together, the two men virtually ruled City Hall and worked successfully to prevent the kind of lurid race-baiting and violence that tore apart so many other towns in the South.

Like Woodruff, Hartsfield had a practical reason for being progressive. In 1946, eight full years before its epochal *Brown* decision, the U.S. Supreme Court outlawed the whites-only Democratic primary in Texas. Hartsfield foresaw the inevitability of voting rights for blacks, and rather than resist to the bitter end he decided to build bridges to Atlanta's black community and seek the support of its leaders. Following a philosophy loosely characterized as "go slow, go easy, but go," he reduced the size of the "WHITE" and "COLORED" signs on the restrooms at the airport until they were almost illegible, then had them removed entirely. He instructed the clerks at City Hall to address mail to blacks using the salutations "Mr." and "Mrs." instead of their first names, a small but unprecedented courtesy.

In 1948, at a time when a quarter of its members were still believed to be closet Klansmen, Hartsfield integrated the Atlanta Police Department He hired eight black officers, and while their duties were severely circumscribed—they had to change into their uniforms at the Butler Street YMCA and were not allowed to arrest whites—their appearance walking the beat in a Deep South city represented a dramatic breakthrough. Thousands of black citizens followed them around on their first day, waving and cheering. A year later 25,000 newly registered black voters helped Hartsfield win reelection.

The mayor called Atlanta "a city too busy to hate," capturing the community's appetite for growth, prosperity, and social acceptability in a fitting phrase that could easily have been modified to express the credo of the Coca-Cola Company as well.

In all of his undertakings, Hartsfield acted only after consulting Woodruff and getting his blessing. Their relationship dated back to the days when Woodruff was a salesman for the General Fire Extinguisher Company and Hartsfield, the son of a foundryman, worked as a male secretary writing up his orders. Even after Hartsfield resumed his studies, passed the bar, became a lawyer, and entered politics, he deferred instinctively to Woodruff. When a tough decision had to be made, Hartsfield would gather the city's business and political leaders in Woodruff's private dining room at Plum Street, and Woodruff would lend his authority to the course of action Hartsfield proposed. "Bill thinks he runs the city," Woodruff once told a visitor, only half-kidding. "Hell, it's my city."

Like so many others, Hartsfield was indebted to Woodruff. Not long after he won his first election as mayor, in 1936, Hartsfield turned to the Coca-Cola Company to redeem $730,000 worth of scrip the cash-strapped city had issued to its employees in lieu of real pay for the last month of the year. Thanks to Woodruff, four thousand city workers and schoolteachers could afford to enjoy Christmas, and Hartsfield took office as a hero. When Hartsfield suffered his only loss at the polls, in 1940, Woodruff quietly paid him a legal retainer that tided him over to the next election, which he won. After that, with Woodruff helping underwrite his campaigns, he carried every election until he finally retired in 1962.

Woodruff could call on City Hall for almost any favor he wanted. Atlanta's chief of police, Herbert Jenkins, patrolled Woodruff's house personally, picked out his burglar alarm system, and ran background checks on his night watchmen. When Woodruff's long-time chauffeur, Lawrence Calhoun, had a heart attack and died, Hartsfield attended the funeral, an unheard-of tribute from a Southern mayor to a black servant. Hartsfield kept a big portrait of Woodruff in his office, where he served Coca-Cola to all his visitors and often called himself the mayor of "Coca-Cola City."

What Woodruff wanted most of all, not surprisingly, was a good atmosphere for business. For all his time spent at Ichauway, Woodruff shared Hartsfield's belief that the fabled glory of the Old South, the picture drawn by Margaret Mitchell in *Gone With the Wind*, was a cruel lie. "The besotting sin of the South is worship of the South," Hartsfield once said. "So many speak of magnolias and beautiful ladies and soft nights, and so many of them had only hookworm and poverty." Woodruff believed in the idea of the "New South," not as some pallid call for regional tolerance but in the same sense meant by Henry Grady, the great editor of the *Atlanta Constitution*, who uttered the phrase for the first time in 1886, the year of Coca-Cola's birth: as an aggressive invitation to investors from the North to build their factories in the South, where low-paid, non-union workers, black and white alike, were ready to turn away from the tired soil, join the assembly line, and start punching a clock for decent wages.

Woodruff served on the boards of several major corporations and was forever browbeating his fellow directors to hold their meetings in Georgia, where he would stage elaborate welcoming demonstrations as if he were a one-man chamber of commerce. In 1950, for instance, he shanghaied the board of General Electric, took them to north Georgia to see the facilities of the Georgia Power Company, fed them an outdoor buffet, gave them a ride on the funicular at Tallulah Gorge, and didn't let up until he had elicited a public promise from GE's president Charles Wilson, that the company would build a plant in the state.

All of Woodruff's ambitions, for his company, his city, and state, the region as a whole, depended on an atmosphere of racial harmony. Every cross-burning and lynching, every whipping of a prisoner on a chain gang, every "WHITES ONLY" sign nailed up by the hammer of the Jim Crow laws, every venal attack on "the Nigra" by the likes of Georgia's father-and-son governors, Gene and Herman Talmadge, fed the image of the South as Tobacco Road and scared off investors. Woodruff wanted desperately for the region to put its best foot forward, but as Hannagan pointedly reminded him, all too often the South "put its stumpy foot forward—the one with hookworm, malaria, and bigotry."

Among his friends and associates, the prevailing view of Woodruff was that he had a sort of split personality, having inherited compassion, charitable instincts, and a keen understanding of human nature from his mother, while his father, who died in 1944, was the source of his intensity and willfulness and hunger to make a profit. For simplicity's sake, people tended to draw a line down the middle of his forehead and divide his "good" and "bad" qualities between his maternal and paternal genes. It was a convenient device (and not entirely off the mark), but it ignored the fact that those traits were inexorably mixed and inseparable within his mind. His vision of a better South, with good hospitals and fine universities, with handsome theaters and museums, public parks and gardens, and a thriving populace, depended on the money that could only come from a vigorous, competitive economy and success in the rough and tumble of capitalism.

In Woodruff's patriarchal view of things, racism was wrong because it was cruel and unnecessary, and most of all because it was bad for business.

Woodruff's drive to seize power and impose his will on Atlanta was without parallel. In no other major American city of the time could an individual businessman be found making so many decisions that affected so many aspects of the community's life.

Not only did Woodruff hold sway over the mayor and Board of Aldermen, he utterly dominated the small group of men who were pleased to call themselves the "power structure" (and who were known to others by the less flattering term "Big Mules"), the heads of the city's law firms, banks, churches, colleges, utilities, and commercial institutions. In a city with no political machine, no organized crime worthy of the name, no large industries or powerful unions, the leaders of the business community had an unusual degree of influence, and they turned to Woodruff as their unquestioned captain.

The key to his strength, of course, was the vast wealth of the Coca-Cola Company. With a market value of more than half a billion dollars, it towered like a colossus over the city's other enterprises. Even though it was a publicly held corporation with some fifteen thousand individual shareholders, Woodruff crafted a way to exercise what amounted to single-handed control over its ownership, giving himself a solitary proxy over the largest pool of capital in the South. He did so, fittingly enough, through a complicated set of arrangements that melded two of his parents' strongest traits, chicanery and charity.

Woodruff shared his mother's ambivalence toward material riches. Certainly he spent abundantly on himself, his wife, Nell, and their friends and family. Especially in Atlanta, where great estates like those of the Rockefellers and du Ponts were unknown, he seemed extravagant enough traveling among his four homes, booking suites with grand pianos on his ocean crossings, throwing lavish parties, and commandeering private railroad cars. But he was not as rich as he appeared. In the early 1950s, he personally held only $19 million worth of Coca-Cola stock, less than 4 percent of the outstanding shares. When Walter Winchell guessed in his gossip column that Woodruff was worth 800 million "bux," more than Henry Ford II, he was off by a factor of 20. With the financial burden of Ichauway, the expenses of spoiling two dozen nieces and nephews, and the drain of a top marginal income tax rate that eventually hit 92 percent, Woodruff often complained in private that he was strapped for cash and would send his secretaries scrambling through his books looking for spare funds. Once one of them found a $37,000 credit tucked away in a brokerage account. "I think you will get by all right," she said in mock seriousness. Two of Woodruff's black servants, taking his frequent expressions of anxiety to heart, put money in a small savings account for him in case he went broke.

Compared with the prodigal spending of some tycoons, Woodruff's habits were relatively modest. "I have never had any desire," he liked to say, "to have a racehorse, a yacht, or a mistress." His friends occasionally teased him, saying, "Two out of three isn't bad," but the fact was he did not indulge in those or other wildly expensive pursuits. When his father chided him for having four homes, he answered, "How many men do you know who have the same woman in each?" Louis Marx, the toymaker, who drove a brand-new Bentley, accused Woodruff of "showing off" by driving around Manhattan in a prewar Chevrolet when he could afford a better car, not realizing that Woodruff simply didn't care.

Woodruff's interest in philanthropy, first stirred by the sight of the old black man's malarial fit at Ichauway, matured quickly with the onset of his mother's final illness. He donated $40,000 to Emory University for a cancer clinic and personally recruited Dr. Elliott Scarborough, an Alabama-born, Harvard-educated oncologist, to run it. More important, he agreed with his mother that her estate should be dedicated to the goal of improving health and education in the South.

In renouncing his inheritance, Woodruff was motivated by more than simple generosity. The disposition of his parents' estate would have an important impact on the control of the Coca-Cola Company, and Woodruff was smart enough to recognize that charity was an instrument he could use to keep that control in his own hands. With no children of his own to provide for, and with little interest in increasing his personal wealth, Woodruff was eager to see his family's fortune used for the betterment of mankind—but only so long as the principal remained in Coca-Cola stock, under his thumb.

Giving money away wisely, Woodruff came to believe, was even harder than earning it in the first place. After long talks with McGill, Emory University's Mizell, Ralph Hayes, and others, he devised the underpinnings of a theory to guide his philanthropy. He wanted to foster progress in the region by improving people's bodies and minds, and he wanted others with wealth to help. If his family sold their Coca-Cola stock to raise money for good causes, Woodruff reckoned, they would be limiting themselves to one-time donations to beneficiaries beyond their control, and they would be doing very little to inspire others to give. Instead, Woodruff envisioned maintaining the family's Coca-Cola stock as a sort of permanent endowment, using the income to make matching grants, challenging others to participate. It soon became a hallmark of Woodruff's style that he would give half—but only half—of the money needed for projects that interested him.

Seeing their potential as a means of maintaining command over the company, Woodruff set out to build a network of charitable foundations whose directors would answer to him and whose duties, in addition to helping people, would include holding on to their shares of Coca-Cola. Woodruff convinced his brothers, George and Henry, to join him in yielding any claim on their patrimony, and he talked his father into creating the Emily and Ernest Woodruff Foundation to maintain and administer the family's estate as a charity. (Misanthropic to the very end, Ernest told a friend he agreed to the plan to give away his money mostly "so that the government would not get it when the final call comes.") Woodruff then appointed himself chairman of the foundation's board of trustees.

Woodruff and his lawyer, Hughes Spalding, led a similar campaign for the disposition of the Whitehead family's fortune. Joseph Whitehead, Jr., the elder of the pioneer Coca-Cola bottler's wastrel sons, died unexpectedly at the age of forty, and much to the surprise of his estranged wife and other relatives his will left everything to the care of orphans. Spalding fended off the widow's threats to "stir up a stink" about Whitehead's private life, sent her off with a $500,000 settlement, and set up a foundation that preserved Joseph Jr.'s Coca-Cola stock.

The second of Whitehead's sons, Conkey, also died young and childless, and he, too, left his estate in a charitable trust administered by Spalding. With her sons gone, and no grandchildren, Lettie Whitehead Evans had a considerable fortune she was willing to dedicate to philanthropic purposes. The problem was, she proved *too* willing. Lonely, susceptible to the importuning of other pleaders, Mrs. Evans frequently changed her will and switched beneficiaries and executors, typically at the behest of the last person who spent time with her. She lived in Virginia, far removed from

Woodruff and the rest of the Coca-Cola family, and Spalding often had to hasten north to dissuade her from some new project, or, as he put it, to chase away "the buzzards who are cultivating Mrs. Evans for their own selfish interests during her declining days."

Woodruff pressed Mrs. Evans to set up a personal foundation to handle her assets and lend discipline to her giving. When she dragged her feet and complained that she had no money to spare to endow such a fund, Woodruff acted on his own and incorporated the Lettie Pate Evans Foundation using $7,500 of his own money. Embarrassed, she agreed to support the foundation, making Woodruff its president and putting him in charge of $10 million of Coca-Cola stock.

Together, the Woodruff and Whitehead family foundations gave Robert Woodruff direct control over more than 10 percent of Coca-Cola's outstanding shares. Yet that was only part of the influence he wielded over the ownership of the company. He also appointed the board of the Coca-Cola International Corporation, the holding company his father had established decades earlier, which still owned more than a quarter of all the outstanding common stock. His father's bank, Trust Company of Georgia, continued to hold the Coca-Cola stock it earned as a participant in the 1919 sale of the company, and the bank also administered scores of individual trust funds and estates with an aggregate of more than half a million shares of common stock, another 10 percent of the outstanding shares.

At any given time, Woodruff had at least half a dozen Coca-Cola directors serving on the bank's board, guaranteeing that the company's interests would be protected. Ignoring the rules of confidentiality, Spalding, a bank director, notified Woodruff whenever an investor planned to sell Coca-Cola stock, and Woodruff would intervene to keep the shares in friendly hands.

When his father's lifelong deputy, Tom Glenn, died in 1946, Woodruff had him replaced as Trust Company's chairman with a loyal friend, John Sibley, Coca-Cola's former general counsel. The bank's concentration of Coca-Cola stock was so heavy some officers privately called it "our problem" and worried they might be sued for failing to diversify. But Woodruff's wishes prevailed and the bank kept its holdings, giving him "working control" of the company.

When it came to preserving Coca-Cola's heritage, Woodruff often used his father's tactics in pursuit of his mother's goals. In 1947, Howard Candler came under legal attack from his sister and brother, who wanted to break up their family's real estate empire and sell the pieces to a New York developer. Hoping to keep the Candler properties intact, Howard turned to Woodruff, who put up the money to have Emory University buy a controlling interest in the Candler Company. Woodruff then sent Spalding to chase off the developer, a task Spalding performed with relish by threatening an endless, financially draining lawsuit that Woodruff would bankroll indefinitely no matter what the actual merits. "These New York fellows scare pretty easily," Spalding declared jauntily after the developer gave up. Then, while Candler was still aglow with gratitude over the rescue mission, Woodruff leaned on him and convinced him to pledge his part of the estate to Emory, a gift worth $5 million.

On a sorrowful note, Woodruff's own brother, Henry, placed his fortune at the service of charity, too. The victim of a series of nervous breakdowns, Henry Woodruff committed suicide on Thanksgiving Day 1947, shooting himself at his parents' old farm outside Richmond, Virginia. His last letter to Nell Woodruff described his agitation over a failed romance. "I haven't asked her to marry me," he wrote. "Am just so afraid we may not get along, and am afraid about many other things. . . ."

Leaving the bulk of his estate to the Emily and Ernest Woodruff Foundation, Henry helped solidify Robert's control over the Coca-Cola Company, but not before Robert came very close to dying as well. Robert blamed himself for the suicide, even though by all accounts he did as much as he could to look after his brother. Henry resisted frequent entreaties to stay with Robert and Nell in Atlanta and their other homes, preferring instead to remain alone on the farm. He had trouble with such mundane matters as buying a car and training a hunting dog, and the courses of treatment he underwent at a sanitarium did not do any lasting good.

Nonetheless, his mother had asked Robert to take care of Henry when she was gone, and he believed he had failed to keep his promise. "It affected him more than anything I've ever seen," said Joe Jones, Woodruff's chief of staff. In the year after Henry's death, Woodruff was moodier and more fitful than ever, frequently falling ill with minor ailments. He began drinking harder and sleeping less. During a stay in New York in August 1948, he was rushed to Roosevelt Hospital with viral pneumonia and a fever of 105. After three touch-and-go days he started a slow recovery, but it was a close call.

McGill, taking a liberty few of Woodruff's other associates dared, wrote him a frank, three-page letter imploring him "to go to the Stork Club less frequently, get more sleep, and quit whipping a tired horse with the number of drinks required to drive tiredness out of the body and mind." McGill urged Woodruff "to conserve yourself for your family, your responsibilities, and your friends," and concluded pointedly, "Mrs. Woodruff is a very charming lady and looks good in any sort of dress or suit, but I don't think she would look good in black."

Recuperating during a long rest-cure at his ranch in Wyoming, Woodruff answered McGill that he accepted the "lecture" and would try to take better care of himself. He did not give up drinking, nor did he shed his perpetual shroud of discontentment, but from then on Woodruff seemed surer about using the wealth and power of his family and his company for public purposes. Somehow his parents' disparate natures consolidated themselves in his mind after Henry's death, just as their estates had been joined in the name of charity. His own brush with mortality strengthened Woodruff's resolve to take the leading role in guiding Atlanta, along with as much of the rest of Georgia and the South as he could, through the rigors of social change that were coming in the 1950s. It would be like a quail hunt, with Woodruff in charge.

But all of it depended on the continuing success of the Coca-Cola Company.

Al Steele bounced back quickly from the failure of Pepsi's "More Bounce" campaign. Seeing that an emphasis on the extra sugar and calories in Pepsi left consumers cold, Steele shifted quickly to a new line of attack. The renegade Coca-Cola man decided to compete with his old company at its own game—quality.

For years, with its "twice as much" theme, Pepsi had been paraded as an inferior substitute for Coca-Cola. Steele turned that image upside down. "Let's get rid of this honkytonk look," he told his top executives one morning. He unveiled a handsome new "Pepsi blue" logo and began applying it on the bottles using paint instead of paper labels. He replaced the company's iron display signs, which tended to rust, with aluminum and strengthened the design of Pepsi's cardboard six-pack, which tended to rip. Most noticeably, he hired Faye Emerson, a statuesque blond actress, to pitch Pepsi on television.

Miss Emerson's show, "Wonderful Town," was not much of a hit with the critics. Debuting on CBS in the fall of 1950, the format called for her to appear for fifteen minutes three times a week solving the "problems" of modern life. The first show featured a lesson on how to ride in a taxi. One of her suggestions was to get in the near door rather than walk around in traffic to the other side—an issue, the *New York Times* observed drily in its review, "that had been worrying a good many of us." She also recommended knowing one's destination and not expecting a cabby to break a $20 bill. But if her advice fell short of the cutting edge, that was beside the point Faye Emerson had a magnificent, arresting bosom, which she displayed to great advantage on Pepsi's behalf in clingy, low-cut evening gowns that suggested a world of sex appeal and glamour.

It was hard to escape the conclusion, the editors of *Advertising* Age wrote, that the program was a vehicle for Miss Emerson's cleavage: "Male viewers can't hear what's said from looking at Faye, and probably don't much care." The star of the show served Pepsi in cut-glass goblets on a silver tray, poured it over cracked ice in a crystal bowl, drank it out of a champagne glass, and generally elevated the product, if not to the level of supreme sophistication, then at least far above the bargain basement

Pepsi's sales recovered and began climbing again. Steele cut costs by going to a smaller bottle and reducing the amount of sugar in his formula, then plowed the savings back into advertising, distribution, and modern plants. "If you want to milk a cow," he explained, "you've got to feed it." He competed with Coca-Cola for a place in the lucrative new field of cup-vending machines, signing agreements to put Pepsi's equipment in movie theaters and army camps and on Pacific cruise liners. He traveled constantly, wooing Pepsi's bottlers.

Most of all, Steele remembered the lesson he learned at the Coca-Cola Company: Soft drinks were not a necessity. "We fill no basic need of man," he liked to say. "Our products don't clean teeth, shine shoes, or add hormones to you." The business depended on salesmanship, first, last, and always. Without constant promotion and catchy, ubiquitous advertising, it would die.

In cataloguing the woes that bedeviled Woodruff and his team at Plum Street, that lesson was a good place to start. They seemed to have forgotten how to sell the product. Radio advertising, never Coca-Cola's strong suit, was in a steep decline. The company's most popular program, a musical variety hour, fell to number 42 among the 126 rated shows, and the others were doing far worse. Singin' Sam had to be dropped, along with the company's soap opera, "Claudia."

Coca-Cola's programs, according to *Sponsor* magazine, became little more than a "clearinghouse" for the clients of Woodruff's friend Sonny Werblin, none of whom had much appeal for younger listeners. The bottlers were supposed to buy air time for Morton Downey on local radio, but they considered his show dull and paid only the bare minimum to put it on low-power stations. Coca-Cola spent $600,000 a year, including Downey's $140,000 salary, producing a show that was doomed to puny ratings.

As for television, the company was willing to experiment—Walt Disney made his first TV appearance on Coca-Cola's Christmas Day special in 1950—but not to make a commitment. At the same time Faye Emerson was using her profile to lift Pepsi's, Coca-Cola's advertising director timidly declined a proposal to sponsor a Western, dismissing TV as "not a national medium."

Nothing was more damaging than the loss of Archie Lee. Weary, saying he needed a complete break, Lee took his wife to Hawaii for an extended vacation in the winter of 1950. When he returned, he learned he was suffering from cancer, and in less than a year he was dead. Lee's lieutenants at the D'Arcy agency failed to uphold his legacy. The man who popularized "the pause that refreshes" was succeeded by a committee of plodders whose idea of a breezy new slogan, unveiled in time for the 1952 season, was the woefully uninspired "What you want is a Coke." Hannagan, the company's press agent, took a stab at creating an ad campaign, but the best he could come up with was a proposal for a TV show featuring "dames who can dance on legs they're not ashamed of."

Coca-Cola seemed to be caught somewhere between the extremes of vulgarity and stodginess. Burke Nicholson, the company's stately senior vice president, proposed a high-school promotion to be known as "Citizens of Tomorrow," in which Coca-Cola would be identified as "a wholesome social binder between young people"—an idea that was, in the argot of the times, hopelessly squaresville.

The company might have limped along indefinitely, avoiding a crisis, had it not been for the squeeze Woodruff put on the bottlers by insisting on holding the retail price at a nickel. The inflationary pressures that had acted on Pepsi finally caught up to Coca-Cola, too, shaving the bottlers' profit margins and in many cases putting them in the red. They had remained fairly stoic as long as they believed their sacrifice would destroy the competition, but now, with every passing day, Steele was proving that consumers would spend 6 or 8 cents, even a dime, for a Pepsi.

As the magic of the nickel wore off, the bottlers grew restive. They were paying 18 cents a gallon for gasoline, up 4 cents from before the war, and costs were rising for bottles, caps, and cases. Their cheap labor was gone, too, thanks to the forty-hour work week and the minimum wage. Some couldn't afford to repaint their trucks. Planning a dinner meeting with a committee of bottlers in the fall of 1950, Harrison Jones warned Woodruff that his guests would be in a rebellious mood and advised that the cocktail period be abbreviated to "prevent any venomous member from having too much false courage."

Woodruff refused to bend. Using persuasion and the subtle threat of reprisals, he got nine of the company's most successful bottlers to write their colleagues a joint letter urging them to hold the line on the nickel. Some of the recipients responded with withering scorn. "It is probably once in a lifetime one receives a letter from nine millionaires all on one sheet of paper," Jeff Martin, the bottler in Lincoln, Nebraska, wrote back. "I think I will have it framed." Unlike them, he explained, he had no spare pile of capital sitting around, and could not afford "a lot of wishful hoping that some miracle would happen. . .to stay at the 5-cent price."

An insurrection was inevitable, and in one respect Woodruff got lucky. His leading adversary, Veazey Rainwater, Jr., son of the early parent bottler, turned out to be a kook. In the weeks leading up to the annual Coca-Cola shareholders meeting on May 7, 1951, Rainwater held a series of "Coke-tail" parties around the country and tried to recruit disaffected fellow bottlers to help him remove Woodruff from control of the company. His effort lost steam when his father disavowed him and his wife sued for divorce, hoping to gain some of his $1 million trust fund before he spent it all on quixotic ventures.

When young Rainwater got up to speak his piece at the annual meeting, he stood alone. Much of his presentation—starting with a proposal that Coca-Cola bottlers wear "drink-o-meters" to verify that at least half of their daily fluid intake consisted of Coke—was laughable. Yet for a company whose annual meetings routinely took fewer than five minutes in an empty boardroom in hard-to-reach Wilmington, Delaware, the spectacle of a bottling scion railing against the management was something quite new and a bit disquieting. The fact was that Rainwater had a long list of suggestions for improvements, many of which were far from ludicrous: quart bottles, Coca-Cola on menus, promotions targeted at housewives, free Cokes in auto showrooms, gift certificates, ads on TV, lightweight coolers for office use.

"Coca-Cola gives us our beautiful homes and fine linens, our gentlemen farms and ranches, our magnificent charities and foundations," Rainwater said at one point, turning an eloquent phrase, "but what are we putting back?" The sheer energy and passion Rainwater brought to his small, feckless mutiny, the boyish enthusiasm of it, seemed to shake loose the cobwebs.

One other interloper made the trip to Wilmington. Woodruff's first cousin, James Waldo Woodruff, Sr., a wealthy and cantankerous businessman from Columbus, Georgia, showed up to complain about stagnation in the value of the common stock. What made his appearance memorable was his opening line. Bill Hobbs, still the president of the Coca-Cola Company, welcomed him to the meeting, and Jim Woodruff asked, "Who are you?"

It was a good question. At the end of his fifth year as president, Hobbs had few duties and rarely made a decision or even a public appearance.

His inaction in the face of the latest health crusade against Coca-Cola was a perfect illustration of the drift in the company's executive suite. In the fall of 1950, a Cornell University professor named Clive M. McCay testified before a select committee in the U.S. House of Representatives that the sugar in Coke caused cavities. And, he said, the phosphoric acid was a dangerous additive. Giving a vivid account that instantly became part of the national folklore, Dr. McCay described how a tooth left in a glass of Coca-Cola would soften and begin to dissolve in a period of two days.

Hobbs was assigned to coordinate the company's response, and his performance can only be described as dithering. Coca-Cola's top chemist, Orville May, explained to Hobbs and the company's other executives that *anything* containing sugar and phosphoric acid—fresh orange juice, for example—would dissolve teeth over a period of time. The point was that people did not hold food and beverages in their mouths for days on end. They swallowed, and their saliva washed away the sugar and acid before lasting damage was done. Otherwise the whole country would be toothless.

Dr. May's argument was sound, but it was just the sort of defensive, unappetizing explanation of the individual ingredients in Coca-Cola that Woodruff had always insisted on avoiding in public. Pope Brock, the company's usually decisive general counsel, admitted he had no ideas "as to just what procedure should be adopted in connection with a reply," saying the question required "mature study and reflection." Hobbs appointed a committee to consider what to do, and its members were still debating several months later.

The bottlers, already agitated over falling revenues, were stirred up anew as their local doctors and dentists and PTAs expressed worry about the possible dangers of Coca-Cola. Adding to the controversy, an article appeared in *Pageant* magazine describing how the "empty" calories in soft drinks displaced "an equivalent number of 'good' calories you need to maintain good health." From his position on the sidelines, Ralph Hayes tried to nudge Hobbs toward a decision. "As an old shuffler myself," he observed, "I'm not decrying paper-shuffling. But the shuffling should finally produce conclusions, policy, and action."

At length Brock and the company's top lobbyist, Ed Forio, pressed Hobbs to take action because "food faddists, communists, crackpots, and the like" were continuing to make news while the company remained silent. Hannagan agreed, suggesting a propaganda campaign that would ridicule Dr. McCay and other nutritionists as advocates of "a Mixmaster diet of worms and castor oil." Still Hobbs stalled.

In the end it fell to the company's elder statesman, Burke Nicholson, to bell the cat and confront Woodruff with the need for change. Nicholson was an unlikely insurgent: He once wrote Woodruff a fawning letter with the salutation "Sir Robert" that said, "Your smile or your frown—each represents for the moment the most important thing in my life. . . ." It was the very improbability of Nicholson as the source of criticism that made his salvo so stinging and effective. The company, he said, was in a state of paralysis, full of "children doing men's work" and old men awaiting retirement. He wrote:

> The flag bearers, holder-uppers of the torch, seekers of the Holy Grail, even the Don Quixotes jousting with windmills, do not seem to be present as of old. Where is the leadership that formerly made people in this institution feel that they belong to a Church to which they gave unquestioned obedience, loyalty and fidelity? Some strong characters must lift up the flag else this Thing recedes into the limbo of just another corporation, just another organized group, and not some great warm moving purposeful crusade.

Nicholson's call to arms left Woodruff shaken. The reproach was aimed at Hobbs, but it plainly included Woodruff, too. A friend who saw Woodruff shortly afterward said it was "the first time in my life I have seen you confused and not knowing just which way to turn."

Woodruff brooded over Nicholson's broadside for several weeks, caught in a mood of lassitude, complaining of headaches and "feeling logy all day," before he finally summoned the will to act. Calling a series of meetings with bottlers around the country, Woodruff announced that he was returning to active management of the company and would be "in the game for keeps." He ordered a new batch of the buff-colored memo cards he used to run the business (literally) out of his pocket, and soon his office at Plum Street was jammed again. One caller complained that visiting him was like "holding a conference with the traffic cop at Five Points at 5 o'clock in the afternoon."

Hobbs was fired. Woodruff installed Nicholson as a caretaker president but made it clear he planned to call the shots himself. He started by outflanking Dr. McCay. If a professor of nutrition at Cornell was bent on maligning Coca-Cola as a health hazard, Woodruff figured, the best way to strike back was to hire a bigger gun who said otherwise. The company's "Chemistry Scholarship Fund" gave a $5,000 study grant to Fredrick J. Stare, chairman of the Nutrition Department at Harvard's School of Public Health, and in due course Dr. Stare wrote an article for *McCall's* magazine advising teenagers to improve their diets by drinking a Coke in the afternoon. With additional grants from the fund fueling his research, Dr. Stare wrote letters to school administrators and other authorities refuting the notion that Coca-Cola caused cavities or dissolved teeth. In time the hubbub subsided.

Resuming command over the company's affairs, Woodruff ordered a variety of changes, including the creation of a long-overdue public affairs office and the purchase of Coca-Cola's first corporate airplane, a DC-3 he christened *Windship* in a play on his mother's maiden name. In Hobbs's wake, Ben Oehlert rejoined the company, and morale in general perked up.

When he turned his renewed energies to the issue of the nickel, however, Woodruff found himself stymied. He grudgingly conceded that many bottlers felt the need to raise prices, but he could see no way for them to do so without dire consequences. If the retail price of a Coke doubled and went to a dime, volume would drop drastically. Consumers might pay 10 cents for a 12-ounce Pepsi, but not for a 6½-ounce bottle of Coca-Cola. And if the price was set in between, at 6 or 7 cents, the logistics would be a nightmare because more and more of Coca-Cola's sales were from vending machines, which were unequipped to deal with pennies. (A bottler in South Carolina tried taping two pennies to the bottom of his bottles and selling them for a dime each, an experiment that fizzled miserably.) The logical move, to a bigger bottle, was an innovation Woodruff obstinately refused to contemplate.

Facing a set of unhappy choices, Woodruff opted for a dramatic long shot. He began exploring the possibility of having Congress authorize the minting of a new, 7½-cent coin.

Woodruff also went to work trying to elect a new president. For the first time in his career, he openly supported a presidential candidate in 1952—his good friend (and the company's wartime benefactor) Dwight Eisenhower.

The two met at a dinner in New York City in the spring of 1945, not long after VE Day, when Eisenhower made a triumphant visit home. The general's affection for Coca-Cola was undimmed. Asked at one stop if there was anything he wanted, he replied, "Could somebody get me a Coke?" And when he'd finished it, he said he had one more request: "Another Coke." He made sure the press corps overheard him, giving the company a nice publicity boost.

Woodruff cultivated a close relationship with Eisenhower and encouraged his budding political ambitions. He was genuinely fond of Eisenhower, but there is no question he also had some very hard-headed, practical reasons for wanting a friend in the White House. If there was any doubt Woodruff's actions had a calculated air, one had only to look at an invitation he sent Ike to visit Ichauway. "Usually our guests are companionable," he wrote, "and in the evening there is bridge, gin rummy or poker." As everyone in his circle knew, Woodruff organized games of gin rummy or poker after dinner every night, but detested bridge and never played. He listed it only because he knew it to be Eisenhower's favorite.

The general visited the plantation in January 1950, and Woodruff lavished attention on him. In later years, Woodruff liked to tell the story of how Eisenhower arose early on his first morning and sent Woodruff's valet, James Roseberry, to tell Woodruff it was time for breakfast. "Mr. Woodruff says down here *he's* the general," Roseberry supposedly replied, "and breakfast will be at eight-thirty." Actually, Woodruff was a good deal more solicitous than that, recognizing in Eisenhower a man whose aura of command surpassed his own. As the 1952 election approached, Woodruff wrote Eisenhower urging him to run, saying his candidacy was "not only essential but inevitable."

Woodruff placed his time, money, and advice at Eisenhower's disposal during the campaign, and even engaged in a rare public quarrel that was reported in the New York tabloids, arguing his candidate's merits over Adlai Stevenson's during a noisy dispute with Averell Harriman one evening at Toots Shor's nightclub.

On election night, Woodruff joined Eisenhower and his top supporters in a suite at the Commodore Hotel in New York to follow the returns and celebrate victory. Around three o'clock in the morning, jubilant but bone weary, Eisenhower circled the room kissing the women goodnight and pumping hands with the men. Woodruff, whose hearing had begun to fade, was bent over with his back turned, engrossed in conversation with Eisenhower's brother, Milton, and failed to respond when Ike spoke to him. Grinning wickedly, the president-elect wound up and kicked Woodruff squarely in the seat of the pants before hugging him and retiring for the night.

At the time, naturally, Woodruff was tickled by the attention, but the episode seemed to be a portent of things to come. In a variety of ways no one could anticipate, Eisenhower's presidency ended up backfiring on the Coca-Cola Company. For starters, the new president showed little enthusiasm about pursuing the company's political agenda. When Woodruff asked him about minting the 7½-cent coin, Eisenhower forwarded the inquiry to the Treasury Department, then dropped the matter as soon as it met resistance in the lower bureaucracy. Even on a trifling issue—Woodruff's request for a change in federal game laws to allow a longer hunting season for mourning doves—the president proved similarly unable or unwilling to help.

The problem was not access. At the behest of Eisenhower's personal secretary, Ann Whitman, the Secret Service issued Woodruff a pass to the White House, a "key to the back door," as he called it, that allowed him to drop in at will. Woodruff typically showed up in the late afternoon for a few cocktails after Ike's golf game at Burning Tree, and he was on the guest list for Eisenhower's regular black-tie stag dinners. Theirs was a warm and lively relationship: After a round of cordials one night, the two were debating so vehemently that Woodruff followed Eisenhower into the family quarters, perched on the side of the president's bed, and badgered him until he changed into his pajamas, climbed under the covers, and ordered Woodruff to leave.

But other than a spirited friendship, and the indisputable propaganda value of having a president of the United States who loved drinking Coca-Cola in front of photographers, it was hard to point to many benefits that accrued to the company because of its close ties to the Eisenhower administration. The costs, meanwhile, proved to be substantial. The president asked a lot of favors of the company, from lobbying help on Capitol Hill to contributions for pet causes. And thanks to the president, Woodruff made a mistake in judgment that drove the company, already in a precarious position, closer to the edge of the cliff.

One of Eisenhower's closest friends was William E. Robinson, the publisher of the *New York Herald Tribune*. A veteran public relations executive and Republican operative, Robinson helped run the campaign and afterward settled comfortably into the president's circle of cronies. As a regular at the White House smokers, he got to know Woodruff and the two hit it off well together.

In the winter of 1953, Steve Hannagan died unexpectedly of a massive heart attack during a trip to Africa, leaving his agency without a leader and the Coca-Cola Company without a publicist. Woodruff arranged to have Robinson take Hannagan's place.

Bill Robinson was an affable man, a good golfer and card player, the sort whose ruddy complexion and slightly hardened features made him look as if his picture might belong next to the phrase "drinking buddy" in the dictionary. And it was after a night of bar-hopping with Woodruff in Manhattan, in fact, that the notion of Robinson running the Coca-Cola Company first cropped up.

Standing in the pantry of Woodruff's River House duplex having a Coke as a nightcap, jabbing the air with a pudgy finger, Robinson began enumerating a long list of criticisms of the way the company was being run. It did not bother him in the least that Burke Nicholson, the president of Coca-Cola, was there, too, listening to the tirade with mounting irritation, nor did it seem to bother Woodruff. "If you think you can do a better job," Woodruff told Robinson, "maybe you ought to have the chance."

The switch was not long in coming. Nicholson was popular within the company—a "harmonizer," in the apt phrase of Ralph Hayes—but hardly a hard charger. A colleague once asked him why he wasn't more aggressive and he replied simply, "I'm doing what the Boss wants me to do." It was obvious, however, that the company could no longer afford to stand pat. By 1954, while Coca-Cola idled, Pepsi's sales had doubled under Al Steele.

As word of the impending promotion circulated through the company grapevine, Robinson's utter lack of experience in the soft drink business raised eyebrows and hackles in the executive suite. Woodruff's senior advisers, including Hayes, urged him to move slowly and tried to warn him that he was repeating the same mistake he'd made with Bill Hobbs. Perhaps, Hayes said, it would be smart to give Robinson at least one interim job as a test before handing him the presidency. Nicholson remarked acidly that he hoped Woodruff would not puff up Robinson as he had Hobbs, "when you almost spoke like the Lord saying of Jesus, 'This is my Beloved Son in Whom I'm well pleased.'"

Nonetheless, on the morning of Saturday, February 5, 1955, two months after he turned sixty-five, Woodruff announced he was retiring. Shuffling seats in the board room, he surrendered his chairmanship to Nicholson, quit the Executive Committee, and gave the presidency of the company to Robinson.

The press reported the changing of the guard as if Woodruff intended to drop from the scene completely. *Time* said Woodruff had "stepped out," leaving the company's affairs in the hands of the "smart, hard-driving" Robinson, and *Business Week* described the move as a clean break equivalent to Asa Candler's sale of the company back in 1919. Woodruff had his furniture removed from 515 Madison Avenue, the company's New York headquarters, and vacated his office in Atlanta, too. Robinson himself clearly believed he'd been anointed, as he granted a series of interviews on his plans before commandeering the corporate DC-3 to fly off around the country and meet the bottlers.

But things were not as they appeared. Two weeks after clearing out of the president's space at Plum Street, Woodruff moved into a bigger office, a suite that was specially built for him, complete with a private kitchen and dining room, in a new wing off the fourth floor of the Coca-Cola building. He continued to come to work as he had before, sitting in a huge leather armchair at a sturdy desk under a portrait of his father, flicking cigar ashes in the general direction of a brass spittoon and punching a set of buzzers on the left leg of the desk that summoned the people he wished to see.

Woodruff, it happened, had retired from New York, not from the Coca-Cola Company. He had come home, determined to spend the rest of his life in Georgia, where his help was needed so badly in politics and philanthropy and where he felt most comfortable. He had no intention of relinquishing power. Retaining his seat on the board of directors, he created a new Finance Committee, appointed himself chairman, and took as firm a grasp on the company's purse strings as his father once had.

"It was a disaster from the beginning," according to Joe Jones. Robinson misunderstood the situation completely, as evidenced by his first gaffe. A few weeks after his appointment, Robinson received a letter from John Sibley asking him to be the guest of honor at a formal dinner in Atlanta, where he could meet the town's leading citizens. It was a command performance, of course, an invitation from Coca-Cola's banker, one of Woodruff's closest friends, politely directing Robinson to present himself for inspection by the men who owned the company and ran the city. The point was lost on Robinson, however, who had his secretary respond curtly that he was too busy traveling.

Actually, had his travels been devoted more to company business, Robinson might have fared better. The bottlers found him charming—"very chatty and friendly," by one account—and his background in advertising and marketing was sorely needed as Coca-Cola clawed to stay ahead of Pepsi. He had a deft wit that helped defuse criticism from the health authorities; the only way Coca-Cola could hurt you, he liked to say, was if a case fell out of the window and landed on your head.

But Robinson was more interested in the golf course and the bridge table than the rigors of running Coca-Cola. After making his inaugural fly-around, Robinson settled back into his old habits and hired an administrator named Curtis Gager (the name rhymed with wager) to be in charge of the company on a day-to-day basis. Gager was a tall, balding man whose steel-framed glasses and flinty expression gave him the appearance of a bird of prey. He had been fired from a top job at General Foods, where he had the reputation of being a hatchet man, and his harsh management style quickly alienated most of his colleagues at the Coca-Cola Company.

"He was a double-barrel, breech-loading son of a bitch," in the description of Delony Sledge, the company's colorful advertising manager, a view that was widely shared. Gager made Sledge, who was known for his vivid, freewheeling speeches, begin submitting his texts for prior approval and editing, and ordered him under penalty of firing to recite them word-for-word. Morale, just beginning to heal after the Hobbs era, plummeted again. Ben Oehlert was given so little work he began reading books in his office.

For their part, Robinson and Gager bemoaned Woodruff's reluctance to innovate. Nicholson's last act as president had been to cajole Woodruff into accepting the idea of larger bottles. Coca-Cola finally came out with a 10-ounce "king-size" and a 26-ounce "family-size," both of which won immediate popularity.* But the old man balked at other necessary changes. Americans had become diet-conscious, yet Woodruff saw no need to compete with the rapidly proliferating ranks of Lo-Cal, Les-Cal, No-Cal, Nu-

---

* As a measure of the newsworthiness of any sort of alteration in Coca-Cola, a cartoon in the *New York Herald Tribune* showed two men marooned on a desert island watching a jumbo-sized Coke bottle wash ashore. "Good heavens," one of them cried, "we're shrinking!"

Thin, Slim-line, and their ilk by marketing a sugar-free cola. Consumers wanted a choice of soft drinks at the vending machine, yet Woodruff vetoed any expansion into other flavors. And while the competition was making huge strides in perfecting cheap, disposable cans, Woodruff resisted the move away from glass bottles.

One difficult but necessary piece of business Robinson carried out with Woodruff's backing was the firing of the D'Arcy agency. No one had surfaced there with even a touch of Archie Lee's creative genius, and Coca-Cola's advertising had begun to provoke derision. When the company unveiled its $15 million ad campaign for 1955, *Business Week* reported, industry insiders mocked its obvious resemblance to Pepsi's. Steele was siphoning away the young adult market with a sophisticated appeal to upscale, urbane consumers, especially fashion-conscious women, and along came Coca-Cola with a pitch to "Bright Young Moderns," using sleek models dressed in designer clothes from B. H. Wragge and Mr. John.

Robinson transferred the account to McCann-Erickson, and after an association of forty-nine years D'Arcy bowed out gracefully with a simple, dignified ad (its best in ages) that said, "We hand it on with pride. . . ." McCann, one of the hottest agencies on Madison Avenue, was expected to make an immediate splash. The problem was that Woodruff had no clear idea about the direction the new ads should take. He wanted "new phrases and mainly new illustrations" but offered little in the way of specific guidelines. Many of his associates in Atlanta were worried about the snob appeal in Coke's and Pepsi's ads. As Sledge, the latest in a long line of home-grown advertising managers, put it, "We are interested in both sides of the railroad track, in both the salon and the saloon. We want to know Rosie O'Grady just as intimately as the Colonel's Lady." It was fine to stress the quality of the product, in Sledge's view, but dangerous to suggest any special quality on the part of the consumers of the product.

Robinson, on the other hand, liked the elevated tone of the most recent ads. Rather than changing tack, he wanted McCann-Erickson to outdo Pepsi at the same game. At Robinson's urging, the agency came up with a fresh slogan, "The Sign of Good Taste," for a series of ads that showed chic, glamorous people drinking Coke in exclusive settings around the world, notably at the Doge's Palace in Venice and the Taj Mahal. The company's greatest strength, in Robinson's mind, was its social cachet and its reputation for being "superior" to other soft drinks. He wanted consumers to associate Coke with people who were "several cuts above the mean or average," according to one in-house memo, and hoped his strategy would persuade hosts and hostesses that "the serving of anything else is a social blunder."

Given the success of the "Pepsi Challenge" several years later, the great irony of Robinson's approach was that it scared Al Steele half to death. Steele was not at all eager to get into a comparison campaign pitting Coke against Pepsi, and even went so far as to issue a public plea to the Coca-

Cola Company not to "turn down the fastest road to universal disaster—that of damning each other's products." Having just managed to ease Pepsi out of the kitchen and into the drawing room, Steele feared his product would finish second in a glamour contest.

Not that Steele personally had much to worry about on the glitz front: In 1955, after ditching his wife, he eloped to Las Vegas with the actress Joan Crawford, his third marriage and her fourth. They set up housekeeping in New York in a penthouse apartment on Fifth Avenue and spent nearly half a million dollars on remodeling. The finished quarters included a cavernous closet for Crawford's 304 pairs of shoes, another room for her cosmetics and pills, a special shampoo and hairdressing basin with spray faucets, and a massage table and whirlpool bath for him. The couple shared a geranium-pink bedroom with a wood-burning fireplace. Guests at "Taj Joan," as *Time* dubbed the duplex, were asked to remove their shoes to keep the pure white shag carpeting in the living room from becoming soiled.

In the eyes of many Americans, of course, the Steeles seemed more gaudy than glamorous, and the larger competition between Pepsi and Coca-Cola struck a false note as well, with the values of Madison Avenue proving to be at odds with those of Main Street. Woodruff had committed the blunder of refusing to see that American life was changing; Robinson made the equally serious error of misinterpreting what those changes were and how the company should meet and exploit them. One reviewer blistered McCann's "Good Taste" series for replacing Coca-Cola's traditional illustrations of "normal, natural, healthy girls and boys, men and women with. . .grotesque and exaggerated caricatures of masculine women and feminine men." McCann, the critic said, "has succeeded in associating Coca-Cola with the dregs and decadent creeps who populate the so-called international set." According to one account, the company commissioned a confidential survey and found that some respondents thought the models looked homosexual.

That was enough for Woodruff. He had already soured on Robinson and Gager, and the "Good Taste" series was the final straw. Woodruff wanted to drop the campaign, but Robinson balked. News of factional fighting within the company leaked to the press, and the Robinson camp fired a salvo in *Sponsor* magazine complaining about "interests that have reached the age of retirement but refuse to give up domination of management," a disparaging reference to Woodruff.

The company's New York and Atlanta offices stopped communicating. In a humiliating mixup, Plum Street ordered the bottlers to change their truck colors from yellow to red-and-white at the same time Robinson's office in New York issued a directive to keep the yellow. As if no aspect of the company's affairs were too petty to bicker over, Robinson seized custody of the new corporate airplane, a Lockheed Ventura, and kept it in New York where Woodruff couldn't use it.

In the spring of 1958, as he prepared to celebrate his thirty-fifth anniversary with the company, Woodruff holed up at the Cody ranch in Wyoming with a few trusted advisers, plotting strategy. One of his guests was Lee Talley, a veteran Coca-Cola man who'd spent most of his career in the Export Corporation. Talley was a Methodist minister's son from Monroeville, Alabama, a five-foot-four bundle of enthusiasm who spoke of his love for the company and its product in the cadences of the pulpit. Woodruff had considered Talley for the presidency before and hesitated, thinking he lacked seasoning. Now, at fifty-six, Talley was as ready as he'd ever be, and Woodruff picked him to be Robinson's replacement.

Talley was expected to break the news to Robinson in person, a task he accepted with pleasure. Like almost every other Southern-bred, lifelong employee of Coca-Cola, he considered Robinson a disastrous president, and there was an element of personal dislike between the two men as well. (Robinson liked to throw an arm around Talley's shoulder, as if the smaller man were a child, a gesture Talley found infuriating.) Returning from the West with Woodruff and Joe Jones, Talley arrived at Penn Station on the *20th Century Limited* one morning, took a limousine directly to 515 Madison Avenue, rode the brass-trimmed elevator up to the eighteenth floor, and hurried to Robinson's office in the back of the suite without pausing to take off his coat or hat. Striding past a secretary without a word, he went to the desk where Robinson was sitting and said, "You're through."

When word reached Plum Street a celebration broke out. "I happened to be up on the executive floor the day Mr. Talley took over from him," a visitor recalled, "and I'm telling you, it was just like the celebration of Independence Day. I mean the atmosphere—you could feel it. He was a family member, Talley was. It was old home week."

It was not an out-and-out firing. Robinson was bumped up to chairman of the board, where he would continue to earn a six-figure salary. But his authority was chopped off completely, and his next assignment on behalf of the company was a trip to Gary, Indiana, to study the can industry and write a report. Gager was demoted and left powerless. The "Good Taste" campaign was restyled entirely and geared toward mainstream Americans. Illustrations of women wearing fur coats gave way to housewives relaxing with a Coke after vacuuming.

Operating with Woodruff's explicit support, Talley took charge. "For the last ten years we have had a pretty dry spell," Woodruff wrote an old friend—but now that spell was over. With his evangelical energy, Talley revived the spirits of the bottlers (who had disliked Gager so much they once booed him at a meeting) and restored the mood of the home office. Talley began making the sort of unapologetic, infectiously overheated pep talks that had been missing since Harrison Jones retired:

> Sometimes I've stood on the deck of a great ocean liner in the North Atlantic on a stormy night as she pitched and rolled in the heavy seas, with her great engines slowed, and she would

be just making way. And as I have stood alone there, peering into the inky blackness of the mountainous seas ahead, I've thought about our business in these changing times....

If the ship is strong and seaworthy, and if the crew is stout-hearted and courageous...she rides out the storm, and the weather clears, and the seas calm, and on the horizon there comes the faint glimmer of another day, and soon a bright streak of morning sun, and the officers train their instruments upon it. Their position is fixed, and a firm voice goes down the speaking tube to the engine room, "Full speed ahead!" And so it echoes throughout the ship, and once more her giant engines quiver and vibrate with life as her bow once more goes crashing through the seas at full speed to her destination.

It was impossible not to mock Talley for such ponderous metaphors, of course, especially when they came from such a diminutive source. He traveled with a custom-built, two-thirds-size lectern he could see over, and his stature made him the subject of considerable teasing. When he went hunting at Ichauway, astride a mount no bigger than a Shetland pony, Woodruff liked to look over at him in the tall grass and yell, "Lee, get on your horse!" And Talley would respond with unfailing good cheer, "I am!"

Yet Talley could be very determined. His sunny disposition and gentle demeanor disguised a tough inner core. An underling remembered asking Talley once for some time to walk around the block and think over a new assignment before accepting. "Well, make it a short block," Talley snapped, his smile disappearing, "because the decision's already been made." Like everyone else who got to the top of the company, Talley was extremely deferential with Woodruff, but he also had the gumption to disagree with him when necessary and push him to change his mind.

"I believe for the first time in a good while Mr. Woodruff is pleased with his management," a friend wrote Ralph Hayes not long after. Talley took over, and it was true. Many years later, contemplating the significance of Talley's rise to the presidency of Coca-Cola, Joe Jones said simply, "He saved the company."

A few months before he became president, Talley gave a speech in Atlanta as remarkable for its time and place as Woodruff's stand against lynching a quarter-century earlier.

The top executives of the Export Corporation were summoned to Plum Street from their posts around the world to attend a special "homecoming" meeting, a gathering meant to demonstrate that the headquarters of the Coca-Cola Company had returned to Georgia once and for all. The point of the assembly was to signal an end to the influence of the New York office, but the striking thing was what Talley had to say about the company's attitude toward race and creed. Speaking in October 1957, in the heart of the Deep South, he told his colleagues, "A man who holds himself out as the head of a business which seeks the patronage of all men—rich and poor, black and white, yellow and brown, Christians, Moslems, Buddhists, and Jews—must be devoid of racial prejudice and religious bigotry."

The men who ran Coca-Cola in Africa, Talley said, had to have "a genuine respect for and a willingness to get along with and understand Negroes." The same was true in India, in Japan and China, in Australia and Cuba and Brazil. The company had to see and appreciate the "best qualities" of the many different peoples of the world, Talley warned, or else it would not be able to do business.

To understand the profound effect Woodruff and his company would have on the unfolding drama of the civil rights movement in Atlanta, it was necessary to look at Coca-Cola overseas. By the early 1950s, more than a quarter of Coke's sales were in foreign markets. "One by one," Jimmy Curtis reported to Woodruff at the onset of the decade, "the many barriers and hurdles that confronted our business when World War II ended are giving way." With grueling effort, the company overcame the welter of health regulations, trademark laws, import duties, and boycotts that blocked its path to the international stage.

The State Department helped, as did the company's lawyers. At one point Coca-Cola had 630 separate infringement cases pending around the globe, the vast majority of which it won. When diplomacy and lawsuits failed, the company occasionally used strong-arm tactics: In one South American city, where a rival bottler threatened to make political trouble, Coca-Cola's field man played private eye, compiled a list of the bottler's mistresses, and had only to recite a half-dozen names before the fellow backed off, saying, "I get the picture." (The company avoided paying bribes for the most part, not so much out of high moral purpose, as Ralph Hayes once explained in a confidential memo, but because a bribed official could always be replaced and the payoff "would be a shining target for review by his successor.")

More than anything else, the Coca-Cola Company succeeded because it granted its bottling franchises to prominent foreign citizens and hired foreign nationals in its workforce. By 1955, the Export Corporation was selling concentrate to 418 bottlers in 92 countries and territories, yet only a handful of its employees—fewer than one percent—were American. Coca-Cola was in effect a French company in France, a Greek company in Greece, a Mexican company in Mexico. Resistance melted because most of the profits remained on foreign soil.

Dealing with partners from other cultures gave Woodruff and his circle at Plum Street a unique perspective and sense of tolerance that was lacking elsewhere in the insular South. What other businessman in Atlanta could boast of receiving a live cheetah as a gift from his managing director in Nairobi? What other company had a photo of Fidel Castro riding a bus in

Havana drinking a bottle of its soda pop? Who else did business in China through an English export house that sold pig bristles? The Coca-Cola Company simply could not afford to be narrow-minded.

The principal owner of Coca-Cola's bottling works in New Delhi, Bombay, and Calcutta was Yadavindra Singh, the Maharajah of Patiala, governor and spiritual leader of India's Sikh population, a close friend of Prime Minister Nehru and a former chancellor of the Chamber of Princes. Known around the world for his work as a diplomat, Olympic sportsman, and philanthropist, the maharajah lived in a cream-white castle the size of Buckingham Palace, with a 10,000-volume library, two square miles of tended gardens, a private army, and a hunting preserve stocked with partridge and wild boar. He was a member of royalty who stood six foot four and wore a turban, and the painful fact of life was that had he visited Atlanta, Georgia, in the mid-1950s, he might well have been considered "colored" and been denied lodging at the Dinkler Plaza Hotel.

Woodruff got to know men like Singh in every corner of the globe and recognized that they simply did not fit into the South's ethos that people could be categorized as either black or white and treated accordingly. When a group of Atlanta businessmen asked Mayor Hartsfield one day when the city's airport would begin getting international flights, his blistering response reflected the concerns of the Coca-Cola Company. "Not until Atlanta becomes an internationally minded city," he said. "What do you plan to do with the Brazilian millionaire who flies in with some money to invest but happens to be black? Send him to the Negro YMCA? Think about it, friends."

With a vast foreign market and millions of American blacks as customers, the company had every reason to want to avoid racial embarrassments in its hometown, especially after the U.S. Supreme Court ruled in *Brown* v. *Board of Education* that segregated schools were unconstitutional. Until 1954, the men of Plum Street and City Hall had been able to move at a slow, gentlemanly pace of their own choosing as they helped ease the bonds of the Jim Crow laws. Afterward, the city of Atlanta—like the rest of the South—was at odds with the law of the land, facing an accelerated demand for change that triggered a countervailing roar of massive resistance.

While Woodruff and his associates could hardly be called bleeding hearts, they seemed to realize almost by instinct that they could not afford to disobey the federal government. "I certainly have never been out for integration," McGill wrote Woodruff at one point, "but whatever my feelings, I am going to try to stay by the law and the courts." Woodruff liked to use an old saying in Negro dialect to explain his position: "Ah tries to cooperate with the inevitable."

Unlike so many of their counterparts in the South, the Coca-Cola crowd grudgingly accepted the fact that delay was futile. One day in the spring of 1955, just after the Masters golf tournament and about a year after *Brown*, President Eisenhower was on his annual visit to Augusta National, with

Bobby Jones along for company. "Mr. President," Jones asked him, "don't you think we're moving a little fast? Couldn't you arrange to give us a little more time?" According to McGill, who recounted the story years later, Eisenhower cocked an eyebrow at Jones and asked how much time he had in mind, and Jones, realizing how he'd sounded, answered sheepishly, "Oh, three or four hundred years, I guess."

Change was coming much faster than that, and fittingly enough one of the earliest breakthroughs involved the public golf course in Atlanta that bore Bobby Jones's name. Three days before Christmas in 1955, Mayor Hartsfield notified the press and TV stations that he'd decided to integrate the course and invited them to cover the event. The night before the new policy took effect, he met with a selected group of black golfers and urged them to tee off the next day at every course in the city *except* Bobby Jones, where he knew the race-baiters would be waiting. "They told me they had promised the television people they would appear," Hartsfield recounted later. "I said, 'Those TV boys aren't interested in watching you hit the ball. They want to get pictures of you getting beat up.'"

As the mayor anticipated, all eyes were on the Bobby Jones course. Vandals struck during the night, scrawling racial epithets in yellow paint on the benches and pavilions. But Hartsfield had a crew out before dawn, and when morning came there was no trace of the graffiti—nor of any black golfers. As the media packed up their cameras and went home empty-handed, blacks desegregated the other courses without incident.

The leaders of Atlanta's black community joined forces with Hartsfield on several occasions, hatching stratagems aimed at achieving change without setting off acts of violence. In the summer of 1957, for instance, a year and a half after Rosa Parks inspired the Montgomery bus boycott, the Reverend William Holmes Borders and his followers decided they could wait no longer to challenge the law that segregated the city's buses. They demanded to be arrested and were, but Herbert Jenkins, the white police chief, sent a black detective who carefully took them into custody and had them booked, bonded, and out of jail in two hours. The door of the detention room was never closed.

"Atlanta Negroes want to see signs of progress," T. M. Alexander, a prominent leader, explained at the time, "but we are not trying to ram it down the white man's throat. The beauty of Atlanta is that there is a liaison between the Negro and the better class of the white community."

Woodruff's attempt to nourish the same kind of moderation on the state level proved less successful, and in many ways he had himself to blame.

The Coca-Cola Company had posted a lobbyist at the Georgia Capitol ever since "Uncle John" Edmondson began working the corridors for Asa Candler just after the turn of the century, buying drinks and dinner for needy legislators. The top priority was to prevent the General Assembly from imposing a penny soft drink tax that would hike the price of a Coke to 6 cents, a job Edmondson and his successors performed with quiet efficiency for decades.

Race did not enter the equation until 1949, and then only indirectly. Senator George, the company's great champion in Congress, had to stand for reelection the next year. Because of his age, seventy-one, and his increasing remoteness from the voters of the state, he was considered vulnerable. The most powerful of his potential challengers was Herman Talmadge, the son and political heir of Eugene Talmadge, the "Wild Man from Sugar Creek," a four-term governor whose fiery oratory, red suspenders, and overt bigotry made him one of the South's most notorious (and popular) public figures until his death in 1946.

In order to keep Herman Talmadge from running against Senator George, Woodruff was prepared to cut a deal. The younger Talmadge had won a special election to finish out the last two years of his father's final term as governor, and Woodruff hoped to persuade him to pass up the Senate race in favor of running for reelection to a full four-year term of his own. Woodruff also wanted the General Assembly to pass a general sales tax that would eliminate once and for all any chance of a special levy on soft drinks. The question was what Talmadge might ask in return.

On a late summer afternoon in September 1949, Hughes Spalding invited Talmadge to his farm on the Chattahoochee River outside Atlanta for a talk. Talmadge confided that he was willing to run for governor again and favored the adoption of a 3 percent sales tax. The problem, Talmadge explained, was that supporting such a tax would hurt him with the voters. He wanted Spalding's promise, and Woodruff's, that the Coca-Cola Company would back him to the hilt for the Senate seat when it came open in 1956, or earlier if George died or retired.

"We will have to make a pretty firm commitment," Spalding reported to Woodruff, "that when a vacancy does occur in the United States Senate we will go down the line for him. That's about the way it stands." Woodruff accepted the terms. Talmadge won the governor's race in 1950 with the company's backing and led a successful fight the next year for passage of the sales tax.

The deal might have been a small footnote of interest only to Georgia's taxpayers, except that it linked the Coca-Cola Company to Talmadge's other politics as well, which included staunch, implacable resistance to the civil rights movement. Unlike his father, Talmadge did not shout the word "nigger" at rallies or point to black children and call them the enemy, but his efforts were no less hostile to the advancement of black people. A lawyer by training, he became one of the South's leading advocates of states' rights and the notion that "separate but equal" could somehow be salvaged in the courts. His famous pamphlet, "You and Segregation," set it all out in black and white.

The company had no leverage at all with Talmadge, and there is no indication Woodruff or Spalding ever tried to get him to soften his views on race. On the contrary, Woodruff praised Talmadge publicly, once toasting him at a formal dinner as "the best governor Georgia ever had, sired by the second best," a line that later caused the Coca-Cola Company a good deal of embarrassment. Talmadge was succeeded as governor by a pair of protegés, Marvin Griffin and Ernest Vandiver, who escalated the segregationist rhetoric and tactics of the state government through the rest of the decade.

In 1956, as Senator George's term was drawing to an end, Talmadge waited for Woodruff and Spalding to make good on the final part of their deal. George was now seventy-eight and ailing, but unwilling to accept the idea of retirement. He had served in the Senate for more than a third of a century and believed he was still invincible at the polls.

As the campaign took shape, most independent observers agreed that George was doomed. While the senator was attending to his duties in Washington, Talmadge had been stumping the state for two full years raising money, locking up commitments and laying the foundation for a powerful challenge. George had scarcely set foot in his home state and was thoroughly out of touch with the electorate.

When the senator belatedly began campaigning, the results were embarrassing. "Old Walter came up here," Willie Barron, the venerable Coca-Cola bottler in Rome, Georgia, reported to the home office, "and I'm one of the few people he still knows. He hasn't been in Floyd County in twenty years." The senator was far from healthy, and he rambled badly in some of his campaign speeches, even breaking down in tears once or twice.

Woodruff spoke to the senator personally, gently urging him to give up gracefully. When the senator failed to heed the message, Woodruff sent an emissary, Robert Troutman, to explain in clearer, more forceful terms that the game was up: There would be no support for another campaign. George reluctantly withdrew from the race, and Woodruff helped arrange a face-saving sinecure, an appointment for George to be President Eisenhower's personal representative to NATO.

The great likelihood is that George would have lost to Talmadge even if Woodruff and the Coca-Cola Company and all the other "Big Mules" in Atlanta had rallied to the senator's side. And it may be that by pushing George into retirement, Woodruff did him a favor. Still, there was a whiff of betrayal to the affair, a feeling that Senator George was being jettisoned in spite of all the favors he'd done over all the years. George's wife, Miss Lucy, never forgave Woodruff. "Pretends to be his friend all this time," she said bitterly to a family member who worked for Coca-Cola, "but look at this!"

George was dead within the year. Talmadge took his hard-line views on race to the U.S. Senate, where he served four terms, leaving behind a statehouse that remained enemy ground to a million black Georgians.

On the evening of Sunday, December 6, 1959, Atlanta held the grandest stag party in its history.

The occasion was Woodruff's seventieth birthday. While a select handful of women, including Woodruff's wife, Nell, listened by intercom from a room on another floor, 147 of the city's top businessmen, lawyers, bankers, and politicians gathered in the Mirador Room of the Capital City Club, where they dined by candlelight on Chateaubriand and supreme of quail, sampled the Coca-Cola mousse that was served for dessert, and then lit cigars and swirled brandy as the program began.

Bobby Jones served as toastmaster. There were three keynote speakers, each taking a different aspect of Woodruff's life as a topic. Ralph McGill spoke on Woodruff the sportsman. Ralph Hayes, joking that "modern Woodruff, like ancient Gaul, is divided into three parts, and I have only a third of him," described his business career. Bob Troutman discussed Woodruff's philanthropy in a text modestly entitled "A Friend to Man."

Among the dinner's other highlights, a life-size, "talking" bottle of Coca-Cola rolled out on the stage and described itself as an emblem of all humanity. "In the far reaches of the free world," a disembodied voice within the robot intoned, "I am mankind. In the everlasting spirit of the struggle upward, I am a power for good. . . . More faith is afforded me than certain sovereign governments."

President Eisenhower, who was away on a state visit to Pakistan, sent a somewhat less dramatic recorded greeting of his own, and the five members of the host committee presented Woodruff with a silver humidor that had a clock on top, along with cameo etchings of their faces. Every guest received a commemorative album, bound in red leather, that contained a scrapbook of Woodruff's life, along with a snapshot (taken earlier that evening and quickly developed) of himself shaking hands with Woodruff in the receiving line.

No one who attended the dinner ever again made the mistake of equating Woodruff's dislike of publicity with a lack of ego. He reveled in the praise until well after midnight, and a few days later he asked all of the speakers go to a studio to repeat their words on tape for posterity. He wrote Eisenhower that the affair "was the best party of its kind I have ever been to."

Had it been a retirement dinner, the lavish accolades might have seemed more commonplace, the kind of soft packing with which men of accomplishment are often crated and sent to the museum. But Woodruff was not retiring, no more than he had been at sixty-five. He gave strict orders before the dinner that no one was to mention his age, and he scrapped plans for a series of reenactments that might have lent the affair the finality of an episode of "This Is Your Life." He declined to receive gifts.

The point of the dinner was power. Woodruff still had power—more of it, in fact, than ever before—and he meant to use it in the pivotal decade at hand, the 1960s. The guests were there to be reminded that they still worked for him.

Ten

POLITICS

In the spring of 1959, Al Steele took to the road trying to sell his jittery bottlers on "The Sociables," a new advertising campaign that continued to present Pepsi as the favorite soft drink of the fox-hunt and dinner-party crowd. Unlike his counterparts at the Coca-Cola Company, Steele still believed in the upscale approach that had brought his product out of the kitchen and, as he put it, "away from poverty."

The bottlers weren't so sure. Faced with a slowdown in sales, they doubted if snob appeal had much further attraction. Sophisticated young adults were a narrow segment of the market, after all, and there were relatively few men in the United States who actually wore top hats, as some of the models did in Pepsi's newest ads.

For six weeks, as he worked his way east from San Francisco through Denver, Dallas, Chicago, Columbus, Albany, and Charlotte, Steele staged an elaborate "Ad-O-Rama" show every night and gave the same high-octane talk over and over, urging the dubious bottlers to help underwrite the campaign. His wife, Joan Crawford, made the trip with him, bringing along twenty-eight pieces of luggage and a supply of Alpine cigarettes and 100-proof Smirnoff vodka. The two kept up a furious pace, drawing mobs of reporters and holding press conferences everywhere they went. "I hate to use my wife to help me sell," Steele admitted, "but let's face it, she does."

Their last stop was Washington, where Steele delivered two speeches, visited Capitol Hill, and taped eleven separate radio interviews before flying home to New York on the company's Lockheed Lodestar. The next night he went to bed early, saying he was exhausted. Crawford found him in the morning, slumped on the floor, dead of a heart attack at age fifty-seven.

To succeed Steele, Pepsi's board of directors turned to a low-key lawyer named Herbert Barnet, a man whose rise through the corporate ranks had been fueled in large part by his efforts to cut costs and put the brakes on Steele's impulsive spending. The antithesis of Steele, Barnet had no appetite for extravagant productions or pretentious ads. One of his first decisions was to fire Pepsi's advertising agency, Kenyon & Eckhardt, and retire "the Sociables" permanently. The day of the top hat was over, much to the relief of the bottlers.

Yet Barnet had little idea what new direction to take. Thanks to Steele, Pepsi had become a full-fledged rival of Coca-Cola, with more than a third of the national cola market and a mandate to compete for an even bigger share. The question was how. When the Pepsi-Cola Company opened its new headquarters on Park Avenue in February 1960, nine months after Steele's death, the *American Soft Drink Journal* hailed the modern, eleven-story glass and aluminum building as "a dramatic symbol of the forward thinking and action which has marked Pepsi-Cola's rise over the past decade." But really it was more of a monument to Steele, a backward salute to his accomplishments that gave no clue how Pepsi planned to cope with the future.

Both companies, Pepsi and Coca-Cola, were confronted with a swiftly changing marketplace where the old verities no longer held. What had been a fairly simple contest between two soft drinks gave way to a modern business climate in which the customers were in charge. After years of telling consumers what they ought to want, the companies found themselves forced to listen.

One of the most urgent challenges arose from the success of vending machines. People liked the convenience of slipping coins into slots to buy ice-cold bottles of Coke and Pepsi, and the machines became a lucrative source of revenue for the companies' bottlers. But people also expected a variety of flavors—root beer, orange, lemon, ginger ale, and grape—in addition to cola. The bottlers were pressing their home offices to develop new lines they could stock. Coca-Cola's New York bottler, a hard-to-manage maverick named Jim Murray, grew so impatient he started selling his own brand of lemon-lime drink called Veep.

Scrambling to regain the initiative, the Coca-Cola Company broke its seventy-five-year tradition and introduced a new product, Sprite, in spite of Robert Woodruff's private misgivings that the citrus flavor was "too sweet, not sharp enough, and possibly has a disagreeable aftertaste." The company also offered a complete line of popular flavors under the brand name Fanta (the name invented by Max Keith during World War II) and began experimenting with Coke in cans. Every idea Woodruff had stubbornly resisted during the 1950s became fact in the early 1960s, all with considerable success.

Pepsi followed the same dictates, launching a lemon-lime drink called Teem and a line of flavors called Patio. For a time, the two companies seemed almost like allies, setting aside their differences while their beleaguered executives tried to figure out where the public was headed. In 1958, diet drinks had accounted for less than one percent of the sales in the nation's $3 billion soft drink industry. Just four years later, in 1962, a public opinion survey found 28 percent of the American people watching their weight. Royal Crown's Diet Rite Cola made a meteoric debut on the supermarket shelves.

At Plum Street, Lee Talley assigned a top priority to "Project Alpha," a crash campaign to develop a competing diet drink. In less than a year, sugar-free Tab was unveiled at a crowded press conference in the auditorium of the Time-Life Building in New York, where a friendly critic said it tasted "like a good, tart Coke." Pepsi kept pace, bringing out Patio Diet Cola for test-marketing in several cities.

What to do about advertising threw both companies for a loop. The creative department at Pepsi's new agency, Batten, Barton, Durstine & Osborn, struggled with the search for a new theme to replace "the Sociables." According to one of the Coca-Cola Company's spies on Madison Avenue, the best the highly regarded BBDO could come up with in the early going was "Relax with Pepsi," a meager effort reportedly "slapped together on a desperation basis at a top-brass level."

Coca-Cola's executives were no happier with their results from McCann. Talley undertook what he called an "agonizing reappraisal" of the company's advertising and concluded it had lost direction. After dropping the high-society approach, Talley wrote in a candid memo:

> We have been selling our product as a light refreshment in a ski lift; we have been selling it as the base for a Coke Float; we have been selling it as the beverage to be consumed with a hot chafing dish of roast beef hash; we have been selling it as refreshment beside the swimming pool; we have been garnishing it with a slice of lemon or lime; we have been selling it as an adjunct to a sandwich snack after a set of tennis; most recently we have been selling it as the chief ingredient in the wassail bowl—a "Cherry Merry" or a "Lemon Grog."
>
> In my humble opinion, we are losing sight of WHAT WE ARE in trying to be all things to all people. . . .

In Talley's analogy, selling Coca-Cola should be like describing an attractive woman. "She is not a piece of lipstick, a bit of eye shadow, a pretty gown, a girdle, a brassiere, a well-turned calf," he wrote. "It is the total ensemble which is a beautiful woman." Ordering the company's advertising director, Delony Sledge, to get busy right away, Talley explained in simple terms what he had in mind for a new theme: "It must reek with quality and beauty. It must ELEVATE THE PRODUCT and PUT IT ON A PEDESTAL." He said he wanted results in weeks, not months.

Pepsi's agency was the first to solve the social riddle and create a successful new advertising campaign. BBDO's president, Charlie Brower, spent four months and untold thousands of dollars on market studies and motivational research surveys that told him what should have been obvious to anyone walking down a sidewalk past a school: America was feeling the results of the baby boom.

The census told the story. In 1952, a typical postwar year, 1,494,000 people died in the United States and 3,844,000 were born, a replacement ratio of more than two and a half to one. A decade later, those children were entering the fifth grade. Like Coke, Pepsi had been gearing its ads toward adults at a time when the biggest wave of young consumers in the nation's history was beginning to surge into the soft drink marketplace.

"Now it's Pepsi for those who think *young!*" declared BBDO's new slogan, abruptly reversing pitches. Unveiling the idea at a Pepsi bottlers meeting, Brower called Coca-Cola an old-fashioned, "fat-headed" competitor ripe for the plucking, a bit of rhetorical swagger that ended the unofficial truce between the companies and signaled the modern stage of a rivalry that continues unabated to this day. A BBDO account executive explained that the point was to portray Coke "as a drink for people who are out of step, out of touch, out of date." It took BBDO another four years to dream up the "Pepsi Generation," but the theme was in place by the early 1960s: Coca-Cola was the drink of the World War II generation, and Pepsi was the drink of their children.

Refusing to answer the competition directly, McCann launched "Things Go Better With Coke," a deceptively simple campaign that worked because it reinforced the idea of Coca-Cola as a mealtime beverage, because it suggested a role for the soft drink as a catalyst in boy-meets-girl encounters and other social situations, and mostly because the company spent a record $53 million putting it in magazines and on television. Coca-Cola was the most heavily advertised product in the country in the early 1960s, and that fact alone helped account for the company's ability to keep ahead of the rejuvenated Pepsi.

Had the budding generational war between Coke and Pepsi been fought and decided in the early days solely on the basis of which company was actually more hip and with-it and attuned to the tastes of America's under-thirty crowd, Plum Street might well have lost Coca-Cola's TV celebrities seemed slightly out of date, a step or two behind the popular curve, as if they belonged in the Smithsonian instead of the studio. Morton Downey and Edgar Bergen stayed on the air long past their prime years, then were replaced by Eddie Fisher, whose "Coke Time" program became obsolete as the rock-and-roll revolution overtook him. In 1965, hitting a sort of trifecta of un-coolness, the company named Anita Bryant, the former Miss America contestant, to be its "Ambassadress of Goodwill," and arranged an appearance for her on "The Lawrence Welk Show," where she sang the title song from *The Sound of Music*.

Happily for the company, however, its performers were not its only means of reaching the public. Coca-Cola's bottlers understood the importance of cultivating the teenage market and underwrote a syndicated radio program called the "Hi-Fi Club," which broadcast a weekly "hop" from various high schools around the country. More than a million teens sent away for membership cards in the club and participated in its prize contests, winning discount coupons for answering such questions as, "Ricky Nelson's mother is named Ozzie, true or false?" Aiming at an even younger audience,

Coca-Cola also sponsored a portion of "The Mickey Mouse Club." L. F. Montgomery, the Atlanta bottler, liked to say that Coca-Cola was there waiting for children as they were weaned off mother's milk, a sentiment that was shared (if not stated quite so bluntly) throughout the organization.

When it came to special events, no one—not even Walt Disney—could match the Coca-Cola Company's knack for mounting an extravaganza. During the planning stages in 1963 before the New York World's Fair, the company sent an executive named Ted Duffield to see Disney about the possibility of collaborating on a pavilion. Duffield recalled being shown into a small office in Los Angeles where Disney offered him a glass of tomato juice, seated him on a brown leather sofa, and presented the concept: a stage filled with foot-tall figurines of the American presidents, starring a mechanical Abe Lincoln standing against a Civil War backdrop reciting a six-minute excerpt from his inaugural address.

Declining politely but emphatically, Duffield hurried back to New York and helped create the "World of Refreshment," an indoor theme park full of startlingly realistic scenes from around the globe, including a village in the Bavarian Alps and a Cambodian rain forest. According to a newspaper report, the exhibit's replica of the deck of a cruise ship was so authentic, down to an underfoot throbbing and the whir of engines, that a visiting teacher shushed her students as they passed by a porthole, saying, "Be quiet now! There are people sleeping in there."

Treating the fair as an occasion of worldwide significance, Coca-Cola published a special newsletter detailing the activities at the pavilion—the number of clippings it generated (more than 1,500), the groups of visitors it drew on a given day (31,500 schoolchildren; 1,500 members of the Daughters of the American Revolution; 200 congressional secretaries), and the names of the celebrities who stopped by: Monique Van Vooren, Paula Prentiss, Jacqueline Kennedy, Gene Tunney, and Art Buchwald. Robert Woodruff made a rare public appearance at the opening ceremonies, accompanied by the reigning America's Junior Miss, Diane Sawyer, who carried a bottle of Coke in her white-gloved hand.

In all the company spent $5 million on the fair, including the installation of the largest carillon in the world, a 610-bell behemoth with 3,600-watt speakers atop a 120-foot tower that played the familiar bars of Coke's ad theme every fifteen minutes, audible for a distance of fifteen miles. Company officials wanted the music to play continuously, but the manufacturer, Schulmerich Carillons of Sellersville, Pennsylvania, balked. "It would have destroyed the dignity of the thing," Schulmerich's musical director explained.

The dignity of the whole undertaking was a matter of interpretation, of course, but the point was that the Coca-Cola Company insisted on having a major presence at the fair. Woodruff, Talley, and every other executive at Plum Street saw Coca-Cola as an American institution, deeply ingrained in the public mind as an idea as well as a product, with a special status that had to be preserved and protected. Advertising alone was not enough.

There were many reasons why the company did well in the early 1960s. For one thing, Pepsi's generational assault triggered a mild backlash among the senior citizenry, who resented the implication that Coca-Cola was for fuddy-duddies. "Frankly," an editorial writer complained in the *Scottsdale* (Arizona) *Daily Progress*, "we're still full of beans, vinegar, and sometimes Coke, and that doesn't make us out of date."

Then, too, there was safety in numbers. Not only were there more consumers than ever before, but they were drinking soda pop at a much faster rate. Per capita consumption of soft drinks in the United States rose steadily from 174 servings in 1954 to 227 in 1963, guaranteeing plenty of demand to meet. And the popularity of Coca-Cola's performers eventually improved. The "Things Go Better" theme song was sung by Nancy Sinatra, Jay and the Americans, and the Supremes, among others, satisfying a wide range of tastes. Going a little too far, perhaps, an ad targeted at black audiences asked, "Why don't somebody lay a Coke on me?"

Mostly, though, Coca-Cola succeeded because it had achieved a special plateau occupied by an elite handful of products that helped define the very essence of what it meant to be American. By 1964, the company could trace a ten-year arc of rising sales that began with the simple expedient of selling the product in bigger bottles and continued with a series of capitulations to the wishes of its customers.

Coke's standing as an icon was an old story, of course. The new wrinkle was the need to keep adapting that icon to the rapid changes taking place in American society. Looking ahead to the next ten years, the challenges promised to be far greater. Not only were tastes evolving, American values were beginning to shift as well, placing all of the nation's institutions in some degree of jeopardy. Like it or not, Coca-Cola was political, and few decades in American history have witnessed greater political upheavals than the sixties.

When researchers aboard the bathyscaphe *Eastward*, combing the ocean floor hundreds of miles off Charleston, discovered a Coke bottle at a depth of 19,200 feet in 1966, news accounts marveled at the ubiquity of the most familiar product on earth. But ecologists despaired.

In spite of all the cunning statecraft practiced by its lobbyists, there had always been one oddly innocent aspect to the Coca-Cola Company's treatment of politics and politicians. Any endorsement was welcome, no matter the source.

For years before and after World War II, the company's publicists blandly repeated the assertion that Hitler liked Coca-Cola, as if to say his taste in soft drinks was the lone humanizing aspect of his personality. From Fidel Castro to King Farouk, any political figure who drank Coke was a welcome sight, friend or foe.

President Eisenhower's fondness for Coca-Cola was so well established as to be taken for granted. When Ike visited New Delhi during his last year in office and posed for photographers sipping a Coke through a straw, Woodruff tossed off a thank-you note to the White House, along with a gentle reminder that the company's long-standing policy was never to show the product being consumed that way. Woodruff believed the use of a straw adversely affected the taste of Coke and implied that the bottle might be unsanitary.

Responding with good humor in a letter marked "Personal—Top Secret," Eisenhower protested. "For the first time I find you somewhat less than understanding," he chided Woodruff. "When I tip up a bottle of Coca-Cola for a good drink it lasts only seconds—with a straw, a lot of talk and more walking, I was able to [attract] more photographs and newspaper correspondents than I could possibly otherwise have done!"

The myth that Coca-Cola was above politics did not survive the 1960s. The trouble began in the summer of 1959, in fact, at the American National Exhibit in Moscow, the scene of Richard Nixon's famous "kitchen debate" with Nikita Khrushchev. The top executives of Coca-Cola Export declined to participate in the trade show, citing their long-running feud with the Communist parties in the Soviet Union and Europe. Bill Robinson argued forcefully that the occasion demanded Coca-Cola's participation, if only to pay the $25,000 cost of publishing a catalogue of American artists whose work would be on display. But he was turned down.

Seeing a rare opportunity open up, Don Kendall, the hard-charging young head of Pepsi's international division, committed his company to provide free soft drinks to every visitor who attended during the show's six-week run.

The decision nearly lost him his job. Just recently rid of Steele, Pepsi's cost-conscious directors had no wish to give away $300,000 or $400,000 worth of free samples, especially when the sale of American products was forbidden behind the Iron Curtain. Kendall saved himself with a visit to the vice president at his hotel in Moscow the night before the exhibit opened. At Kendall's urging, Nixon came by the Pepsi booth the next day and brought Khrushchev with him. Staging a small debate of his own, Kendall got the Soviet premier to taste two kinds of Pepsi, one bottled in the United States and one in Moscow. Naturally Khrushchev said he preferred the Russian version, but what mattered was the photograph that went out over the wires showing him guzzling Pepsi. "Khrushchev Learns to Be Sociable," the caption said, using Pepsi's old slogan one last time with fine, unwitting irony.

Kendall's coup infuriated Woodruff and the other executives at Plum Street, not least because of the vice president's complicity in bringing it off. As the number two man in the Eisenhower administration, Nixon was presumed—wrongly, it seemed—to be part of the team. In the fall, when Nixon launched his own bid for the presidency, he asked Woodruff to meet with him, talk things over, and consider supporting his candidacy. The session did not go well.

Nixon and his wife, Pat, arrived in south Georgia to spend the weekend at a plantation near Ichauway owned by Jim Hanes, the underwear mogul. Woodruff drove over to spend Saturday with the vice president and was immediately struck, unfavorably, by the fact that Nixon did not hunt. Pat Nixon went out and actually got a bird, Woodruff reported later to Eisenhower, but her husband was "not a shooter," and that was a bad sign.

Making matters worse, Nixon committed a gaffe when he sent a follow-up note a few days later thanking Woodruff for giving him a jar of Ichauway's sorghum syrup. As any halfway attentive Yankee visitor should have known, the plantation's special delicacy was pure Georgia cane syrup, not sorghum, and Woodruff (whose life's work, after all, centered on syrup) was always irritated if someone failed to make the distinction. "There is a very great difference," he wrote Nixon, "between our syrup and sorghum, which is generally a heavy, bitter-sweet substance." Perhaps, Woodruff added, "I will get you down here sometime and teach you more about these specialties of the Deep South."

Privately, Woodruff dismissed Nixon as a man lacking a sense of humor. "They never had any rapport," Joe Jones recalled. "That's the best way to put it, I think. Nixon just wasn't his kind of folks."

During the primary season, Woodruff threw his support behind Lyndon Johnson, and then sent Morton Downey to serve as an unofficial ambassador to Hyannisport after John F. Kennedy gained the Democratic nomination. Ever since the Coolidge administration, Woodruff had tried to maintain a cordial relationship with the occupant of the White House, and if that was not possible he found intermediaries to build bridges and look after the company's interests. Woodruff detested Kennedy's father, Joseph, for his wheeling and dealing in general (and specifically for trying to pressure the company into giving him bottling franchises in South America during World War II), but that did not prevent the offer of an olive branch. Hedging his bets, Woodruff also remained courteous toward Nixon and even helped him set up a few fund-raisers in Georgia, just in case.

Once the election was decided, though, Nixon was shunned. The crucial moment came two years later, after he lost the California governor's race. With his hopes of reviving his political career lying in apparent ruins, Nixon sounded out the Coca-Cola Company about a job, using an old navy friend, DeSales Harrison, as the go-between. Don Kendall had approached Nixon about handling Pepsi's legal business, Harrison told his colleagues at Plum Street, but Nixon was interested in representing Coca-Cola, the top company in the industry. The subject was taken up at a meeting in Lee Talley's office, according to one of the participants, "and everybody said, 'No, we don't need that son of a bitch on the payroll.'" The decision to reject Nixon was forwarded to Woodruff, who concurred.

No other political decision in the company's history proved as consequential. For all its battles with Dr. Wiley and his fellow reformers in the federal government, for all the gut-level lobbying the company did at the

Capitol and in statehouses across the land, Coca-Cola had managed for nearly eight decades to avoid a partisan label. Now it got one overnight. Nixon became the senior partner in Pepsi-Cola's outside law firm, and from that moment on the fight between Pepsi and Coke became a fight between Republicans and Democrats.

Because of the overwhelming tragedy that took place later the same day in the same place, few people remember that Nixon was in Dallas on November 22, 1963, attending a Pepsi-Cola bottlers' convention.

In his speech to the group, Nixon deftly maneuvered to push a wedge between the president and vice president. It appeared highly likely, Nixon said, that Kennedy would drop Johnson from the ticket as a liability in 1964—a prediction designed to taunt and embarrass the Democratic administration in Johnson's home state. Seeing Nixon's purpose as soon as the UPI story on his speech clattered across the teletype, an executive at Plum Street arranged to send a copy to Johnson.

But Johnson required no prodding to demonstrate his affinity for Coca-Cola. As vice president, he often drank Cokes in public, and he continued the practice when he became president. Visiting the World's Fair, for instance, he posed for a photograph tipping a bottle to his lips. On another occasion he and his daughter Lynda Bird drank Cokes together while the cameras clicked. Johnson was fully aware of Nixon's association with Pepsi and went out of his way to even the score. During the campaign of 1964, he told reporters Coca-Cola was the soft drink of choice on *Air Force One*.

Never one to ignore a political alliance, LBJ maintained warm relations with Woodruff and rarely missed a chance for a friendly gesture. One of the company's top lobbyists, Ovid Davis, recalled standing under the porte cochere in front of the Sheraton Carlton Hotel in Washington one morning waiting for a cab when a small motorcade of three black limousines came roaring by from the White House:

> The president was in the middle one, and he whipped back around—varroom! You can imagine what that did to the car in front and the one in back. It caused the damndest confusion. And the president stuck his head out and said, "Good morning, boy, how're you?" I said, "I'm very fine, thank you, Mr. President." He said, "How's Bob? Tell him I said howdy." By then the whole street was really in a mess.

Johnson helped the company in tangible ways as well. One of the strangest, longest-running bureaucratic battles in the history of the Food and Drug Administration was resolved in Coca-Cola's favor during Johnson's presidency—more than a quarter of a century after it began.

In 1938, Congress passed a law requiring ingredient labeling for most foods and beverages, a reform the Coca-Cola Company fought tooth and nail. The problem was not so much protecting the secret formula, since the flavorings in Merchandise No. 7X were exempt from the disclosure requirements, but rather in having to certify the presence of caffeine and other controversial additives the company preferred not to acknowledge. ("Coca-Cola," a company official wrote at the time in a candid in-house memo, "can never be explained to the average consumer so that the consumer will be benefited by this explanation.")

When Congress agreed to a brief delay in imposing the law on the soft drink industry, Coca-Cola's lobbyists went to work and quietly managed to stretch the postponement all the way into the 1960s. Consumers' groups eventually raised a ruckus, and the FDA announced belated plans to create regulations putting the law into effect. Treating the matter as a full-scale crisis, the company responded by launching a furious campaign meant to strip the labeling requirement of all meaning.

Ben Oehlert, whose brazen attempt to make Coca-Cola a military necessity had succeeded so brilliantly during World War II, spearheaded the company's effort. Summoning new powers to bend logic, Oehlert first argued that the company could satisfy the law by putting a label on its bottles that said simply, "Contains Coca-Cola syrup and carbonated water." The lone ingredient in Coca-Cola, Oehlert reasoned, was Coca-Cola syrup. This the FDA refused to buy.

Next, Oehlert tried a volley of assertions. Since Coca-Cola was 99½ percent sugar and water, he told the FDA, the remaining ingredients were too minor to merit disclosure. People already knew what was in Coca-Cola, he added, and if they didn't it was because they didn't care. And besides, the only significant difference between Coke and other colas was in the flavorings, which were exempt from disclosure anyway. These pleadings also fell on deaf ears.

Oehlert's final argument was a masterpiece. Since Coca-Cola had always contained caffeine, he asserted, it was by legal definition a "caffeinated" soft drink, and thus there was no reason to list caffeine on the label. Just as it was unnecessary to identify caffeine as an ingredient in coffee, Oehlert said, it was understood that caffeine was a constituent element of cola beverages, and proclaiming that fact on the side of the bottle would be redundant

The government was unmoved. Oehlert arranged a private luncheon in Washington with George Larrick, the FDA commissioner, who confided that he planned to rule against Coca-Cola. If the company wanted to keep caffeine off its label, Larrick said, it would have to pursue an appeal in a public hearing. Reporting the conversation to Woodruff a few days later, Oehlert advised strongly against asking for such a hearing, since "every crackpot and screwball would rush to [attend] and would not confine their comments to the labeling of caffeine but instead would in every way possible libel our product. . . ."

Oehlert's warning was not without basis. The most recent edition of *Fact* magazine, a left-leaning journal published by the activist Ralph Ginzburg, had announced on its cover that Coca-Cola caused "tooth decay, headaches, acne, nephritis, nausea, delirium, heart disease, emotional disturbances, constipation, insomnia, indigestion, diarrhea, and mutated offspring." The text of the article claimed the existence of a "massive dossier of medical evidence indicting Coca-Cola as one of the most poisonous beverages ever found in a bottle that doesn't bear a skull and crossbones." There wasn't much the company could do to prevent such attacks, Woodruff believed, but at least it could deny its accusers a public forum. There would be no hearing.

Using various stalling tactics, the company continued to hold the FDA at bay, until at last a tidy solution presented itself. Commissioner Larrick, a holdover from the Kennedy administration, retired, which gave President Johnson the opportunity to name a successor, Johnson was happy to consult with the Coca-Cola Company before making the appointment, and in due course he picked James Goddard, an assistant surgeon general who happened to be the director of the Centers for Disease Control in Atlanta, where he was on friendly terms with several company officials.

Eleven days after his appointment (and twenty-eight years after the original enactment of the law), Dr. Goddard published a proposed final order in the Federal Register that said caffeinated soft drinks did not have to list caffeine as an ingredient. Coca-Cola had won.

Only it wasn't quite that simple. In attempting to explain exactly what constituted a caffeinated soft drink, the FDA stumbled into the thicket of pretense that underlies Coca-Cola's mystique, with Alice-in-Wonderland consequences. By law, the FDA said, a caffeinated soft drink was any beverage that had the word "cola" as part of its brand name, or that contained caffeine made from the kola nut.

An objection was raised by the makers of Dr Pepper. Had the caffeine in Dr Pepper actually been derived from kola, the seed of the African tree, there would have been no problem. But contrary to the fable created by the Coca-Cola Company over the decades, kola had never been the natural source of caffeine in any soft drink. At the behest of Dr Pepper, the FDA ruling was amended so that all "natural caffeine-containing extracts" were added to the definition.

The absurdity of the situation took a moment to sink in. The federal government now said, in effect, that *any* soft drink that contained caffeine was automatically exempt from saying so on its label. This led inevitably to a new tangle when the manufacturer of Kickapoo Joy Juice, a soft drink that did not resemble a cola at all but was laced with caffeine, asserted a right to protection under the labeling law. With the FDA threatening to reexamine the whole issue, Oehlert negotiated a settlement that allowed Kickapoo to call itself "the original Dog Patch cola," thereby qualifying under federal law as a caffeinated cola drink, free of the requirement of listing caffeine on its label.

Putting an end to one of the company's less edifying episodes, Oehlert had a letter mailed to all Coca-Cola bottlers urging them to let the FDA ruling become final without further objection. It was sound advice, and they took it.

As part of the mania for mergers that swept corporate America in the early 1960s, Coca-Cola acquired the Minute Maid Corporation, the Orlando-based manufacturer of frozen orange juice. Along with thousands of acres of citrus fields, the deal provided Plum Street with the services of an eccentric financier named William Appleton Coolidge.

A small man in his early sixties with a fringe of flyaway gray hair, Coolidge was the heir to a large New England textile fortune. He had invested heavily in the research that led to Minute Maid's breakthrough in frozen citrus processing, and after the merger he wound up with more than $2 million in Coca-Cola common stock and a seat on the board of directors.

A lifelong bachelor, Coolidge collected fine art, including a Rubens and a Van Gogh, which he kept in a dusty old mansion outside Boston that was so dark the paintings had to be viewed with a flashlight. As a cum laude graduate of Harvard College and Harvard Law, with a stint at Oxford's Balliol College in between, Coolidge believed Woodruff and the other members of Coca-Cola's board would welcome his brilliant insights into running the business. He was mistaken.

At Minute Maid, Coolidge was accustomed to leisurely board meetings that went on for two or three days at a time, with members encouraged to brainstorm together, sharing their musings and daydreaming aloud. The atmosphere at Plum Street, where Woodruff ran tight, no-nonsense sessions that rarely lasted a morning, came as a surprise to Coolidge, and a genuine disappointment. He liked Woodruff and was drawn to him, as so many people were. He wanted to discuss his ideas and give counsel.

Woodruff considered Coolidge little more than an overgrown pixie, according to Joe Jones, and teased him for wearing his wispy hair down to his shoulders. Coolidge was unquestionably bright, but he knew nothing about the soft drink business, and Woodruff resisted his attempts to create a more intimate relationship.

One day at lunch in Plum Street's private dining room, chatting informally with the board members, Woodruff let down his guard. Muttering darkly, he criticized the "beatniks" and other outsiders who were coming into Mississippi and the rest of the Deep South, agitating for civil rights reform and stirring up dangerous passions among blacks and whites alike. Southerners of both races felt resentment at being told what to do, Woodruff said, especially by adventurers from the North who seemed more interested in provoking trouble than bringing about worthwhile change.

Coolidge was offended. Responding in a letter a few days later, he said he was "grieved" by Woodruff's attitude. "The horrible tragedy of this whole business," he wrote, "lies in the feeling that fine Southerners like yourself have—that the coloured man does not really seek for his self-respect. I do not know how that is going to be brought home to you. I only hope it is not through bloodshed. . . ." As for his own politics, Coolidge added, "I am always tempted, myself, to join in some such type of protest but have felt that, when the time came, my influence would be greater if I had not committed myself that way."

Coolidge's letter triggered a fury in Woodruff that had rarely been seen before. Emotionally, he reacted as if some wild-eyed nineteenth-century abolitionist had appeared from a time machine and accused him of slave-holding. "I wouldn't want to go into the matter of who profited the most from the practice of hauling Negroes from Africa and selling them to Southern planters," Woodruff fumed, dictating a response to Coolidge. "My impression is that money received from this business formed the basis of several New England, especially Massachusetts, family fortunes. . . ."

Before putting his answer in the mail, Woodruff stopped to review his activities of the past several years. Perhaps he could have done more, he reflected, but certainly he had no apologies to make to a liberal egghead from Boston, especially one who declared with such rectitude that he was denying himself the experience of public involvement in the civil rights struggle. Woodruff hadn't had that luxury.

In 1960, Governor Ernest Vandiver had faced a serious problem. Elected two years earlier on the slogan "No, not one"—meaning not one black child would be allowed to integrate Georgia's public schools—Vandiver found himself under federal court order to desegregate Atlanta's city schools and the state's other public schools and colleges or see them closed. He was looking desperately for a nimble way of breaking his promise when his executive secretary, Griffin Bell, then a young lawyer fresh from King & Spalding, came up with an inspiration. If the Georgia General Assembly created a blue-ribbon commission to hold hearings around the state on the question, Bell was confident the people would think carefully about the consequences and arrive at the conclusion that the schools must remain open, even if it meant integration. The perfect chairman would have to be found to lead the group, and Bell suggested one of his mentors, John Sibley.

Sibley undertook the job with Woodruff's complete support. There was no question of persuading white Georgians that sending their children to school with blacks was a good idea. The only goal was to keep the governor from being arrested and the schools from being padlocked. "Regardless of whether or not we like it or don't like it," Sibley said on WSB radio, accepting his appointment, "we are all bound by it"—the authority of the federal courts.

With no police guard, not even a sergeant-at-arms, Sibley worried that he and his fellow commissioners might end up the victims of a riot, but he pressed ahead and scheduled hearings in all ten of Georgia's congressional districts, allowing everyone to let off steam. John Greer, a liberal state legislator from Atlanta who served on the commission, recalled a rural colleague rushing up to him during one of the hearings: "And he demanded, 'What's all these niggers doing in here?' I said, 'They came to talk, Senator.' And he said, 'Well, that ain't the way I understood it. I thought we were just going around the state and let the whites talk it over, decide what we'd do and then we'd tell the niggers about it.'"

But he understood wrong. The commission worked exactly as Sibley anticipated. After hearing from more than 1,600 witnesses, black and white, its members voted to obey the federal authorities and keep the schools open, a decision the public grudgingly supported.

A few months later, Mayor Hartsfield put out a call to Sibley, Woodruff, and others in the business leadership, asking their help in resolving the most serious showdown yet between the races, over the desegregation of the city's lunch counters. In October 1960, Martin Luther King, Jr., who had largely bypassed Atlanta in his crusades up to then (and who praised his home town for having "a power structure willing to engage in dialogue"), joined a group of students from the Atlanta University Center and staged a sit-in at the Magnolia Room, the popular restaurant on the sixth floor of Rich's downtown department store. Fearful of a backlash from the Klan if he failed to act, proprietor Richard Rich personally had King and the others arrested for trespass.

The ensuing escalation of tensions became a well-known chapter in the civil rights movement, as a segregationist judge in nearby DeKalb County sent King to the maximum security state prison at Reidsville on an old traffic citation, and John and Robert Kennedy intervened to help gain King's release. Hartsfield was left with the delicate task of brokering a long-term solution between the black community and the city's white merchants. King was free, but the students arrested with him had refused bail and were still in jail. "John," the mayor wrote Sibley, with a carbon to Woodruff, "the top twenty-five people of this community—the men, not the boys—have just simply got to cancel a few out-of-town engagements, get together and help me decide what to do."

Like aging Mafia dons, Sibley and Woodruff had been looking around for some time for younger men they could groom to run the city in the next generation. As a test, they gave the assignment of resolving the sit-in impasse to Ivan Allen, Jr., a patrician businessman who ran Atlanta's biggest office supply company and was serving as president of the Chamber of Commerce. Allen opened the negotiations by inviting two lawyers, Bob Troutman, who represented Rich's, and A. T. Walden, a venerable black leader known as "the Judge," to meet with him in his office.

A small but decisive moment occurred during one of the first sessions when Walden asked to use the bathroom. Allen realized with immediate embarrassment that the facilities in his own business were segregated. He could not send Walden into a whites-only toilet without risking an incident with one of his employees. "All hell would have broken loose," he said later. Yet neither did he dare ask Walden to use the poorly maintained black employees' washroom in the basement. Instead, giving an early display of his knack for artful compromise, Allen showed Walden into his own private bathroom.

Over the next few weeks, Allen helped arbitrate a written agreement in which the executives of two dozen of the city's leading businesses agreed to full desegregation of their facilities, including the lunch counters, and the leaders of the black community responded by calling off their boycott. It was not nearly as easy as it sounded. The agreement included a delay of several months in implementation that offended many in the black community, and opposition began growing as soon as the terms were announced. The danger that the truce might unravel came to a dramatic head one night at the Wheat Street Baptist Church, when an angry crowd threatened to spill out the doors and take its protest to the streets.

Dr. King walked in as his father and other older leaders were being jeered. Commanding silence by his mere presence, King told his listeners they had "a contract with the white man, the first written contract we've ever had with him. . .after waiting one hundred years and having nothing to show until now." If anyone broke that contract, he warned, it would not be black people. The deal held.

Other changes followed at an accelerating pace. Hartsfield was ambivalent about seeking another term in the 1961 mayor's race. At seventy-two, he was divorcing his wife of nearly fifty years to marry a younger woman, a step likely to provoke scandal and cost votes. He feared the embarrassment of losing, and he was worn out by the draining political fights of recent years. He stepped aside in favor of Allen, who campaigned on a platform of continuing the seamless relationship between City Hall and the business community.

If anything, Allen proved even more reliant on Woodruff's support than Hartsfield had been. Running with thousands of dollars in contributions from Woodruff and his circle, Allen defeated the arch segregationist Lester Maddox in a runoff in the fall election, winning the city's wealthiest white precincts and taking the black, vote 21,611 to 237.

One spring afternoon a few months after he took office, Allen was relaxing on his front porch at home with his wife, Louise, when a big sedan eased up the driveway.

Emerging from the passenger side, Woodruff joined the Aliens for a drink, made small talk for a few minutes, and then pulled an envelope out of his coat pocket In it was an offer of $4 million to help the city build a public garden and arts center at Piedmont Park.

Woodruff had ambitious plans for Atlanta. For years, he'd been showering Emory University with largesse, underwriting its expenses and expanding its facilities until the medical school and hospital gained national renown. Once, in the 1950s, when the Ford Foundation named him to an advisory board to help dispose of $90 million in grants to medical schools,

Woodruff urged that the money be distributed to as many schools as possible. "But don't worry about Emory," he added. "I can take care of Emory myself."

Now he wanted to transform Piedmont Park, the city's central green space, into a cultural mecca. Woodruff hired a full-time philanthropic consultant, a retired educator named Philip Weltner, who drew up the blueprint for a complex that included a theater, symphony hall, and museum, to be centered around a giant fountain in the midst of formal gardens, playgrounds, and restaurants. Weltner envisioned his design as an "outdoor living room" for Atlanta as well as a national tourist attraction, and he christened it with the suitably grand title of "Bois d'Atlante." A second phase called for a funicular, crystal palace, planetarium, and library for the fine arts. Woodruff offered to put up $4 million, anonymously, if the city would include $2 million for the center in an upcoming bond referendum. Mayor Allen quickly agreed.

Atlanta had reached an important turning point. The population of the metropolitan area hit the million mark, the airport became a vital transportation hub, and the rest of the country began to regard the city as the capital of the Deep South. In a perceptive cover story in *Holiday* magazine, writer Frances Gray Patton said Atlanta wanted

> progress and gracious living, big industries and a system of super highways—and it wants to keep its trees. You feel, as you sometimes do when you watch a young boy blossom with strong and contradictory impulses, that for this city any moment could be the crucial one. An idea that captures the civic imagination, a principle embraced or rejected, an act of wisdom or a silly blunder might make all the difference.

The voters rejected the bond issue. To Woodruff's utter shock, they turned down the park plan, along with improvements in the schools, streets, and sewers. It was, he confided to a friend, "quite difficult for me to understand." Yet the explanation was not so elusive. Black voters had reviewed the list of civic projects and concluded that it mostly benefited whites, while whites had seen the Bois d'Atlante as a fancified conspiracy to integrate Piedmont Park.

Nothing involving race could ever be taken for granted in Atlanta. The levels of distrust were too high. The mayor blamed himself for failing to campaign heavily enough for the bond issue, and Weltner bemoaned "the grave danger. . .of finding our town drift into the hands of ill-tempered race mongers and blackguards." To both of them, Woodruff counseled patience. They would try again, when tempers had cooled off.

Crucial moments seemed to arrive almost every day in 1962. In *Baker* v. *Carr*, the Supreme Court affirmed the notion of "one man, one vote" and swept away the system that gave residents of tiny rural counties in Georgia more clout at the polls than people in Atlanta, Columbus, and the state's other big cities. With urban voters newly empowered, Woodruff and his friends saw a chance to elect a moderate as governor and threw their support behind Carl Sanders, a state senator from Augusta. Sanders became a fixture in Woodruff's suite, using Plum Street as a field office where he could raise money and organize his campaign. "I'd come to work, say eight o'clock in the morning, sometimes sooner," Joe Jones recalled, "and Sanders would be sitting there, out in the lobby on the telephone, calling up people asking them for their vote, their support." Sanders came by so regularly he was finally given his own key to Woodruff's private elevator.

Backed by Woodruff and the Atlanta business community, Sanders defeated Marvin Griffin, who was making a comeback try with the backing of the Klan, and put an end to the string of staunch segregationists in the governor's office. A change in the boundaries of Atlanta's congressional district gave Woodruff an opportunity to defeat another ardent segregationist, and he helped recruit Philip Weltner's son, Charles, a thirty-four-year-old liberal lawyer, to run for the seat. When young Weltner won, Woodruff could count the governor of Georgia, the mayor of Atlanta, and the local congressman as progressives who owed their jobs and political allegiance in large part directly to him.

A final moment of truth occurred just after the election. Just as an ornate and oversized hotel, the Kimball House, had symbolized Atlanta's aspirations a century before, the city's new landmark was the Commerce Club, a private facility for members of the Chamber of Commerce built atop a six-story parking garage. The board of the Commerce Club represented the governing elite of Atlanta, its oligarchy of businessmen, all of them white.

For years, the Chamber had entertained the members of the Atlanta delegation to the Georgia General Assembly at a dinner before the annual session of the legislature. In the aftermath of the 1962 elections, as he looked over the invitation list, Mayor Allen realized he had a problem. The city had just elected its first black state senator since Reconstruction, Leroy Johnson, and the club's rules flatly forbade black guests.

Convening a meeting of the board, which included Woodruff, Allen stood and described the dilemma, then made a motion to change the rules and allow blacks to attend events at the club as guests. In the complete silence that followed, Allen failed to gain a second for his motion. "I just stood there," he recalled years later. "Not a word was said." Then Woodruff leaned over and said in a loud whisper, "Ivan, you're absolutely right." The motion was seconded and carried unanimously.

There were, of course, limits to what Woodruff hoped to accomplish. He could do nothing, for instance, to lift the heavy hand of racial oppression in Baker County, which surrounded his plantation and earned the nickname "Bad Baker" among civil rights proponents. The chief election official there once refused to let a black teacher register to vote, warning her—in front of a *New York Times* reporter—that she would be fired if she tried. The U.S. Office of Education issued a report that said integrating Baker County's schools was the "hardest nut in Georgia to crack," as only seven black children had been admitted by the mid-1960s. The sheriff, L. Warren "Gator" Johnson, routinely terrorized blacks throughout the county, including Ichauway.

Woodruff's overseer, Guy Touchtone, was part of the problem. A heavy drinker, Touchtone began abusing Ichauway's black tenants, forcing his attentions on some of the women who lived on the plantation, and inviting Sheriff Johnson on the property to help him enforce his authority when there was trouble. Eventually the blacks complained directly to Woodruff that the situation was "intolerable," and he responded by pensioning Touchtone off.

It was clear to Woodruff that other parts of Georgia were not ready to move as fast as Atlanta. In 1963, President Kennedy called Mayor Allen at his City Hall office and asked him to come to Washington to testify in favor of the public-accommodations bill that was meant to end segregation in the South's hotels and restaurants. Allen, anxious to go but believing it might cost him his political career, turned to Woodruff for advice. "I know it's going to be a very unpopular thing to do," Woodruff said. "But you've made up your mind and you're probably right about it, and I think you should go." At Woodruff's suggestion, Allen recommended a delay in imposing the law in small towns, but even so he was the only elected official in the South to speak publicly in support of the act.

The ensuing criticism of Allen was withering, and some of Woodruff's friends questioned his judgment, if not his sanity, for encouraging the mayor to testify. They also warned him to muzzle his friend Ralph McGill, whose columns in the *Atlanta Constitution* endorsed Allen's position and advocated racial progress. Woodruff, who had steadied McGill for years with a standing job offer at Coca-Cola if the newspaper fired him, fended off the hard-liners. "You'd better keep yourself flexible," he told them. "Things are not going to be like they were."

Coolidge's letter chiding Woodruff about his racial attitudes arrived not long afterward. As he refined his response, Woodruff gradually calmed down. He set aside the draft with its bitter recriminations about the origins of slavery and tried a softer rebuke. "I am sorry," he said, "that you do not seem to have a better understanding of the subject we were discussing." At length he abandoned even that mild answer, and instead sent Coolidge a simple acknowledgment that he'd received his letter, adding, "Thanks so much for sending it along."

When Martin Luther King, Jr., won the Nobel Peace Prize in the fall of 1964, two of Atlanta's white religious leaders, Rabbi Jacob Rothschild and Archbishop Paul Hallinan, arranged a celebration dinner at the Dinkler Plaza Hotel and invited the cream of the city's business leadership to attend. No one accepted.

At the time the invitations went out, Woodruff was at Ichauway recovering from a harrowing riding accident in which his horse had stumbled, thrown him, and then fallen on top of him. At seventy-five, he counted himself lucky to have escaped serious injury with only cuts and bruises. During his recuperation, one of his visitors was Allen, who told him about the dinner and expressed concern that the city would be humiliated if the white community boycotted it Woodruff agreed. He asked Allen and the new president of Coca-Cola, Paul Austin, to return to Atlanta and convene a meeting to rally the troops.

As was the custom in those days, the businessmen held their gathering at the exclusive, all-white Piedmont Driving Club, entirely oblivious to the irony of the circumstances. Austin, the heir apparent to Lee Talley as top executive at Coke, cut an impressive figure. A former Olympic rower, he stood six foot three and was still physically powerful in his forties. As a graduate of Harvard and Harvard Law, he was intellectually imposing as well. He told the assembly of two dozen bankers, lawyers, and businessmen in forceful terms that he wanted them to buy tickets and support the dinner. In case anyone missed the point, he added that he was speaking on Woodruff's authority.

Listening to the grumbles of reluctant assent that greeted Austin's remarks, Allen sensed that not even the weight of the Coca-Cola Company was going to be enough to guarantee a successful turnout at the dinner. Most of the men would buy tickets, he figured, but they would make excuses and send underlings to the Dinkler Plaza ballroom on the night of the event. There would be a scattering of white faces at the tables, but the absence of the elite would be an obvious affront to Dr. King. "Most of y'all will be out of town or sick," Allen predicted, his voice rising in accusation. "But don't you worry. Your mayor will be there."

What happened next was a chain reaction worthy of Rube Goldberg. One of the men at the meeting, a banker, responded angrily to the pressure and began making phone calls urging his colleagues not to buy tickets at all. Among the people he called was Lou Oliver, the head of Sears, Roebuck in the Southeast, a man of progressive sensibilities who was angered in turn by the banker's open racism. "Who does he think he's talking to?" Oliver spluttered, and he recounted the conversation to his secretary. She went out to dinner that night with her husband and another couple and repeated the story, and as it happened the other man was a stringer for the *New York Times*.

On December 29, 1964, the *Times* ran a story from Atlanta under the headline, "BANQUET TO HONOR DR. KING SETS OFF QUIET DISPUTE HERE." Now the dispute was no longer quiet. The article reported that an unnamed "leading banker" was making calls strongly objecting to the dinner and discouraging participation. By coincidence, the government of Haiti was negotiating a loan at the time with Atlanta's Citizens & Southern Bank, and a representative of President-for-Life François "Papa Doc" Duvalier called from Port-au-Prince in a huff demanding to know if Mills Lane, the head of C&S, was the banker in question. As Lane assured everyone who would listen, he was not the culprit. And to prove it, he bought a block of tickets to the dinner.

Within the next few days, the organizers sold out all 1,500 tickets to the dinner, and the occasion is remembered to this day as a high point of comity between the races in Atlanta. As more than a hundred top businessmen looked on, Dr. King accepted a crystal Steuben bowl inscribed with a dogwood blossom, the city's symbol, and gave a speech calling forth the goodwill of millions of Southern whites "whose voices are yet unheard, whose course is yet unclear, and whose courageous acts are yet unseen."

Several Coca-Cola officials attended, and though Woodruff did not, it seems fair to say he was there in spirit.

For those who believed in portents, Woodruff's horseback spill made a trenchant metaphor. Through the first half of the sixties, the Coca-Cola Company was riding high in the saddle, enjoying financial returns commensurate with its successes in politics and marketing. The common stock was split 3-for-1 in 1960 and 2-for-1 in 1965, as share prices rose handsomely. Annual sales neared the $1 billion mark.

A cycle of bad fortune seemed inevitable, and fittingly enough it began on April Fool's Day 1966. On that date a businessman named Moshe Bornstein called a press conference in Tel Aviv and accused the Coca-Cola Company of refusing to do business in Israel for fear of reprisals and loss of profits in the Arab world. A week later in New York, the Anti-Defamation League of B'nai B'rith released a statement backing up the charges, triggering headlines across the country.

Responding with a touch of panic, the company hurriedly put out a statement over Jim Farley's signature saying the allegations were "unfair and unfounded," and claiming the real reason it did not have a bottling plant in Israel was because the market was too small.

That was not true. As the tangled details of the story emerged, the company was caught in a lie, with predictable, damaging results. In 1949, Coca-Cola had tried to open a bottling plant in Israel, and the government there had blocked the franchise, citing the same foreign exchange worries that affected many other countries in the postwar era. Once the refusal was part of the record, however, the company treated it as a convenient excuse to avoid doing business in Israel, just as its critics charged.

In 1961, a misunderstanding occurred that threatened to stir up a hornet's nest of religious animosities. A civil servant in Cairo named Mohammad Abu Shadi ordered a Coke and was served a bottle manufactured in Ethiopia. Mistaking the Amharic lettering on the label for Hebrew, Shadi publicly accused the company of doing business with Israel. Hoping to douse the ensuing furor and fend off the threat of an Arab League boycott, the manager of Coca-Cola's Egyptian bottling operations assured the press that the company would never allow the Israelis to have a franchise. It was then, in denying their bottler's impolitic statement, that company officials first invented the rationale that Israel was too small a market for a franchise—blithely ignoring the fact that nearby Cyprus, with only a tenth of Israel's population and a lower standard of living, supported a bottling plant quite nicely.

Meanwhile, Moshe Bornstein, the Israeli businessman, was hard at work selling his countrymen a beverage he called Tempo-Cola. His trademark, which used the same Spencerian script as Coca-Cola's, drew the attention of the company's lawyers, who elected to file suit claiming infringement. They won, but it was truly a Pyrrhic victory. Bornstein was understandably angry. The Coca-Cola Company had no interest in a franchise of its own in Israel, yet it was happy to take him to court and saddle him with the trouble and expense of changing the lettering on his bottles. Hoping to get even, he traveled to New York, engaged a lawyer with ties to the Anti-Defamation League, and ventured to the Coca-Cola Export office to demand a bottling franchise. When he was turned down, he returned to Tel Aviv and held his press conference.

The exposure of Coca-Cola's checkered history in Israel was deeply embarrassing to the company. The administrators of Mount Sinai Hospital in Manhattan announced they would stop serving Coke, and the owners of Nathan's Famous Hot Dog Emporium on Coney Island threatened to follow suit—just the sort of angry gestures the company dreaded. Leaders of the Jewish community in Atlanta called on Woodruff and Fillmore Eisenberg, a vice president who was the company's highest-ranking Jewish officer, pressing for explanations.

Within days, after a flurry of high-level meetings in Atlanta and New York, the company announced it was negotiating a bottling franchise in Tel Aviv with Abraham Feinberg, a prominent Manhattan banker and president of the Israel Development Corporation. Working at damage control as furiously as if they were dancing the hora, company officials enlisted an outside public relations agency, Ruder & Finn, for advice about how to "counteract any lingering ill effects on the American Jewish community." An immediate recommendation was the release of photographs of Jim Farley meeting with Feinberg and Georgia-born Morris Abram, the president of the American Jewish Committee. Over the long term, Ruder & Finn proposed in a confidential memo, Coca-Cola should underwrite a pamphlet on ecumenism, open accounts at Israeli-owned banks, and provide free soft drinks at American colleges with high Jewish enrollments.

If the strategy smacked a bit of pandering, it nonetheless signaled the company's desperation to avoid accusations of anti-Semitism. One of Coca-Cola's publicists warned privately that the key was to "minimize the impression that we have either reversed our policy or have knuckled under." But of course that was exactly the impression the company gave (since it was exactly what the company *did*), and the Arab League struck back with swift retribution by moving to place Coca-Cola on its boycott list. The price of peace with Israel and American Jews, it seemed, would be economic war with the Arab states.

The focus shifted quickly to efforts to escape the boycott. Lee Talley directed the preparation of an official "presentation" designed to impress Egyptian President Gamal Abdel Nasser with the benefits Coca-Cola was providing his country. Alex Makinsky, the company's manicured diplomat, was brought out of retirement and dispatched from Paris to work his charms in Cairo. But he failed miserably. The fact was, Makinsky reported back, Coca-Cola did not generate much economic activity in Egypt. Even though sales were robust, the company's profits were small because of a pricing squeeze, and most of the revenues were returned to the United States. The Egyptians considered Coca-Cola a symbol of America, Makinsky said, and it was one they could afford to make a target for retaliation.

Turning to the Johnson administration for a favor, Ben Oehlert persuaded the president to aid the company's effort to escape punishment. Oehlert held a luncheon in Washington for Mustafa Kamel, the ambassador from the United Arab Republic, and invoked Johnson's name in urging at least a postponement in imposing the boycott. Later Oehlert showed Kamel the three bound volumes of news clippings from the French affair of 1950, warning him of the "outcry" the Arab League risked in attacking Coca-Cola. Kamel expressed a desire "to be helpful to our problem," Oehlert reported, but was able to arrange only a temporary delay.

By fall, with the deadline approaching for the league to begin its boycott, a sense of futility took over at Plum Street. Not even the intervention of the White House could stall the matter for long, it appeared, and company officials sat back and awaited the loss of their Arab markets. One day in October, an unsolicited letter arrived addressed simply to "The president, Coca-Cola." It came from one David Heaton, sales manager of Heavyweight Champion Brands, Incorporated, suggesting that Coca-Cola might alleviate some of its troubles in the Middle East by marketing a fruit drink embossed with the likeness of boxer Muhammad Ali. Paul Austin, who received the letter, sent it along to two of his marketing executives.

"This is one of those things that is so ridiculous it almost makes sense," Austin said in an accompanying memo. "Hopefully, you will find that it is, in fact, ridiculous. Or is it?"

It was. Yet as many of his colleagues at Plum Street were beginning to notice, J. Paul Austin had a very unorthodox way of looking at things. He explained once to a writer from *Forbes* magazine that he liked to "pull all the legs off the centipede and see what he's really like," which was another way—an unusual way—of saying he kept an open mind.

Austin grew up in LaGrange, Georgia, and went to work for Coca-Cola in 1948 on the recommendation of his father's boss, textile manufacturer Cason Callaway. Callaway was a good friend of Woodruff's, and his sponsorship earned Austin, a thirty-three-year-old lawyer at the time, a place on the fast track for advancement. After the requisite brief apprenticeship loading cases of Coca-Cola on trucks (and outperforming the younger men working beside him), Austin was assigned to the company's Chicago office negotiating bottler franchises.

His colleagues could tell he was marked for a quick rise through the ranks. George Lawson, who later served the company as general counsel, started work in Chicago on the same day Austin did and noticed that their superiors "were sort of circling lightly around Paul," as if anticipating he might be the boss one day. As another associate put it, Austin "came in as more or less a member of the family."

For his own part, Austin sensed that Woodruff was testing him for bigger things. Woodruff paid a rare visit to a bottlers' convention in Chicago not long after Austin's arrival there and made a point of introducing him to the men. The theme of the gathering was the Old South, and without any warning Woodruff surprised Austin by asking him to get up and give a talk on Negro spirituals. As it happened, Austin had studied the subject—it was his senior thesis at Harvard, in fact—and he was able to speak comfortably and knowledgeably for nearly forty-five minutes without notes, leaving the bottlers suitably impressed. Later he told his family he had no idea if Woodruff knew ahead of time about his expertise in the matter.*

Before leaving Chicago, Austin married Jeane Weed, a secretary in the Coca-Cola office. They made a striking couple—she was pretty enough to be a model, and he was handsome, with a resemblance to the actor Robert Preston. Their next stop was New York, where Austin worked in the Coca-Cola Export office. In 1954 he was assigned to South Africa, where he impressed the home office by turning a dismal market into one of Export's sales leaders. By 1958, when Lee Talley took the presidency of Coca-Cola, Austin was the consensus choice to replace him as the head of Export.

The testing continued. Woodruff and Talley liked to sit in the back of the company plane after flights home, sipping martinis in the twilight and talking about company business. It was quiet and secluded out on the tarmac, far from ringing telephones and eavesdropping ears. In 1961, they decided to make Austin the executive vice president of Coca-Cola—Talley's understudy, in effect—with a wide range of new responsibilities that included Tab, the World's Fair, syrup pricing, and advertising.

It also fell to Austin to decide whether to cooperate with the producers of the movie *One, Two, Three*, a sharp-edged comedy starring Jimmy Cag-

---

* Austin never learned just how closely Woodruff was watching him. Before putting him on the payroll, Woodruff hired a private investigator who compiled a confidential report on Austin's background, disclosing among other things that he had a C-plus average at Harvard, that he voted Republican, and that he was well liked and highly regarded. Woodruff knew perfectly well that Austin was a whiz on spirituals. He was giving him a chance to shine, seeing if he would take it.

ney as an ambitious Coca-Cola manager in West Germany. Oddly enough, the movie worried Austin more than the other projects. He gave the go-ahead, but as the completion date approached he grew nervous. As with all matters affecting the company's image, the film was of intense concern to Woodruff. Austin sat next to him during a private screening in Atlanta a few days before the general release in theaters, fretting that he'd made a mistake. He was greatly relieved to see a broad smile on Woodruff's face when the lights came up, and later he told a friend it was the moment he believed he finally had it made.

Six months afterward, on May 8, 1962, Austin was named president of the Coca-Cola Company. His rise to the top was so fast and smooth it naturally aroused the resentment of men who had been with the company longer. Ben Oehlert, bitter over the loss of his own chance to be president, told people he thought Austin must be Woodruff's bastard son. Others were not so inventive or wicked, but Austin rekindled the same misgivings that had greeted so many of Woodruff's impetuous choices over the years—all of those comets, like Bill Hobbs, who'd burned so brightly, only to flare out.

This time around, Woodruff seemed to understand the wisdom of breaking in the new president slowly. Talley continued to serve as chief executive officer, exercising final authority over Austin and acting as a buffer between him and Woodruff. It proved to be a useful arrangement, because Austin brought an idiosyncratic style to the job that caught people by surprise. After gaining permission to pump an extra $1.5 million into the advertising budget in the summer of 1962, for instance, Austin grandly announced "Operation Flood" and gave a speech to the bottlers explaining, "There is a tide in the affairs of men, which, taken at the flood, leads on to fortune. . . ." Even by the hortatory standards of Talley and Harrison Jones, quoting Shakespeare to the bottlers was considered a bit much, especially over a relatively paltry sum of money.

Austin's intellectualism caused chafing at Plum Street, as did his aptitude and appetite for publicity. Unlike Woodruff, Austin cultivated financial writers and granted interviews; he posed for the cover of *Business Week*. He dispensed his erudition freely, explaining to reporters that management was a "pseudo-science" in which executives could improve themselves by pursuing advanced courses, preferably at Harvard. Woodruff found he had to keep Austin on a tight tether and remind him occasionally who was boss. When the S&H Stamp Company invited Austin to serve on its board, he asked Woodruff and Talley for routine permission, and they brought him up short by saying no.

For the time being, Woodruff decided to keep Talley in place as CEO, holding the younger, more energetic Austin in check. Talley's younger brother, John, was promoted to head of Export, sandwiching Austin and trimming his authority over the company's field managers. Most frustrating to Austin, his ideas for change ran into resistance. Dissatisfied with selling only beverages, he wanted to expand into the food business, and when he got a feeler from Atlanta-based Frito-Lay, the snack company, he pushed hard for a merger. Woodruff and Talley turned him down, a decision that became all the more exasperating when Don Kendall struck again and acquired Frito-Lay for Pepsi. PepsiCo, as the combined business was known, proved to be an immediate success, and Austin made sure the business press in New York found out he was not the one who had dropped the ball.

For the first time since he'd taken the reins of the company forty years earlier, Woodruff found his absolute authority over Coca-Cola's affairs under challenge. Austin turned out to be a tireless, guileful infighter, as adept at office politics as he was ambitious. He kept constant pressure on Talley, who finally began to show the signs of wear and tear. In 1966, when he turned sixty-five, Talley told Woodruff he wanted to retire as CEO and "take a seat on the bench." Nothing Woodruff said could persuade him to change his mind. Talley's wife, Marge, had never liked the round-the-clock demands Woodruff put on her husband. She wanted him to spend his remaining years in peace, sailing the yacht they kept on Chesapeake Bay, and he was ready to go.

Talley was the last of the Coca-Cola executives who could serve both Woodruff and the company with equal, undivided loyalty. Without a trace of embarrassment, he wrote a farewell letter calling Woodruff a "genius" and likening him to Jesus Christ for his "power to draw all men unto you." Woodruff returned the sentiment, presenting Talley with a crystal stone that encased a golden sword. Like King Arthur, Woodruff said, Talley had been the only president in the company's long history able to pull Excalibur from the rock.

Austin's vantage point was entirely different. He paid the appropriate courtesies to Woodruff, but as he looked around the company he saw serious, chronic problems that demanded fixing, many of them Woodruff's fault. The business suffered from the inevitable cronyism that crept in whenever one man ruled an institution for so many years, Austin believed. He saw the Talleys as part of a vein of nepotism that ran through the management, thwarting the careers of abler men.

As he neared his goal of becoming CEO, Austin made a conscious decision that he could no longer afford to be friendly with his colleagues. Knowing he had stables to clean out, he adopted an unsmiling demeanor and began keeping his distance, almost to the point of rudeness. The act was so effective that a reporter described him in a profile as a "gaunt, grim" man, when in truth he was quite upbeat and flamboyant by nature.

Not surprisingly, Woodruff's ardor toward Austin cooled. "You can always tell a Harvard man," Woodruff began needling him, quoting an old saw, "but you can't tell him much." Austin's ego became the topic of pointed jokes among Woodruff's inner circle. One night over drinks in his cabin at Augusta National, Woodruff unloaded on Austin at length, pounding home the point that business leaders ought to display a sense of humility.

Afterward, a friend said, "Paul came back. . .with smoke coming out of both ears."

Yet Woodruff still admired the younger man's abilities, and the fact was that no one else had been groomed to take Talley's place. Had he wished, Woodruff could have blocked Austin's promotion to CEO, but he did not. Other members of the board believed the company needed the kind of fresh blood Austin represented, and Woodruff conceded they might be right.

When the board elevated Austin to his new post, the *Wall Street Journal* reported the news under the headline, "AUSTIN, MAN BEHIND COCA-COLA CO.'S 'ROUGH' COMPETITIVE HUSTLE, NAMED CHIEF OFFICER." The coverage disturbed Woodruff, who was unaccustomed to public assessments of the company's personnel and corporate personality. The *Journal's* story quoted an unnamed, veteran board member who "gleefully" described Austin as a "son-of-a-gun," another breach of protocol that ruffled Woodruff's feathers. Hoping to reassure Woodruff, Hughes Spalding suggested that the article, while "a little out of character for us," might well have a positive impact.

Instead, Woodruff's qualms continued to multiply. One of Austin's first acts as CEO was to circulate the draft of a letter informing Morton Downey that his contract would be dropped when it expired at the end of 1966. Appalled, Woodruff summoned Austin to his office. "You have to talk to him about this first," Woodruff insisted. If it made good business sense, Woodruff said, Austin was free to terminate Downey's long association with Coca-Cola. But doing so by mail was heartless. These things had to be handled with grace, Woodruff said, not just for Downey's sake but for the reputation of the company.

Austin shrugged. In his view, Downey typified the company's difficulties. He was on the payroll solely because he was one of Woodruff's old chums. Politely or otherwise, Austin believed, these people had to be dismissed.

More than a matter of temperament, the root of the friction between Austin and Woodruff was a fundamental rift over the question of ownership. Austin saw the Coca-Cola Company as a publicly held corporation, answerable to its thousands of shareholders and subject to the scrutiny of Wall Street. The books were full of unusual arrangements—a pension for the widow of one of Woodruff's outside advisers, for instance—that could not pass muster under the rules of modern business practice.

Woodruff's view, the polar opposite, was that he owned Coca-Cola himself. An instructive moment came in 1964, during the transition in management, when an opportunity arose to liquidate Coca-Cola International, the old holding company that still owned 23 percent of the outstanding shares of Coca-Cola common stock. Woodruff declined to do so. He had a memo prepared explaining that "the reasons which dictated the creation of International forty-two years ago are just as valid today"—a roundabout way of saying he still shared his father's desire for one-man working control over the company's destiny.

Settling into an uncomfortable stalemate, Woodruff gave Austin day-to-day command of Coca-Cola's affairs, but at the same time he promoted Fill Eisenberg to chief financial officer and assigned him to look over Austin's shoulder and watch how he spent Coca-Cola's money. "Our cash is on budget," Austin protested in a memo to Woodruff. And Woodruff shot back, "I see that our cash is 'on budget' at the end of October. How about the end of the year?"

Given his unhappiness with Austin, Woodruff might have been expected to turn his back on Cason Callaway, the man who sponsored Austin in the first place. Instead, in an odd twist of events, Woodruff spent time, energy, and money in 1966 trying to get Callaway's son elected governor.

With the state constitution barring Carl Sanders from running for a second consecutive term, Woodruff settled on Howard "Bo" Callaway as an attractive successor. In 1964, Callaway had become the first Republican in modern times elected to Congress from Georgia, serving a district south of Columbus. He was good-looking, moderate on race, and pro-business, and as the governor's election approached Woodruff urged him to run. Woodruff also promised to raise $100,000 for him, and Callaway duly announced his candidacy. In theory his chances appeared excellent, since Barry Goldwater had carried Georgia for the GOP in 1964.

But it turned out there was a problem. Callaway was an utterly inept campaigner. The first sign of trouble came when he began telling people about the money. Woodruff's financial backing was supposed to be kept confidential, as even the greenest of Georgia politicians understood, yet Callaway was traveling around the state blabbing indiscreetly, saying Woodruff was supporting him and quoting figures. Ovid Davis, Coca-Cola's lobbyist, was sent to hush Callaway and help polish his stump style, a job that proved difficult. "Old Bo," Davis recalled ruefully, "was a hard-headed S.O.B."

Callaway's shortcomings did not seem terribly alarming at first. The leading Democratic candidate, Ellis Arnall, was a liberal ex-governor who had served in the 1940s and enjoyed a national reputation for enlightened views on race. He would not embarrass the state if he won. The dark horse, however, was Lester Maddox, who had gained his most recent notoriety for chasing black customers out of his Atlanta restaurant wielding a pick handle. In the Democratic primary, Maddox finished a surprising second (just ahead of a little-known state senator named Jimmy Carter), forcing Arnall into a runoff election to decide the nomination.

Events overtook the campaign. On the afternoon of September 6, 1966, a week before the voters returned to the polls, an Atlanta policeman shot and wounded an auto theft suspect during a chase through Summerhill, one of the city's most impoverished black neighborhoods. In an ensuing riot, 16 people were injured and 75 arrested. Thanks to white backlash, Maddox won the runoff easily and became the Democratic nominee for governor.

With Maddox in line for the Governor's Mansion, the outcome of the November general election took on a new urgency. Believing a victory for Callaway was imperative, Woodruff poured more of his resources into the campaign. A private meeting was arranged with some of Atlanta's black leaders so Callaway could make a pitch for their support. Ovid Davis helped coach him on what to say: "Work for me on election day, and I'll work for you for four years." But Callaway made a botch of it. As a couple dozen of Atlanta's most prominent black citizens filed into the room, he blurted, "Come on in, boys," a choice of phrase that was met with stony silence. Then he told them, "I want you to know, I'm going to treat you just like I treat everybody else." It was hardly an inspiring promise.

Davis's frustration with Callaway grew as election day neared. Callaway "is about as cocky as anybody I ever saw," Davis reported to Woodruff. "Bo feels like he has the election won going away." Try as he might, Davis could not convince Callaway that Maddox had a prayer of defeating him. "It got to the point," Carl Sanders remembered, "where Mr. Woodruff and John Sibley and some of them finally just threw up their hands in utter despair because they couldn't get Bo to comprehend. Hell, he had the race won. He should have won it in a walkaway."

Davis did what he could, spreading money here and there, planting a few unfriendly questions for the media to ask Maddox at forums, and trying to keep Mayor Allen and Maddox's other critics from excessive attacks that might backfire. But his efforts were not enough.

When the votes were counted, Callaway failed to gain an outright majority of the popular vote, as required by Georgia law. He finished first, but a write-in campaign for Arnall held Callaway below the 50 percent threshold needed for victory. The outcome of the election would have to be decided by the Georgia General Assembly, where the membership was overwhelmingly Democratic and almost certain to pick Maddox.

"The implications of our world-wide business and Maddox are, of course, absolutely incompatible," Davis wrote in a memo, summing up the thinking at Plum Street. The only hope was to persuade the courts to order another election. In that case, Davis noted, a renewed effort would be made to secure the black vote. "We have the apparatus to get them out," he told Woodruff, "and it has been financed."

But the courts left the matter in the hands of the legislature, whose leaders made it clear they would rather operate with Maddox as a weak, pliant governor than spend four years waging battle with a Republican. At length Davis concluded that further efforts to block Maddox would be futile. So far, he noted, the only whisper of the company's involvement had been a single newspaper report that said "progressive business interests" in Georgia were opposed to Maddox. Better to leave it that way.

Closing the books on a disastrous election, Davis looked ahead four years and recommended that Woodruff buy $100 worth of tickets to an appreciation dinner for Jimmy Carter. "I do not think this boy has a political future," Davis wrote, "but he might."

Then there was Vietnam.

When the escalation of the American military commitment in South Vietnam began in earnest in 1965, company officials had every reason to think Coca-Cola could "go to war" with the GIs as it had in the past. The army requisitioned 382,000 cartons of Coke in cans and established a standing refill order of 9,000 cartons every two weeks. With the availability of 17-day express shipping from San Francisco to the ports on the Vietnamese coast, getting the product to the war zone promised to be fairly easy, and the company hoped to start selling Fanta, Sprite, and Tab to the servicemen as well as Coke.

By the summer of 1966, though, as the buildup of American forces reached full velocity, the unique difficulty of waging war in Southeast Asia became apparent. Unlike World War II, ground won in battle in Vietnam did not remain secure under American control. Guerrilla attacks disrupted every facet of life.

The company's experience trying to provision the troops closely paralleled the frustrations of the military itself. Heavy fighting blocked the supply lines to several cities, holding up shipments of soft drinks and other refreshments. At Da Nang, the post exchange ran out of Coke and beer for two weeks, and the servicemen were complaining.

The company sent a field observer, David Brann, to investigate, and he reported a pattern of "feast or famine." Supplies were plentiful where the U.S. Army swept the highways and maintained the perimeters, he said, but sparse elsewhere. "An area [is] only secure as long as the troops are physically present," Brann explained to Plum Street. "Once they are moved to another area in their 'seek and destroy' operations, the Viet Congs [sic] return to cut the arterial roads and transportation comes to a virtual standstill."

His assessment might have served as a synopsis of the failure of the entire American military enterprise. Vietnam was a helicopter war, with no established front lines, only bases and villages that were American turf one day and Viet Cong the next.

Under the circumstances, there seemed little point in trying to associate Coca-Cola with the war effort, since support for it in the United States was just as evanescent. Company officials avoided the kind of publicity they'd encouraged during World War II, and they began looking forward to the day when, as Austin put it, "the Vietnam affair grinds to a halt."

Austin turned his energies to the war of commerce Coca-Cola was waging elsewhere around the globe with Pepsi. The competition between the two cola giants spread to every continent in the 1960s, with Pepsi emerging the victor more often than not.

In Venezuela, where the Coca-Cola bottler had grown especially lax, Don Kendall launched a sales campaign so effective the word "Pepsi" became a synonym for all carbonated soft drinks, including Coke. Trying to recoup, Coca-Cola Export organized a sampling program in Caracas and other major cities and gave youngsters free Cokes and school supplies. But much to their chagrin, the Coca-Cola field men discovered that no matter what they handed out, the children invariably responded, "Thank you for the Pepsi!"

Brazil and Uruguay were not much better, and there was one bleak point during the decade when none of the company's operations in South America made a *centavo* of profit. Before he retired, Lee Talley prepared a memo outlining the company's trouble spots. The "Imitator," as he insisted on calling Pepsi, was "gaining ground" not only in South America, but in Canada, France, England, and the Philippines. Pepsi's export sales quadrupled between 1959 and 1963, and kept rising.

The cola wars extended behind the Iron Curtain as well. At Austin's urging, the company got a quiet okay from the Johnson administration and took the first halting steps toward selling Coke in the Soviet Union. But the process of negotiating the logistics, including trademark protection, quality control, and the shipment of syrup through Brussels (with payment secured by letters of credit from a Belgian bank), threatened to drag on forever. Even then, sales would be limited to foreign visitors at Intourist stops. With Pepsi making inroads among the civilian populations in Yugoslavia and Rumania, it appeared Coca-Cola might fall behind in the Communist world as it had elsewhere.

Doing business overseas seemed to grow more complicated and treacherous with every passing year. In Greece, not long after a group of colonels seized power in a coup, news accounts disclosed that Coca-Cola's press agent in New York, Tom Deegan, had accepted a retainer of nearly $250,000 a year to represent the junta and tidy up its image. Although Austin moved swiftly to dismiss Deegan, the revelation inflicted severe injury on Coke's standing with the Greek public. When the colonels were overthrown, the new democratic government retaliated by imposing a special tax on the company's Athens bottler.

Deegan, meanwhile, went to work for Pepsi.

At home, Coca-Cola's office politics proved almost as byzantine, as Austin moved to consolidate his strength inside the executive suite. One of his gambits in particular became the stuff of legend.

Austin had reached the conclusion that Ben Oehlert ought to leave the company. The situation had been tolerable while Oehlert was stationed in Orlando, running Minute Maid. But after he returned to Atlanta as a senior vice president in 1965, Oehlert made a habit of second-guessing Austin's decisions on everything from lobbying to mergers to marketing, filing memos that poked holes in every project Austin undertook. Once a master of tact, Oehlert experienced a personality change and became, as one of his children put it, "too big for his britches." He held Austin in disdain and grew unguarded about showing how he felt.

Like a frontier town too small to accommodate a pair of gunslingers, Plum Street proved inadequate to contain the two men. Their clashing egos became a major concern within the company, until Austin found an adroit solution: He arranged to have President Johnson appoint Oehlert ambassador to Pakistan.

When Oehlert expressed reluctance about taking the remote posting, Woodruff stepped in personally and persuaded him to go, arguing that the job would be the perfect capstone to his career.*

Woodruff's intervention sent a clear message. In spite of his uneasiness, he had decided his new CEO deserved a chance to manage the company free from constant sniping. Austin took full advantage of the running room. While he had once been forced to seek permission for even the smallest decisions, he now behaved largely as he saw fit. He joined the board of General Electric as an outside director, and when he was named Man of the Year by the International Advertising Association, he told Woodruff he would be flying to West Berlin to accept. He didn't ask.

Forbes, long a source of lavish praise for Woodruff's guidance of the company, reported approvingly in a cover story in 1967 that he had retired for good. "When Robinson and Talley were president," the article said, "Woodruff still made all the final decisions. Now he stands aside and lets Austin make them. . . . Austin is boss." In fact, *Forbes* said, the top executives at Plum Street rarely mentioned Woodruff's name anymore.

The article infuriated Woodruff's old friend Dick Gresham, the minister. "I hate to see your great business acumen flouted by a showman," he wrote. But Woodruff held his tongue. Never one to seek publicity even in the rosiest of circumstances, Woodruff withdrew further behind the curtain that shielded him from the eyes of the public.

As the decade drew to a close, Woodruff suffered a draining series of personal losses that left Austin and many others convinced that his career, and perhaps his life, too, had reached a final stage.

As happens to all people who live into their late seventies, Woodruff watched many of his friends die or grow enfeebled. The worst sight was

---

* As it turned out, Oehlert liked Islamabad and deeply appreciated all of the trappings of high diplomatic office. In his later years, retired and living in Palm Beach, Florida, he had himself listed as "Ambassador Oehlert" in the phone book and drove around town in a secondhand Rolls-Royce with an American flag mounted on the front fender. But he never forgave Austin. If he could, he told his family, he would have killed the man.

Bobby Jones, the great athlete, once the master of a golf stroke so fluid it seemed a work of art, crippled by a bone spur that dug into his spinal column and left him in constant pain, paralyzed and confined to a wheelchair. Woodruff visited Jones's house most Sunday mornings and could see him wasting away.

More and more, Woodruff gave in to his "sense of futility," as Gresham called it, the dark mood that had gnawed at him all his life. He took more comfort than ever in liquor, so much so that his friends, fearing he might stumble and fall on the winding staircase in his house on Tuxedo Road, had an elevator installed to carry him up to his bedroom at night.

Woodruff's greatest concern, more worrisome to him than politics or business, was the proper disposition of his fortune. Determined to make the wisest use of his money, he came to detest pressure for donations from any source, no matter how worthy. "It always gives me pleasure to do something for somebody, without being asked," he explained once. "I don't like to be asked." His words were misinterpreted by some as evidence of quiet beneficence, when in fact he meant exactly what he said: He did not like to be asked.

Millions of dollars in grants from the Woodruff and Whitehead foundations flowed to Emory and the new Atlanta Arts Center and other causes, but at Woodruff's request the Atlanta newspapers agreed to report that a man known only as the Anonymous Donor was at work. One reason for Woodruff's secretiveness was a desire to protect his brother George, who had three daughters and several grandchildren and feared a kidnapping. More than security, though, Woodruff's goal was to shield himself from the distress of turning down supplicants. Every time his wealth was mentioned, he was swamped with requests for money. He did not like to be asked, because he did not like having to say no.*

Woodruff's demand for privacy took on outsized proportions. When a driver on the City Slicker bus tour, wheeling tourists past the mansions of Buckhead, pointed out Woodruff's house and described him as having "buckets of money" available for philanthropy, the remark was reported to the Coca-Cola Company and treated as a serious violation of civic decorum. The bus company instructed all its employees, in writing, that Woodruff's name was never to be uttered again.

One morning Woodruff opened his copy of the *Atlanta Constitution* and was surprised to see a story in the business section that detailed his holdings

---

* Woodruff's papers include scores of letters from people begging for money. Most of their stories are tales of horrific tragedy and genuine need—sick or injured children, impending evictions, pleas for scholarships and church contributions—while a few are marvels of ambition and unmitigated gall. One man sought financial backing for his invention, an upholstered wheelchair equipped with a fold-out cot, toilet, and lunch tray. Another wrote, "To get straight to the point of this letter, sir, I have this obsession to become a millionaire.

of Coca-Cola stock. The information came from a proxy statement—in effect a public document—but Woodruff was livid nonetheless. A day or two later, he ran into Jack Tarver, the publisher, waiting for an elevator at the Commerce Club. "Let me tell you something," Woodruff said, openly angry. "I will not have anything written about my wealth in the newspaper." He had moved the Coca-Cola Company out of Atlanta once before, Woodruff added pointedly, and he was prepared to do so again.

Lucille Huffman, Woodruff's longtime secretary, tried to coax him out of his doldrums. He had always been subject to bouts of unhappiness, she reminded him, but in the past he'd treated his low points as an incentive to gather strength and rally. Now, she said, he was giving in to depression. "It is a lonely reward to be placed on a pedestal," she wrote him in a personal note, "but there you are in the lives of so many people, many more than you will acknowledge, and so your right to live as you want to live becomes less and less at your disposal."

Before he could answer her challenge, Woodruff suffered the harshest blow of all. On the night of January 22, 1968, Nell Woodruff was watching television at Ichauway when she began to feel weak. She needed help from one of the servants to get out of her chair and into the bedroom. Moments later she suffered a massive cerebral hemorrhage. She died the next afternoon.

"I have lost my partner," Woodruff said, over and over. "I have lost the one I could count on to be on my side." Her death was shattering to Woodruff. He had been the dominant partner throughout their fifty-five-year marriage, yet in many ways he depended on her. "I tied myself to the tail of a kite," Nell often remarked, and the metaphor could be extended to say that she served to steady him in strong winds.

As with most powerful, magnetic men, Woodruff drew his share of female admirers over the years, but Nell found a clever, gentle way of disarming them: She drew them in as friends of her own, close enough to watch carefully. The Woodruffs' union, by all accounts, was a strong one. His life, she wrote in a birthday letter to him a month before she died, "is a constant inspiration to me. . . . God has been good to me and I am grateful. You have my love—all of it. Your 'little girl.'"

Other burdens fell on Woodruff's shoulders. On Thursday afternoon, April 4, 1968, he and Carl Sanders were visiting the White House, having a drink with Lyndon Johnson. It was a somber occasion, coming just five days after the president's announcement that he would not seek reelection. As they talked, an aide entered the Oval Office and handed Johnson a slip of paper saying Martin Luther King, Jr., had been shot. Later that night, after King died, Woodruff put a phone call through to Ivan Allen in Atlanta, offering to write a blank check to cover any extraordinary expenses the city incurred in connection with King's funeral.

Allen remembered Woodruff's exact words. "Ivan," he said, "the minute they bring King's body back tomorrow—between then and the time of the funeral—Atlanta, Georgia, is going to be the center of the universe. I want you to do whatever is right and necessary, and whatever the city can't pay for will be taken care of. Just do it right." Allen said later it was only in listening to Woodruff that he realized how many mourners—and members of the media—would be descending on the city. Five days later, as Governor Maddox cowered in his office at the Capitol with the blinds drawn, 200,000 people marched through the middle of downtown Atlanta without incident, following the mule wagon that carried King's body, crying and singing "We Shall Overcome."

In the months before and after his wife's death, Woodruff helped bury several friends and intimates: Eisenhower, Elliott Scarborough, Harrison Jones, Hughes Spalding, Ralph McGill, Gene Kelly, and Mattie Heard, the cook with the sweet voice from Ichauway. The grief seemed to overwhelm him. His drinking got seriously out of hand, and his surviving associates began to wonder about his will to live. He aged visibly from month to month, turning gray and looking like an old man for the first time.

One of Woodruff's contemporaries, Red Deupree, the retired chairman of Procter & Gamble and a former outside director of Coca-Cola, liked to tell the story of visiting his doctor for treatment of a case of rheumatism. The medicine he was given irritated his stomach, and he complained on his next trip to the office. "How long do I have to keep taking this stuff?" he asked.

"How old are you?" the doctor inquired.

"Eighty-four," Deupree replied.

"In that case," the doctor said, "not long."

Woodruff appropriated the story and started telling it himself. He laughed when he got to the punch line, but he seemed perfectly serious about the point. He didn't think he had long to go.

Eleven

"OCTOGENARIANS!"

There were several people who could share credit for Robert Woodruff's gradual recovery of spirit.

His new doctor, Garland Herndon, moved into a house next door in Atlanta and began stopping by for breakfast every morning, monitoring his health. At Herndon's insistence, Woodruff cut back steadily on his drinking and set himself toward a goal of quitting completely, an accomplishment Herndon promised would give him "comfort, health improvement, and pride in a feat few are able to accomplish."

Woodruff's old friends rallied to his side and worked tirelessly to cheer him up. Red Deupree swore he actually had Woodruff giggling one night at Ichauway as they sat up playing gin rummy and telling old stories.

And Martha Ellis, one of Nell's nieces, brought the spark of female companionship back into his life. Petite, pretty, and vivacious, Mrs. Ellis had been a favorite of Woodruff's for years. When she was widowed, a year after Nell died, she and Woodruff found themselves drawn together, seeking solace.

Theirs was not exactly an adolescent romance. Woodruff turned eighty in 1969, and she had her sixty-fifth birthday the next year. He found one of her most attractive attributes to be a clear, mellifluous speaking voice, which he could understand easily in spite of his increasing deafness. Yet neither was their relationship entirely geriatric. They liked to ride horseback over the endless trails at Ichauway, as she recalled, "checking the collards and onions, searching for turkey tracks, pausing at the Orange Hole and Alligator Bend to wonder if the creek is rising or falling." In the evenings, they sat by the fire in their robes and pajamas, comfortable with each other, talking in a philosophical vein.

She would write him notes occasionally, reflecting the affection that deepened between them. "Your good opinion of me is a great treasure," she told him after one visit "Your high regard means more to me than you know. . . . God be with you through your sometimes sleepless nights." He kept a photograph of her on his dresser, a picture from her younger years when she wore her hair long and had a flirtatious look in her eyes.

They talked of marriage, and though Mrs. Ellis demurred in the end (fearing an utter loss of independence if she moved into the big mansion on Tuxedo Road), she became his consort and unofficial hostess and steered him back on the social circuit.

For all the positive elements that helped rekindle Woodruff's will to live, however, it seemed the strongest of his motives was a dark determination to keep watch over Paul Austin and make sure he did not ruin the Coca-Cola Company. Woodruff went to his office every day, where he insisted on reviewing the major decisions that affected the business.

Austin proved to have undeniable talent in many of the disciplines necessary to run the company, chief among them an ability to foresee social trends. The environmental movement was especially worrisome to Austin, because he empathized with critics who charged that the company was, as he put it, "littering the landscape." With its mountains of non-returnable bottles, fleets of trucks, and acres of billboards, Austin believed Coca-Cola made an "ideal target" for protest. As the first Earth Day approached in the spring of 1970, he predicted trouble.

Unhappily for the company, Austin's skills did not always extend to finding solutions for the problems he diagnosed. His answer to Earth Day, for instance, was to deliver a speech with the prodigious title "Environmental Renewal or Oblivion. . .Quo Vadis?" to a glassy-eyed group of Southern bankers. He also moved to acquire Aqua-Chem, Incorporated, a water-purification company he thought could be billed as a subsidiary devoted to pollution treatment. The Aqua-Chem merger came with a hefty price tag of 1,754,000 shares of Coca-Cola common stock, an amount Woodruff and the board could hardly believe and approved only with the gravest misgivings.

One of Austin's brainstorms was the development of Saci, a high-protein drink made from cocoa and soy beans, which he hoped to begin marketing in the Third World as a diet supplement In the supercharged political atmosphere that prevailed at the time, the idea backfired. Appearing before Senator George McGovern's Select Committee on Nutrition and Human Needs, consumer advocate Ralph Nader accused the company of plotting to export a healthful drink to other countries while continuing to sell cola—a product with "absolutely no vitamins or proteins"—in the United States. When the company declined to provide a witness to testify at the hearings, Nader taunted, "Coca-Cola has a great many reasons for not appearing. If you ever get them to appear, you will see some of the most shocking deceptions and power plays in the history of this country."

When Austin delegated the responsibility for curing the company's ills, he got better results. He believed, for example, that the round, red Coca-Cola logo had grown overly familiar and needed a facelift. Launching "Operation Arden," named for the Elizabeth Arden line of cosmetics, he assigned a team from the firm of Margulies & Lippincott to come up with a new design. Their creation, a curving ribbon called the "dynamic wave," served in effect to underline the trademark and make it catch the eye again. The company's advertising agency, McCann-Erickson, revived an old, World War II-era slogan, "The Real Thing," and turned it into a hugely successful campaign.

Austin's greatest moment occurred when he ignored his own judgment and deferred to McCann on the concept for a new radio and TV commercial. Hoping to capitalize on the mood of the times, the agency gathered some two hundred youngsters of various nationalities on a hillside in Italy and had them lip-sync the words to a sweet, pacifistic tune, "I'd Like to Buy the World a Coke." When he listened to a recording of the song (which was actually performed by a British group, the New Seekers), Austin found the words and sentiments treacly and seriously considered killing the ad. But he relented, explaining, "That's why we have an advertising department."

Aired in 1971, the song became a sensation, so popular the public began calling radio stations and asking them to play it for free, just as they'd once clamored for Pepsi's "Twice as Much" jingle. The New Seekers and other groups recorded a fresh version, stripped of references to Coke, called "I'd Like to Teach the World to Sing," which eventually sold more than a million copies. Austin got a firsthand indication of the tune's impact a few months later at a White House dinner, when the Ray Coniff Singers performed it as the final number in a medley of their favorite songs. Aware that President Nixon was a Pepsi man, several guests winked and nodded at Austin, and one whispered, "How much did you pay for that?"

Reporting the episode to Woodruff later, Austin joked breezily that he was lucky not to have been marched out by a Marine guard. But it was one of few light exchanges between them. Woodruff was growing more and more concerned about Austin's stewardship of the company. Many of his innovations, notably the purchase of a shrimp farm in Mexico, struck Woodruff as eccentric at best and possibly as evidence that Austin had lost his senses. Instead of swallowing hard and approving Austin's plans, Woodruff and his allies on the board began turning thumbs down.

In a move that misled many outsiders, Austin assumed the title of chairman in addition to president and CEO, but he was deprived of the full power that typically went with those jobs, since Woodruff continued to control the votes of a majority of the directors. Austin kept waiting for Woodruff to resign from the board, or at least to give up his chairmanship of the powerful Finance Committee, neither of which Woodruff showed the slightest inclination of doing.

Early in 1972, Woodruff suffered a pair of strokes that weakened his right side, but he refused to let Dr. Herndon put him in the hospital. Determined to conceal the seriousness of his condition, Woodruff went to Ichauway to recuperate, and later he gave Dr. Herndon and Mrs. Ellis gifts of $1 million each for helping in his recovery. Though his right hand remained limp and he had difficulty walking, Woodruff stubbornly insisted on going back to work, where he had a document prepared asserting that his capacity to serve the company was undiminished.

Tensions reached a head in 1973 when Austin proposed an expensive, complicated land deal in partnership with D. K. Ludwig, the billionaire investor, and Japan's giant Mitsubishi Corporation. Austin wanted to create a joint venture and buy thousands of acres of farmland in Brazil to grow, sugar, citrus, and other agricultural products the company used in its soft drinks. He then planned to sell most of Minute Maid's groves in Florida to developers for a sizable profit.

Woodruff's response, in a word, was no. Without lingering over the details, Woodruff concluded that it was dangerous policy to rely on the political stability of the Brazilian government, and he had a general dislike for taking on partners. Mostly he thought Austin was in over his head, risking $20 million of the company's money on a piece of financial derring-do when he ought to be out selling more soda.

Austin pursued the debate face-to-face during a visit to Woodruff's house in Atlanta. This was a golden chance to raise profits by cutting the cost of ingredients, he said. The military junta in Brazil was "in the saddle," as he put it, and would stay there for at least the next ten years. Brazil was a "treasure house" of raw materials. Ludwig had connections in the right places, and he'd make an excellent partner. Austin reminded Woodruff of his own defiance of the board fifty years earlier in expanding the foreign end of the business. "I'm not in a position to help my directors in quite the same way," Austin added tartly, but he swore his idea was a good one. His parting comment—that he didn't plan to "strong-arm" Woodruff by taking their dispute to the full board—was a curious remark that managed to convey a tone of surrender and insubordination at the same time.

There was no dramatic breach when Woodruff reiterated his veto of the Brazilian project. Not a word of their disagreement was breathed in the financial press. Only a few people in the executive suite were even aware of it. But from that point on, in the language of divorce, the relationship between Woodruff and Austin was irretrievably broken.

Woodruff had been pushing Austin for several years to groom a successor, and now he stepped up the pressure. Coca-Cola had acquired Duncan Foods, a Houston-based coffee company, during the 1960s, in a deal many analysts considered a poor bargain. A joke made the rounds at Plum Street that the only genuinely valuable asset Duncan Foods brought to the table was Charles Duncan, Jr., the attractive young president and scion of the family. As it happened, life imitated humor: Duncan caught Woodruff's attention and became his newest protegé.

With Woodruff's backing, Duncan rose through the ranks of Coca-Cola Export, following the same career path as Austin, who was ten years his senior. In the summer of 1970, Duncan was promoted to executive vice president of Coca-Cola, and the *New York Times* proclaimed him the "rising star" of the company. Duncan moved into an office on the fourth floor at Plum Street and became a fixture at the daily luncheons in Woodruff's private dining room.

"I think that was the kiss of death," Joe Jones said, looking back. Seeing Duncan as a direct threat, Austin unleashed a plague of annoyances on him, some petty, some major, all designed to make his life unpleasant. Austin cut

Duncan out of the information loop, gave orders behind his back, undermined him with other executives, and generally engaged in the corporate equivalent of poking a sharpened stick in his cage.

Duncan's response to the pressure came as a disappointment to Woodruff. Thanks to his personal wealth, Duncan was close to Woodruff in ways Austin could never hope to be.* When Woodruff decided to sell his ranch in Wyoming, he turned to Duncan, asked him to buy it, and named a price. Duncan wrote a check the next day. But that same wealth turned out to be the cause of Duncan's undoing. He was simply too rich to put up with Austin's harassment. Duncan looked to Woodruff to protect him and smooth his way, and when that did not happen he resigned. He went back home to Texas in the spring of 1974, when Woodruff thought he should have stayed in Atlanta and kept scrapping.

For his own part, Austin came to view Woodruff as an obstructionist, a recalcitrant old man who demanded flattery and hand-holding, and whose whims held back progress. With his chief rival gone, Austin gained a little breathing room, yet as he looked at his board of directors he found himself captive to a group of men born in the nineteenth century. Woodruff, John Sibley, Jim Farley, and Abbott Turner, the son-in-law of W. C. Bradley, were all in their eighties. "Octogenarians!" Austin would mutter under his breath, wondering what Wall Street made of a soft drink company with youthful customers, youthful commercials, and a board that belonged in a museum display case. Austin began circulating occasional memos on the subject of a mandatory retirement age for board members, which Woodruff and the others ignored. Once, when Austin raised the subject directly and prodded him to resign, Woodruff replied curtly, "I can't do that."

On a trip to London around that time, Woodruff was greeted by the company's top European officer, Klaus Putter, and his family. Putter's little girl curtsied when she met Woodruff, as if she were being presented to a monarch. And that was pretty much how Austin saw it. Woodruff was a doddering old king who planned to cling to the crown until the day he died.

To replace Duncan, Austin turned to a sweet-natured, low-key veteran named J. Lucian Smith, a native Mississippian who'd been with the company since 1940. Luke Smith's first supervisor had joked that he was "too nice" to advance very far, and for years he had toiled in the middle ranks of management, running the New England bottling operations.

Eventually Smith rose to the presidency of the company's new domestic sales division, Coca-Cola USA, where it appeared he would finish his career. Austin considered him the ideal choice for the role of a caretaker president: He had no enemies, had never shown much ambition—and he

---

* After the merger with his family's company, Duncan held 220,825 shares of Coca-Cola common stock worth nearly $30 million and was given a seat on the board.

was fifty-five years old, just three years younger than Austin, unlikely to mount a campaign to unseat him as chairman and CEO.

Woodruff approved the promotion, and a measure of calm was restored to Plum Street, at least superficially. Throughout its long existence, the Coca-Cola Company had managed to present a cheerful, sunny face to the world no matter what mischief was erupting in the executive suite, and in 1974 it lifted that tradition to a new plateau. With the nation convulsed over Watergate and the slow disengagement of U.S. forces from the war in Vietnam, Coca-Cola unveiled a series of commercials called "Look Up, America," designed to bolster the country's mood with patriotic music and pictures. "It struck the creative team," a company official said, "that there was almost a yearning among a large segment of the population to hear something good about our country."

Even more than the "Back to Normal" ads of the 1930s, which encouraged a feeling of recovery from the Depression, the new commercials asserted a role for Coca-Cola in shaping the national psyche—quite a remarkable declaration for a soft drink manufacturer. The executive who oversaw the campaign, Don Keough, was named Adman of the Year by the magazine *Advertising Age*, which seemed a fitting tribute.

Yet no sleight-of-hand could divert attention for long from the contentious atmosphere that prevailed on the fourth floor of Plum Street. Like jealous siblings, Woodruff and Austin feuded over Smith, even though (or perhaps because) he went out of his way to be agreeable with both of them. When Woodruff began inviting Smith to join his lunch group, Austin fumed and finally ordered him not to go anymore. When Woodruff prodded Austin to give Smith a raise, Austin balked, arguing that his $225,000 salary was adequate.

A more heated conflict broke out over Fill Eisenberg. As chief financial officer, Eisenberg reported directly to Woodruff and the Finance Committee, bypassing Austin. Like Woodruff, Eisenberg tended to be old-fashioned about the company's balance sheet, satisfied to keep a large surplus of $100 million or more on the books as a hedge against hard times. He literally sat by Woodruff's side at meetings, passing judgment on Austin's proposals, routinely recommending against them. Naturally Austin was looking for a way to eliminate Eisenberg, and in 1974 he thought he'd found one.

Eisenberg shared Woodruff's aversion to Wall Street analysts and the business press, a prejudice that flowered into full-scale loathing when the Coca-Cola Company's financial condition took a turn for the worse in the mid-1970s. Inflation drove up the price of ingredients, putting a severe bite on Coca-Cola's revenues, and skittish investors started a sharp run on the company's common stock, driving its value down further and faster than any time since the 1930s.

As the company's stock tumbled—from a high of 127¾ a share all the way down to 44⅝—Eisenberg got angrier and angrier. His phone was ringing two or three times a day, with one Wall Street specialist after another demanding to know why Coca-Cola was performing so badly, until at last he blew his stack and refused to answer at all. He issued a formal statement announcing that he had decided "to stop all direct contacts with security analysts," pending further notice.

The outcry that resulted was harsh, albeit predictable. Using a word full of freight at the time, *Institutional Investor* magazine accused the company of "stonewalling," and quoted an unnamed source as saying Eisenberg "always treated the Street like dirt anyway." The criticism was leveled not just at Eisenberg personally, but at the Coca-Cola Company's "ancient tradition of secrecy," dating back to the days of Doc Pemberton. The timing of the decree was atrocious, one analyst said, because "confidence in the company is at a low ebb." Eisenberg responded by extending his blackout to business reporters as well.

Austin could see all the goodwill he'd cultivated with financial writers and investment houses drying up overnight. Eisenberg's gag order struck him as embodying everything that was wrong with the old approach, starting with the presumption that the shareholders and the public were to be told almost nothing about the inner workings of the business. This time, Austin believed, Eisenberg had gone too far.

On his next birthday, in March 1975, Eisenberg would turn sixty-five. Austin circulated a memo proposing not only that Eisenberg retire then, but that the corporate by-laws be amended to eliminate his job. Instead of having an executive vice president for finance who reported to Woodruff as chairman of the Finance Committee, there would be two new positions, treasurer and controller, both reporting to Austin, the CEO. Austin even nominated his own pick for treasurer, Charles Lord, and noted pointedly that Lord's first act would be to reverse Eisenberg's policy on contact with Wall Street.

While couched in dry language, Austin's gambit was the closest thing to an outright coup attempt at the Coca-Cola Company since Sam Dobbs had tried to outmuscle Woodruff's father more than half a century earlier. And the result this time was no less certain. Woodruff kept Eisenberg in the job and had him continue reporting to the Finance Committee, which remained a burial ground for Austin's ideas.

When the air at Plum Street grew too stifling, Austin often availed himself of the company plane and took off for faraway ports of call. Like Woodruff, he was drawn to the international side of the business, and he loved the physical sensation of flight, the sense of swift passage through inky nights across great distances.

Often he flew alone, with only the pilots for company. Austin also shared Woodruff's taste for alcohol, and he liked to board the company's new jet-powered Gulfstream, slip off his suit, put on a sweater, and roam the back of the plane, having a drink or two, sometimes more, trying to relax. Ralph Whitworth, the company's senior pilot, once flew Austin straight through from Tokyo to Paris, with refueling stops in Anchorage and Greenland, spending eighteen hours in the air. "He wanted to go places and do things," Whitworth explained.

In addition to his flair for divining social change, the other great gift Austin brought to running the Coca-Cola Company was a keen faith in the importance of foreign markets. Austin became CEO around the time Coca-Cola's export sales caught and began to surpass the domestic side, a trend he thought was inevitable and worked hard to encourage. The company enjoyed considerable growth in Germany, Japan, Brazil, and South Africa during Austin's tenure, and the *New York Times* reported Coke was "fast on its way" to becoming a national drink in India as well.

Austin took a worldly approach to world affairs, hiring an avowed communist as a plant manager in Chile during Salvador Allende's presidency, and currying favor with Imelda Marcos in the Philippines by giving her $35,000 worth of equipment for a nutrition center. Looking at the largest untapped market of all, Austin inaugurated contact with officials in Red China, hoping his membership on the Smithsonian Institution's board of regents would gain him a visa and a visit. He also contemplated the end of the Cuban embargo and sent an emissary to Havana to open talks. Later he went himself and held a clandestine meeting with Fidel Castro.

Inevitably, Austin began to supplant Woodruff as the company's top political operative, both overseas and at home. The election of Richard Nixon in 1968 marked a change of parties—and soft drinks—in the White House. Woodruff no longer had a pass at the gate or a standing invitation to drop by the Oval Office at "milking time," as he called it, for a casual cocktail. In 1972, Nixon made news (and cemented his place in the Plum Street rogues' gallery) by negotiating Pepsi's entry into the Soviet Union.

Austin's route into national politics had its origins in the 1970 governor's race in Georgia. With the one-term limit still in effect, Lester Maddox had to leave office, and the contest to succeed him quickly took shape as a two-man race between Carl Sanders, the immediate past governor, and up-and-coming Jimmy Carter. Aware of Woodruff's friendship with Sanders, Carter sent word through his top adviser, Charles Kirbo, that he would like to visit Ichauway and make a pitch for support from the Coca-Cola crowd. According to Coca-Cola's lobbyist, Ovid Davis, Carter's nose was "still a little bit out of joint" because the business community had spurned him four years earlier. Woodruff replied by suggesting a talk in Atlanta, not at the plantation, which Carter interpreted—correctly—as a brush-off.

Woodruff and his circle backed Sanders to the hilt, leaving Austin the job of building bridges to the governor's office when Carter won. Austin did so gladly, forming a close friendship with the new governor and giving him access to the company's resources, notably its fleet of planes and its network of international contacts. In the fall of 1974, as he began his improbable bid for the White House, Carter fended off suggestions of inexperience and provincialism by tying himself directly to the company.

"Georgia has a particular advantage over some states," Carter said, "in that we have our own built-in state department in the Coca-Cola Company. They provide me ahead of time with much more penetrating analyses of what the country is, what its problems are, who its leaders are, and when I arrive there, provide me with an introduction to the leaders of that country in every realm of life."

The notion of a one-term Georgia governor running for the presidency with a foreign policy built on "penetrating analyses" from the Coca-Cola Company sounded pretty far-fetched at the time, and some officials at Plum Street laughed up their sleeves. Yet Austin stuck with Carter and encouraged his candidacy, and even went so far as writing a letter to several top national businessmen, including Frank Cary, the chairman of IBM, urging support of Carter as "a person of destiny who can and will become a great president."

In the years since then, fearing the taint of partisan politics, the company has tried to play down Austin's association with Carter, suggesting it was little more than a matter of corporate courtesy for a hometown politician. But the fact was that Austin gave early and enthusiastic backing to the Carter campaign, highlighted by a luncheon he threw at New York's "21" Club, along with Henry Ford II and Seagram's Edgar Bronfman, to "introduce" Carter to the national business community.

When Carter won, it appeared Austin had gambled successfully and could reap the rewards that came from having a friend in the Oval Office. Even before the inauguration, Austin and his wife accompanied Rosalynn Carter on a state visit to Mexico. Speculation swirled in the media that Austin was in line for a top job in the administration, possibly even secretary of state, until he made a point of placing a call to Kirbo in Washington withdrawing his name from consideration. Austin sent Woodruff a memo apologizing for the "unsettling effect" his political involvement had created in Coca-Cola's executive suite, when of course he'd enjoyed it thoroughly.

The early days of Carter's presidency were marked by several small kindnesses toward the Coca-Cola Company. According to *Newsweek* magazine, Bert Lance, the budget director, discovered a secretary drinking a Pepsi and told her, "You know, ma'am, our crowd likes a good old Democratic drink—Coke." The president's son Jack found a Pepsi in a White House refrigerator and had it removed.

The title over the *Newsweek* article called Austin "Carter's Chum from Coke" and explained that he was one of the president's closest friends and advisers. Austin protested, saying the two were "not bosom buddies," but he also dropped a delicious tidbit about a recent trip he'd made to see the Egyptian president, Anwar Sadat. "At the end of the conversation," Austin recounted, "I said, 'Do you want this to remain confidential, or do you want me to report directly to my government?' He said, 'I'd like very much if you would report it. That's the reason for our conversation.'"

It was all heady stuff. John Sibley's son Jimmy, a lawyer with King &

Spalding, was on the company jet with Austin when it touched down in Cairo. A band was in place, playing on the tarmac, Sibley recalled, and Austin rushed out the door to accept the greeting. It turned out the tune was the "Marseillaise," being played in recognition of a French dignitary who was leaving at the same moment, but that was beside the point. Coca-Cola was doing business in 139 countries, and its CEO gloried in having the stature of a minister of state.

Woodruff found himself completely eclipsed. His direct involvement in city politics ended when Ivan Allen retired as mayor in 1970, and he had only a passing acquaintance with George Busbee, the governor who followed Carter.

Instead of giving guidance, Woodruff had to satisfy himself with making the city and state the recipients of his philanthropy. In 1971, he presented Allen's successor, Sam Massell, with $9.9 million worth of Coca-Cola stock to purchase a two-acre tract for a park in the middle of downtown Atlanta. The *Atlanta Constitution* dutifully concealed Woodruff's role in the transaction, reporting only that the city's "Anonymous Donor" was at work again.

But the idea of anonymity had begun to chafe at Woodruff. In earlier years, as Mayor Hartsfield once put it, Woodruff's role as a philanthropist was "the worst-kept secret in town." Every citizen of consequence knew about his gifts, and among the people who mattered to him he got the credit he deserved. Any time the Atlanta newspapers reported a nameless donation, Woodruff was assumed to be the source. Once, seeing a story about an anonymous gift that actually had come from the Campbell Foundation, Woodruff rebuked his staff, saying, "I don't remember approving that grant."

Now, however, his lifelong insistence on privacy gave way to a yearning for recognition. In 1974, he agreed to accept the city's highest honor, the Shining Light award, and showed up in person to collect it, walking uncertainly with a cane and clutching the arm of his valet. "Business genius, counselor of presidents, sportsman, humanitarian, benefactor of education, medicine, and the arts," the plaque called him. Six years after accosting the publisher of the Atlanta newspapers with a demand that his name never again appear in print, Woodruff consented to a story on the front page under the headline, "CITY'S 'ANONYMOUS DONOR' REVEALED TO BE WOODRUFF."

Once the dam broke, there were dozens of tributes, and Woodruff savored them all. Some days he would ask Joe Jones, "What's in the paper this morning?" Jones recognized Woodruff's new vanity as more than an acceptance of mortality or an interest in his place in history. Woodruff had been at the center of things for half a century, Jones thought, and wanted to stay there. He craved affirmation of his vitality and importance. Jones tried to tease him, saying he'd outlived his enemies, but Woodruff's true fear was outliving his usefulness. A friend found him crying one day, fretting that his life had lost its purpose.

To Woodruff, old age brought absolutely no benefits whatsoever. He hated being feeble, hated growing deaf. His eyesight got worse and he began complaining that he was blind. A friend wrote to suggest books with oversize print, and he dictated a stark rejoinder: "I never cultivated the habit of reading books. My preference has been to concentrate on doing things myself rather than read about other people doing things."

He became crotchety, ill-humored much of the time. Joe Jones, who had served him loyally for four decades as a male secretary and all-purpose factotum, gradually assumed a far larger role as chief of staff, handling many of Woodruff's affairs and occasionally reminding him of the realities of his advancing years. In the winter of 1975, as the city of Atlanta languished in the grip of recession, one of its business leaders, Billy Sterne, the president of Trust Company, called on Woodruff to "reenter the scene" and give counsel again as he had in the Hartsfield and Allen years. After Sam Massell's lone term, City Hall had passed to Maynard Jackson, Atlanta's first black mayor, and relations between the administration and the business community were strained.

"There's no way for you to 'reenter' the scene," Jones told Woodruff. The city's reigning businessmen were the sons and grandsons of his old friends, and he hadn't even met the latest batch of politicians. "In what way would you become involved?" Jones asked. "What would be the text of your remarks at, say, a Commerce Club board meeting?" Trying to become active again would be a burden on Woodruff, Jones said, implying the corollary that Woodruff was also in danger of making himself a burden on others.

Ignoring the advice, Woodruff agreed to speak to the directors of the Commerce Club, in the same room he'd once helped desegregate. He told the old Red Deupree story—"Not long!"—and urged his listeners to get busy, form a committee, and become involved. The speech was not an embarrassment, yet it had little impact. Aside from a white paper produced by a local think tank, nothing came of it. The day of the Big Mules had ended.

Woodruff made one final, graceful gesture before exiting the political stage. At a time when most businessmen refused to have anything to with Mayor Jackson, Woodruff went to a meeting and made a point of shaking his hand and posing with him for a newspaper photographer. "What would mother and Aunt Emie say if they could see Atlanta's Negro mayor sitting beside you?" one of Woodruff's cousins wrote him, astounded at the tableau that appeared in her copy of the afternoon *Atlanta Journal*. "Guess I was born too soon!"

A little over a year later, when the editors of the *Journal* compiled a list of the ten most powerful people in Atlanta, they included Paul Austin. But they left Woodruff off, explaining that he'd taken "a few steps down" the ladder.

Looking back, trying to pinpoint the onset of the terrible sicknesses that drained Austin of his energy and memory, and that eventually claimed his mind, some of his colleagues remembered the General Electric board meeting that took place in March 1975.

At the peak of his career at the time, with no hint that anything might be wrong, Austin joined in a discussion with his fellow GE directors about the outlook for the national economy over the next few years. No one in the room was very optimistic, but the "Austin scenario," as he called it, stood out as a grim vision of apocalypse.

The recession would continue and worsen, Austin said. Millions of Americans, most of them black, would be left unemployed. When their unemployment benefits ran out, the inner cities would go up in flames, consumed by riots far worse than anything seen in the summers of the 1960s. Police and firemen, helpless to protect themselves, would abandon their posts en masse. The U.S. Army would have to restore order at bayonet point. All three branches of the federal government, the White House, Congress, and the courts, would cease functioning, and a high-ranking army officer would seize command. Taking Charles de Gaulle as his model, he would impose a form of limited dictatorship on the country.

When he finished talking, Austin was greeted by silence. Word of his performance leaked back to Plum Street, where he was pressed for an explanation of the "disturbing" nature of his prophecy. There was nothing at all unusual about his lecture, he insisted, defending himself in a memo that was circulated around the top levels of the company. If the other GE directors were quiet after he spoke, he said, it must have been because they agreed with him.

There were other episodes, notably a talk in which Austin predicted that half of the country's colleges would soon close, never to reopen. But he was a florid man by nature, an Ivy League intellectual who loved to play iconoclast, and his earliest lapses were dismissed as Austin being Austin, dabbling in sociology, making breathless pronouncements just for the shock value. Perhaps a martini or two at lunch accounted for the occasional extra dose of melodrama.

Two or three years passed before Jeane Austin began noticing clues that something was seriously wrong with her husband. Usually brimming with energy, he started tiring easily and going to bed early. His golf game deteriorated. He had trouble remembering things. One day he brought home a stack of memory improvement books and placed them by his armchair.

Perhaps, if the company hadn't been in such turmoil, Austin's condition might have been diagnosed and treated. But he was bent on maintaining power, so he stayed away from the doctors who could have helped him, denying there was any problem. Most of his associates assumed he was drinking more, succumbing to the pressures of the executive suite. No one knew he had developed a treacherous pair of diseases, Parkinson's and Alzheimer's, and that he stood on the verge of a swift, ghastly descent

Coca-Cola's corporate health seemed to be following Austin downward, as if it were susceptible to some strange malady of its own. In April 1975, with the company still reeling from the plunge in its stock prices a year earlier, Pepsi unveiled an odd piece of mischief, the "Pepsi Challenge," in Dallas. With a meager market share there of only 6 percent, trailing not only Coke but Dr Pepper as well, Pepsi officials were desperate enough to try an off-the-wall approach. Combing, the city, they rounded up several dozen professed Coca-Cola drinkers and conducted a taste test, asking them to choose between sodas marked "Q" and "M." As a hidden camera rolled, slightly more than half the participants chose "M" and were surprised to discover it was Pepsi. Their responses were then fashioned into commercials and aired on local TV.

The scientific validity of the Pepsi Challenge was open to interpretation, of course. Its original purpose was merely to show that more than 6 percent of the population of Dallas would like the taste of Pepsi, a perfectly reasonable theorem. Nationally, Coca-Cola and Pepsi enjoyed rough parity in supermarket sales, so the results of the challenge should not have been considered earth-shattering. Yet for some reason the commercials had a memorable impact. "More Coke drinkers like Pepsi than Coke," the tag line went, and it made for effective television.

The Coca-Cola Company's response bordered on the irrational. Instead of pretending to ignore the competition—its policy for more than three decades—the company churned out a bewildering set of statements and commercials aimed at disparaging Pepsi's results, starting with a claim that people had a psychological preference for the letter M over the letter Q, unfairly skewing the outcome. Pepsi's agency, BBDO, hit back immediately with a new set of taste tests using the letters L and S that also detected a preference for Pepsi. Coca-Cola answered that salvo with a faux-comic spot in which people explained why they liked the letter L better than the letter S. Then, for reasons that defied logic, the company ran another commercial claiming that people preferred Fresca to Pepsi, a comparison of differing flavors that the *National Observer* dismissed with one word: "silly."

Taking on a life of its own, the Challenge spread to eleven cities over the next year, boosting Pepsi's sales in most instances and frightening Coca-Cola's bottlers half to death. The term "Cola Wars" came into popular usage, as puzzled observers tried to figure out the rationale behind the sniping and hard-sell tactics in an industry that had long relied on pleasant words and pictures and more or less peaceful coexistence. The affair was a "taste bud donnybrook," *Time* said, a case of "sheer zaniness." Rance Crain, the editor of *Advertising Age*, called publicly for a cease-fire, saying the ads were "confusing, silly, and derogatory," and likely to damage Madison Avenue's tender credibility.

The long-term results of the Challenge were hard to measure, since the two companies typically competed with price-cutting and other marketing tactics at the same time, affecting the sales figures. By most accounts Coca-Cola suffered little lasting, tangible damage. Its share of the national cola market held steady while Pepsi enjoyed modest gains at the expense of smaller, lesser-known cola labels. As a matter of psychology, however, Pepsi inflicted a severe wound to the Coca-Cola Company's self-esteem. For years, the "Imitator" had been disparaged around Plum Street not just as an inferior product but as the embodiment of moral laxity, a copycat bent on stealing Coke's good name. Now Pepsi claimed it was better than Coke, and consumers seemed to be agreeing. Finding no effective way to respond to the Challenge, Coca-Cola announced in late 1976 that it would simply stop trying.

The company's advertising, veering away from the "Real Thing" in search of a fresh angle, stumbled along with a passive, forgettable slogan, "Give me a smile with everything on it, and I'll pass it on."

As if to punctuate the notion that Coca-Cola had lost its handle on the nation's taste, Austin committed the company to be the sole backer of a Broadway musical, *1600 Pennsylvania Avenue*, which opened to terrible reviews in the spring of 1976 and closed after only three performances, losing $1 million. "Tedious and simplistic," Clive Barnes wrote unsparingly in the *New York Times*, as the company sheepishly declined comment.

On the international front, Coca-Cola suffered the loss of an important market when Indira Gandhi lost power in India in 1977. Moving to appropriate the profits from Coca-Cola's syrup factory and twenty-two bottling plants, the new Indian government ordered the company to cede majority ownership to local shareholders, a step that jeopardized the secrecy of the formula. Rather than take the risk, the company spent $2 million grinding up its bottles and pulled out of a market with sales of 900 million drinks a year. The one positive note in the episode was a spate of publicity about the sanctity of the formula—modest consolation for having to abandon a subcontinent.*

At the same time it was suffering a spate of reversals in public, the company embarked on a campaign of internal change, one that would have been painful and wrenching enough in the best of circumstances, even if its two top men hadn't been incapacitated and at odds with each other. As it was, Plum Street started a battle with its bottlers that grew almost as bitter as the civil war Ernest Woodruff set off in 1920.

Once again, the price of ingredients played a central role in the hostili-

---

* Woodruff's lifelong aversion to change had calcified, reaching the point that it included his own dwindling weight When he stepped on the scales in the morning and asked his valet, Cal Bailey, to kneel down and check the reading, the soft-spoken black man would call out dutifully, "One seventy-five, Mr. Woodruff, same as always!"—even though the needle had fallen below 150 pounds.

ties. Under the perpetual contracts they'd preserved in court in the 1920s, the bottlers paid the company a fixed amount for Coca-Cola syrup. Sugar was subject to a sliding scale, depending on domestic prices, but the other "merchandises" remained at the same level set more than half a century earlier. In theory, at least, as the inflation of the late 1970s pushed costs up higher and higher, the day was coming when the bottlers could force the company to sell them syrup at a loss.

As a practical matter, most bottlers recognized the futility of driving their parent company into bankruptcy and were willing to discuss modifications of the old arrangement. The devil was in the details. Foremost on everyone's mind, the Federal Trade Commission had begun an attack on the very concept of exclusive territories for the bottlers. In 1971, the FTC filed antitrust complaints against Coca-Cola, Pepsi, and six other soft drink companies, charging that the licenses they gave their bottlers were in effect local monopolies that reduced competition and led to higher prices.

While they stood shoulder-to-shoulder with the bottlers battling the FTC, company officials also believed that the fear of losing their franchises would make the bottlers more malleable and likelier to give ground. Luke Smith was assigned the challenge of getting the contracts amended, and he surprised his colleagues with the determination he brought to the task.

At first, Smith enjoyed swift, steady progress. He traveled across the country holding meetings with the bottlers, explaining in his soft-spoken, earnest manner that the home office simply couldn't afford to keep selling syrup at the old fixed price while inflation drove the cost of ingredients through the roof. As one bottler recalled, Smith argued convincingly "that they couldn't live with what we had, and the system was going to go down the drain."

Most of the bottlers trusted Smith and appreciated his reasoning. Many agreed to amend their contracts, even though those contracts had been in their families for generations, handed down like heirlooms from parent to child to grandchild. Eventually, though, Smith ran into resistance. Some of the big bottlers, led by Charles Millard, the chairman of the New York bottling company, balked at giving the company so-called "free-will" pricing, insisting instead on limited increases tied to the consumer price index. One of the most influential old-line bottlers, Crawford Johnson III of Birmingham, Alabama, joined forces with Millard, placing Smith's project in jeopardy. Soon the discussions between Smith and the bottlers grew heated—"bombastic," in the description of one participant—as positions on both sides hardened.

With the issue moving swiftly from a technical dispute to a company-wide crisis, the one thing Smith desperately needed was a clear set of instructions from the top, a bargaining position ratified and supported by the chairman and board of directors.

He got the opposite.

In the spring of 1978, Woodruff and Austin were barely communicating. Neither man was in complete possession of his faculties. A morbid contest had begun to see which one would outlast the other, with control over the Coca-Cola Company as the prize.

At eighty-eight, Woodruff still commanded the loyalty of the "Old Guard" on the board, having fended off most of Austin's attempts to appoint directors of his own. Making a show of strength, Woodruff arranged to have Dr. Herndon, his personal physician, placed on the board, while turning down the names of several proposed outside members, including Henry Kissinger and Shirley Temple Black.

Yet Austin remained the chairman and CEO. He still ran the company on a daily basis. He finally succeeded in pushing Fill Eisenberg into retirement, opening the door for approval of some of his projects by the Finance Committee. On Austin's recommendation, the company went into the wine business, bought a plastic bag company called Presto Products, and undertook plans to invest in several independent Coca-Cola bottling operations.

As far as the outside world could tell, Austin's health was fine. He capped years of work on the international front by gaining exclusive rights to supply soft drinks at the 1980 Olympic Games in Moscow, then topped his coup by announcing that Coca-Cola would become the first American consumer product sold in China. Austin's friendship with President Carter seemed to be flourishing, so much so that the *Washington Star* hinted at impropriety. Not only had the White House paved Coca-Cola's way into the Soviet Union and China, the newspaper charged, but it also had given $300 million in foreign aid to Portugal, which in turn lifted a fifty-year ban on the sale of Coke.

Insiders, of course, could see that Austin was behaving erratically. But they didn't know why. A friend recalled meeting Austin for lunch at the Piedmont Driving Club in those days, "and he wouldn't make any sense at all. Then he'd have a couple of martinis, and he'd begin to make a little bit more sense. . . ." Apparently, his friend surmised, the problem was advancing alcoholism.

For the company's executives, life became a high-stakes guessing game. Austin was sixty-three, facing the prospect of retirement on February 14, 1980, his sixty-fifth birthday. To everyone's amazement (and without a word of explanation) Woodruff abruptly asked the board to give Austin an extra year. But would he stay on after that? And if not, would he be able to pick his successor?

Luke Smith wasn't the only one wondering. A half-dozen ambitious men had risen to prominent positions within the company, and they'd begun mapping strategy and plotting allegiances, calculating their odds of getting to the top, partly as a matter of personal aspiration but also because the Coca-Cola Company genuinely, desperately needed new leadership.

Wall Street observers, sniffing change and trying to handicap the field, put their money on Don Keough. A broad-faced Irish Catholic with an easy, beatific smile, Keough had joined the company in the Duncan Foods merger and was now a vice president in charge of operations in the Western Hemisphere. Born on a farm in Iowa, possessed of a gift for public speaking that rivaled Harrison Jones's, Keough seemed to personify Coca-Cola's all-American appeal. When he spoke of the "shared experience" Coke represented in people's lives, it had the ring of truth. At fifty-one, he was young enough to run the company for a decade.

But who could say? For more than half a century, the one immutable certainty about advancement at the Coca-Cola Company had been the need to play up to Woodruff. Since the days of Bill Hobbs, Woodruff's weakness for buttery words and adulation had been obvious to everyone. He was conscious of it himself. "I've had a hell of a time," Woodruff admitted to a nephew, "picking the right people for big jobs in my company." In a way it was understandable. The people who flattered Woodruff usually believed what they were saying, or at least tried very hard to make themselves believe it, since that was human nature. No one wanted to be a hypocrite.

Smith's wife, Claire, became very fond of Woodruff, even going so far as to write him a thank-you note when he accepted an invitation and came to their house. "We not only respect and admire you," she gushed afterward, "but most of all, *WE LOVE YOU*. Thank you for sharing your time with us!!!"

Keough matched the effusion. When he was invited to Ichauway, he lavished his host with gratitude. "I'm a very lucky man, Mr. Woodruff," he wrote, "for a great many reasons. One very special reason, which will always be special, is that I have been privileged to know you—and therefore to know all the best of human character."

Looking back, it was easy to mock the flowery excesses of the time, but careers turned on the whims of a man who craved attention and kind words, and who returned those feelings and often rewarded them in material ways.

With little else to guide him beyond Woodruff's adamant insistence on preserving the Coca-Cola empire, Smith took an extremely hard line in his negotiations with the bottlers. He refused to consider the pricing index suggested by Millard, the New York bottler, and eventually their talks broke off. The campaign to amend the contracts reached an impasse.

Frustrated, Millard approached Keough, who saw no reason for being so obstinate. Keough thought a sliding scale for syrup afforded the company adequate protection, and he quickly reached agreement on a compromise that satisfied Millard and most of the other holdout bottlers. Going behind Smith's back, Keough took the deal to Austin, who approved it and got Woodruff and the board to give their assent. That was that. Over the next few months, scores of bottlers signed new, amended contracts.

Understandably, Smith felt betrayed. He blamed Austin for switching the rules on him in the middle of the game. He stopped speaking to Austin, making an already uncomfortable situation even more strained. The resolution of the bottling imbroglio should have brought peace to the Coca-Cola Company. Instead, like the sharp noise that triggers an avalanche, it set off a series of repercussions that changed the business forever.

Austin's condition began to worsen at an accelerated pace. His judgment grew impaired. Early in 1979, he told Woodruff he planned to switch the date of the company's annual meeting so he could attend a party in celebration of Coca-Cola's fiftieth anniversary in Germany. Woodruff pointed out that the day of the annual meeting was fixed in the corporate by-laws, and could only be changed by a vote of the board. Doing so, he said, "would be unwise and unfortunate."

Then, just two years after naming his own man, Charlie Lord, as chief financial officer, Austin announced that he wanted to make a change. He was unhappy with Lord, he told Woodruff, and planned to install another man above him as an executive vice president in charge of finance. Woodruff asked what was going on, and Austin replied defensively. He'd been running the company for years, he reminded Woodruff, making "adjustments" in the corporate hierarchy. There had been "no Black Fridays, just evolutionary moves here and there." There was no cause for alarm.

The press began speculating about Austin's tenure. The hometown newspaper, the *Atlanta Journal-Constitution*, reported that Austin was "silent" about a successor and "leaves the impression that he is in no hurry to let an heir apparent emerge, even though such an attitude inevitably has encouraged a lot of rumor-spreading in the business community and a bit of jockeying for position within the company."

In fact, Austin did have a successor in mind. During his posting in Johannesburg twenty years earlier, he'd hired a white South African named Ian Wilson to be his chief accountant, and the two men had become fast friends. In the years since, the aggressive, sharp-edged Wilson had proven himself a skilled manager. He took over Coca-Cola's operations in Canada and spruced up the balance sheet there, then moved to Atlanta as an executive vice president, adding the Far East to his growing portfolio of responsibilities.

Wilson understood the importance of currying Woodruff's favor if he hoped to advance. Displaying perfect deference (if not perfect grammar), he wrote after one visit, "You left both Sue and I different people, touched by the special, and very human attitude and approach you convey." When they entertained visiting bottlers from Japan and Thailand, the Wilsons occasionally invited Woodruff to dinner, knowing he would command the esteem of the Asians by dint of his great age.

For his part, Woodruff seemed fond enough of Wilson. He invited him to Ichauway and included him in his luncheon group from time to time. But Woodruff gave no sign of readiness to make Wilson the next head of the Coca-Cola Company. When Austin suggested putting Wilson and another executive on the board of directors, Woodruff declined. Luke Smith remained first in the line of succession, with every likelihood of becoming chairman and CEO. Stymied, seeing that he needed more time to fashion the outcome he wanted, Austin began entertaining the idea of postponing his retirement indefinitely.

For a while, he had his way. In July 1979, Woodruff suffered a loss of lucidity and then contracted pneumonia. When he went into Emory Hospital, many in his circle assumed he would not come out. His brother George, who had always been leery of the lawyers and trustees who would gain control of the family fortune when Robert was gone, took steps to liquidate the Emily and Ernest Woodruff Foundation. After living all his life in the shadow of Robert's legendary philanthropy, George arranged to make a gift of the entire corpus of the trust fund—Coca-Cola stock worth more than $100 million—to Emory University. It would be the largest single gift ever given to a school, a fitting farewell.

"Everyone thought he was dying," Woodruff's private nurse, Edith Honeycutt, recalled. The overseer at Ichauway called the staff together to tell them their boss had seen his last quail season.

And, back on Plum Street, Austin fired Luke Smith.

Physically and mentally drained after his war of attrition with the bottlers, Smith began a two-week vacation in August 1979. He spent the time relaxing on his houseboat on Lake Lanier, an hour north of Atlanta, and was about to return when he got the word. On the day he was due back at work, Austin put out a press release announcing that for "personal reasons," Smith had decided to take early retirement and would resign immediately as president. With no avenue of recourse, Smith was forced to accept the verdict.

Only Woodruff did not die. His medical crisis eased. His pneumonia gradually began clearing up, and he was able to return home to his bedroom in Atlanta to convalesce. In the fall, he was taken to Ichauway, where he regained some of his strength, improving bit by bit until at last he got up, got dressed, and insisted on mounting a horse.

He remained a very frail old man. Two men had to hoist him into the saddle, and he could ride only a few paces. When he tried going on a quail hunt, Joe Jones remembered, "he couldn't see or hear well, or turn quickly enough to hit anything." A handler had to hold him up so he wouldn't fall. The important point, though, was that he lived. The events that ensued were a mystery to outside observers, and incomprehensible at times to the participants themselves—which was hardly surprising, since the two main players were suffering from the ravages of age and dementia—yet the key to it all was quite simple: Woodruff lived.

Austin acted first. With his nemesis Smith out of the way, he moved to assimilate power. At the company's regular board meeting in November

1979, Austin proposed the appointment of six vice chairmen, all reporting to him, with the understanding that one of them would emerge as his successor. While Woodruff looked on, still a little muddled from his illness, the board accepted the plan.

Everywhere, from Wall Street to *Business Week* to the Coca-Cola Company's own cafeteria, people scrambled to make sense of the unexpected developments. The main challenge was sorting through the six contenders: Keough, Wilson, and senior managers Al Killeen, Claus Halle, Roberto Goizueta, and Ira "Ike" Herbert. Only Keough was well known outside the company, and the press anointed him the front-runner. A handful of insiders recognized Wilson as Austin's personal favorite and placed their bets accordingly. The others were considered long shots.

Of all the names on the list, the most obscure belonged to Goizueta (pronounced Goh-SWET-uh), a reticent, aristocratic Cuban who'd joined the company in Havana in 1954 as a chemical engineer. After fleeing Castro for the United States in 1961, Goizueta worked his way up through the technical side of the business and eventually earned an executive vice presidency, taking charge of the legal department and general administration as well as the laboratory.

The *Wall Street Journal*, which kept close tabs on the succession battle, gave Goizueta little chance of winning, noting that he was "at a disadvantage because he has never managed one of the company's soft-drink units." In fact, he had no marketing experience at all. He had never worked on an ad campaign, never roused the bottlers with a speech, never fought for shelf space at a supermarket. He'd never sold a single bottle of soda.

For those who liked portents, however, it seemed noteworthy that alone among the vice chairmen, Goizueta knew Coca-Cola's secret formula. By policy of the board, only the company's top two chemists were allowed to memorize the "strategic information," as it was called. Goizueta had undergone the rites of initiation in 1974, replacing a senior vice president who suffered a heart attack on a trip to London.

Goizueta's new status brought him closer into Woodruff's circle. Along with the other acolytes, Goizueta began attending the 12:30 luncheons, and before long Woodruff asked him for a photograph to add to the collection of favored executives he kept at his Tuxedo Road home. As he gained further promotions, Goizueta had the good sense to thank Woodruff each time, knowing the old man had given his approval. When he traveled, Goizueta sent Woodruff postcards.

To those who knew him, Goizueta's rise was not surprising. He could seem a little shy when he first met people, ill at ease with small talk, quick to light a cigarette and turn the conversation to a safe, familiar topic. Yet he had a keen, observant eye and an understanding of human nature not always found in men of science. Once, he recalled, he and Austin were in Woodruff's office, engrossed in a discussion about the business, when Woodruff abruptly interrupted, turned to Joe Jones, and barked, "Joe!

How many shares of Coca-Cola do I have?" Jones answered with the exact number, and Austin observed later that Woodruff must be slipping further, losing his memory and ability to concentrate. Goizueta responded that he thought it was simply Woodruff's way of reminding both of them he still owned a big chunk of the company.

Like others in the company with ambition, Goizueta cultivated a close relationship with Woodruff. He told people unblushingly that Woodruff reminded him of his father, and he beamed when Woodruff began calling him "partner"—even though Woodruff referred to most of his junior associates that way. But Goizueta also had genuine admiration for Woodruff, an appreciation of the extraordinary skills, now dimmed by age, that he'd displayed running the company for so many years. "He was a *sponge*," Goizueta said, marveling at Woodruff's capacity to listen intelligently and draw information out of others.

Goizueta tried to learn from Woodruff. He was struck, for instance, by the way Woodruff rarely set a deadline when he gave an underling a project. Instead, Woodruff would ask the man how soon he could finish, and most times, in his eagerness to please and impress the boss, the fellow would place himself "on the hook" by volunteering to meet the earliest possible completion date.

At a time when some executives began referring to their visits to see Woodruff as "the duty," Goizueta actually looked forward to spending a half-hour with him every other day or so. Woodruff received guests at home most afternoons in a sitting room with a fireplace on the second floor of his Tuxedo Road mansion. Goizueta stopped by frequently, drawing out Woodruff's thoughts and reminiscences, sipping a vodka and tonic while they chatted. Woodruff often reached forward and clutched his visitor by the forearm, holding him with a surprisingly strong grip, and Goizueta guessed he did so because touch was his only remaining active sense, now that his eyesight and hearing and appetite were all but gone.

Woodruff's conversation often consisted of little more than his favorite aphorisms—"The world belongs to the discontented"—and some of his listeners concluded he'd grown senile. Only a handful, including Goizueta, realized that he possessed a sort of subterranean awareness, a lasting, deep-seated interest in the company's welfare that had scarcely subsided a bit

In the winter months of January and February 1980, Woodruff was unhappy. The dismissal of Luke Smith gnawed at him, reviving his bad memories of the ouster of Charles Duncan. The company's continuing financial difficulties bothered him, especially a steady shrinkage of the cash reserves.

And he hated the new Coca-Cola skyscraper Paul Austin was putting up.

At a Finance Committee meeting in 1974, Austin had unveiled plans for a twenty-six-story tower to accommodate the company's burgeoning workforce.

The old brick home on Plum Street and a newer eleven-story structure, a utilitarian glass-and-concrete box that went up next door in the late 1960s, were proving inadequate as the payroll hit 1,500 employees and kept growing. The new tower, Austin predicted, would meet the company's needs for at least a decade, perhaps longer.

In a sunnier frame of mind at the time, Woodruff gave his approval. "I guess it looks all right," he said. Then he joked, "I don't suppose John Sibley and I will have much interest in what's going on by then anyway."

"Mr. Chairman," Sibley shot back, only partly amused, "I'll speak for myself on that subject!"

As it happened, they'd both lived on into their nineties, and now the building was nearing completion. The day approached when Woodruff would have to be moved out of his familiar, beloved suite on the fourth floor of Plum Street into new quarters. Suddenly it was no longer a laughing matter.

Joe Jones called the architects and designers together and explained carefully that they would have to reproduce Woodruff's office, dining room, kitchen, and conference room *exactly*, in precise scale, with every last detail identical, or else the old man would become confused and agitated, which would mean serious trouble for everyone.*

Duplicating Woodruff's suite wouldn't be possible, one of Austin's men said. There would be slight variations because of the tower's shape, and the layout of rooms would have to be reversed. In that case, Jones replied, he would need an advance set of blueprints and drawings, so he could begin the long, difficult process of acclimating Woodruff to the idea of innovation. But the design team let the matter lapse.

By the time the tower was ready for occupancy, Austin had placed his wife, Jeane, in charge of decorating. She got her first hint of Woodruff's simmering displeasure one morning when she called Jones to ask a question about the furnishings for the new conference room. Woodruff, Jones warned, had not been inside the new building, had not been shown the floor plans, and wanted nothing more or less than to remain in the same surroundings he'd had for the past quarter-century.

On March 3, 1980, Woodruff was escorted into his new suite on the penthouse level of the tower. By any standard of taste, the architects had created a spectacular space atop the new building: a three-story atrium with a skylight, fine art on the walls, and offices overlooking a panorama of Atlanta's skyline and forested neighborhoods. To Woodruff, though, the

---

* After the Coca-Cola Company's withdrawal, a state-owned enterprise began selling an ersatz cola called "77," in honor of the year of political change. Its poor flavor and lack of popularity led a cartoonist for an Indian newspaper to depict a tube of "78 Toothpaste" under a sarcastic announcement, "Great Things to Come." Limited supplies of smuggled Coke began selling for 35 cents a bottle, triple the previous price.

light and paintings and pretty views meant nothing. He prowled his rooms like a detective combing the scene of a crime. The lighting, he grumbled, was too dim in the office and dining room. The kitchen was too small and in the wrong place. The dining room was too small. The portrait light on his favorite dog painting needed to be brighter.

Then Woodruff went into the bathroom, shut the door, and tried his new toilet. It was several inches lower than the old one, too close to the floor for comfort. It annoyed him tremendously.

Joe Jones dutifully recorded all of Woodruff's complaints and forwarded them immediately to Mrs. Austin and her design consultant, John Chaloner. They responded within days by installing new lighting, but as Chaloner explained with exquisite patience, they couldn't very well change the sizes of the rooms, since those were governed by the dimensions of the building. As to the toilet, he said, modern plumbing technology and federal health regulations required the use of the lower models. Chaloner said he would be happy to make further inquiries on the subject and take up the matter with Paul Austin when he got a chance, but he offered little hope of a solution.

Chaloner's answer was perfectly reasonable (if a bit patronizing), but it was emphatically not what Woodruff wished to hear. He picked up the phone and rang Goizueta, who listened carefully and dispatched a carpenter and a plumber to Woodruff's suite that very morning, where a riser was built under the toilet, lifting it to the exact, precise, identical height of the old one. Woodruff was assuaged. The metaphor, that by fixing Woodruff's throne, Goizueta had placed himself one step closer to inheriting the company's, was too good to miss.

Austin, meanwhile, was oblivious. With his diseases progressing, the move to the tower left him even more disoriented than Woodruff. He wandered through the wrong door one morning and demanded of a startled colleague, "What are you doing in my office?" Once an impressive speaker, he began stumbling through his public appearances. His facial expression grew wan and uncertain. In an episode that quickly made its way through the grapevine, he had the company pilots fly him to New Orleans, only to forget why he'd wanted to go after he landed.

His wife tried to protect him. She began spending her days at the company, working out of his office. The tower stood as the signature piece of Austin's regime, almost literally the capstone of his career, a granite monolith with the familiar Spencerian script of Coca-Cola's trademark carved into the peak of the facade, illuminated in red, visible for miles across Atlanta. With a good eye for art (though no formal training), Mrs. Austin tried to make the interior just as distinctive. She commissioned a set of four-seasons tapestries for the lobby, found a pair of seascapes for the boardroom, and covered the walls with Russian, Moroccan, and South American oil paintings from a dealer in New York. In all she spent $6 million, and when she was done every room in the building bore her touch.

She made the tower into quite a symbol, and of course that meant it was a target, too.

The problem was the proprietary attitude Mrs. Austin developed toward the new complex and the house rules she began issuing. Word spread that she was trying to run the business as well as decorate it. No sooner had Woodruff's commode been fixed than his chauffeur was shooed away and told he could no longer park in front of the building, on Mrs. Austin's orders. One of the company's top administrators, Charles Adams, resigned in frustration, citing her interference with his duties.

Her worst blunder was an edict banning Coca-Cola's secretaries from eating their brown-bag lunches (and drinking their Cokes) in the little landscaped plaza across the street. A secretary herself when she'd met her husband, Mrs. Austin seemed to want to keep the clerical help tucked away out of sight, where they would not tarnish her neat and tidy showplace. Her explanation—that she was worried about attracting pigeons from the Varsity, a landmark drive-in restaurant a half-mile away on the other side of Georgia Tech—brought ridicule. Someone tacked up a sign in the lobby asking wickedly, "Why worry about pigeons in the park when there are turkeys in the tower?"

One of the company's veteran secretaries, disturbed by the stuffy atmosphere and worsening morale, wrote a stinging letter of complaint to Austin on behalf of "the little people" and mailed a carbon copy to Woodruff, who responded by issuing an order of his own. From that moment on, he said, Austin's wife was forbidden to enter the building.

The final straw came shortly afterward, when Austin proposed a $100 million debt offering to help pay for the tower, whose price tag had reached $120 million. For nearly sixty years, Woodruff had prided himself on keeping the company liquid. It was an old-fashioned notion, perhaps, but the idea of borrowing money, especially for a needless luxury that contributed nothing to Coca-Cola's earnings, struck him as crazy. "You must be broke," he told Austin.

The clock on Austin's extra year as chairman and CEO had begun ticking on February 14, 1980, his sixty-fifth birthday. Barely three months later, Woodruff decided the selection of a successor could not be postponed any longer. John Sibley, at ninety-one a year older than Woodruff, convinced him it was essential to put new management in place before they and the other old-timers died. Woodruff agreed. He asked Austin to recommend one of the six vice chairmen for the post of president, which had remained vacant since Luke Smith's departure.

Austin nominated Ian Wilson, setting off a crisis. Wilson had detractors throughout the company, men he'd offended in one way or another with his brusque personality, or who feared that a white South African would damage the company's image—or who thought Wilson might perpetuate Austin's reign, depriving them of a chance to start their own. The company's deputy financial officer, Sam Ayoub, a native Egyptian, was openly contemptuous of Wilson. "Everybody knows he's sharp," Ayoub said, "but he didn't have the quality of being a human being."

Confident that Woodruff would accept his choice, Austin and his wife took the Wilsons out for a celebratory dinner in Atlanta, and afterward Wilson left town for a month-long tour of the Far East, where he dropped hints to his managers that they could look forward to following him up the ladder.

In his absence, Joe Jones and others set to work trying to persuade Woodruff to pick someone else. Jones ridiculed the memo Austin prepared in support of Wilson's qualifications, noting that it placed business acumen near the bottom of the list, below Wilson's golf game. On a more serious note, questions were raised about Wilson's legal residency in the United States and whether he'd pulled strings improperly in obtaining his green card from the Immigration and Naturalization Service.

As recently as the previous winter, Woodruff had entertained Wilson at Ichauway, praising him effusively as they sat and had cocktails in the gun room. But now Woodruff began hearing vigorous objections to Wilson from a variety of quarters, including Dr. Herndon and other members of the board. His enthusiasm dimmed. "Mr. Woodruff," Ayoub explained, "had a very strong feeling that an executive has to take care of his people. And he felt [Wilson] was going to create problems, and there would be friction between people, and morale would go to hell."

Woodruff summoned Austin to his office and told him Wilson was unacceptable.

Had his health been better, Austin might have challenged Woodruff, but the fact was Woodruff still held sway over the board. Remarkably, after fourteen years as CEO of Coca-Cola (and a decade as chairman), Austin could command the votes of only three or four directors. Woodruff controlled the rest. His brother and doctor were on the board. So were a pair of Austin's most virulent enemies, Luke Smith and Fill Eisenberg. Two of the oldest members, Sibley and Abbott Turner, had retired, but they'd been replaced by their sons. The membership, typified by George Craft, a son-in-law of Hughes Spalding and former chairman of Trust Company, was a microcosm of the rich families and ruling institutions whose holdings constituted millions of shares, and whose loyalty to Woodruff spanned generations.

Instead of Wilson, Woodruff and his inner circle decided they wanted Goizueta to be the new president, and Austin was instructed to convene a special meeting of the board to make the choice official. As they gathered in the new pecanwood-paneled boardroom of the Coca-Cola tower on the afternoon of Friday, May 30, 1980, a few of the outside directors were puzzled. No one had bothered to tell them the succession fight was over. Austin made a motion to elect Goizueta president, Woodruff signaled his concurrence, and in minutes the session was over, without discussion, debate, or dissent. Goizueta entered the room afterward and made his way around the long, narrow table, shaking hands.

Wilson, who had just returned to Atlanta after his travels through Asia, was utterly mystified by the sudden collapse of his fortunes. He went to see Joe Jones to find out what had happened, and Jones replied, "Ian, you'd have to go ask Mr. Woodruff about that." Wilson made a trip out to Tuxedo Road to see Woodruff, who was polite but vague, revealing nothing to Wilson about the campaign that had been waged against him.

The *Wall Street Journal* described Goizueta's ascension as "another confounding executive shuffle," a phrase that neatly summed up the confusion prevailing among Coca-Cola's employees and bottlers, the financial media, the investment community, and the public at large. The company no longer formally boycotted security analysts and business reporters, as it had under Eisenberg, but an aura of secrecy continued to surround its affairs. Over the weekend that followed the special meeting, a spokesman declined to arrange interviews with Goizueta and the other principals, explaining, "They just don't have time right now."

The first order of business, inside the company and out, was to get a handle on Goizueta. He did not make it easy.

When he sat down with reporters in the coming weeks, he seemed to delight in striking an enigmatic air, one moment sounding like a technocrat and the next like a South American novelist with a metaphysical bent. As a manager, he told the *Atlanta Journal-Constitution*, his goal was "to be in the midst of a crowd, but to have the independence of solitude." To illustrate the importance of skepticism, Goizueta handed out lead coasters that a flim-flam artist once sold him as silver at an airport in Mexico. He spoke in aphorisms. In his new job, he said, "I'm like the golfer who has to keep his head down and concentrate on his follow-through."

His foreign birth did not sit well with all members of the Coca-Cola family. Arguing that "this is an American company, manufacturing an American product, in the American way," the bottler from Huntsville, Alabama, wrote Woodruff urging that Don Keough be given the presidency instead. Coca-Cola, the bottler said, needed "the strong leadership of a dynamic American salesman." Others questioned Goizueta's abilities in the marketplace. "The man's never done anything," the Memphis bottler complained. "His big claim to fame was that he ran the United Way in Atlanta."

In one important sense, of course, the doubters had it completely wrong. Coca-Cola had long since ceased being an "American" company. Seventy percent of its revenues now came from foreign sales. Far from being alien, Goizueta was a sort of citizen of Coca-Cola, born in Havana (where the first offshore shipment of syrup had arrived in 1899) and naturalized in the United States after the revolution in his homeland. His education included a year at a New England boarding school, where he learned impeccable English. He earned his degree in chemical engineering from Yale.

As a company man, Goizueta's pedigree included working with the legendary Gene Kelly, the pioneer organizer who helped set up Coca-Cola's fledgling operations around the world. Goizueta remembered the tight-fisted Kelly visiting Havana in the fifties, refusing to stay in a decent hotel or hire a private car. Kelly rode the streetcar and would bury his face in the newspaper when the conductor came around, so that Goizueta had to pay the nickel fare for him.

By any measure, including his custodianship of the secret formula, Goizueta qualified as an insider. In the company's highest councils, his was a familiar face. One reason Goizueta beat out Keough and the other marketers was that they spent a great deal of their time on the road, selling, while he remained in Atlanta, attending to Woodruff and his advisers and gaining their trust.

In the final analysis, Goizueta's selection turned out to be the oldest story in business: He appealed to the owners. No one had ever counted up the number of Coca-Cola millionaires in Atlanta, but they were legion. Georgians owned more than 40 percent of the outstanding shares of common stock. As the *New York Times* once put it, the company was a "Southeastern money tree."

At the time Goizueta became president, the value of Coca-Cola stock had shrunk by half. All across Atlanta, shareholders waited impatiently for a hike in dividends and an improvement in stock prices. At Emory, Trust Company, King & Spalding, in the Whitehead foundations, and among scores of families, the old worry about overconcentration in Coca-Cola common stock stirred again.

Goizueta tried to warn reporters not to mistake him for a mere "technical man." His mission was strategic, he said—to cope with inflation, recession, and foreign exchange, to boost earnings in the company's divisions, to smooth relations with the bottlers, to expand into new, profitable product lines and enterprises, and most of all to improve the performance of the stock. "Finance, technical, marketing, and team spirit," he told a visitor, waving his hand in a circle to accentuate the sweep of his duties.

As reports of the tension in Coca-Cola's boardroom filtered into the newspapers in the days after his election, Goizueta found himself portrayed in some accounts as a compromise pick in a showdown between Woodruff and Austin. He bridled at the suggestion that he might have been a second choice, or that he was someone's puppet "I've always taken a great deal of pride in being my own man," he said. "I've gotten to this position by being my own man and I expect to be my own man from now on."

But he wasn't his own man yet.

When Woodruff first suggested making Luke Smith the new chairman of the board, some of the other directors thought he was kidding. "We won't have to pay him much," Woodruff observed, noting that Smith had been given a large financial settlement and consulting fee when he was ousted as president Before long it became clear Woodruff was serious. He wanted Goizueta to be president and CEO, but not chairman. In years gone by, Woodruff had recycled some of his retired officers—Burke Nicholson, Bill Robinson, Lee Talley—as figurehead chairmen who presided at meetings without wielding any real influence over the company's affairs. He proposed doing so again. It was his way of preserving the clout of the Finance Committee.

Having roused himself to action, it seemed, Woodruff intended to keep exercising his old prerogatives, signing off on the company's major decisions. His renewed desire for involvement alarmed his closest associates. John Sibley, in particular, believed the whole point of naming Goizueta president was to elevate him quickly to the chairmanship and place him in complete charge. "I think Sibley wanted to be sure...that Austin was in fact retiring," Joe Jones recalled.

Woodruff and Sibley had a complicated relationship. Sibley felt enormous respect for Woodruff, but he'd also earned a large measure of independence during their sixty years working together, and he thought it was time for Woodruff to give the next generation (or more accurately, the one after it) a chance to take over.

Instead, Woodruff's interest in Luke Smith added a new layer of uncertainty to the succession question. With Austin's extra year as chairman due to run another nine months, through March 1981, Sibley foresaw the potential for continued maneuvering and jostling among the board members and upper management. He argued in favor of designating Goizueta as chairman-elect, and got the leaders of Trust Company to send a message of endorsement by electing Goizueta to their board of directors.

For his own part, recognizing he was not yet home free, Goizueta continued a personal crusade for Woodruff's approval. He lavished attention on the old man, papering him with upbeat memos and even sending him an occasional poem. Running what amounted to a political campaign, Goizueta also solicited the backing of the bottlers and sent some of their wives gifts of porcelain boxes. "It never does any harm to get on the good side of our main bottlers," he explained to Woodruff, as if reciting his lessons.

A battle of leaks broke out in the press, with one faction of unnamed sources speculating that Austin might leave before his year was up and another that he might stay on afterward. Caught in the middle, the company's public relations office declared neutrality, releasing a formal statement that said Austin would serve the period scheduled, no more, no less.

In a page-one story with a memorable headline—"'THE CIGAR' HAS COME BACK"—the *Wall Street Journal* divulged many of the background details of the split between Woodruff and Austin, painting a vivid portrait of Woodruff's dissatisfaction with the new tower, the debt offering, and Mrs. Austin's decorating. The question of the chairmanship, the newspaper reported, remained wide open. The article treated Woodruff benignly, but as Austin had warned so many times, the company nevertheless suffered the embarrassment of appearing to be in thrall to the stubborn impulses of a ninety-year-old man.

A little more than a month later, on July 19, 1980, the stalemate was broken with abrupt finality when Luke Smith died of a heart attack at the age of sixty-one. The loss appeared to deflate Woodruff. With his personal candidate for chairman gone, he quickly acquiesced in the decision to promote Goizueta to CEO and chairman. Observing proprieties, the board allowed Austin to retain the titles until his year was up, but his career was effectively over. The company announced Goizueta's accession with great fanfare, leaving no ambiguity. He was the new boss.

The aura of confusion hanging over the company began to lift. At the same time he gave his blessing to Goizueta as Coca-Cola's new leader, Woodruff also agreed to the liquidation of Coca-Cola International, the old holding company that had given him (and his father before him) working control over the business. Coca-Cola International still owned 15 percent of Coca-Cola's common stock, and its dissolution was a sign that Woodruff had abandoned any further intention of wielding a one-man proxy.

Now Goizueta would get to be his own man. In a small step with big implications, the board voted to make Goizueta a member of the Finance Committee—without bothering to tell Woodruff. The change offended Woodruff, who complained that expanding the committee was "contrary to his concept" of how things should be done. But the board declined to reverse its action.

Goizueta, meanwhile, went about the task of consolidating his authority. As his first act, he decided to tackle Woodruff's fabled distaste for incurring debt. The Coca-Cola bottling company in New York, an independent, publicly owned corporation, appeared ripe for an unfriendly takeover. Like most bottling operations, it was vulnerable to being "milked" by a raider who would hike prices and slash the advertising budget for short-term profit, ignoring the long-term consequences. Goizueta wanted to buy a controlling interest in the company, take it private, and then resell it to friendly owners. To do so, he would have to borrow more than $200 million.

Firmly, patiently, Goizueta outlined the plan to Woodruff, explaining why it made sense to pay interest so long as the return on the investment was higher. To Goizueta's considerable surprise, Woodruff grasped the point easily and gave his approval. The deal went through in December 1980, before Goizueta had formally assumed his new position.

In a fresh round of interviews, Goizueta began speaking with a stronger voice. "It is the curse of the engineer," he told the *Financial Times*, "that the fellow who drives the locomotive and the fellow who designs it are both called engineers." He had more in mind, he seemed to be saying, than just running the Coca-Cola Company. He planned to redesign it as well.

If anyone missed the point, he repeated it in plain English. "We're going to take risks," he said. "What has always been will not necessarily always be forever."

Twelve

NEW COKE

On his first trip to Ichauway, mistakenly believing the plantation was a grand country estate, Roberto Goizueta showed up wearing a yellow ascot and not knowing how to shoot. He spent his first afternoon at the skeet range taking target practice on Coke cans, then went out quail hunting the next morning, properly attired, and bagged a couple of birds.

He was a quick study in business, too. As he prepared to take command of the Coca-Cola Company, Goizueta conducted what came to be known as the "Spanish Inquisition," a two-week interrogation of top managers in every area of the business. He prowled the tower asking questions, critiquing the system at the same time he learned it. "I used to get mad at him," Sam Ayoub, the financial officer, recalled. "He wanted to know everything that was going on in the company."

By the time Paul Austin's final month as chairman and CEO expired at the end of February 1981, Goizueta was itching to take over. He commissioned studies by several outside consultants, all of whom confirmed the conclusions he'd already reached. Coca-Cola's executives were paralyzed by indirection, and the company's operations and financial policies were outmoded, in some cases almost medieval.

Goizueta hastened to assemble his own management team. A year earlier, over drinks at the bar of the St. Regis Hotel in New York, he and Don Keough had agreed that if one of them rose to the top spot, the other would serve as his number two man. Keeping his end of the bargain, Goizueta got the board's approval to offer Keough the jobs of president and chief operating officer.

Keough accepted, but not before giving the matter careful thought. Because of his quick smile and warm, ebullient nature, Keough was often underestimated and seen as a sort of corporate greeter, a gifted public speaker who had little to contribute when it came time for the harsh realities of the business. Nature had conspired to give him a face that closely resembled Ed McMahon's, as if he were born to play the perfect sidekick. Even Woodruff misjudged him. "Use Keough to handle the bottlers," Woodruff once advised Goizueta, a remark that stung Keough's feelings. That was how Woodruff had used Harrison Jones.

The comparison of Goizueta and Keough to Woodruff and Jones—a taciturn boss and a glad-handing front man, "Mr. Inside" and "Mr. Outside"—was inevitable (and accurate up to a point), yet it shortchanged Keough. True, he could tell an audience an old joke and make them laugh anew, and he gave inspirational speeches worthy of the pulpit. But he could also be very steely, as he showed in outflanking Luke Smith during the negotiations with the bottlers. He knew marketing inside out and had strong ideas about strategy for the company's future. The nice-guy portrait that emerged frustrated him so much he prodded reporters to give him a sharper edge in their stories. Quoting an unnamed source, one account in the hometown *Journal-Constitution* described Keough as "rough, tough, not Mr. Smooth." And a bottler said, "Don Keough is just plain tough. He's just as mean as he has to be. If you get in his way, he'll eat you alive."

Several years later, contemplating the succession from the vantage point of retirement, Keough said the decision to pick Goizueta as chairman had been "absolutely correct." If he did not think so at the time, if he resented finishing second, he nonetheless appreciated how his skills and Goizueta's might dovetail and benefit them both. The package he was offered—president and chief operating officer, with a seat on the board of directors—promised to elevate him to a near partnership with Goizueta, and he took it.

Looking at the two men, it was easy to see the study in contrasts: Goizueta with his dark good looks and tall, slender frame, his tailored suits and fastidious habits and syrupy Spanish accent; Keough with his open, jolly manner, his double chins, and the flat, nasal voice of the American Midwest. Their personalities were different, too. On an early venture together, inspecting the company's assets, they spent a day in Lebanon, Pennsylvania, watching the assembly of steam boilers at a plant owned by Aqua-Chem, the subsidiary Paul Austin had insisted on buying. Goizueta was fascinated by the manufacturing process and the quality of the engineering, while Keough, failing to suppress a yawn, pronounced the whole thing an awful bore. Yet they had no disagreement whatsoever about what to do with the plant. It wasn't making enough money, and they agreed it had to be sold. Aqua-Chem's other line, they noted ruefully, was the manufacture of desalinization plants—machinery whose purpose, providing fresh water for bottling in desert nations, made little sense for Coca-Cola in light of the Arab boycott.

Their differences aside, both men were intense, impatient, and absolutely focused on the bottom line. During the year they'd spent as vice chairmen (being paraded around like "prize bulls," in Keough's cutting phrase), they had formed an alliance of necessity. To appreciate how crazy things had become, Goizueta liked to say, shaking his head, one had only to reflect on the fact that Austin assigned Keough, the company's greatest natural salesman, to administer affairs in Latin America, while Goizueta, a native of Cuba, was given a range of merchandising tasks. "Don and I had to get very close," Goizueta explained, "because all of a sudden he was traveling Latin America and I was dealing with marketing issues, and it didn't make any sense." And so they had teamed up, with nothing less in mind than picking the company apart and rebuilding it from ground zero.

During the Austin years, the Coca-Cola Company had accumulated quite an assortment of unrelated enterprises, including inland shrimp farms, private-label coffee, and factories that made plastic straws, moist towelettes, and carpet shampoo. The "cats and dogs," as Goizueta called them, were diverting time and energy from the main job of selling soft drinks. Few of the sidelines made money, and Goizueta put out the word that all of them were for sale.

Overseas, Goizueta discovered that in many countries the company was warehousing more than a year's worth of inventory—bottle caps, ingredients, and other items—under an outdated policy meant to protect against shortages of Coca-Cola if shipments arrived late. In the past twenty years, he determined, not a single major delay had occurred, yet in the meantime the capital cost of maintaining the huge stockpiles had risen to $22 million a day.

At home in the United States, the company's bottling system was antiquated, dating back to the days when route salesmen drove their trucks from one small mom-and-pop store or gas station to the next, chatting with the proprietors, writing up orders, and unloading cases of Coke by hand. Now the major outlets were supermarket chains, whose executives negotiated million-dollar orders directly with the home office in Atlanta. "The guy on the truck," Keough observed drily, "didn't see the head of Winn-Dixie very often."

The FTC's attack on exclusive franchises had frozen the bottlers in place for nearly a decade, making it impractical for them to consolidate their territories or invest in modernizing their equipment. Not until the summer of 1980, when Congress approved special legislation exempting the soft drink industry from the antitrust laws, was the way finally cleared for widespread restructuring.

Other challenges abounded. Surprisingly, for a company that prided itself on doing business in more countries than belonged to the United Nations, Coca-Cola's sales reports from overseas often took weeks to arrive in Atlanta, defeating any hope of hedging against foreign currency fluctuations. The board, nervous about the company's growing reliance on foreign earnings, wanted Goizueta to concentrate on enhancing domestic revenues. Yet demographers in the United States were making ominous predictions of a falloff in soft drink consumption in coming years, as the baby-boom generation grew older and grayer.

Not even the company's apparent successes were spared scrutiny and gimlet-eyed criticism. In 1979, McCann-Erickson had produced one of the most popular TV commercials of all time, a vignette in which "Mean" Joe Greene, the Pittsburgh Steelers' glowering defensive lineman, broke into a dazzling, sunny grin after a little boy insisted on giving him his bottle of Coca-Cola. Two years later, the new management team decided to cancel the "Coke and a Smile" campaign, deeming it pleasant but ineffective, too feeble a response to the Pepsi Challenge.

At the center of things, fueling the mood of crisis, was a stark statistic:

During the past decade and a half, Coca-Cola's market share had remained stagnant while Pepsi's kept rising. In supermarkets, where shoppers had an unrestricted choice of soft drinks, Pepsi had actually climbed ahead of Coke as the preferred cola, and only its greater availability in vending machines and at fast-food outlets (led by McDonald's) kept Coca-Cola in first place overall.

On March 28, 1981, just four weeks after becoming chairman, Goizueta summoned fifty of the company's top managers to a resort in Palm Springs, California, where he hoped to convince them the time for radical change had arrived. His demeanor was a handicap. Like Woodruff, he felt uncomfortable giving speeches and tended to rely on slogans and aphorisms that concealed his inner fire. He distributed a written "Strategy Statement" that appeared at first glance to be a garden-variety sermon on the virtues of hard work, intelligent risk-taking, and the need to keep an eye on the bottom line.

It was only when Goizueta began denouncing the company's "sacred cows" that his listeners pricked up their ears and recognized how passionately he meant what he said. He recalled the 1950s, when the company had stubbornly refused to offer consumers a larger bottle, and vowed that no fixed rules or corporate commandments would ever again hogtie the Coca-Cola Company. There would be no more taboos. For emphasis, perhaps just for the shock value, he said he was even prepared to change Coca-Cola's secret formula.

In one of his earliest meetings with Woodruff, Goizueta recalled, someone raised the question of using synthetic caffeine from mineral sources in Coca-Cola to save money. "We only have one formula," Woodruff replied stiffly, slamming the door on the subject.

Goizueta did not share the old man's unyielding constancy. He felt no particular reverence toward the formula. Learning it hadn't awed him. Old Doc Pemberton, he liked to say, had not necessarily created the best-tasting soft drink in the world back in 1886. As a chemical engineer, trained in the laboratory, Goizueta approached the business of making soft drinks with a practical attitude, almost literally with a sense of clinical detachment. If he could improve the syrup or cut the cost of manufacturing it, no shiver of sentimentality was about to stop him.

At the time he gained the chairmanship, Goizueta had been running the company's technical division for seven years. He'd already won a campaign to replace half the cane sugar in Coca-Cola with a new, cheaper form of sweetener called high-fructose corn syrup, or HFCS, a move that saved the company more than $100 million a year. When Woodruff fretted about making the change, Goizueta enlisted John Sibley as an ally, and Sibley reminded Woodruff that they had used other sweeteners in the past when necessity demanded, notably beet sugar during World War II. "This is just another kind of sugar, Bob," Sibley argued, carrying the day.

Now, as the man in charge, Goizueta gave the green light to a far more dramatic venture. Starting in 1975, under the code name "Project Triangle," company officials had begun experimenting with a new diet cola to replace Tab. Though it had performed well since its debut in 1963, perennially leading the diet market, Tab suffered a serious flaw—its name. Because of the legal superstitions still gripping the company at the time, no one had dared christen the drink Diet Coke or Diet Coca-Cola. In fact, since it contained no caffeine and no kola extract, the Legal Department was afraid to call it a cola at all. The name Tab was a nice play on the idea of people who wanted to keep "tab" on their weight, and it passed muster with a computer programmed to weed out words that might give offense in other languages. But there was no getting around that fact that it failed to mention the most powerful trademark in the world.

Goizueta, Keough, and their deputies figured a diet drink bearing the name Coke would soar automatically to a huge share of the market—a view bolstered by a clever field test. When asked to taste plainly marked samples of Tab and Diet Pepsi, consumers preferred Tab by a narrow margin, 52 percent to 48 percent. When those same consumers were given Tab in a can labeled "Diet Coke," however, their enthusiasm jumped and they favored it more than three to two. Meanwhile Goizueta had the chemists in his lab working on a new formula for the diet drink, so it would taste better in fact as well as fancy.

In the spring of 1980, the company was poised to launch Diet Coke when Austin suddenly got cold feet. Keough, who was traveling in Buenos Aires at the time, received a telex from Atlanta abruptly canceling the project without a word of explanation. Perhaps, he speculated, Austin simply wasn't up to the rigors of introducing a new product. Goizueta believed that another executive, Al Killeen, had frightened Austin about the legal consequences of putting the Coca-Cola trademark on a diet drink. Others thought Austin's big worry was a threat that the new product would "cannibalize" sales of Tab and Coke. Whatever the case, Austin's last important act as CEO had been to kill Diet Coke.

Goizueta meant to reverse the decision. He went to work on Woodruff, hoping to persuade him that introducing Diet Coke was a good idea. The two had begun joking with each other about who wielded the ultimate authority in the company. "You're the boss," Woodruff would say, and Goizueta would answer that he was not, that he was merely the chairman. "The boss," he told Woodruff, "is the one who *names* the chairman."

In reality, as Woodruff recognized, Goizueta had assumed power quickly and was moving to dismantle the old regime. The octogenarians on the board had to be retired, Goizueta felt, not just to avoid embarrassment on Wall Street, but because of the very real threat of legal liability in the event the company's directors were shown to be incapable of hearing and understanding the matters they voted on. After arranging final three-year terms for Woodruff and a few of the other elders, Goizueta had the board adopt new by-laws that prevented the reappointment of directors after their seventy-first birthday.

Growing more infirm every day, Woodruff dropped off the Finance Committee in the spring of 1981 and stopped coming to the office except on rare occasions. Yet Goizueta went out of his way to continue cultivating Woodruff's support. Every other day or so, Goizueta made the pilgrimage to Woodruff's house to visit with him in his sitting room and keep him informed about the affairs of the business. Woodruff was his "greatest ally," he said years later, and he never lost his instinctive desire to please the old man and gain his approval. One of Goizueta's favorite stories was the time he said to Woodruff, "I think we're going to have a good year," and Woodruff answered, "No, no, you *will* have a good year." Rather than finding the remark fatuous, Goizueta respected Woodruff's positive attitude. If the old man spoke in bromides, well, Goizueta's grandfather did, too. So did Goizueta, for that matter.

The corporate climate began changing with gathering speed, as old attitudes and practices were abandoned. John Hunter, one of the company's brightest field men, came in from the Philippines complaining about the poor performance of Coca-Cola's independent bottler there, San Miguel Breweries, whose owners were far more interested in selling beer than Coke. Invited to attend a meeting of the Finance Committee, Hunter proposed spending $30 million for a 30 percent stake in San Miguel and a joint-operating agreement. Tight-fisted Fill Eisenberg, who still served as a director and member of the Finance Committee, expressed shock. "Thirty million in the Philippines!" he erupted. "Of all the places!" But Goizueta cut him off. "Yes," he said firmly, "in the Philippines."

In the early summer of 1981, the company's chief financial officer, John Collings, died of a heart attack and was replaced by his deputy, Sam Ayoub, the Egyptian-born mathematical wizard. Ayoub shared Goizueta's personal affection for Woodruff and also Goizueta's belief that Woodruff could be persuaded to lend his support to almost any undertaking so long as it made sense and was carefully explained. In days gone by, Austin and Eisenberg had often clashed in front of Woodruff, with Austin pursuing new ventures and Eisenberg checkmating him by keeping the corporate purse snapped shut. Now Goizueta and Ayoub filled those jobs, and they took a completely different approach—they cooperated.

As the company's need to borrow money ballooned, Ayoub sought to reassure Woodruff that the return on their investment would surpass the interest they were paying. When Woodruff gave his assent, Ayoub recalled, "everybody was surprised. [But] all he wanted to know was what are you going to do with the money, and how are you going to do it?" The fact that two men with foreign backgrounds and alien accents found it easy to explain themselves to Woodruff, when that goal had proven so elusive to Austin, a fellow Georgian, was a fine irony. Within a year, the company pumped more than half a billion dollars into bottling operations.

By the autumn of 1981, Goizueta, Keough, and Ayoub had developed a comfortable working relationship. They perfected what amounted to a stage act and took it on the road, traveling from coast to coast to dramatize the company's new mission for audiences of investors, business writers, and financial analysts. At one session in Los Angeles, after Goizueta and Ayoub had spoken first, Keough opened his remarks by saying, "I'd like to apologize for my accent. I hope it doesn't detract from the international flavor of the company."

Ayoub was particularly effective. Putting an end to years of the silent treatment from Eisenberg, Ayoub opened up and talked candidly about the company's financial challenges, notably its difficulty in recovering overseas earnings at a time when foreign currencies were weakening against the dollar. "In a country with inflation like Argentina's," Ayoub told one group, drawing chuckles with his frankness, "you can lose money if you have a flat tire on the way to the bank." The way he handled the problem, he explained, was by modernizing Coca-Cola's reporting system—and by gambling on his instincts and speculating in the exchange markets. "My foreign currency department is right here," he told an interviewer, patting his belly. "I rely on my gut feelings."

As intended, the presentations from the new triumvirate grabbed the attention of the financial world, "NEW TOP EXECUTIVES SHAKE UP OLD ORDER AT SOFT-DRINK GIANT," proclaimed a headline in the *Wall Street Journal*, over a story that said Austin's dour, remote style had given way "to an enthusiasm akin to that of schoolboys released from a long detention period." Describing the swift, far-reaching changes they were instituting, Goizueta gushed to a reporter, "Frankly, I didn't think it would be so much fun." His mood, he said, was one of exhilaration.

As long as he took care to fashion a convincing argument, Goizueta found, he could count on securing Woodruff's blessing for virtually all of the new ideas he had in mind. The key was to use logic, couched in terms Woodruff found familiar. Anxious to gain a go-ahead for the Diet Coke project, for instance, Goizueta went to see Woodruff armed with a pile of statistics showing the steady, continuing growth in demand for diet drinks. "Mr. Woodruff," he said, "slowly but surely your company—the Coca-Cola Company—is turning into the Tab Company." The only way to keep that from happening, he said, was to put the trademark on a diet cola. Woodruff understood and agreed. The planning proceeded.

In advertising, Goizueta and Keough decided they wanted a fresh message, something short and punchy and memorable. They pressured Coca-Cola's long-time agency, McCann-Erickson, into hiring John Bergin, the celebrated adman who'd invented the "Pepsi Generation" ads of the 1960s, and Bergin oversaw the development of a campaign—"Coke Is It!"—that met all the criteria. Once again, though, Goizueta had Woodruff's reaction to consider. Calling Coca-Cola "it" had been on the Legal Department's forbidden list since John Sibley's heyday in the 1930s. Goizueta explained that the point was to use the fewest words possible, and Woodruff surprised him by giving his approval.

Goizueta's wife, Olguita, found it almost impossible to believe that Woodruff, who had utterly dominated the company and its executives for more than half a century, would willingly cede so much of his power, and she feared some kind of backlash. Others wondered as well, remembering the many times Woodruff had withdrawn briefly from the company's affairs in the past, only to throw off the cloak of retirement and resume command. His one-man control over ownership was effectively finished, but the specter remained of "the Cigar" returning one last time, agitating the handful of old-timers who still served with him on the board, testing the allegiances of the younger generation of leaders at Trust Company, King & Spalding, Emory University, and other Atlanta institutions with large Coca-Cola portfolios, and perhaps igniting a crisis on Wall Street.

As if to test that possibility, Goizueta and Keough set off on their boldest tangent yet, taking the company completely beyond the soft drink business. They decided to buy a movie studio.

The origin of the deal was perfectly simple.

If the Coca-Cola Company hoped to boost its earnings in the United States, it would have to diversify.

The tricky part was figuring out what to buy. One of Goizueta's outside consultants, Arthur D. Little, recommended acquiring either a drug company or a film studio, on the more or less reasonable theory that the executives of a soft drink company, having had experience with lab work and advertising, would feel a natural affinity for pharmaceuticals or entertainment

Ruling out the medical industry because of the lengthy periods required for research and development, Goizueta and Keough quickly settled on Hollywood, and their advisers picked Columbia Pictures as the only major independent studio likely to be available. Keough made the initial approach to Columbia's chairman, Herbert Allen, at a private dinner at the "21" Club in Manhattan in November 1981.

Allen, the scion of an investment banking family in New York, was in no particular hurry to sell out. He'd put $2.5 million into the studio eight years earlier, when it was struggling, and now Columbia was doing well, riding the success of *Close Encounters of the Third Kind* and a string of other hits. He listened politely as Keough explained Coca-Cola's interest in acquiring Columbia, and said he would think it over. But he warned that the price would be high. "It will knock your eyes out," he said.

In the next session, with Goizueta and Ayoub in attendance, Allen and Francis "Fay" Vincent, Columbia's president (later the commissioner of baseball), laid out a glowing picture of the studio's financial health, putting special emphasis on the stream of revenues that came from the television division. Columbia produced TV series as well as movies, Allen explained, and the syndication fees for such popular reruns as "Barney Miller" and "Charlie's Angels" brought in tens of millions of dollars a year. The film library, with some 1,800 titles, was a precious asset.

Goizueta, making no effort to conceal his eagerness, agreed with Allen that the two sides should "run the numbers" and meet again within a month to negotiate the terms of the deal. First, however, Goizueta had the Coca-Cola Company's board of directors to contend with. All of his decisions had been rubber-stamped so far, in part because he'd taken care to coax Woodruff into supporting them. Buying Columbia would be different. The company would be entering a glamorous new world, full of potential controversy, at a cost likely to dwarf all previous ventures. One very real concern was that the merger might result in the Allen family having more Coca-Cola stock than Woodruff, which Goizueta feared might make the old man angry and unhappy.

In early January 1982, Goizueta collected Ayoub and flew to Ichauway to brief Woodruff about the transaction. It tickled Ayoub enormously that after Goizueta spent half an hour over breakfast earnestly explaining the details of the deal and outlining its benefits, Woodruff withheld his blessing until he'd heard an okay from his "money man," as he called Ayoub. Woodruff's old habit of running any and all proposals past his chief financial officer, no matter what the CEO wanted, hadn't changed.

On Sunday, January 17, 1982, after several hours of spirited negotiations in Atlanta, Goizueta agreed to acquire Columbia for a price of $75 a share, or nearly $750 million in cash and Coca-Cola stock. Columbia stock had been trading at about $40 a share in recent weeks, which meant Coca-Cola would be paying almost double the market value to obtain the studio.

When the terms of the merger were announced two days later, Wall Street erupted with criticism. Goizueta believed he might have overpaid slightly, if only to close the deal quickly before other parties sniffed an opening and started a bidding war, but the financial community reacted as if he and Keough and Ayoub were green country boys who'd had their pockets picked clean in the big city. "We were *punished*," Keough said later, still awed at the ferocity of the response. Within a week, Coca-Cola stock fell $5 a share, losing about 10 percent of its value.

Woodruff was deeply disturbed. For three nights in a row, according to his valet, Cal Bailey, he prowled around Ichauway, sleepless, and agitated, complaining that he didn't know "a damn thing" about the Columbia transaction. He sought continual reassurances that he would remain Coca-Cola's largest Coca-Cola shareholder (which was, in fact, how Goizueta deliberately structured the deal). As a practical matter, Woodruff could no longer read, could barely hear, and had trouble concentrating on any subject for more than a few minutes at a time.

But by the time of the next directors' meeting, Woodruff had made up his mind. He backed Goizueta. Shortly after the meeting started, he made the formal motion to acquire Columbia. The inherent drama of the situation was undone somewhat by Woodruff's behavior: After making the motion, he stood up in evident confusion and tried to leave the boardroom, and when Goizueta gently sat him back down he greeted the ensuing highlight of the day's activities, a presentation by Columbia's studio chief, Frank Price, with a giant yawn. Yet Woodruff's role was decisive. The board gave unanimous approval to the deal.

For Goizueta, the Columbia merger became a defining moment. First and foremost, it cemented his control of the company. Woodruff's gesture served as an unmistakable signal that the new management could look forward to operating with a free hand. The board meeting turned out to be the last one Woodruff ever attended, and the motion he made was the final piece of official business he conducted for the Coca-Cola Company. During a chat not long afterward, he took Olguita Goizueta's hand and told her he was counting on her husband "to run my company for many, many years."

Just as important, the reaction to the deal convinced Goizueta that the financial community liked to engage in ruthless second-guessing, typically without bothering to give the participants the benefit of the doubt. He'd spent the better part of two years cultivating the goodwill of business reporters and financial analysts on Wall Street, only to be savaged the first time he poked a toe beyond the narrow confines of the soft drink industry. The experience made a lasting impression. Years later, Goizueta was unable to keep the scorn out of his voice when he talked about the media. "You know," he said, "if the press gets surprised, then *you're* wrong."

Many observers believed the Coca-Cola men got the short end of the stick because they were unfamiliar with the kind of rough-and-tumble haggling practiced in Hollywood and New York. One account of the Sunday negotiating session described how Goizueta, Keough, and Ayoub left the room after hearing Herb Allen's first offer, huddled together to consider their response, and then returned to make a counteroffer. As Ayoub opened his briefcase, the story went, Fay Vincent got a glimpse inside and saw a stack of envelopes, which he assumed meant the other side was prepared for the bidding to reach higher levels. As Ayoub started to hand an envelope across the table, Vincent won an important psychological victory by saying, "Forget that one, Sam, and go on to the next envelope."

The point of the story was plain enough, and valid as far as it went. Goizueta conceded his team wasn't as seasoned at the game of poker as the men across the table. Yet the truth was the Columbia deal turned out to be good for *both* sides. What infuriated Goizueta was Wall Street's insistence that every transaction had to have a winner and loser. Most of Coca-Cola's previous bargaining had been with its own bottlers—bitter clashes, as often as not, but contests that were carried out privately and tidied up politely afterward, with no one's head carried around on a pole as the vanquished foe. In the culture of Coca-Cola, the distasteful aspect of Fay Vincent's conduct wasn't so much that he'd picked up an extra dollar or two by clever dickering, but that he later told people about it.

Over the next few months, Goizueta enjoyed the considerable pleasure of swift vindication. Columbia released two critical and financial hits in 1982, *Gandhi* and *Tootsie*, and the studio entered into an immensely lucrative joint production venture with Home Box Office (HBO), the pay-cable outlet owned by Time, Incorporated. A new studio, TriStar, was opened in partnership with HBO and CBS. During the first year, the Coca-Cola Company made $90 million in operating profits from its new entertainment subsidiary, more than Wall Street—or Goizueta himself—had imagined possible.

Unlike the Columbia deal, no one expressed a bit of surprise when Diet Coke became an immediate, unqualified success.

In August 1982, the company rented Radio City Music Hall, hired the Rockettes, and literally kicked off the new product with a song and dance extravaganza. Sales surged from day one. "There was no way, in diet-conscious America, that such a drink could fail," an envious Pepsi executive claimed later. Goizueta seemed to agree. He gave the go-ahead for Diet Coke, he liked to say, without conducting a single market test. "Market testing is to see whether you are going to succeed or fail," he explained. "But as far as I was concerned, failure was just not an option."

Certainly the *idea* of Diet Coke was popular. After years of studying consumers' attitudes (by staging "purchase intent" games at shopping malls, among other methods), Coca-Cola's research department had established beyond a reasonable doubt that people wanted a sugar-free brand of Coca-Cola. On Wall Street, the prevailing wisdom was that virtually any dark-colored liquid bearing the name "Diet Coke" was bound to perform well, simply by exploiting the value of the Coca-Cola trademark. The company even decided to spell the word "diet" in the product's brand name with a lowercase *d* in order to place greater emphasis on Coke.

Yet the notion of preordained victory ignored the extraordinary effort Goizueta and his chemists put into perfecting the taste of Diet Coke. Most soft drink manufacturers, including Pepsi, made their diet versions by removing the sugar from their regular syrup, substituting a synthetic sweetener, and then adjusting the ingredients until they came as close as possible to the original flavor. The result usually fell short of the mark, typically because of an unpleasant aftertaste.

In formulating Diet Coke, Goizueta's technicians tinkered with the formula until they created an entirely new flavor, one that was "smoother" than the original, with less phosphoric acid (the ingredient that gave Coca-Cola its characteristic bite), and had a different blend of oils. There was no need for traditional market testing as such, because the recipe was refined in the laboratory and subjected to hundreds of taste tests, until Goizueta satisfied himself that Diet Coke was as good as its namesake, perhaps better.

Instead of relying on the traditional selling point of low calories, the advertising campaign for Diet Coke was built around a claim of intrinsic quality. Though the point might seem obvious in hindsight, the company recognized that consumers now wanted sugar-free beverages that pleased their palates. The account was given to McCann's innovative sister agency, SSC&B/Lintas, whose writers captured the idea perfectly with the memorable slogan, "Just for the taste of it, Diet Coke!"

By the end of 1983, Diet Coke had become not only the nation's leading sugar-free beverage but the fourth best-selling soft drink in the whole market, trailing only Coca-Cola, Pepsi, and 7-Up—a consensus choice as the most successful new product in the history of the industry. "If you go around here," Goizueta said several years later, waving a hand around the offices atop the Coca-Cola tower, "you're going to find at least ten people who say [Diet Coke] was their idea."

The same was not true of New Coke.

After fielding the question for years and years, at forums and after speeches, in interviews and during conversations with friends, Don Keough finally came up with the ideal explanation of his role in the creation of New Coke: "I was on vacation at the time."

Actually, as New Coke became a part of America's folklore, a synonym for marketing futility and boneheadedness rivaled only by the dreaded Edsel, Keough and Goizueta and dozens of other executives at the Coca-Cola Company grudgingly accepted the fact that they would have to spend the rest of their lives defending their participation in a fiasco. Almost to a man they asked only one kindness—that they not be accused of acting carelessly or capriciously, or without having given the matter a great deal of thought. It was a fair request.

New Coke began incubating in 1975 with the advent of the "Pepsi Challenge." In city after city, as Pepsi claimed to be winning head-to-head taste tests, Coca-Cola officials rushed to conduct tests of their own. The results came as a sharp disappointment. Coca-Cola could not prove its superiority. In several instances Coke *lost*. The numbers were kept under wraps, but word swept quickly through the ranks of the Coca-Cola family that the product had a taste problem.

In one very important respect, as it happened, the test results were misleading. By their very nature, blind tests sought to strip away the psychological influence of a product's image in order to gauge its underlying merit, when in the cola business such an exercise was virtually meaningless: There were no real-life circumstances under which image and taste could be divorced. A youngster did not sit down at a soda fountain one day, order a glass of Pepsi and a glass of Coke, sniff the bouquets, take a sip of each, and announce a favorite for life. Product loyalty was far more complicated.

It was a tricky point. Pepsi could say it tasted better than Coca-Cola, but actual consumers could never make a fair, clinical determination of the accuracy of the claim—they couldn't decide for themselves—because their taste buds would always be compromised by the thoughts and emotions and associations that the name of the product conjured up in their minds. Knowing what they were drinking would always affect the taste.

The outcome of the Pepsi Challenge reflected the eccentricities of the business. Pepsi's sales improved slightly, but not at the expense of Coca-Cola. Some consumers, swayed by the impression that Pepsi had achieved parity with Coca-Cola, switched to Pepsi from *other* colas, yet there was no evidence that Coke suffered any significant, lasting defections. Ultimately, the campaign had the effect of turning the Cola Wars into a contest between two giants, benefiting both companies at the expense of smaller competitors. John Sculley, the president of Pepsi-Cola in the early 1980s, liked to argue that the rivalry was not "some gladiatorial contest where one of us has to leave on a stretcher. We're both winning."

Not surprisingly, Coca-Cola officials failed to share Sculley's benign view. They loathed the Challenge and tried desperately to debunk the notion that Pepsi had emerged as an adversary of equal standing. Bill Cosby performed in a series of commercials ridiculing Pepsi as a lowly pretender. In one TV spot, the comedian said, "If you're number two or three or seven, you know what you want to be when you grow up"—he held up a can of Coke—"the number-one soft drink in the world."

While presenting a public facade of bravado, though, the men in the Coca-Cola tower were growing more and more worried. They could ill afford to ignore Pepsi's gains, no matter how difficult it might be to pinpoint the causes. The stark fact was that Coke's market share had been shrinking for several decades, from 60 percent just after World War II to less than 24 percent in 1983. The main reason was "segmentation," the proliferation of diet drinks, citrus flavors, caffeine-free colas, and other new beverages that flooded the soft drink market and lured consumers away from sugar colas like Coke and Pepsi. (The very phrase "sugar cola," in fact, was a retronym, like "real turf," necessary to place an old drink in a new category in the expanding soft drink market.) The Coca-Cola Company was marketing many of these new products, of course, and profiting from the trend.

Yet the mediocre performance of Coca-Cola could not be blamed entirely on segmentation. In spite of the limitations of product testing, company officials devised new, increasingly sophisticated methods that sought to measure Coke directly against Pepsi. Roy Stout, the scholarly director of the company's marketing research department, piled up a small mountain of graphs, charts, computer printouts, and other data, all of which suggested that taste was the lone plausible reason for Coca-Cola's stagnation in the market "If we have twice as many vending machines, dominate fountain [outlets], have more shelf space, spend more on advertising, and are competitively priced," Stout asked pointedly, "why are we losing share?"

Others asked the same question. The head of Coca-Cola USA, a hard-charging Argentine named Brian Dyson, one of Keough's protegés, became almost evangelical on the subject. The testing persuaded him that consumers' tastes had changed over the years, and he believed they'd begun to prefer Pepsi's sweeter, smoother flavor over Coke's. His nightmare was that Pepsi might catch and surpass Coke while he was in charge. "I'm not going to sit on my ass and watch that," he told an interviewer.

Goizueta, too, suffered "complete frustration," as he put it, "that after everything was done, we kept losing market share." As early as 1979, well before taking over the company's top job, Goizueta directed his technical division to begin experiments with the secret formula, looking for a new taste that would beat Pepsi in the blind tests. At the time, he was in no position to commit the apostasy of changing the formula, but four years later things were different.

Goizueta gave Dyson formal permission to undertake a project aimed at reformulating Coca-Cola. Dyson, in turn, assigned day-to-day responsibility for the job to Sergio Zyman (pronounced ZEE-man), a Mexican native and former Pepsi manager who had joined Coca-Cola USA and risen quickly to become head of marketing. Zyman, fresh from his highly praised work helping to launch Diet Coke, threw himself enthusiastically into the task.

In the aftermath of New Coke's rise and fall, the nationalities of the men involved came into question, as if by foreign birth they must have lacked a homegrown appreciation of the place Coca-Cola occupied in the American social fabric. That view was easily dismissed with a reminder that many unmistakably "American" executives at the Coca-Cola Company, chief among them Don Keough (reared in Sioux City, Iowa), concurred in the decision. Yet the cultural backgrounds and experiences of Goizueta, Dyson, and Zymian did, in fact, play a significant part in the way the project unfolded.

Two and a half years into his chairmanship, Goizueta could point to an unbroken string of successes in reshaping the business. Understandably, his confidence had grown. He did not for a minute believe he'd become infallible, but he thought he deserved some credit for having taken the necessary risks. His favorite proverb, loosely translated from Spanish, was, "Just because a man is courteous, don't think he isn't brave." For all his natural reserve and shyness, there was a bit of the matador about him. He enjoyed taking chances.

"I had a very large home with servants when I was growing up," he told an interviewer once, describing his family's sugar plantation in Cuba. "I lost everything I had when I was thirty-one, and hell, here I'm chief executive of one of the premier companies in the U.S." After the Cuban Revolution, the possibility of a business reversal or two held little fear for him.

At the same time, Goizueta thought many of the men around him took themselves and the business too seriously. In his annual report for 1982, Goizueta remarked that the Coca-Cola Company was providing *"panem et circenses*" for its customers—bread and circuses—through its refreshment and entertainment divisions. The phrase had a slightly contemptuous ring, coming (as Goizueta, trained in classic Latin, knew it did) from Juvenal, the Roman cynic who believed his countrymen were too easily distracted and satisfied by such superficial things. On other occasions, Goizueta expressed the thought more directly, saying company officials needed to get off their high horses and recognize that "we are selling only a little moment of pleasure."

Dyson, for his part, fit perfectly into the company's new, aggressive management style. A fitness buff who participated in triathlons, Dyson loved to compete, intellectually as well as physically, and he took the lead in pushing through many of the changes that transformed the business. At Keough's request, he'd come to Atlanta from South America in 1978 to help prod the bottlers into signing amended contracts, a job he performed with such tenacity he earned a reputation within the company for highhandedness. His approach to Pepsi bordered on the bloodthirsty. "We believe in two eyes for an eye and two teeth for a tooth," he once vowed with awkward, biblical fury, "and if our competitor swats us in the face, we will turn around and knock [the] hell out of him."

The grandson of English emigrants, Dyson grew up on a 4,400-acre *estancia* in the remote countryside of Argentina, and though he presented little of a macho stereotype in appearance, his behavior seemed to be modeled directly on Luis Firpo, the boxer known as "the Wild Bull of the Pampas." Edgy, unable to sit still, Dyson stayed in constant motion and craved constant change. He believed in acting while others were still worrying about the consequences, a hurry-up attitude that was captured nicely by his motto: "Ready, fire! aim."

Zyman, too, brought an exotic background to the Coca-Cola Company—not so much his upbringing in Mexico but the years he spent working for Pepsi. Smart, impeccably tailored, multilingual (and so assertive he earned the nickname "the aya-cola"), Zyman was one of several executives lured away from Pepsi in the late 1970s as Coke's troubled management searched for an answer to the Challenge. Unlike some of the old hands in Atlanta, Zyman had no difficulty at all believing that Pepsi was beating Coke in taste tests, and he had no qualms about advocating a change in flavor to solve the problem.

When he was assigned to oversee the reformulation, Zyman picked the name "Project Kansas" for the operation, as if to mock the sanctity of Coca-Cola's traditions. The reference was to William Allen White, the Kansas editor whose letter to the company in the 1930s lavished praise on Coca-Cola as a "sublimated essence of all that America stands for, a decent thing honestly made, universally distributed, conscientiously improved with the years." With supreme irreverence, Zyman invoked a homily from the American heartland, one that had come to stand for Coca-Cola's durable virtues, as he set out to change the secret formula.

"We had done bold things," Keough said later, "and we had a full plate of activity after more than a decade of inactivity, and we were— My guess is we were feeling our oats."

Despite their impatience and zest for action, Goizueta and his team moved with surprising caution as Project Kansas got under way. Before they could replace the old Coke, they first had to find a superior substitute, and the search proved more difficult than expected.

The chemists in the technical department had been tinkering with the formula off and on for four years, brewing up variations of the familiar cola flavor, but so far nothing had beaten Pepsi. Roy Stout, the marketing research director, received a steady supply of experimental syrups, which he dutifully submitted to consumer panels for blind sampling. The best result to date had been a tie.

In a fluke of timing, Pepsi dropped the Challenge in the fall of 1983, just as Project Kansas was starting. For all its evident success, the campaign provoked mixed feelings at PepsiCo headquarters in New York. Roger Enrico, Pepsi's new president, thought the Challenge was stale and wanted to return to the tried-and-true success of the Pepsi Generation theme. Nationally, many of Pepsi's bottlers disliked the Challenge because it spurred pricing wars and advertising skirmishes in their local markets. Don Kendall, the chairman of PepsiCo, had never felt much enthusiasm for the strategy, and after an eight-year run it was quietly shelved.

Yet the search for a new Coca-Cola formula went on. By now the taste question had become a cause célèbre throughout the company, a convenient scapegoat to explain Coca-Cola's lackluster performance. "Human nature being what it is," Keough said, "once you find a handy problem . . . you can build it up and [exaggerate] it. I think there was a little of that. If a bottler was having difficulty with his market share, he could say, 'We've got this taste issue.'" The ranks of those advocating a change in the formula swelled to include many of Coca-Cola's longtime bottlers, men and women whose families had been selling the product for nearly a century.

While the technicians worked in the lab, the market researchers struggled with a pricklier subject: what to do with the new, improved formula if and when it finally arrived. Unlike Diet Coke, which struck almost everyone who heard of it as a good idea, "*New* Coke" had an alien ring. If Coca-Cola was an ideal product, as the company had been proclaiming for so many years, then a "new and improved" version seemed to be a contradiction in terms. Should the company simply change the formula without fanfare? What if consumers noticed the difference? What if they *didn't*? How about selling two versions, Coke and Coke Two? What would happen to the trademark?

To their credit, the leaders of Project Kansas labored mightily to think through all of the implications of what amounted, in the business world, to a metaphysical conundrum. They tried, through hundreds of interviews and tests, to measure the public's likely response to the idea of a change in the way Coca-Cola tasted. Contrary to some accounts, they discerned in advance that many lifelong Coca-Cola drinkers would be reluctant to contemplate any change at all, even for the better. But they had no convenient way of calculating the depth and breadth of that reluctance. They could not afford to ask consumers too many direct questions without giving away their mission—and as the paper-shredder in Zyman's office attested, secrecy was a top priority.

As far as the outside world knew, the company was blooming with renewed financial health. At the end of 1983, *Dun's Business Month* pronounced Coca-Cola one of the five best-managed companies in the country. Columbia's revenues, fueled by the box-office popularity of *The Big Chill* and *Ghostbusters*, grew at a rate of 30 percent a year. Goizueta sold off several of the company's less profitable subsidiaries, including Aqua-Chem, the private-label coffee line, and the wine business. When Edgar Bronfman of Seagram's called to ask about buying the state-of-the-art winery, Goizueta recalled, "I had to sit down, 'cause I didn't think anybody wanted it. . . . I said to myself, 'Wow, this is my lucky day!'" Operating profits for the next year, he calculated, might pass $1 billion for the first time.

Goizueta might have been forgiven a bit of gloating, having showed up his doubters on Wall Street, but some act of providence held him back. In a highly flattering profile in the *New York Times* in 1984, he issued a prescient warning. "There is a danger when a company is doing as well as we are," he said, "and that is to think that we can do no wrong. I keep telling the organization: 'We can do wrong and we can do wrong big.'"

According to Goizueta and others, the breakthrough in Project Kansas came from Diet Coke. In simple terms, the company's chemists tried reversing the traditional method of making diet drinks. They substituted sugar, in the form of high-fructose corn syrup, for the artificial sweetener in Diet Coke, and after a year of fiddling they believed they'd perfected a new formula for Coca-Cola that would beat Pepsi in blind taste tests. Like Diet Coke, the most noticeable change in the new formula was its smoother taste, brought about by a reduction in the amount of Merchandise No. 4, phosphoric acid. By adding citric acid, which was less biting, the chemists also gave the new formula a slightly more lemony scent.

There were several other changes, including adjustments in the amounts of caramel, caffeine, and vanilla, and the elimination of Merchandise No. 5, the source of the vestigial traces of coca and kola. Merchandise No. 7X, the super-secret blend of flavoring oils, was also altered. Aside from smoothness, the most conspicuous difference in the new formula was its greater sweetness, resulting from an extra ten calories' worth of HFCS per 12-ounce serving.

With the new recipe in hand, Stout and Zyman arranged to conduct blind taste tests—not just a few sips by a few panels of consumers, but an exhaustive battery of 190,000 tests costing $4 million in all, with respondents from every age group and every region of the country. The results were dramatic and seemingly conclusive. After losing to Pepsi in in-house taste tests for years, by margins as high as 10 to 15 points, the new Coke beat Pepsi by 6 to 8 points. The new Coke also beat regular Coke.

The minute he saw the numbers, Dyson began pressing to reformulate Coca-Cola, the sooner the better. But Goizueta and Keough hesitated. First they had to make a series of preliminary decisions, answering a succession of questions that could not be resolved by testing. They began by agreeing that any change in the formula would have to be announced openly. Aside from the matter of public trust, the company had legal obligations to its bottlers that required the disclosure. It followed, then, that there would be a "new" Coke and an "old" Coke—and thus a dilemma whether to keep both on the market.

At first glance, the idea of two Coca-Colas had a logical appeal. Consumers with evolving tastes would have a new product tailored to their palates, while loyalists could continue drinking what was, after all, still the most popular soft drink in the land. But on closer reflection, offering two Cokes threatened to defeat the very purpose of the exercise: By splitting its share of the sugar cola market, the Coca-Cola Company would almost certainly put Pepsi in first place, with attendant bragging rights. As a more elusive concern, Goizueta and Keough assumed that the new Coke would quickly begin outselling the old version, leading to the potential embarrassment of having a product called Coke Two outperforming the flagship brand. They concluded that the old Coke would have to be retired and taken off the shelves.

In the closing months of 1984, surveys showed Coke's lead in the sugar cola market narrowing until Pepsi trailed by fewer than three points, the closest margin ever. Those numbers, along with the results of the taste tests, finally convinced Goizueta and Keough to go ahead. During the holiday season at the end of December, they met with Dyson and Ike Herbert, the director of corporate marketing, and resolved to proceed with the reformulation.

Setting the wheels in motion, Herbert and Zyman ventured to New York for a hush-hush meeting with the top executives of McCann-Erickson, the company's advertising agency. In a secluded office nicknamed "the bunker," the men from Atlanta divulged the news of their decision and assigned John Bergin, McCann's president, to start work on a campaign to launch the new Coke. The target date was April, just four months off. If any word of the project leaked prematurely, Herbert said, leveling a direct threat, the agency would be fired. Meanwhile, back home, Dyson widened the membership in Project Kansas to include Coca-Cola's top marketing and public relations officials, who were given the monumental (and totally confidential) task of coordinating New Coke's debut.

One other consideration remained, and that was the issue of what, if anything, to tell Woodruff. Goizueta has always maintained that he flew to Ichauway, explained the decision to Woodruff, and received his blessing for the new formula—an account that provoked skepticism at the time and continued to raise eyebrows many years later. Actually, Goizueta recalled in an interview for this book, he had been briefing Woodruff for several years on Coca-Cola's shrinking market share and poor performance in taste tests with Pepsi. "I was bringing him along as to what we were doing," Goizueta recounted, clarifying the sequence of events, and "I said, 'You know, we've tried everything. We have the best commercials. We've tried everything and nothing works. We may have to, um, we may have to kind of change the formula.'"

Goizueta's conversation with Woodruff about the company's plans, that is, was not quite as explicit as he first suggested. Certainly Goizueta did not look the old man in the eye and tell him point-blank that the sacred secret formula was being junked in favor of a version that tasted more like Pepsi. There would have been no purpose in doing so. "He'd have hit me over the head," Goizueta said. Besides, Woodruff's permission wasn't necessary. The change in by-laws restricting the age of directors had caught up with Woodruff in the spring of 1984, and his retirement from the board ended his formal association with the company after sixty-one years.

As a farewell honor, Woodruff was named director emeritus and awarded a "consulting" fee of $20,000 a year, which he accepted as a supplement to the income from his $250 million in Coca-Cola stock. (He cashed his monthly Social Security check, too.) But in fact he was no longer able to advise anyone about anything. By the time of his ninety-fifth birthday, on December 6, 1984, Woodruff's deterioration was painfully obvious, and most of his visitors could tell death was close. If he was aware of the impending drama of New Coke, he failed to mention it to Joe Jones or Martha Ellis or any of the others in the small circle of intimates who helped shepherd him through his final days.

Toward the end of the quail season in February 1985, Woodruff lost his appetite and stopped eating. He grew confused at times, thinking his wife, Nell, was still alive. His nurse, Edith Honeycutt, the same woman who had cared for his father nearly half a century earlier, sat at his bedside and reminisced with him about old times. She would recite his favorite poem, "If," and the Twenty-third Psalm, and she got a nephew with a strong baritone voice to record a selection of hymns Woodruff liked. He asked to hear them again and again. Woodruff went into Emory University Hospital on February 25, 1985, and died ten days later, on March 7, holding Edith Honeycutt's hand, listening to "Just a Closer Walk with Thee."

Paying tribute, Goizueta closed Coca-Cola's worldwide offices on the following Monday, March 11, 1985.

In the outpouring of eulogies that followed, during ceremonies in Atlanta and on the grounds of Ichauway and elsewhere, one remark in particular stood out. Praising Woodruff's high standards, Dr. James Laney, the president of Emory, reminded the mourners at a campus memorial service that Woodruff's earliest decision at the Coca-Cola Company had been to visit Will Bradley in Columbus and insist on "no tampering" with the formula. What made the comment so intriguing, in hindsight, was that Laney had recently joined Coca-Cola's board of directors and obviously had no idea that a reformulation was in the works. Incredibly, Goizueta had yet to inform the board members about the Kansas Project.

At the time of Woodruff's death, Goizueta still had the option of slamming on the brakes and changing his mind about New Coke. On April Fools' Day, 1985, he and Keough listened for several hours as Dyson and Zyman made a final presentation outlining the status of the venture and reiterating their arguments for proceeding. Looking back, Keough believed the key defect in their preparations was a failure to conduct tests anticipating the public's response to the disappearance of old Coke. "All through the discussion," he said later, "you always had that in your head—what is the fundamental, unresearchable reaction going to be?" New Coke might be the best-tasting cola in the world, but what would the American consumer think about losing an old, familiar friend?

To Goizueta, though, there was little point asking hypothetical questions of people. "I don't think you can [do] market testing and measure emotions," he explained. "To ask the average housewife whether she likes a product she can't touch or see is just trying to measure emotions." The one tangible, inescapable fact, in his view, was the twenty-year slide in Coca-Cola's market share, and the urgent need to do something about it. Goizueta had sampled the new formula himself and liked the way it tasted (he was still drinking New Coke years later, singing its praises as "the best-tasting sugar cola on the market"), and his judgment was backed up by the results of the taste tests. After sleeping on the decision overnight, he gave New Coke the formal go-ahead.

The planning for New Coke's introduction, already feverish, grew frenzied. Dozens and eventually hundreds of people—board members and bottlers, ad writers and typesetters, employees in almost every division of the company—were brought in on the project and sworn to secrecy, lest the news slip out prematurely. A variety of small but crucial choices had to be made, starting with exactly what to call the product. Ike Herbert's instinct, shared by Goizueta and Keough, was simply to retain the name Coca-Cola and avoid using the word "new" at all. But Dyson, Zyman, and some of the bottlers believed the change in flavor had to be emphasized in order to grab the public's attention, and their position carried the day. "New Coke" went on the label.

Next, the Project Kansas team had to fashion an explanation for changing the formula. After years of pooh-poohing the Pepsi Challenge, no one at the Coca-Cola Company had the least intention of admitting that the new taste was similar to Pepsi's. To say so would be tantamount to waving a white flag of surrender. Indeed, even as the work on New Coke neared completion, the company ran television commercials with Bill Cosby exalting Coca-Cola as *less sweet* than Pepsi, with more of a "real" cola taste—a campaign that made absolutely no sense whatsoever, coming as it did on the eve of the introduction of a sweeter drink.

Goizueta and Keough planned to unveil New Coke at an elaborate press conference in New York City on Tuesday, April 23, 1985. As he scripted his remarks, Goizueta intended to say the new formula had beaten Pepsi in blind taste tests, a straightforward claim of superiority he thought might eliminate the need for any further discussion of the reason for the change. But Herbert and others raised a warning. If someone asked how the *old* Coke had fared in taste tests with Pepsi, Goizueta would have to confess it had lost, the very admission everyone in the company sought to evade. Goizueta "caved in," as he put it, and agreed to delete any mention of Pepsi or the Challenge or the relative merits of the two colas—a decision, he concluded later, that was a mistake.

Invitations to the press conference went out to news organizations on the afternoon of Friday, April 19, 1985, four days in advance of the event. Perhaps, as they put the final touches in place and prepared to announce an action they could not explain and for which they could provide no ready rationale, the leaders of the Coca-Cola Company should have known they were exposing themselves to a counterattack from Pepsi. Even so, they had no way of anticipating just how swift and stinging the response would be.

Driving home in New York on the Friday evening before Coca-Cola's press conference, Joe McCann had a brainstorm so strong he nearly swerved off the highway. Like everyone else who worked for Pepsi, McCann, the director of corporate public relations, had heard the rumors that Coke was on the verge of announcing a new formula. Like the others, he was scared Pepsi's rival might be about to score a great coup.

Suddenly he realized he was "looking at it the wrong way." The Coca-Cola Company was not introducing a new product, he decided, it was pulling an existing product off the market and conceding. As soon as he arrived home, he put in a call to Roger Enrico, Pepsi's president. "They're admitting defeat!" he said excitedly. "The most famous product in the world is coming off the shelves. They're leaving the battlefield, folding their tents. *Roger, we just won the Cola War!*" All Pepsi had to do, McCann advised, was claim victory.

Enrico thought it over and agreed. On Monday morning, the day before Coca-Cola's announcement, he wrote an open letter to all of Pepsi's employees and bottlers asserting that after nearly a century of competition, "the other guy just blinked." Proclaiming that the new Coke had been reformulated to taste "more like Pepsi," Enrico crowed that "victory is sweet" and announced that the whole company would celebrate by taking a day off on the coming Friday. Then he arranged to have the letter placed as a full-page advertisement the next day in major newspapers across the country, including the *Atlanta Journal-Constitution*.

Pepsi's preemptive strike caught Coca-Cola by surprise. While Goizueta and Keough went through the final dress rehearsal for their joint appearance, Pepsi executives were working the telephones, calling business reporters to stress the idea that New Coke had been made to taste more like Pepsi. Giving out statistics about Pepsi's rise in market share, they planted unfriendly questions designed to throw the Coca-Cola men on the defensive. In a series of radio, print, and TV interviews, Enrico hammered away at the theme that Coca-Cola was surrendering.

By eleven o'clock Tuesday morning, when Goizueta and Keough took the stage at the Vivian Beaumont Theater in New York's Lincoln Center, the two hundred members of the media in the audience were primed and ready to challenge every assertion in the presentation. Ordinarily, journalists pay great deference to executives of the caliber of Goizueta and Keough, but this crowd seemed more like the Washington press corps, waiting to pick apart an injured president.

The lights were dimmed, a song with a martial cadence rang out from the speakers—"We are, we will always be, Coca-Cola, All-American history!"—and a giant screen above the stage flickered with images of cowboys, athletes, the Statue of Liberty, the Grand Canyon, families with children, Eisenhower and Kennedy, wheat fields, all interspersed with old Coca-Cola commercials. Goizueta then went to the lectern and, plainly nervous, announced that Coca-Cola had a new taste. "The best," he said, "has been made even better." He described the discovery of the new formula during the research for Diet Coke, explained that consumers preferred New Coke over old Coke in taste tests, and said the management had decided to "buy the world a new Coke." Keough followed, detailing the company's successes launching Diet Coke, Sprite, and Cherry Coke. "The best," he said, "never rest." Neither man uttered a word about Pepsi.

After a preview of the commercials that had been filmed for New Coke, the floor was opened for questions, and the assault began. The first question set the tone. "Are you a hundred percent certain," a reporter asked, "that this won't bomb?" The next query, simple and direct, exposed the fragility of the company's whole strategy. What was the difference, a journalist asked, between the old Coke and the new Coke?

"When you describe flavor," Goizueta responded, sounding practiced and thus evasive, "it is a matter better left to the poets or copywriters or members of the press. Why don't you try it, and you yourself make the judgment?"

The plan, carefully crafted beforehand, was for Goizueta and Keough to avoid characterizing New Coke. The press, they figured, would report Pepsi's gain in market share in recent years and speculate that New Coke was a response. But there was no reason for the company's top two executives to confirm that scenario, nor for them to discuss whether New Coke tasted more like Pepsi. Unhappily for Goizueta, though, the plan unraveled in a matter of minutes. When another reporter persisted in asking about New Coke's taste, he hemmed and hawed and answered, "I would say that it is smoother, uh, uh, rounder, yet, uh, yet bolder—it has a more harmonious flavor. . . ."

Here was the chairman and CEO of the Coca-Cola Company, a chemical engineer by training, sounding utterly flustered at the prospect of describing the flavor of his new product. Some of the journalists broke into open snickering. Next, as if prompted by Enrico, the press asked if New Coke was a response to the Pepsi Challenge. "Oh, gosh, no," Goizueta said, his credibility bleeding away. "The Pepsi Challenge? When did that happen?"

The siege lasted an hour, and when it was over Goizueta and Keough had managed to sound less like businessmen than artless, dissembling politicians. Rather than admit Coca-Cola's erosion in market share, Keough said Coke and Pepsi had been in a "horse race" for the past twenty years, running roughly even. Goizueta suggested that the company's recent ads touting Coke as less sweet than Pepsi were a "good diversionary tactic," deliberately designed to help keep New Coke a secret. Asked if New Coke had been made sweeter, Goizueta danced around and ducked the question.

In the hubbub, one vital point was nearly overlooked: the fate of the faithful Coca-Cola drinker who liked the old formula. The company's blind taste tests had demonstrated that consumers preferred New Coke over old Coke by ten points, 55 percent to 45 percent. Even more significant, additional tests in which consumers were permitted to see the labels yielded a *stronger* preference for New Coke, 61 percent to 39 percent. Thus Goizueta and Keough had reason to think the idea of a new formula would appeal to people, an argument they made emphatically during the press conference.

But what, a reporter asked, about the 39 percent who favored the old Coca-Cola? Giving perhaps the most infelicitous answer of the day, Keough said smugly, "Well, 39 percent of the people voted for McGovern." As it happened, Keough and some others in the company's high command thought they might have to reissue old Coke in a year or so, perhaps during the company's centennial celebration in 1986, if enough customers kept clamoring for it. But instead of simply saying so, Keough fueled the sense that the company intended to scrap old Coke forever—and that anyone who disagreed had no more sense than a supporter of the hapless George McGovern.

Much to the delight of Enrico and his colleagues, the initial stories from the press conference focused on Coca-Cola's evident capitulation to Pepsi. On television that night, David Letterman joked, "Coke's decided to make their formula sweeter—they're going to mix it with Pepsi."

The real news, however, turned out to be the shudder of betrayal that began stirring somewhere deep in the hearts of a large segment of the American populace. Like the faint, sinister vibration at the nuclear power plant in the movie *China Syndrome*, it signaled an impending meltdown.

Long before they had ever tasted a sip of it, millions of Americans decided they *hated* New Coke.

All across the country, and especially in the South, people responded to the change in formula as if the company had committed an act of parricide, killing off a beloved member of the family. The surge of emotion over old Coke defied all reason. Hundreds and then thousands of angry callers began inundating the company's 800 number in Atlanta, and the remarkable thing was that many of them weren't Coca-Cola drinkers at all. They were simply American citizens, upset and feeling a profound sense of loss.

In the media, writers and cartoonists treated the management of the Coca-Cola Company not as businessmen who were trying to improve a popular product, but as vandals who wanted to deface a national treasure. "Next week," Michael Kernan wrote in the *Washington Post*, "they'll be chiseling Teddy Roosevelt off the side of Mount Rushmore." A New York newspaper announced, "The new drink will be smoother, sweeter, and a threat to a way of life."

The reaction was almost exactly the same as the eruption that greeted the French government's attempt to ban Coca-Cola in 1950. Only now the culprit was the company itself. One of the clippings carefully preserved in Woodruff's old scrapbooks was an article written in 1980 by Bob Greene, the syndicated columnist, who gushed, "I love Coca-Cola. It is the finest product manufactured in the United States, and America's most noble ambassador to the world. . . ." Like a keeper of the sacred flame, Greene helped lead the assault on New Coke, labeling it a failure and deeming Goizueta and Keough "soda jerks."

Protests sprouted up everywhere. A songwriter in Nashville, playing mischief with the company's slogan, dashed off a ditty called "Coke *Was* It" that became a popular hit on radio stations. In city after city, die-hard Coke drinkers began stockpiling supplies of the old soft drink, often with local TV crews on hand to record the activity and showcase it on the nightly news. The company's mailroom filled with sacks of letters from irate consumers. "Changing Coke," one writer said, "is like God making the grass purple or putting toes on our ears or teeth on our knees."

Making the most of an adversary's disarray, Pepsi officials concocted a brilliant TV commercial that depicted a distraught Coca-Cola loyalist, a teenage girl who gazed sadly at a can of Coke and asked, "Can somebody out there tell me why they did it? They said they were the real thing. They said they were it. And then they changed." After picking up a can of Pepsi and taking a long, satisfied gulp, she brightened and said, "*Now* I know why."

Years later, indulging in a bit of wishful thinking, Goizueta theorized that it might have been smarter to try introducing New Coke exclusively in cans and bottles, and not at fountain outlets. As it was, he said, many people sampled the new formula at fast-food restaurants, movie theaters, or ballparks, where the taste fluctuated. "If you go to a fountain outlet and you order a Coke," he explained, "most of the time they put in too much ice, or the carbonation is not as it should be, but you have ordered a Coke and you drink it and you don't think about it. [Then] we changed the formula, and you go to that same fountain outlet and all of a sudden you become a wine-taster"—a finicky critic ready to pounce. Had consumers compared New Coke in cans or bottles with old Coke from the fountain, Goizueta believed, "they would have said, 'God, this New Coke tastes better.'"

Yet the fact was many people didn't *want* to like New Coke. They were unable to give it a fair chance, because they were angry over its very existence. Some of them were taking bottles and cans of it into the streets and pouring it down storm drains. During the month of May 1985, the company staged "rolling out" parties for New Coke in forty-five cities and gave away a million cans of the product, and in almost every instance their reward was a spate of negative publicity focused on consumers demanding the return of old Coke.

Company officials recognized they had a crisis on their hands. Just as Lyndon Johnson realized the Vietnam War was a lost cause when Walter Cronkite finally criticized the American effort, the top brass at Coca-Cola knew they were on the ropes when Paul Harvey, the voice-of-the-heartland syndicated radio commentator, pronounced New Coke a failure and urged the company to apologize and bring back the old product They began considering the idea.

Don Keough's epiphany, oddly enough, took place on foreign soil. One night in Monaco, during a convention of Coca-Cola bottlers, he and Goizueta took their wives to a small Italian restaurant overlooking the Mediterranean. During dinner the owner, hoping to make a friendly gesture, brought over a basket with a velvet cover and made a small ceremony of presenting them a vintage 6½-ounce bottle of Coke—"The original," as he proudly put it. Keough was struck anew by the veneration accorded the old product and the place of honor it occupied around the world. For the first time, he began to worry about the permanent damage the company might be doing to its goodwill if it continued to defy the wishes of its customers.

Not long afterward, Goizueta recalled, he and Keough were chatting in the private dining room next to Goizueta's office on the twenty-fifth floor of the Coca-Cola tower in Atlanta, "and I don't know how it came up—it could have been him who said it first, or it could've been me—but one of us said, 'Why should we be taking all this aggravation?' Really, that was the extent of the conversation. I don't know who said it: 'Let's just bring it back and call it Coca-Cola Classic.'"

Goizueta chuckled at the recollection, yet he found very little amusing in the consumer rebellion that raged around him at the time. The TV commercials for New Coke backfired, irritating viewers so much their scheduling had to be cut back. Articles appeared suggesting that the prime motive behind New Coke was to cut costs by using cheaper ingredients (including synthetic vanilla), which lent credence to accusations that the new product was some sort of counterfeit. One of the final straws was a letter that arrived asking for autographs from Goizueta and Keough, the "two dumbest executives" in America. When Brian Dyson and others at Coca-Cola USA argued for more time to establish the market for New Coke, Goizueta answered, "You're not the fellows who are being called names. I am." Even Goizueta's own father questioned his judgment, asking him, "What have you done?"

On July 11, 1985, Goizueta and Keough returned to the stage—this time without fanfare, in the auditorium of the Coca-Cola USA building in Atlanta—and announced the return of Coke Classic. Actually, the news had leaked the day before, when Peter Jennings of ABC News interrupted the soap opera "General Hospital" to break the story on national television. Headlines filled the front pages of newspapers across the country the next morning, heralding what company insiders called "the Second Coming."

Goizueta spoke first, telling consumers simply, "We have heard you." It was Keough who summoned the oratory that raised the occasion to a higher level:

> There is a twist to this story which will please every human-
> ist and will probably have the Harvard professors puzzling
> for years. The simple fact is that all the time and money and
> skill poured into consumer research on the new Coca-Cola
> could not measure or reveal the deep and abiding emotional
> attachment to original Coca-Cola felt by so many people. . . .
>
> The passion for original Coca-Cola—and that is the word
> for it: passion—was something that caught us by surprise. . . .
> *It is a wonderful* American mystery, a lovely American enigma,
> and you cannot measure it any more than you can measure
> love, pride, or patriotism.

Some might accuse the company of retreating, Keough continued. "How I love that! We love any retreat which has us rushing toward our best customers with the product they love most." Then, anticipating the question of the hour, he uttered his most memorable line of all: "Some critics will say Coca-Cola made a marketing mistake. Some cynics will say that we planned the whole thing. The truth is we are not that dumb and not that smart."

That day the company's hotline recorded 18,000 calls, and for the first time in two and a half months, they came from people who had kind words to say. "You would have thought," Ike Herbert said later, "we had invented a cure for cancer." Outside Goizueta's office, a small plane circled by trailing a banner that said, "Thank you, Roberto."

It was left to Sergio Zyman to poke a hole in the warm curtain of reverence that threatened to close the episode. A few days after the Classic Coke announcement, he breezed into a meeting at McCann-Erickson in New

York, where the agency's executives and creative types were still smarting from the heated disputes and bruising work that had gone into creating the advertising campaign for New Coke.

"Disregard all previous instructions," he said.

Recovery from the New Coke calamity did not occur overnight.

First came the ridicule. "Coke *Are* It!" cried the comedians. Roger Enrico, Pepsi's president, held a press conference to ask if his rival planned to start up a "Cola-of-the-Month Club," and wondered wickedly if the nation's grocery shelves would have enough space for New Coke, Coke Classic, new Diet Coke, old Diet Coke, new caffeine-free Coke, old caffeine-free Coke, new Tab, old Tab, caffeine-free diet Old Cherry Coke, and so forth.

The taunting raised a legitimate point. All along, Goizueta and his colleagues had been driven by the fear that Coca-Cola, their flagship product, would tumble out of first place as the nation's most popular soft drink, leaving Pepsi the winner. With New Coke and Coke Classic splitting the sugar cola category, that fate now appeared certain, and it provoked a complete about-face in corporate posture. After ninety-nine years of jealous insistence that the trademark "Coca-Cola" referred exclusively to one individual brand of soft drink—a "single thing coming from a single source," in Justice Holmes's famous phrase—the company now reversed position and declared that "Coca-Cola" was a "mega-brand," a broad designation covering all the soft drinks it manufactured.

In essence, the Coca-Cola Company tried to muddle the rules of competition. What mattered now, Goizueta and Keough decreed, was not how any one product fared in the soft drink market, but how *all* of a company's products fared together.

Naturally Pepsi cried foul. As 1985 drew to a close, market surveys showed Pepsi-Cola as the number one brand in the United States, ahead of New Coke and Coke Classic combined. Enrico set to work on a book with the triumphant title *The Other Guy Blinked: How Pepsi Won the Cola Wars*.

But the numbers revealed something else of far greater significance. Coca-Cola Classic was proving phenomenally popular. Against all expectations, Classic immediately began outselling New Coke, and much to everyone's surprise it kept right on rising until it overtook Pepsi again early in 1986. By the time the paperback version of Enrico's book came out, he'd renamed it *The Other Guy Blinked: Dispatches from the Cola Wars*. He no longer claimed victory.

Keough, straining to explain the craze over Coke Classic, told the *Wall Street Journal*, "It's kind of like the fellow who's been married to the same woman for 35 years and really didn't pay much attention to her until somebody started to flirt with her." It was a nice analogy, yet it glossed over the absolute bewilderment Keough and everyone else in the Coca-Cola tower felt over the outcome. No one could explain the renewed appeal of the old formula. New Coke was supposed to be the top cola, with Classic satisfying the demands of the traditionalists. Instead, New Coke pulled a disappearing act (shrinking quickly to a paltry 3 percent market share), while Classic began selling better than the original.

Teenagers, who had demonstrated the most enthusiasm for Pepsi's smoother, sweeter taste in blind tests, now displayed a preference for Classic. The company ran a separate ad campaign for New Coke aimed directly at youngsters—a series of arresting, postmodern TV commercials featuring a video-generated character named Max Headroom who exhorted viewers to "C-c-c-c-catch the Wave!"—and the logic-defying response was a boom for *old* Coke in the youth market.

Years later, still pondering what happened, Keough said he thought perhaps the psychological impact of Coke Classic's rebirth had been so powerful it actually altered people's tastes and revived the appeal of the celebrated "bite" in Coke. Other theories seemed equally plausible, among them the likelihood that the ad campaigns for Coke and Pepsi affected how people, especially young people, *thought* the two colas tasted. When Michael Jackson touted Pepsi as the "choice of a new generation," Pepsi's standing with teenagers soared, and then Max Headroom came along and made Coca-Cola seem hip again, all part of an ebb and flow that continues to this day. Another theory was that blind taste tests, by registering people's reactions after only a sip or two, reflected an undue preference for sweeter drinks.

One intriguing subplot involved Diet Coke. In 1983, the company began using aspartame, a new, vastly superior artificial sweetener in Diet Coke, and sales skyrocketed. Already successful, Diet Coke leapfrogged 7-Up to become the third best-selling soft drink in the country. With its smoother taste and high-quality sweetener, Diet Coke bore a close resemblance to New Coke, and as New Coke vanished the company's marketers began positioning Diet Coke as the "flanker" cola meant to appeal to Pepsi drinkers. Thus Diet Coke *became* New Coke, in a sense, and helped answer the need New Coke was supposed to meet.

Whatever the reasons, the company survived New Coke with surprising ease. The only lasting damage was to the egos and reputations of the men involved. Goizueta, already impatient with the media for their shoot-first criticism of the Columbia deal, still harbored feelings of anger and disdain years later, complaining that no one had ever reported the rationale for his decision (when, in fact, Thomas Oliver, an *Atlanta Journal-Constitution* business writer, had written a finely detailed, evenhanded book on the subject, *The Real Coke, the Real Story*). The business press, Goizueta said, unfairly accused the company of tampering with a highly successful product. "We changed the formula of a highly loved product," he argued, "but let's face it, it was losing market share for twenty years."

If he felt the media failed to appreciate his actions, at least Goizueta could take comfort in Wall Street's response. Even in the midst of the firestorm against New Coke, the company's stock price rose. Coca-Cola common closed at 84½ a share at the end of 1985, up more than a third for the year. In the early months of 1986, as the fallout from New Coke cleared away, the price shot all the way up to 117 ⅛, a record high. As he prepared to preside over the company's centennial celebration, in May 1986, Goizueta was also approaching his own fifth anniversary as CEO, and he could point with pride to a tripling in the value of the stock during his tenure.

In separate interviews eight years after the summer of New Coke, Goizueta and Keough both volunteered the same reason for the company's quick recovery from the fiasco: their careful cultivation of Wall Street's financial analysts and portfolio managers. Vowing never to repeat Fill Eisenberg's mistake of giving the investment community the cold shoulder, Goizueta and Keough held thirteen different meetings with representatives of some four hundred institutions during 1985, and they made a convincing case that they would do whatever was necessary to protect the interests of the shareholders.

It was a good thing they succeeded, too, because the next event in the company's storied history was the release of a blockbuster movie from Columbia Pictures called *Ishtar*.

Defying the odds that govern business disaster, the same people who thought up New Coke also produced one of the biggest flops in Hollywood history, a plodding desert comedy with Dustin Hoffman and Warren Beatty that earned back only a fraction of the $30 million-plus it cost to make.

Ishtar marked a symbolic turning point for Coca-Cola, the place in the road where the company reversed direction and headed back to its origins peddling soda pop. As a practical matter, of course, in a corporation with annual revenues of more than $7 billion, the losses on any single movie were a mere pittance. Columbia suffered a string of box-office failures in 1986 and 1987, yet the studio still made money syndicating reruns and distributing films and TV shows in association with various partners. After acquiring Merv Griffin Enterprises in 1985, Columbia also gained a steady stream of impressive revenues from the game shows "Jeopardy!" and "Wheel of Fortune."

The problem, in Goizueta's view, was the inordinate amount of attention drawn to the movie end of the business. Financial reporters, already in Goizueta's doghouse, irritated him anew by harping on the poor performance of Columbia's films and ignoring the studio's strength in other areas. "I don't know how many times we told them that [Columbia's earnings] were growing faster than any segment of our business," he complained, "but by God, *Ishtar* didn't make money, so it must have been a lousy business."

As it grew, the studio put more and more of a strain on management in Atlanta. Every aspect of the film business was monumentally complicated, and Goizueta concluded that Columbia had grown too big and time-consuming to remain under the parent company's umbrella. In a sophisticated refinancing maneuver in 1987, Coca-Cola bundled its movie and TV properties together into Columbia Pictures Entertainment and sold off 51 percent for about $1.5 billion. Two years later, post-*Ishtar*, Japan's Sony Corporation bought the other 49 percent for another $1.5 billion, extricating the Coca-Cola Company from its troublesome show business venture while yielding a tidy windfall of more than $1 billion. "HOLLYWOOD ENDING," declared a *Wall Street Journal* headline.

Goizueta moved to restore simplicity to Coca-Cola's affairs. By his own admission, he and Keough and their lieutenants "took our eye off the ball" while diversifying during the first half of the 1980s. Now they rededicated themselves to the job they knew best, selling soft drinks around the globe.

There was more to the shift than a chastened management pulling in its horns and giving up adventurism after a spate of bad decisions and bad luck. The soft drink business itself has changed, presenting new opportunities. The dollar began to weaken against foreign currencies, making overseas sales highly profitable once again. And the company now had far greater control over its bottlers, through part ownership and other means, so that more of the profits came back to Atlanta.

A few simple truths reanimated the Coca-Cola Company. Fully 95 percent of the world's population, five billion people, lived outside the United States. Unlike Americans, they were a largely untapped audience. "When I think of Indonesia," Keough liked to say, "a country on the Equator, with 180 million people, a median age of eighteen, and a Moslem ban on alcohol, I feel I know what heaven looks like." China, which opened its doors to Coca-Cola in 1979, had a billion people and a per capita consumption of one—one lone soft drink a year. In America, on average, every man, woman, and child gulped down three hundred servings a year. That made the United States a $46 billion market, one Coca-Cola and Pepsi would try forever to divide and conquer. But in the meantime, if Coca-Cola could boost per capita consumption around the rest of the planet even a little, there were billions of dollars to be made.

In many instances, the company's new crusade in the global marketplace was carried out using old-fashioned methods Asa Candler would have recognized. In Bordeaux, France, a stubborn piece of turf where Coca-Cola had never caught on, a team of fresh-faced salesmen and saleswomen in bright red jackets hit the streets in the autumn of 1988 and plastered 35,000 Coca-Cola stickers on every outdoor surface they could find, then gave away thousands of cups of Coke in a sampling campaign much like the ones Candler's nephews ran before the turn of the century.

Elsewhere the company tried futuristic approaches. In Japan, where consumers were accustomed to buying a wide variety of goods from vending machines, Coca-Cola installed hundreds of thousands of state-of-the-art automated dispensers, an average of two for every square kilometer in the country, some of them equipped to take credit cards, and collared an amazing 85 percent share of the soft drink market.

When the Berlin Wall collapsed in 1990, the company rushed into East Germany, where a consumer survey showed 99 percent of the people still knew the name Coca-Cola, even though the product had not been for sale there since World War II. As the Soviet Union broke apart, Goizueta and Keough opened new plants throughout the newly capitalist nations of Eastern Europe, finding that Coca-Cola was welcomed both as a source of cash and a symbol of Western freedoms. In Warsaw, a crowd broke into spontaneous applause at the sight of a Coke delivery truck coming down the street.

Guided by the policy "think globally, act locally," the company tried to tailor its production and marketing practices to the indigenous cultures everywhere it operated. When the 1996 Summer Olympics were awarded to Atlanta, a reporter asked Keough if he was excited about having the Games come to the company's backyard, and he responded gently, "We have a very large backyard."*

Almost everywhere, the renewed emphasis on international sales bore spectacular results. As ever, the company's soft drinks were distributed mostly by truck—only now the vehicles in the system numbered more than 100,000, by far the largest commercial fleet in the world. The "gee-whizzers," the statistics Coca-Cola people loved to toss out to illustrate the immense size of their business, grew even more breathtaking. By 1994, the company and its bottlers had 650,000 employees on the payroll, and they were selling more than 685 million soft drinks a day. If all the Coke ever produced were placed in traditional 6½-ounce hoopskirt bottles, the public relations department calculated, two and a half *trillion* bottles would be filled, and those bottles, laid end to end, would reach around the globe at the Equator 12,000 times (or a third of the way to Saturn).

The money was just as impressive. The run-up in the price of Coca-Cola common stock, fueled by Wall Street's rekindled confidence in Goizueta's and Keough's stewardship, created a new order of wealth that simply overwhelmed the legacy of the Woodruff era. The stock was split, split again, and then a third time, and still the price went up, until the value of the company reached $56 billion in the early 1990s, up *fourteen times* over its worth in 1980. Coca-Cola became the sixth most valuable public corporation in the country.

At Emory University and Trust Company of Georgia, old holdings of Coca-Cola stock swelled in value to more than a billion dollars each. One of the bank's directors told a friend, "Our dumbness in not being smart enough to diversify has been the smartest thing any dumb people ever did."

---

* Disappointed suitors from the other bid cities accused the company of collusion, but company officials made a strong case that having the Games in Atlanta would be as much a nuisance as an opportunity. When Atlanta's Olympic mascot, "Whatizit," was unveiled at the end of the 1992 Summer Games in Barcelona, Coke executives were shocked at its primary color—Pepsi blue.

Woodruff's personal fortune was converted into a foundation by the terms of his will, and the endowment grew to $1.5 billion, the tenth largest in the nation. In a satisfying completion to his life's labors, Joe Jones became chairman of the Woodruff Foundation and continued the benefactions of his old boss. The cumulative contributions of the Woodruff and Whitehead family philanthropies reached the $900 million mark.

All told, Georgians held 17 percent of the Coca-Cola Company's equity, worth almost $10 billion. Someone who'd bought a single share of common stock from Ernest Woodruff for $40 in 1919 now held a piece of paper worth $102,000. If he'd reinvested all the dividends over the years by buying more stock, his original stake would have grown to more than $2 million. Latecomers did well, too. Warren Buffett, the famed investor from Omaha, Nebraska (who had a five-Cherry-Cokes-a-day habit), began buying Coca-Cola stock in 1989 and saw his $1 billion investment quadruple in value to $4 billion in three short years. By the year 2020, Buffett predicted, Coca-Cola would be the most valuable company in the United States.

As he prepared for the company's annual meeting in Atlanta in April 1992, Goizueta was deeply concerned about a potential shareholder protest over the size of his own executive compensation package. Three years earlier, when the price of stock was considerably lower, the shareholders had agreed to give him one million shares if he stayed on as CEO until his scheduled retirement in 1996. It was a very generous award—vastly more than the stock options given to Paul Austin in his time—and suddenly those shares had skyrocketed in value to *$83 million*. Some headline writers made him sound like a plunderer.

Yet on the day of the meeting, there was not a single peep of criticism from the four thousand shareholders gathered in the audience, for the plain and simple reason that Goizueta had made all of them rich, too.

In March 1991, Wayne Calloway, the chairman of PepsiCo, was inducted into the National Sales Hall of Fame. In his speech, he described a dream he'd had the night before. He found himself wandering the sands of Iraq, he said, where he came, upon General Norman Schwarzkopf, the hero of Desert Storm, carrying a Diet Pepsi in his hand. Then Schwarzkopf faded away and Saddam Hussein appeared, drinking a Coke.

Obviously, the Cola Wars were showing no signs of cooling off. One of the Coca-Cola Company's great victories in the aftermath of New Coke was the "mega-brand" concept. Roger Enrico joked that the proliferation of splinter Coca-Cola brands would choke the nation's supermarket shelves—and that was exactly what happened. Along came caffeine-free Coke, caffeine-free Diet Coke, diet Cherry Coke, diet Sprite, Lymon, Mello Yello, Mr PiBB, Fresca, and diet Fanta, a cascade of new soft drinks that crowded other manufacturers out.

Only Pepsi had the muscle to compete, and the two giants of the soft drink industry soon had the shelves almost entirely to themselves. Through rebates and discounts (and one or two instances of outright price-fixing), Coke and Pepsi bottlers gained a sort of dual monopoly on space in the soft drink sections of convenience stores and supermarket chains across the United States. Royal Crown, their closest pursuer in the sugar cola category, clung to a tiny market share of only 3 percent.

Just as the Coca-Cola Company wished, the beverage industry embraced total soft drink sales as the standard measure of performance. With 41 percent of the overall U.S. market, Coca-Cola's brands outsold Pepsi's by eight points, a comfortable margin that held steady into the mid-1990s.

In the glow of Coke Classic's inexplicable success, Keough and Ike Herbert, the company's top marketing executive, tried to rethink the whole question of advertising. They were spending several hundred million dollars a year on TV commercials, but somehow that did not seem to be enough. For the price of two primetime spots on NBC, Keough figured, the company could buy exclusive rights to serve Coke in a hotel chain, and over the course of a year the population of guests who saw Coke's display ads would be the equivalent of a good-size city.

To Herbert, the key word was presence. Coca-Cola had to be a physical part of people's lives, not just an evanescent name that flashed by on the TV screen. At home and abroad, from the Academy Awards to the World Cup, Coca-Cola had to be seen as a participant in special events. In amusement venues from Walt Disney World to the San Diego Zoo, it had to play an integral role in the activities. The company's long-standing concession to serve soft drinks at the Olympics became a license to fly blimps, install huge inflated Coke cans atop buildings, paint benches Coca-Cola red, and stick Coca-Cola umbrellas over the tables at snack bars and cafes throughout a host city. By the last decade of the twentieth century, it was difficult to attend a sporting event or a circus or a festival anywhere in the world without finding Coca-Cola in the sightlines.

Naturally there was no ignoring the air war on TV with Pepsi. In a memorably fey commercial, Pepsi showed the rap star M. C. Hammer sipping a Coke and breaking into a lugubrious rendition of the lounge song "Feelings." That, along with Ray Charles's spirited ditty, "You got the right one, baby, *uh-huh*," revived Pepsi's generational appeal and frightened Coca-Cola into shaking up its forty-year-old relationship with McCann-Erickson. In 1992, Michael Ovitz, the powerful Hollywood agent, took over the creative reins and scored a critical success with "Always, Coca-Cola," a campaign best known for a spot in which a group of polar bears watched the Northern lights together while sipping Cokes.

As in any hundred-years' war, the fortunes of the two soft drink rivals surged back and forth, attracting intense interest from Wall Street and the financial press. Don Keough retired in the spring of 1993, leaving the Coca-Cola presidency vacant, and a financial wizard named Doug Ivester, the architect of the company's restructuring strategy, emerged as his likely successor. Sergio Zyman, who left the Coca-Cola Company in the wake of New Coke, returned in the summer of 1993—"he has reformulated himself," Goizueta explained—sparking speculation that Coke's marketing would take another turn and find a new direction. Two new products, Fruitopia and OK Soda, were introduced in 1994.

As for Goizueta, he remained in firm command of the company, and the future looked bright enough to him that he predicted another tenfold growth in stock values by the year 2000.

Coca-Cola's unique place as the most American thing in America continued, undiminished by New Coke or any of the other buffeting winds of the 1990s.

The *idea* of Coca-Cola, for so long an elusive entity that had existed separate and apart from the soft drink itself, became more tangible. The company built an attraction in downtown Atlanta called the World of Coca-Cola, a museum and arcade with an old-fashioned soda fountain and a display of futuristic vending machines, which began drawing paying visitors at the rate of a million a year (at $2.50 apiece for adults and $1.50 for children). In New York, the company opened a retail store on Fifth Avenue to sell Coca-Cola souvenirs and memorabilia. More than 3,000 people swarmed in on opening day to look over items that ranged from postcards for 75 cents to a neon sign for $6,000. A fast-growing Coca-Cola collectors' club claimed 6,700 members in 23 countries.

At times it was hard to make sense of people's thinking about Coca-Cola. Buying antique trays and lamps was one thing, but now they began spending their hard-earned money on brand-new promotional gimcrackery as well, the sort of clutter Asa Candler once labored to give away. Ordinarily sensible men and women walked around in Coca-Cola clothes, looking like moving billboards, and paid for the privilege of doing so. By placing a price tag on the appeal of the trademark, it seemed, the company might be running the risk of undermining the century-old goodwill of Coca-Cola's good name.

Yet if one felt a nip of derision coming on, there was another side of Coca-Cola's mystique to contemplate, too. Earl Leonard, the company's top lobbyist, a fellow little given to soft sentiment, pulled out a letter one day to show a visitor. A father had written to describe his child's battle with cancer. The little girl had undergone extensive chemotherapy, losing all her hair. She was embarrassed by her appearance, and other children had laughed at her, until her father had the inspiration of giving her a bicycle helmet embossed with Coca-Cola's familiar trademark. For some reason the father couldn't explain, his daughter felt normal when she ventured out in public wearing the helmet, and she was treated normally wherever she went. It was as if the name Coca-Cola simply could not appear where something was wrong.

In her novel *The Blessing*, written in 1951, Nancy Mitford had a character speak of Coca-Cola using the language of Moslem mysticism, with its legend of the djinn, or genie: "When I say a bottle of Coca-Cola," Mitford wrote, "I mean it metaphorically speaking, I mean it as an outward and visible sign of something inward and spiritual, I mean it as if each Coca-Cola bottle contained a djinn, and as if that djinn was our great American civilization ready to spring out of each bottle and cover the whole global universe with its great wide wings. . . ."

Nearly half a century later, Coca-Cola remained the same: a simple drink of sugar and water, with a name that transcended the commerce of the marketplace and held the power to conjure memories and stir emotions and affect the human heart.

IMAGE GALLERY

Doc Pemberton (*left*) invented the syrup, but his partner, Frank Robinson (*right*) gave Coca-Cola its most valuable asset—its name. They served their new drink for the first time at a soda fountain in Jacobs' Pharmacy in Atlanta (*below*) in 1886.

Asa Candler with his wife and five children. His eldest son, Howard, is at top center.

Candler took control of Coca-Cola and in 1899 opened a new factory, which he called "sufficient for all our needs for all time to come." The company's entire workforce could fit on the front steps.

Promotions, including a tray featuring opera singer Lillian Nordica (*left*), and give-away items like those clogging the company's New York office (*right*) drove sales up so fast Coca-Cola had to move into a bigger home just ten years later.

The dawn of the automobile age and the advent of general circulation magazines gave rise to a new generation of Coca-Cola ads typified by the motoring party in the *Saturday Evening Post* of August 8, 1905. The promise that Coke would "quicken the tired brain" harkened back to the patent medicine era.

Asa Candler's ambitious nephew, Samuel Dobbs (*left*), took charge of advertising in 1906, and gave the account to William C. D'Arcy (*right*), whose appreciation of sex appeal led to the creation of an early bathing beauty poster in 1914 (*below*).

The earliest of this series of Coca-Cola bottles (*above*), the wire-and-loop Hutchinson stopper, left, was unsanitary and often exploded, forcing bottlers (*below*) to wear masks. The invention of the bottle cap improved the product and led to sudden prosperity.

The Coca-Cola bottlers held their first convention, complete with a "Joke Contest," in Atlanta in 1909.

Coca-Cola's lawyer, Harold Hirsch, urged development of the distinctive hoopskirt bottle in 1915.

Independent bottlers in Knoxville (*above*) and across the country gained even greater wealth, provoking sharp tensions with fountain salesmen (*below*) and other employees of the home office.

Asa Candler (*left*) gave the Coca-Cola Company to his children, who sold it in 1919 to a group of investors secretly headed by Ernest Woodruff (*right*), a man Candler detested. After fighting the Candler family and the bottlers for four years, Woodruff gave the presidency of the company to his son, Robert, who would run it for the next half century.

Robert, age 2 ½ (*top left*), grew up to be a poor student who barely paused on his way from the Georgia Military Academy (*top center*) to a job shoveling sand in a foundry (*top right*). He settled down after marrying Nell Hodgson (*bottom left*) in 1912, but still found time to hang out with his friend Ty Cobb (*below*) at New York's Polo Grounds.

Robert Woodruff in 1923, the year he took over as president of the Coca-Cola Company.

Woodruff gave the advertising account to Archie Lee (*left*), who created the "Ritz Boy" billboard (*bottom*).

Lee tapped into people's desire for a "Pause That Refreshes" at work (*left*), and urged a weary populace to cheer up during the Depression (*center*), while Norman Rockwell's art associated Coke with America's rural innocence (*right*).

Some of Coca-Cola's ideas, like Haddon Sundblom's Santa Claus, were wildly popular.

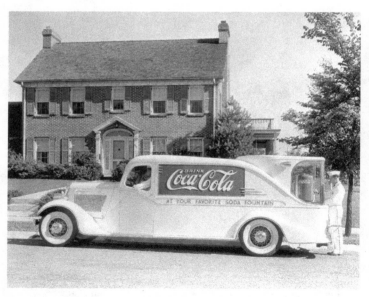

Others, like the "home sampling" van of 1934, flopped.

The company built a spectacular soda fountain at the Chicago World's Fair of 1933.

Harrison Jones, holding Woodruff in a headlock, was the company's outgoing "Mr. Outside." But Woodruff actually relied on Ralph Hayes (*center*) and John Sibley (*right*) as his top lieutenants. Belying his meek appearance (outfitted here for a day at Woodruff's plantation in 1936), Sibley was a combative lawyer who tried to destroy Coca-Cola's competitors, notably Pepsi, in court.

Coke was popular in Havana (*top left*) from the turn of the century. But elsewhere, despite determined sales efforts in China (*bottom left*) and Holland (*middle*), the American soft drink was slow to catch on.

As World War II approached, the company's only widespread success was in Nazi Germany.

Woodruff visited London in 1938 and asked German manager Max
Keith to look after Coca-Cola's interests during the impending
hostilities.

The company's ads created images that fused Coke with the American war effort.

Coca-Cola officials persuaded Winston Churchill's daughter Mary (*left*) to christen a bomber with a bottle of the soft drink, but there was nothing staged about the deep affection GIs felt for Coke in the foxholes (*below*).

Postwar innovations included serving Coke on airliners. But sticking to the nickel price and small bottle hurt the company in the marketplace.

Two of Woodruff's show business friends, bandleader Xavier Cugat and "the Oomph Girl," actress Ann Sheridan, posed with a bottle of Coke in the Starlight Room of the Waldorf-Astoria.

Enlisting the pigeons of Venice to advertise Coca-Cola in the Piazza San Marco (*above*) and lining up a fleet of trucks in front of the Colosseum in Rome (*below*), the company offended European sensibilities and provoked the French parliament to try outlawing the American soft drink.

Prince Alexander Makinsky took charge of the company's defenses.

Woodruff was happiest at his plantation, Ichauway, with his wife, Nell (*above left*), or napping after lunch with close friend Bobby Jones, the golfer (*below left*). Woodruff loved quail hunting (*above*), but he also used the plantation to cultivate important alliances.

He shared a Coke with soon-to-be-president Eisenhower in 1950.

Journalist Ralph McGill, left, and ventrilo-quist Edgar Bergen (who endorsed Coke on radio) were among the celebrities to come to the plantation for a turkey hunt.

Woodruff sometimes wept listening to gospel songs by the Ichauway choir, led by a Mattie Heard, the cook.

His chauffeur, Lawrence Calhoun, kept a small savings account for Woodruff in case he went broke giving away money.

This scene from the fields, where a handler named Julian held three pointers, could have come from a century before.

Woodruff and his close friend, Atlanta Mayor William Harsfield, left, had practical reasons for encouraging progressive race relations.

Hartsfield integrated the city's police department and won black support at the ballot box. Coca-Cola had millions of American blacks as customers.

Coca-Cola president Lee Talley urged his employees to practice racial moderation. Company officials supported the 1964 dinner in honor of Martin Luther King Jr.'s Nobel Peace Prize. Coretta Scott King and Mayor Ivan Allen Jr., Hartsfield's successor, sat next to King.

Woodruff opposed the political aspirations of Lester Maddox, who is pictured with his son, Lester Jr., chasing the Rev. Albert Dunn away from his restaurant, the Pickrick. Note the pistol in Maddox's hand.

Maddox won the Georgia governor's race in 1966 after an arrest sparked a riot in Atlanta's Summerhill neighborhood.

Vice President Richard Nixon showed his loyalty to Coke at a 1958 picnic. But, when the company spurned his request for a job in 1963, he went to work as a lawyer for Pepsi.

Lyndon Johnson responded by making Coke a Democratic drink. Later, as president, Nixon arranged Pepsi's entry into the Soviet Union.

At home and abroad, Coca-Cola aimed its pitch at teenagers. The bottler in Boston sponsored a Hi-Fi Club hop.

Japanese lanterns decorated a dance in Japan in 1962.

Nothing delighted company officials more than a celebrity endorsement, and in the 1960s no one was hotter than the Beatles.

Paul Austin, right, gained Woodruff's confidence and became president of Coca-Cola in 1962.

Woodruff spoke at Lee Talley's retirement dinner in 1966. Talley, left, stepped down as chairman, pleading exhaustion after relentless fighting with Austin in the executive suite. Woodruff then promoted Austin, right, to chairman and CEO.

Under Austin's guidance in the late 1960s and early 1970s, Coca-Cola captured the mood of the times with a gentle tune, "I'd Like to Teach the World to Sing" (*above*), and marketed bellbottom beach pants embossed with the company's new slogan, "It's the Real Thing" (*below*).

In 1979, after years of personal diplomacy, Austin finally succeeded in returning Coke to China.

Woodruff remained vital into his eighties. As a widower, he enjoyed the social companionship of Martha Ellis.

But by 1978, Woodruff had turned eighty-eight and was debilitated by age. He and Austin, left, who suffered undiagnosed cases of Parkinson's and Alzheimer's diseases, clashed bitterly over business issues and the question of Austin's successor.

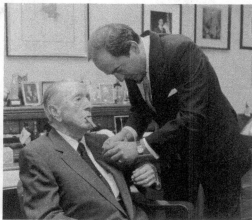

' Woodruff's longtime chief of staff, Joseph Jones (*left*), maneuvered to make Roberto Goizueta (*right*, giving Woodruff a sixty-year service pin in 1983) the company's new boss.

Goizueta and Don Keough survived the New Coke fiasco and later opened the World of Coca-Cola.

Coca-Cola's advertising continued to capture the public's fancy into the 1990s, with whimsical TV commercials that depicted animated polar bears enjoying the pause that refreshes. But the idea was not new.

Unbeknown to the company's creative team, an artist had conjured up the very same image in Paris in the 1920s, giving an unintended boost to the slogan "Always, Coca-Cola."

NOTES

Abbreviations Used In Notes

CC	Coca-Cola Company
CCA	Coca-Cola Archives
RWP	Robert W. Woodruff Papers
ESC	Emory Special Collections
RHP	Ralph Hayes Papers
ACP	Asa Candler Papers
AHC	Atlanta History Center
HSP	Hughes Spalding Papers
EL	Eisenhower Library
NYT	*New York Times*
AP	Associated Press
AC	*Atlanta Constitution*
AJ	*Atlanta Journal*
AJC	*Atlanta Journal-Constitution*
UP	United Press
UPI	United Press International
WSJ	*Wall Street Journal*
int	Interview by author
int/CCA	interview in Coca-Cola Archives
RWW	Robert W. Woodruff
EW	Ernest Woodruff
JJ	Joseph W Jones
HS	Hughes Spalding

LEGAL CASES CITED IN NOTES

Bottling—The Coca-Cola Bottling Co. v. *The Coca-Cola Company,* Fulton County Superior Court, 1920. Also, *The Coca-Cola Bottling Co.* v. *The Coca-Cola Co.,* U.S. District Court, Delaware, 1920. (*The Bottling* case records were made available to the author by the Atlanta law firm of Sutherland, Asbill & Brennan. Except as noted below, other case records are from the Coca-Cola Archives.)

Chattanooga or *40 Barrels—United States* v. *Forty Barrels and Twenty Kegs of Coca-Cola,* 241 U.S. 265, 289. (Record of appeal from the Federal Records Center, East Point, Ga.)

Chero-Cola—The Coca-Cola Company v. *Chero-Cola Company,* 273 F. 755, D.C. Circuit. [1921.]

Diet Coke—Coca-Cola Bottling Co. of Shreveport, Inc., et al. v. *The Coca-Cola Company.* (More than a dozen judicial opinions were published in connection with this and a related case, *Coca-Cola Bottling Co. of Elizabethtown, Inc., et al.* v. *The Coca-Cola Company,* also known as the *E-town* case.)

Dixi-Cola—Dixi-Cola Laboratories, Inc., et al. v. *The Coca-Cola Company,* 117 Fed. (2d) 352.

Koke—The Coca-Cola Co. v. *Koke Company of America,* 254 U.S. 143, 41 Sup. Ct 113. [1920.]

Loft—The Coca-Cola Company v. *Loft, Inc.* and *The Coca-Cola Company* v. *Happiness Candy Stores, Inc.,* 167 A. 900. [1933.]

Nashville—Nashville Syrup Co. v. *The Coca-Cola Company,* 215 F. 527, 6th Circuit [1914.] (Federal Records Center, East Point, Ga.)

Pepsi—Coca-Cola Company of Canada, Ltd. v. *Pepsi-Cola Company of Canada, Ltd.,* 1938 Ex. C.R. 263, Court of the Exchequer, Ottawa, Canada; 1940 S.C.R., 1942 All E.R. 615.

RC Cola—The Coca-Cola Co. v. *Nehi Corp.,* 25 Atl. (2d) 364.

Roxa-Kola—Coca-Cola Co. v. *Carlisle Bottling Works,* 43 Fed. (2d) 119, 6th Circuit, 1930. Cert. denied 282 U.S. 882.

Rucker—Henry A. Rucker (Collector of Internal Revenue) v. *The Coca-Cola Company,* U.S. Circuit Court, District of Georgia. (Trial and Appeal Record, Federal Records Center, East Point, Ga.)

Taka-Kola—.Coca-Cola Company v. *Old Dominion Beverage Corp.,* 271 Fed. 600, 4th Circuit, 1921. Cert denied, 256 U.S. 703, 41 Sup. Ct. 624.

INTRODUCTION: RED SCARE

Description, background of Makinsky: Memo, Phil Mooney to Bill Pruett, 8/28/79; H. Burke Nicholson, Jr., and Don Sisler ints, both 8/16/91, in bio file, CCA. Dinner party: Kahn, *Big Drink,* p. 27. Makinsky holding court Sisler int. Coalition of Communists: Minutes, French National Assembly, 12/1/49, translated in CCA. (A scholarly analysis of the French political landscape appears in *Seducing the French,* by Richard F. Kuisel, University of California Press, 1993.) Details of the Coca-Cola Company's internal handling of the situation are from a file of correspondence kept by Stephen Ladas and made available to the author by the company.

Makinsky worried: Memo, Makinsky to Talley, 1/17/50. Five investigations: Letter, Makinsky to Ladas, 2/7/50. Secret Police surveillance and dossiers: Letter, Talley to Ladas, 3/5/50. Lawyer afraid: Memo, Makinsky to Talley, 12/12/49. Chilling incident: Alfredo Schvab int. "Imminent peril": Letter, Makinsky to Ladas, 2/7/50.

Pope Brock description: Wells, *First Hundred Years*, p. 149, photo, p. 159. Field man in Colombia: Duffield memoirs, CCA. Foreign income and profits: *Advertising Age*, 10/17/55; memo, Austin to RWW, 4/17/73, RWP. "Alarm" at Coca-Cola Export: Letter, Brock to Ladas, 2/3/50. Brock's temperament and dislike of Curtis: Confidential source. Brock rallying company officials and sending Ladas to Paris: Letter, Brock to Ladas, 2/13/50. Description of Ladas: Sisler int. Description of transatlantic flight: Nicholson int. Ladas's mood and actions in Paris: Letter, Ladas to Brock, 2/24/50. Rolland's request: Memo, Rolland to Ladas, 3/11/50.

Fadayev's speech in Rome: AP, Rome, 10/30/49; *New York Herald Tribune*, 3/2/50. Widespread European resistance to American products: *The Sphere*, London, 3/25/50. Story and headline in *L'Unita* described in *Time*, 8/22/49. Hungarian magazine described in *Newsweek*, 11/28/49. "Cocacoliques": NYT, 3/1/50. Vienna beating: Article, *Top Secret* magazine, undated, RWP. Seething at Chiclets: *Le Monde*, 12/30/49. Swiss newspaper editor: *Pittsburgh Post-Gazette*, 10/17/49. Barge in Venice: *Time*, 8/22/49. Quote from *Le Monde*: *The New Yorker*, 1/11/50.

List of Asa Candler's giveaway items: Munsey; Garrett essay, 2/14/57, CCA; Coca-Cola *Bottler*, Apr. 1959. "Most American thing . . .": Hayes, RWW birthday speech, 12/6/49. Sundblom Santa: *Chicago Tribune* magazine, 12/21/69; *Insight* (D'Arcy publication), Dec. 1980. "World's friendliest club": 1946 ad, cited by Garrett, 2/14/57 manuscript, CCA. For details of Coca-Cola's participation in World War II, see chapter 7 notes. Requisition for Tokyo: U.S. Navy order, 6/6/45, CCA.

Scott: Cited in Bell Papers. "United Taste": Handwritten memo, unidentified but probably coined by Steve Hannagan, Coca-Cola's publicist, ca. 1950, RWP.

Ladas's meeting with Bruce: Letter, Ladas to Brock, 2/24/50. Bruce's actions of Dec. 1949: Letter, Ladas to Fred Morrison, 12/2/49; NYT, 12/30/49. French scientists' belief Coca-Cola was aphrodisiac: Memo, Prof. E. J. Bigwood, 6/2/50, CCA. Laws against phosphoric acid: Order, Tribunal of the Seine, 3/31/41; decree by Judge M. L. Crenn, 11/19/42. Belgium: Letter, Makinsky to Carl West, 9/16/52. "Swiss formula" and "smoke screen" quote: Letter, Brock to Ladas, 2/3/50. Makinsky advocated pretending to be "shocked": Letter to Ladas, 1/21/50.

Ladas's argument to Bruce: Letter presented to Bruce at meeting, 2/23/50. A good overview of the U.S. Embassy's negotiations with France is found in *Foreign Relations of the United States*, 1950, State Department, U.S. Government Printing Office, Washington; also described in memo, Makinsky to Ladas, 2/7/50. Bruce "too much" a diplomat: Letter, Ladas to Brock, 2/24/50. "Slippery": *Ibid.* Boulet bill on agenda, "frantic" efforts: Letter, Ladas to Brock, 3/6/50. Schneiter: Minutes, National Assembly, CCA.

Hannagan's retainer: JJ int; *Time*, 7/30/45. Business conditions at CC: See chapter 8 notes. News appeared next morning: NYT, 3/1/50. (Except as noted, news clips are from three scrapbooks titled "The French Problem, Publicity," CCA.) AP: 2/28/50. "Coca-Colamity": *New York Herald Tribune*, 3/2/50. "Superior French habit": *Washington News*, 3/2/50. Cut off aid: New York *Daily News*, 3/2/50.

Sevareid: Text, 3/1/50 commentary, WCBS. Morgan: Text, WNBC broadcast, undated but 3/1 or 3/2/50, CCA. Farley background: Oral history, 10/18/75, CCA.

Farley statement Text, CCA. Farley on TV: Transcript, CBS, 7/28/50. CC's name more popular than Stalin's: Report, Leo Dolan to Hannagan, 8/14/52, RWP. Ed Sullivan: New York *Daily News*, 3/4/50. Billy Rose column: Text, CCA. (417 newspapers: Clippings collected in "Publicity" scrapbooks.)

French embassy complained: Press release, CCA. Bonnet ushered Farley and Curtis into office: Letter, Farley to Bonnet, 3/24/50. Ladas answered Rolland: Letter to Rolland, 3/16/50. Communists stormed rostrum, cried out AR 3/3/50.

Judge took two-month honeymoon: Letter, Talley to Ladas, 3/7/50. Bonnet invited Farley back: Memo, Ladas to file, 3/25/50. Farley made appeal: Press release, 6/15/50. Deal with Louis Descamps: Memo, Curtis to RWW, 11/28/50, RWP.

Oehlert and Kamel: Letter, Oehlert to Vernon G. Hoppers, undated but 1966, RWP. New Coke background is taken from Oliver, *The Real Coke, the Real Story*. "Organoleptic properties": Preclusion order, *Diet Coke IV*, p. 375. A dozen alterations: *Diet Coke I*, 563 F. Supp. 1122, p. 1131.

ONE: STIRRINGS

Description of Pemberton: Photo and oil portrait, CCA. For general background on Pemberton, the author is indebted to Monroe King, an Atlanta historian who maintains an extensive collection of documents known as the Pemberton Archives. Forty-gallon kettle: Deposition of Sam Dobbs, 7/27/14, Examiner of Interferences, *Koke* case, CCA. Frank Robinson description: Photo and portrait, CCA; Cecil Stockard, Jr., Frank M. Robinson (II) ints.

Pemberton paid for license: Catalog, Southern Botanic-Medical College; article, "The History of Education in Monroe County," T. E. Smith, 1934, Pemberton Archives. Thomson's theories, indictment for murder: *Reform Medical Practice*, M. S. Thomson, Georgia Telegraph Steam Power Press, 1857, Pemberton Archives.

Pemberton settled in Columbus, married: Monograph, Mrs. Mercer (Ernestine) Sherman (Pemberton's great-niece), 1947, RWP; AC, 8/19/69. Opened business: *Columbus Directory*, 1859-1860, CCA. Old ad: CCA. Borrowed $10,000: Article by Mrs. J. S. Newman (Pemberton's sister-in-law), *Confederate Veteran* magazine, July 1929, CCA. "No chemist": Affidavit, Sherman quoting C. L. Newman, 9/13/51, CCA.

Pemberton in Civil War: King int; Sherman monograph; "List of Field Officers, Regiments and Battalions in the Confederate States Army, 1861-1865," Pemberton Archives. Sold nutmeg: King int. Conditions in postwar South, three *Ms*: Savitt and Young, pp. 162-63. Stadiger's Aurantii, Dr. Dye's Voltaic Belt Ads, AJ, May 1885.

Pemberton moved to Atlanta: *Dictionary of Georgia Biography*, vol. II, p. 785. (The year is given as 1869 in AC, 8/19/1969.) Description of Atlanta: Garrett, *Atlanta and Environs*, vol. I. City Code: *Ibid.*, p. 850. Opera House completed: *Ibid.*, p. 840. Atlanta as center of commerce: *Ibid.*, pp. 828-29. Kimball House: AC, 10/18/1870. Pemberton ended up at Kimball House: H. Candler, *Asa Griggs Candler*, p. 63. Pemberton's inventions: Letterhead, Pemberton Chemical Co., 7/13/1887, CCA.

Pemberton gained prominence, served on board, had "pleasant, benign face": AC, 4/18/1886. Could not be trusted: *A. F. Merrill v. John S. Pemberton*, 1875, Circuit Court, Atlanta, Case 777, Box 16, Federal Records Center, East Point, Ga. Other suits, Pemberton's business practices and health: King int. "A sense of increased intelligence": Text, Pemberton speech, Georgia Pharmaceutical Association, Apr. 1887, CCA.

Grant bit into peach: Julia Dent Grant, *Personal Memoirs*, p. 329. Grant's lingering death: Articles, AJ, 3/3/1885 and several others in Mar. 1885. Enterprising reporter: McFeely, *Grant*, p. 509. Grant moved to Mount McGregor: *Ibid.*, p. 507, and photo, p. 516. Grant dribbled soup: UP, 3/22/1885. Newspaper called it "cocoacine": AJ, 3/9/1885.

Mariani provided cocaine: Booklet, *Coca and Its Therapeutic Application*, by Angelo Mariani, published by J. N. Jaros, NY, 1890, CCA. Mariani began promoting coca in 1871: Article, "Vin Mariani," *Pharmacy in History*, by William Helfand, vol. 22, no. 1, 1980. Endorsements: Book, *Portraits from Album Mariani*, Mariani & Company, 1893, CCA. Footnote: *Ibid.* Mariani's formula was 1/10 grain: *Collier's*, 6/8/1907. Dosage of three glasses, 22 proof: Helfand.

Parke Davis: Musto, p. 7. Pemberton created French Wine of Coca: Ad, AJ, 3/10/1885. Pemberton "followed...French formula": Article, AJ, 3/10/1885. (Newspapers often ran an interview to accompany paid advertising. The ad and story appeared during the same month the *Journal* was carrying lengthy reports on Grant's suffering.)

Pemberton set up at 59 South Broad: AJ, 3/10/1885. Sold flint bottles for $1 apiece: Ad, Talbot County, 1884, CCA. Pemberton sold 888 one day: King int. Needed fresh capital, moved into Holland house: Unpublished memoir, George Lowndes, Nov. 1929, CCA. "Old rookery": Dobbs deposition, *Koke* case. Description of Pemberton setup: Sherman monograph, quoting Pemberton's nephew.

Background of Robinson and Doe: Frank M. Robinson deposition, *Koke* case; profile, Wilbur G. Kurtz, Jr., Jan. 1954, ESC; Stockard, Robinson ints; Robinson obit, *Bottler*, Aug. 1923. Robinson, Doe, Pemberton, and Holland made deal: Receipt, Robinson to Pemberton Chemical, 1/19/1886; ledger entry, Robinson, 1/1/1886, CCA, showing transfer of shares of Pemberton Chemical to Robinson family members.

Robinson description: Photos, CCA. "Little dried-up fellow": John S. Candler deposition, *Koke* case. Rocked on boots to add height: Stockard int. (Other details: Entry in *A Standard History of Georgia and Georgians*, vol. VI, by Lucian Lamar Knight, Lewis Publishing, 1917, in the possession of Frank M. Robinson, great-grandson and namesake of Frank Robinson.)

Local prohibition: Garrett, *Atlanta and Environs*, vol. II, pp. 95-99. (The mistaken speculation comes mainly from an unpublished 1952 memoir, "The True Origin of Coca-Cola," written by Howard Candler, who wrongly asserted that Coca-Cola evolved from French Wine of Coca. An ad for French Wine Coca appears in AJ, 6/9/1886, after Coca-Cola's debut.)

Five soda fountains: Memo, Bell to Garrett, 5/2/66, CCA. Greater profits from sale by glass: Young int. Origin of soft drink industry, Riley, pp. 9-10, 118. Background of kola, claims on its behalf: Series of articles in *The New Idea*, house publication of Frederick Stearns Co., 1892-1894, CCA.

Pemberton's inspiration: Sam Brown int (quoting Hirsch and H. Jones); memo, Bell to C. W. Adams, 5/9/67, CCA. (An unpublished manuscript titled "Corporate History," ca. 1932, CCA, calls Coca-Cola "day-time coffee.") Kola tasted bitter: Testimony, A. L. Chasen (CC chemist), *Dixi-Cola* case, 2/9/40. "Awful mixture": Lowndes memoir, CCA. Pemberton used caffeine from Merck: Inventory, 7/21/1887; text, Pemberton speech, Apr. 1887, CCA.

Steps in making Coca-Cola: Contrary to numerous claims over the years, no single document with the "original" formula for Coca-Cola exists. Pemberton's ingredients and recipe, however, are substantiated by 1) a letter, John Candler to Fred Beall, 9/26/1907, setting out Coca-Cola's contents and manufacturing process, CCA; 2) an inventory of materials transferred by Pemberton to Lowndes and Venable, 7/21/1887; 3) the testimony of H. Candler and J. C. Mayfield, *Koke* case; 4) a letter, W. P. Heath to RWW, re No. 5 and Sicilian oil, 3/3/31, RWP; 5) a letter, Curtis to RWW, re cassia, 2/25/37, RWP; 6) a memo, C. R. Bender to file, re visit of FDA inspector to Atlanta syrup plant, 7/22/57, RWP; 7) the confidential files of Ralph Hayes (detailed in chapter 8 notes), RHP; 8) a formula apparently written by Frank Robinson, currently in the possession of his great-grandson.

(A recipe marked "X" contained in Pemberton's formula book, available in CCA, is not in Pemberton's handwriting and is thought to date from the 1940s. The celebrated secret formula that remains locked in a vault at Trust Company of Georgia dates from the sale of the company ,in 1919, and reflects several changes in the recipe made during the Candler era, as detailed in later chapter notes.)

Pemberton dispatched runners: Robinson deposition, *Koke* case. "Soda Water King": Card, 4/11/1887, CCA. Plan from outset was to carbonate: Ad, AJ, 5/29/1886 (discovered by Bell in 1966). Robinson recalled: Robinson deposition, *Koke* case. Venable had to write down the name: Dobbs deposition, *Koke* case.

Pemberton fell ill: Lowndes memoir. Footnote, re "dope fiend": Murphey, Mayfield depositions, *Koke* case. C. Pemberton died: Obit, AC, 7/4/1894, CCA. 25 gallons sold: Pamphlet, "What Is It?" Jan. 1901, *Rucker* case, Federal Records Center. Doe left, Robinson gave Coca-Cola a second chance, collaborated with Ridge: Robinson deposition, *Koke* case. Woodcut by Harrison: "What Is It?" Sampling tickets: Dobbs deposition, *Koke* case. Endorsement by Venable: Card, 4/11/1887. Advertising materials: Inventory, 7/21/1887. Woolfolk Walker hired: Dobbs deposition, *Koke* case. Logged nearly thousand orders: Account sheet, 7/22/1887, in possession of Frank Robinson. Pemberton applied: Document, U.S. Patent Office, CCA.

Pemberton called Lowndes: Lowndes memoir. Pemberton sold two thirds: Contract, 8/8/1887, CCA. "Sales day" encounter with Candler, Candler visit to Pemberton: Candler deposition, *Koke* case. Candler introduced Pemberton to Asa: Stockard int.

Candler family description: H. Candler, *Asa Griggs Candler*; genealogy, A D. Candler, 1902; bio files, CCA. Asa's childhood, arrival in Atlanta, early employment, and marriage: *Candler*. "Bury the hatchet": Letter, Howard to A Candler, 11/24/1978, ACP. Sole proprietor: Letterhead, ACP.

Lowndes and Venable sent dray, "orders began," production ceased: Lowndes memoir. Walker asked Mrs. Dozier for money: Deposition, Mrs. M. C. Dozier, *Koke* case. Dozier bought two-thirds share: Contract, 12/14/1887.

Robinson pitched CC to Asa, pointed to wagon: Waiters, p. 22. Asa unenthusiastic: *Ibid.*; Stockard int. (In an article titled "How I Won and Lost an Interest in Coca-Cola," *Drug Topics*, July 1929, Joseph Jacobs, the proprietor of Venable's soda fountain, claimed to have held a brief ownership position with Candler, but existing documents offer no substantiation.)

Candler changed mind: Letter, Asa to Warren Candler, 4/10/1888, ACP. Canceled $550 debt: Memoir, Dan Candler, Oct. 1929, CCA. Paid Walker and sister $750: *Illustrated Profile*, p. 8.

Pemberton died: Obit, AC, 8/18/1888, CCA. Candler sent dray: Dobbs deposition, *Koke* case. Candler hoisted demijohn: *Candler*, p. 85. Marcus Aurelius's motto: Text,

Candler speech to bottlers, 1916, CCA. High-pitched voice: Garrett int. Robinson named superintendent: *Candler*, p. 86. Refining the formula: Howard Candler, 'True Origin," 1952; Dobbs article, AJ, 11/23/1908 (reprinted from *Advertisers' Magazine*). Cut coca extract to trace: Slack Report, 6/24/1891, cited in "What Is It?" pamphlet, *Rucker* case. Kola nuts cost $20 per pound: "What Is It?" CC contained little of either ingredient Letter, Asa to Howard Candler, 7/27/1908, ACP.

Candler paid Walker and Dozier $1,000: *Illustrated Profile*, p. 8. Walker skipped town for Hot Springs: Testimony, Mrs. Dozier, *Koke* case. "Sole proprietors": Ad, AJ, 5/1/1889, CCA. CC as "Refreshing!" and "brain tonic": Munsey, p. 38. Botanic Blood Balm ad: Booklet titled "Coca-Cola," undated but ca. 1890, CCA. Sampling campaign: Letter, Asa to Warren Candler, 4/10/1888, ACP; memo, Price Gilbert, Jr., to Bell, 2/22/39, CCA. Sales of 8,855 gallons: Annual Sales report, CCA.

Candler full-time into proprietary medicines: AC, 1/25/1891, CCA. Description of 42½ Decatur St., production process: Memoirs of Dan Candler ("A Brief History of Coca-Cola") and Sam Willard (untitled), both ca. 1929, CCA. Sold 19,831 gallons: Annual Sales report, CCA. "Big-footed Negro": Waiters, p. 35. Single full-time salesman, George Little: *Candler*, p. 88. Details of stock offering: Dan Candler memoir.

TWO: DOPE

Salesman gave away sampling tickets, Asa quote: Letter, J. J. Willard to Carl Jones, 3/12/49, CCA. Sales reached 281,000: Annual Sales report, CCA. Factory moved and expanded: Folder, "Coca-Cola Homes," Wilbur Kurtz, Sr., CCA. Nicknames for CC: Testimony, Dobbs and F. W. Green, *Koke* case; lecture, "The Story of Coca-Cola," Dr. Robert C. Wilson, 11/15/65, at the Southern College of Pharmacy.

Slack report: 6/24/1891, cited in "What Is It?" pamphlet, *Rucker* case. "Ordinary dose" as one grain: Brief, CC to 5th Circuit Court of Appeals, undated but ca. 1902, *Rucker* case. Candler believed name had to be descriptive: Candler's testimony, *Ibid*. Candler and Robinson devised new Merchandise No. 5, called "tea": Memoir, "Thirty Three Years with Coca-Cola, 1890-1923," Howard Candler, CCA.

Candler claim CC provided "mental clearness," "vigor of the intellect": "What Is It?" pamphlet, *Rucker* case. Candler sang "Onward Christian Soldiers": Memoir, "As I Remember," Ross Treseder, Jan. 1973, CCA. "I do not propose to vend a poison": Letter, Candler to J. W. Quillian, 8/20/1898, CCA. Candler told *Daily World*: Issue of 5/16/1892, CCA. Jacobs believed CC contained cocaine: Article quoting Jacobs's grandson, Sinclair Jacobs, in *Atlanta Jewish Times*, undated but ca. 1990, CCA.

Details of Candler's suit challenging the federal stamp tax: Record, *Rucker* case, 5th Circuit Court of Appeals, No. 1239, Federal Records Center, East Point, Ga. Candler declared new building "sufficient. . .for all time to come": "Coca-Cola Homes," Kurtz, CCA. Sales neared 500,000 gallons: Annual Sales report, CCA. Branch factories: Memo, CC's tangible assets, marked "early 1913," CCA; letter, Asa to Howard Candler, 2/25/1909, ACP. "If our collections are as good": Letter, Asa to Howard Candler, 4/15/1902, ACP. Ran out of urns: Letter, Dobbs to H. Candler, 4/21/1899, CCA.

Episode of drunken New York salesman: Letter, Asa to H. T. Applewhite, 6/2/1902, ACP. Account of trial: Transcript, *Rucker* case. Jury deliberated fewer than fifteen minutes: Motion for retrial, 2/24/1902. Scare over cocaine spread through South: Musto, p. 6 (and Musto's chapter notes, pp. 254-55). Belief that cocaine gave blacks "superhuman" powers: *Cocaine: A New Epidemic*, Chris-Ellyn Johanson, Chelsea House Publishers, 1986, p. 57. "Kolafra" pamphlet: Johnson & Johnson archives. Warning re "white-skinned peoples": William Rosser Corbett, quoted in article, "Ruin in the Kola Nut," clipping identified only as *Times Herald*, undated, CCA.

Doctor in Augusta warned of "fiends": *Augusta Chronicle*, 2/4/1900, CCA. *Wilson Daily News:* Undated clipping, ca. 1903, CCA. Laws against cocaine: Text, bill in Pennsylvania legislature, 1903 session, CCA. Attack on CC in Virginia: Letter, Asa Candler to Howard, 8/7/1902, ACP.

Candler called on Schaefer to remove cocaine: Letter, Asa Candler to W. B. Reeves, 3/2/1904, RHP. (In the letter, Candler says Coca-Cola never contained cocaine "to any appreciable extent.") Schaefer's process: Testimony of Dr. Charles Caspari, *Koke* case. Adams's articles from *Collier's*, 12/2/1905 and 6/8/1907, reprinted by P. F. Collier & Son, 1907.

"Punch a hole in it": Affidavit of Lettie Evans, 6/5/20, *Bottling* case. Wiley's background: "Three Southern Food and Drug Cases," Dr. James Harvey Young, *Journal of Southern History*, Feb. 1983; "A Reply to Dr. Harvey W. Wiley's 'The Coca-Cola Controversy,'" pamphlet by Harold Hirsch, 1912, CCA; *History of a Crime Against the Food Law*, Harvey W. Wiley, Arno Press, 1976; and *Harvey W. Wiley, An Autobiography*, Harvey W. Wiley, Bobbs-Merrill, 1930.

War Department banned CC: Leavenworth, Kansas, *Daily Times*, 6/28/1907, CCA. John Candler protested, waited, went to Washington and saw Wiley: Letters, J. Candler to Asa Candler and Dobbs, both dated 9/17/1907, CCA. "Poison squad": *New York World*, 10/31/1907, CCA. Wiley re "Coca-Cola habit": Wiley, *History*, pp. 376-82. Wiley's view of South, Civil War experience: Wiley, *Autobiography*, pp. 69-75.

Wiley sent Kebler: Young, "Three Cases," p. 11. Wiley's weakness, ban on benzoic acid: *Ibid.* Wiley's exchange with Roosevelt, appointment of Referee Board: Wiley, *Autobiography*, p. 241. Candlers approached Secretary Wilson: Letter, J. Candler to Dobbs, 10/11/1907, CCA. Wiley submitted analysis: Telegram, J. Candler to Asa, 10/16/1907, CCA. Army lifted ban: Order, E. C. Ainsworth, adjutant general, War Department, 10/28/1907, CCA. Wiley's report, accusations against CC: Letter, J. Candler to Asa, 10/17/1907, CCA. Asa's response: Letter to Fred Beall, 10/21/1907, CCA. Asa declined to publicize victory: Letter, Dobbs to J. Candler, 11/1/1907, CCA.

Garrett recalled boys asking: Garrett int. "Money-making machine": Letter, Asa to Howard Candler, 9/21/1901, ACP. "Don't indulge SELF": Letter, Asa to Howard, 3/21/1902, ACP. ". . .not arrived to be stylish": Letter, Asa to Howard, 9/21/1901, ACP. Asa saved paper: Kahn, *Big Drink*, p. 58. "I never keep money": Letter, Asa to Warren Candler, 1/13/13, ACP. "Dear sweet fish": Letter, Asa to Lucy, 5/22/1897, CCA. Asa made sons share kit: Candler, p. 197. Asa kept chickens: Waiters, p. 23.

Candler built skyscrapers: Real estate inventory, 12/31/15, CCA. Tom Watson denounced "dope": Letter, Asa to J. Candler, 9/23/1907, CCA. Methodist church dropped ads, Warren Candler returned share: Bell Papers. CC attacked by both Temperance leaders and liquor manufacturers: Letter, Asa to Warren Candler, 8/5/1907; A. M. Biedenharn, Sr., int/CCA. Treseder memoir, CCA. Editors shook down CC for ad space: Letter, Dobbs to Ben Thomas, 6/21/1905, exhibit in *Bottling* case.

Idea that CC contained, cocaine enraged Candler: Text, Candler speech to bottlers, 1916, CCA. "It is not dope!": Waiters, p. 43. Candler wanted to perform public service: Letter, Asa to Howard Candler, 17/23/13, ACP.

Selling CC a pursuit with a "narrow compass": Watters, p. 116. Asa wanted Howard to attend medical school: Letter, Asa to Howard, 5/30/1899, ACP. Asa offered Howard a job with CC: Letter, Asa to Howard, 5/29/1897, ACP. Asa instructed Howard to assess European conditions: Letter, Asa to Howard, 7/6/1900, ACP. Asa asked Howard to attend school in New York: Letter, Asa to Howard, 7/12/1900, ACP. Howard leaves medical school: Letter, Howard to Asa, 9/21/1901, ACP.

Asa called New York "bottomless pit": Letter, Asa to Howard, 5/9/1901, ACP. Sidewalk vendors undercut CC: John H. Power int/CCA. Howard disliked commerce: Letter, Howard to Asa, 3/12/1903, ACP. Howard described "Holy of Holies": H. Candler, "Thirty Three Years," CCA. Howard was five nine and 135 pounds: H. Candler's pocket diary, 1902, CCA. "As soon as possible": Letter, Asa to Howard, 7/25/1908, ACP. Asa encouraged Howard to "master its details": Letter, Asa to Howard, 2/25/1909, CCA.

Asa sounded out Samuel Brown: Depositions of Asa Candler and Ernest Woodruff, 1/27/25, *United States of America* v. *Coca-Cola Company*, No. 738, U.S. District Court for the Northern District of Georgia, Federal Records Center, East Point, Ga. Brown liked euchre: Samuel Brown (grandson) int. Name was anglicized: Teena Watson int. What Brown had in mind: from a file of legal correspondence involving Samuel Brown, Harold Hirsch, and others in the archives of Kilpatrick & Cody, successor to the law firm of Candler, Thomson & Hirsch.

Howard Candler returned from lunch and discovered Kebler and Lynch: H. Candler's testimony, *Chattanooga* case. Asa roared: Testimony of Lynch, *Ibid.* Wiley ached to bring charges, was held in check, episode with Seely: Wiley, *Autobiography*, pp. 261-62; Wiley, *History*, pp. 376-82.

Participants trooped into Chattanooga, stayed at Patten: Letter, Asa to Howard Candler, 3/17/11, ACP; diary of Anna Kelton Wiley, Wiley Papers, Library of Congress (copy in CCA). Description of Anna Wiley: Wiley, *Autobiography*, p. 281. Emily Watson sang "My Wee Bird": *Chattanooga Times*, 3/24/11. Wileys' room overlooked post office: Mrs. Wiley's diary.

Government had two main charges: libel filed by government, *Chattanooga* case. Lynch's testimony: Trial transcript, *Ibid.*, CCA. Unless otherwise noted, accounts of the trial are taken verbatim from the trial transcript. "Even the bumblebees love" CC: *Chattanooga Times*, 3/14/11. Wiley and wife went shopping: Mrs. Wiley's diary. Asa "anticipated a mean-nasty case": Letter, Asa to Howard Candler, 3/14/11, ACP. "That liar," Asa fumed: Letter, Asa to Howard Candler, 3/15/11, ACP. (Asa vehemently denied having taken the Lord's name in vain.)

Kebler said caffeine made heart hard: *Chattanooga Times*, 3/16/11. CC experts snickered: Young, "Three Cases," p. 14. "U.S. has about exhausted its rat . . . evidence": Letter, Asa to J. J. and Sam Willard, 3/21/11, ACP. Corry back-ground: Deposition and affidavits on file with trial record, Federal Records Center, East Point, Ga.

"Have you ever written a book?" anecdote: *American Food Journal*, 4/15/11, CCA. (A scholarly treatment of the expert testimony re caffeine appears in the *Journal of the History of the Behavioral Sciences*, Jan. 1991.) Testimony of James "Jeems" Gaston:

Chattanooga Times, 3/23/11. Government optimism "dwindling": *Chattanooga Sunday Times*, 4/2/11. Wiley left for Cornell: *Chattanooga Times*, 3/25/11. Wiley's "old style" dinner: *Chattanooga Sunday Times*, 3/26/11.

Hirsch worried about directed verdict Hirsch deposition, *Koke* case. Sanford's thinking: Transcript and Sanford's order, *Chattanooga* case. "Case Is Practically Thrown Out": *Chattanooga Times*, 4/7/11. "Irresponsible faddist": *Food Journal*, 4/15/11.

Candler and Brown agreed on $8 million: Letter, Hirsch to Sam Brown, 8/23/11, Kilpatrick & Cody files. Wiley resigned, became editor of *Good Housekeeping*. "Too good to be true": Letter, Hirsch to Colby, 3/14/12. Brown gave up: Letter, Sam Brown to Hirsch, 6/14/13. Company had record $8.8 million revenues: Sales chart, D'Arcy archives.

Griffith film: Videotape at CCA (discovered by Professor Martin S. Pernick, University of Michigan). "Truth, Justice and Coca-Cola": CCA. Hirsch found capital "saturated with the idea" that CC contained cocaine: Letter, Hirsch to Sam Brown, 2/14/12, Kilpatrick & Cody files. "I have forgotten the books": Letter, Asa to Howard Candler, 7/23/13, ACP.

THREE: DOBBS

Dobbs on his deathbed: Letter, Eleise Wrenne to RWW, 7/19/50, RWP.

Dobbs's early days with CC: Dobbs deposition, 7/27/14, *Koke* case. Dobbs grew up poor: CC obit, undated, CCA; AJ, 11/1/50. Called "Sammie": Letter, J. J. Willard to Frank Rowsey, 4/10/56, CCA. Dobbs spotted Matthews bottling machine: Memoir, Dobbs as told to Frank Harrold, 10/13/33, CCA. Description of bottling process: Riley, pp. 83-86. Dobbs sold syrup for bottling, argued with Asa: Memoir, 10/13/33. "There are too many folks who are not responsible": Deposition of Veazey Rainwater, 6/3/20, *Bottling* case.

Dobbs took charge of shipping: *Candler*, p. 86. Job required precision: Watters, p. 37. Dobbs studied with Warren Candler: CC obit. Photo of Dobbs: CCA.

CC of Gay Nineties employed twenty people: Photo, 1899, CCA. Process of making syrup: Letter, Sam Willard to H. Candler, 10/2/29, CCA. Candler deployed nephews: Memoir, "A Brief History of Coca-Cola," by Dan Candler, 1929, CCA. Dan Candler anecdote: Watters, p. 46.

Early promotions, Grant, Couden: Memo, Price Gilbert, Jr., to Bell, 9/22/39, CCA. Asa saw sign in McKinley's cortege: Text, Asa Candler speech to bottlers, 1916, CCA. Russell photo: *Benjamin J. Falk* v. *The Coca-Cola Company*, 9/5/1895, Case 7304, U.S. Circuit Court for the Northern District of Georgia, Federal Records Center, East Point, Ga. (Falk, the photographer, sued Candler for copyright infringement.) Japanese fans: Garrett manuscript on advertising, 2/14/57, CCA. Mooney int. Howard passed out fans in Kansas City: "Thirty Three Years," H. Candler, CCA.

Dobbs took over sales: Letter, Dobbs to H. Candler, 4/21/1899, CCA. Metal-bound trunks: J. J. Willard memoir, 3/3/66, CCA. Nephews viewed Dobbs with trepidation: Sam Willard memoir, 1929, CCA. Robinson's forgiving nature: Obit, *Coca-Cola Bottler*, Aug. 1923, CCA. Stockard, Robinson ints. Robinson's concern about salesmen: Letter, Robinson to H. Candler, 4/21/1899, CCA.

Dobbs had harder edge: Garrett, Kurtz ints. Trebilcock attended WCTU meetings: Memoir, Oliver Allstorm, 4/22/56, CCA. Locomobiles: Letters, Howard Candler to

Asa, 6/2/1902, and Asa to Howard, 2/25/1909, both ACP. Metalurgique: Treseder, p. 28. Salesmen made $12.50: Watters, p. 47. Company paid expenses: Treseder, pp. 9-10. Dobbs became "only contact point": Memoir, Sam Willard, 1929, CCA. Dobbs as "immensely attractive": Treseder, p. 13.

Asa railed against "pirates" and "scoundrels": CC minutes, annual meeting, 12/9/1896, CCA. John H. Power: Oral history, 3/3/66, CCA. List of imitators: *National Bottlers' Gazette*, 1/5/17, CCA. *Opinions, Orders.* Dobbs wanted to sue infringers, complained of "flagrant" violations: Letter, Dobbs to RWW, 5/4/37, RWP.

Dobbs became jealous of Robinson: Letter, J. J. Willard to Frank Rowsey, 4/10/56, CCA. Ad in *Munsey's:* Letter, Price Gilbert, Jr., to Bell, 9/22/39, CCA. Dobbs and Robinson bickered, went to board: Robinson, Stockard ints; Watters, p. 93. Hiring of St. Elmo Massengale: Massengale deposition, 10/4/11, *Nashville* case. Jack Prince ad: AJ, 12/27/1903, CCA. Nap Lajoie ad: *Philadelphia Bulletin*, 1905, CCA.

Massengale showed theatergoers: *Saturday Evening Post*, 6/3/1905, CCA. Massengale's automobile ad: CCA. Dobbs wanted ads to "attract the eye": Letter, Dobbs to B. E Thomas, 4/2/1907, exhibit in *Bottling* case. Asa Candler was "chief policy officer": Letter, J. J. Willard to Frank Rowsey, 4/10/56, CCA. Cousins feared Dobbs's ambition: Memo, Howard Kurtz, Jr., to Delony Sledge, 4/10/56, describing interview with J. J. Willard and Sam Willard, CCA. Asa made Dobbs advertising manager: Dobbs deposition, 1/20/16, *Koke* case.

Description of D'Arcy: *Between Us* magazine (a publication of D'Arcy-MacManus & Masius), 75th anniversary; *Insight* (also an agency publication), Dec. 1980; *Tide*, 10/15/45; Jack Taylor, James Payne ints. Dobbs, D'Arcy introduced by Willard Cox: Memoir, Robin Smith, 3/17/77, D'Arcy archives. Dickel ad: *Tide*, 10/15/45. Dobbs gave D'Arcy $4,602 in billings in 1906 and $25,000 in 1907: CC minutes, cited by Wilbur Kurtz, Jr., in memo, 4/10/56, CCA.

D'Arcy looked like banker or minister: Oral history, Eddie Miller, undated, D'Arcy archives. D'Arcy likened relationship to doctor and patient: "The Business of Modern Advertising—As We See It and Practice It," brochure, ca. 1920s, D'Arcy archives. Ad in St. Louis directory: Mooney int. Ty Cobb ad: CCA. Hosiery ad anecdote: Miller oral history.

Sam Willard re early illustrations: Waiters, p. 52. D'Arcy introduced bathing beauty: *Bottler*, Apr. 1959. Animated billboard, dirigible: Waiters, p. 59. D'Arcy got $225,000 in 1910: CC minutes, quoted in Kurtz memo. Magazines CC used: Memo, J. Robert Mudd, 9/21/61, D'Arcy archives. Massengale lost the account: C. C. Pangman, quoted *Bottler*, Apr. 1959.

Hirsch's background: *Atlanta and Environs*, vol. II, p. 770; obit, AJ, 9/26/39; *Bottler*, Apr. 1959; photo file, CCA. The Trade-Mark Act of 1905: Hopkins, Appendix E, pp. 549-50. South Carolina bottlers case: *The Coca-Cola Company* v. *H. G. Bailey and E. B. Donald*, 1906, reported in *Opinions, Orders*, pp. 284-90. Toca-Cola, Ko-Kola, and Kos-Kola cases: *Ibid.* "Genuine" ad campaign: Garrett manuscript on advertising, 2/14/57, CCA.

Dobbs in Chicago with druggists: Letters, Dobbs to John Candler, 9/19/1907 and 9/21/1907, and to Fred Beall, 9/20/1907, CCA. Dobbs became president of Associated Advertising Clubs: Pamphlet, "The Fight for Truth in Advertising," Round Table Press, 1936, CCA. Footnote: *Ibid.* Dobbs's call for "clean . . . publicity": Text, address in 1911 in Boston, CCA. Local committees became Better Business Bureaus: *Greater Philadelphia* magazine, Aug. 1961, CCA.

Howard Candler's visit to Schaefer lab: Letters, Asa to Howard Candler, both 7/27/1908, ACP. Dobbs called CC "my child": Letter, Dobbs to RWW, 5/4/37, RWP. Dobbs made $8,000: Memo marked "early 1913," Kilpatrick & Cody files. Dobbs called son "Candler": Dobbs bio file, CCA.

Howard seen as "quiet, kind": Treseder, p. 13. Asa told Warren he planned to retire: Letter, 1/13/13, ACP. Landers's account: Memoir, "My 38 Years with the Coca-Cola Company," William A. Landers, unpublished, 1950, CCA. "I do not want to make money": Letter, Asa to Howard Candler, 7/23/13, ACP.

Cotton prices collapsed; Asa's loan guarantee: *Atlanta and Environs*, vol. II, pp. 637-40. War "has almost scared the life" out of business in South: Letter, Asa to J. J. Willard, 10/14/14, ACP. Asa's $1 million gift to Emory: Letter, Asa to Warren Candler, 7/16/14, ACP; *Atlanta and Environs*, vol. II, pp. 641-44. Candler underwrote $3 million bond issue: *Ibid.*, vol. II, pp. 662-63.

Howard became president: CC minutes, 1/21/16. Howard speculated: *Candler*, pp. 144-48. Footnote: CC minutes, 1/22/14. Candler issued public notice: Copy, 2/1/16, ACP. Dobbs changed address to New York: Letter, Dobbs to H. C. Spence, 2/5/16, CCA.

Asa held 391 shares: Special dividend distribution, CC minutes, 4/8/14. "I vote my shares against that": *Fortune*, July 1931. Hughes's Supreme Court ruling: *Chattanooga* case, CCA. Howard recalled reaction: *Candler*, p. 150. Candler ran for mayor: *Atlanta and Environs*, vol. II, pp. 695-97.

Candler proposed selling CC for $25 million, cited terms: Letter, Hirsch to Sam Brown, 3/3/16, Kilpatrick & Cody files. Involvement of Max Pam: Letter, Hirsch to Sam Brown, 8/15/11; letter, Pam to Hirsch, 5/31/13, Kilpatrick & Cody files.

Candlers rejected Pam deal: *Candler*, pp. 152-53. Clue that suggests what happened: Letter, John Candler to Hirsch, 1/6/17, Kilpatrick & Cody files. (Candler states the deal failed "because of the transfer of a considerable part of the real estate that was desired in this trade.") Asa Candler, Jr., background: Sibley, pp. 153-54; obit, AP, 1/12/53; *Time*, 4/9/51. Asa, Jr., owed $100,000: Letter, Asa Sr. to Warren Candler, 1/13/13, ACP. "He is such a child": Letter, Asa to Howard Candler, 4/15/1902, ACP. Asa Sr. arranged to sell and remove real estate: CC minutes, 12/21/16.

Candler signed agreement with Edward Brown and Colby: CC minutes, 1/15/17. Colby threatened suit: AJ, 4/27/20. Candlers moved to Candler building, Asa urged William to visit plant: Letter, Asa to Howard Candler, 9/22/17, ACP.

"We are finding it exceedingly difficult": Letter, Dobbs to W. H. Gallaway, 4/24/17, CCA. "Don't let lack of material worry you": Letter, Asa to Howard Candler, 9/22/17, ACP. Howard paid "enormous prices" for caffeine: Letter, H. Candler to Dobbs, 10/25/17, CCA. Colorless CC: Statement, H. Candler to Kurtz, 5/1/53, CCA.

Hoover decreed half quota: Letter, Dobbs to H. Candler, 3/14/18, CCA. "Making a Soldier of Sugar": CCA. D'Arcy's meeting with Hoover: Letter, D'Arcy to RWW, 2/4/42, RWP. "Privilege" to sacrifice: Ad, *Pictorial Review*, June 1918, CCA. Sales dipped, then rose: Sales report, D'Arcy archives. "Victory's Reward": Ad, CCA.

Hirsch settled case: Bell Papers; *Opinions, Orders*, p. 31. Wiley complained bitterly, footnote: *Good Housekeeping*, May 1922. Candlers bought North Avenue tract: CC minutes, 2/12/19; memo to IRS, King & Spalding, 12/11/46, RWP. Candler divided stock on Christmas 1917: Graham and Roberts, p. 88. New stakes, reorganization:

CC minutes, 2/14/18. Ownership "corralled": Asa Candler deposition, 1/27/25, *United States* v. *Coca-Cola Co.*, No. 738, Federal Records Center, East Point, Ga.

Asa to retire: *Bottler*, Dec. 1918, CCA. Wife gravely ill: Graham and Roberts, p. 87. Audit: CC minutes, 9/13/19; Atlanta *Georgian*, 4/27/20.

Trust Company's charter gave "right to do almost anything": Text, Thomas K. Glenn speech, 5/19/36, AHC. Woodruff formed Atlantic Ice and Coal: Martin, *Three Strong Pillars*, pp. 32-33. Woodruff sat on porch with shotgun: Text, Bobby Jones speech, 12/6/59, CCA. Atlanta Steel Company affair: Glenn speech. Rand & Leopold rolltop: The author was permitted to examine the desk, which still occupies a room at Trust Company (and contains some of Woodruff's papers, including documents detailing his trade for the paper mill).

Joel Hurt background: Martin, *Three Strong Pillars*, pp. 15-17; Edge, *Joel Hurt*. Streetcar fight: J. Martin, *Mule-to-MARTA*, vol. I, p. 59 *et seq.* Hurt and Woodruff ripped up rails: *Ibid.*, p. 68. Spalding found cufflink: Confidential source; rumor confirmed by King & Spalding senior partners Robert L. Steed, Bradley Hale. Woodruff replaced Hurt as Trust Company president; relations strained: Edge, pp. 274-75. Woodruff reputedly not "altogether on the up and up": Garrett int, quoting Richard Courts. Woodruff knew Candler disliked him: Woodruff deposition, 1/27/25, *United States* v. *Coca-Cola Co.*, No. 738, Federal Records Center, East Point, Ga.

Dobbs elected president of chamber, spoke at Woman's Club: AJ, 2/25/19. Dobbs joined board of Trust Company: *Men of the Trust Company of Georgia*, vol. V. Dobbs told Woodruff he was "willing to sell out": Dobbs's testimony, *Bottling* case. Dobbs and Woodruff met at Waldorf: *Ibid.* Bank's net worth was $2 million: Bank letterhead, 10/17/19, CCA.

Stetson background: Bond, p. 42 *et seq.* Stetson gave impression Guaranty Trust was lead institution: CC minutes, 9/9/19. Dobbs enlisted Hirsch as ally, worked to persuade family: Letter, Dobbs to J. J. Willard, 8/2/19; letter, Hirsch to Hunter, 8/8/19, CCA. Alston obtained signatures: Deposition of H. Candler, 5/3/20, *Bottling* case; Trust Company minutes, 8/13/19; Woodruff deposition, 1/27/25, *United States* v. *Coca-Cola Co.*

Asa was "profoundly shocked": *Candler*, p. 184. Footnote: *Kansas City Times*, 4/7/21, CCA. Woodruff called special meeting: Trust Company minutes, 8/2/19. Directors insisted on legal reassurance, backing of "solvent" persons: *Ibid.* Details of transaction, $5 shares: Deposition of William C. Wardlaw, 4/28/20, *Bottling* case; letter, Guaranty Trust to Trust Company, 9/13/19, CCA.

Woodruff sent telegram complaining, "Impossible . . .": Trust Company minutes, 8/19/19. Woodruff sent letter marked "Strictly Confidential": *Ibid.*, 8/13/19. Text of letter: Copy received by H. Candler, dated 8/22/19, CCA. Woodruff drafted letter: Trust Company minutes, 8/19/19. Woodruff had showdown in New York: Letter, William Wardlaw to RWW, 9/10/40, RWP.

Trust Company shareholders raised $2 million: Wardlaw deposition, 4/28/20, *Bottling* case. Payne made motion: Trust Company minutes, 8/21/19. Newspapers reported sale: AC, 8/22/19. One-day subscription: Wardlaw deposition, *Bottling* case. Prospectus said "present management . . . will continue": Prospectus offered by Trust Company, Aug. 1919, RWP. Voting Trust: AC, 5/4/20.

FOUR: BOTTLED-UP ANGER

Howard Candler was upset, had "nothing to do" with syndicate: H. Candler deposition, 5/3/20, *Bottling* case. Howard married to Flora Glenn: Bio, *Men of the Trust Company*. Howard's share of proceeds: Author's calculations. Meeting of 9/16/19, Howard Candler's motions: CC minutes.

Woodruff and bank made money: Wardlaw deposition, 4/28/20, *Bottling* case; letter, Guaranty Trust to Trust Company, 9/13/19, CCA. Trust Company minutes, 8/13/19 and 9/23/19; Trust Company report prepared Jan. 1965 by W. Bethel Minter. "He would meet 'em walking": Gordon Jones int. Price Gilbert, Sr., anecdote: Delony Sledge oral history, 3/11/81, CCA.

Description of W. C. Bradley: Obit, *Columbus Ledger-Enquirer,* 7/27/47. "Very palatable": *Ibid.* (Memoir of W. C. Woodall). Nunnally: McKee Nunnally, Sr., McKee Nunnally, Jr., ints; letter, H. Spalding to RWW, 12/1/67, listing CC holdings of Winship Nunnally's estate, RWP. Bulow Campbell: Letter, Campbell to RWW, 11/2/37, RWP. Smaller investors: Margaret Thrower, Bill Turner, Betty Corn ints. 1,500 individuals participated: AJ, 4/28/20.

CC world's largest user of sugar: Harrison Jones speech, 1924; manuscript titled "The Coca-Cola Company," D'Arcy archives. Price was 9 cents per pound in WWI: Third affidavit of H. Candler; draft agreement dated 2/12/20, *Bottling* case. Sugar futures began to rise: WSJ, 3/15/21; letter, Dobbs to Rainwater and Hunter, 11/18/19, *Bottling* case.

Woodruff set up executive committee, made Bradley chairman: CC minutes, 11/10/19. Howard Candler given green light; board adopted policy of sixty-day supply: CC minutes, 12/15/19. Formula given as collateral: AJ, 4/27/20.

Thomas and Whitehead arranged introduction to Candler: *Bottler,* Dec. 1946. "Gentlemen," Candler told the Chattanoogans: Text, Candler speech to bottlers, 1916, CCA. Candler proposed deal: Asa Candler deposition, *Bottling* case. Thomas hastened to room at Piedmont Hotel: Affidavit of John Candler, *Ibid.* Contract: Copy, *Opinions, Orders.* "If you boys fail": Veazey Rainwater memoir, *Bottler,* Apr. 1959.

A "stunner": Deposition of Veazey Rainwater, 6/3/20, *Bottling* case. Thomas plant "crude," keg showered Hardin: *Bottler,* Dec. 1946. Plant in poor neighborhood: Letter, DeSales Harrison to Bell, 8/8/66, CCA. Masks: Photos, CCA. Hutchinson bottle: Riley, p. 97; ad, W. H. Hutchinson & Son, Inc., *National Bottlers' Gazette,* Sept. 1965. Shelf life of CC: Affidavit of J. T. Lupton, 6/3/20, *Bottling* case.

Thomas and Whitehead became "parent" bottlers: Second affidavit of George T. Hunter, 6/3/20, *Bottling* case. Thomas and Whitehead drew line across map: Veazey Rainwater oral history, 3/18/65, CCA. Lupton enjoyed bragging: Letter, Lupton to RWW, 10/7/31, RWP. Lupton bought half Whitehead's interest: Rainwater oral history.

Invention of crown cap: *Columbus Ledger,* 5/28/61; Riley, p. 102. "Pouring it into the Oconee?": Rainwater memoir, *Bottler,* Apr. 1959. Plant openings: Garrett article, *Ibid.* "Dope wagon": Ralph Langford int/CCA. CC and chianti: Arthur Pratt article, *Bottler,* Dec. 1959. Josephine: Photo, *Bottler,* 1909. Deaths of Whitehead and Thomas: *Bottler,* Apr. 1959.

Convention at Aragon Hotel: AJ, 1/20/1909. "There is money in it": Hoy, p. 43. Parents paid 92 cents a gallon: Letter, Asa Candler to Thomas, 1/14/1907, *Bottling* case.

NOTES | 437

"WATERMELONS": Letter, DeSales Harrison to RWW, 9'/13/49, RWP. Royalty approached $1 million: Dobbs deposition, *Bottling* case.

Dobbs considered Lupton venal: Letter, Dobbs to D'Arcy, 4/20/20, CCA. Lupton asked, "Who's going to pay?": Rainwater oral history. Hunter considered a slow mover: Letter, Acklin to RWW, 10/4/41, RWP. Whitehead sons had bad reputations: Garrett int. Robinson, Dobbs, and Hirsch wanted to bottle: Stockard int; Dobbs deposition, *Bottling* case.

Rainwater invented fresh job: Rainwater oral history. Anecdote about D'Arcy and Montgomery: Delony Sledge oral history, 3/11/81, CCA. Invoice for "some trouble" in Texas: Letter, W. O. Mashburn to Rainwater, 2/15/11, *Bottling* case. Other states: Letter, Mashburn to Rainwater, 5/11/12. Crawford Johnson asked, "Harold, can you keep us going?": Hirsch testimony, *Koke* case. Wiley case cost $250,000: Lupton affidavit, *Bottling* case.

"Strange elements," origin of Bottlers' Association: Ralph Beach article, *Bottler,* Apr. 1959. Perry Wilbur Fattig: Kahn, *Big Drink,* p. 94. Rainwater sought quality: Rainwater article, *Bottler,* Apr. 1959. Origin of distinctive bottle: Clyde Edwards oral history, 8/15/49, CCA. Edwards picked cacao pod: Mooney int. Hirsch wanted to give royalty of 25 cents per gross: Edwards oral history; Hirsch deposition, *Bottling* case. Root ended up wealthiest man in Indiana: Kahn, *Big Drink,* p. 156.

Hunter wired Hirsch: Telegram, Hunter to Hirsch, 8/7/19, *Bottling* case. Hirsch responded, "Powerful interests": Letter to Hunter, 8/8/19, *Ibid.* Rainwater and Hunter received a panicky letter: Letter dated 11/18/19, *Ibid.*

Executive committee meeting of 12/15/19: CC minutes; AJ, 4/27/20. "Boys, I have. . .bad news": Rainwater deposition, 5/11/20, *Bottling* case. Hirsch and Rainwater drafted a document spelling out every "merchandise": Document dated 2/12/20, filed as exhibit in *Bottling* case. Bitter, all-night session: Letter, Dobbs to D'Arcy, 8/6/20, CCA. Candler wrote letter terminating contracts: Letter dated 3/2/20, *Opinions, Orders.*

Woodruff intended to "emasculate and supersede" the board: Letter, Dobbs to D'Arcy, 8/6/20, CCA. Woodruff guilty of "butting-in": Letter, Dobbs to D'Arcy, 4/26/20, CCA. Negotiating session with company's final offer: H. Candler affidavit, 3/6/20, *Bottling* case. Hunter vowed to pull CC down with him: Rainwater affidavit, *Bottling* case.

Conkey Whitehead hired King & Spalding: Spalding, *The Spalding Family,* vol. II, p. 169; letter, H. Spalding to father, 12/4/35, HSP. Sibley picked as lead counsel: Wells, *First Hundred Years,* p. 143. Parent bottlers filed suit: Application for injunction, 4/14/20, Montgomery Papers, AHC; AJ, 4/14/20.

Dobbs saw Rainwater's strategy unfolding: Letter, Dobbs to D'Arcy, 4/20/20, *Atlanta Constitution:* Issue of 4/15/20. Rainwater disclosed Voting Trust AJ, 4/18/20. Account of hearings from transcripts, *Bottling* case. Hirsch's clash with Phillips: AJ and *Atlanta Georgian,* 4/27/20.

Dobbs told Woodruff "the lawyers were trying the case": Letter, Dobbs to D'Arcy, 4/26/20, CCA. Woodruff was "as busy as a mangy dog": Letter, Dobbs to D'Arcy, 5/18/20, CCA. Dobbs complained to Bradley: Letter, Dobbs to D'Arcy, 4/28/20, CCA. Hirsch discovered "exclusive license" evidence; "four-teen-inch shell": Letter, Dobbs to D'Arcy, 5/21/20, CCA. Candler testified on company's behalf: Candler deposition, *Bottling* case. Judge Pendleton's grandson joined Hirsch's firm: AJ, 5/1/20.

Plaintiffs withdrew suit Telegram, Dobbs to D'Arcy, 5/31/20. Sugar reached 28 cents a pound: *Atlanta Georgian*, 5/4/20. Howard Candler exercised contracts, court fixed temporary price at $1.57 a gallon: AJ and *Atlanta Georgian*, 2/15/21.

"I would start a vigorous advertising campaign": Letter of 8/6/20, CCA. Executive committee meeting of July 1920: *Ibid*. Sugar prices plummeted: *Atlanta Georgian*, 2/15/21. Company committed to spend $8 million, H. Candler prayed for storm; "the company might not be able to carry on": Landers memoir. Hilton docked safely: AJ, 12/15/20.

"Woodruff and Bradley are very fond": Letter, Dobbs to D'Arcy, 8/6/20, CCA. Dobbs counted Glenn in his corner: *Ibid*. Dobbs stepped off train, was asked to see Hirsch: Letter, Dobbs to D'Arcy, 10/5/20, CCA. Executive committee meeting in September: CC minutes, 9/20/20. H. Candler became president, Bradley became chairman: AC, 10/26/20.

Dobbs packed bags, went to Canada: AC, 10/26/20. Stock hit low of 27⅛: *Atlanta Georgian*, 10/11/20. *Atlanta Journal* reported board would skip dividend: Issue of 10/11/20. Cost of syrup went up to $1.81: *Atlanta Georgian*, 2/15/21. Judge Morris ruled for parents: *Opinions, Orders*.

Supreme Court heard oral arguments: AJ, 12/7/20. Mayfield made Yum-Yum: Testimony of A. O. Murphey, *Koke* case. Footnote: Pamphlet, "A Document in Evidence," copyright 1912, by Diva Brown. "A humbug and a fake": *National Bottlers' Gazette*, undated. Background of *Koke* case: Brief, Coca-Cola Company, on appeal before the Commissioner of Patents, U.S. Patent Office, CCA. "Cheap and common swindle": *Ibid*. Ninth Circuit held CC ineligible for relief: Order, 2/24/19.

CC stock fell to 17⅞: Garrett int; AC, 7/18/35. Businessmen asked Candler to save them; he could not sleep: Letter, Onezima de Bouchel to A. Candler, 11/23/19.

Holmes ruled: *Opinions, Orders*. "A distinct feeling of optimism": AJ, 12/7/20.

Howard Candler was in New York City: Letter, Howard to Asa Candler, 1/31/21, ACP. Woodruff complained about wage scale: Memo to file, H. Candler, 4/20/21. "Continued picayunish interference": *Ibid*. Investors put stock in play: WSJ, 2/24/21. Stock prices began creeping up: WSJ, 3/15/21. Voting Trust in jeopardy: Boman int; H. Candler memo, 4/20/21.

Candler urged overseas expansion at board meeting: Letter, H. Candler to Bradley, 3/2/21, CCA. Woodruff engaged in flurry of moves: King & Spalding memo re IRS audit of Ernest Woodruff's estate, 12/11/46; affidavit, James W. Woodruff, Sr., 7/30/53, HSP. Woodruff tried to bully Candler into releasing false report; stock prices had "rapid and unusual advance": H. Candler memo, 4/20/21. Woodruff willing to sell out: *Ibid*. Stock price went up despite gloomy report: *New York Sun*, 4/27/21.

Judge in Philadelphia urged settlement: Memo, Brock to Kurtz, 7/22/74, CCA. Stetson and Spalding negotiated in Atlantic City: AJ, 6/19/21. Royalty set at 12½ cents per gallon, ratified by board: CC minutes, 7/25/21. Dividend resumed: AJ, 12/4/21. KO closed at 41⅜: AJ, 12/10/21. Sales were $28.5 million; Candler chided bottlers: Annual report, cited in *Atlanta Georgian*, 2/27/22.

"Steady accumulation" of KO by New York investors: WSJ, 12/9/21. Woodruff accumulated stock: Trust Company report, prepared Jan. 1965 by W. Bethel Minter; balance sheet, Piedmont Securities, 10/15/25, RWP.

Howard Candler tried to send official to Central America: Letter, Culpepper to H. Candler, 4/15/22, CCA. Woodruff organized CC International: Memo, Ray Bowling to RWW, 5/11/49, RWP. Directors' meeting of 11/27/22: AJ, 11/27/22. New directors: Minter memo. New Yorkers stunned: CC minutes, 2/26/23. Wall Street investors blocked trading: AJ, 2/9/23.

FIVE: "GET YOUR READINESS"

Woodruff's fable about joining CC: Numerous sources, including a memo, JJ to Kurtz, 5/20/72, CCA (making the myth part of the company's official archives). Description of the bottlers' meeting, 3/6/23 through 3/8/23, and text of speeches: Transcripts, CCA, and D'Arcy archives. Description of H. Jones: Bio file and photos, CCA; Sledge int/CCA. "Thirst Knows No Season" ad: *Bottler*, Apr. 1959.

Hearing loss: Kahn, *RWW*, p. 21; letter, RWW to S. Jones, 9/21/67. George Waldo's ear trumpet: Illus., Wells, *A Life*, p. 6. Woodruff lineage: Genealogy by Annie Lucille Woodruff Swift, 1947, RWP. George Waldo invested in Confederate currency: *Columbus Ledger*, 5/26/63. War ruined Woodruff, he rebuilt Wells, *A Life*, p. 5, citing *Columbus Enquirer* obit, 11/5/11; letterhead, Empire Mills, RWP.

Ernest went to work, hated weather: Letters, EW to Ernie, 5/23/1884 and 7/12/1884, RWP. Unless otherwise noted, details of Ernest and Ernie's courtship are from their correspondence, RWP. (In a letter to a friend, 3/13/1880, Emie stated she weighed ninety-four pounds.) Winship genealogy: Bio file, CCA; personality file, AHC.

Ernie's parents fled: Correspondence file, Mary Frances and Robert Winship, 1864, RWP. Sideboard stolen: JJ int. (The sideboard is now in the dining room at Ichauway.) Winships' gentility: Garrett int. Wedding and honeymoon: Letter, Emie to mother, 4/26/1885.

Ernest joined Joel Hurt: Edge, pp. 115-16. Ernest called "Chief": Letter, Wardlaw to RWW, 5/4/39, RWP. "Exacting master," routine at Trust Company: AJ, 6/5/44. Ernest five eight Passport, RWP. "Wisdom of Sages": Copy sent to RWW by Eugene Gunby, 7/25/72. Woodruff's frugality: *Fortune*, Sept. 1945. Restored phones: Martin, *Pillars*, p. 30. Train to Baltimore, crackled like diplomas: McGill, AC, 9/22/41, RWP. Glenn "always let him have his own way": Speech, 5/19/36. Ernest wanted saloon: Martin, *Pillars*, p. 25. Mother's letter: 5/23/1896, RWP.

"Main spring": Draft letter to IRS, Robert Troutman, Jr., undated, RWP. Woodruffs' house in Inman Park: Wells, *A Life*, pp. 21-23. Ernest bought Oldsmobile: *Ibid.*, pp. 30-31. Mammy Lou: Photo, RWP. Robert a poor student, "I got four": Letter, RWW to parents, 5/4/1900, RWP. (Except as noted, all correspondence of Woodruff and parents is from RWP.) Entertained at aunt's house: Elliott, p. 80. Pony anecdote: Text, Hayes speech, RWW's seventieth birthday, RWP.

Woodruff suffered dyslexia: JJ, Ellis ints. (Grace Adkins, wife of Ichauway's superintendent and a specialist in learning disabilities, concurs in the speculation.) Underbite: JJ int. Presence of "Kid" Woodruff: George C. Woodruff, Jr., int. Woodruff flunked out of Boys High: Elliott, p. 81. Description of Georgia Military Academy: Text, Col. Woodward speech, 1932, RWP; William Brewster, Jr., int. Robert blossomed, was leader: Letter, Brewster to Huffman, 9/7/62, RWP; *Parade Rest*, 1908. Joined fraternity: Invitation, 11/3/1906, RWP. "I didn't have to go to classes": Elliott, p. 83. Woodruff made impression: Letter, Gresham to RWW, 5/8/34; letter, Richardson to RWW, undated but ca. 1932, RWP.

Woodward told Ernest, "Don't send him": Elliott, p. 87. Ernest wanted Robert to be banker: Letter, E. W. Gans to W. White, 10/8/13, RWP. Robert "studying my head off": Letter, RWW to EW, undated but 1908. Doggerel poem: Undated, RWP. Hanging around Kappa Alpha, Stone's: Elliott, p. 87. Helen Payne: Letter, Emie to RWW, 11/20/1908.

"I trust I shall always be a comfort": Letter, RWW to mother, 1/22/1907. Emie monitored his condition: Letter to RWW, 9/12/1906. Ernie's sick headache: Letter, EW to RWW, 2/2/1906. Postcard: 10/4/1908. Robert sneaked back to Atlanta, father's response: Letter, EW to RWW, 10/15/1908.

Dickey wrote back, dismissing Robert: Letter, Dickey to EW, 2/2/1909. "Shirtsleeves": McGill article, "The Multimillionaire Nobody Knows," *Saturday Evening Post*, 5/5/51.

Robert put on overalls: Photo, RWP. Employment history: Hayes speech, seventieth birthday; Elliott, pp. 89-90. "Good old muscle jobs": *The City Builder*, May 1923, RWP. Trip west: Itinerary, photos, RWP. Description of Nell: Kennedy, *Devotedly*. Ernest hired Robert: Elliott, p. 90. Robert set off for Asheville: McGill, AC magazine, 9/8/40.

Robert met White, bought trucks: *The Sandbag* (White Company publication), 10/25/29, RWP. Wedding "most brilliant": AJ, 10/18/12. Gift of $1,000: List of gifts, EW to RWW, RWP. Baker anecdote: Elliott, pp. 92-93. "He thought I was making a mistake": Profile by Medora Field Perkerson, AJ, 5/27/23. Penitentiary held bankers: Elliott, p. 93.

White had reason for hiring Woodruff: Letter, Gans to White, 10/8/13. "I don't waste time": Elliott, p. 94. Woodruff re Yellowstone Park: *Ibid.*, p. 89. Woodruff promoted, made $300 a month: Memorandum of Occupation, RWP. Woodruff hired Roseberry: Roseberry folder, RWP. Woodruff golfed with Bobby Jones, hunted with Ty Cobb: Photos, Ichauway and RWP. Deed to house: Letter, EW to RWW, RWP. Letter from White salesmen: RWP. "Woodruff gives credit": *The Albatross* (White Company publication), Jan. 1918, RWP. Photo: *Georgian American*, 1/7/17, RWP.

Woodruff designed truck body: Letter, Lt. Col. H. J. Gallagher to RWW, 8/23/17, RWP. Woodruff cultivated older men, joined Nonas: Folder, "Norias Hunting Club Finances," RWP; JJ int. Potter arranged loans: JJ, Yearley ints; loan statements, Guaranty Trust, RWP. Teagle befriended Woodruff: Unpublished manuscript, biography of Teagle, Nicholas A. Curry, May 1992.

Ernest confided envy: Letter, Edith Honeycutt to RWW, 7/9/70, RWP. Abie Cowan anecdote: Elliott, pp. 65-66. Ernest treated Robert's wife "like dirt": M. Hodgson, Jr., int. Footnote: Kahn, *RWW*, p. 43. Ernest flicked woman with strop: Letter, James D. Allen to RWW, 5/28/51, RWP. Robert hired George: Wells, *A Life*, p. 87. Robert promoted, drew attention: Letter, W. R C. Smith to RWW, 8/4/21, RWP. CC ordered 30 trucks: Letter, H. Jones to RWW, 8/8/21, RWP. Robert had world on a string: Letter, J. D. Allen to RWW, 8/8/21, RWP.

Ernest signed over 1,000 shares: List of gifts, J. W. Brown to RWW, 4/7/23, RWP. Robert didn't know how much CC he owned: Letter, RWW to Ilah Warner, 4/9/23, RWP. Concern over nepotism: Letter, Wardlaw to RWW, 5/4/39. Howard hated traveling: Manuscript, "My Thirty Three Years with Coca-Cola, 1890-1923," H. Candler, CCA. Asa and Mrs. de Bouchel: AC, 2/1/24 and 2/5/24; *Onezima de Bouchel v. Asa G. Candler*, Case No. 619, GI 8090, Federal Records Center, East Point, Ga.

Schoolboys chanted: Garrett int. Candler married May Little Ragan: NYT, 2/10/24, quoted in Graham and Roberts, p. 123.

Dobbs's associates purged: Letter to W. C. Bucher, 12/12/21, CCA. Jones re bottles: Text, speech ca. 1919, CCA. Bradley, Glenn, and Wickersham visited Robert in New York: Elliott, p. 118. Teagle promised job: Manuscript marked "John Love" but otherwise unidentified, ca. 1930, RWP. "A pig knows about Sunday": JJ int. "Hang the chart": "Love" manuscript. Robert tried counteroffer: Elliott, pp. 118-19.

"Having a very difficult time": Letter, RWW to Warner, 4/9/23. Dividend hiked: Minutes, CC board, 11/27/22. $4 million in treasury: Atlanta Georgian, 1/24/23. Flora Candler upset, Woodruff went to Callanwolde, "I need help": JJ int. William anxious to protest; Howard calmed him: Letter, H. Candler to Charles Culpepper, 4/16/23, CCA. Preliminary step: Minutes, CC shareholders meeting, 2/26/23. Hirsch made general counsel: Minutes, executive committee meeting, 2/26/23. Special session: Minutes, board meeting, 4/28/23.

Woodruff redecorated office: Treseder memoir, CCA. Woodruff hired friends: Friendly Hand (CC publication), 12/3/23, CCA. Description of CC building: Treseder. Woodruff hired Key as "vice president": Kahn, RWW, p. 46. Woodruff in Moose Jaw: Los Angeles Express, 2/1/24; minutes, executive committee meeting, 10/29/23. Montreal, New Orleans consumption levels: CC annual report, 2/1/28.

D'Arcy calculations: Printer's Ink, 11/24/21, D'Arcy archives. Fountains peaked at 115,000: Text, J. Jones speech, ca. 1924, CCA. "Arm's length": Term paper, Holland Judkins, Jr., Jan. 1948, CCA. Woodruff's emphasis on quality: Bottler, Oct. 1924. Rowland anecdote: Rowland, pp. 30-31. "Mean squint": M. Hodgson, Jr., int. Woodruff never asked if orders were carried out Goizueta int. Joseph Jones quotes: JJ int. "Eight O'clock Club": Letter to RWW, 4/30/25, RWP. Board of Control: Treseder memoir. Woodruff picked sales team: Friendly Hand, 12/3/23.

Woodruff reopened Chero-Cola case: Minutes, Advisory Committee meeting, 8/14/23. Footnote: Chero-Cola Booster, Apr. 1923, CCA. Anecdote of Harrison Jones and father: Dorsey int. Alterations to formula: Diet Coke I, p. 1131. Woodruff drove to Columbus, got Bradley's promise: JJ int; Elliott, p. 217. "Sell the company as an institution": Printer's Ink, 9/18/24, D'Arcy archives. "Charm of Purity": Memo, "Analysis of Coca-Cola Advertising, 1915-1925," CCA.

Woodruff retrieved formula: Minutes, CC board meeting, 2/23/25; Elliott, p. 127; W. A. Heath int/CCA. Rules re formula: Minutes, CC board meeting, 4/27/25; affidavit of Robert Keller, Diet Coke III, p. 294.

"I've just been lucky": Perkerson profile, AJ, 5/27/23. Woodruff's fear of being misunderstood: McGill observation, Saturday Evening Post, 5/5/51. White anecdote: Printer's Ink, Sept 1929, RWP. Woodruff's bromides: Detroit News, 6/29/23; Edward Thierry's syndicated column, ca. 1923. Woodruff interviewed reporters: B. C. Forbes column, Atlanta Georgian, 3/2/28. "Thoughts" in Friendly Hand, issue of 10/1/23. Woodruff's code: Folder marked "Codes: Personal," RWP. Origin of Acmaro's name: JJ int. Not as tough as father: Elliott int.

Woodruff and D'Arcy: M. Hodgson, Jr., int. Lee description, background: Advertising Age, 1/1/51. Lee's letter to mother: 4/5/17, CCA. Adept with rifle: St. Louis Post-Dispatch, 12/23/50, CCA. "Best work I have ever done": Letter, Lee to father, 3/8/21, CCA. Gray Saturday in Oct. 1921: Letter, Lee to father, 10/29/21, CCA. Woodruff gave Lee the White account Letter, Lee to mother, 7/7/22, CCA.

"We wanted to promote": RWW quoted in Bell Papers. Woodruff as best man: Louis and Yazijian, p. 44. Lee "bridged the gap": Letter, Gresham to RWW, 1/6/63, RWP. Sundblom background: *Chicago Tribune* magazine, 12/21/69; *Insight* (D'Arcy publication), Dec. 1980; *Advertising Age*, 3/22/76. "I hadn't the slightest idea": Letter, Sundblom to Kurtz, 12/5/55, CCA. Dobbs's dilemma: Testimony, 1/20/16, *Chero-Cola* case, U.S. Patent Office, CCA. A million calendars, 17 million napkins, etc.: Testimony of B. S. McCash, *Ibid*. Lee wanted "family resemblance": Paper, Roland Krebs, 1960, D'Arcy archives.

Lee re Winnie the Pooh: Letter to RWW, 8/25/31, RWP. "Ritz Boy" ad: CCA "An idea like free enterprise or democracy": Proposal, Lee to RWW, 11/14/49, RWP. "American youth and romance": "Analysis of Coca-Cola Advertising, 1915-1925."

SIX: SHORT SALES

Woodruff sent man on secret mission: Letter, Horsey to RWW, 12/16/24, RWP. Woodruff wanted to develop Europe: Letter, Horsey to Powers, 9/3/29, CCA. Candler sent salesman in 1899: Bell Papers. CC "followed flag": Mooney int. Early expansion: Watters, p. 179. Howard nagged board: *Bottler*, Sept. 1926.

Sales restricted to Americans: Letter, Horsey to Kelly, 7/13/33; speech, Burke Nicholson, Jr., 12/4/73; Nicholson int. Candler promised "invasion": 1913 newspaper interview, cited in Bell Papers. Linton episode: Letter, Dobbs to J. J. Willard, 7/22/19, CCA; letter, Delcroix to H. Candler, 8/4/21; M. Hodgson, Jr., int.

Horsey's findings in London: Report, Horsey to RWW, 12/31/24, RWP. Woodruff given $150,000 limit for Mexico: Minutes, CC board meeting, 1/26/25.

Woodruff claimed clandestine Foreign Department: Elliott, p. 127; Kahn, *RWW*, p. 69. Office opened at 111 Broadway: Text, article by Russ McCracken, 1/9/59; memo, Curtis to Hayes, 7/11/41, CCA. Curtis typed like machine gun: Bacon memoirs, CCA. Ocean liners: Transcript, Bell int with Charles P. Swan, 3/21/66, CCA. Order for freight-car load; expansion in 1926 and 1927: Bell Papers. Woodruff used concentrate and beet sugar: *Refresher*, vol. 8, no. 3, 1976, RWP.

Foreign Department was amateurish: Swan int. Horsey spoke only English: Letter, Horsey to RWW, 12/20/35, RWP. Horsey tried to do too much: Memo, H. Jones to RWW, 9/20/29, CCA. French sales were $94.22: Folder, "Foreign Sales," May 1931, RWP. Woodruff's trip to Europe: Letter, "Eight O'clock" members to RWW, 4/30/25, RWP. Harrold's expenses: Memo, W. S. Kell to Horsey, 8/26/25, RWP; Kahn, *RWW*, pp. 62-63. Woodruff at Monte Carlo: *Ibid.*, p. 154. Power of attorney: Minutes, board meeting, 4/27/25, CCA.

"The cash register rang": Text, H. Jones speech, CCA. "Gee-whizzers": Watters, p. 3. Power caught in crossfire: Bell int with John H. Power, 3/3/66, CCA. Study of intersections, use of billboards: *Advertising Club News*, 12/15/30, D'Arcy archives; Armbruster int.

CC's radio program, contest: *Bottler*, Apr. 1959. Woodruff fired salesmen: *Printer's Ink*, 12/6/28, RWP. A replica of Woodruff's office, with the original furniture, is maintained on the twelfth floor of the Coca-Cola tower. "Bitsy" Lott: Mrs. Lott refers to herself as "fat folks" in a telegram to Ina Good, ca. 1935, RWP. Woodruff declined bonus: Transcript, meeting of RWW, Sibley, and others, 10/20/33, Sibley

Papers. "My prosperity": Letter, Kelly to RWW, 2/10/26, RWP. CC's financial condition: Unpublished article titled "Corporate History," 2/5/32, CCA.

Ernest operated pool, speculated: Balance sheet, Piedmont Securities, 3/26/25. Big buy in Oct. 1926: Letter, S. E Boykin to RWW, 11/8/26, in folder marked "Mr. RWW—Securities—Coca-Cola #1," RWP. Ernest's syndicate engaged in short sales: Balance sheet, Piedmont Securities, 10/15/25, RWP. Dan Rountree anecdote: Bradley Hale, John H. Boman, Jr., ints. Ernest's holdings worth $4 million, Robert's worth $1 million: Financial statements, RWP. Robert and Nell went on cruise: Itinerary, RWP. "Only time I felt rich": JJ int; Elliott, p. 140.

Woodruff's gambling: Folder marked "Bets," RWP. Woodruff bet passengers, beat them home: AJ, 6/19/27, RWP. Bennett had "empty feeling": Letter to RWW, 5/17/39, RWP. White situation: Transcript, meeting of RWW, Sibley et al., 10/20/33, Sibley Papers. Woodruff and White decided to quit Nonas, buy own plantation: Letter, RWW to Frances Arnold, 8/30/77, RWP; JJ int. Groomsman anecdote: Elliott, pp. 98-99. Price tag on buyout plan: Memo, 2/5/29, White Company folder, RWP.

Woodruff executed short sales, using surrogates: Brief to IRS, John E. McClure, 5/10/37, Sibley Papers; legal memo to file, Homer Hendricks, 5/17/37, RWP.

Statistical Department warned: Report, "Coca-Cola Economic Position," 10/23/26, with memo by H. B. Garner, 10/21/26, CCA. Movement against narcotics: Memo, H. Jones to file, 10/29/29, CCA; Musto, pp. 197-205. Woodruff leased cocaine plant in Peru: Letter, Hayes to Stuart J. Fuller, Far Eastern Division, U.S. State Department, 4/28/37, RHP. Footnote: Letter, Hayes to M. J. Hartung, 8/6/62; Hartung's unpublished memoirs, 6/1/66, RHP.

Stock prices recovered: NYSE listings, AC, 1927 and 1928. Freeman's sales: Letter, Rainwater to RWW, 1/16/28, RWP. "Sad guess": McClure IRS brief. EW's holdings: Trust Company digest, 5/25/20, AHC. Ernest chided Robert Letter, EW to RWW, 12/21/27, RWP. Ernest "always comes through": Pat Martin, quoted in letter, Glenn to EW, 3/13/33, RWP.

Ernest put CC stock in play: Memo, Piedmont Securities, 4/17/28, RWP. (Trust Company of Georgia's general ledger indicates 4,972 shares of Coca-Cola common stock were sold between Dec. 1927 and 3/31/28: Report prepared Jan. 1965 by W. Bethel Minter.) Price of common reached $130: AC stock listings. Wall Street grew curious: R. L. Barnum syndicated column, "The Day in Finance," 2/2/28.

Forbes saw Woodruff, Woodruff's quotes: Forbes column, *Atlanta Georgian*, 3/2/28, RWP. All-time high: AP, 4/3/28. 'Terrific punishment": Barnum, 4/3/28. "Sensational climb": AP, 4/9/28.

Hopkins background: Article by Medora Field Perkerson ca. 1936 and other clippings in a scrapbook lent to the author by Lindsey Hopkins III. First airmail: AC, 10/2/11. Hopkins description: Lindsey Hopkins III int. "Divine spark": Letter, Thornton Fincher to Hopkins, 4/22/34, scrapbook.

Hopkins leaked: AP, 4/10/28. Borrowed $1 million: Canceled note, dated 4/9/28, scrapbook. Anecdote of Ernest calling Hopkins: McKee Nunnally, Sr., int. Hopkins demanded list of shareholders: NYT, 4/18/28. Hopkins accused insider crowd, labeled ringleader: AC, 4/18/28. Ernest decided to sell for good: AC, 4/26/28. Glenn letter to shareholders: 4/16/28, RWP. Bradley said, "Let the other fellows do the talking": AC, 4/18/28.

Board meeting of 4/30/28: AC, 5/1/28. Ernest boarded *Crescent Limited:* AC, 5/3/28. Ernest met Stetson, discussed Canada Dry merger: *Fortune,* June 1937, CCA; report marked BP-II 289, Harvard Business School, RHP. "Greatest trader": Bond, p. 78. Discussions with Saylor, Canada Dry up $7: AC, 5/9/28. Deal was dead, Woodruff went home: AC, 5/10/28. Glenn wrote another letter: 6/13/28, RWP. Hopkins wrote letter: 6/14/28, RWP. Hopkins paid off loan: Scrapbook.

Woodruff boarded ocean liner: Itinerary, RWP. Gave camera to Boy Scout: Photo, June 1928, RWP. Cooler: Rainwater speech, Mar. 1929, CCA. Kelly went to Asheville: Staton int/CCA. Sales committee meeting: Minutes, 9/25/28, CCA. Horsey tried to get okay: Letter, Horsey to Powers, 9/28/28, CCA.

"I have gotten poor": Letter, RWW to White, 1/24/28, RWP. Glenn and Hirsch lent shares: Hendricks memo. Footnote, Woodruff sold Class A: On 9/24/31, 9/28/31, and 9/29/31, RWW sold $819,000 worth of Class A shares, according to telegrams in RWP. (Woodruff's oft-repeated statement that he'd never sold any Coca-Cola stock thus was not accurate.)

"Troubles and afflictions": Letter, RWW to Harry Hodgson, 11/3/28, RWP. Ichauway: Observations based on author's visits, Dec. 1989 and Feb. 1991. Debate over lodge: JJ int. Woodruff offered bounty for snakes: AJ, 7/16/29, RWP. "Malaria": Numerous sources, including McGill column, AC, 12/12/49. 40 percent suffered: *Albany Herald,* 8/31/37. Quinine: Ozzie Garrett, Mae Bailey ints. Bud Walker's leg: *Baker County News,* 8/2/29. "Get on top": Letter, Gresham to RWW, 9/21/66, RWP.

White's accident: Unidentified clipping, 9/29/29, RWP; Elliott, p. 142. Woodruff arranged to be made president: Elliott, pp. 143-44; correspondence with Virginia White, RWP. "I'll live in a Pullman": NYT, 10/3/29, RWP. *Time* item: 10/14/29 issue. World Series: RWP. *Cleveland Plain Dealer,* undated clipping, RWP. White Motor stock fell: Stock listings, AC.

Meeting at White Building: *Bottler,* Mar. 1930, reprinted from *Printer's Ink,* RWP. Woodruff dissolved pool, "not a howling success": Letter, RWW to Teagle, 11/14/29, RWP. "Sound Your Horn": Letter, Rainwater to RWW, 11/24/31, RWP. Woodruff stopped at every light: Letter, Gresham to RWW, 12/2/40, RWP.

"Corporation presidents . . . dream": *Chicago Daily News,* 2/6/30, RWP. "Pause That Refreshes" ads: CCA. Chemists conducted test, found ecgonine: Transcript, hearing before Senate Agriculture and Forestry Committee, 6/24/30, CCA. "Coca-Cola addiction": Testimony of W. G. Campbell, *Ibid.* Hirsch assigned Heath to double-check, Heath found cocaine: Report marked "confidential," Heath to Hirsch, 7/12/28, RHP. Chemists forwarded findings to Col. Nutt: Campbell testimony.

Gortatowsky sold nineteen kilos of cocaine: Affidavit by Gortatowsky, Oct. 1928; minutes, meeting of Permanent Central Opium Board, League of Nations, Geneva, 8/14/33, and copy of report titled "Traffic in Opium and Other Dangerous Drugs," all RHP.

Predicament involving imports, Merck allowance: Memo, H. Jones to file, 10/29/29, CCA. "Mr. Woodruff has been phoning": Letter, H. Jones to Hirsch, 11/27/29, CCA. Nutt agreed to hold off: H. Jones memo, 10/29/29. Woodruff lined up Crisp: Telegram, H. Jones to Crisp, 3/10/30. Porter listened with sympathetic ear: Letter, Crisp to H. Jones, 4/7/30. Porter's agenda: Musto, p. 205. Porter agreed to amend: Letter, Crisp to H. Jones, 3/10/30, CCA.

Ways and Means Committee: Transcript, hearings 3/7-3/8/30; letter, Schaefer to Hirsch, 3/15/30, CCA. State Department roadblock: Letter, Crisp to H. Jones, 4/8/30, CCA. Woodruff called in favor from Edge: Letter, Hayes to RWW, 1/21/58, RWP. Secretary of State Cotton: Undated article, the *N.A.R.D. Journal*, citing letter from Cotton to Senator Smoot, 4/24/30, CCA. CC suspended use of Lima plant: Letter, Hirsch to U.S. State Department, 1/15/33, RHP. No. 5 to $1.11 per pound: Memo, H. Jones to RWW, 7/28/30, CCA.

Woodruff's schedule, lunch of sardines: *Fortune*, July 1931. German situation: Study, written by Powers, 12/11/29; memo, Horsey to Kelly, 5/18/33, CCA. Powers "struggling along": Letter, Powers to Horsey, 6/20/29, CCA. Powers called on Woodruff: Powers study, 12/11/29. Workman barked *"Eine!"* Letter, Powers to H. Jones, 5/13/30. Woodruff gave loan, took mortgage: Contract, 2/10/30, CCA.

CC "operating illegally": Horsey memo, 5/13/30. Holding companies: Audit, 1/18/36, CCA. Ernest found opposing Robert "distasteful," boycotted meetings: Letter, EW to RWW, 4/4/31, RWP. Powers asked for $5,000 more: Letter to H. Jones, 4/2/30, CCA. Powers's books "appalling," Horsey warned home office: Horsey memo, 5/18/33. Woodruff invested $100,000: Memo, Curtis to file, 6/9/39, CCA.

Kelly assigned to Germany: Letter, Acklin to Kelly, 4/10/33, CCA. Kelly description: M. Hodgson, Jr., Ellis ints. Kelly kept manuals: "A Sales Manual for European Coca-Cola," ca. 1935, CCA; brochure, "It's Always Summer Indoors," RWP. Put governors on accelerators: Letter, Kelly to RWW, 10/3/33, RWP. Kept record of every round of golf, dressed well, drank champagne: M. Hodgson, Jr., int. Rumor that he jumped from woman's window: Ellis int.

Kelly brushed Powers aside: Letter, Powers to RWW, 2/14/31, RWP. *Seufzertasche:* Bell Papers. Materials: "Sales Manual," CCA. Sold 4,000 cases: Letter, Powers to Acklin, 4/13/32, CCA. More than 60,000 cases in 1932: Keith oral history, CCA.

Coca-Cola golf balls: Letter, Wayne Kell to RWW, 3/27/31, RWP. Drivers used tongs and shoulder pads: Tom Watson Brown int. Jones's view of vending machines: Memo to RWW, 10/18/29. *Fortune:* July 1931 issue.

Repeal affected stock prices: AP, 12/18/32. Strategy backfired, stock prices fell: Listings, AC. Ernest revived syndicate: Folder marked. "Coca-Cola Trading Account," 1932, RWP. "Lower class 'tipster sheets'": Letter, EW to RWW, 4/25/32, RWP. "Sweating blood," buy order: Speech text, Glenn, 5/19/36, AHC.

Averted "sectional panic": Draft letter, McClure to IRS, 11/27/39, RWP. "Break the tension" ad: AC, 7/7/32. Bottom at 68½: AC, 12/18/32. "Strenuous" days: Letter, EW to RWW, 4/25/32. Sold short while "holding the bag": Letter, EW to RWW, 6/20/32, RWP.

Barrage of suggestions: Letter, EW to RWW, 2/5/33, RWP. Bradley backed Robert: Letter, Bradley to EW, 2/25/32, RWP. Bradley said "my friends," turned red: *Columbus Ledger*, 2/12/60, CCA. Robert Woodruff "nervous and depressed": 2/25/33 letter, RWP. Visit from Gresham and Richardson: Letter, Gresham to RWW, 2/7/34, RWP. Woodruff announced extra $1 million: *Editor & Publisher*, 11/26/32, D'Arcy archives. H. Jones recommended beer: Memo to RWW, 7/5/32, RWP. Dobbs recommended investing: Letter to W. C. Bucher, 12/29/32, CCA.

SEVEN: PEPSI

Billboard owners gave free space: Memo, H. Jones to RWW, 10/27/33, RWP. *Ann Vickers:* Letter, Lee to RWW, 3/29/33, RWP. Coca-Cola appeared on 20,000 walls, etc.: Memo, unsigned, 2/25/32, CCA. Description of illustrations: From Munsey, *Collectibles.* Allen booklet: Garrett manuscript, 2/14/57, CCA. "Junior League": Letter, Sundblom to Kurtz, 12/5/55, CCA. Mrs. Wigglesworth: Letter, Forbes to RWW, 9/20/34, RWP.

Dayton bottler: Report, H. Bell, 5/23/30, CCA. Conveyor belt: Talley speech, 6/25/58, RWP. Brother John's: *Advertising Age,* 8/29/31, D'Arcy archives. Sundblom Santa: *Insight* (D'Arcy magazine), Dec. 1980; Wally Armbruster, int. "Dear Santa, Please Pause Here": Munsey, p. 236. "On his fanny": *Rolling Stone,* 1/3/74.

Turner Jones campaign: Memo, T. Jones to RWW, 8/15/33, RWP. "Back to Normal" ad: 1933, CCA. "Innocent. . .healthy child viewpoint": Jones memo, 8/15/33. Bolton memo: 9/26/33, D'Arcy archives. Ladies on diving board: Ad, *Ladies Home Journal,* Aug. 1934, CCA. *Dinner at Eight* ad: CCA. CC "intoxicating": Quoted in *Good Health,* Jan. 1931, D'Arcy archives. Hirsch got Seal of Approval: Bell Papers. Lee quote: Letter to RWW, 3/39/33, RWP. Stock price: AC, 7/18/35.

Hirsch's lawyers filed suits: *Opinions, Orders.* Activities of Trade Research Department: *Fortune,* July 1931; Kahn, *Big Drink,* pp. 125-27; Treseder memoir, p. 55. Footnote: *Coca-Cola* v. *Mrs. P. K. Xeppas, Coca-Cola* v. *G. W. Seignious,* and other cases filed in U.S. Circuit Court, District of Georgia, Federal Records Center, East Point, Ga.

Guth background, description: Bio, "Six and One Half Decades with Charles G. Guth," prepared by CC lawyers, 3/26/41, CCA. "The Strange Case of Loft vs. Guth, the Great Pepsi-Cola Mystery," 1939, Coming Events, Inc., RWP. "He wore spats": Lunsford int.

Guth and Loft; Guth's meeting with Harris: Transcript, Guth's testimony, *Pepsi* case. Guth's acquisition of Pepsi; Pepsi's history: "Report on Pepsi Cola 1939," Frank Troutman and J. Rogers, CCA. Footnote re Pepsi-Nola: Testimony, J. C. Mayfield, *Koke* case. Hirsch wanted to make Pepsi a target: Hirsch deposition, *Koke,* 3/16/18, CCA. Hirsch changed mind: Letter, Hirsch to H. Candler 4/14/22; letter, Sibley to RWW, 1/11/38, RWP, containing Hirsch's testimony in *Chero-Cola* case.

Taka-Kola: "Report on Pepsi Cola 1939"; *Taka-Kola* case. Investigators spat out Pepsi: AP dispatch, undated but ca. 1933; New York *American,* 1/11/33, CCA. Tried to prove substitution: *Loft,* case. Guth knew law: Guth's testimony, Exchequer Court, Ottawa, 3/31/37, CCA.

$10,000 reward and claim: AP, 5/10/32, CCA. CC filed suit, Guth claims threat of destruction: NYT, 5/5/32. "BEVERAGE BATTLE OF THE CENTURY": *New York Journal,* 5/17/32. First courtroom engagement: AJ, 6/7/33; ruling, *Loft* case, 6/6/33, CCA. Lunsford int. Court costs of $60,000; Guth turned to bottling: Guth testimony, Ottawa. Guth doubled amount, sold $450,000 worth: "Strange Case."

Woodruff re "chiselers": Letter, B. C. Forbes to RWW, 7/28/38; DeSales Harrison memo, 10/23/40, RWP. CC officials called Pepsi "Imitator": Memo, Oehlert to RWW, 8/16/57, CCA. Guth hired Hawkes: Smart's argument, Ottawa.

Woodruff out of debt—RWW paid off the final $350,000 of a loan with Guaranty Trust in Oct 1934 and a $425,000 loan from his family 7/31/34: File, Accounts & Notes Payable, RWP. Ernest gave $1 million gifts: Transfer statement, 6/4/32, RWP.

Woodruff lost patience with Lupton: Memo, RWW to file, 8/4/31, RWP; letter, RWW to Lupton, 11/18/31, RWP. Lupton belittled "kindergarten": Letter to RWW, 12/22/32, RWP.

Whitehead sons were hellions: B. Jones, Garrett ints; correspondence of Hughes Spalding and his father, Jack, HSP. Account of Conkey Whitehead and Frances Porter, photo: AC, 1/12/30. Whitehead divorced again: *Chicago Tribune*, 8/23/33. Detective found him drunk, turning blue: Jimmy Sibley int. "Big streak of mean": Letter, Jack Spalding to Hughes Spalding, 11/11/38, HSP. Spalding visited Pierre: Letter, H. Spalding to father, 12/7/36, HSP.

Whiteheads agreed to sell: Memo, Hirsch to RWW, 12/28/32, RWP; memo, Brock to RWW, 9/21/59, CCA. Ernest criticized, "in a jam": Letter, EW to Acklin, 3/8/33, RWP. Hirsch's bad blood toward Sibley: Letter, Acklin to RWW, 6/27/37; letter, 4/29/37, Hirsch to CC directors, RWP. Woodruff asked advice, relied on Sibley: Memos, Sibley to RWW, 3/30/33, 8/4/34, and 10/25/34, RWP. Woodruff gave car: Letter, Sibley to RWW, 12/27/34. Sibley considered for CC presidency: Letter, Jack Spalding to Hughes Spalding, 2/15/36, HSP.

Sibley's song at Woodruff anniversary: Program, RWW anniversary dinner, 10/17/36, RWP. Woodruff arranged motorcade: Letter, Hughes Spalding to father, 3/31/37, HSP.

CC moved to Delaware, Hirsch reluctant to go: Exchange of letters, Sibley and Hirsch, 8/22/35, RWP. Plum Street looked "forsaken": Letter, Lott to Holmgren, 10/11/34, RWP. Woodruff bought tickets: Patterson int. Hirsch and Sibley disagreed; Hirsch wanted to fight Pepsi: 4/29/37, Hirsch to CC directors (resigning as general counsel). Sibley took a dim view: Letter, Sibley to RWW, 5/17/37, RWP.

CC filed suit; Herridge's exchanges with Judge MacLean: Transcript, Exchequer Court, CCA. Hirsch and Smart blundered: Privy Council decision, 1942 All E.R. 615, 5/19/42, CCA. *Cola Call*, Oct 1985, CCA. Background of trademark law: *Corpus Juris Secundum*, vol. 87, "Trade-Marks, Etc."; *The Law of Trademarks, Tradenames and Unfair Competition*, James Love Hopkins, W. H. Anderson Company, 1917; *The Law of Unfair Competition and Trade-Marks*, Harry D. Nims, Baker Voorhis & Company, 1947. Ko-Co-Lem-A Mitch-O-Kola decisions: *Opinions, Orders*. Roxa-Cola: *Roxa-Cola* case.

Hayes description: Biographical pamphlet, New York Community Trust, 1976; NYT, 6/22/77. "Anyone who thinks": Memo, Hayes to RWW, 12/13/37, RWP. "Great American drink": Letter, Hayes to RWW, 11/17/38, RWP. "American as Coca-Cola": *Music News*, 7/13/39; *Washington Post*, 6/24/39. Hayes gave McGill $500: Memo, T. Jones to RWW, 10/7/36, RWP.

"Kings have abdicated": Draft, Hayes essay, Jan. 1937, RWP; reprinted, *Bottler*, Apr. 1959. Hayes wanted to leave "quieter. . .backwaters": Letter, Hayes to RWW, 7/30/53, RWP. Hayes history: Bio pamphlet; memo, Marion Allen, Jr., to JJ, 2/18/75, RWP. Woodruff wanted to hire Hayes: Manuscript, marked "John Love" but otherwise unidentified, ca. 1930, RWP. Hayes as prolific correspondent: Author's examination of RHP.

Lawyer raised questions about No. 5: Report, Hayes to RWW, 4/28/37, RWP; letter, Hayes to Anslinger, 4/20/37, Anslinger Papers, Pennsylvania State University, University Park, Pa. Assignment "full of maggots": Letter, Hayes to RWW, 12/21/35, RWP. Hayes flattered Anslinger: Letter, Hayes to Anslinger, 3/21/36,

Anslinger Papers. Mayes misled Anslinger: Letter, Hayes to Anslinger, 4/23/37, RHP. Anslinger authorized export, gave "benediction": Letter, Hayes to Anslinger, 4/20/37, Anslinger Papers. New Studebaker: Letter, Hayes to RWW, 1/21/58, RWP.

William Allen White letter: 3/9/38, RWP. (Elsewhere in the company's archives the second paragraph is deleted.) Sibley/Hayes exchange, "given the gods a giggle": Memo, Hayes to Sibley, 5/6/36, RWP.

CC's market value: *Barron's*, 11/7/38. Sales doubled: Report, Continental Insurance Company, Oct. 1938, RWP. Woodruff's complaint about the New Deal: Letter, RWW to H. H. Johnson, 2/2/34, RWP. Description of Senator George: AJ, 12/20/42; *Time*, 7/19/43 (cover story); JJ, Lawson ints. "Bob, come back in my room": JJ int. Loans totaling $8,000: Letters, Senator George to George Adams, 10/8/36 and 1/7/38; Adams affidavit, 1/24/44 (in folder marked "confidential"), RWP. Sen. George's actions re sugar tax: Memo, Hayes to file, 6/25/36, RWP.

D'Arcy quote: Letter to RWW, 6/18/36, RWP. Chicago World's Fair: Letter, Clint King to RWW, 10/5/65, RWP. Howard Candler walked up: Letter, H. Candler to RWW, 11/12/34, RWP. Black-tie dinner: Speech text, 5/19/36, AHC. Woodruff subjected to criminal investigation: Brief to the IRS, Sibley, 5/10/37, Sibley Papers. Footnote: Yearley int.

"He was God": Patterson int. "Skillful navigating": Letter, H. Jones to RWW, 1/2/34, RWP. Porters' smiles: Letter, Good to Acklin, 11/18/36, RWP. Striding corridor with head down: Patterson int. Description of H. Jones's birthday: Memo, D. Harrison to Bechtel, 5/24/37; scrapbook, "When Harrison Jones Was Fifty," CCA.

"Easy to see down into the valley": *Saturday Evening Post*, 5/5/51. "I belong to the discontented": Text, RWW speech, 4/7/53, RWP. "Big voice": Letter, Lott to Good, 10/22/35, RWP. Acklin cracked: Letter, Hayes to RWW, 8/5/33. Woodruff "wearing out the hired hands": *Ibid.* "Thank goodness": Letter, H. Spalding to father, 12/7/37, HSP.

Beer-only regimens: Letter, Sibley to RWW, 12/17/36, RWP. Recuperate at White Sulphur Springs: Letter, RWW to Rainwater, 7/14/31, RWP. Trick knee: Letter, M. Hodgson, Sr., to RWW, 2/9/37, RWP. "Twitching": Letter, A. D. Whiteside to Hayes, 4/28/39, RHP. "Urgent, wistful need": Letter, Gresham to RWW, 1/23/36, RWP. Why pray only once a week: Letter, RWW to M. Hodgson, Sr., 2/13/37, RWP.

Nell unable to have children: Dorothy Jones int. Cousin (John Bratton) killed: Letter, RWW to Connally, 4/17/35, RWP. Ernie misdiagnosed: Letter, Fischer to RWW, 6/2/39, RWP. Nurse remembered Robert "like a little boy": McCurdy int. Woodruff and McGill: Letter, McGill to RWW, 1/19/66; letter, RWW to McGill, 1/22/66, RWP. "I'm going crazy": Ellis int.

Ernest Woodruff held up, Moyers case: AC, 1/14/37; letters, H. Spalding to father, 11/21/36, 11/28/36 and 1/15/37, HSP. "Some day," Woodruff told Hayes: Letter, 6/21/39, RWP. Hayes answered: 6/27/39, RWP. Truck in New Orleans: Letter, Boykin to RWW, 11/27/34, RWP.

Hirsch withdrew: Letter, 4/29/37, Hirsch to CC directors, RWP. Sibley drew up plan: Memo, Sibley to RWW, 12/22/37, Sibley Papers. Chicago sting operation: Lunsford int. "More goods for the money": Memo, Kelly to RWW, 2/22/38, RWP. "Bed bugs just crawl in": Memo, H. Jones to RWW, 8/15/41, CCA. D'Arcy hamstrung: In-house memo, 1/19/39, D'Arcy archives.

"New kind of beverage," Sibley's response: Letter, Sibley to RWW, 3/6/40, RWP. Sibley detested "filching": Sibley's 12/22/37 memo. Bucknell: Memo, Sibley to RWW, 2/26/41, RWP. Lawsuit a week: Memo, Sibley to RWW, 3/6/40, RWP.

Woodruff sided with Sibley: Sibley's 12/22/37 memo. (Woodruff also gave Sibley a $30,000 bonus at the end of 1937.) Woodruff kept "Fresh Syrup" file: Note, Curtis to Kelly, 11/25/33. Woodruff "expressed himself": Letter, D. Harrison to Carl Thompson, 7/3/35, RWP. Sundblom left canvases unfinished: Armbruster int.

MacLean ruled: Opinion, Exchequer Court, CCA. Sibley pleased, quote re "unprincipled concern," Pepsi's countersuits: Letter, Sibley to RWW, 8/8/38, RWP. Guth lost Loft case: *New York Herald Tribune*, 9/20/38. Description of Mack: Biographical study, compiled by CC investigators, 10/26/40, RWP. Guth notebook: "Six and One Half Decades with Charles G. Guth," RWP. (Mack's partner Wallace Groves was a friend of Ernest Woodruff: Letter, Groves to EW, 10/11/38, RWP.)

Nims conducted survey: Sibley memo, 12/22/37. Sibley fainted: Letter, H. Spalding to father, 11/5/38, HSP. Mack initiated contact after "Guth out of the way": Letter, Mack to RWW, 6/26/39, RWP. "Minimum of acrimony": Handwritten note in Mack file, RWP. Dixi-Cola suit Opinion, 3/5/40, U.S. District Court, *Dixi-Cola* case. Surprise witness in Royal Crown case: AP, 11/11/40; *RC* case. Canadian Supreme Court reversed: Order, Supreme Court of Canada, 12/9/39, CCA.

Mack's sales techniques: *Pageant*, undated but 1946, CCA. "Pepsi and Pete": *Tide*, 1/15/41, CCA. Fifteen-second jingle: *West* magazine, 2/9/69, RWP. Aired 300,000 times: Enrico, p. 18. *New Yorker* cartoon: 1/20/40 issue. Twenty-eight million radios: Memo, 2/13/40, D'Arcy archives. "Sound as parsnips": Letter, Hayes to Lee, 2/10/41, RWP. Woodruff "not wholly sold": Letter, RWW to Rathbun, 2/21/30, RWP. Comedian "steals the show": Letter, Lee to T. Jones, 1/19/35, RWP. Singin' Sam: Memo, Lee to T. Jones, 10/12/36, CCA. Kostelanetz: *PM* magazine, 4/13/41.

Consumer Union Reports: "The Battle of the Colas," Aug. 1940 issue. Bride with calla lilies: June 1939 issue. Brenda Frazier: New York *Sun*, 12/28/38, RWP. Hayes alarmed: Letter to RWW, 11/17/38, RWP. H. Jones discussed 12-ounce drink: Memo to RWW, 8/15/41.

CC won Dixi-Cola: Opinion, U.S. District Court, Baltimore, CCA. Fourth Circuit overturned Dixi-Cola: Ruling, 1/11/41, 48 U.S.P.Q. 164, CCA.

"Quite disappointing": Telegram, Sibley to RWW, 1/11/41, RWP. Turkey at Sing Sing: Undated, handwritten note, Hayes to RWW, RWP. Mack had visited, sent new proposal with secretary: Memo, RWW to file, 9/18/41, RWP. Sibley objected: Letter to RWW, 1/21/42. Sibley drafted resignation: Draft letters, 12/15/41, Sibley Papers. Sibley took trolley: Lunsford int.

Woodruff settled with Mack: Agreement, Mack and H. Jones, 5/13/42, RWP. Sibley ventured to London: Memo to RWW, 1/21/42; Jimmy Sibley int. Lord Russell's quotes: Transcript, Privy Council ruling, CCA. Lords held trademarks upside down: Jimmy Sibley int.

EIGHT: WAR

Account of Carl West's flight: Wartime diary kept by West, CCA. Powers set records: Report, Brown Brothers Harriman & Co., 8/18/44, RWP. "Back of each bottle a Nazi": Powers to Acklin, 4/5/33, CCA. Blumhoffer spread rumors: Memo, Sibley to

RWW, 10/7/36; memo, H. Jones to RWW, 8/28/37, CCA. Hebrew lettering: Bell Papers; *Top Secret* magazine article, ca. 1937, RWP.

Hayes called on Borchers: Memo, Hayes to RWW, 6/23/38, RWP. Salesmen encountered hostility: M. Hodgson, Jr., int. McGill trip, description of convention: Letter, McGill to RWW, 3/23/38, RWP. CC considered smuggling: Memo, unsigned but probably Acklin, 2/16/40, RWP. Powers asked McGill to smuggle money, episode on train: Letter, McGill to Austin, 5/4/66, RWP. Powers died: Cable, Max Keith, 12/14/38, RWP; Bell Papers. Keith background: Keith oral history, CCA. Woodruff wanted "little better understanding": Letter, Acklin to RWW, 2/18/39, RWP.

FTC communication: File compiled by DeSales Harrison, CCA. Ben Oehlert background: Bio, CCA; memo, Sibley to RWW, 1/27/38, RWP. Oehlert suggested discontinuing bonuses: Letter, Oehlert to RWW, 1/4/40, RWP. Oehlert's wartime strategy: Memo, Oehlert to H. Jones, 7/3/41, CCA. Lunacy: Memo, H. Jones to RWW, 5/28/42, RWP. Oehlert tried Hayes: Memo, 7/15/41, RWP. "Folly": Memo, 3/26/42, RWP

Gilmore cable: Apr. 1941, RWP. CC as "morale food": Letter, Hayes to B. Osier, 11/12/41, RWP. War Department asked for supply in Iceland, Woodruff gave green light: Memo to file, Curtis, 11/4/46, CCA. Hickam Field: Photo, "Importance of Rest-Pause," CCA.

OPM order: Order M-55, 12/13/41, CCA. CC asked to return sugar: Letter, C. Roberts to RWW, 4/19/44, RWP. Woodruff led contingent Memo, Oehlert to file, 1/3/42, RWP. Public complained: Letter, Bobby Jones to RWW, 1/3/42, RWP.

Singin' Sam ad: Text, 2/10/42, RWP. Woodruff killed ad: Memo to Oehlert, 2/11/42, RWP. "Importance of Rest-Pause": Copy, CCA. Government had claim on molasses, etc.: Letter, Oehlert to Office of Price Administration, 4/7/42, RWP. Senator George killed profits tax: Memo, Oehlert to RWW, 5/20/41, RWP; *PM* magazine, 9/19/40. Forio to WPB: Memo, Forio to Acklin, 5/4/44. Oehlert's definitions: Memo, Oehlert to OPM, 2/12/42, RWP. Interest in training camps, Chester, S.C.: Heath int/CCA. Sales down 16 percent: Neilsen survey, RWP. H. Jones warning: Memo to RWW, 12/30/42, RWP. Pepsi sales rose: Neilsen survey, RWP.

Mizell suggested sugarless CC: Letter to RWW, 2/26/42, RWP. Woodruff okayed sugar substitute: Letter to Acklin, 10/2/42, RWP. Caffeine prices: Letter, Hayes to RWW, 5/5/54, RHP. Guano, urea: Memo, Hayes to RWW, 9/1/42, RWP. New process for No. 5: Memo, RWW to Hayes, 3/30/40, RWP. Curtis and cassia: Letter to RWW, 2/25/37, RWP. Footnote: Memo, 10/24/46, RHP. Shortages: Memo, W. G. Lamb, 5/31/43, CCA. RWW quote: Letter to Gordon, 6/12/42, RWP.

"American cola": Memo, Troutman to Acklin, 7/15/42, RWP. Keith placed in charge: State Department communiqué, 10/3/41, RWP. Keith sent word, loyalty doubted: Memo, Nicholson to RWW, 3/13/42. Description of Keith: Burke Nicholson, Jr., int.

Company mythology: CC archivists are unable to find any written reference to the "anywhere for a nickel" policy. First mention is a 5/10/44 memo marked "confidential" in RWP, written by George R. Jackson, Jr., sent to RWW by Cliff Roberts. Agronsky comment: Text, 5/30/42. Oehlert report: 6/1/42.

Invitation from Eisenhower: Cable, 6/29/43, CCA. Men preferred CC over beer: Eisenhower's testimony before Senate subcommittee, AP, 2/3/51. "I wish I could be home": Unidentified newspaper clipping, sent by Oehlert to War Food Administration, 8/9/43, RWP. Curtis scoured, got AA-3 rating: Letter, Curtis to Fowler, 8/24/44, RWP. Pepsi complained: Curtis, memo to file, 3/21/44, RWP. Marshall ordered: War Department Circular No. 153, 7/5/43, CCA.

Thomforde's experience: Oral history, 12/8/65, Bell Papers. Quartermaster said space meant for "bullets, guns": Bacon memoir, CCA.

GIs wanted mail, cigarettes: Unpublished manuscript re CC in wartime, 1945, James Kahn, CCA. Spitfire pilot: *Los Angeles News*, 1/29/42, CCA. Casablanca plant: *Stars and Stripes*, 11/2/43, CCA. Monte Cassino: Photos, War Picture Pool, 3/16/44, CCA; photo, *Des Moines Register*, 3/20/44. Mauldin cartoon: 7/7/44, United Feature Syndicate. Pyle re auction: *St. Louis Post-Dispatch*, 1/26/44. "Little things": Bell Papers. Dietrich: UP, 10/12/42. Japanese radio and Tokyo Rose: Bell Papers.

West crept back into Brussels: West diary. CC's attempts to join Normandy invasion, Bacon's escapades in Europe: Bacon memoir; Bacon oral history, CCA. Cooke into China: TO dispatch, 2/25/45, CCA. Braendle in Philippines: Bell Papers. Okinawa incident: UP, *Wheeling* [W. Va.] *Intelligencer*, 6/17/45.

Brussels liberated: West diary. TOs crossed Rhine, went to Frankfurt, Stuttgart, Essen: Bacon oral history. Meeting with Keith: *Ibid.*, and Keith oral history, CCA.

Curtis grew suspicious, sent investigator: Report, Walter J. Derenberg to Ladas, 1/14/46, CCA. Keith preserved Mrs. Powers's coat: Letter, Dr. Hertha Curtius to Keith, 12/16/45, CCA. Keith kept plants open: Keith oral history. Curtis re "more satisfactory": Report on Germany, 11/6/45, CCA. Keith named administrator, went back to work: Keith oral history.

CC spent $5.5 million: Curtis memo, 10/17/46, CCA. Survey in *American Legion* magazine: Memo, Oehlert to Steele, 10/10/45, RWP. D'Arcy wrote: Letter to Sibley, 5/21/42, RWP. Gilbert memo: 9/1/42, RWP. Gilbert banished: Sledge int/CCA. Marx's suggestion: Letters to RWW, 8/20/46 and 9/8/46; Woodruff's response, 9/23/46, RWP. Woodruff at Pebble Beach: Letter, Thompson to RWW, 3/16/44, RWP. Woodruff predicted: Memo, H. Jones to RWW, 9/1/44, RWP.

Acklin drank, had breakdown: JJ int. Mizell warned: Memo to RWW, 6/20/45, RWP. (Woodruff's response is scribbled in the margin.) McCollum story: Elliott, p. 29. Hobbs named president: CC press release, 5/6/46, CCA.

Hodgson's, Inc.: Extensive files, HSP. $450,000 loan: Letter, Scott Candler to Emil Schram, director of RFC, 8/5/38, RWP. (Woodruff used "helpful influence" to obtain the loan: Letter, Spalding to RWW, 6/21/56, RWP.) "Walls of Jericho": Letter, Hughes Spalding to Harry Hodgson, 8/20/47, RWP. Spalding admired Hobbs: Letter, Spalding to RWW, 9/22/49, HSP.

Hobbs's soft shoe: Lunsford int. "Great listener": Kurtz int. Woodruff "enamored": Lawson int. "Ass-kisser": M. Hodgson, Jr., int. Trouble signs: Kurtz int. "Legree": Letter, Hayes to Hobbs, 3/6/47, RWP. "Old farts": Lawson int. Brock criticized Sibley: Letter, Brock to Sibley, 11/17/43, Sibley Papers. Hobbs and Bacon clashed: Bacon oral history.

Woodruff called Hobbs: JJ int. Woodruff left for trip, asked for boots: Memo, RWW to Nicholson, 5/27/46, RWP. "Touch of the jitters": Letter, RWW to Gresham, 8/29/46, RWP. "I have retired": Letter, RWW to Hayes, 11/7/46, RWP. Hedda Hopper: *Los Angeles Times*, 7/12/47. Hobbs getting along "by and large": Memo, H.

Jones to RWW, 6/10/46, RWP. Took away company cars: Letter, RWW to Thompson, 7/20/46, RWP. Fought Brock: Letter, Brock to Hobbs, 3/13/47, RWP. Failed to work with Lee: Letter, Lee to RWW, 10/10/46, RWP.

RWW re "swan song": Text, 5/22/47, RWP. Woodruff returned: Letter, RWW to Teagle, 6/28/46, RWP. "Trouble with Hobbs" joke: Lawson int. "One of the mistakes": JJ int. Hayes criticized: Letter, Hayes to Hobbs, 9/22/47, RWP. Spalding watched in discomfort: Jimmy Sibley int. Woodruff reluctant to dismiss: JJ int. Hayes quit: Letter, Hayes to P. Brown, 1/7/48, RHP. Oehlert quit: Letter to RWW, 1/8/48; memo, 2/27/48, RWP.

Steele description: Photos, bio file, CCA. Called people "Pal": Memo, John Springer, 3/17/77, D'Arcy archives. Carny's trick: Confidential source. Grew up around world, devised "Sono-Meter": *Coffeyville* [Kan.] *Journal*, 6/29/54, CCA. Steele discovered Downey: Werblin int. Woodruff at clubs: Photos, CCA; Jack Spalding int; letter, *New York Daily Mirror* columnist Nick Kenny to RWW, 7/9/46, RWP. Hannagan and Sheridan: Sheilah Graham column, 2/17/49.

Woodruff hired Steele as vice president: CC memo, 6/16/45. Convention description: *Bottler*, Apr. 1948. "Maestro": Telegram, Nicholson to Ina Good, 4/4/46, RWP. "Tent pole": Letter, Hannagan to RWW, 9/17/46, RWP. D'Arcy survey: Letter, Nicholson to RWW, 1/12/45, RWP. Steele's vision of future: *Fortune*, June 1950; *Forbes*, 6/15/51. More ideas than "dog has fleas": Charles Adams int/CCA. Expense account: *Ibid.*

Lamb memo: 12/2/37, RWP. Steele complained: Springer memo, D'Arcy archives. Nicholson took dim view: Burke Nicholson, Jr., int. Nicholson slashed Steele's budget: Adams int/CCA. Breezy day, Oak Room: *Investor's Reader*, 4/20/53, RWP. "Sweet-smelling" S.O.B.: Whitworth int.

Mack out of ideas: *Tide*, 5/18/51. Mack losing money, prices up: Memo, Brock to RWW, 11/13/50, RWP; *Forbes*, 6/15/51. "And better, too": *Fortune*, Jan. 1947. Stock fell: *Forbes*, 3/1/49. Steele hired CC men: JJ int. Steele put books in order: *Investor's Reader*, 4/20/53. "I'm going to put you in Cadillacs": Tedlow, p. 99. Pepsi's appeal to poor, "kid trade": *Forbes*, 6/15/51.

"Bounce to the Ounce" campaign: Ad, NYT, 1/10/50. "No comment": *Tide*, 1/20/50. "Damning indictment": Memo, Hayes to Nicholson, 1/20/50, RWP. Pepsi sales fell: *Sponsor*, 9/2/52, RWP. Bra factory: AP, 12/19/51; undated memo, Hobbs to RWW, RWP. *Time* cover, quotes: 5/15/50. Pepsi complained: Export Sales *Bulletin*, undated, RWP. Winchell: *New York Daily Mirror*, 5/17/50. Copps quote: Memo to RWW, 6/1/50.

"Fatal error": Letter, RWW to Brock, 11/13/50. "Half as much": Export Sales *Bulletin*. 5-cent fares gone: Unidentified newspaper clipping; *Fortune*, Jan. 1951. Holding the Alamo: Memo, Hobbs to Hannagan, 1/21/50, RWP.

NINE: BLACK AND WHITE

Except as otherwise noted, descriptions of Ichauway and its routines are from the author's two visits there, in Dec. 1989 and Feb. 1991. Woodruff ate first: JJ int. Woodruff's homes: Various descriptions in RWP. Dogs' diets: Edgar Duncan int. "I never heard the Boss overtalk": Adkins int. Woodruff asked two questions: JJ int. Gardner thanked: Letter to RWW, 12/19/38, RWP. Guest found arrowhead: Burke Nicholson, Jr., int.

Saturday evenings at Ichauway: JJ int; photos at Ichauway. Ichauway baseball team: Cal Bailey int. Ozzie Garrett anecdote: Garrett int. Huffman census, "dat'll do" quote: Bailey int. Lynching, footnote: Pinkerton report to RWW, 6/28/33, RWP. Woodruff spent $60,000: Memo, R. W. Bowling to RWW, undated but ca. 1951, RWP. "Foolish idea": Pinkerton report. Letter thanking God: Elliott, p. 38. Funeral for Lloyd George: Letter, RWW to Rose Davis, 4/14/64, correcting description in an undated newspaper column, "About Dogs," ca. 1939, RWP. Woodruff provided dogs medical care, quote, asked overseer: Adkins int. Black residents bemused, shake heads: Cal Bailey int. Bergen's visit, magic show: AC, 2/1/48, RWP. McGill re "Yonder Comes Day": undated column (ca. 1934), AC, RWP.

Farley's speech: 11/21/50, described in statement of complaint from National Fair Play Committee, Jan. 1951; *Daily Worker,* 12/18/50, RWP. Hannagan warned, quotes: Letter to. RWW, 8/22/46, RWP. Hayes echoed: Letter to RWW, 1/1/51, RWP. New York plant hired first black: *New York Courier,* 5/5/51, RWP.

Number of blacks in United States: Letter, Hayes to RWW, 5/8/53, RWP. Mack directed scholarships: *Pageant,* undated but 1946, RWP. Mack launched "Leader": *Printer's Ink,* 9/9/49, RWP. Woodruff asked Hayes to do "a little bit more"; Hayes suggested: Letter, Hayes to Goodloe, 9/12/50, RWP.

Crackers' exhibition, Klan threat: AP, 4/8/49 and 4/11/49; letter, Hayes to Hobbs, 4/18/49, RWP. Maddox's warning: Letter, Maddox to Montgomery, 8/17/63, RWP. Woodruff joined Tuskegee: Letter, Hayes to Hobbs, 9/19/50, RWP; *Bottler,* Dec. 1950. Footnote: Text Washington's address, RWP. Woodruff's view, re "hooey": Letter, RWW to Glenn, 6/28/43, RWP.

Release sent to sixty-three black publications: Press release, Hannagan, 10/30/50, RWP. Company advertised in black magazines, hired Kendrix: Memo, Coste to Hobbs, 12/12/51, RWP. CC hired Hampton, Jackson: Washington, D.C., *Nite Life,* 2/13/53, RWP. Hiring policy was timid: Memo, Coste to Hobbs, 12/12/51. Woodruff invited bankers, had to take train, Aldrich anecdote: Ivan Allen, JJ ints. Visit to Tuskegee: Allen int; *Bottler,* May 1953; *Ebony,* Feb. 1953.

Hartsfield as progressive, re 1946 Supreme Court decision: Martin, *Hartsfield,* p. 50; Herbert Jenkins, quoted in AJC, 1/18/81. "Go slow" philosophy: Martin, *Hartsfield,* p. 48. Reduced size of signs, addressed blacks as "Mr.": *Ibid.,* p. 49. Quarter of Police Department thought to be Klansmen: *Newsweek,* quoted by Jenkins in AJC, 11/17/79. Hartsfield integrated police: *Ibid.* Thousands cheered, voters helped: Martin, *Hartsfield,* p. 51. "Too busy to hate": Allen, p. 21. Hartsfield consulted Woodruff, deferred: Martin, *Hartsfield,* p. 8; *Washington Star,* 1/21/79; also, photos show Hartsfield listening obediently to RWW during luncheon, 10/5/61, RWP. "Hell, it's my city": Lawson int.

Hartsfield indebted, scrip: AC, 12/3/36, RWP. Woodruff paid retainer: Martin, *Hartsfield,* p. 35. Jenkins's favors: Letter, Charles Eberhart to Jenkins, 8/30/57, RWP. Hartsfield attended Calhoun funeral: AC, 11/17/45. Hartsfield kept portrait of Woodruff, etc.: Elliott, p. 187.

"Besotting sin": *Time,* 8/17/62. Woodruff's vision of better South: *Forbes* column, 8/12/37, RWP; McGill article, AJC magazine, 8/19/56, RWP. Woodruff shanghaied GE board: AJ, 4/16/50, RWP. Woodruff's split personality: McGill, *Saturday Evening Post,* 5/5/51.

CC worth more than half a billion dollars: Report, Continental Insurance Company, Oct 1938, RWP. CC had 15,000 shareholders: Letter, Turner Jones to George Adams, 8/6/45, RWP.

Woodruff's suite with grand piano: Snapshot, RWP. Woodruff held $19 million worth: Financial statement, 7/31/53, RWP. Winchell guessed: *New York Daily Mirror*, 11/10/47, RWP. Top marginal rate: IRS Public Affairs Office, Washington, D.C. Secretary found $37,000 credit: Memo, Holmgren to RWW, 3/20/45, RWP. Servants kept savings account: JJ int. "Never had any desire": Multiple references; origin probably in text by McGill, ca. 1939, RWP. "Two out of three": attributed to Henry Troutman, Tarver int. Louis Marx story: AJC magazine, 12/20/81, RWP.

Woodruff founded cancer clinic: Press release, July 1937, RWP. Woodruff recruited Scarborough: Isabelle Scarborough int. Woodruff on giving money away wisely: McGill column, AC, 10/22/63, RWP. Woodruff's created foundation: Proxy statement, 4/11/46, RWP. Ernest told friend: Letter, Fischer to EW, 6/23/38, RWP. Woodruff and Spalding led campaign for Whitehead fortune: Extensive correspondence, RWW and Hughes Spalding, HSP. "Stir up a stink": HS to Jack Spalding, 12/4/35, HSP. "The buzzards": Letter, HS to RWW, 9/17/53, HSP. Woodruff used $7,500 of his own money: B. Jones int.

Woodruff appointed board of Coca-Cola International: Correspondence, R. W Bowling and RWW, RWP. Woodruff replaced Glenn with Sibley: Wells, *First Hundred*, pp. 180-81; letter, HS to RWW, 5/23/46, HSP. "Our problem": Letter, Craft to RWW, 4/21/49, HSP. Howard Candler anecdote: Letters, Hughes Spalding to RWW, 7/19/47 and 7/25/47, HSP. Henry's suicide: AJ, 11/28/47. Letter to Nell: 10/25/47, RWP. Robert looked after Henry: JJ int. Illness in New York: Letter, Hughes Spalding to Mrs. Evans, 8/28/48, HSP; JJ int. McGill letter: Aug. 1948, RWP. Woodruff accepted "lecture": Letter, RWW to McGill, 8/28/48, RWP.

Steele's strategy: *Fortune*, May 1961. "Let's get rid of this honkytonk look": *Forbes*, 6/15/51. New logo: *Fortune*, May 1961. Faye Emerson's show: NYT, 9/29/50; photo, *Tide*, 10/13/50. Editors of *Advertising Age*: 1/22/51 issue, RWP. "If you want to milk": *Forbes*, 6/15/51. Steele competed with CC: Letter, Thompson to RWW, 4/18/51, RWP. "Don't clean teeth": *Bottling Industry* magazine, 12/6/55, RWP.

CC's radio fell to 42nd, shows canceled: Memo, Oehlert to Hobbs, 2/27/48, RWP. Programs were "clearinghouse": *Sponsor*, Mar. 1949, RWP. Problems with Downey show: Memo, Toigo to CC executives, 6/1/50, RWP. Disney's first appearance: Disney press release, 11/2/50. CC turned down Western: Memo, Coste to RWW, 3/27/51, RWP.

Lee tired: Letter, Lee to RWW, 12/30/49, RWP. Lee's death: Obit, UPI, 12/22/50. "What you want": Munsey, p. 317. Hannagan re "dames": Letter to Morse, 10/28/52, RWP. Nicholson proposed "Citizen" program: Memo, Nicholson to RWW, 6/1/50, RWP. Bottlers grew restive: Memo, C. W. Hodgson to RWW, 11/18/50, RWP. Harrison Jones warned: Letter to RWW, 10/30/50, RWP.

Letter from nine bottlers, dated 1/9/51; Martin's response, 1/30/51: Montgomery Papers, AHC. Veazey Rainwater, Jr.'s "Coke-tail" parties: Telegram of invitation, 3/31/51, RWP. Father disowned, wife sued: AJC, 4/29/51. Rainwater at annual meeting: Transcript, 5/7/51, RWP. James Woodruff quote: Letter, Hughes Spalding to RWW, 6/11/51, HSP.

McCay testified: Memo, Hayes to May, 9/27/50, RWP. May explained: Statement, 9/19/50, RWP. Brock admitted he had no ideas: Memo to RWW, 10/3/50, RWP. *Pageant* article: Oct 1951 issue. Hayes tried to nudge Hobbs: Memo, 11/17/50, RWP. "Faddists": Memo, 3/25/52, RWP. "Mixmaster diet": Memo, Hannagan to RWW, 3/25/52, RWP.

Nicholson re "Your smile": Letter to RWW, 10/7/55, RWP. Nicholson memo: 7/17/51, RWP. Woodruff "confused": Letter, Thompson to RWW, 9/12/51, RWP. Woodruff brooded, felt logy: Letter, RWW to Hayes, 9/22/51, RWP. Woodruff "in the game": Letter, C. W. Hodgson to RWW, 4/18/52, RWP. Woodruff ordered cards: Letter, Hayes to JJ, 7/11/52, RWP. "Traffic cop": Letter, L. F. Montgomery to RWW, 6/11/52, RWP. Hobbs fired, Nicholson installed as caretaker: Burke Nicholson, Jr., int. Dr. Stare: Folder, RWP; *McCall's*, Mar. 1954.

Christened plane: JJ int. Pricing problems: Letter, Hayes to RWW, 10/22/51, RWP. Woodruff explored possibility of 7½-cent coin: Kahn, *RWW*, p. 133; letter, Hayes to RWW, 10/22/51, RWP. (A handwritten note by RWW suggests he also contemplated a 3-cent coin.)

Woodruff met Eisenhower at dinner Invitation, Waldorf-Astoria, 6/19/45, RWP. "Another Coke": *Washington Times-Herald*, 6/19/45, RWP. "Poker after dinner": Letter, RWW to Eisenhower, 12/1/48, EL. Roseberry anecdote: The closest contemporary account is McGill in the *Saturday Evening Post*, 5/5/51. Candidacy "essential": Letter, RWW to Eisenhower, 11/1/51, RWP. Argument with Harriman: *New York Post*, 10/22/52. Election night anecdote: Letter, RWW to author, quoted in AJC, 4/16/77; text, Tex McCrary radio broadcast, 11/5/52. Eisenhower dropped coin request Kahn, *RWW*, p. 133. Mourning doves: JJ int.

Special pass: Letter, Ann C. Whitman to RWW, 2/11/54, RWP. Woodruff showed up after golf; argument after stag dinner: JJ int. President asked favors: Drew Pearson column, Feb. 1956, RWP; JJ int; *New York Herald Tribune*, 6/22/59.

Robinson background: *Look*, 6/1/54, RWP. Hannagan died: Obit, *Bottler*, Mar. 1953. River House nightcap anecdote: JJ int. Nicholson as "harmonizer": Letter, Hayes to RWW, 7/13/54, RWP. "What the Boss wants": JJ int. Pepsi's sales doubled: Shearson, Hammill & Co. report, May 1955, RWP. "Beloved Son": Memo, Nicholson to RWW, 11/8/56, RWP. Woodruff "stepped out": *Time*, 2/14/55. *Business Week*: 1/12/55 issue. Woodruff created Finance Committee: Letter, Hughes Spalding to RWW, 11/24/54, HSP. "Disaster": JJ int. Sibley invitation: 3/10/55, RWP. Robinson "chatty": Letter, Hughes Spalding to RWW, 9/25/55, HSP. If a case fell: *Fact*, Nov. 1964. Gager: Bio, CCA. "Double-barrel" SOB: Sledge int/CCA. Oehlert read books: Ben Oehlert III int. Footnote: Cartoon in *New York Herald Tribune*, 1/13/57, RWP.

Insiders mocked CC campaign: *Business Week*, 2/12/55. D'Arcy bowed out: D'Arcy archives. Woodruff wanted "new phrases": Letter, RWW to Hayes, 10/11/56, RWP. Sledge quote: Text, Sledge speech, 5/19/52, CCA. Robinson thought CC "superior": Memos, Robinson to RWW, 9/16/58 and 9/17/58, RWP. Steele worried: *Bottling Industry* magazine, 12/6/55. Steele's apartment: *Time*, 5/19/58.

Reviewer blistered McCann's ads: Newsletter, John Redmond Kelly, 11/1/57, RWP. Robinson's salvo: *Sponsor*, 12/1/56. Truck color mixup: Letter, L. F. Montgomery to RWW, 7/3/56, RWP. Robinson kept plane: Whitworth int. Woodruff holed up, turned to Talley; Talley told Robinson, "You're through": JJ int. Celebration at Plum

Street: Broyles int. Robinson sent to Gary: Letter, Robinson to RWW, 6/25/58, RWP. "Dry spell": Letter, RWW to Ty Cobb, 4/26/59, RWP. Talley's energy, speech: Text, 6/25/58, RWP. Lectern: Charles Adams int/CCA. "Lee, get on your horse": JJ int. "Make it a short block": Adams int/CCA. Woodruff pleased: Letter, Garlington to Hayes, 8/26/60, RHP. "Saved company": JJ int.

Talley speech on race: Text, Oct. 1957, RWP. "One by one": Letter, Curtis to RWW, 8/8/50, RWP. 630 lawsuits: Letter, Brock to Hobbs, 1/5/50, RWP. Field man played private eye: Confidential source. Company avoided bribes: Letter, Hayes to Shillinglaw, 1/12/59, RWP. 418 foreign bottlers: Letter, Robinson to RWW, 1/19/56, RWP. Cheetah: Letter, C. J. Manussis to RWW, ca. 1951, RWP. Pig bristles: Letter, Horsey to RWW, 12/7/33, RWP. Description of Maharajah: Program and photos, dinner, Links Club, 12/14/56; unpublished memoir, Frank Harrold, RWP; NYT, 1/21/57. Hartsfield re Brazilian millionaire: *Fortune*, Sept. 1961, RWP.

"Never been. . .for integration": Letter, McGill to RWW, 9/26/58, RWP. "Ah tries": *Fortune*, Sept. 1945. Bobby Jones anecdote: Letter, McGill to Hayes, 9/2/66, RHP. Hartsfield integrating Atlanta golf courses: *The Reporter*, 7/11/57. T. M. Alexander: *Ibid.*

Woodruff's deal with Talmadge: Letter, Hughes Spalding to RWW, 9/14/49, HSP. "Best governor": *Time*, 6/26/50. George in political trouble: *U.S. News*, 4/29/55. "Old Walter": Ovid Davis int. Senator cried: Talmadge int. Woodruff sent emissary: Bell, Davis ints. Miss Lucy's quote: Lawson int.

Woodruff's birthday: Program, speech texts, AHC; Ellis, JJ, Garrett ints. Speakers go to studio: Letter, Bobby Jones to RWW, 12/29/59, RWP. Wrote Eisenhower: Letter, 12/8/59, RWP.

TEN: POLITICS

Steele's tour and "Ad-O-Rama" campaign: *Bottling Industry*, 5/5/59; Crawford, p. 193. "Sociable" campaign: *Editor & Publisher*, 3/26/60. "Away from poverty": Laidlaw & Co. study, 1963, RWP. Pepsi bottlers disliked campaign, Steele's itinerary: *Fortune*, May 1961. Crawford's luggage: unidentified clipping, RWP. "I hate to use my wife": WSJ, 5/9/59. Steele's death: Crawford in *American Weekly*, 7/31/60. (Crawford gives a somewhat more melodramatic account in her autobiography, pp. 195-96.) Barnet's succession, firing Kenyon & Eckhardt: *Fortune*, May 1961.

Pepsi's new headquarters: *American Soft Drink Journal*, 2/4/60. "Sign of Good Taste" dropped: Memo, Sledge to RWW, 12/30/59, RWP. Success of vending machines, Murray anecdote: NYT, 1/29/61. Introduced Sprite, RWW harbored misgivings: Letter, RWW to Kelly, 9/29/61. Fanta: WSJ, 9/9/60. Teem, Patio: NYT, 1/29/61. Rise of diet market, survey findings, Project Alpha, description of press conference: *New Yorker*, 3/14/63. Patio Diet Cola: AC, 5/21/63. BBDO struggled: Memo, Sledge to L. Talley, 7/13/60, RWP. Talley's reappraisal: Memo, Talley to Austin, Sledge, 10/6/62, RWP.

Brower's campaign for Pepsi: *Fortune*, May 1961. Census numbers: "The Philosophy of Coca-Cola Advertising," Sledge, Feb. 1954. McCann's "Things Go Better" campaign, $53 million: *Time*, 10/18/63; Laidlaw & Co. study. CC's celebrities out-of-date: Memo, Toigo to Nicholson, 6/1/50, RWP. Fisher: Letter, Robinson to RWW, 1/19/56, RWP. Bryant on Welk: CC press release, 9/10/65. "Hi-Fi Club": Sample text, radio broadcast, 1958, RWP. Montgomery quote: Letter, Montgomery to RWW, 5/22/52, RWP.

Duffield's visit to Disney: Unpublished Duffield memoir, "As I Recall," RWP. World of Refreshment description, teacher anecdote: *New York World-Telegram & Sun*, 5/20/64, RWP. Newsletter: World of Refreshment Bulletin, No. 4, CCA. Diane Sawyer: Photo, RWP. Carillon description, Schulmerich anecdote: WSJ, 3/24/64. Editorial in Scottsdale newspaper: 1/20/66. Per capita rose: E. F. Hutton report, Sept. 1964. Sinatra, Supremes: *Dun's Review*, Oct. 1964. "Why don't?": WSJ, 9/20/65. Bathyscaphe: *Dun's Review*, Oct. 1964.

Hitler liked Coke: UPI, 10/12/42. Castro: Photo sent to RWW from R. M. Thomas, 3/23/59. Farouk: Duffield memoir. Eisenhower in Delhi: Photo, *New York World-Telegram*, 12/12/59, RWP. Woodruff's note: RWW to Ann Whitman, 12/23/59, RWP. Eisenhower's reply: Letter to RWW, 12/26/59, EL.

Nixon in Moscow: Full account in *London Sunday Times*, 11/26/72. Robinson argued: Memo, Robinson to RWW, 6/8/59, RWP. Kendall nearly lost job: NYT, 4/11/65; *New York Journal American*, 4/22/59. "Khrushchev Learns": Enrico, p. 21. Nixon asked to meet: Invitation, Nixon to RWW, 9/14/59. Nixon at Hanes plantation: Letter, RWW to DDE, 12/14/59, RWP. Nixon's gaffe: Letter, RWW to Nixon, 12/21/59, RWP. No rapport with Nixon: JJ int. RWW supported Johnson, sent Downey to Hyannisport: *Ibid*. RWW detested Joseph Kennedy: *Ibid*. Kennedy wanted bottling franchises: Letter, Archie Lee to RWW, 11/30/42, RWP.

Nixon sounded out CC about a job: Memo, Lucille Huffman to RWW, 8/20/68, RWP; Ovid Davis int. Kendall approached Nixon: Memo, Charles K. Holmes to Luke Smith, 10/4/63, RWP. Meeting in Talley's office, rejection of Nixon: Davis int.

Nixon speech in Dallas: UPI, 11/22/63. Copy to Johnson: Memo, Austin to Oehlert, undated, RWP. Johnson's affinity for Coke: Photos, 5/13/64 and 9/12/64, RWP. Coke on *Air Force One:* Transcript, World News Roundup, 10/12/64, RWP. Johnson motorcade: Davis int.

Background of FDA labeling affair: Memo, Oehlert to RWW, 6/13/61; letter, Thomas F. Baker, American Bottlers of Carbonated Beverages, to George Larrick, FDA commissioner, 8/29/61; memo, Forio to RWW, 5/11/65. CC "can never be explained": Letter, DeSales Harrison to RWW and Acklin, 4/17/39, RWP. Ginzburg: *Fact*, Nov.-Dec. 1964. Larrick retired: NYT, 11/16/65. Johnson consulted with company on successor: Memo, Oehlert to Austin, 1/25/66. Goddard's decision: Federal Register, 1/27/66. Objection by Dr Pepper: Letter, Dr Pepper to FDA 2/19/66. Kickapoo agreement: Letter, Oehlert to National NuGrape Co., 2/25/66. Oehlert had letter mailed: Letter, Forio to borders, 2/11/66, RWP.

Coolidge description: CC bio; *Saturday Review*, Feb. 1981. Coolidge accustomed to leisurely board meetings: JJ int. Wanted to give counsel: Letters, Coolidge to RWW, 3/13/61 and 3/8/62, RWP. Woodruff considered Coolidge a pixie: JJ int; letter, Coolidge to JJ, 3/30/84, RWP. Woodruff criticized "beatniks": Memo, RWW to file, 8/26/64, RWP. Coolidge "grieved": Letter, Coolidge to RWW, 8/25/64, RWP. Letter triggered fury: Draft, letter of response, RWW to Coolidge, 8/26/64, RWP.

Vandiver in 1960: Vandiver, Bell, Jimmy Sibley ints. John Sibley on WSB radio: Text, AJ, 2/19/60. Sibley worried, Greer story: ATC, 8/6/77, RWP; Waiters, p. 242.

Hartsfield called on Sibley: Letter, Hartsfield to Sibley, 11/16/60. King praised hometown: AC, 11/8/63. Sit-in at Rich's, aftermath: Allen, *Mayor*, pp. 36-37. Sibley and Woodruff assigned impasse to Allen, anecdote about Walden and bathroom: Allen, p. 37; Allen int. Scene at Wheat Street church, King's quote: Allen, pp. 41-42.

Hartsfield divorcing, worried about scandal: Martin, *Hartsfield*, p. 131. Allen ran with Woodruff's support: Allen int. Black vote: Allen, p. 60.

Allen on his porch: Allen int. Ford Foundation anecdote: *Fortune*, 12/17/79, RWP. Weltner's design: Letters, Weltner to RWW, 5/17/62 and 5/27/62, RWP. Story in *Holiday:* May 1961 issue. Voters rejected: Allen, p. 70. Woodruff confided "quite difficult": Letter, RWW to D. Harrison, 8/3/62, RWP. Weltner re "grave danger": Letter, Weltner to RWW, 8/7/62, RWP. Woodruff counseled patience: Allen int.

Woodruff supported Sanders: Sanders int. Fixture in suite: JJ int. Key to elevator: Letter, Sanders to Lucille Huffman, 11/29/65. Woodruff supported Charles Weltner: Ovid Davis, Gerald Horton ints. Commerce Club description: AJC, 9/18/60. Leroy Johnson incident, Woodruff's intervention: Allen, pp. 94-95; Allen int. Baker County election official refused: Memo, unidentified, re story in NYT, ca. Mar. 1960, RWP. Baker as "hardest nut": U.S. Office of Education, quoted in NYT, 12/20/65. Sheriff terrorized blacks: Branch, p. 528. Touchtone drank, abused tenants: Memo, JJ to RWW, 5/30/62. Pensioned Touchtone off: JJ int.

Kennedy called Allen: Allen, p. 106. Woodruff's quote: *Ibid*, p. 108; Allen int. Woodruff's friends' criticism, his protection of McGill, quote: Martin, *McGill*, p. 75; letter, Martin to JJ, 5/8/72, RWP. Drafts of Woodruff's replies: 8/26/64, Coolidge file, RWP.

Rothschild and Hallinan invited: Letter, hosts to RWW, 12/16/64, RWP. No one accepted: AJ, 12/29/64. Woodruff's riding accident: Letter, RWW to Bekker, 4/7/65, RWP. Allen discussed dinner with Woodruff and Austin: Allen, Jeane Austin ints. Austin description: Bio, CCA. Austin told group to buy tickets, Allen's quote: Allen, p. 97. The chain reaction re government of Haiti: Author int with Helen Bullard, 1977; a slightly different version is recounted in *My Soul Is Rested*, by Howell Raines, Putnam, 1977. *New York Times* headline: 12/29/64 issue. Description of dinner: AC, 1/28/65.

Stock splits: Press releases, CCA. Sales neared $1 billion: *Miami Herald*, 2/6/66. Moshe Bornstein press conference: Memo, Austin to file, 4/8/66, CCA. B'nai B'rith: NYT, 4/8/66. Farley statement 4/12/66, CCA. Situation in 1949: WSJ, 4/18/66. Incident in 1961: NYT, 1/11/61, cited in ADL release. Plant in Cyprus: Bornstein in NYT, 4/14/66. Suit against Tempo: Austin memo, 4/8/66. Mount Sinai and Nathan's: *Time*, 4/22/66. Jewish leaders called on Eisenberg: Memo, Edwin Fisher to Charles Adams, 4/27/66, CCA. Negotiations with Feinberg: WSJ, 4/18/66.

Ruder & Finn advice: Memo, Ruder & Finn to Thomas J. Deegan Inc., 4/28/66, CCA. "Minimize impression": Memo, Deegan to CC, 4/15/66. Arab League boycott: Memo, Oehlert to Austin, 5/16/66, RWP. Presentation to Nasser, Makinsky experience: Letter, Vernon Hoppers to J. Talley, 6/30/66; letter, Makinsky to L. Talley, 7/9/66, RWP. Oehlert's lunch for Kamel, Kamel's desire to be "helpful": Letter, Oehlert to LBJ, 8/23/66, RWP. Heaton letter: 10/19/66, CCA. Austin's response: Memo, 10/26/66, CCA.

"Pull all the legs off: *Forbes*, 5/15/71. Austin's background: Confidential report, Proudfoot's Commercial Agency, forwarded to RWW by Dun & Bradstreet, 6/2/49, RWP. Austin marked for rise: Lawson int. Austin came in as "member of the family": Stuart Watson, quoted by Austin in letter to RWW, 6/16/65, RWP. Austin's talk on Negro spirituals: Tolleson int. Footnote: The Proudfoot report. Austin's marriage, promotions: Jeane Austin int. Woodruff and Talley sat on plane: Whitworth int. Austin's promotion: CC press release, 5/2/61. Austin's responsibilities: Memo, L. Talley to Austin, 11/14/61, RWP. Austin and movie: Jim Montgomery int.

Austin named president: AJC magazine, 6/24/62. Oehlert's remarks: Ben Oehlert III int. "Operation Flood": Text Austin speech, undated but summer of 1962, RWP. Austin posed for cover: *Business Week*, 8/24/63. "Pseudo-science": *Dun's Review*, Oct. 1966. Asked to join S&H, denied: Memo, Austin to RWW and L. Talley, 9/24/65, RWP. John Talley promoted: JJ, Ayoub ints. Pushed Frito-Lay merger: Jeane Austin int. (According to Ayoub, Austin blamed Fill Eisenberg for killing the deal and told reporters so.) Talley retired, quote: Letter, Talley to RWW, 6/20/66, RWP. Talley's wife wanted: JJ int. Talley likened RWW to Christ: Letter, Talley to RWW, 6/20/66. Woodruff presented sword: Text, RWW at Talley dinner, 6/9/66, RWP.

Austin saw problems: JJ, Jeane Austin ints. Unsmiling demeanor: JJ, Tolleson ints. "Gaunt": WSJ, 5/4/66. Harvard joke: JJ int. Austin with "smoke coming out": Letter, S. C. Van Voorhis to RWW, 5/2/84, RWP. WSJ headline: 5/4/66 issue. Spalding suggested: Letter to RWW, 5/6/66, RWP. Memo re dropping Downey: Austin to RWW, 9/16/66, RWP. Woodruff's response: RWW's memo to file, approximately same date, RWP.

Pension for widow (of Emory's Robert C. Mizell): JJ int. RWW declined to liquidate International: Memo, JJ to RWW, 9/30/64, RWP. Exchange re budget: Handwritten note, Austin to RWW, 12/3/67, with RWW's response, RWP.

Woodruff settled on Bo Callaway: Ovid Davis int; memo, Callaway to RWW, 1/21/66. Woodruff promised to raise $100,000, Callaway blabbed: Memo, JJ to RWW, 3/23/66, reporting gossip from former Governor Vandiver, RWP. Callaway "hard-headed": Davis int. Events of 9/6/66: NYT magazine, 10/16/66.

Woodruff poured more resources, Callaway meeting with black leaders: Davis int. Callaway "cocky": Memo, JJ to RWW, reporting Davis remark, 10/25/66, RWP. Sanders quotes: Sanders int. Davis spread money, unfriendly questions: Memos, Davis to RWW, 10/13/66 and 10/29/66, RWP. "Implications" of Maddox and CC: Memo, Davis to RWW, 12/15/66, RWP. Effort "has been financed": Memo, Davis to RWW, 12/5/66, RWP. Only mention was "progressive" interests: Memo, Davis to RWW, 12/13/66, RWP. Davis on Carter: Memo to RWW, 11/21/66, RWP.

Vietnam situation: Memo, J. Talley to JJ, 8/11/65, RWP. Problems in 1966: Trip report, David Brann, 6/24/66, CCA. Affair "grinds to a halt": Memo, Austin to RWW, 9/27/71, RWP.

Situation in Venezuela: Letter, R. M. Thomas to RWW, 5/8/61. No profits in South America: Letter, Thomas to RWW, 11/5/65. Pepsi "gaining ground": Memo, Talley to Austin, 10/5/65. Pepsi's export sales quadrupled: E. F. Hutton report, Sept. 1964, RWP.

Attempts to sell in Soviet Union: Memo, Austin to RWW, 1/5/67, RWP. Pepsi in Yugoslavia and Rumania: Letter, Farley to Austin, 12/21/66, RWP. Greece, Deegan: *Newsweek*, 3/18/68. Austin dismissed Deegan: Letter, Austin to Deegan, 9/17/68. Deegan went to work for Pepsi: Letter, Deegan to RWW, 12/12/68.

Austin at odds with Oehlert: Memos, Oehlert to Austin, 8/25/65 and 8/30/65; Leonard int. Oehlert "too big": Ben Oehlert III int. Austin had Oehlert appointed ambassador: Leonard, JJ, Ben Oehlert III ints; letter, Oehlert to Austin, 6/28/67. Footnote: AP, 2/5/70. Oehlert would have killed Austin: Ben Oehlert III int.

Austin flew to Berlin: Memo, Austin to RWW, 6/10/68, RWP. *Forbes* story: 8/1/67 issue. Gresham: Letter to RWW, 8/26/68, RWP. Bobby Jones's condition: Elliott int. Sunday visits: Atlanta Athletic Club bulletin, May 1978. "Sense of futility": Letter, Gresham to RWW, 6/21/62, RWP. Elevator installed: Isabelle Scarborough int.

"I don't like to be asked": AJC magazine, 5/9/76. George Woodruff's fear of kidnapping: Wells, *A Life*, p. 106. Footnote: Letters observed by author; names withheld for reasons of privacy. Bus driver: Memo, Jeanne Garrett to CC, 11/10/65, RWP. Bus company's instructions: Letter, Henry Taylor to Franklin Garrett, 3/11/66, RWP.

Story in *Atlanta Constitution*: 4/30/68 issue. Woodruff ran into Tarver: Witnessed by Jimmy Sibley. Huffman tried to coax: Letter, Huffman to RWW, 12/6/67, RWP. Nell's death: JJ int. "Lost my partner": Kennedy, pp. 152-53. "Tied myself to. . .a kite": *Ibid*, p. 56. Nell disarmed admirers: Ellis int. Birthday letter: Nell to RWW, 12/6/67, RWP.

Woodruff and Sanders at White House: Sanders int. (The aide was Tom Johnson, later president of Cable News Network.) Woodruff called Allen: Allen, p. 205. Allen realized: Allen int. Maddox cowered: Allen, p. 216.

Woodruff's drinking got out of hand: Elliott int. Woodruff's appearance: Snapshots, Apr. 1968, RWP. Deupree story: JJ int.

ELEVEN: "OCTOGENARIANS!"

Herndon moved next door: JJ int. "Comfort, health": Letter, Herndon to RWW, 7/15/69, RWP. Deupree swore: Letter, Deupree to RWW, 12/9/69, RWP. Ellis a favorite: Ellis int. Riding at Ichauway, robes and pajamas: Letter, Ellis to RWW, 3/10/71, RWP. "Your good opinion": Letter, Ellis to RWW, 9/13/70, RWP. Photo on dresser: Author's observation during Ichauway visit. Ellis demurred: Ellis, JJ ints. Woodruff went to office every day: Letter, JJ to Mrs. Dixie Dorian, 4/17/70, RWP.

"Littering the landscape": Memo, Austin to RWW, 11/28/69. Predicted trouble: Memo, JJ to RWW re Austin phone call, 4/22/70, RWP. "Quo Vadis" speech: Text, Georgia Bankers Association speech, 4/16/70, CC Collection, ESC. Aqua Chem description and price: Letter, Austin to RWW, 1/22/70. Misgivings: JJ int.

Saci, McGovern select committee: Memo, Ovid Davis to RWW, 7/15/69, RWP. Nader quote: Transcript, RWP. Operation Arden, "Real Thing": *Business Week*, 4/25/70; *Tropic* magazine, 8/26/73. "I'd Like to Buy": Munsey, p. 231; Doran int. Considered killing ad: Tolleson, Doran ints. White House dinner description: Memo, Austin to RWW, 2/4/72, RWP. Woodruff's worry about shrimp farm: JJ, Oehlert ints; memo, Austin to RWW, 12/22/77, RWP.

Austin becomes chairman, 5/5/70, CC release. Waited for Woodruff to resign: Jeane Austin int. Woodruff's strokes: JJ, Ellis, Elliott ints. Seriousness kept quiet: Honeycutt int. Gifts of $1 million: JJ, Yearley ints. Document: 2/15/72, RWP. Ludwig deal, argument with Woodruff: Memos, Austin to RWW, 4/17/73 and 5/4/73. The second memo describes their face-to-face meeting. Woodruff's misgivings: JJ int.

Woodruff pushing for successor: Letter, John Sibley to RWW, 11/13/70. Joke about Charles Duncan as asset, becoming protegé: JJ int. "Rising star": NYT, 1/10/71. Austin's meddling with Duncan: JJ, Ayoub, Jimmy Sibley ints. (Duncan declined to cite any specific complaints against Austin, but confirmed the unpleasant relationship.) Woodruff disappointed: JJ int. Footnote: Proxy statement, 1974, CC. Duncan bought ranch: Duncan int.

Austin's view of Woodruff, "octogenarians": JJ, Jeane Austin ints. Circulating memos: Charles Adams memo, 1/10/74. (John Sibley volunteered to retire after Woodruff accused him of "mumbling," but Woodruff asked him to stay on: Memo, Sibley to RWW, 10/5/71.) "I can't do that": JJ int. Trip to London: Letter, RWW to Putter, 10/23/73, RWP.

Luke Smith resume: CC bio. Smith "too nice": Jim Fowler, quoted by confidential source. Austin's view of Smith became apparent later, upon Smith's firing. "Look Up" commercials, quote, and Keough's honor: *Advertising Age*, 12/16/74.

Woodruff and Austin feuded: JJ, Elliott ints. Salary dispute: Memo, Austin to RWW, 11/11/75, RWP. Conflict over Eisenberg: JJ, Ayoub ints. Stock values: *Institutional Investor* magazine, Dec. 1974. Eisenberg's decision "to stop all direct contacts": Letter, Eisenberg to Robert W. Kirkpatrick, Jr., carbon to CC board of directors, 11/26/74, RWP. Criticism by *Institutional Investor*: Dec. 1974 edition, article titled "Stonewalling It at 'Coke.'"

Austin's criticism of Eisenberg and proposal he retire: Memo, Charles Adams to Austin, 11/12/74, RWP. Woodruff's refusal: Memo, Austin to Eisenberg, 2/3/75, RWP.

Austin's habits on company plane: Whitworth int. Export sales catch domestic around 1961: AJ, 10/16/63. CC strong in Germany, Japan, etc.: Memo, Austin to RWW, 5/4/73, RWP. "Fast on its way": NYT wire service, AJC, 8/8/71. Hiring communist: Memo, W. O. "Billy" Solms to RWW, 8/18/72, RWP. Marcos gift: Memo, Austin to RWW, 9/16/76, RWP. Contact with China: Letter, Austin to Harold Martin, 7/10/74, RWP. Contact with Havana: Memo, Austin to RWW, 2/13/74. Clandestine meeting: Patterson int.

"Milking time": Letter, RWW to Nixon, 3/7/69. Pepsi allowed into Soviet Union: *London Daily Mail*, 11/18/72; Louis and Yazijian, p. 203 (quoting *Time*, 11/27/72).

Re 1970 governor's race, Carter wrote Woodruff 1/8/69 asking to come to Ichauway "and talk about quail, bird dogs, and one or two other less important matters." Woodruff declined 1/13/69, saying, "I am in and out of the plantation and when I am here usually have a house full of guests." Carter's nose "out of joint": Memo, Ovid Davis to RWW, 10/5/70, RWP. Woodruff backed Sanders: Adamson, Leonard, Sanders ints.

Carter's statement: AC, 11/12/74. Austin letter to Cary: 4/14/76; RWP. Luncheon at "21": Guest list, 7/22/76, RWP. Austin trip to Mexico, Cabinet speculation: *Newsweek*, 2/7/77. Austin called Kirbo, withdrew name: Memo, Austin to RWW, 11/16/76, RWP. Lance and Jack Carter anecdotes, headline, Sadat story: *Newsweek*, 2/7/77. Austin in Cairo: Jimmy Sibley int.

Woodruff's gift of $9.9 million: AJ, 7/6/71; Massell news release, 7/6/71; and Massell int. The land was originally assembled by a pair of developers using a dummy corporation called TWFB, Incorporated, an acronym that was said to stand for "The Whole F***ing Block." When they were unable to complete the deal, Woodruff saw a chance to create a green space and at the same time provide a showcase for the facade of the new headquarters of his father's bank, Trust Company. In an interview for this book, Massell disclosed for the first time that Woodruff later approached him and offered to let him decline the gift if he thought the park might attract derelicts and become a political liability.

Hartsfield on "worst kept secret": Elliott, p. 60. "I don't remember": Text of Bois-feuillet Jones speech to Atlanta Rotary Club, 9/11/78, RWP. Shining Light: Program, 7/11/74. "'Anonymous Donor' Revealed": AJ, 7/12/74. "What's in the paper?": JJ int. Found him crying: Jimmy Sibley int.

Woodruff complained he was blind: JJ int. "I never cultivated": Letter, RWW to Frances Arnold, 2/21/79, RWP. Sterne called on Woodruff: Memo, Austin to RWW, 2/26/75. "There's no way for you to 'reenter'": Letter, JJ to RWW, 3/3/75. Woodruff's speech: Letter, Sterne to RWW, 3/7/75. White paper: Letter, Jimmy Sibley to RWW, 1/28/76. Woodruff's final gesture: Letter, Mrs. Willaford Leach to RWW, 7/4/76. *Journal* list AJ, 3/29/78.

Austin at GE board: Memo to file by Austin, 3/21/75, RWP. Austin predicted half the colleges would close: JJ int. Jeane Austin noticed clues: Jeane Austin int. Austin's drinking: Ayoub int, numerous other sources. Pepsi Challenge: Oliver, pp. 52-53. Tag line: *Business Week*, 6/12/78. Coca-Cola's response: Oliver, p. 55. Faux-comic spot, Crain quote: *Newsweek*, 8/30/76. (*Newsweek's* headline was "The Cola War.") People prefer Fresca: *National Observer*, 7/31/76. *Time* magazine quotes: 7/26/76 issue. Coke announced it would stop trying: Keough, AC, 11/16/76.

"Give me a smile": WSJ, 3/5/80. Musical folds: NYT wire, 5/8/76. Barnes review, NYT, 5/6/76. Loss of India: *India Today*, Sept 1-15, 1977, RWP. CC spent $2 million grinding bottles: *Far Eastern Economic Review*, 12/7/79, RWP. Footnote: Cartoon in *The Statesman*, 10/21/77.

Battle with bottlers: Background in *Diet Coke* opinions; Hames int. FTC attack: 1979 *CQ Almanac*, p. 389. Luke Smith assigned: Oliver, p. 34. "System. . .down the drain": Charles Brightwell int/CCA. Millard and Johnson resisted, discussion grew "bombastic": Crawford Johnson III int/CCA.

Barely communicating: Jeane Austin, Ayoub ints. Woodruff turned down Kissinger and Black: Memos, Austin to RWW, 3/11/76 and 7/12/76, RWP. Austin pushed Eisenberg into retirement: Memo, Austin to RWW, 1/5/77, RWP. Wine, Presto Products, bottling: Goizueta int. Moscow Olympics: *Advertising Age*, 3/20/78. China: CC press release, 12/19/78. *Washington Star* allegations: 1/21/79 issue. Friend meeting Austin for lunch: Yearley int. Woodruff gave Austin extra year: JJ int.

Wall Street money on Keough: NYT, 4/9/78; AJC, 7/30/78; *Business Week*, 9/10/79. Keough on "shared experience": Keough speech text, Foresees Club, 12/10/73, RWP. "Hell of a time": M. Hodgson, Jr., int. Claire Smith letter: 6/23/77, RWP. Keough letter: 12/20/77, RWP. Smith, Millard talks broke off; Millard approached Keough; Austin approved deal: Oliver, pp. 35-36; Keough int.

Austin wanted to switch annual meeting: Memo, Austin to RWW, 1/10/79. RWW's response: 1/10/79, RWP. Austin unhappy with Lord, explanation: Memo, Austin to RWW, 2/12/79. Press speculation, "leaves impression": AJC, 7/30/78. Austin wanted Ian Wilson: Ayoub, JJ, Jimmy Williams, Jeane Austin ints. Wilson description: Ayoub, JJ ints; *Fortune*, 6/1/81. Wilson's thank-you letter: To RWW, 10/20/75. Wilson invited Woodruff: Letter, Wilson to RWW, 8/19/76. Austin suggested putting Wilson on board: Memo, Austin to RWW, 8/24/76.

Woodruff lost lucidity: JJ, Honeycutt ints. Brother acted to liquidate foundation: Boisfeuillet Jones int. "Thought he was dying": Honeycutt int (Joe Jones did not think Woodruff was dying, but agreed that others thought so). Overseer's prediction: Elliott, p. 281. Austin fired Smith: CC press release, 8/22/79, CCA. Smith at lake:

Memo, Smith to Austin, 7/31/79, RWP. RWW's recuperation: JJ int; letter, John Sibley to RWW, 10/15/79, RWP.

Austin named vice chairmen: WSJ, 3/5/80. Goizueta description: AC, 5/31/80; WSJ, 6/2/80. Goizueta "at a disadvantage": WSJ, 3/5/80. Goizueta's rites of initiation: Memo, JJ to RWW, 2/7/74, RWP. Goizueta attended lunches: Goizueta int. Woodruff asked for photograph: Letter, Goizueta to RWW, 3/3/78.

Observation of Goizueta: From author's int. "How many shares?" story, etc.: Goizueta int. Woodruff was unhappy: JJ int; Elliott, p. 275.

Austin unveiled plans, Woodruff joked: JJ int. Jones called the architects: JJ int; memo, JJ to John Chaloner, 3/3/80. Footnote re Woodruff's weight: Goizueta int. Design team let matter lapse: Memo, JJ to Jeane Austin, 5/17/79. Hint of displeasure: *Ibid.* Description of tower: Author's observations. Woodruff prowled, complained: Memo, JJ to Chaloner, 3/3/80. Chaloner responded: Memo, Chaloner to RWW, 3/6/80. Woodruff phoned Goizueta, repair of toilet: Goizueta int.

Austin in wrong office: Ayoub int. Flew to New Orleans: Carlton Curtis int. Mrs. Austin's decorations: Jeane Austin int. Spent $6 million: WSJ, 6/10/80. (Mrs. Austin said she spent only $250,000 on art.) Woodruff's chauffeur shooed: Ayoub, Bailey ints. Adams resigned: Mooney int. Edict banning secretaries: WSJ, 6/10/80; Jeane Austin int. Secretary's letter to Woodruff: WSJ, 6/10/80. $100 million debt, "You must be broke": *Ibid.*

Woodruff decided a successor needed, Austin nominated Wilson: JJ, Ayoub, Jimmy Williams ints; WSJ, 1/16/81. Wilson's detractors: Jimmy Sibley int. Austin-Wilson dinner: Ayoub int. Jones ridiculed memo: JJ int. Questions about legal residency: NBC News, reported in AJ, 6/10/80. Woodruff entertained Wilson: Letter, Wilson to RWW, 2/5/79; *Fortune*, 6/1/81. Objections: JJ, Ayoub ints. Woodruff summoned: JJ int. Board membership: Roster of directors, CCA. Description of board meeting of 5/30/80: WSJ, 6/10/80. Wilson saw Woodruff: JJ int. "Confounding executive shuffle," spokesman's quote: WSJ, 6/2/80.

Goizueta's goal to be "in the midst": AC, 6/13/80. Handed out coasters: WSJ, 6/2/80. "Like golfer": WSJ, 6/11/80. Huntsville bottler: Letter, Robert Wilkinson to RWW, 6/5/80, RWP. Memphis bottler: WSJ, 8/7/80. Two thirds of revenues foreign: NYT, 8/7/80. Goizueta background and Kelly anecdote: Goizueta int. Goizueta gained trust: Confidential source. "Money tree": NYT, 1/10/71. Goizueta not "technical man," describes mission: WSJ, 6/11/80. Goizueta as "own man": AC, 6/11/80.

RWW suggested Smith as chairman: AJ, 7/15/80; Jimmy Sibley int. RWW alarmed Sibley: JJ int. Goizueta elected to Trust Company board: Memo, Goizueta to RWW, 6/9/80, RWP; NYT, 7/9/80. Goizueta lavished attention: Memos, Goizueta to RWW, 7/16/80 and 7/21/80, RWP. Public relations declared neutrality: AC, 7/16/80. "'Cigar' Has Come Back": WSJ, 6/10/80.

Smith died: Obit, CC, 7/20/80. Goizueta's accession announced: AC, NYT, WSJ, all 8/7/80. Liquidation of CC International: AC, 8/1/80. Goizueta joined Finance Committee, Woodruff upset: Memo, JJ to Garth Hamby, 9/19/80, RWP. Goizueta persuaded RWW to borrow $200 million: Memo, Goizueta to RWW, 11/11/80. Goizueta's stronger voice: *Financial Times*, 10/1/80.

TWELVE: NEW COKE

Wearing an ascot: Photos, Feb. 1981, RWW scrapbook No. 33. Skeet range: Letter, Jimmy Williams to RWW, 3/2/81, RWP. "Inquisition": Goizueta int. "I used to get mad": Ayoub int. Executives were paralyzed: Goizueta int. Over drinks: Oliver, p. 65; Keough int. Keough accepted: Keough int. "Use Keough": Goizueta int. "Not Mr. Smooth . . . eat you alive": AJC, 9/28/80. "Absolutely correct": Keough int. Unless otherwise noted, the descriptions of conditions within the company are from Goizueta and Keough ints.

Antitrust legislation: 1980 *CQ Almanac*, pp. 381-82. Baby boom older and grayer: *Business Week*, May 1977. Ads considered ineffective, Pepsi ahead at supermarkets: WSJ, 3/6/80. Goizueta summoned, "sacred cows": Oliver, pp. 72-75; Goizueta int; CC video, 11/12/93.

Early meeting with Woodruff, change to HFCS, Sibley quote: Goizueta int. "Project Triangle": Opinion, *Diet Coke VII*, 6/28/91, p. 149. Naming Tab: Press release, CC, 3/28/63; *Atlanta* magazine, May 1963. Legal Department afraid: Letter, Lee Talley to James Murray, 3/28/63, RWP.

Clever field test: Oliver, p. 105. Austin got cold feet Keough, Goizueta ints. Joking with Woodruff: Goizueta int. Woodruff dropped off Finance Committee: CC news release, 5/5/81, CCA. Goizueta cultivated Woodruff: Goizueta, JJ ints. Hunter and Philippines: Goizueta int. Ayoub replaced Collins, reassured Woodruff: Ayoub int

Stage act, quotes from Keough, Ayoub, and Goizueta, headline: WSJ, 11/6/81. Ayoub on "gut feelings": WSJ, 8/3/82. Woodruff okayed Diet Coke: Goizueta int. Pressure McCann: WSJ, 11/6/81. Olguita Goizueta's fear: Goizueta int.

Little recommended: Oliver, p. 82. Unless otherwise noted, the account of CC acquiring Columbia is from Oliver, and from Goizueta, Keough, Ayoub, and JJ ints. Woodruff disturbed: Cal Bailey int. How Goizueta structured the deal: Goizueta quoted in Nick Poulos column, AJC, 3/10/85. Woodruff unable to concentrate: Letter, Tom Jackson to Mrs. Graham Jackson, 8/2/82, RWP. Woodruff's behavior at board meeting: Goizueta int. Ayoub's briefcase: Oliver, p. 92. Critical hits, joint production, profits: WSJ, 4/24/86.

Diet Coke launch: Oliver, p. 111. "No way. . .drink could fail": Enrico, p. 7. Goizueta on market testing: NYT, 3/4/84. Use of lowercase *d:* Paul Pendergrass int. Most manufacturers: Enrico, p. 65. Less phosphoric acid: *Diet Coke I*, p. 1132. Ads for diet Coke: Oliver, p. 108. Diet Coke in fourth place: *Ibid.*, p. 111. "If you go around here": Goizueta int.

"I was on vacation": Keough int. Coca-Cola test in Houston: Oliver, pp. 56-57. Word swept quickly: Keough int. Pepsi sales: Oliver, pp. 58-59. Sculley quote: WSJ, 11/6/81. Cosby ad: Oliver, pp. 59-60. Unless otherwise noted, the figures on market share are from Oliver. Stout quote: Oliver, p. 118. Dyson quote: *Ibid.*, p. 119. Goizueta's "frustration": Goizueta int. Goizueta assigned Dyson, Zyman: Oliver, p. 121. Goizueta's favorite proverb: Goizueta int. "I had a very large home": WSJ, 11/6/81. *"Panem et circenses"*: Letter, 3/30/83, Goizueta to board of directors (with 1982 annual report), CCA. "Moment of pleasure": *Financial Times*, 10/1/80. Dyson description: Oliver, pp. 36-37; WSJ, 3/6/80. Reputation for high-handedness: Hames int. "Two eyes for an eye" and "Ready, fire!": 1984 bottlers meeting, CCA. Zyman description: Enrico, p. 50. "Feeling our oats": Keough int.

Search for new formula: Oliver, p. 61. Pepsi dropped the Challenge: Enrico, p. 89. "Human nature": Keough int. Bottlers wanted change: Hames int. Questions about New Coke: Keough, Goizueta ints. Best-managed: *Dun's Business Month*, Dec. 1983, RWP. Columbia growth: WSJ, 4/24/86. Goizueta sold: Divestiture list, CC. "Lucky day": Goizueta int. Might pass $1 billion: Letter, Goizueta to RWW, 12/6/84, RWP. "There is a danger": NYT, 3/4/84.

New formula: AC, 6/18/85, quoting a chemical analysis made by a Royal Crown "flavorist." The company admitted changing Merchandise No. 7X to something called "7X-100," in honor of Coca-Cola's upcoming centennial. Extra ten calories: Oliver, p. 165. Battery of tests: Goizueta remarks, press conference, 4/23/85. New Coke beat Pepsi: Oliver, pp. 126-27. Goizueta and Keough hesitated. . .resolved to proceed: Goizueta, Keough ints.

Herbert and Zyman to New York: Oliver, pp. 130-32. Goizueta and Woodruff: Goizueta int. Woodruff's consulting fee: Letter, Goizueta to RWW, 4/19/84, RWP. (The fee arrangement was not publicly disclosed.) Woodruff's final days: Photos, RWP; JJ, Honeycutt ints. (Cal Bailey said Woodruff's pet Labrador, Bobo, stopped eating the same day as Woodruff.) Offices closed: Statement, Goizueta to CC employees, 3/8/85. Laney's speech: Text, RWP. April Fools' Day meeting: Oliver, p. 145. Description of plans for unveiling New Coke: Goizueta, Keough ints.

Joe McCann anecdote and quotes, Enrico's ad: Enrico, pp. 203-4. Pepsi employees working the phones: *Ibid.*, p. 213. Press conference quotes from transcript in Oliver. Letterman: Enrico, p. 216.

Callers to 800 number, media response: Oliver, pp. 172-74. 1980 Greene clipping: *Florida Times-Union*, 4/2/80, RWP. Greene's assault on New Coke: Oliver, p. 175. Songwriter: *Ibid*, p. 13. Letter: *Ibid*, p. 187. Pepsi ad: Enrico, p. 220. Goizueta theorized: Goizueta int. "Rolling out" parties: Oliver, p. 190. Paul Harvey: *Ibid.*, p. 191. Keough's epiphany: Keough int. Goizueta's meeting with Keough: Goizueta int. TV commercials backfired: Oliver, p. 196. New formula cut costs: *Atlanta Business Chronicle*, 7/1/85. "Two dumbest": NYT, 1/21/91. "Being called names": Goizueta int. Goizueta's father: Oliver, p. 185. Jennings interrupted: *Ibid.* p. 212. Press conference transcript from Oliver. "Cure for cancer": Oliver, p. 217. Plane with banner: Goizueta int. Zyman anecdote: *Adweek*, 8/2/93.

"Coke *Are* It!": Numerous sources. Enrico press conference: Enrico, p. 239. "Megabrand": *Ibid.*, p. 238. Classic overtook Pepsi: Oliver, pp. 225-26. Keough quote: WSJ, 4/24/86. New Coke to 3 percent: *Beverage Digest*, 5/7/86. Boom for old Coke and reasons for it Keough int. Diet Coke became New Coke: Ralph Doran int. Goizueta's complaints: Goizueta int. CC stock prices: Oliver, p. 227; WSJ, 4/24/86. *Ishtar* description: Leonard Maltin's *TV Movies and Video Guide*, Plume, 1990, p. 546. Columbia failures: WSJ, 4/24/86. Inordinate attention to movies: Goizueta int. Refinancing: WSJ, 10/8/87. More than $1 billion: Pendergrass int. "Hollywood Ending": WSJ, 2/26/89.

"Eye off ball": Goizueta int. CC's refocus on international sales: NYT, 5/21/90; Goizueta, Keough ints; PR packet for portfolio managers' meeting, 3/15/94. Bordeaux, Japan: *Journey*, Feb. 1989. East Germany: NYT, 5/3/91. Eastern Europe: *Fortune*, 5/31/93. Keough and Payne: AJC, 2/28/93; Curtis int. Footnote: Confidential source.

"Gee-whizzers": Fact sheet, CC Media Relations Department. Stock price rise: AJC, 4/15/92. "Our dumbness": Ivan Allen, Jr., quoted in AJC, 2/28/93. Cumulative contributions: Letter, Linda Lee Saye to JJ, 11/23/92. Buffett *Fortune*, 5/31/93. Buffett's prediction: Confidential source.

Goizueta's concern over $83 million compensation, description of annual meeting: AJC, 4/16/92. Calloway dream: *Consumer Reports*, Aug. 1991. Pepsi and CC dominating supermarkets: *Ibid.* CC's 41 percent: WSJ, 10/1/91. Keough on hotel rights: Keough int. Herbert on presence: *Journey*, Dec. 1988. Hammer and Charles ads: WSJ, 8/2/91.

Ivester as successor: *Fortune*, 5/31/93, and many other sources. But John Hunter, the veteran international manager, was seen as a possible rival: AJC, 2/28/93. Goizueta predicted: Goizueta int.

World of Coca-Cola: Author's visit. Retail store: NYT, 11/24/91. Letter from man: Leonard int. Mitford quote: *The Blessing*, Random House, 1951, p. 207, RWP.

BIBLIOGRAPHY

BOOKS
Only books cited in Notes are listed.

Allen, Ivan, Jr., with Hemphill, Paul. *Mayor: Notes on the Sixties*. New York, Simon & Schuster, 1971.

Bond, Adrienne Moore. *Eugene W. Stetson*. Macon, Ga., Mercer University Press, 1983.

Branch, Taylor. *Parting the Waters: America in the King Years, 1954-1963*. New York, Simon & Schuster, 1988.

Candler, Charles Howard. *Asa Griggs Candler*. Atlanta, Emory University, 1950.

Coca-Cola Company, The: An Illustrated Profile of a Worldwide Company. Atlanta, The Coca-Cola Company, 1974.

Crawford, Joan, with Jane Kesner Ardmore. *A Portrait of Joan*. New York, Doubleday, 1962.

Dictionary of Georgia Biography. 2 vols. Athens, Ga., University of Georgia Press, 1983.

Dietz, Lawrence. *Soda Pop*. New York, Simon & Schuster, 1973.

Edge, Sarah Simms. *Joel Hurt and the Development of Atlanta*. Copyright Sarah Simms Edge, 1955 (originally written for the *Atlanta Historical Society Bulletin*).

Elliott, Charles. *Mr. Anonymous*. Atlanta, Cherokee Publishing Company, 1982 (originally published as *A Biography of "The Boss."* Copyright Robert W. Woodruff, 1979).

Enrico, Roger, and Kornbluth, Jesse. *The Other Guy Blinked*. New York, Bantam Books (paperback), 1988 (Hardcover: Bantam, 1986).

Garrett, Franklin. *Atlanta and Environs*. 2 vols. Athens, Ga., University of Georgia Press, 1954.

Graham, Elizabeth Candler, and Roberts, Ralph. *The Real Ones*. Fort Lee, N.J., Barricade Books, 1992.

Grant, Julia Dent. *The Personal Memoirs of Julia Dent Grant (Mrs. Ulysses S. Grant)*. New York, Putnam, 1975.

Hopkins, James Love. *The Law of Trademarks, Tradenames and Unfair Competition*. 3d ed. Cincinnati, W. H. Anderson Co., 1917.

Hoy, Anne Hoene. *Coca-Cola: The First Hundred Years*. Atlanta, The Coca-Cola Company, 1986.

Kahn, E. J., Jr. *The Big Drink*. New York, Random House, 1959.

_____. *RWW.* Atlanta, The Coca-Cola Company, 1969.

Kennedy, Doris Lockerman. *Devotedly, Miss Nellie*. Atlanta, Emory University, 1982.

Kuisel, Richard F. *Seducing the French*. University of California Press, 1993.

Louis, J. C, and Yazijian, Harvey Z. *The Cola Wars*. New York, Everest House Publishers, 1980.

Martin, Harold H. *Ralph McGill, Reporter.* Boston, Atlantic Monthly Press, 1973.

_____. *Three Strong Pillars*. Atlanta, Trust Company of Georgia, 1974.

_____. *William Berry Hartsfield, Mayor of Atlanta*. Athens, Ga., University of Georgia Press, 1978.

Martin, Jean. *Mule-to-MARTA*. 2 vols. Atlanta, Atlanta-Historical Society, 1975.

Martin, Milward W. *Twelve Full Ounces*. New York, Holt, Rinehart & Winston, 1962.

McFeely, William S. *Grant: A Biography*. New York, Norton, 1981.

Munsey, Cecil. *The Illustrated Guide to the Collectibles of Coca-Cola*. New York, Hawthorn Books, 1972.

Musto, David E, M.D. *The American Disease: Origins of Narcotic Control*. Yale University Press, 1973.

Oliver, Thomas. *The Real Coke, the Real Story*. New York, Random House, 1986 (author's citations from paperback edition, Penguin Books, 1987).

Opinions, Orders, Injunctions, and Decrees Relating to Unfair Competition and Infringement of Trade-Mark. Atlanta, The Coca-Cola Company, 1923.

Raines, Howell. *My Soul Is Rested*. New York, Putnam, 1977.

Riley, John J. *A History of the American Soft Drink Industry*. Washington, D.C., American Bottlers of Carbonated Beverages, 1958.

Rowland, Sanders, with Terrell, Bob. *Papa Coke: Sixty-five Years Selling Coca-Cola*. Asheville, N.C., Bright Mountain Books, 1986.

Savitt, Todd L., and Young, James Harvey. *Disease and Distinctiveness in the American South*. Knoxville, University of Tennessee Press (paperback), 1988.

Sibley, Celestine. *Peachtree Street, U.S.A.* New York, Doubleday, 1963.

Spalding, Hughes. *The Spalding Family*. Vol. II. Atlanta, Stein Printing, 1965.

Tedlow, Richard S. *New and Improved: The Story of Mass Marketing in America*. New York, Basic Books, 1990.

Thomson, M. S. *Reform Medical Practice*. Macon, Ga., Georgia Telegraph Steam Power Press, 1857.

Watters, Pat. *Coca-Cola: An Illustrated History*. New York, Doubleday, 1978.

Wells, Delia Wager. *The First Hundred Years, A Centennial History of King & Spalding*. Atlanta, King & Spalding, 1985.

_____. *George Woodruff: A Life of Quiet Achievement*. Macon, Ga., Mercer University, 1987.

Wiley, Harvey W. *Harvey W. Wiley: An Autobiography*. Indianapolis, Bobbs-Merrill Company, 1930.

_____. *History of a Crime Against the Food Law*. New York, Arno Press, 1976 (first published by de Vinne-Hallenbeck Co., New York, 1929).

MANUSCRIPT COLLECTIONS

Anslinger Papers, Historical Collections & Labor Archives, Pattee Library, Pennsylvania State University.

Hunter Bell Papers, Coca-Cola Archives, Atlanta.

Asa Candler Papers, Emory Special Collections, Emory University, Atlanta.

D'Arcy archives, D'Arcy Masius Benton & Bowles, St. Louis.

Eisenhower Papers, Eisenhower Library, Abilene, Kans.

Ralph Hayes Papers, Ms No. 4000, Western Reserve Historical Society, Cleveland.

Arthur and L. F. Montgomery Papers, Atlanta History Center, Atlanta.

John A. Sibley Papers, Emory Special Collections, Emory University, Atlanta.

Hughes Spalding Papers, Ms No. 1665, Rare Books Department, University of Georgia, Athens, courtesy of the Spalding family.

Robert W. Woodruff Papers, Emory Special Collections, Emory University, Atlanta.

INTERVIEWS

Among the 130 people who granted interviews for this book, the following provided quotes, anecdotes, facts, or confirmations that are cited in the Notes:

Terry Adamson, Bill Adkins, Ivan Allen Jr., Wally Armbruster, Jeane Austin, Sam Ayoub, Cal Bailey, Mae Bailey, Griffin Bell, John H. Boman Jr., Sam Brown, Tom Watson Brown, Vernon Broyles, William R. Brewster Jr., Betty Corn, Carlton Curtis, Ovid Davis, Ralph Doran, Jasper Dorsey, Charles Duncan, Edgar Duncan, Charles Elliott, Martha Ellis, Franklin Garrett, Ozzie Garrett, Roberto Goizueta, Bradley Hale, Bill Hames, Morton Hodgson Jr., Edith Honeycutt, Lindsey Hopkins III, Gerald T. Horton, Boisfeuillet Jones, Dorothy Jones, Gordon Jones, Joseph W. Jones, Donald Keough, Monroe King, Wilbur Kurtz Jr., George Lawson.

Also: Earl Leonard, Julius Lunsford Jr., Sam Massell, Alice Horton McCurdy, Jim Montgomery, Philip F. Mooney, H. Burke Nicholson Jr., McKee Nunnally Sr., McKee Nunnally Jr., Benjamin H. Oehlert III, Elizabeth "Red" Patterson, James K. Payne, Paul Pendergrass, Frank M. Robinson (II), Isabelle Scarborough, Alfredo Schvab, Carl Sanders, Jimmy Sibley, Don Sisler, Jack Spalding, Robert L. Steed, Cecil Stockard Jr., Herman Talmadge, Jack Tarver, Jack Taylor, Margaret Thrower, Diane Tolleson, Bill Turner, Ernest Vandiver, Teena Watson, David A. "Sonny" Werblin, Ralph Whitworth, James B. "Jimmy" Williams, George C. Woodruff Jr., Alexander Yearley IV, James Harvey Young.

The following individuals, although not cited in the Notes, gave interviews that contributed guidance, insights, and background information: Miles Alexander, Grace Adkins, Rosa Mae Bailey, Ferd Bellingrath, Henry Bowden, Richard Y. "Bo" Bradley, Sebert Brewer Jr., Paul Brown, John S. Candler II, Joe Cavanaugh, Rob Chambers, Herbert Elsas, Bill Emerson, Harold S. Gulliver Jr., William Helfand, Maynard Jackson, Willis Johnson, Boiling Jones III, Marshall Lane, James T. Laney, Bill Mathis, A. A. McNeill, W. Bethel Minter, Lee Molesworth, Hal Northrop, John Ott, William Pressley, Josephine Robinson, Jack Sibley, Ted Simmons, U.S. Sen. Alan K. Simpson (R-Wyoming), Hughes Spalding Jr., Robert Strickland Jr., June Tillery, William C. Waters III, C. E. "Bud" Webster, Delia Wager Wells, Charles Weltner, Richard Wright.

INDEX

ACKNOWLEDGMENTS

During the research and writing of this book, I've been borne along by the willingness of others to give freely of their time and help.

My first and greatest debt is to Joseph W. Jones, the executive aide who spent half a century at the right hand of Coca-Cola's longtime boss, Robert Woodruff. Jones threw his full support behind my project from the outset, sat patiently through dozens of hours of interview sessions, and persuaded many of the members of Woodruff's inner circle—including his nurse, pastor, doctor, stockbroker, pilot, plantation overseer, and personal valet—to speak openly and candidly with me.

Thanks to Jones, I was able to make two visits to Ichauway, Woodruff's beloved plantation in south Georgia, where I relived the old-fashioned rituals of the quail hunt, enjoyed the bounties of the dinner table (and lost a few dollars at night playing gin rummy). If there are any factual errors in this account, they have occurred despite Joe Jones's scrupulous efforts to set the record straight.

Dr. Linda Matthews, the head of Emory University's Special Collections Department, and the department's archivists—Beverly Allen, Ginger Cain, Kathy Knox, Barbara Mann, and Ellen Nemhauser—gave me guidance, sound advice, and unfailing good company during the year and a half I spent examining Robert Woodruff's private papers (which comprise an estimated 200,000 pages of documents) and several other manuscript collections.

At the Coca-Cola Company, my thanks begin with chairman and CEO Roberto Goizueta, who allowed me generous access to the company's extensive repository of corporate records. Phil Mooney, manager of the Archives Department, his deputy, Joanne Newman, and their assistant, Laura Jester, extended every imaginable courtesy to me during the weeks I spent combing the files. Carlton Curtis and Paul Pendergrass of the Corporate Communications office answered my inquiries and helped steer me through the executive labyrinth.

Some of the most revealing material I uncovered was in the private papers of Ralph Hayes, a Coca-Cola executive who spent nearly thirty years in charge of procuring the most sensitive ingredients in the secret formula; I appreciate his decision to preserve the documents and donate them to the Western Reserve Historical Society of Cleveland, and I thank the staff there for assisting in my review of the material.

The sons of Hughes Spalding—Jack, Hughes, Jr., and Phinizy—gave me permission to review their father's papers at the University of Georgia, which yielded a wealth of fresh information on Woodruff's political dealings and also disclosed how Woodruff used the instruments of philanthropy to maintain rigid control of the Coca-Cola Company.

On the legal front: At the firm of King & Spalding, I received help and guidance from Bob Steed, Griffin Bell, Bradley Hale, and Delia Wager Wells. Miles Alexander of Kilpatrick, Cody helped me gain access to a cache of correspondence from the early 1900s that shed new light on Asa Candler's early attempts to sell Coca-Cola. Bill Hames of Sutherland, Asbill & Brennan arranged to let me review an important case record.

Elsewhere in Atlanta, Willis Johnson, the venerable public affairs officer at Trust Company of Georgia, provided background information and introduced me around the executive suite. I thank bank chairman Robert L. Strickland, Jr., for letting me look through the papers in Ernest Woodruff's old rolltop desk.

In St. Louis, Jack Taylor and Jean Kammer of D'Arcy Masius Benton & Bowles, the advertising agency that handled the Coca-Cola account from 1906 to 1955, opened their files to me, and Margaret Goode helped me photocopy a small mountain of surveys, in-house reports, and oral histories that shed light on the agency's creative processes.

Other librarians and archivists were equally helpful and gracious: Arlene Royer of the Federal Records Center, East Point, Ga.; Elisabeth S. King of Johnson & Johnson, New Brunswick, N.J.; Dwight Strandberg of the Eisenhower Library, Abilene, Kan.; Liz McBride of the Emory University main library, Atlanta; and Dr. Jeanette C. P. Eisenhart of the Historical Collections and Labor Archives, Pattee Library, Penn State.

A good deal of my newspaper research was done at the Atlanta History Center, which afforded me numerous chances to converse with Franklin Garrett, the city's redoubtable historian, who among many other contributions was able to describe Asa Candler's high-pitched voice, which Garrett remembered from the day Candler spoke to his third-grade class more than seventy-five years ago. Ted Ryan, the center's visual arts archivist, directed me to several photographs that appear in this book.

Rob Aaron of Aaron-Smith Associates, Inc., in Atlanta, assisted capably and promptly with some of my research.

Monroe King, who has made a lifelong study of John Pemberton, shared his extensive collection of documents with me. I was unable to agree with King's assessment of Pemberton as one of the great unsung men of science of the nineteenth century; nonetheless, the papers gave valuable details about Pemberton's education, career, and family life.

For information and scholarly guidance, I thank Dr. James Harvey Young of Emory, the nation's leading authority on the patent medicine era, and William Helfand, who has studied the life and work of Angelo Mariani.

A list of the 130 people I interviewed appears in the Bibliography. I am grateful to all of them, but especially to Herbert Elsas, Beth Minter, Jimmy

Sibley, and Jimmy Williams for help in piecing together the background of several confusing episodes in the company's history. Any flawed conclusions are mine, not theirs. Charles Elliott, Woodruff's official biographer and long-time hunting companion, generously shared his insights into what made Woodruff tick.

John Huey of *Fortune* magazine was an early, enthusiastic backer of this project. He directed me to his literary agent, Kristine Dahl of International Creative Management, who championed my cause with determination and skill. Her colleagues at ICM—Heather Schroder, Elizabeth Bennett, Gordon Kato, and Dorothea Herrey—have encouraged me and worked hard to make this book a success.

At HarperCollins, I thank editor Rick Kot, who has since departed, for buying my book and bolstering my confidence when I needed it most. His successor, Virginia Smith, and her assistant, Joshua Rutkoff, have shepherded me through the arduous process of putting my prose between covers and on the shelf. Frank Mount's suggestions for editorial improvement were sharp-eyed and thoughtful, and I accepted most of them. Copy editor Erin Clermont and production editor Trent Duffy fixed my mistakes and groomed my grammar. Text designer Jessica Shatan and cover designer Lawrence Ratzkin made the package attractive, while production manager Tracy Dene got the book out in record time. Publisher Jack McKeown gave this book his personal attention, which I deeply appreciate.

I could not have written *Secret Formula* without a corps of faithful friends and advisers who gave advice, shared their knowledge, read the manuscript, or simply volunteered to listen when they had better things to do: Helen Cooper, Bob Coram, Nick Curry, Cliff Graubart, Terry Kay, Pam Meredith, Dawn and Doug Mullins, Tom Oliver, Judy Tabb, and Stuart Woods. Colleagues at CNN who aided and abetted me include Gail Evans, Bob Furnad, Chris Guarino, Tom Hannon, and Carol Kinstle. My fellow panelists from "Sunday News Conference"—Jeff Dickerson, Marilyn Geewax, Tom Houck, Bill Shipp, and Dick Williams—have kept my sails filled with breeze. Shipp deserves special thanks for setting up my computer and word processor, and then finding Jeff Berry to make it work. Williams served as my daily sounding board.

My brother-in-law, Bennett Kight, has given me excellent legal and literary guidance. He makes having a lawyer in the family a privilege. His wife, Judy Kight, has been a friend of this book.

Finally, my greatest appreciation is for my wife, Linda, whose good counsel and unflagging support have buoyed me throughout this undertaking. Her keen eye and ear for language have improved the writing in this book in countless ways, and her judgment is present in every word of the content. The selection and layout of the book's photographs is a direct result of her skill at design.

It seems all spouses suffer at the hands of an author at work, and mine is no exception. I thank Linda for her patience with my ups and downs, and I love her with all my heart. She is my best friend, and, I hope, severest critic.

ABOUT THE AUTHOR

Frederick Allen was an award-winning reporter and political columnist with the *Atlanta Journal-Constitution* from 1972 to 1987, after which he joined CNN as chief analyst and commentator covering the 1988 presidential election. His essays for the program *Inside Politics* earned CNN a CableACE Award, and Allen was called the "best political analyst" by the editors of the *Hotline*.

Allen is the author of three books. His history of the Coca-Cola Company, *Secret Formula*, was published in 1994 and has been translated into seven languages. *Atlanta Rising*, a history of modern Atlanta, was published in 1996 and is taught at several colleges. *A Decent, Orderly Lynching*—an account of the vigilantes of Montana—was published in 2004, and Allen was honored by the Western History Association with the inaugural Michael P. Malone Award for his research into vigilante symbolism. He is currently working on a book about Theodore Roosevelt.

Allen graduated from Phillips Academy (Andover) and earned a BA in journalism from the University of North Carolina, Chapel Hill. He and his wife, Linda, live in Atlanta, and Big Sky, Montana.